THE ENCYCLOPEDIC SOURCEBOOK OF

NEW AGE RELIGIONS

THE ENCYCLOPEDIC
SOURCEBOOK OF

NEW AGE
RELIGIONS

EDITED BY
JAMES R. LEWIS

Prometheus Books

59 John Glenn Drive
Amherst, New York 14228-2197

BP
605
.N48
E53
2004

Published 2004 by Prometheus Books

Inquiries should be addressed to
Prometheus Books, 59 John Glenn Drive, Amherst, New York 14228–2197
VOICE: 716–691–0133, ext. 207; FAX: 716–564–2711
WWW.PROMETHEUSBOOKS.COM

08 07 06 05 04   5 4 3 2 1

Library of Congress Cataloging-in-Publication Data

The encyclopedic sourcebook of New Age religions / edited by James R. Lewis.
    p. cm.
Includes bibliographical references and index.
ISBN 1–59102–040–9 (alk. paper)
1. New Age movement—Encyclopedias. I. Lewis, James R.

BP605.N48E53 2003
299'.93—dc21

2003043185

Every attempt has been made to trace accurate ownership of copyrighted material in this book. Errors and omissions will be corrected in subsequent editions, provided that notification is sent to the publisher.

Printed in the United States of America on acid-free paper

CONTENTS

Christianity and the New Age

Spiritual Commodification and Sociological Issues

PART II

Theosophy

"Christianized" Theosophy

Spiritualism/New Thought

The Asian Influence

Other Forerunners

1987

INTRODUCTION

The last traces of sunlight from another lazy Santa Barbara day had just faded out of the western sky. From the darkened street some twenty yards away, we heard occasional car noises and the muffled voices of passing pedestrians, but these sounds felt distant, as if our little gathering was mysteriously insulated from the outer world. A large, low window along the wall we faced made the office room in which this meeting was held seem less businesslike than usual, a transformation enhanced by the dim lighting, which created a séancelike atmosphere. Seated on folding chairs in a loose semicircle around an entranced, heavy-set medium, we relaxed as best we could in what was supposed to approximate a meditative state. Our outward calm, however, belied the intense expectancy with which we awaited the arrival of the spirit who would possess the sleeping channel's body.

Soon, she began to "twitch" in a peculiar way, indicating that a disembodied entity had taken control of her body. Gradually opening her eyes, the possessed medium began by addressing us in the unidentifiable accent so common to most New Age channels: "Greetings to you, Masters! How are you in your bodies this evening?" This odd salutation was the lead-in to a lively session in which the medium channeled a number of entities, from St. Germain to the Archangel Michael. Judging from the dialogue, these elevated beings showed remarkable interest in the mundane affairs of our small group (fewer than a dozen participants).

The claims of elevated spiritual authority, the unnatural accents, and the uncanny impression that we might actually be communicating with discarnate spirits were all pretty standard fare. These accoutrements, familiar to anybody

11

who has experienced New Age spiritualism first hand, recalled similar performances from channeling's heyday in the late 1980s. In those heady days, when the premier medium/entity J. Z. Knight/Ramtha could chum around with Merv Griffin on national television, channelers' messages were bolder and their prophecies more dramatic: Rather than picturing the New Age dawn in fuzzy pastels, Ramtha and others painted the future with stark colors of apocalyptic destruction. Imminent "earth changes" were confidently predicted—earthquakes and other natural disasters that would radically change the face of the planet and usher in a New Age civilization.

Times have, however, changed. Enterprising channelers attracted far larger audiences in the late 1980s. The medium whose workshop I briefly described above initiated her public work in Santa Barbara a year or two *after* channeling began declining in faddishness around 1988, and, despite four years of steady promotional work, infrequently brought in audiences of more than a few dozen. By way of contrast, Penny Torres, a comparable New Age medium from Santa Barbara who began her work in 1986, was able to draw national attention to Mafu (a disembodied entity critics described as a "Ramtha clone") and parlay her channeling business into a prosperous New Age church.

The channeling phenomenon exemplifies the aspect of the New Age movement that became the focus of media attention—and media ridicule—in the late 1980s: It was showy and dramatic and lent itself to caricature. The media blitz, by focusing on these spiritual sideshows, obscured deeper, more serious aspects of the New Age. Also, by focusing on such phenomena as channeling and crystals—and regarding them as somehow embodying the essence of the New Age—the decline of the channeling fad, the crystal fad, and other fads seemed to indicate that the New Age was fading away by the end of the decade. This impression was reinforced by the many participants in New Age spirituality who, largely because of media ridicule, stopped identifying themselves as *New Agers*. As a result, certain outside observers were quick to pronounce the movement dead.

The New Age had not, however, passed from the scene; its participants simply moved on to new interests like shamanism, American Indian spirituality, angels, and so forth. This ongoing change of focus from one topic to another characterizes what we might think of as the *surface structure* of the New Age subculture. The *deep structure* of New Age spirituality constitutes such constants as belief in the evolution of the soul through successive incarnations, monism, karma, the basic goodness of human nature, the power of the mind to transform reality, and so on. These relatively stable notions derive from the occult-metaphysical tradition that gave birth to the New Age, particularly as that tradition was embodied in the Theosophical movement. Other aspects of the New Age, such as channeling and angels, become overnight sensations, occupy center stage for a few years, and then are themselves swept aside (though never cast away entirely) by the next fad. When viewed in this way, it is clear that, far from waning into obscurity, the New Age has been enjoying a steady expansion.

What does the growth of an alternative religious subculture mean for society as whole? There have been a variety historical periods during which religious innovation flourished. In the West, there was a proliferation of a new religious consciousness in the late classical period, as well as in the wake of the Reformation. In the United States, historians have noted a recurring pattern of religious awakenings beginning with the Great Awakening of the 1740s.

The most general observation we can make is that periods of renewed spiritual activity occur in the wake of disruptive social and economic changes: The established vision of "how things work" no longer seems to apply, and people begin searching for new visions. In previous cycles of religious experimentation, innovative forms of Protestantism often formed the basis for these new visions. As revivalist fervor died down, new or reinvigorated Protestant denominations became the pillars of a new cultural hegemony.

The most recent period of religious innovation occurred in the decades following the demise of the 1960s counterculture. However, unlike previous cycles of revival, the religious explosion that occurred in the 1970s and 1980s has not provided a basis for a new spiritual and cultural synthesis. While there has been a growth in conservative Protestant denominations during this period (a growth parallel to the pattern of earlier Awakenings), there has also been a marked growth in "metaphysical" religion. The most visible manifestation of this latter strand of spirituality has been the New Age movement, which offers a fundamentally different vision of the world from traditional Christianity. Both conservative Christianity and nontraditional ("New Age") spirituality continue to expand and show no sign of slowing in the immediate future.

For the most part, the growth of conservative, traditionalist religiosity has attracted more public attention than the expansion of nontraditional religiosity. The principal exception to this general pattern was, as mentioned earlier, a short period in the late 1980s when the New Age was in the public spotlight. Interest rapidly waned, however, and alternative spirituality was dead as a hot topic for the media circus well before the decade had drawn to a close.

As is often the case, scholars did not become interested in the New Age as a subject for academic analysis until well after its demise in the media. What they discovered, among other things, was that the so-called New Age was but the most visible manifestation of a significant spiritual subculture that had developed out of a preexisting occult-metaphysical strand of religiosity. (Prior to the emergence of this subculture, this form of religiosity had been embodied in such diverse movements as Theosophy, Spiritualism, and New Thought.) The first scholarly anthology to examine this subculture—published in 1992 under the title *Perspectives on the New Age*—was co-edited by the present writer and J. Gordon Melton. In time, the New Age became an acceptable category of study. Papers on the movement are now regularly presented at conferences, and articles on the New Age are now published in academic journals. European scholars, particularly in the United Kingdom, have generated a substantial academic literature on this subculture.

As a pioneering study, *Perspectives* was never meant to be the definitive work in this area. And in the years that have passed since its publication, I have often given thought to what was left out of that volume. For example, one of the points on which Melton and I disagreed was the form in which the New Age movement would persist. Based on his deep familiarity with American religious history, Melton anticipated that the New Age would die out as a broad cultural movement. What would remain instead would be a set of new denominations shaped by the New Age movement, much as new denominations had arisen in the wake of the Pentecostal movement.

I, on the other hand, anticipated that the residue of the New Age movement would be an expanded, decentralized spiritual subculture loosely held together by such institutions as "metaphysical" bookstores, alternative periodicals, New Age gatherings, and independent spiritual teachers. I downplayed the importance of New Age religious organizations, particularly the ones that recruited members, and viewed them as playing at most a peripheral role. This point of view helped to shape *Perspectives*, and none of the chapters in that collection focuses on specific religious organizations.

As it has turned out, both of us were right, or—if one prefers—both of us were wrong. As I predicted, an alternative spiritual subculture has continued to exist as a decentralized phenomenon. However, as Melton predicted, a plethora of nontraditional religious groups have arisen that, in important ways, provide stable points of reference for the larger subculture. Partially as a way of correcting my earlier de-emphasis on religious organizations, many chapters of the present collection focus on specific groups and movements that have arisen out of the New Age movement.

In *Perspectives on the New Age*, I also presented a reasonably detailed argument for retaining "New Age" as an etic category, despite the fact that most participants in this diffuse subculture rejected the designation *New Age* following the widespread negative media exposure the movement received in the late 1980s. While I seriously doubt that my advocacy was directly responsible, it has, in fact, been the case that academic specialists have adopted this convention—as reflected in the set of scholarly papers contained in the first part of the present volume.

The present collection brings together some of the best recent scholarship on the New Age movement. In addition to chapters on specific organizations influenced by the New Age movement, other chapters look at the movement's historical roots and examine certain broader issues. Also, and in distinction from all other works in this area of study, the volume presents selections from some of the more important historical movements that directly influenced the New Age movement plus a selection of the literature from contemporary spiritual groups.

PART ONE

PART ONE

HISTORICAL INFLUENCES

I
ESOTERICISM AND THE NEW AGE

Christoph Bochinger

First, a description of my position: I do not speak from "within" my topic. Apart from some sympathies, I am not part of the New Age or esotericism. Rather, I am presenting this topic from the discipline of religious studies. The role of people in religious studies who occupy themselves with contemporary issues is quite often one of a peeping Tom. Using mostly the qualitative methods of the social sciences, we try to gain insight into a mainly foreign world. We do participatory observations or interviews, analyze this data according to specific methods, and thereby attempt to reconstruct the participants' emic understanding of their religion, their activities, and their worldview. If we do our job properly, it is not we who are the experts but our interview partners, "experts of themselves," as we call them.

We are dealing with a phenomenon that does not easily comply with such efforts. There is, in central Europe, a centuries-old tradition of enlightenment and rationalism, which is a very good reason for substantial criticism of religion. Churches and theology, to the best of their abilities, have had a good look at modern criticism of religion and have come to live with it. Suddenly, however, a boom of irrationalism is emanating from an unexpected corner, which seems to resist all those achievements. It is not even clear if it is, in fact, a religious phenomenon. In current times, should not people who make decisions using pendulums, or who sort themselves and their contemporaries into the nine categories

Written for this anthology.

of the so-called Enneagram, be classified as nutcases? Or perhaps their attempts should be regarded as the psychological phenomena of regression? Such explanations are not permitted from the standpoint of religious studies. We should not explain the phenomenon causally but regard it—following Max Weber—in its subjectively intended way. I would like to begin by making some assertions about the term "New Age"; then, in the second part, I offer statements about *esotericism*, and in the last part, I conclude with certain systematic reflections.

1. WHAT IS THE NEW AGE?

Since the 1980s, I have been dealing with the strange phenomenon of increased secularization and alienation from mainstream religion in Germany, which simultaneously coexists with a boom in alternative forms of religiosity there. The term *New Age* was, for a number of years, the heading for new religious developments of various kinds, but it soon disappeared totally. Today, it is simply a terminus technicus for a scientific or a theological-apologetic. In fact, except for Berlin, it never got a foothold in the eastern states of Germany at all. Nonetheless, I regard it as useful to present the history of this term because it tells us much about the characteristics of contemporary alternative religions.

In the mid-1980s, this term was on everyone's lips. At the same time, I realized that regardless of its presence in the media and New Age publications, there was hardly anyone who identified with that term. Even authors whose book covers prominently displayed "New Age" in their titles told me that they did not identify with that term and that it had been the editor's idea. A *member* finally told me that in order to understand New Age, I should read three books: Marilyn Ferguson's *The Aquarian Conspiracy* (German: *Die sanfte Verschwoerung*), Fritjof Capra's *Wendezeit*, and finally, an anthology of texts, compiled by a pastor, which he regarded as New Age. With time, I found that this represented a very typical constellation. New Age was a quite diffuse heading for various alternative movements. In part, these had existed in different subcultures for a long time and did not require a term like *New Age* at all. When, in 1983–84, the paperback publishing industry discovered this topic and the need for a generic term for its series, this expression suddenly became fashionable. And, only a short time later, theologists and other observers began writing books about New Age. Thus, this unusual phenomenon achieved its contours. Fritjof Capra, regarded as its key author due to his similar-sounding book title *Wendezeit* (*Time of Change*), does not use the term, however, and most of the participants had a similar experience. "New Age," at that point, was a virtual heading for any number of manifestations whose representatives saw, perhaps, a network-like connection but did not have any interest in unifying their ideas.

There were some exceptions to this, namely, in circles close to the science journalist Marilyn Ferguson. In her book, she linked alternative attempts of the feminist, ecological, Christian, Eastern, and other movements in a visionary framework that she called "Conspiracy in the Age of Aquarius." In this, she refers back to a development in esoteric astrology: the point of the sun in the spring moves slowly back in the sky and in this way circles the zodiac in about 26,000 years. This astronomical fact, known in antiquity, was interpreted in an astrological sense around 1890 in the circle of the Theosophical Society. They understood this as the Age of Christianity that corresponds to the zodiac sign of the fish, which after two thousand years was followed by the Age of Aquarius. This age was linked to a maturation of humanity and a new form of religion that would replace Christianity in its regular form. Under modern conditions, religion, in and of itself, was not going to disappear but Christianity, as an outdated form of religion, was going to be transformed or was going to die. This image of a religiously interpreted Age of Aquarius reached the American hippie movement in 1970, and from there, Marilyn Ferguson's book transported it to Europe.

However, usage of the term *New Age* has a longer history than does the image of the Age of Aquarius, which is, typically, a modern myth. By the middle of the nineteenth century, there were several English and American magazines with this title, which had an alternative, religious focus. Astrology did not play any role in that. It was probably William Blake, the Romantic poet and copperplate engraver, who coined the term. He used it in 1804 in the sense of a "New Church" as depicted by the alleged ghost-watcher, Emmanuel Swedenborg. New Age is, therefore, used to express the expectation that there will be a new, alternative form of religion after Christianity.

2. ESOTERICISM AND THE NEW AGE

The term *esoteric* is easier to define in its context and is, in contrast to *New Age*, also used by insiders. It derives from the Greek *esoteros*, comparative of *eso*, inside. In its meaning, it denominates an "inner circle" of initiates in contrast to the *ignorants,* outside. That is, it is linked to the Arcane Discipline and transmittance of a special knowledge. Contemporary esoterics define it, however, quite often in the sense of an internalized form of religion, an inner path in principle open to anyone.

Esoterica are widespread. Although it is difficult to assess correct numbers, it is quite probable that in Germany there are more active esoterics than there are active churchgoers. In addition, there are striking overlaps between church-affiliated Christian and esoteric orientations. Within our Bayreuth Institute of Research of Contemporary Religious Culture, in Oberfranken (a region in Bavaria), we are currently carrying out a project financed by the DFG (German Research Society), interviewing Protestant and Catholic Church members in regard to their spiritual orientation. Oberfranken is a rather rural region, largely shaped by the churches. Nonetheless, it contains a rainbow of esoteric and other religious beliefs, ideas, rituals, and so forth. In contrast to major cities, many local residents participate in both church-affiliated and non-church-related religious avenues of experience. They have individual paths.

For instance, there is the professor who has a fortune-teller read the cards for him and takes her lifestyle suggestions seriously. Or the woman who has come a long way. She has been influenced by Buddhist thought and rituals but has been in contact with new religious groups for quite some time. At the same time, she is part of the local church choir and is convinced that the purest resonance (as she puts it) exists only in the Christian beliefs. Thus, she is using a typically esoteric play of words and does not see her path in the sense of having left Buddhism behind her.

There are many more examples, but such generalizations should not include all the church members. Rather, it has become clear that esoteric and new religious orientations are widespread, and the relations between these and mainstream religion are much more complex than initially indicated. Although the religious character of any experience is unclear, it is clear that so-called esoteric ideas and actions sometimes reach far into the cultural areas of Christian religiosity.

Therefore, some people in religious studies conclude that *esotericism* is a specific form of religion that has always existed as a subcategory within Christianity and other religions and has always been in relatively open contrast to the official church and its dogma.

Consequently, they find *esoterica* in Christian and Islamic mysticism, as well as in Taoism. Thus, in final analysis, every deeper form of religiosity and spirituality should be seen as potentially esoteric. This implies a religious "left-over" category for shallow dreamers, which transforms into the nutshell of religiosity, the essence of religion. In the end, the official church and theology also represent only a sort of shell—in the best case, a shell filled with "real" religion; in the worst case, the spirit has long gone. This approach is as faulty as marginalizing the esoteric from religion because a separation of shell and kernel does not do justice to the multitude of possible orientations.

The French historian Antoine Faivre offers a more differentiated definition of esotericism. Esotericism is not something uniform but a loosely defined concept. He sees it as a specific way of thinking characterized by specific moments, and he traces its amalgamation to the Renaissance. Faivre lists the following elements as essential to the esoteric way of thinking:

1. The teaching of corresponding relations between heavenly and earthly worlds ("as above so below"), between the world and humans, between macrocosms and microcosms, and so forth.

2. The belief that all of nature, in all its aspects, is animate.

3. The possibility of attaining knowledge of hidden aspects of the world through symbolic or ritual means (divination, tantric, intuition, etc.).

4. The experience of "transmutation," that is, a tight connection between knowledge and inner experience, recognition, and a religious path, which leads one through situations of crisis and culminates after the experience of rebirth in a special enlightened knowledge.

3. ESOTERICISM AS RELIGIOUS MOBILITY: A STRUCTURAL APPROACH

I believe that an approach originating in the history of ideas and thoughts is quite sensible, even though I myself favor a more structural one that originates later in history and is grounded in religious studies and sociology. In my mind, esotericism is, foremost, a modern manifestation of religion and religiosity. Indeed, its characteristics include the high mobility and permeability of its members and the resonating ideas that are loosely held together by certain foundational beliefs. This type of religion is linked to the new possibilities but also to the threats of modern times. Its spiritual precursors may have already been visible during the Renaissance, but only under modern conditions do they unfold their full impact.

In the development of our modern culture and life, people faced new problems understanding their position in the world. Even Isaac Newton made intensive explorations of things both metaphysical and occult—right alongside his more famous pioneering scientific works. In contrast to (meta) physicists of earlier times, these two sides are conflicting in him, something that can almost only be explained psychopathologically. One of his pupils was Emanuel Swedenborg, a leading scientist in Sweden during the first part of his life. After a profound personal crisis, he became a visionary of the spiritual world. He did not see this as leaving behind the sciences but as one of two faces of a new, progressive time. I call that the reverse side of enlightenment.

It is characteristic that the noun *esotericism* came into being only in the nineteenth century. With the effects of the Enlightenment, and especially with the scientific-technical progress in single esoteric traditions (that might go back to antiquity), the term became a noun in the minds of people affected by it.

This development has continued up until now. The outer framework of contemporary existence is characterized by a high level of mobility. Even from an external point of view, this creates a precarious situation for the deep-rooted structures of the major religions. Traditional Christian values, such as faithfulness or the binding nature of membership to a parish, are challenged from the outside by today's rapid pace. On the other hand, esoteric religion has—apart from the previously mentioned beliefs in its common framework—some characteristics that seem to fit the time-specific needs of the modern individual and community as well: for example, the widespread esoteric concept that all religions contain, in their essence, the same message and that differences are merely external (this belief allows for a permeability between different religious systems). Esoteric religion also allows criticism of all dogma and emphasis on the individual experience (motto: "knowledge instead of belief"). However, knowledge does not mean merely intellectual knowledge, rather a certainty in its entirety, including on the emotional level.

4. PERSPECTIVES

Is esotericism the religion of the future and of peace? That would be generalizing too much, at least for someone in religious studies. The history of the modern esoteric movement contains the same precipices as does the history of more conventional religions. Mainly two venues of criticism have to be mentioned: First, some esoteric patterns of thought and action are shaped by totalitarian ideologies. Much has been unearthed in this regard through research on Nazism. Even more dangerous, nowadays, might be a sort of esoteric neo-Liberalism that uses the power of spiritual leaders and exploits the impotence of others. Second, in today's esotericism, there is widespread consumerism, which renders turning to materialism into a caricature of spiritual values. A critic once, very appropriately, called it a finely textured materialism. In this regard as well, esotericism is something quite modern: The possibility of attaining everything, of combining everything whimsically, and when finished, of throwing it away—this possibility has a seductive, as well as a destructive side.

Thus, approaching esotericism from religious studies, as I do, reaches its limits. I am not in a position to judge whether esotericism is good or bad. I am allowed, though, to point out that it is a typically modern form of religion, which to my mind, shares all the positive and negative points of other religious systems.

THEOSOPHY AND THE THEOSOPHICAL SOCIETIES

An Overview

James A. Santucci

THEOSOPHY

The modern Theosophical movement is represented today in the United States primarily through six organizations: the Theosophical Society, headquartered in Adyar, Madras, India; the Theosophical Society, headquartered in Pasadena, California; the United Lodge of Theosophists, formed in Los Angeles, California; the Temple of the People, with headquarters at Halcyon, near Pismo Beach, California; the Word Foundation of Dallas, Texas; and Point Loma Publications in San Diego, California. Of these groups, the Adyar T.S. is considered by most (though not by all) Theosophists to be the parent organization. All claim to disseminate Theosophy, a term popularized and defined by Helena Petrovna Blavatsky (1831–1891) to denote the Wisdom of the Ages, embodying "higher esoteric knowledge"—hence, a "Secret Doctrine"—partially recoverable in

This is a revised and updated version of a paper that has already been published in *Syzygy* 6, nos. 1–2 (winter–fall 1997): 221–45; *The Encyclopedia of Cults, Sects, and New Religions*, ed. James R. Lewis (Amherst, NY: Prometheus Books, 1998), pp. 388–89 ("Point Loma Publications"), 480–83 ("Theosophical Movement"), 476 ("Temple of the People"), 483–87 ("Theosophical Society"), 503–505 ("United Lodge of Theosophists"), and 527–28 ("The Word Foundation"); *The Encyclopedia of Cults, Sects, and New Religions*, 2nd ed. (2002), pp. 573 ("Point Loma Publications"), 722–23 ("Temple of the People"), 727–30 ("Theosophical Movement"), 730–34 ("Theosophical Society), 760–62 (U.L.T.), 802–803 ("The Word Foundation"), and *Odd Gods*, ed. James R. Lewis (Amherst, NY: Prometheus Books, 2001), pp. 270–89.

imperfect and incomplete form in those portions of the scriptures of the world's great religions that express mystical teachings and in those philosophies that display a monistic or pantheistic bent.

HISTORY

The Theosophical Society was founded in New York City in 1875 with Henry Steel Olcott (1832–1907) becoming its first president, H. P. Blavatsky becoming its first corresponding secretary, George Henry Felt and Seth Pancoast the vice presidents, and William Quan Judge (1851–1896) the counsel for the society. First proposed on September 7 by Colonel Olcott,[1] the society—titled "The Theosophical Society" on September 13—was inaugurated on November 17. Less than three years later, in May 1878, the Theosophical Society affiliated with a reformist Hindu organization known as the Ârya Samâj under the leadership of Svâmî Dayânanda Sarasvatî (1824–1883), whose promotion of the Vedas—the ancient compositions of the north Indian Âryan tribes composed between 1600 and 500 BCE—as the font of Truth served as the basis of his attempt to return Hinduism to a more pristine form devoid of later corruptive teachings and practices such as polygamy, child-marriage, caste, satî, and polytheism. Due to differences that arose within a few months of affiliation—one of which was the Svâmî's adoption of a personal Supreme God, a position that was not acceptable to many members of the Theosophical Society—it was decided to modify the association by distinguishing three bodies: (1) the Theosophical Society; (2) the Theosophical Society of the Ârya Samâj of Âryâvarta, that is, a "link society"; and (3) the Ârya Samâj. Separate diplomas existed for each, with only members of (2) belonging to both (1) and (3). By 1882, all affiliations were broken because of Svâmî Dayânanda's attacks on the Theosophists for their leaders Olcott and Blavatsky associating with Buddhists and Parsis and for their formally converting to Buddhism in Ceylon (Sri Lanka) by taking pânsil (pañcasîla), "the Five Precepts," in May 1880. Around this time, the headquarters of the T.S. in the persons of Olcott and Blavatsky moved first to Bombay in early 1879 and then to Adyar, Madras, in December 1882.

During the 1880s, four significant events occurred in Theosophical history: the Coulomb affair (1884); the formation of the Esoteric Section of the T.S. under Mme Blavatsky on October 9, 1888;[2] the publishing of the *Secret Doctrine*—the seminal work of the Theosophical Movement—in 1888; and the joining of the T.S. in May 1889 of Annie Besant (1847–1933), the second president of the T.S. (Adyar) and certainly the most prominent Adyar Theosophist in the twentieth century. Regarding the Coulomb affair, Emma Coulomb, a housekeeper at the Adyar headquarters, charged that Blavatsky had produced fraudulent psychic phenomena and was responsible for writing letters in the name of her Masters or Mahatmas. She was investigated by Richard Hodgson on behalf of the Society for Psychical Research (S.P.R.), whose well-known 1885 report (this was the second report issued by the S.P.R.: the 1884 preliminary report of the S.P.R. was more neutral) charged that she committed these misdeeds, thus calling to question her claim that Masters or Adepts actually existed. Though the Hodgson Report was accepted by the S.P.R. at its general meeting held on June 26, 1885, it was never the official or corporate opinion of that organization.[3] As such, it could not withdraw a report that it had never issued. What it had done was to "make amends for whatever offence we [the S.P.R.] may have given."[4] The damage was done, however. Ill at the time, Blavatsky departed from Adyar. She eventually settled in London, where she

William Q. Judge, founder of the Theosophical Society in America. (*Reprinted with permission of the American Religion Collection*)

instituted—at the suggestion of Willian Q. Judge—the formation of the Esoteric Section under her leadership as outer head (the inner heads being the Mahatmas). It was an organization designed to "promote the esoteric interests of the Theosophical Society by the deeper study of esoteric philosophy" (Notice of "The Esoteric Section of the Theosophical Society," October 9, 1888). Although it had no institutional connection with the T.S., it was only open to its membership; furthermore, all teachings and activities were conducted in secret.

With the death of H. P. Blavatsky on May 8, 1891, the leadership of the Esoteric Section (by this time called the Eastern School of Theosophy) passed to Judge and Besant. A few short years later, charges were brought against Judge that he was "misusing the Mahatmas' names and handwriting"—in other words, claiming that he received messages from the Master, or, as Besant put it, "giving a misleading material form to messages received psychically from the Master." Although the charges were dropped in July 1894 by Besant and Colonel Olcott, they were reopened toward the end of 1894 by Besant, who proposed a resolution during the December 1894 convention of the T.S. at Adyar that President Olcott "at once call upon Mr. W. Q. Judge to resign" his vice presidency of the society. The resolution having been passed, Judge refused to resign. Later, at the Convention of the American Section of the T.S. in Boston (April 28–29, 1895), delegates voted for autonomy of the American Section from the Theosophical Society at Adyar, with Judge elected president for life, calling itself "The Theosophical

Society in America." Whether this separation is to be interpreted as a schism—the position of the Adyar T.S.—or simply the recognition that there was never any legal connection between the Adyar T.S. and the original New York T.S. in the first place (according to the interpretation of "The Theosophical Society in America")[5] is a matter of opinion. The vote on the part of the American Section was followed by the expulsion by Colonel Olcott of Judge and all who followed him. This included more than five thousand members in the United States and affiliated societies elsewhere, including lodges in England and Australia.

After Judge's death on March 21, 1896, Ernest Temple Hargrove (d. 1939) was elected president of Judge's T.S. in America. The Eastern School of Theosophy (the new name of the Esoteric Section as of 1890) had also "split" on November 3, 1894: one group remaining in the Adyar Society, with Annie Besant as outer head, and one within Judge's society under an outer head whose name was to have been kept secret until 1897, but in May 1896 it was revealed (in the *New York Sun* [May 27–28] and *Theosophy* [June 1896])[6] that it was Katherine Tingley (1847–1929) who was to be Judge's successor. Tingley followed and further developed the direction that Judge pursued in the latter years of his life, emphasizing less theoretical and more practical applications of Theosophical teachings in the area of social and educational reform. In February 1897, she laid the cornerstone of a community in Point Loma, San Diego, which was to become the new international headquarters of the T.S. in America (the old headquarters being in New York). In the same year, she founded the International Brotherhood League with herself as president, which was designed to carry on a number of humanitarian functions ranging from educational to philanthropical. Furthermore, all the lodges of her society were closed to the public in 1903.

By the latter part of 1897, Hargrove became disenchanted with Tingley's activities and also perhaps with her unwillingness to share her power with him or with anyone else. He resigned the presidency and attempted to gain control of the 1898 convention held in Chicago, but he was unsuccessful both at the convention and in subsequent court action. As a consequence of Hargrove's intense opposition at the convention over the contents of the new constitution composed by Tingley (about which he knew nothing until its introduction at the convention),[7] Hargrove left the society and formed his own organization with about two hundred former members of Tingley's T.S. in America. Hargrove's New York–based reformed Theosophical Society in America later renamed itself the Theosophical Society in 1908,[8] with A. H. Spencer becoming the acting president. It remained a viable organization for many years until the society, and possibly its own Esoteric School of Theosophy,[9] entered a period of "indrawal" from active work.[10] The direction and forceful quality of Tingley's leadership led to two dissenting bodies: The Temple of the People, founded in 1898, and the United Lodge of Theosophists, established in 1909 by Robert Crosbie and others in Los Angeles.[11]

In 1898, Tingley renamed the T.S. in America the Universal Brotherhood and Theosophical Society, and as its "Leader and Official Head" she pursued her activities in applied Theosophy, including an ambitious educational program, called Raja Yoga, that was initiated in 1900, which emphasized an integration of physical, mental, and spiritual training and education. From the earliest student population of five, the number quickly jumped to one hundred by 1902, two-thirds of whom were Cuban, owing to her abiding interest in Cuba arising from the Spanish-American War in 1898 and the support by Mayor Bacardí of Santiago of Tingley's objectives. In 1919, the educational program was expanded with the establishment of the Theosophical University. With the closing of the lodges in 1903, most of the committed and talented members were now at Point Loma, engaging not only in this formal educational experiment but also in related activities such as agriculture and horticulture, writing, researching, publishing, and dramatic and musical productions.

By the 1920s, however, these activities began to taper off due in the main to financial problems. With Tingley's death in 1929, the direction under its more intellectual and scholarly leader Gottfried de Purucker moved once again in the direction of theoretical Theosophy, with emphasis on the teaching and study of the core Theosophical works. Renaming the U.B. and T.S. the Theosophical Society, Dr. de Purucker embarked on a fraternization movement—partly owing to the hundredth anniversary of the birth of H. P. Blavatsky in 1831 approaching—with the ultimate aim of reuniting all the societies. Unification, however, was not possible, but conventions and other cooperative activities between Adyar and Point Loma were held throughout the 1930s. Toward the close of de Purucker's tenure, he made the practical decision of selling the community holdings at Point Loma, called Lomaland, and moving the society to Covina, a small community east of Los Angeles. In that same year (1942), de Purucker died, and the society was led by a cabinet for the next three years until a new leader, Col. Arthur Conger, was elected in 1945. According to one dissident account, shortly after his election, those members of the cabinet who did not acknowledge Colonel Conger's esoteric status as "mouthpiece for the Masters"—thereby claiming the same status as H. P. Blavatsky—were stripped of all responsibilities in the T.S. These former officers and several other individuals in the United States and Europe eventually left the T.S. headquarters: some voluntarily resigning their memberships, others having their memberships involuntarily canceled. The work of the Point Loma tradition established by Tingley was continued by an organized number of groups in the United States and Europe. One such group was Point Loma Publications, chartered in 1971 as a nonprofit religious and educational corporation.

In the meantime, the Theosophical Society in Covina remained under the leadership of Colonel Conger until his death in early 1951.[12] William Hartley (1879–1955), a longtime resident member of the society, was the chosen successor of Conger, but James A. Long (1898–1971) was accepted by the cabinet of the T.S. instead. Long was appointed because only a photostatic copy, not the original document, of Colonel Conger's designated appointee was produced.[13] Hartley, together with his followers, left Covina[14] and established his own Theosophical Society, now headquartered in The Hague, Netherlands.

James Long continued to head the Theosophical Society. A number of significant events took place during his leadership. The Theosophical University and all the lodges (chartered during the tenure of Dr. de Purucker) were closed;[15] the Swedish property in Visingsö was sold; and *Sunrise*, a monthly magazine, was established. Long also went on extensive lecture tours overseas and set about visiting the membership both within and outside the United States. Upon his death in 1971, Grace F. Knoche became the leader of the Theosophical Society.

During the eventful year of 1898, another Theosophical organization came into existence with the founding of the Temple of the People by Dr. William H. Dower (1866–1937) and Francia LaDue (1849–1922), who believed that they were following the instructions of the "Master" to separate from the Tingley-led Universal Brotherhood and T.S. and, according to its own declaration, to lay the "mental, physical, and spiritual foundations of the coming sixth race." Arising out of the Syracuse (New York) Lodge of the U.B. and T.S., they and their group moved to California in 1903, where they settled on land east of Oceano, establishing the headquarters known as Halcyon. By 1904, Dr. Dower had opened the Halcyon Hotel and Sanatorium in order to continue his medical practice, treating such maladies as tuberculosis, nervous disorders, alcoholism, and drug addiction. The following year (1905), the Temple Home Association was incorporated, which laid out a town plan and sold or leased house sites, thus organizing a cooperative colony, with LaDue, also known as Blue Star, becoming the first head—guardian in chief—of the temple. In 1908, the temple was incorporated under the title "The Guardian in Chief of the Temple of the People, a Corporation Sole." After LaDue's death in 1922, Dr. Dower became the second head of the temple, supervising the construction of the Blue Star Memorial Temple. Begun in 1923 and completed in 1924, the Blue Star Memorial Temple was built in accordance with mathematical and geometrical symbolism illustrating the Unity of all Life, or the Higher Self. Upon Dr. Dower's death in 1937, Mrs. Pearl Dower became the third guardian in chief, who organized the property according to its present specifications, a ninety-five-acre property consisting of fifty-two homes, thirty of which are owned by the temple, and the William Quan Judge Library, which also houses the temple offices and an apartment for visitors. The successor to Mrs. Dower in 1968 was Harold Forgostein, who, at the request of Dr. Dower, had painted in the early 1930s twenty-two pictures depicting the Native Americans' contributions to understanding the balance in nature and scenes from the life of Hiawatha, both important in temple teachings. These paintings are now in the temple's University Center. Forgostein remained head of the temple until 1990; the present guardian in chief is Eleanor L. Shumway.

Another association, the United Lodge of Theosophists, was organized by a former member of the U.B. and T.S. at Point Loma and Hargrove's Theosophical Society. Robert Crosbie (1849–1919), a Canadian living in Boston who became a Theosophist under the influence of W. Q. Judge, originally lent his support to Tingley as Judge's successor. Around 1900, he moved to Point Loma to help in the work she initiated there. In 1904, losing confidence in her leadership and methods for private reasons, he left Point Loma and moved to Los Angeles, where he associated for a time with Hargrove's Theosophical Society and with a number of Theosophists who were later to support the U.L.T., John Garrigues among them. In 1909, Crosbie, with these same interested acquaintances who shared his view that only the Source Theosophy of Blavatsky and Judge carried the teachings of Theosophy as it was intended to be delivered in modern times (i.e., in the latter decades of the nineteenth century and beyond), formed the United Lodge of Theosophists in Los Angeles. What set this group apart from other Theosophical societies was (and continues to be) its stress only on Source Theosophy and such writings as are in accord philosophically with those of Blavatsky and Judge (but excluding the letters of the Masters K.H. and M. written between 1880 and 1886[16] to the prominent Theosophical writer, vice president of the T.S. and rival to Blavatsky, A. P. Sinnett, because private letters were no substitute for the actual Theosophical teachings),[17] the rejection of leaders and teachers (all associates in the U.L.T. are described as students), and the stress on anonymity for those writings on behalf of the U.L.T. Even Crosbie himself claimed no special status, although he is held in high esteem by associates. After Crosbie's death, the lodge in Los Angeles established the Theosophy Company in 1925 to serve as fiduciary agent for the associates. No leader was recognized, but Garrigues was acknowledged as a major figure in the Los Angeles U.L.T. until his death in 1944, along with Grace Clough and Henry Geiger, but students in the U.L.T. insist that the principle of anonymity outweighs its disadvantages. The U.L.T. developed into an international association of study groups through the efforts of another important figure in the Theosophical Movement, the Indian Parsi B. P. Wadia (1881–1958). Originally a member of the Adyar T.S., which he joined in 1903 and where he served in a number of capacities—including that of Annie Besant's secretary—he resigned in 1922 because of his perception that the Theosophical Society "strayed away from the 'Original Programme.'" From 1922 to 1928, he remained in the United States and assisted in founding U.L.T. lodges in New York; Washington, D.C.; and Philadelphia. Following his departure for India via Europe, he encouraged local students to found U.L.T. lodges, including those in Antwerp, Amsterdam, London, Paris, Bangalore, and Bombay. At present, U.L.T. lodges and study groups are located throughout the United States and in Belgium, Canada, England, France, India, Italy, Mexico, the Netherlands, Nigeria, Sweden, and Trinidad (West Indies). Because of the considerable contributions of Wadia, he is the only person, with the exception of Crosbie, within the U.L.T. who is identified by name.

Turning now to the Theosophical Society (Adyar), the largest society by far (despite the loss of most of the original American Section in 1895),[18] the work that was conducted primarily by Colonel Olcott, and also to a lesser extent by Blavatsky during her abbreviated stay in India, adopted an activist stance with their championing of Hinduism and Buddhism upon their arrival in India in 1879. Colonel Olcott was especially active in helping to initiate a Buddhist revival in India and Sri Lanka and to upgrade the position of the outcasts in India. As the first American to convert to Buddhism overseas in 1880, he worked with great enthusiasm for the cause of Buddhism not only in Sri Lanka but also in other Buddhist nations: promoting the foundation of Buddhist schools, writing the *Buddhist Catechism*—which attempted to unite northern and southern Buddhists—and helping to design a Buddhist flag that all Buddhist nations could adopt as their universal emblem symbolizing Buddhist unity. In India, Colonel Olcott established "Pariah schools" for the uplifting of the depressed classes. One such school, known today as the Olcott Memorial School in the vicinity of Adyar, celebrated its one-hundredth anniversary. The purpose was to offer free education for the children of these classes in skills that would provide self-sufficiency, such as tailoring, gardening, carpentry, and printing. One further contribution made by Colonel Olcott was the establishment of the Oriental Library in order to preserve Indian manuscripts from neglect and to keep them in India. The manuscripts were housed in the newly built Adyar Library, formally opened in December 1886.

His activist role was continued by the second president of the T.S., Annie Besant, who became involved in numerous activities both within and outside the society, including such diverse activities as occult investigations, education, politics, social reform, and the introduction of ritual within the society. Among her numerous contributions, Besant was instrumental in founding the Central Hindu College in Benares in 1898, and she became active in Indian politics, serving as president of the Indian National Congress, forming the Home Rule League, and later drafting the Home Rule Bill (1925). Within the Theosophical Society, she founded the Theosophical Order of Service in 1908, which was intended to administer the first object of the society—to form a nucleus of the universal brotherhood of humanity—by carrying out works of compassion and alleviating suffering, including such activities as the giving of goods, medicine, clothes, and such to the needy and advocating the abolition of the cruelty of animals. Besant's activities within the society during her presidency are closely associated with another prominent though controversial Theosophist, Charles Webster Leadbeater (1854–1934). In large part, under his influence, teachings were introduced in the T.S. that were considered by Blavatskyites to have deviated from the original teachings of Blavatsky and her Masters. Derisively called "Neo-Theosophy" by F. T. Brooks, a Theosophical writer and the tutor of Jawaharlal Nehru in the early years of the twentieth century, these teachings were considered by those who limited themselves to the writings of Blavatsky and Judge to be heretical, judging from the opinions that appeared in Theosophical literature of the 1920s. "Neo-Theosophy" included two highly significant and innovative actions: Leadbeater's discovery, in 1909, of the physical vehicle for the coming World Teacher—known as Maitreya or the Christ—Jiddu Krishnamurti (1895–1986) and the alliance with the Old (later, Liberal) Catholic Church from 1917 under the direction of Bishops Leadbeater and James Wedgwood. As if this were not controversial enough for many within the Theosophical movement, the man behind these innovations, Leadbeater, was himself under a cloud of scandal. In 1906, charges were raised

Charles W. Leadbeater, Theosophical writer and leader.
(Reprinted with permission of the American Religion Collection)

by the secretary of the Esoteric Section in America, Helen Dennis, that he was teaching her young son and other boys masturbation as a form of occult practice. This charge, which raised the specter of pederasty in the eyes of his accuser, led to Leadbeater's resignation from the society. Upon his reinstatement in 1908, with the help of Besant, Leadbeater soon thereafter discovered J. Krishnamurti, a young Hindu boy who he said was to be the vehicle for the coming World Teacher. Much of the work of the society revolved around the training of the boy and preparing the way for the World Teacher's coming. In 1911, another organization known as the Order of the Star in the East (O.S.E.) was founded in Benares by George Arundale—which soon became a worldwide organization with Besant's help—specifically for this purpose.[19] Not long thereafter, the general secretary of the German Section, Rudolf Steiner, disenchanted with the O.S.E. and displeased with Besant's presidency, caused the General Council of the T.S. to advise the president to cancel the German sectional charter and to issue a new sectional charter to the German lodges.[20] Fifty-five out of sixty-nine German lodges followed Dr. Steiner, who laid the foundation for the Anthroposophical Society in early 1913. Despite the defections of Steiner and others, however, the Theosophical Society gained more members than it had lost. The promise of the imminent coming of the World Teacher in the vehicle of Krishnamurti contributed to both unprecedented controversy within, and popularity of, the Theosophical Society until 1929, when Krishnamurti renounced his role and left the society. Thereafter, the society never regained the popularity that it had in the 1920s.

The second event that generated controversy was the promotion of the Old Catholic, later Liberal Catholic, Church by members of the society. This promotion was primarily the brainchild of C. W. Leadbeater, who, with James Ingall Wedgwood (1883–1951), helped to establish the Church. Theosophists, especially those belonging to non-Adyar groups, viewed the L.C.C. ritual and the acceptance of the apostolic succession, on which the bishopric is authenticated, as having no place in Theosophical teaching. As the 1920s progressed, there was an attempt to combine the claims centering on the World Teacher with the ritual of the L.C.C., including the selection of twelve "apostles" for Krishnamurti, but ultimately the whole plan dissolved with Krishnamurti's rejection of that role.

After 1929, the T.S. retrenched and returned more to those teachings generally associated with Theosophy. After Besant's death in 1933, the presidency passed on to George Arundale (1934–1945), who continued the activism that was so typical of Besant's term. During his tenure, his wife, Srimati Rukmini Devi (1904–1986), established the International Academy of Arts on January 6, 1936 (later known as Kâlakshetra, "the Field or Holy place of Arts"), having as its objects (1) "[t]o emphasise the essential unity of all true Art"; (2) "[t]o work for the recognition of the arts as vital to individual, national, religious and international growth"; and (3) "[t]o provide for such activities as may be incidental to the above objects." Associated with the second purpose of Kâlakshetra was to revive and develop the ancient culture of India. To Dr. Arundale, Indian dance revealed occult ritual, in his words, "the occultism of beauty."

Following him was a protégé of Leadbeater's, C. Jinarâjadâsa (1946–1953), who, among his many contributions to the society, displayed an active interest in publishing many documents relating to the history of the society from the early years of the T.S. As one of the foremost Theosophical authors, Jinarâjadâsa displayed a distinctly scholarly bent in his published works and, in order to carry out the third object of the society, inaugurated in 1949 the School of the Wisdom at the International Headquarters of the Theosophical Society at Adyar on the anniversary of the society's own inauguration, November 17.[21] In his inaugural address, Jinarâjadâsa stated that the school's purpose was "to equip its students to become, each according to his temperament and aptitude, philosophers, scientists, ethical teachers, artists, givers of economic law, statesmen, educators, town planners and every other possible type of server of humanity."[22]

Following Jinarâjadâsa were N. Sri Ram (1953–1973), responsible for building the current Adyar Library building; John S. Coats (1973–1979); and the present international president of the T.S., Radha Burnier (1980–).[23]

BELIEFS/PRACTICES

The teachings promulgated by the Theosophical societies are ultimately those that have secured the attention of its members as well as what individuals understand Theosophy to be. As a rule, most Theosophists associate the basic teachings with the "three fundamental propositions" contained in the Proem of H. P. Blavatsky's magnum opus, *The Secret Doctrine*, published in 1888. These propositions are:

1. The existence of an Absolute, Infinite, Reality or Principle,

2. The cyclic nature or periodicity of the universe and all therein, and

3. The fundamental identity of the soul with the Universal Oversoul and the pilgrimage of all souls through the cycle of incarnation in accordance with Karmic law.

At the inception of the society, it is most likely that the founders had differing views of the term according to their own understanding. Thus, according to Olcott, "theosophy" was chosen to represent the aspirations and objects of the society because it reflected the contents of a lecture given by George Henry Felt on September 7, 1875, titled "The Lost Canon of Proportion of the Egyptians." In that lecture, Felt claimed to have discovered the Egyptian and Greek Canon of Proportion and, as a by-product of this understanding, how to cause "elementals" or "creatures evolved in the four kingdoms of earth, air, fire, and water" to manifest. The definition of "theosophy" that represented this knowledge matched that found in the American edition of Webster's unabridged dictionary (published ca. 1875), which reads as follows: "supposed intercourse with God and superior spirits, and consequent attainment of superhuman knowledge by physical processes as by the theurgic operations of ancient Platonists, or by the chemical processes of the German fire philosophers."[24]

Based on Felt's alleged discovery, Olcott proposed the formation of a society for the expressed purpose of obtaining "knowledge of the nature and attributes of the Supreme Power and of the higher spirits *by the aid of physical processes*." Such was the statement in his inaugural address as president of the society:

[H]ow can we expect that *as a society* we can have any very remarkable illustrations of the control of the adept theurgist over the subtle powers of nature?

But here is where Mr. Felt's alleged discoveries will come into play. Without claiming to be a theurgist, a mesmerist, or a spiritualist, our Vice-President promises, by simple chemical appliances, to exhibit to us, as he has to others before, the races of beings which, invisible to our eyes, people the elements. . . . Fancy the consequences of the practical demonstration of its truth, for which Mr. Felt is now preparing the requisite apparatus!

In other words, the original purpose of the Theosophical Society was—in the words of the minutes taken on September 8, 1875—"for the study and elucidation of Occultism, the Cabala &c . . . ," or to state this more forcefully: to demonstrate, by what passed as "scientific" means, the existence of hidden worlds, replete with occult forces and beings therein. Taken in this light, the society's original 1875 objects ("to collect and diffuse a knowledge of the laws which govern the universe") take on enhanced meaning.

Also recognized at the time of the society's founding was the opinion that this "Occultism," "Cabala," or "theosophy" existed from the dawn of humanity, preserved and transmitted by great teachers such as Pythagoras, Buddha, Krishna, and Jesus from its inception to the present and ascertained in the myths, legends, and doctrines of the historical religious traditions, such as Christianity, Judaism, Hinduism, Buddhism, and Islam, and lesser-known mystery cults.[25] Thus Charles Sotheran, in his paper on "Ancient Theosophy," states:

> From the beginnings of the Christian and Mahometan eras to this day the "fire" has never burnt out, the "light" has never been extinguished, and a perfect "illumination," has ever been kept scintillating with more than a faint glimmer. As a beacon, it has shed its rays far and wide in eventful epochs in history. Whether in the persons of the Gnostics, or Cabalists, or Templars, or Albigenses, or Rosicrucians, or Illuminati, or the Carbonari of our days, an impetus has been given by the unseen Theosophists, who, directing or controlling, have influenced the cause of freedom and shed enlightenment not alone in the schools of the metaphysicians, but on social and political strongholds.[26]

This view is accepted by Blavatsky, who offers much the same opinion in her articles, "A Few Questions to 'HIRAF'"[27] and "What is Theosophy?"[28] Thus, Theosophy reflected a lineage going back to earliest time whose content reflected the collected wisdom of Western esotericism, with roots going back to Egypt, the Hebrews, and Greece. The inclusion of Eastern wisdom—which is increasingly recognized from the early nineteenth century well before Blavatsky popularized it in her interpretation of the Ancient Wisdom—is acknowledged by 1875 not only by her but by her contemporaries as well. Although Eastern— especially Hindu and Buddhist—wisdom becomes increasingly prominent in Blavatsky's writings during her advancing years, the basis of her teaching is still primarily Western esotericism. This becomes especially apparent in a work written just a few years prior to her death in 1891, *The Secret Doctrine*, but there is abundant evidence that Eastern wisdom was recognized many years before.

Blavatsky's first book-length expression of this wisdom and of the Theosophical Society's original (1875) objects was her *Isis Unveiled*, published in 1877. In the ensuing two years, over ten thousand copies were sold, making it one of the most popular books of its kind in the nineteenth century. It continues to have considerable influence in Theosophical circles, with over one hundred fifty thousand copies sold since its publication.

It is quite clear that *Isis Unveiled* contained a more Western bent than the books that followed. Indeed, the preface states that *Isis* "is a plea for the recognition of the Hermetic philosophy, the anciently universal Wisdom Religion, as the only possible key to the Absolute in science and theology." This Wisdom Religion is identified with magic, considered in ancient times "a divine science which led to a participation in the attributes of Divinity itself." *Isis Unveiled* appeared in two volumes, with the first volume devoted to the hidden and unknown forces of nature, discussing subjects such as phenomena and forces (chapter 2), elementals and elementaries (chapter 7), cyclic phenomena (chapter 9), psychic and physical marvels (chapter 11), and the Inner and Outer Man (chapter 10), all accompanied with a vast array of supportive and incidental knowledge—ancient and modern, Western and Eastern, esoteric and exoteric. Volume two discusses similarities of Christian scripture, doctrine, history, and personalities with non-Christian systems such as Buddhism, Hinduism, the Vedas, and Zoroastrianism, all based on the notion that they share a common origin referred to as the "primitive 'wisdom-religion.'"

This wisdom described in *Isis Unveiled* was given a more "Oriental" (i.e., Indian) flavor in the 1888 publication of Blavatsky's *The Secret Doctrine*, wherein the above-mentioned three propositions serve as the starting point for most Theosophists. Theosophy, in this sense, took on a nondualistic or monistic view of ultimate reality, manifested or emanated in a dynamic complementarity and evolutionary progressionism. These general "propositions" presented by Blavatsky were restated in more specific teachings in *The Secret Doctrine* and elsewhere, some of which may be summarized in the following statements:

1. The evolution of the immortal individual continues through innumerable lives, such continuity made possible through reincarnation: the entrance of Self—the trinity of Spirit, Soul, and Mind—into another (human) body;

2. The complement of reincarnation is that force, known as the "Law of Cause and Effect (Karma)," that fuels future rebirths and determines the quality of the experience therein;

3. The structure of the manifested universe, humanity included, may be viewed as septenary in composition and cooperative in all relationships;

4. Humanity evolves through seven major groups or periods called Root Races, each of which is divided into seven subraces. At the present time, we humans belong to the fifth Root Race, known as the Aryan (Sanskrit "Noble") Race. The term, however, is not limited here to "Indo-European" peoples; it has a much broader meaning;

5. The individual is in actuality but a miniature copy or microcosm of the macrocosm;

6. The universe—and humanity—is guided and animated by a cosmic hierarchy of sentient beings, each having a specific mission to fulfill.

While most Theosophists would subscribe to all or part of the above statements, one should keep in mind that the above statements may take on various interpretations, depending on the understanding of each Theosophist. Furthermore, although some commentators emphasize the presence of Eastern (Hindu and Buddhist) philosophy in Theosophical teaching after 1880 when Blavatsky and Olcott arrived in India, this does not preclude the presence of important Western (Kabalistic, Christian, Masonic, and pre-Christian) teachings and myths and doctrines after 1880 or the presence of Eastern thought prior to 1880 as evidenced in *Isis Unveiled*.

ORGANIZATION/MEMBERSHIP

As of the end of 2002, the Theosophical Society, with its international headquarters in Adyar (Chennia), Madras, India, had a worldwide membership of about 32,000, distributed in almost seventy countries; the Theosophical Society in America, one of its sections, had a national membership of 5,410 (2002–2003). It considers itself to be the parent Theosophical Society and thus goes back to its New York origins in 1875, although the Theosophical Society (Pasadena) takes the position that the original Theosophical Society divided in 1895, with each T.S. having equal claim to the 1875 New York origins.

The Theosophical Society (Adyar), incorporated at Madras in 1905, is currently under the presidency of Radha Burnier. It comprises forty-seven national societies or sections, the oldest being the American Section (the Theosophical Society in America as it is now known), formed in 1886, and the British Section (chartered in 1888),[29] and the most recent being the Regional Association in Slovenia formed in 1992. The sections are composed of lodges. The governing body of the T.S. is the General Council, consisting of the president, vice president, secretary, and treasurer, all elected general secretaries of the national sections, and up to twelve additional members nominated by the president and elected by the General Council. The international president is elected by popular vote every seven years. The national president of the American Section is similarly elected every three years. An international convention is held annually, usually at Adyar. The society has a magnificent library on the grounds of the headquarters that houses original manuscripts in Sanskrit and other Asian languages and books and journals on Theosophy, philosophy, and religion. The archives of the society are currently housed in the headquarters building and contain many thousands of documents, including the important scrapbooks of Blavatsky and the Olcott diaries. The Theosophical Publishing House also functions in Adyar and produces a number of pamphlets and books, written primarily by its members, and continues to issue the oldest Theosophical periodical, the *Theosophist*. In addition, the quarterly *Adyar Newsletter* is published by the society, as is the respected *Adyar Library Bulletin*, a scholarly journal specializing in oriental research. The Theosophical Society in America is headquartered in Wheaton, Illinois, which is also the site of a rather extensive lending and research library. It also publishes a number of works, including Quest Books, through the Theosophical Publishing House (Wheaton). The T.S.A. also publishes the *American Theosophist* for its members and *Quest* magazine for the general readership. Although organizationally not a part of the T.S., the Esoteric Section is closely associated with the T.S. Its headquarters in the United States is in Ojai, California, at the Krotona Institute. On its grounds is the Krotona School of Theosophy, whose principal purpose is to serve as an educational arm of the society, to promote its work, and to implement the three objects of the T.S. These objects (according to the international society's wording) are

1. To form a nucleus of the universal brotherhood of humanity, without distinction of race, creed, sex, caste, or color.

2. To encourage the study of comparative religion, philosophy and science [the Theosophical Society in America has "comparative study of religion"].

3. To investigate unexplained laws of nature and the powers latent in man [the T.S.A. substitutes "humanity" for "man"].

Members of The T.S. are expected to approve and promote these objects. They are also expected to search for Truth through study, service, and devotion to high ideals. As the society states: "All in sympathy with the Objects of The Theosophical Society are welcomed as members, and it rests with the member to become a true Theosophist."

The Theosophical Society, now headquartered in Pasadena, is the direct descendant of the Theosophical Society in America, of which Judge was the first president, followed by Tingley's Universal Brotherhood and Theosophical Society. It is currently described as a worldwide association of members "dedicated to the uplifting of humanity through a better understanding of the oneness of life and the practical application of this principle." Membership figures are not given out; the number, however, is low, perhaps a few thousand. Members are known as Fellows of the Theosophical Society (F.T.S.); their only obligation is the acceptance of the principle of universal brotherhood and a willingness to try to live it. Fellows are received as probationary fellows; full fellowship is implemented with the issuance of a diploma, signed by the leader and secretary general, which is issued by the International Theosophical Headquarters. Other groups within the T.S. include branches, formed by three or more F.T.S. who apply for a charter, and national sections, the latter headed by a national secretary. The head of the T.S. is designated as Leader—at present it is Grace F. Knoche—who serves for life and who is also responsible for appointing a successor. The general officers include the members of the cabinet, the secretary general, treasurer general, and the national secretaries, all of whom are appointed by the leader. The leader has the power to remove from office any officer of the society. The publishing arm of The T.S. is the Theosophical University Press, which publishes the bimonthly *Sunrise: Theosophic Perspectives* and over forty book titles written by H. P. Blavatsky, Katherine Tingley, Gottfried de Purucker, A. Trevor Barker, William Q. Judge, James A. Long, Charles J. Ryan, and others. The Theosophical Society (Pasadena) has initiated correspondence courses, library centers, public meetings, and study groups and overseas translation and publishing agencies in the Netherlands, the United Kingdom, Sweden, Australia, Germany, South Africa, and Finland. The objects of The T.S. are as follows:

1. To diffuse among men knowledge of the laws inherent in the Universe.

2. To promulgate the knowledge of the essential unity of all that is, and to demonstrate that this unity is fundamental in Nature.

3. To form an active brotherhood among men.

4. To study ancient and modern religion, science, and philosophy.

5. To investigate the powers innate in man.

The United Lodge of Theosophists is "a voluntary association of students of Theosophy" founded in 1909 by Robert Crosbie and others, having as its main purpose the study of Theosophy, using the writings of Blavatsky and Judge as their guide. Because personality or ego is considered to have negative effects, "associates" pursue anonymity in their Theosophical work. Regarding this work, the U.L.T. Declaration, the only document that unites associates, states that its purpose "is the dissemination of the Fundamental Principles of the philosophy of Theosophy and the exemplification in practice of those principles, through a truer realization of the SELF; a profounder conviction of Universal Brotherhood." It regards as Theosophists all "who are engaged in the true service of Humanity, without distinction of race, creed, sex, condition or organization." The work of the U.L.T. is mainly practical and educational, conducting meetings and classes on various Theosophical subjects and publishing books, pamphlets, and magazines. Lodges and study groups exist, with lodges typically consisting of between twenty and one hundred associates and study groups of five to thirty associates. Associates can voluntarily participate in the work of a study group or lodge, ranging from attending or teaching classes in the public dissemination of Theosophical teachings. All activities are voluntary. In addition, there are associates who do not belong to any lodge because they live in countries and regions that have no proximate U.L.T. center. No leader exists in the U.L.T., nor is there any formal organization, although the Theosophy Company serves as fiduciary agent for the U.L.T. and its publications. All lodges and study groups are independent of one another but are united in a common goal, the individual goal of pursuing the three objects of the U.L.T., which are nearly identical to the objects of the Adyar T.S. (Adyar object (1) = U.L.T. object (1): "To form the nucleus of a Universal Brotherhood of Humanity, without distinction of race, creed, sex, caste, or color"; (2): "The study of ancient and modern religions, philosophies and sciences, and the demonstration of the importance of such study; and (3) the investigation of the unexplained laws of Nature and the psychical powers latent in man.") The work of the lodges focuses on the dissemination of source Theosophy. Those who are in accord with the U.L.T. Declaration are considered "associates." They express their sympathy with the work of the U.L.T. in the following manner: "Being in sympathy with the purposes of this Lodge, as set forth in its 'Declaration,' I hereby record my desire to be enrolled as an Associate, it being understood that such association calls for no obligation on my part, other than that which I, myself, determine."

The number of associates is uncertain because renewable or "sustaining" memberships do not exist, nor is there a published list of associates. The only figure supplied by an associate in Los Angeles is that "many thousands of associates" have belonged to the U.L.T. since 1909, but the figure today is not more than a few thousand worldwide. Lodges and study groups exist in Los Angeles but also in other parts of the United States, Canada, Belgium, England, France, India, Italy, Mexico, the Netherlands, and Sweden. Publications include the works of Blavatsky and Judge; compilations of articles, letters, and talks by Robert Crosbie, titled *The Friendly Philosopher*; his commentary and discussion on Judge's *The Ocean of Theosophy*, titled *Answers to Questions on "The Ocean of Theosophy"*; and a small book, *Universal Theosophy*. The Theosophy Company also publishes works that are associated with ancient theosophy (such as *The Bhagavad-Gîtâ*, Patañjali's *Yoga Sûtras,* and *The Dhammapada*), and the magazines *Theosophy,* the *Theosophical Movement* (Bombay), and *Vidya* (Santa Barbara, California).

The Temple of the People as a religious society and the village of Halcyon are both currently under the leadership (known as guardian in chief) of Eleanor L. Shumway, who was selected by her predecessor. Besides this office, there is a seven-member board of officers, selected each year by the guardian in chief. On the board is an inner guard and treasurer, both reserved for women; an outer guard and a scribe, both reserved for men; and three delegates at large, selected from members not living in Halcyon. Membership of the temple is neither solicited nor closed to any individual; the only responsibility of the member is his or her own development. Of the total of some two hundred fifty members worldwide, about eighty reside at Halcyon. An annual convention that lasts about a week begins on the first Sunday of August. The objects of the temple are

1. To formulate the truths of religion as the fundamental factor in the evolution of the human race. And this does not mean the formulation of a creed.

2. To set forth a philosophy of life that is in accord with natural and divine law.

3. To promote the study of the sciences and the fundamental facts and laws upon which the sciences are based which will permit us to extend our belief and knowledge from what is known to the unknown.

4. To promote the study and practice of art on fundamental lines, showing that art is in reality the application of knowledge to human good and welfare, and that the Christos can speak to humanity through art as well as through any other fundamental line of manifestation.

5. The promotion of a knowledge of true social science based on immutable law, showing the relationship between one human being and another, and between human beings, God, and nature. When these relationships are understood we will instinctively formulate and follow the law of true brotherhood: the unity of ALL life.

The Word Foundation, Inc., was established in 1950 "to make known to the people of the world all books written by Harold Waldwin Percival, and to ensure the perpetuation of his legacy to humanity." Percival's books include *Thinking and Destiny*; *Adepts, Masters, and Mahatmas*; *Masonry and Its Symbols*; *Man and Woman and Child*; and *Democracy Is Self-Government*. Percival (1868–1953) was born in Bridgetown, Barbados, British West Indies. He came first to Boston then to New York City with his mother after the death of his father. There he joined the Theosophical Society in 1892; eventually established the Theosophical Society Independent, which emphasized the study of the writings of H. P. Blavatsky and Eastern "scriptures"; and from 1904 to 1917 published the *Word* magazine. In addition, he established the Theosophical Publishing Company of New York. In 1946, the Word Publishing Co., Inc., was constituted, and it was under this aegis that Percival's books were first published and distributed. The foundation is run by a board of directors consisting of the president, vice president, treasurer, and secretary. Mr. Arnold E. Menze is the current president. In addition to publishing the works of Percival, it also has introduced in 1986 a new series of the *Word* magazine, published quarterly. The foundation claims a worldwide membership of about one thousand as of 1994. The purpose of membership is to support the foundation's publishing activities and to facilitate "student-to-student" study groups.

Point Loma Publications, Inc., is not a society but an independent publishing firm whose aim is to carry on the literary legacy of members of the Point Loma Theosophical Society (now the T.S., Pasadena). It was established on January 22, 1971, by former members of the cabinet of the T.S. who refused to acknowledge the esoteric status of Colonel Conger, the new leader of the T.S., in 1945. The former chairman of the cabinet of the T.S., Iverson L. Harris, became the president and chairman of the board of directors. In the 1950s, disaffected members started to organize and give public lectures in San Diego, California. The importance of the name "Point Loma" in the history of the Theosophical Movement, however, led eventually to the establishment of P.L.P. in San Diego, as is evident in the Articles of Incorporation:

> [T]o publish and disseminate literature of a philosophical, scientific, religious, historical and cultural character, faithful to the traditions and high standards maintained by the Theosophical Society with International Headquarters formerly at Point Loma, California, under the leadership of Katherine Tingley from 1900 to 1929, and of Gottfried de Purucker, from 1929 to 1942: to pursue and perpetuate the aims of the original T.S., founded in New York City by Helena Petrovna Blavatsky, Col. H. S. Olcott, Wm. Q. Judge and others, as enunciated by them on October 30, 1875.

P.L.P. remained under the leadership of Mr. Harris until his death in 1979. W. Emmett Small (1903–2001) became the new president that year and remained so until his retirement in 1993. The current president is Kenneth R. Small. Branches of P.L.P. are in The Hague, Netherlands, and Costa Rica. There are no members belonging to P.L.P., only associates or "friends" who support the work of the corporation. As a side note, other organizations based on the original work of Point Loma T.S. arose in Europe. One group is the Theosophical Society–HPB, which was founded by William Hartley after James Long was recognized as leader by the cabinet (see above). This society now functions in The Hague, the site of its international headquarters, under the presidency of Herman C. Vermeulen. England and Germany also have small groups following the Point Loma tradition.

PUBLICATIONS/EDUCATIONAL OUTREACH

The first magazine of the Theosophical Society, the *Theosophist*, was initiated with the October 1879 issue in Bombay under the editorship of H. P. Blavatsky. The periodical, published at the international headquarters in Adyar, Madras, continues to this day and is the official organ of the international president of the T.S. (Adyar). Also published are the *Adyar Newsletter* and *Adyar Library Bulletin*. The *American Theosophist* and the *Quest* are both published by the T.S. in America, and journals are published by each of the forty-seven national sections of the society. In addition to periodical literature, the T.S. carries on an active publishing program through the

Theosophical Publishing House in Adyar, India, and Wheaton, Illinois, the head-quarters of the Theosophical Society in America. The T.P.H. of the T.S. in America also publishes Quest Books, books devoted to a variety of subjects that reflect the Theosophical viewpoint in its broadest perspective.

The Theosophical Society (Pasadena) publishes the magazine *Sunrise*. Its publishing arm, Theosophical University Press, features the source literature and classics of Theosophy, including the works of Blavatsky, Judge, Tingley, Purucker, and others.

The Theosophy Company, the fiduciary agent of the United Lodge of Theosophists, publishes the journal *Theosophy*. In addition, *Vidya* is published by students at the Santa Barbara Lodge U.L.T., California, and the *Theosophical Movement*, founded by B. P. Wadia, is published in Bombay, India. Both the Theosophical Society (Pasadena)—through its Theosophical University Press—and U.L.T.—through the Theosophy Company—publish the major works of Blavatsky (*The Secret Doctrine* and *Isis Unveiled*) and Judge (*The Ocean of Theosophy*), as well as a variety of other works. The Temple of the People pub-lishes the quarterly the *Temple Artisan* at Halcyon, as well as several works unique to its organization: *Theogenesis, Temple Messages, Teachings of the Temple*, and *From the Mountain Top*.

The Word Foundation publishes the *Word*, revived in 1986, as well as the works of Harold W. Percival, mentioned above.

Point Loma Publications published the *Eclectic Theosophist*, at first a bimonthly journal, later a quarterly, under the joint editorship of W. Emmett Small and Helen Todd (until her death in 1992). After W. E. Small's retirement, the mag-azine came under the editorship of Kenneth R. Small. Publication ceased, how-ever, in 1995. Point Loma Publications currently publishes a variety of works that were originally issued during the Point Loma years of the Universal Brotherhood and Theosophical Society, as well as a number of original works, including *The Buddhism of H. P. Blavatsky* by H. J. Spierenburg, *The Way to the Mysteries* by L. Gordon Plummer, *T. Subba Row: Collected Writings*, *The Hill of Discernment* by A. Trevor Barker, and *Introduction to Sanskrit* by Thomas Egenes.

NOTES

1. This is Colonel Olcott's version as contained his *Old Diary Leaves: First Series, America 1874–1878*, 2d ed., vol. 1 (Adyar, Madras: Theosophical Publishing House, 1941), pp. 117–18 (originally pub. 1895). Although this is the accepted version of what happened on the night of September 7, a letter by William Quan Judge suggests otherwise. This letter, written to Sarah Cape in October 1893, reads as follows:

In 1874, thought of looking up spiritualism and finding Col. Olcott's [1875] book 'People from the Other World'. I wrote him asking for the address of a medium. He replied that he did not then know one, but had a friend Mme Blavatsky who asked him to ask me to call. I called at 46 Irving Place New York and made her acquaintance. Very soon after at a gathering of people there H. P. Blavatsky asked me to ask Col Olcott then at the other side of the room to found a Society. I asked him and then called the gathering to order assumed the chairmanship and nominated Olcott as permanent chairman, as which he was elected. He then took the chair and nominated me as secretary and I was elected. This was the beginning of the Theosophical Society.

This letter is located in the archives of the Theosophical Society of America (Wheaton, IL) and is quoted in Sylvia Cranston, *HPB: The Extraordinary Life and Influence of Helena Blavatsky, Founder of the Modern Theosophical Movement* (New York: G. P. Putnam's Sons, 1993), p. 140. I thank Will Thackara of the Theosophical University Press (Pasadena) for this information.

This is not the only opposing account. Both H. P. Blavatsky and Henry J. Newton also claimed to have been the founders of the Theosophical Society.

2. So declared in the anonymously written (most likely Annie Besant) "The Eastern School of Theosophy: Historical Sketch," reprinted in *Theosophical History* 6, no. 1 (January 1996): 11. It was, however, printed in Madame Blavatsky's journal, *Lucifer* 3, no. 14 (October 15, 1888).

3. Hodgson wrote most of the report, but it was the product of a committee consisting not only of Hodgson but also of E. Gurney, F. W. H. Myers, F. Podmore, H. Sidgwick, J. H. Stack, and Mrs. H. Sidgwick.

4. So stated in the editorial note to Vernon Harrison's article "J'Accuse," *Journal of the Society for Psychical Research* 53, no. 803 (April 1986): 286. The article begins with a strong statement:

> The Report of the Committee appointed to investigate phenomena connected with the Theosophical Society (commonly called the Hodgson Report) is the most celebrated and controversial of all the reports published by the Society for Psychical Research. It passes judgement on Madame H. P. Blavatsky . . . ; and the final sentence in the *Statement and Conclusions of the Committee* has been quoted in book after book, encyclopaedia after encyclopaedia, without hint that it might be wrong. It runs:
>
> "For our part we regard her neither as the mouthpiece of hidden seers, nor as a mere vulgar adventuress; we think that she has achieved a title to permanent remembrance as one of the most accomplished, ingenious and interesting impostors in history."

Harrison goes on to demonstrate that the "case against Madame Blavatsky in the Hodgson Report is NOT PROVEN—in the Scots sense."

5. This is discussed by W. Q. Judge in his article "The Theosophical Society," *Path* 10 (May 1895): 55–60 and reprinted in *Echoes of the Orient: The Writings of William Quan Judge*, vol. 2, compiled by Dara Eklund (San Diego: Point Loma Publications, 1980), pp. 197–202.

6. The *Path* changed its name to *Theosophy* in April 1896.

7. Discussed in Emmett Greenwalt, *California Utopia: Point Loma: 1897–1942* (San Diego: Point Loma Publications, 1978), pp. 37–40.

8. John Cooper, "The Esoteric School within the Hargrove Theosophical Society," *Theosophical History* 4, nos. 7–8: 179.

9. The last document ascribed to the E.S.T. is *Aids and Suggestions*, no. 18, dated December 7, 1907. See Cooper, "The Esoteric School within the Hargrove Theosophical Society," p. 185.

10. The "indrawal" most likely took place in the latter part of 1938, although Cooper ("The Esoteric School," p. 180) considers 1935 to be the actual date. The *Theosophical Quarterly*, the major magazine of the society, ended its publication run in October 1938.

11. According to Jerry Hejka-Ekins in a private communication (February 20, 1996), the U.L.T. actually broke off from the Hargrove Society, since Crosbie joined the latter after he left Tingley's Universal Brotherhood and Theosophical Society. Hejka-Ekins adds, however, that "it [the U.L.T.] appears to be more of a reaction to the Point Loma Society [the U.B. and T.S.]."

12. One of the last official acts of Colonel Conger was to move the printing and publishing activities, headquarters, and library to Altadena and Pasadena in 1950–1951.

13. Will Thackara (Theosophical University Press in Pasadena) has informed me that although Colonel Conger did sign a document appointing Hartley as his successor, Hartley was not recognized as leader by the cabinet.

14. One of the final acts of Colonel Conger was to move the headquarters to Altadena and Pasadena in 1950–1951. I thank Will Thackara (Theosophical University Press) for this information.

15. The Theosophical University was chartered in 1919 by Katherine Tingley and became inactive in 1951. Its charter, however, has been kept current by its trustees. My thanks to Will Thackara of the Theosophical University Press (Pasadena).

16. The letters referred to here are included in *The Mahatma Letters to A. P. Sinnett from the Mahatmas M. and K.H.*, transcribed, compiled, and introduced by A. T. Barker, 2d ed. (London: Rider and Company, 1926). The letters contained in A. P. Sinnett's *The Occult World* are accepted, however, as is the letter from the Maha Chohan.

17. Many U.L.T. members also consider that the letters were never intended for publication.

18. The Adyar Theosophical Society's American Section, though substantially decreased in members, quickly regained its strength under the leadership of Alexander Fullerton (?1895–1907) and with the 1897 tour of the American Section of Annie Besant and Countess Constance Wachtmeister (1839–1910), a close associate of H. P. Blavatsky and enthusiastic worker for the Theosophical cause. This and subsequent tours by Charles Webster Leadbeater beginning in 1900 and by Colonel Olcott and Countess Wachtmeister in 1901 led to a membership increase from 281 in 1896 to 1,455 as of May 1901. The American Section continued as a major player within the Theosophical Society under a number of general secretaries (or presidents as the leaders were later called). Following Alexander Fullerton were Dr. Weller Van Hook (1907–1912), who moved the headquarters of the section from New York to Chicago; A. P. Warrington (1912–1920), who is responsible for establishing the new headquarters at Krotona, Hollywood; L. W. Rogers (1920–1931), under whose stewardship the cornerstone of the new headquarters building at Wheaton, Illinois, was laid in 1926, and membership of the section reached 8,500 by

1927; Sidney A. Cook (1931–1945), who presided over the society at a time when its membership declined to a low figure of about 3,000 in 1941, due in part to Krishnamurti's dissolving the Order of the Star and in part to the Depression; James S. Perkins (1945–1960); Henry Smith (1960–1965); Joy Mills (1965, acting national president, and 1966–1974, president), Ann Wylie (1974–1975, acting president); Dora Kunz (1975–1987); Dorothy Abbenhouse (1987–1993); John Algeo (1993–2002); and Betty Bland (2002–).

19. In the official organ of the Order of the Star in the East, the *Herald of the Star* (vol. 1, no. 1 [11 January 1912]), J. Krishnamurti (or whoever wrote on his behalf) notes that George S. Arundale, the principal of the Central Hindu College, was the true founder of the order, known at the time of its formation (January 11, 1911) as the "Order of the Rising Sun." Its purpose was "to draw together those of his [Arundale's] scholars who believed in the near coming of a great Teacher, and were anxious to work in some way to prepare for Him" (pp. 1–2).

20. *Theosophist* (February 1913): 637.

21. Called the International Centre of Theosophical Studies in the 1970s but renamed The School of the Wisdom in 1985.

22. "The School of the Wisdom: Inaugural Address Delivered on November 17, 1949," *Theosophist* 71, no. 3 (December 1949): 156.

23. John Coats died on December 26, 1979. From January to June 1980, Surendra Narayan became the vice president in charge. Burnier took office in July 1980.

24. The term, though adopted in the light of this definition, was not unknown prior to this period (September 1875). Blavatsky employed the term in February 1875 in a letter to Professor Hiram Corson ("theosophy taught by the Angels") and in her "A Few Questions to 'Hiraf'" ("Theosophic Seminary"). The first mention comes close to the "angelophany" discussed in Arthur Versluis, *Theosophia: Hidden Dimensions of Christianity* (Hudson, NY: Lindisfarne Press, 1994).

25. This is stated by another founder of the T.S., Charles Sotheran (1847–1902), in a lecture, "Ancient Theosophy," presented on November 21, 1875, just four days following the inauguration of the society. For further information, see James Santucci, "Does Theosophy Exist in the Theosophical Society?" in *Ésotérisme, Gnoses and Imaginaire Symbolique: Mélanges Offerts à Antoine Faivre*, eds. Richard Caron, Joscelyn Godwin, Wouter J. Hanegraaff, and Jean-Louis Vieillard-Baron (Leuven, Belgium: Peeters, 2001), pp. 471–89.

26. As it appears in the *Spiritual Scientist* (Boston) 4, no. 12 (May 25, 1876): 140.

27. This article first appeared in the *Spiritual Scientist* (Boston) 2, no. 19 (July 15, 1875): 217–18, 224, and no. 20 (July 22, 1875): 236–37. Reproduced in the *H. P. Blavatsky Collected Writings*, vol. 1: 1874–1878, 3d ed., comp. Boris de Zirkoff (Wheaton, IL: Theosophical Publishing House, 1988), pp. 101–19.

28. *H. P. Blavatsky Collected Writings*, vol. 2: 1879–1880, comp. Boris de Zirkoff (Wheaton, IL: Theosophical Publishing House, n.d.), pp. 89–90. The article was originally published in *Theosophist* 1, no. 1 (October 1879): 2–5.

29. After the separation of Judge's society from Adyar in 1895, Colonel Olcott canceled the charter of the American Section. A new charter was issued, with the San Francisco Lodge serving as temporary headquarters, in the same year for the American Section Adyar T.S., making the charter retroactively valid to 1886 (*Theosophist*, supplement of the October 1895 issue).

REFERENCES

Blavatsky, H. P. *Collected Writings*. Comp. Boris de Zirkoff. Vols. 1, 2, 4. Wheaton, IL: The Theosophical Publishing House, 1988 (vol. 1, 3d ed.), 1967 (vol. 2), 1969 (vol. 4).

———. *Isis Unveiled*. 1877; repr., Los Angeles, CA: The Theosophy Company, 1982.

———. *The Secret Doctrine*. 1888; repr., Los Angeles, CA: The Theosophy Company, 1974.

———. *Some Unpublished Letters of Helena Petrovna Blavatsky*. Introd. and commentary Eugene Rollin Corson. London: Rider and Co., n.d.

Campbell, Bruce F. *Ancient Wisdom Revived: A History of the Theosophical Movement*. Berkeley: University of California Press, 1980.

Cooper, John. "The Esoteric School within the Hargrove Theosophical Society." *Theosophical History* 4, nos. 7–8 (April–July 1993): 178–86.

Cranston, Sylvia. *HPB: The Extraordinary Life and Influence of Helena Blavatsky, Founder of the Modern Theosophical Movement*. New York: Jeremy P. Tarcher/Putnam Book/G. P. Putnam's Sons, 1993.

Gomes, Michael. *The Dawning of the Theosophical Movement*. Wheaton, IL: Theosophical Publishing House, 1987.

———. *Theosophy in the Nineteenth Century: An Annotated Bibliography*. New York and London: Garland Publishing, 1994.

Greenwalt, Emmett A. *California Utopia: Point Loma: 1897–1942*, 2d ed. San Diego: Point Loma Publications, 1978.

Harrison, Vernon. "J'Accuse: An Examination of the Hodgson Report of 1885." *Journal of the Society for Psychical Research* 53, no. 803 (April 1986): 286–310.

Judge, W. Q. "The Theosophical Society." *Path* 10 (May 1895): 55–60 Repr. in *Echoes of the Orient: The Writings of William Quan Judge*, vol. 2. Comp. Dara Eklund. San Diego: Point Loma Publications, 1980, pp. 197–202.

Jinarâjadâsa, C., ed. *The Golden Book of the Theosophical Society: A Brief History of the Society's Growth from 1875–1925*. Adyar, Madras: Theosophical Publishing House, 1925.

———. "The School of the Wisdom: Inaugural Address Delivered on November 17, 1949." *Theosophist* 71, no. 3 (December 1949): 153–60.

Kell, Wane. "B. P. Wadia: A Life of Service to Mankind" (unpublished).

Krishnamurti, J., ed. *The Herald of the Star* 1, no. 1 (January 11, 1912), and 6, no. 3 (March 1917).

The Mahatma Letters to A. P. Sinnett from the Mahatmas M. and K.H. Transcribed, comp., and with introd. A. T. Barker. London: Rider and Company, 1926.

Melton, J. Gordon. *Encyclopedia of American Religions*, 4th ed. Detroit: Gale Research, 1993.

Olcott, Henry Steel. *Old Diary Leaves*, 6 vols. Adyar, Madras: Theosophical Publishing House, 1972–75.

"Preamble and By-Laws of the Theosophical Society" (October 30, 1875).

Ransom, Josephine, comp. *A Short History of the Theosophical Society: 1875–1937*. Adyar, Madras: The Theosophical Publishing House, 1938.

Ross, Joseph E. *Krotona of Old Hollywood*, vol. 1, 1866–1913. Montecito, CA: El Montecito Oaks Press, Inc., 1989.

Ryan, Charles J. *H. P. Blavatsky and the Theosophical Movement*. San Diego, CA: Point Loma Publications, Inc., 1975. Also published as a 2d ed., Grace F. Knoche, ed. Pasadena, CA: Theosophical University Press, 1975.

Shumway, Eleanor L. *The Temple of the People: A History*. Pamphlet distributed by the Temple of the People, P.O. Box 7100, Halcyon, CA 93421.

Taylor, Anne. *Annie Besant: A Biography*. Oxford: Oxford University Press, 1992.

"Theosophical Endowment Corporation" (A nonprofit corporation chartered by the State of California, U.S.A., September 16, 1942). Document of the Theosophical Society (Covina, later Pasadena).

"Theosophical Endowment Corporation" (Certificate of Amendment of the Articles of Incorporation, July 23, 1953). Document of the Theosophical Society (Covina, later Pasadena).

The Theosophical Society: Constitution (as amended August 27, 1971).

"The Theosophical Society: Inaugural Address of the President Delivered Before the Society November 17th, 1875."

U.L.T. "Biochronology of Robert Crosbie" (unpublished).

———. *The International Theosophical Year Book: 1938*. Adyar: The Theosophical Publishing House, 1938.

———. *The Theosophical Movement: 1875–1950*. Los Angeles: The Cunningham Press, 1951.

———. "The United Lodge of Theosophists: Its Mission and Its Future." Los Angeles: Theosophy Company, n.d.

Versluis, Arthur. *Theosophia: Hidden Dimensions of Christianity*. Hudson, NY: Lindisfarne Press, 1994.

Wadia, B. P. *To all Fellow Theosophists and Members of the Theosophical Society*. Los Angeles, 1922.

3

RUDOLF STEINER, ESOTERIC CHRISTIANITY, AND THE NEW AGE MOVEMENT

Roger E. Olson

Misconceptions about the so-called New Age movement abound. One of the primary ones is that it represents a Westernized form of Hinduism and originated in the oriental spiritual influences brought to America and Europe by emissaries from the East such as Swami Vivekananda, Paramahansa Yogananda, and Maharishi Mahesh Yogi. Few if any experts on the New Age movement labor under this illusion—recognizing that while Hinduism, Buddhism, Sikhism, and Sufiism all play significant roles in the eclectic blend that makes up the movement, even more important in its overall recipe are ingredients drawn from the Western esoteric tradition, including "esoteric Christianity." To these two key sources must be added, of course, that uniquely American phenomenon called "New Thought," with all its diversity. Without any one of these three main sources, the New Age movement would not be what it is and would lack much of its dynamic attraction and appeal. As the movement develops and matures, however, one of the three sources is emerging as dominant—at least in Britain and America—and deserves especially careful scrutiny from scholarly interpreters. It is the esoteric source— labeled the "alternative reality tradition" by Robert Ellwood[1] and superbly described and analyzed by Carl Raschke in *The Interruption of Eternity: Modern Gnosticism and the Origins of the New Religious Consciousness.*[2]

To the uninitiated, "esoteric Christianity" may sound like an oxymoron. After all, is not the gospel open and for all? How can it be "esoteric"? However,

---

Written for this anthology.

there has always been a loosely knit community of people who consider themselves Christian but identify more with the Gnostic tradition than the dominant Orthodox theologies of Roman Catholicism, Eastern Orthodoxy, and Protestant denominations. They hark back to the ancient wisdom of the mystery schools of the Hellenistic world; the Valentinian and Basilidean schools of Gnostic Christianity; the Kabbalistic speculations of medieval occultists, alchemists, and magical fraternities; the Albigensians and Cathari; the Renaissance and Reformation Neoplatonists and mystics; and the Rosicrucian brotherhoods and initiatory lodges loosely linked with early Masonry. Their heroes of the faith tend to be Meister Eckhart, John Tauler, Paracelsus, Swedenborg, and Rudolf Steiner more than Augustine, Aquinas, Luther, and Schleiermacher. Their worldview contains monistic more than monotheistic impulses and emphasizes the eternality of the divine spark that constitutes the human soul or spirit. Redemption is spiritual evolution, and the universe for them is filled with gradations of beings that are either friendly or hostile to the spirit's journey to its true home in the Fullness of Divine Being.

For such Christians, the human person is a microcosm of the divine macrocosm, reflecting, even embodying, within itself the structure of the spiritual world from which it has fallen into dense matter. The revealing of this correspondence and the unlocking of its power is the great accomplishment of the Christ, who appeared as the Buddha spirit in Gautama and then supremely and uniquely in the greatest human initiate of all, Jesus of Nazareth. To them, esoteric Christianity is the highest expression of the occult wisdom of the ages because it contains the secret of redemption—the power of the Christ-spirit working within the alienated and alienating mass of dense matter to free consciousness from imprisonment and release the spirit to continue on its evolutionary journey into the Aquarian age and beyond.

Of course, not every adherent of esoteric Christianity agrees with every detail of this composite world picture. Furthermore, since the enormously influential contribution of Helena Petrovna Blavatsky's *Secret Doctrine*, most esoteric Christians would add reincarnation and some doctrine of karma to it. In spite of diversity, twentieth- and early twenty-first-century esoteric Christianity displays an amazing degree of conceptual unity. Even a cursory reading of Blavatsky's *Secret Doctrine*, Annie Besant's *Esoteric Christianity*, Rudolf Steiner's *Christianity as Mystical Fact*, Max Heindel's *The Rosicrucian Cosmoconception*, Guy Ballard's *Mysteries Unveiled*, and Alice Bailey's *The Externalisation of the Hierarchy* reveals a basic consensus regarding the fundamental nature of reality—rooted heavily in the Gnostic-Hermetic tradition. Defoliate some of the exotic jungle of terminology drawn from that tradition and you find striking parallels between these esoteric Christian manifestos and recent New Age teachings. The channeled entities seem to have read them and translated them into the jargon of the seventies and eighties. The worldview remains the same.

Some of the most perceptive interpreters and scholars of the New Age movement have discerned this connection with esoteric Christianity. Although her perceptivity may be questionable, Constance Cumbey recognized the New Age movement's indebtedness to esoteric Christianity in her two books *The Hidden Dangers of the Rainbow*[3] and *A Planned Deception.*[4] In both cases, she tended to overstress the role of Alice Bailey, however. Earlier, and more sympathetic to the New Age movement, Theodore Roszak dedicated an entire chapter of his pioneering study of the budding phenomenon titled *Unfinished Animal*[5] to three "occult evolutionists" whom he regarded as seminal prophets or apostles of the "Aquarian Frontier": Blavatsky, Steiner, and George Gurdjieff. In some of his writings on the New Age movement, J. Gordon Melton has correctly identified the crucial significance of esoteric Christianity (often labeled "the occult/metaphysical tradition") for understanding its background and origins. He mentions Blavatsky, Besant, Bailey, Charles Leadbeater, Andrew Jackson Davis, and Guy Ballard as important channels of that tradition's influence to the New Age movement.[6]

Among those who so rightly identify and explore this connection between esoteric Christianity and the New Age movement, however, there is a marked tendency to ignore or neglect the role of Rudolf Steiner (1861–1925). Russell Chandler, for instance, discusses the key role played in the formation of the New Age movement by Blavatsky and her "successors"—Annie Besant, Guy Ballard, and Alice Bailey.[7] Like many others, he fails even to mention Steiner. This common neglect of Steiner flies in the face of Carl Raschke's statement that "Steiner may be remembered as the occult theologian *par excellance*, summing up and synthesizing after the fashion of a Gnostic Thomas Aquinas many disparate strands of hitherto secret tradition. Steiner stitched together the main fibers of hermeticism, Rosicrucianism, theosophy, and Eastern mysticism. He displayed the quintessence of the modern Gnostic attitude."[8]

The relative truth of this assessment of Steiner's significance as an esoteric theologian must be assumed rather than defended here. However, anyone who will take the time to read British sociologist Geoffrey Ahern's book *Sun at Midnight: The Rudolf Steiner Movement and the Western Esoteric Tradition* (Aquarian Press, 1984) will find there a very credible and convincing defense of Raschke's claim. Circumstantial evidence for Steiner's power and influence as the West's premier esoteric leader may be found in his legacy in worldwide anthroposophy. The Anthroposophical Society and its related organizations are growing, according to Ahern. The anthroposophical network around the world includes the very prestigious Waldorf Schools, which have produced over 25,000 graduates in the United States alone. The Waldorf system represents the second-largest private school system in North America. Also included are agricultural communes based on Steiner's "biodynamic" methods of farming, clinics based on his homeopathic theories of health care, the "Camphill Community" network of homes for the mentally impaired, and the denomination of churches known as the

Christian Community. There are also the publishing houses, Rudolf Steiner Press and the Anthroposophical Press, which publish hundreds of books by Steiner and his followers. A number of colleges in Germany, Great Britain, and the United States place Steiner's teachings at the center of their curriculums. Some of his books are published by nonanthroposophical publishers, such as Harper and Row (e.g., *The Essential Steiner* and *Cosmic Memory*).

Steiner's followers include a number of very influential people, including British philologist Owen Barfield; Church of England canon A. P. Shepherd; Carl Louis von Grasshoff (later known as Max Heindel), founder of the Rosicrucian Fellowship; and the "father of the British New Age Movement," Sir George Trevelyan. Although there is some debate about whether Rudolf Hess was an Anthroposophist, there is no doubt that his wife was a member of the German society. Steiner's influence also touched the artistic and literary communities through Wassily Kandinsky, Frank Lloyd Wright, and Saul Bellow. According to his biographers Wilhelm and Marion Pauck, Paul Tillich was genuinely interested in Steiner and anthroposophy during the 1920s. Without doubt, then, Steiner's influence has extended far beyond the bounds of the actual membership of the Anthroposophical Society itself, which includes only about 25,000 persons.

But has it extended to the New Age movement ? If so, where is that influence found? One must be very careful here. Although Steiner claimed to base his worldview and cosmology directly on his "Spiritual Science," in which he conducted sense-free research into the spiritual realms through, for instance, clairvoyant "reading" of the Akashic chronicles, much of his information closely parallels the metaphysical beliefs of other esoteric Christians such as Blavatsky, Besant, and Bailey. He was the head of the German branch of the Theosophical Society from 1903 until his famous falling out with Annie Besant in 1913 over her promotion of the "Order of the Star of the East" and of Krishnamurti as the new "World Teacher." He always claimed, however, that his own teachings arose independently of his theosophical connection and belonged to the greater tradition of Rosicrucian wisdom. Bruce Campbell's judgment on this dispute may be the best conclusion that can be drawn: "Perhaps a fair estimation of the influence of Theosophy on Steiner and Anthroposophy would be to say that the Theosophical Society offered a home to an independent-minded occultist during a crucial period of his development, and that while his predominantly Western emphasis differed from that of Theosophy the effects of the latter were real and lasting."[9]

The problem this early connection with Theosophy presents for estimating Steiner's influence on the New Age movement is obvious. In many cases, New Age writers do not specifically acknowledge any human source of their teachings, preferring instead to claim "Higher Knowledge" as their source. Scholarly attempts to trace them back to some occult thinker can easily run afoul of the tangled lines of influence among these various esotericists. The common stock of ideas contained in this tradition is so broad and deep that it is nearly impossible to pin down a con-

Rudolf Steiner, founder of the Anthroposophical Society. (*Reprinted with permission of the American Religion Collection*)

temporary New Age idea to any single source within it. Some have attempted to argue that Blavatsky's *The Secret Doctrine* is the fountainhead of it all. Others, however, have demonstrated quite convincingly that this supposedly seminal source of modern esoteric Christianity borrowed heavily from earlier and contemporary sources such as Spiritualism, Rosicrucianism, and other miscellaneous Hermetic writings.[10] The point is that one cannot discount the relative originality of Steiner's esoteric teachings simply because they happen to parallel those of other occultists of the time. However, equally important is that one cannot claim them as the source of some New Age idea unless Steiner is specifically mentioned or is the only possible source within the modern esoteric tradition.

The key to Steiner's influence on the New Age movement is the "Findhorn Connection." The well-known Findhorn Community in Scotland was founded by British esotericists Peter and Eileen Caddy and Dorothy MacLean in 1962. During the sixties and seventies, it became a Mecca for those journeying along Roszak's "Aquarian Frontier" and came to be considered by many of them the prototype of the new planetary community, a center of light, even the "garden that will save the world."[11] Among many other pioneers of the New Age, William Irwin Thompson made the pilgrimage to Findhorn in the early seventies and came back transformed.[12] Perhaps the most influential member of the community during its formative years was David Spangler (b. 1945), who arrived there as a young man in his twenties in 1970 with a load of esoteric Christian baggage. *The New Age Encyclopedia* calls him "a major spokesperson for the emerging New Age Movement"[13] and describes his book *Revelation: The Birth of a New Age* as "not only . . . the manifesto for the Findhorn Community, but one of the most cogent statements of the goals and ideals of the entire New Age Movement."[14] James Parks Morton, dean of the Cathedral of St. John the Divine, where Spangler subsequently served as "resident mystic," has endorsed him as "a highly regarded advocate of spiritual empowerment, a recognizable influence in the so-called 'New Age' movement."[15]

In his lectures and books, Spangler unequivocally places himself in the tradition of esoteric Christianity and attempts to turn the New Age movement in that direction. That is not to say that he denigrates the value of the oriental influence, but only that his own orientation, which he finds most useful for the New Age movement as a whole, is distinctly Western and Christian. Without any doubt, Rudolf Steiner represents Spangler's master-teacher in spite of the fact that Spangler claims to have received his ideas through communications with spiritual entities such as "Limitless Love and Light" and "John." (Spangler claims that he has never been a "trance channeler," but that seems to fly in the face of the facts, depending on how one defines that phenomenon.) Spangler's books, many of which are composed of "messages" and lectures delivered at Findhorn during the seventies, are liberally sprinkled with typically esoteric ideas and terms and communicate a view of the cosmic and individual spiritual evolution that directly parallels Steiner's. The clearest example of Steiner's influence on Spangler lies in the latter's teachings on the Christ. But does Spangler acknowledge this influence? Sometimes. For example, in his autobiography, *Emergence: The Rebirth of the Sacred*, Spangler mentions a number of ideas and people who influenced him and the rest of the Findhorn community: astrology, evolution, Nostradamus, Edgar Cayce, the Theosophical Society, and Lucis Trust (Alice Bailey's publishing house). Yet the tribute to Steiner overshadows all:

> Another source is anthroposophy, a spiritual doctrine that grew out of the teachings of the Austrian mystic and scientist Rudolf Steiner. While Steiner's writings do not discuss the idea of a New Age as explicitly as some of the other sources mentioned, in his innovative integration of spiritual perception and insights with such fields as education, agriculture, medicine, the care of the retarded, and practical politics he prefigured many of the attitudes and techniques that a New Age culture might embody.[16]

In personal correspondence with this writer, Spangler acknowledged his indebtedness to Steiner while at the same time playing it down somewhat: "Back in the middle Sixties, upon the advice of friends who felt that much of what I was then experiencing and teaching reminded them of Rudolf Steiner, I read a bit of Dr. Steiner's work, primarily his book *Knowledge of the Higher Worlds* and one or two others dealing with the Christ."[17] Before ever reaching Findhorn, then, Spangler was already aware of Steiner's esoteric philosophy and was no doubt incorporating it into his own New Age belief-system. In his first book, *Revelation: The Birth of a New Age*, he explicitly names the Anthroposophical Society as a major avenue of the public release of the ancient mystery teachings into the New Age.[18] Interestingly, William Irwin Thompson, in his book *Passages about Earth*, says that at Findhorn Spangler struck him as a "philosopher in the tradition of a Rudolf Steiner" (p. 163).

A frequent visitor to and strong supporter of the Findhorn Community was British educator and anthroposophist Sir George Trevelyan. Trevelyan gained a reputation for expertise in the field of adult education as principal of Attingham

Park from 1948 until his retirement in 1971. He also gained great prestige among British occultists for his visionary leadership in founding and directing the Wrekin Trust, an educational charity concerned with the spiritual nature of man and the universe. As an anthroposophist, of course, Trevelyan is committed to the spiritual teachings of Steiner and has popularized them in his two books *A Vision of the Aquarian Age* (Stillpoint, 1984) and *Operation Redemption* (Stillpoint, 1985). He came into contact with Spangler through Findhorn, with which he had strong ties, and eventually wrote the foreword to Spangler's first book. If one reads Spangler's and Trevelyan's books together, one will recognize a significant amount of "cross-fertilization" in terms of concepts as well as language. Although he has been called the "Father of the New Age" in Britain, Trevelyan's influence on the American New Age movement is growing through his two books and his influence on the Findhorn Community, which in turn has had such an influence in America.

What are some *specific* concepts borrowed by Spangler and Trevelyan from Steiner? Their versions of the esoteric worldview are heavily laden with specifically Steinerian elements. Trevelyan especially follows closely Steiner's cosmology with its complex heirarchies of cosmic periods, cosmic beings (angels, archangels, powers, principalities, etc.), stages of earth evolution, and bodies of human beings (physical, etheric, astral, ego). For example, Steiner taught that an especially dark and dense period of human spiritual evolution called "Kali Yuga," lasting for about five thousand years, ended in 1899 (or thereabouts). He placed a great deal of significance on this as it signalled the beginning of a new period of spiritual evolution which would gradually lead humans out of their captivity to dense matter and ego-isolation into direct knowledge of higher worlds.[19] Trevelyan reproduces the basic outlines of this view of present earth evolution faithfully.[20]

Trevelyan also follows Steiner closely in his description of higher spiritual entities that help or hinder the human spirit in its evolution—especially between physical incarnations. For both men, these include *not* the "Great White Brotherhood" of Theosophy but angels, archangels, archai, and other hierarchies including Gabriel, Michael, Lucifer, and Ahriman. The first pair are held by Steiner and Trevelyan to be positive and the latter pair negative, although none are essentially evil.[21]

Spangler is more eclectic than Trevelyan, but he too appears to borrow heavily from Steiner's unique twists on theosophical cosmology. For Spangler, as for Steiner, humanity's plight and opportunity for spiritual advancement lie in the increasing "fall" into matter, including the physical body. Such materialization, while good and necessary in itself as a part of evolution of spiritual freedom and higher consciousness, became too intense due to essentially good forces of materialization and individualization having too much power (Lucifer and Ahriman). The birth of the New Age is linked with the increasing influence of spiritual energies from within and outside of the earth—especially the cosmic Christ—overcoming and balancing these negative powers.[22]

The central theme tying all three men together and setting them apart from other esoteric influences on the New Age movement is their common view of the Christ. Steiner broke away from the Theosophical Society largely over the issue of Christology. Annie Besant, in keeping with Blavatsky, envisioned the Christ as a cosmic principle of spiritual consciousness that appears repeatedly in earth evolution in especially enlightened initiates. Besant recognized Buddha as the highest such Christ-initiate and Jesus as the second highest. Like others in the theosophical tradition, she looked for the next great initiate, the "World Teacher," who would in essence be Christ's incarnation for this age. She identified the young Krishnamurti as this person. Later, Alice Bailey and followers such as Benjamin Creme continued the watch for the next incarnation of the Christ.

Steiner was violently opposed to this interpretation of Christ, as he believed it demeaned Jesus and represented a materialistic notion of Christ. For him Christ, or the Christ impulse, the "Cosmic Ego"[23] incarnated only once and through that incarnation in Jesus of Nazareth, entered into the etheric sphere of the earth imparting energies that will lead humanity eventually to recognize its true Christ-nature.[24] The once-for-all incarnation of Christ in Jesus was considered by Steiner to be *the* turning point in human spiritual evolution. He conceived the Second Coming of Christ as a time in which humans would regain their lost capacities to see into the etheric realm of earth where Christ now resides and recognize him there: "The return of Christ thus will come to pass for humanity through the fact that human beings will advance to the faculty of beholding Christ in the etheric."[25] Steiner warned against "materialistic minds" that would proclaim another physical incarnation of Christ[26] and more than hinted that this evil would arise again and again in the "brotherhoods of the West and East," by which he meant Theosophy.[27]

Steiner considered the work of Christ through Jesus unique, unrepeatable, and unsurpassable. Of course his interpretation of the incarnation was distinctly gnostic: "In Christ [Jesus] alone do we find a divine-spiritual being in direct connection with a physical body. This means that the I of Jesus abandoned his physical, etheric, and astral sheaths, and the Christ incarnated Himself as the I within those sheaths so that the I of every human being can have a connection with the Christ."[28] Through Jesus, Christ taught the great spiritual truth of humanity's inner divinity. Again, his message was essentially gnostic. According to Steiner, Christ taught that "If man can . . . elevate himself . . . he can perceive within himself that drop of the divine, his I; through his purified consciousness soul he can behold God."[29] The Christ's mission in Jesus was not just to teach this esoteric truth of humanity's divinity, however. It also included death and resurrection. Through Jesus' death on the cross, Steiner claimed, the "etherized blood of Jesus" entered into the earth and began transforming it, imparting spiritual energies that will eventually spread new moral impulses and clairvoyant powers. Through the resurrection of Jesus' etheric body the Christ, still united with it, entered into the etheric body of the earth and began imparting spiritual energies to humanity from there.[30] For Steiner, then, the influence of Christ is absolutely central to the spiritualization of humanity in the New Age and Jesus was the unique vehicle by which the Christ impulse entered into this ministry. No future incarnation of Christ is necessary or desirable, for if it were to happen, it would prove that "humanity has made no progress at all in the last 2,000 years."[31]

Steiner's Christology is echoed almost exactly by both Spangler and Trevelyan. Once again, Trevelyan's account is closest to Steiner's. He compares Steiner to Paul: "As Paul must be seen as the first discoverer of the Cosmic Christ, so Steiner rediscovered Him and became His apostle for our century."[32] Like Steiner, Trevelyan sees Jesus as the human sheath for the indwelling Cosmic Christ. The incarnation was a gradual takeover of Jesus by the Christ, which was only fully accomplished at the baptism. This Christ was the very same one that appeared earlier, in a less intense fashion, in the Buddha, but his appearance in Jesus was qualitatively different because it was an incarnation.[33] According to Trevelyan, the death of Jesus on the cross transformed the earth because "a God experienced human death. At the moment when the blood ran into the earth from the body on the cross, the whole aura of the earth changed."[34] Jesus' physical body disappeared, but his "etheric body," filled with Christ, rose from the tomb and entered into the etheric body of the earth from which it is now in contact with the etheric bodies of all humans. Because of the Christ-event in Jesus, "Each man has his Higher Self or spiritual principle, and this is Christ-filled."[35] As for Steiner, so for Trevelyan, there is no need for Christ to incarnate again because "The Christ is now overlighting all mankind. He is present everywhere in the etheric. If men can lift their consciousness into this supersensible, invisible realm, they will find Him. In this sense, the Second Coming has already happened. It is for us to bring it to individual consciousness and realization."[36]

Several times Trevelyan repeats that Christ does not need to incarnate again. For him, the Second Coming is the coming of a new consciousness, not the physical reappearance of another human "Christ." There is a curious passage in *Operation Redemption*, however, in which Trevelyan seems to wish to synthesize Steiner with Alice Bailey. That he has read and been influenced by Bailey is clear from his frequent references to her and his quotations from the "Great Invocation." However, the basic pattern of his Christology is drawn from Steiner, not from Bailey, who stood in the tradition of Besant in prophesying the reappearance of Christ in a physical form as another World Teacher. She fully expected him to come in person and "walk among men" as he did before.[37] Her disciple Benjamin Creme continues this expectation.[38]

Trevelyan suggests that *perhaps* Christ may someday "reappear" on television, for instance.[39] However, he quickly returns to the basically Steinerian orientation by expressing the Second Coming primarily as a mystical experience in which all humanity will one day participate: "If we can raise our thinking and awareness into the etheric field, there we shall find Him. We should then, as far as we are individually concerned, experience an aspect of the Second Coming by lifting a preexistent condition into consciousness."[40]

Spangler also follows Steiner rather than the Besant-Bailey tradition in thinking about Christ.[41] Like Steiner and Trevelyan, he admits that the Christ expressed himself (or, in Spangler's terms, "itself") in Buddha who was "the first one of humanity to fully awaken to the level of the cosmic Christ."[42] However, according to Spangler, "this cosmic force [Christ] literally entered the vehicles of Jesus and took them over, and used those vehicles as a means of making a very important link with the Earth."[43] The effect of Christ's incarnation in Jesus was "to literally impregnate the etheric structure of the Earth. . . ."[44] This happened because in and through the death of Jesus and the outpouring of his blood "the life-energy of the Christ released within this relative world of form as never before."[45]

Like Steiner and Trevelyan, then, Spangler sees the Christ-event in Jesus as *the* unique turning point in the spiritual evolution of the earth and of humanity itself. Because of it, the New Age is inevitable: "The New Age is essentially a time in planetary history when the fruits of revelation given and anchored by Jesus come into being. In human terms, this means it is a time when we learn to *be* at one with God ourselves, to be Christs ourselves" (p. 29). Reading Spangler's *Reflections on the Christ* immediately after reading Steiner's *The Reappearance of Christ in the Etheric* is an interesting experience. Nowhere in the book does Spangler mention Steiner by name. However, most of its concepts almost exactly echo ones contained in Steiner's book. Toward the end, like Trevelyan, Spangler attempts to accommodate the Besant-Bailey view by suggesting that there may be some sort of reappearance of Christ in a personal form in the future.[46] Nevertheless, the basic pattern of his thought leaves no need for such an event. For him, because of Jesus' life, death, and etheric resurrection, Christ now dwells in the earth as "the soul of the universe, the synthesizing, guiding, evolving energy, and presence that links the spirit of God . . . with the divine life manifesting through the infinite variety and complexity of forms that make up creation as we know it."[47] Christ is uniting microcosm and macrocosm. He (It) is Christing the universe. For Spangler, then, the Second Coming is a "universal experience, not confined to any one person or group of people."[48] Ultimately, the Second Coming is the realization made possible by Christ that "we can be divine incarnations because in essence, that is what we are."[49] This obviates the need for any further physical appearance of the Christ.

There are many more parallels between Steiner and Trevelyan and Spangler. In fact, the latter two, who are widely recognized as leading spokesmen for the New Age movement, could rightly be considered little more than translators and popularizers of Steiner's anthroposophical worldview. While they are not the only ones influenced by Steiner, they represent that influence in its purest and most easily recognizable form. Through them and others like them, countless New Age communities (often patterned after Findhorn), "teachers," and individuals have been touched by Steiner's esoteric Christianity so that it must now be recognized as a major influence on America's New Age movement.[50]

NOTES

1. Robert Ellwood and Harry Partin, *Religious and Spiritual Movements in America*, 2d ed. (Englewood Cliffs, NJ: Prentice-Hall, 1988).

2. Carl A. Raschke, *The Interruption of Eternity: Modern Gnosticism and the Origins of the New Religious Consciousness* (Chicago: Nelson-Hall, 1980).

3. Constance Cumbey, *The Hidden Dangers of the Rainbow* (Shreveport, LA: Huntington House, 1983).

4. Constance Cumbey, *A Planned Deception* (n.p.: Pointe Publishers, 1985).

5. Theodore Roszak, *Unfinished Animal: The Aquarian Frontier and the Evolution of Consciousness* (New York: Harper & Row, 1975), pp. 125–37.

6. J. Gordon Melton, *Encyclopedic Handbook of Cults in America* (New York: Garland Publishing Co., 1986), pp. 108–10. See also the articles "An Overview of the New Age Movement" and "New Thought and the New Age" (presumably written by Melton) in J. Gordon Melton, Jerome Clark, and Aidan Kelly, *The New Age Encyclopedia*, 1st ed. (Detroit, New York, and London: Gale Research, 1990), pp. xiii–xxxiii and 326–31, respectively, and J. Gordon Melton, "A History of the New Age Movement" in *Not Necessarily the New Age*, ed. Robert Basil (Amherst, NY: Prometheus Books, 1988), pp. 35–53.

7. Russell Chandler, *Understanding the New Age* (Dallas: Word Publishing, 1988), p. 47.

8. Raschke, *The Interruption of Eternity*, pp. 124–25.

9. Bruce Campbell, *Ancient Wisdom Revived: A History of the Theosophical Movement* (Berkeley: University of California Press, 1980), p. 158.

10. During Blavatsky's own lifetime, her writings—primarily *Isis Unveiled* and *The Secret Doctrine*—came under heavy attack for supposed plagiarism. Her main critic in this regard was a spiritualist scholar named William Emmette Coleman, who published books and articles attempting to expose the true sources of her supposedly inspired writings. Discussion of this controversy and of Coleman's arguments may be found in Campbell, *Ancient Wisdom Revived*, pp. 32–48. See also J. Stillson Judah, *The History and Philosophy of the Metaphysical Movements in America* (Philadelphia: Westminster, 1967), pp. 92–102.

11. For information on the background, history, and present status of the Findhorn Community, see the article on it in *The New Age Encyclopedia*, pp. 171–74. Also see Paul Hawken, *The Magic of Findhorn* (New York: Harper & Row, 1975).

12. William Irwin Thompson, *Passages about Earth: An Exploration of the New Planetary Culture* (New York: Harper & Row, 1981), pp. 150–83.

13. *The New Age Encyclopedia*, 1st ed., p. 174.

14. Ibid., p. 123.

15. James Parks Morton, "Introduction," in David Spangler, *Emergence: The Rebirth of the Sacred* (New York: Delta/Dell, 1984), p. ix.

16. Spangler, *Emergence*, p. 19.

17. Excerpt from personal letter dated August 1, 1990.

18. David Spangler, *Revelation: The Birth of a New Age* (Forres, Scotland: Findhorn Foundation, 1976), p. 124.

19. Rudolf Steiner, *The Reappearance of Christ in the Etheric* (Spring Valley, NY: Anthroposophic Press, 1983), pp. 9–12.

20. George Trevelyan, *A Vision of the Aquarian Age: The Emerging Spiritual World View* (Walpole, NH: Stillpoint Publishing, 1984), pp. 30 ff.

21. For Steiner's view of spiritual hierarchies, see *The Essential Steiner: Basic Writings of Rudolf Steiner*, ed. Robert A. McDermott (San Francisco: Harper & Row, 1984), pp. 299–300. For Trevelyan's view, see *Operation Redemption. A Vision of Hope in an Age of Turmoil* (Walpole, NH: Stillpoint Publishing, 1985), pp. 57–74.

22. Compare Spangler, *Revelation*, pp. 100 ff., and *Reflections on the Christ* (Forres, Scotland: Findhorn, 1978), pp. 2–3 and 33 ff., with Steiner, *Reappearance of Christ*, pp. 9–12 and p. 78, on "Ahriman." See also Geoffrey Ahern, *Sun at Midnight: The Rudolf Steiner Movement and the Western Esoteric Tradition* (Wellingborough, Northamptonshire: The Aquarian Press, 1984), p. 110.

23. Like most esoteric Christians, Steiner is quite vague about the exact nature of the "Christ." Sometimes he describes Christ in very personal terms, almost as if he were referring to the second person of the orthodox Christian Trinity. At other times, and more in keeping with occult tradition, he describes the "Christ-Being" in universal, impersonal terms. He equates him (or it) with the "Sun Logos," the "spiritual Being of the Sun," the Holy Spirit, "The Universal Ego, the Cosmic Ego" (*The Essential Steiner*, p. 277). Overall, it seems that Steiner conceived the Christ as the universal, cosmic, group I or Ego, which is the Self connecting both microcosm and macrocosm. It is humanity's true Higher Self, lost and forgotten, but being rediscovered through the event of Jesus Christ.

24. Steiner, *Reappearance of Christ*, pp. 17–18.

25. Ibid., p. 42.

26. Ibid., p. 19.

27. Ibid., pp. 151–55.

28. Ibid., p. 103.

29. Ibid., p. 94.

30. Ibid., pp. 127–28, 69–88.

31. Ibid., p. 106.

32. Trevelyan, *Operation Redemption*, p. 33.

33. Ibid., pp. 75–88.

34. Ibid., pp. 38–39.

35. Ibid., p. 41.

36. Ibid., p. 42.

37. Alice Bailey, *The Externalisation of the Hierarchy* (New York: Lucis Publishing Co., 1957), pp. 602 ff.

38. Benjamin Creme, *The Reappearance of the Christ and the Masters of Wisdom* (London: Tara Press, 1980).

39. Trevelyan, *Operation Redemption*, p. 51.

40. Ibid.

41. Spangler's Christology has been the subject of a doctoral dissertation. See Ron Rhodes, "An Examination and Evaluation of the New Age Christology of David Spangler" (Dallas Theological Seminary, Th.D. dissertation).

42. Spangler, *Reflections on the Christ*, p. 6.

43. Ibid.

44. Ibid., p. 7.

45. Ibid., p. 28.

46. Ibid., p. 130.

47. Ibid., p. 21.

48. Spangler, *Revelation*, p. 122.

49. Spangler, *Reflections on the Christ*, p. 86.

50. Is Matthew Fox's "Creation Spirituality" a permutation of esoteric Christianity? Especially in his most recent book, *The Coming of the Cosmic Christ* (San Francisco: Harper & Row, 1988), Fox writes about the "Christ" in a way very reminiscent of esotericists such as Steiner, Spangler, and Trevelyan. For him, the Cosmic Christ is "the pattern that connects" all things with each other, including the microcosm and macrocosm (pp. 142–44). Although Fox nowhere mentions Steiner, he does include David Spangler in his "family tree" of creation-centered spirituality in *Original Blessing: A Primer in Creation Spirituality* (Santa Fe: Bear & Co., 1983), p. 314. It seems that at present Fox stands somewhere between contemplative Christianity and esoteric Christianity, moving toward the latter.

4
PARADIGMS OF NEW THOUGHT PROMOTE THE NEW AGE

Gail Harley

INTRODUCTION

New religious movements (NRMs) in America are significantly important because they are uniquely innovative and substantially different from the more mainstream Protestant, Catholic, and Jewish religious traditions. Innovative religions, including the kindred factions of the Harmonial family, such as New Thought and Christian Science, are collective expressions and creative responses to conventional, traditional, and legitimated ideas of what society holds to be "real." Harmonial religions specifically address spiritual serenity, physical and mental healing, and prosperity principles.[1] A person's relationship with the cosmological harmony of the universe is a central focus that allows the positive attributes of life to flow through them and manifest as tangible results in the finite world. These NRMs critique while they create new religious and spiritual paradigms based on current cultural designs and social organization. Danny Jorgensen, sociologist of religion, states that the New Thought movement and other alternative religions serve to advance and support diverse ways of thinking, feeling, and behaving about sacred issues that are considered to be of ultimate cosmic significance. Innovative religious movements and groups are subjective responses to traditional religion, culture, and society and many times are reactions to the established religions and the social structure of society that is supported and promoted by them.[2]

New religions are potently expressive because they constitute a tremen-

Written for this anthology.

dously powerful means of *resisting* and/or *promoting* fundamental changes in human cultures and society. Religious innovations challenge conventional images of reality as well as the basic structure and organization of the established society by promoting not only fresh and creative but many times extremely radical and revolutionary viewpoints.[3]

Year after year, the world continues to be disenchanted by secularization because of the rapid encroachment of modernity. The technological processes connected with rationalization, industrialization, urbanization, and individualization have undermined much of the power of religion in contemporary cultures. New Thought emerged as a positive response to this diverse secular culture that promoted the development of a large middle class in America. Its early acceptance into the mainstream milieu was a middle-class phenomenon. According to Dell de Chant, historian of religion, this was "religious idealism packaged for popular consumption by an optimistic, self-confident, self-made society." Because of the significant advance in the technological worldview, New Thought's pragmatic approach to life could be easily framed into a schematic blueprint based on scientific methodology, or as de Chant notes, "a religious technology."[4]

In contrast, an astonishing number of would-be new religions appear with regularity in the United States, and most do not survive the initial years. It is rare for them to attract a substantial number of followers, and an even smaller number of new groups outlive their founders. New religions walk a theological tightrope. If they are viewed as a genuine alternative to existing religions, they will attract publicity and followers. Yet when considered far too radical from the normative culture, they don't attract as many adherents or become as popular. In order to survive, a new religion must gather sufficient human populations with substantial economic resources to create a viable, enduring social organization. This has happened with New Thought over the last century.

Mormonism, Seventh-Day Adventism, Jehovah's Witnesses, Scientology, Christian Science, Spiritualism, Holiness–Pentecostalism, and New Thought are particular products of American culture and society. Of these, Christian Science and New Thought, as members of the Harmonial family, provide exciting insights into religion in America and the sociocultural milieu that produced them. New Thought, one of the major innovators, has been the most neglected by scholars. Reasons for this may be: (1) its teachings and practices have not been perceived as especially offensive to traditional religions or the larger society; (2) it has not generated much public protest or opposition; and (3) it commonly is viewed as part of a larger, highly complex, and very diffuse metaphysical movement.[5] Despite its low profile for the past one hundred years, research conducted in the 1980s and 1990s has revealed New Thought and the Harmonial family to be one of the more successful and significant new religions produced in the United States. New Thought by its very unobtrusive nature has obliquely projected its cardinal precepts into the mainstream culture to serve as a foundation for the New Age movement.

HISTORICAL ANTECEDENTS OF NEW THOUGHT

New Thought in this hemisphere has roots in European and Asian thinking and has branched out profusely since its beginning. With significant gaps in the historicity one could even hark back to ancient Gnosticism or Neoplatonism. However, New Thought's philosophical antecedents can be more readily traced to the ideas of Emanuel Swedenborg (1688–1772), a noted scientist and inventor who postulated that events in the supernatural realm were correlated with phenomena in the finite world. This law of correspondence and its variations are found in the Native American and Roman Catholic religious traditions. The thought of Ralph Waldo Emerson and the Transcendentalists was influenced by this idea, and presupposition of correspondence between the two worlds became widely held in all metaphysical groups such as Spiritualism, Theosophy, and New Thought.[6] The Transcendentalists also incorporated the sacred texts of the East, which embraced a monistic theology that proposed God was not only in everything but everyone (immanent). Their religious viewpoints were a decided departure from Western notions of the Holy that were primarily monotheistic, presupposing that God was an anthropomorphic and a transcendent deity significantly different from humans and the world, which were his creations.

The mental healing practice of Phineas Parkhurst Quimby (1802–1866) of Belfast, Maine, sparked new ideas regarding the power of the mind. Quimby, a skilled clock maker, believed that sickness was the result of erroneous thinking and a cure could be obtained by changing one's belief system. Quimby's work was secular and did not have an overtly religious orientation, yet he developed a deep and abiding spirituality from his healing practice. His pioneering ventures made unique contributions to the religion of healthy-mindedness, or the "mind cure" movement, as William James termed it, at the turn of the twentieth century.[7] This mental or metaphysical healing movement would later evolve into New Thought. Among Quimby's clients were Julius and Annetta Dresser, Warren Felt Evans, and Mary Baker Eddy, all of whom became vital forces in the growth of metaphysical healing.

Next to Quimby in importance to the then-embryonic New Thought was Warren Felt Evans (1814–1889), a former Methodist minister who had embraced the teachings of Swedenborg and joined the Swedenborgian Church of the New Jerusalem. In 1863 he was healed by Quimby's methods and wrote prolifically from 1869 onward about spiritual healing. He employed Quimby's technique of positive affirmation and avoided the use of negative terms. Evans was primarily a writer and like Quimby, he founded no church or institution.

Mary Baker Eddy was injured in a fall shortly after Quimby died in 1866. Without him as her personal physician, Eddy sought healing from reading and reflecting on biblical scriptures. She regained her health and thought her miraculous recovery occurred as a sole revelation to her from Divine authority—God. As she

Emanuel Swedenborg, an important contributor to New Thought. (*Reprinted with permission of American Religion Collection*)

grappled with the complexity of integrating religion and health, she began to formulate a preeminent technique for healing that could be consistently replicated and taught to others. Her book *Science and Health with Key to the Scriptures* developed as a result of her revelation. By 1879 she had attracted enough adherents to found the Church of Christ, Scientist, in the Boston area.[8] Eddy was subsequently accused by Julius and Annetta Dresser of pirating Quimby's healing work and partially creating her church doctrine based upon his healing principles. For a number of years, the highly charged emotional responses and intense paper warfare generated between Eddy and her staunch supporters and the Dressers and their fractious affiliates served to keep public attention focused on the dramatic debates and the specific people promoting mental healing in the New England area. Consequently, the significant historical foundations of New Thought that were rapidly evolving in the Midwest, in Chicago, and points farther west in Colorado and California were largely ignored at this time due to the Quimby controversy.[9] Polemics attempting to delineate Eddy's particular contributions to spiritual healing have raged for one hundred years or more.

On closer examination of the original writing of both Quimby and Eddy, it is evident that there is an essential difference in their respective teachings. Yet both were engaged in a unique struggle to hammer out a definitive terminology that would provide structure and format to mental healing. Part of the early controversy over Eddy's movement seems to have stemmed not only from her rejection of conventional medical practice but also from her boldness as a woman in a patriarchal culture to found a new religious tradition. However, Eddy's vigilant protection of what she perceived to be Divine Revelation led to her inability to allow strong women to remain in her movement.[10] Many of the men and the more compliant women of her entourage remained under her autocratic control. Yet it was Eddy's success as an administrator and religious paragon that gave permission to women to organize and establish institutionalized forms of new religious movements.

ORGANIZED NEW THOUGHT
FOUNDED BY EMMA CURTIS HOPKINS

While the New Thought and Christian Science movements have been historically related, today they operate along widely divergent avenues. New Thought was founded pragmatically and organizationally by the charismatic Emma Curtis Hopkins (1849–1925).[11] Emma Curtis was born on September 2, 1849, in Killingly, Connecticut. She was a schoolteacher and the oldest of nine children of a prominent family of New England colonial heritage. She married George Hopkins, also a schoolteacher, in 1874 and had a son, John Carver, in 1875. Hopkins had studied with Eddy (1883) in Boston and had served as editor of the *Christian Science Journal* in 1884–85. After being discharged from her editorial position and excommunicated by Eddy in 1885, Hopkins and another student, Mary Plunkett, relocated to Chicago and founded the Emma Curtis Hopkins College of Christian Science in 1886. It was not long before Hopkins had secured the pacesetter position in promoting New Thought.

Like Eddy, Hopkins perceived the universe to be based in a religious idealism that saw God as Good, Truth, Love, Substance, and First Cause. Evil was not an embodied reality but a facet of erroneous thinking. God was Divine Mind, a universal principle, not an anthropomorphic deity. Also like Eddy, Hopkins used personal terms to talk about the integral components of God, such as Father, Mother, God. Unlike the founders of Theosophy and Spiritualism, Hopkins first attempted to interpret her metaphysical principles within the framework of ecclesiastical Christianity. Originally believing Christian Science to be the spirit of the newer ideas and specific methods for divine healing that heralded the Second Coming of Christ in the world, Hopkins and others of her time used the term Christian Science in a generic way to denote the metaphysical healing process. Of course, this widespread use of the term a century ago has served to confuse people since that time who have become accustomed to think that orthodox Christian Science was the sole purveyor of that term. Actually, the coupling of the two words "Christian" and "Science" was first used in 1850 in a book by the Reverend William Adams, titled *The Elements of Christian Science*, so neither Quimby nor Eddy was the first to coin the term.

A significant feature that early New Thought shared with several other new American religious groups, such as Spiritualism, Theosophy, and the Holiness movement, was its openness to the leadership of women that had been forbidden in mainstream denominations. Concomitant with this new freedom, women assumed pivotal positions as editors, owners, and publishers of early New Thought journals and magazines. It was Hopkins who orchestrated the paradigm shift and decidedly feminist bent of early New Thought. This pioneering spirit encouraged women to seek pulpits of power and prestige that had previously been denied them. Hopkins not only ordained women, empowering them to teach, preach, and heal, but declared the Holy Spirit, the third person of the Trinity, to be female. Hopkins's assertion of a threefold principle that she developed in an essay titled "Trinity" denotes the age of the Father as a patriarchal rulership. The time of Jesus as the Son is depicted in the Gospels, and the age of the Holy Spirit is believed to be the unfolding of the centuries since the death of Jesus. The age of the Holy Spirit or Comforter is the era when feminine energy would be recognized and celebrated. She saw the metaphysical movement as a significant historical signpost that this was indeed happening. Not writing for a scholarly audience, Hopkins did not use citations, so it is difficult to tell whether she knew of a similar trinitarian paradigm developed by Joachim of Fiore in the twelfth century.

Through Hopkins's teachings at her college of Christian Science, the Hopkins Metaphysical Association was created and named for her by an initial class of students, many of whom journeyed to Chicago to study with her. By 1887 these Hopkins's associations were linked together in a loosely affiliated coast-to-coast network of about twenty-one individual groups. However, conflict developed. Some of the early graduates wanted to use the alternative healing methods as marketable strategies for economic support in their private practices. As a result of this secularization, Hopkins reassessed her sacred commitment to divine healing. Several notable issues fostered a change in plans. First, in response to the millennial ideas circulating in her day, Hopkins interpreted the third era of the time of the Holy Spirit to mean a great and definitive change would occur in the world. She used the rapidly shifting roles of women as an example of the emergence of this New Age that empowered women. In an autobiographical statement, she declared that "woman, the bearer . . . is stepping . . . out of her character or role . . . with such force" that her associates stand by with astonishment.[12] Second, during her childhood on her parents' farm, she had experienced a vision to found a hospital for poor, sick children. This led her to study with Eddy and explore her controversial healing modality. Hopkins, a practical visionary, embraced spiritual healing in order to promote a more ideal world. Believing Christian Science to be a divinely inspired, age-old spiritual process, she consequently bridged the gap between college and seminary while emphasizing the holiness of her ministry.

Hopkins was an innovator whose ideas were not cloned from either Quimby or Eddy. Certainly, the radical feminist viewpoints that she quickly implemented in her network of ministries bear little or no resemblance to these forebearers. Quimby was preoccupied with the healing of the individual. Eddy was preoccupied with creating institutional Christian Science. Hopkins's focus was the dissemination of Christian Science Truth as a catalyst for spiritual, social, and economic change. Consequently, she founded the Christian Science Theological Seminary in Chicago in 1888. Its mission statement included:

> The Bibles of all times and nations are compared: Their miracles are shown to
> be the results of one order of reasoning, and the absence of miracles shown to

be the result of another order of reasoning. . . . At this Seminary the teachings of inspired writers are proved to be identical with the native inspirations of all minds in common. . . . We perceive that inherently there is one judgment in all mankind alike. It is restored by the theology taught here. With its restoration we find health, protection, wisdom, strength, prosperity.[13]

Her students would matriculate on two levels. The first-level students were practitioners. Only those taking the advanced course taught personally by her would be ordained as ministers. Her graduates, first of the college and then the seminary, earned for her the epithet "teacher of teachers" of the New Thought movement. At the first graduation ceremony, Hopkins spoke "against the old dispensation and with one voice declared for a new and a true, wherein the poor may be taught and befriended, women walk fearless and glad, and childhood be safe and free."[14] A New Thought publication called *Christian Science*, founded and edited by Ida Nichols, one of her able students, became a key publishing arm with Hopkins as the star writer. An abundance of New Thought periodicals and schools, many founded by women, sprang up from San Francisco to Boston.[15] Until the advent of her student organizations, there was no clearly developed and organized New Thought movement. Individual schools or particular groups were lone enterprises limited to single locations. It was her prophetic vision and administrative ability, coupled with a strong commitment to New Thought, that fortified the network enough to give the movement its pivotal foundation. She believed that the reemergence of the metaphysical tools of spiritual healing, its principles of prosperity, harmonious living, and spiritual serenity would transform the world.

From 1888 until 1895, she managed her theological seminary and dispatched missionaries not only to outreach locations throughout the country but to serve as advocates for social, economic, and educational justice for the disenfranchised. She sent delegates and advisers to the Women's Christian Temperance Union (WCTU) and the Women's Federal Labor Union in Chicago. One of her early students, Frances Lord, author of *Christian Science Healing: Its Principles and Practices* (1888), carried the word abroad to England. Mary Plunkett withdrew from Hopkins's ministry in 1888, taught in New York City, and became a missionary to New Zealand in 1890. In 1893 Hopkins journeyed to England and lectured there. These and other mission journeys made New Thought an American export.

Hopkins was a prodigious writer, publishing in pamphlet form, in New Thought journals, and in the *Chicago Inter-Ocean* newspaper. Her texts, including *Class Lessons 1888* and *Scientific Christian Mental Practice*, written during her Chicago years, continue to be read and studied by healing practitioners today. Hopkins's rigorous training program insured that New Thought was firmly entrenched and deeply etched on the theological map of America. Hopkins, in a revolutionary stance, had forthrightly assumed the role of a bishop and ordained the founders of the first generation of New Thought ministries into a new religion.

Her seminary had graduated over 350 people, primarily women, and had ordained another 111 people as advanced graduates who were personally tutored by her and qualified as ministers. Her graduates, first of the college, then the seminary, included Kate Bingam, teacher of Nona E. Brooks and Fannie James, who with Malinda Cramer began Divine Science in Denver, Colorado, and Annie Rix and Charles Militz, who founded Homes of Truth on the West Coast. The most influential of her ordinands were Charles and Myrtle Fillmore, the cofounders of the Unity School of Christianity in Kansas City, Missouri, who were ordained in 1891. Unity is the largest New Thought ministry today.[16] Toward the latter part of her life, Hopkins (by then a reclusive mystic who saw students only one on one) taught a young Ernest Holmes her newer ways, and he subsequently established Religious Science in Los Angeles, California. Another of her graduates, Charles Burnell, who met and married Mary Lamereaux while matriculating at Hopkins's seminary, has had an endowed chair dedicated to his memory in the Religious Studies Department at Stanford University in Palo Alto, California.

HOPKINS'S LATER YEARS

In 1895, Hopkins, weary after a nine-year sojourn as founder and CEO of a new religious movement, closed the doors of her theological seminary in Chicago and relocated to New York. Content that her bright, energetic students and able lieutenants would continue to sow the pragmatic seeds of New Thought, she turned her attentions to a different type of ministerial effort. She continued to send her "International Bible Lessons" to the *Chicago Inter-Ocean* newspaper, where they were published until 1898. Countless numbers of religious people read her metaphysical scriptural interpretations throughout the eight years she wrote her newspaper column. Hopkins, reclusive by nature and mystical by temperament, continued her ministry in New York with a different format. She no longer used Christian contexts as much for a springboard to promote her doctrines. Her thinking had become more eclectic.

Throughout her remaining years, she lived in several elegant residential hotels in Manhattan, renting a suite of two or three rooms, where she taught her twelve lessons in mysticism and saw her students during private appointments. Her last abode was the Iroquois Hotel, where she mentored and ministered to the intelligentsia who were the avant garde of art, literature, and drama. Her students included radical journalist Hutchins Hapgood (writer for the *New York Globe*), and his wife, Neith Boyce, feminist writer and playwright for the Provincetown Players, who were pacesetters in modern theater,[17] as well as Elizabeth Duncan, the older sister and teacher of Isadora, and the founder of the progressive Duncan school for children. Another student, Mabel Dodge Luhan, was an upper-class socialite turned social reformer who married Antonio Luhan, a Native American from the pueblo near Taos, New Mexico. Together, they fought for social justice and Native American rights. Mabel Luhan, strongly encouraged by Hopkins to write, became an important chronicler of not only the lives of these avant-garde personages but their immense contributions to sociohistorical progress.[18]

A parallel avenue of the introduction of New Thought into avant-garde culture came through the Heterodoxy Club of Greenwich Village in New York. This organization was a secular collective for radical women who openly flouted the status quo. They were actively involved in labor reform, suffrage, and settlement house projects. Several of its members, including Mabel Dodge Luhan, were closely associated with New Thought, as well as Florence Woolston Guy, editor of the *Woman Voter*, who was married to writer David Seabury.[19] Seabury was the younger son of Julius and Annetta Dresser, whose older brother Horatio authored the first *History of the New Thought Movement*, published in 1919. Seabury, a psychologist, wrote in the genre of New Thought and used his mother's maiden name to distinguish himself from his celebrated family.

Other prominent students of Hopkins were Robert B. (Bobby) Jones, who was a gifted stage designer and business partner of Eugene O'Neill; Emilie Hapgood, a tireless worker for African American rights who sponsored the first all-black theater troupe to perform on Broadway; Maurice Stern, a gifted Russian-born artist; and Selena Chamberlain, the teacher of Emmet Fox (1886–1951), one of the most celebrated and successful New Thought writers and ministers of all time. His pamphlets and texts continue to be reprinted and sold in metaphysical bookstores.

Hopkins continued to write and teach until 1923, when her health began to deteriorate from congestive heart failure. Afterward, her ability to work became more sporadic. She was busy in those New York years, with private appointments from early in the morning until late at night. The only times she did not schedule private appointments were the days she lectured in Boston and Philadelphia. Much like a good general, she saw herself on duty at headquarters for as many hours as she could be available for the troops. A quintessential mystic, she perceived herself to be married to God and her work to be a corollary of God's will on Earth. Her marriage to George Hopkins had begun to flounder in 1886, when she moved to Chicago. After initially making the move with her, George Hopkins soon returned to New England, where he resumed his career as a high school teacher. Putting God before man, she never returned to him, and he finally divorced her in 1900 for abandonment. Her son, John Carver, died in 1905.

Hopkins, the mystical idealist, fulfilled her early childhood vision to found a hospital for sick, destitute children. The world became her hospital without walls and its inhabitants the poor, sick children. Her particular therapeutic modality was the healing and prosperity precepts of the newer ways administered through silent communion to the multitudes who suffered, seeking peace from their problems. Most important, she taught, mentored, and ordained those who, as exemplary role models and dedicated missionaries, would take these spiritual principles around the world and extend them into the upcoming century and next millennium. In a moment of prophecy, several years before her death, she spoke enthusiastically of the spirit of the New Age and those who embodied the spirit. The quest for spiritual healing and prosperous, harmonious lifestyles became especially embodied in the equalitarian ideals of the New Age movement through the indelible spiritual imprint of the enigmatic mystic who was married to God. Hopkins passed away quietly on April 8, 1925, in Killingly, Connecticut, her birthplace. Her writings and teachings were kept alive for some years by the High Watch Ministry, under the direction of her younger sister Estelle Darrow Carpenter.

Hopkins's role as master teacher, organizer, and mentor helped power the processes of idealistic thinking that fueled new modes of iconoclastic behavior. Her teachings as a monist and perennial philosopher demonstrated an intuitive and experiential awareness of cosmic unity. These teachings were appreciably different from the consensus reality of the societal norm. Hopkins shared with others of the time, such as William James, and with the much earlier Transcendentalists, philosophical ideas that stretched the parameters of human imagination. Today, research unveiling new dimensions and perspectives of consciousness is being reported in quantum and relativity physics. These fresh paradigms present serious challenges to the Newtonian-Cartesian worldview that supports ideas of a mechanistic universe based upon a Newtonian understanding of linear causality. Current research indicates that on a cellular level, cosmic unity may be somewhat more than just the experiential awareness of some mystics. An example of a New Age organization that resonates to a wedding of ancient mystical thought with that of quantum and relativity physics is the American Gnostic School under the direction of J. Z. Knight, near Yelm, Washington. The students are encouraged to delve into both science and spirituality as salient avenues for self-transformation.

INSTITUTIONALIZED NEW THOUGHT

In 1899 in Hartford, Connecticut, proponents of metaphysical religion held a convention that was the forerunner of the International New Thought Alliance (INTA), organized in 1914 and still active today. With an infancy running parallel with growth explosions in the social and medical sciences and other interdisciplinary areas, the INTA encouraged and supported individualism among its members. A blending of principles has resulted in a synthesis with these other fields, adding exciting dimensions to the health sciences and strengthening the global ambiance of New Thought as a forerunner in universal and multidimensional thinking.

New Thought, by its independent nature, continues to foster innovative development within the American religious arena. For instance, in 1992 the Unity-Progressive Council was established in Clearwater, Florida. This council is not a member of the Association of Unity Churches (AUC) or affiliated with the Unity School of Christianity. This organization has founded the Unity Progressive Seminary, which is committed to equalitarian principles and has classes open to people of all faiths. Their motto is *Libertas et Veritas*—Freedom and Truth. This particular group intends to prepare its graduates to pursue the highest spiritual ideals in order to become outstanding leaders in both secular and religious areas.[20] They have also received a charter to begin the Emma Curtis Hopkins College of the Liberal Arts.

There are many smaller independent New Thought–type churches that are not affiliated with the more well-known arteries of New Thought. Some of these truth teachers and pastors are eclectic in view and choose the themes of their ministries from a multiplicity of New Thought ideas, some synthesizing with New Age or Spiritualists' precepts. An example of this type of integration is the ministry of the Reverend William L. Lamb of the Lighthouse of Truth in Tampa, Florida. Now semiretired after more than thirty years of service to humanity, he devoted his educational ministry to the spiritual healing precepts of New Thought, specifically through the work of Emma Curtis Hopkins and some of her ordinands, such as Charles and Myrtle Fillmore of Unity. He also incorporated Spiritualists' beliefs and integrated the teachings of independent Theosophist Alice A. Bailey, who founded the Arcane school, as well as those of earlier Theosophists. He grounded these metaphysical principles in the latest pragmatic theories in psychology and psychiatry, such as the work of Robert Assagioli and contemporary psychotherapists Alice Miller and J. Konrad Stettbacher. His students, many following the model established by Hopkins's seminary a century earlier, studied locally and moved on. For some years, his students could choose from a wide spectrum of personally prepared class lessons and tapes through correspondence courses. These students have circumnavigated the globe, a significant number of them committed metaphysical practitioners drawn from the fields of education and medicine. Lamb, a collector of antique books, has assisted in the republishing costs of keeping Hopkins's books in print and also has been a longtime affiliate with the Spiritual Frontiers Fellowship association. Today, while semiretired and similar to Hopkins in being somewhat reclusive, he selectively mentors an inner circle of dedicated advanced graduates, who astutely challenge the cultural norms, while serving on the frontlines of the human service professions. Other comprehensive ministries that follow models of synthesis acknowledge the cross-fertilization process that has occurred between New Thought and New Age tenets.

In contrast to an eclectic ministry, there are those in New Thought who seek to reinforce the boundaries that segregate and separate them, hoping to retain the original purity of principles contained in early New Thought. The Ministry of

Truth, International, in Chicago, under the direction of the Reverend Marge Flotron, a former executive in the advertising industry, is one such organization. Flotron does not have a congregational ministry, yet has dedicated her nation-wide outreach programs specifically to the teachings from Hopkins's books. Her ministry has republished an extensive list of Hopkins's works that are available through mail order. Flotron guest lectures and sponsors seminars drawn solely from Hopkins's metaphysical lessons and has dedicated her life to preserving the "priceless works" of Hopkins. She maintains a membership in the International New Thought Alliance. Other New Thought ministries operate at varying degrees along this continuum from synthesis to segregation.

REFLECTIONS OF NEW THOUGHT
IN THE SOCIOCULTURAL MILIEU

Perhaps more important to American culture than the communal forms of New Thought expression is the way its modalities of healing, prosperity, and positive thinking have been carried into other more mainstream sacred and secular spheres of society. Ralph Waldo Trine's (1866–1958) *In Tune with the Infinite* has sold over two million copies since it was published in 1897. The message of universal religion permeates all his works. The oneness with Infinite Life and the Power that funds this life was one of his significant messages. Trine was not an innovator; perhaps for this reason he has attracted a following far and beyond most New Thought writers. According to historian of religion Charles Braden, Henry Ford is reputed to have credited his reading of Trine's book with his over-whelming success as an entrepreneur, and "he gave hundreds of copies of it to other industrialists."[21] Norman Vincent Peale (who as a young man read much of the work of New Thought writers such as Ernest Holmes) wrote the *Power of Positive Thinking*, first published in 1952. A much later work, *The Positive Power of Jesus Christ* (1980), teaches a distressed woman to thank God for helping her now instead of hysterically imploring him to begin do so. (This is a variation of decreeing that was introduced by Hopkins.) Robert Schuller, pastor of the Crystal Cathedral in Anaheim, California, offers a variation of positive thought based on Peale's work in his promotion of "possibility thinking" as a prescription for individual and collective advancement. Substantial material from Hopkins's text *High Mysticism* (1923) and her earlier works was used in the teaching manual for the International Order of St. Luke the Physician, a group dedicated to spiritual healing, founded by Dr. John Gayner Banks, an Episcopal priest. Many Americans as adults today grew up to the positive proclamation poetry of Ella Wheeler Wilcox. Writer Charlotte Perkins Gilman lived by New Thought principles, although she never formally affiliated with a ministry. The novels of Lloyd C. Douglas, especially the film *Magnificent Obsession* (1929) taken from the novel, did much to promote positive thinking and New Thought ideals among a secular population.[22] Tent-preacher-turned-television-evangelist Oral Roberts has been quick to jump on the bandwagon for harmonious positive thinking. His "something good is going to happen to you, today" has consistently reverberated over the airwaves for a number of years with the broadcasts of the electronic church.

FEMINIST SPIRITS IN REBELLION[23]

Many religious groups connect healing with divine intervention. However, the spiritual healing espoused by New Thought that is done silently or forthrightly is not to be confused with the faith-healing phenomenon associated with Pentecostal-type churches or the miraculous healing tradition found in Roman Catholicism. Faith-healing in America is normally associated with the Pentecostal family of religion, a decidedly Protestant concept that does not make use of sacred shrines, holy sites, and saints, as Roman Catholicism does. It is an emotional and sometimes flamboyant religious expression based on the holiness concept of the nineteenth century that understands transformation to take place as a form of conversion or spiritual renewal.[24] J. Gordon Melton, historian of American religious movements, documents that the revivalism of the holiness movement gave women permission to speak and lead prayer. In fact, during the later part of the nineteenth century, "no religious movement . . . was so open to female leadership."[25] (This movement led into the Pentecostal movement of the twentieth century.) In an extensive theological treatise penned in 1859, Phoebe Palmer defended the God-given right of women to preach when women were forbidden to speak in public. Palmer and other firebrands like her in the holiness movement, according to Melton, "pioneered the ordination of women." When Hopkins mobilized and empowered largely middle-class women to teach, preach, and heal and assumed the authority of a bishop to ordain clergy, a great deal of sociotheological agitation promoting the right of women to speak God's word had already occurred.

DECREES, AFFIRMATIONS, AND PROSPERITY

In New Thought, the divine goodness of the world is manifested through health, prosperity, joy, and love. To mentally deny the opposites causes them to disappear. Hopkins also added creative visualization as a process to promote change. To allow a poverty-stricken child a glimpse of a prosperous lifestyle would replace visions of lack and give the child the images of abundance needed to reshape her or his world. Hopkins had a mystical belief that a decree verbalized at noon occurred at a time of cosmological balance. When the sun cast no shadow, the opposite of the decree would not also be called forth in an attempt at balance in a universe governed by dualism. Many of her services that were open to the public at her theological seminary were scheduled for noon. This practice of decreeing is stronger and more intense than an affirmation. For that moment, each person, no matter how plebeian her lifestyle, becomes nobility. The power of royal imperative transforms the consciousness of the speaker to take charge and shape events in his or her life.

For example, Hopkins stated: "We have no business to have sickness or pain or poverty of unhappiness . . . when Christians are poor do they talk as if they had chosen poverty . . . they are poor because they can't help it and their whining is pretty good evidence. . . . Do not allow yourselves to believe in misery . . . decree against it. . . . There shall nevermore be any poverty known among us."[26]

Hopkins's student Frances Lord systematically organized and correlated Hopkins's work about prosperity in her previously mentioned book published in 1888. This was the first introduction of selectively chosen prosperity concepts that specifically affirmed abundance to a New Thought audience. Consequently, early New Thought proponents were quick to wed sound business practices with metaphysical principles. This pragmatic union produced prosperity and abundance. Successful businesspeople tend to follow those guidelines either deliberately or intuitively. Affirmations quickly became a theological foundation of the New Thought movement, where they were considered to be types of prayers. "I now have wealth and abundance" would be affirmed by someone who had a rapidly diminishing or depleted savings account. In New Thought, only God and Divine Reality are real. People suffer lack through erroneous ideas that manifest as viable in the mundane world. By affirming health, prosperity, or whatever needs transforming, one is changing the ideas and creating the perfection of what already is perceived to be metaphysically real.

In this view, illness and poverty are not a genuine part of God's world. Instead, abundance in health, success, and financial structure can be affirmed, as this is believed to be what God wants. Affirmations directly link New Age thinking with New Thought as the theological antecedent. In fact, as psychology fought for its inclusion as a legitimate science, it too absorbed positive affirmations from New Thought that could be used to train the mind. The idea that the unconscious shaped the conscious world and deliberately constructed affirmations could be used to reorder and remake the unconscious world developed. The conscious mind reprogrammed its repository of ideas by replacing images of lack through mentally or verbally creating positive thoughts that re-created for the individual more balanced and harmonious cognitive thought processes. Someone who needed to diet would affirm and visualize a slim, trim, healthy body, as if already thin.

Other groups in this century seized the idea of decreeing and this precept became a prominent feature of the "I AM" group started by Guy Warren Ballard in the 1930s. From there it became diffused throughout more contemporary groups such as the New Age Church of Christ and the Church Universal and Triumphant, where a verbal variation developed in the cadence in which it is spoken.[27] Groups that interface psychology and religion, particularly those dedicated to self-help, also set up workshops and seminars to teach the transformational journey through the power of affirmation and creative visualization. Very few teachers of the contemporary therapeutic process know the exact origins of the precepts they have established these self-help and educational programs by.

CONCLUSION

While the New Age seems new, it is not. It is constructed on the building blocks of the occult and metaphysical religious traditions, namely, New Thought, Spiritualism, and Theosophy. The mental healing sciences enjoyed a concurrent development with academic explosions in scientific knowledge that melded a "religious technology" for aggressive, ambitious Americans. According to Melton, the movement called New Age is a social product of the later 1960s that emerged around 1971.[28] While accepting religious tenets from the Eastern traditions, the New Age owes much of its heritage to roots deeply embedded in the philosophy and lifestyles of Western culture. The New Age emerged as a primal force for transformation and the seminal method to ordain change was healing, whether healing the individual of various physical or psychosomatic ailments or healing the natural environment from the sustained assaults of industrialization upon fragile ecosystems. Because of the innovative ideas about healing, the metaphysical movements, particularly New Thought, produced dramatic alternatives to societal norms. These resourceful principles appeared to defy conventional medical practice and in many cases diminished the power of the medical community to control individual patients. For example, allopathic medical treatment based on a germ theory of illness that treated the site of disease and not the total person was challenged by holistic precepts of mind, body, and spirit integration.

This much remains clear: the harmonious and egalitarian principles of New Thought expressed the individualist quest for meaningful religious experience. Profound optimism and positive affirmations toward prosperity and health blended quite readily into mainstream culture, providing the building blocks for a New Age religion. However, there has been a downside for New Thought. As a response to the initial challenge of grandparenting the New Age, several older, institutionalized branches of New Thought have very recently disavowed specific New Age teachings, such as astrology, pyramid power, and trance channeling, in an attempt to protect and insulate their foundational teachings. Examples of this recent reticence to merge more closely with New Age developments has resulted in new policy decisions taken by the International New Thought Alliance, the Association of Unity Churches, and the Unity School of Christianity. Recent critical discourse has targeted New Thought traditions as contrary to (in some cases) and different from (in other cases) New Age thinking. What the theological future holds for these two movements is unclear. Both are young in terms of their longevity (1880s for New Thought), with New Age being by far the younger (1970s). Perhaps the dialectical and theological tension between the two movements indicates that the initial transmission of idealist precepts and methodologies from the older New Thought tradition to fund the dynamism of the New Age has been exhausted. New Age occult encroachment upon the mystical and pragmatic parameters of New Thought fuels the current controversy. The fear seems to be that the religious idealism of New Thought[29] will be seriously altered, or worse, subsumed by the more pervasive New Age movement. However separate or intermeshed the two movements become in the future, the herald of harmonious living embodied in the healing tenets and prosperity principles of the New Thought movement from the 1880s until the present has provided a significant *Zeitgeist for* the New Age.

NOTES

1. Sidney Ahlstrom, *A Religious History of the American People* (New Haven: Yale University Press, 1974), p. 1019.
2. Danny Jorgensen, quoted by Gail M. Harley in *Emma Curtis Hopkins: Forgotten Founder of New Thought* (Syracuse, NY: Syracuse University Press, 2002).
3. Ibid., p. v.
4. Dell de Chant, "New Thought and the New Age," *New Age Encyclopedia* (Detroit: Yale Research Institution), p. 222.
5. Jorgensen, *Emma Curtis Hopkins*, p. vi.
6. Shawn Michael Trimble, "Spiritualism and Channeling," in *America's Alternative Religions*, ed. Timothy Miller (Albany: State University of New York Press, 1995), p. 331. This article is a brief discussion about the historical developments of Spiritualism in American culture. See also a short discussion of Theosophy in Robert Ellwood and Catherine Wessinger, "The Feminism of Universal Brotherhood: Women in the Theosophical Movement," in *Women's Leadership in Marginal Religions: Explorations Outside the Mainstream*, ed. Catherine Wessinger (Urbana and Chicago: University of Illinois Press, 1993), p. 69.
7. William James, *The Varieties of Religious Experience* (New York: Penguin Books, 1982), p. 94.
8. John Simmons, "Christian Science and American Culture," *America's Alternative Religions* (Albany: State University of New York Press, 1995), p. 65. This short article offers some interesting discussion about the historical contributions of Christian Science.
9. The first book about New Thought history, titled *The History of the New Thought Movement*, was written by Horatio Dresser (Crowell, 1919). The book is problematic because Dresser was a philosopher, not a trained historian. He ignored the signif-

icant development of organized New Thought in the West and Midwest. For details, see J. Gordon Melton, "New Thought's Hidden History: Emma Curtis Hopkins, Forgotten Founder," *META* 1, no. 1 (1993). Also in Harley, *Emma Curtis Hopkins.*

10. Stillson Judah in *The History and Philosophy of the Metaphysical Movements in America* (Philadelphia: Westminister Press, 1967) discusses this, as does Charles Braden in *Spirits in Rebellion* (Dallas: Southern Methodist University Press, 1963), p. 138.

11. The definitive biography of Hopkins, *Emma Curtis Hopkins: Forgotten Founder of New Thought*, written by Gail M. Harley, was published by Syracuse University Press in 2002. This biography attempts to correct all errors in previous literature. Every single book, document, article, or essay that contained even scanty information about Hopkins held significant errors in birthdate, number of children in family, date and place of death, date and year of leaving Christian Science, ownership of periodicals or establishment of a church, etc. The fact that so much confusion has existed about her demonstrates that her immense contributions to American religious history have been eclipsed.

Hopkins, the enigmatic mystic, believed she was married to God and that the cause of metaphysical healing to which she dedicated her life was more important than self-promotion. She did not write an autobiography or leave a paper trail about her personal life that would make it easy for scholars to reclaim her. Yet snippets of information emerge sporadically. It is to be hoped that with the newer research findings in print that more material about her and the understudied New Thought movement in America will be recovered.

12. "The Trinity, Isaiah 51," *Christian Science* 1, no. 4 (December 1888): 77–82, and its conclusion one month later in *Christian Science* 1, no. 5 (January 1889): 109–13.

13. *Christian Science Seminary Catalogue*, year ending November 30, 1893. This is the only year for which an original document has been recovered. It is housed in the archives of the Institute for the Study of American Religion (ISAR) in Santa Barbara, California, and has been shared with this writer by Dr. J. Gordon Melton, director. A complete citation of the mission statement is also quoted in Harley, *Emma Curtis Hopkins.*

14. The entire addresses given by a number of prominent women, such as Elizabeth Boynton Harbert, women's editor of the *Chicago Inter-Ocean* newspaper, are reported in *Christian Science* 1, no. 6 (February 1889), and *Christian Science* 1, no. 7 (March 1889). The most complete collection of these periodicals is found in the ISAR archives.

15. For a complete enumeration of the astonishing number of schools and periodicals, see Gary L. Ward, "The Feminist Theme of Early New Thought," ISAR Occasional Paper no. 1 (Santa Barbara: Institute for the Study of American Religion, 1989,) pp. 18–19. Also quoted in Harley, *Emma Curtis Hopkins.*

16. For a brief summary, see Harley, "New Thought and the Harmonial Family" in *American's Alternative Religions*, pp. 324–28. For a thorough discussion of Myrtle Fillmore and Unity, see Dell de Chant, "Myrtle Fillmore and Her Daughters: An Observation and Analysis of the Role of Women in Unity," in Wessinger, *Women's Leadership*, p. 102.

17. Hutchins Hapgood at that time had written *The Autobiography of a Thief* (New York: Fox Duffield, 1903; reprinted, New York: Johnson Reprint Corporation, 1970) and *The Spirit of the Ghetto* (New York: Funk and Wagnall, 1902; reprinted, Cambridge: Harvard University Press, 1967), and he is probably best remembered for *A Victorian in the Modern World* (New York: Harcourt Brace and Co., 1939). Neith Boyce was the author of various works, including *The Folly of Others* (1904; reprinted, Freeport, NY: Books for Libraries Press, 1970). She originally worked for Lincoln Steffans at the *Commercial Advertiser.*

18. Mable Dodge Luhan, *New York Movers and Shakers*, vol. 2 of Intimate Memories Series (New York: Harcourt Brace and Co., 1933). She devotes chapter 17 to Hopkins, although references to her are peppered throughout the book.

19. Judith Schwarz, *Radical Feminists of Heterodoxy* (Norwich, VT: New Victoria Publishers, Inc., 1986).

20. Harley, "New Thought," in *America's Alternative Religions*, p. 327.

21. Braden, *Spirits in Rebellion*.

22. Ahlstrom, *A Religious History*, pp. 1030–1031.

23. The subhead is taken from Charles S. Braden's groundbreaking book, *Spirits in Rebellion* (Dallas: Southern Methodist University Press, 1963). Material recently recovered indicates that Emma Curtis Hopkins was the founder of organizational New Thought. Without this documentation, Braden states that it was probably her mysticism that influenced New Thought more than anything else. This is partially true. Her pragmatic ability to translate New Thought to a missionary movement and her quintessential mysticism are inextricably linked, the former to organizational development and the latter to the spirit of New Thought.

24. David Kinsley, *Health, Healing, and Religion: A Cross-Cultural Perspective* (Upper Saddle River, NJ: Prentice Hall, 1996), pp. 119–48. Kinsley gives an interesting overview of faith healing that relates it to shamanic forms of healing in various cultures. He does not address the healing concepts in New Thought or Christian Science, which would have made an intriguing comparison.

25. J. Gordon Melton, "Emma Curtis Hopkins: A Feminist of the 1880s and Mother of New Thought," in *Women's Leadership*, pp. 88–101.

26. Hopkins, "Hopkins Metaphysical Association," *Christian Science* 1 (October 1888): 40.

27. J. Gordon Melton, Jerome Clark, and Aidan A. Kelly, *New Age Almanac* (New York: Visible Ink Press, 1991), p. 306.

28. Ibid., p. 4.

29. De Chant, "New Thought," p. 222.

REFERENCES

Ahlstrom, Sidney. *A Religious History of the American People*. New Haven: Yale University Press, 1974.

Braden, Charles. *Spirits in Rebellion*. Dallas: Southern Methodist University Press, 1963.

Harley, Gail. *Emma Curtis Hopkins: Forgotten Founder of New Thought*. Syracuse, NY: Syracuse University Press, 2002.

Judah, Stillson. *The History and Philosophy of the Metaphysical Movements in America*. Philadelphia: Westminster Press, 1967.

Melton, J. Gordon, Jerome Clark, and Aidan A. Kelly. *New Age Almanac*. New York: Visible Ink Press, 1991.

Miller, Timothy, ed. *America's Alternative Religions*. Albany: State University of New York Press, 1995.

Wessinger, Catherine, ed. *Women's Leadership in Marginal Religions: Explorations Outside the Mainstream*. Urbana and Chicago: University of Illinois Press, 1993.

NEW AGE GROUPS AND RELIGIONS

5

EDGAR CAYCE AND REINCARNATION

Past-Life Readings as Religious Symbology

J. Gordon Melton

When Edgar Cayce (1877–1945) died, he left behind a unique resource: complete transcripts of over sixteen hundred readings he had given in the last decades of his life to the hundreds of people who came to him for help and advice. Subsequently, under the leadership of his son Hugh Lynn, the Association for Research and Enlightenment and the Edgar Cayce Foundation mobilized thousands of people to explore and study the transcripts, which were cross-indexed and proved the inspiration for numerous books that have attempted systematically to present the information and teachings scattered in bits and pieces haphazardly through the readings. Thus, by compiling the many life readings on Atlantis, association writers developed a coherent picture of what Cayce taught about that lost continent.

In more recent years, the publication and spread of the Cayce literature became a major factor in the emergence of what is loosely termed the New Age movement. For example, one can trace the speculation on crystal power, which has emerged as such a prominent teaching among New Age groups, directly to the compilation into a booklet of Cayce's rather meager and scattered references to crystals in the readings.

Among the major themes in the writings are several other key New Age concerns, including alternative health (possibly the most explored material in the Cayce readings), astrology (the least explored in relation to the significant amount of attention Cayce devoted to it), and reincarnation. Reincarnation, as developed in the hundreds of past-life readings given by Cayce, could be seen as the single most

Written for this anthology.

prominent concern of the Cayce materials. For over thirty years, Cayce went into trance and offered people information on "previous lives lived in planet earth" while interpreting their significance for present existence. These life readings, along with readings that specifically asked for elaboration on the material given in the life readings, presented a cosmic metaphysics that many have accepted and used for guidance in their lives.[1] The importance of the reincarnation theme in the Cayce readings has taken on added dimensions in this present generation, with over 20 percent of the American public now professing a belief in reincarnation.

THE EMERGENCE OF REINCARNATION AND CAYCE'S PAST-LIFE READINGS

The idea of reincarnation and the possibility of exploring past lives did not just suddenly emerge in the Cayce readings. Cayce demonstrated his psychic talents on many occasions and had gained some reputation nationally. That fame brought Arthur Lammers to his door. Lammers, a wealthy printer from Dayton, Ohio, walked into Cayce's Selma, Alabama, studio in 1921. He is described by Cayce biographers as a man interested in and a deep student of metaphysics, the occult, esoteric astrology, and Eastern religion. Tibet, Theosophy, and the Great White Brotherhood were his intellectual playground. Initially, Lammers questioned Cayce about these matters only to handle the skepticism of the Bible-believing Christian that Cayce then was.

In November 1923, Lammers paid for Cayce to come from Selma to Dayton, Ohio, along with his wife, Gertrude. Lammers supplied a stenographer while Cayce gave two readings a day for a week. It was at the end of the third of these readings that the famous quotation concerning Lammers appeared: "Third appearance on this plane—He was a monk." In between readings, there were extensive conversations on Lammers's favorite subjects. The final reading consisted of the three life readings (the first of many that Cayce would later give)—for Lammers, Cayce, and a third participant. As a result of the readings and conversations with Lammers, Cayce became quite familiar with his theosophical cosmology, which began to fit conveniently into his other psychic work. Beginning during the week in Dayton, the role of past lives assumed an ever-increasing prominence in Cayce's psychic work and his readings, often under the questioning of those present when he went into trance, enlarged upon themes first mentioned in the past-life readings.

RESEARCHING THE CAYCE MATERIAL

While encouraging this vast amount of writing concerning the Cayce readings, the association has offered little encouragement to what might be termed scholarly treatments of Cayce and his readings. The material remains virgin territory to the intellectual historian ready to discover the many elements of metaphysical/occult thought that Cayce, largely unknowingly, synthesized into the teachings now lodged within the readings. We are completely lacking data of a social scientific nature. Sociologists have neither collected data on the current membership of ARE nor attempted to use the tools of the social sciences in examining the highly quantifiable material Cayce left behind. The motivation to examine critically the Cayce readings is provided by the extraordinary claims made by the leadership of the Association for Research and Enlightenment for Cayce's abilities, as well as the continuing popularity of Cayce's teachings.

Also, while much of the Cayce material is purely metaphysical speculation and hence primarily a matter of faith, the readings do make a number of claims concerning many points of prehistory and medical advice, which are subject to at least some level of independent verification. Reincarnation is an area in which the metaphysical assertions and the more mundane verifiable claims overlap. Thus, individuals may adhere to the basically theosophical worldview of the readings on purely philosophical grounds (primarily a solution to the problem of evil in the concept of karma). However, many members of the association were initially attracted to the readings and now support the acceptance of the metaphysical perspective because of claims of the confirmed accuracy of the more mundane material in the readings that concern historical events or medical advice, only a minuscule part of which have ever been subjected to critical scholarly scrutiny.

One major discouragement to scholarly research is the very bulk of the Cayce records, which consist of the verbatim transcripts from several decades of readings. To make sense of the records, a substantial number would have to be read and analyzed.

The association has, to be sure, conducted some important research as attempts to gain some *external validation* of the teachings. Researchers have asked how the Cayce material conforms to independently verifiable data from other areas of knowledge. Such attempts follow closely the pattern set in the "search for Bridey Murphy" as attempts were made to track down the truth of Bridey Murphy's previous existence and gather any information about her life in Ireland.[2] Parallel research with the Cayce material has centered on information gleaned from the life readings, especially claims about Atlantis and the Holy Land in the time of Jesus. One researcher, following the Bridey Murphy pattern, tracked the evidence suggestive of a possible return of nineteenth-century feminist-prohibitionist Frances Willard.[3]

Attempts to verify the Cayce material in this manner have always followed a fairly consistent pattern. Much *general* data has a high correlation, while *specific* data is neither falsifiable nor verifiable due to the lack of records. (Such proved true in Bridey Murphy's case also).[4] Such a lack of specifics is most evident in the Atlantis material. No single relic exists of Atlantis, though it remains a speculative possibility. There is no record of one RaTa, a priest of Egypt and major recurring character in the Cayce life readings, yet there is also no list of Egyptian priests to check it against. The evidence is *consistently inconclusive.*

Research has also sought to highlight discovered patterns of *internal consistency* within the Cayce readings. Does it present an internal wholeness in its philosophy and content that, in spite of its speculative nature, is a reasonable and satisfying approach to life? The philosophy and worldview found in the readings and articulated through the ARE literature has proved satisfactory to many, but, for those who lack a previous interest in theosophical or Eastern worldviews, is of no particular interest. After all, numerous other psychics have "channeled" a consistent workable speculative cosmology and ethic. The metaphysical speculations become interesting primarily because of the independently verifiable material on such topics as healing, Atlantis, and past lives.

A variety of ways could be suggested to test the Cayce material. However, in spite of its name, with a few rare exceptions, the Association for Research and Enlightenment has demonstrated little interest in, and on occasion even discouraged, "research" in the commonly understood sense of that term. Rather it has behaved in ways more consistent with what we generally think of as a "religious" organization. It has devoted its energies to evangelical (spreading the teachings of Edgar Cayce), organizational (recruiting individuals into study groups), and educational activities (through seminars emphasizing the spiritual metaphysical and practical life-situation implications of the teachings). It has even encouraged several major apologetic volumes to handle the problem of those incidents in which Cayce's psychic abilities undeniably failed him.[5]

Understanding Cayce essentially as a religious teacher (and a myth maker) and the Association for Research and Enlightenment as a religious body suggests a way to move beyond a mere exposition of Cayce's teachings and at the same time to resolve some of the problems in the readings that arise as soon as they are taken literally as presenting either historical or scientific information. Thus laying aside for the moment the immediate question of the factual nature of Cayce's assertions concerning, for example, ancient history or modern medicine, this chapter focuses on the elements of the readings that have emerged as religious symbols and attempts to suggest the manner in which these symbols function.

The great majority of Cayce's readings were for individuals and included (besides an astrological reading) the delineation of (usually) four past lives, each of which was having some karmic effect in the present. As one begins to read a sample of the life readings, it is soon evident that the number of different settings of the past lives presented in Cayce is relatively small. That is, in giving readings to his clients, Cayce chose from a limited number of points in time and places on the world—what I have termed a *time-culture slot*. Further reading reveals not only a repetition of particular time-culture slots but of actual content, so that after a cursory reading of several past-life accounts, one could begin to predict the content. When a person is told that he or she once lived in, for example, ancient Rome, the reader would know immediately what effect that life will have on the person presently. The time-culture slots function as basic symbols to carry the message of the readings.

The high level of repetition in the life readings makes them ideal subjects for a quantitative approach, and quantifying elements of the readings proved immensely useful in uncovering the underlying patterns within the readings and thus revealed some of the symbology employed by Cayce. The quantifying effort began with a count of the total number of past incarnations discussed in the Cayce transcripts and then a selection of a smaller sample for closer scrutiny.

Table1: Settings of incarnations[a]

	Total	Sample
Egypt	1300+	60
America	1200+	64
Colonial Settler		31
Revolution		19
Other		14
Persia	600+	31
Atlantis	500+	19
New Testament	500+	36
Old Testament	400+	19
Ezra and Nehemiah		9
Nebuchadnezzar		3
Other		7
Rome	400+	16
England	300+	13
France	250+	23
Greece	250+	8
Crusades	139	14
India	97	2
Peru	79	0
Gobi	73	9
Scandinavia	74	3
Troy	52	0
German	52	1
Yucatan	41	4
Spain	34	1
All Others	173	5
Total 6514		316

Total column shows the number of incarnations in the life readings #1400–1599 that were used as a representative sample.

[a]The figures were taken from the index card file at the Edgar Cayce Library. Numbers below 150 are exact counts. Those above 150 are approximations made by measuring the thickness of the index cards. They are not exact but close enough for this study.

PATTERNS: THE BASIC DATA

The ARE's efforts to cross-index the Cayce readings greatly assisted the process of dealing with the material in a quantitative way. Table 1 is a table of incarnations.[6] It shows the locations of all the incarnations noted in all the life readings.

By *time-culture slot* is meant the particular place and moment in time and history that an incarnation takes place. Cayce's readings show an extremely limited number of time-culture slots. For example, the largest number of incarnations are listed for Egypt, but they do not cover Egypt's whole history. They are limited to Egypt during the time when RaTa was the main priest. The second entry shows a slight variation in the time-culture slot in that these incarnations vary over America's precolonial history, but they always represent the incarnated person as a settler. The remaining time-culture slots are presented in descending order, Persia during the reign of Uljtd, and so on.

There was one difficulty in quantifying the material in that some countries are mentioned only in connection with another country. Thus, Peru and the Yucatan are significant as locations for incarnation only as the places to which Atlanteans migrated when their homeland was destroyed. Some Grecian incarnations relate to Uljtd's rule in Persia. Thus, a mere fifteen time-culture slots account for approximately 90 percent of all the incarnations that Cayce recounted. Also of note, Cayce asserted that the most recent incarnation mentioned of each sitter was, in almost all cases in which it was mentioned, in America.

The basic symbology of the life readings is the time-culture slots that provide the settings for the particular incarnation and the message that incarnation was said to contain. As will be seen, the variety of messages given in relation to any time-culture slot is equally limited.

THE SAMPLE

The task of covering the life readings of the more than sixteen hundred individuals would be a monumental one, both statistically and in the time consumed in study. The possibility of giving statistical consideration to the whole of the material is open only to someone who is capable of a lengthy stay at Virginia Beach, which has not been possible for this author.

In lieu of a general survey, a more modest project was conceived. A representative sample consisting of all life readings between numbers 1400 and 1599 was selected to be quantified. Singled out for special consideration were the Atlantean and Egyptian incarnations.

Results of this survey indicate that the sample followed the overall pattern of the reading's incarnations. It was from these incarnations that some of the patterns in Table 1 emerged. First, American incarnations were discovered to be divided three ways: those identified as settlers in some part of colonial America, those who took part in the Revolutionary War, and others who include a number involved in either the Gold Rush of 1849 or the New England witchcraft trials. Second, the Old Testament references are primarily from two eras, the time in which Ezra and Nehemiah rebuilt the Wall of Jerusalem and the time of Nebuchadnezzar.

Noticeably absent from the life readings are references to incarnations outside the mainstream of Western cultural history (fewer than 100 out of 6,516), including neglect of Africa south of the Sahara, China, Russia, and Latin America.

Since the vocation followed during the past incarnations was a noticeable, consistent bit of information in the life readings, it was singled out as an item of interest. Because the largest number came from the RaTa period of Egypt, and because of the paucity of published material on this era, it was used as an illustration.[7]

The general picture of Egypt presented in the readings is of a time of civil war in which the pharoah's brother revolted but was defeated. Egypt was the recipient of immigrants from Atlantis. Much of the real power was in the hands of RaTa the high-priest (Edgar Cayce in a former life), who ran the Temples Beautiful and the Temple of Sacrifice. RaTa attempted to "organize religious practices and bring the people to the idea of the one creative principle through the symbology of the sun and the continuance of individual life."[8] The people who supposedly survived from this era to seek a Cayce reading fall roughly into three categories as pictured below in Table 2.

Table 2: Types of incarnations in Egypt

RaTa Incarnations	Number	Percentage
Total in sample	60	100[a]
King's household	20	33
Prince(ss)	(6)	10
Temple	23	38
Priestess	4	6
Other	14	23
Hospital	(4)	6
Granaries	3	5

[a]Percentages have been rounded off and do not add up to 100.

The sample indicates that over three-fourths of these incarnations were either of the king's household, ruling officials and royalty, or temple workers. Of the remaining 23 percent, two occupations, hospital work and being in charge of granaries, took up half. In the relatively small sample, three people are designated as ruler over the granaries.[9] The designated vocation also served as a symbol, and people with the same vocations were given essentially the same information. For example, people who were told that they were priests in their Egyptian incarnation would also be told that they had educational abilities and would find present happiness in an activity that included instructing others.

Beyond the general vocational patterns, a more important pattern of repetition occurs when two individuals were given the same exact reading. This happened more than once. Just in the representative sample, three different men were told that they were the ruler of the granaries of RaTa's Egypt. (No count is available of how many others this happened to.) Significantly, in several occasions, two people were specifically identified as a particular person. The subject of reading number 1432 was identified as the woman taken in adultery in the famous biblical story, and number 295 was also identified as this personage. Two different people were identified as the central figure in the biblical story of the rich young ruler (#2677 and #1416). These patterns indicate the symbolic nature of the material in the life readings.

Further illustration of vocational material came from the most publicized segment of incarnations, those concerned with Atlantis. To give added information, all references in chapter 3 of the popular book *Edgar Cayce on Atlantis* were added to the sample. A picture of Atlantis according to Cayce can be found in this book. These incarnations are listed in Table 3.

Table 3: Types of incarnations in Atlantis[a]

	Chapter 3	#1400-1599	Total	Percentage
Total in Samples, Chapter 3	47	19	66	
Prince(ss and Ruler)	9	6	15	23
Priest and Temple Officials	10	6	16	24
Technicians	14	2	16	24
Other	8	3	11	17
Unknown	6	2	8	12

[a]Total number of Atlantean incarnations: 500+

In Atlantis as in Egypt, there are a large number of rulers and priests, though the significantly large number of technicians and engineers manifests a difference from Egypt. Little or no recognition in the literature published by previous writers on Cayce is given to the vast percentage of references to royalty in the Atlantean readings. In like measure, the writers on Cayce and Atlantis seem to have missed the connection between the vocation and the repetition of what is said to different people who received the readings.[10]

PATTERNS OF DEVIATION

Even though 90 percent of the incarnations fit into fifteen time-culture slots, a total of 537 (out of 6,516) do not fit. In the sample, twenty-three of these deviating incarnations appear (out of 316). The question was asked, is there some reason for the variation? Unfortunately (for the researcher), there is a cloak of anonymity thrown around those people whose readings are on file. (This anonymity, while frustrating, is a necessity for the protection of those who sought a reading). Because of the anonymous nature of the material, the search for patterns ended almost before it was begun. However, from the little bit of biographical data given (date and place of birth), one correlation appeared so often that it could not be ignored. Where there was a deviation in the time-culture slot pattern, *it was often related to the place of birth* of the individual (which may account for the large number of American incarnations). In the representative sample, number 1476 has a Polish incarnation. Number 1476 was born in Poland. The other Polish incarnation was for number 1869, who was born in Warsaw. Many of the Norwegian and "Scandinavian" incarnations are of Norwegian birth (or in one case of Norwegian ancestry). Numbers 1431, 1437, and 1450 are such cases. The Norwegian incarnations are in most cases also related to either Eric the Red or Lief Erickson (the only Norwegians of whom most Americans have even heard).

While a biography of each person who received a life reading would be a researcher's delight, at least one pattern of deviation relative to the present life of the sitter was revealed. *Deviating incarnations are tied to the present birth place of the individual.* The deviating incarnations revealed the symbolic nature of the first life Cayce tended to note in giving a life reading. It occurred in the land where the client was born in this life.

GLAMORIZATION OF THE PAST

As a by-product of reading over a hundred of the past-life readings in order to quantify them, one further reflection emerged from the study. It is quite common in the psychic community for psychics to receive mediumistic revelations from the famous. These revelations have most often come through mediums supposedly channeling from famous personages. This author has known numerous mediums who regularly channeled from the likes of Elvis Presley, Martin Luther King, Albert Schweitzer, and Gandhi. There is a noticeable attempt to enhance the medium by an association with the famous. Since Cayce was not a traditional medium and hence did not contact spirit entities, this process is absent.

However, there is present in Cayce material a similar occurrence in the enhancement of the subjects for whom life readings were given by either identifying them or associating them with famous personages in past incarnations. This process began with the very first reading in which Lammers was identified with Hector (of the Trojan War). A more recent instance was a young woman who was identified with Frances Willard and about whom a book was written. There are, of course, several hundred incarnations that identified people as being among the very elite few mentioned in the Bible.

One might expect a famous person or two to appear in the over six thousand incarnations, but one becomes suspect when there are so many. The number of the famous is further highlighted by the percentage of royalty and other elites (priests, generals, etc.) in the readings (as high as 50 percent in some time-culture slots).

CONCLUSION: TOWARD A NEW WAY TO UNDERSTAND THE CAYCE MATERIAL

Reincarnation scenarios offer a rather dramatic setting in which to place an otherwise mundane psychic reading. Cayce's adoption of reincarnation and past lives as the religious symbols through which advice and counsel were offered to his clients also provides some insight into the development of his talents. They seem to have emerged as the very suggestible Cayce encountered the strong-willed Lammers. Once Lammers' ideas were lodged within that part of Cayce that came to the fore when he was in trance, they were allowed to expand and grow. Elaboration on the material was continually encouraged by the entranced Cayce being questioned on specific issues by those who were present for his reading sessions.

The understanding of the reincarnation material as symbolic, not literal, does much to explain the repetitions in the Cayce readings. When Cayce clairvoyantly picked up certain data about present conditions of the sitter (either psychically or from readily available information), such data would be translated symbolically into a certain time-culture reincarnation slot. A foreign birth was translated into a previous incarnation in that land. The symbolic understanding also explains why the fifteen time-culture slots concentrated on those relatively well known to the average American in the early twentieth century. Cayce was using those eras about which he had been taught by his public school education, church school, and the theosophist Lammers. Thus, American pioneers, the Crusaders, the fall of Troy, Old Testament times, Jesus' era, mystic Egypt, and occult Atlantis all appear. Even the Essene material is directly derivative of two occult best-sellers—*The Aquarian Gospel of Jesus Christ* by Levi Dowling[11] and the Rosi-crucians' *The Mystical Life of Jesus* by H. Spencer Lewis.[12]

The reincarnation material functions as a convenient tool to self-awareness, a fact being exploited by a number of present-day counselors.[13] By highlighting facts about a sitter through a reincarnation symbol, one can, to many people, reveal self-truth in a way that is acceptable to the conscious ego. The insight about the sitter's state is accepted as true, and because the self is picking up a strain from a past life, the self is responsible for the situation and bears the responsibility for overcoming it. At the same time, since the cause of the situation is from a past life, it comes as an intruder into this individual existence. The conscious self (the personality?) is not responsible and thus can resign itself to paying a karmic debt.[14]

This modest study does suggest several needed areas of further research. A full, quantified survey of the life readings touching on the several other elements besides vocation would, of course, provide valuable information as well as con-firmation of the symbolic nature of the readings. Second, a search for like pat-terns in the astrological and medical readings should also prove fruitful. The medical readings especially need to be subjected to some critical review, as they have become the source for a broad program of medical advice to ARE members and friends.

Finally, a study of the sources that elaborate on certain time-culture slots could prove most enlightening. A study initiated contemporaneously with the work reported on in this paper has found that the material on the Essenes in the Cayce readings also has a mundane source, some popular nineteenth-century psychic books. The furtherance of studies of the extensive Cayce records will have as a long-term payoff an understanding of this one important psychic figure and also make a major contribution to our understanding of the process by which a public psychic operates.

NOTES

1. Cayce, unlike many of his professional psychic contemporaries, did not go into trance in order to contact spirits. Rather, in trance, he was able to read what was termed the akashic records (a idea derived from Hindu thought), believed to be a cosmic record bank of data on all past events. Information on Cayce, life readings, and the cosmology can be found in the several general works on Cayce, the best of which are Thomas Sugrue's *There Is a River* (New York: Dell Books, 1967), and Hugh Lynn Cayce's *Venture Inward* (New York: Harper and Row, 1967). Both are easily obtainable in paperback editions.

2. Morey Bernstein, *The Search for Bridey Murphy* (New York: Doubleday & Company, 1956).

3. Jeffrey Furst, *The Return of Frances Willard* (New York: Coward, McCann & Geoghegan, 1971).

4. Cf. the symposium on the Bridey Murphy case in *Tomorrow* 4, no. 4 (summer 1956): 4–49.

5. See Edgar Evans Cayce and Hugh Lynn Cayce, *The Outer Limits of Edgar Cayce's Power* (New York: Harper & Row, 1971), and Lytle W. Robinson, *Is It True What They Say about Edgar Cayce?* (New York: Berkley Books, 1979).

6. By "incarnation" is meant a reference to one particular past life about which a person is told. In the average Cayce reading, four previous incarnations or past lives are recounted.

7. The major item on Egypt is a booklet by Mark Lehner, *The Egyptian Heritage* (Virginia Beach, VA: A.R.E. Press, 1974, 1981). Cayce's life as RaTa is covered in W. H. Church, *Many Happy Returns: The Lives of Edgar Cayce* (New York: Harper & Row, 1984).

8. Life reading #294-153.

9. Life readings #1442-1, #1574-1, #1587-1.

10. Though large numbers of the Atlantean royalty's readings are quoted in Edgar Evans Cayce's *Edgar Cayce on Atlantis* (New York: Paperback Library, 1968) almost no reference to their subject's princely state is made (a fact that accounts for the large number of eclipses in the text). Also, the Atlantean random sample (from #1400–1500) indicates a much higher percentage of royalty and religious functionaries than the quotations from chapter 3. This additional fact would tend to call into question the reliability of *Edgar Cayce on Atlantis* as a source for understanding the actual content of the Cayce material.

11. Levi Dowling, *The Aquarian Gospel of Jesus the Christ* (Los Angeles: Leo W. Dowling, 1911). This volume has been frequently reprinted.

12. H. Spencer Lewis, *The Mystical Life of Jesus* (San Jose: AMORC, 1929).

13. Cf. Morris Netherton and Nancy Shiffrin, *Past Lives Therapy* (New York: Ace Books, 1978); Edith Fiore, *You Have Been Here Before* (New York: Coward, McCann & Geoghegan, 1978); and Denys Kelsey and Joan Grant, *Many Lifetimes* (Garden City, NY: Doubleday & Company, 1867).

14. This should not be interpreted as an attack on a belief in reincarnation in general, merely as a suggestion that basing a belief in reincarnation on the Cayce material is basing a significant part of one's worldview on weak ground. This says nothing about a belief in reincarnation based on other research—hypnotism (which has its own problems), the remembered past life research of Ian Stevenson, and the testimony of spirit entities through mediums. Each of these methodologies must rise or fall on its own.

6

A COLONY
OF SEEKERS
Findhorn in the 1990s
Steven Sutcliffe

INTRODUCTION

This paper offers a thumbnail sketch of the Findhorn community. Deliberately, it depends largely on ethnographic reportage in the belief that such a methodology is an important and often undervalued component in the study of religion. Indeed, it seems particularly suited to the field of posttraditional religious practice—specifically the dissident and vernacular spiritualities of "New Age" and Paganism[1]—where the performance of freshly devised and mixed-and-matched rituals to express composite worldviews assembled from heterodox sources lies at the heart of the phenomenon. But there are still comparatively few ethnographies available:[2] hence this account. I begin with an overview of Findhorn and end with a brief analysis.

FINDHORN: AN OVERVIEW

> We provide a training ground for spiritual seekers wishing to understand and express their own unique spirituality (Walker, 1994:17).

From *Journal of Contemporary Religion* 15, no. 2 (2000): 215–31. Copyright © 2000 by the Journal of Contemporary Religion. Reprinted in a slightly revised form by permission. http://www.tandf .co.uk/journals/carfax/13537903.html.

Findhorn[3] is a substantial settlement of spiritual "seekers" (Sutcliffe 1997) on the northeast coast of Scotland, which since 1962 has hosted three generations of seekers engaged in the exploration of alternative spiritualities, psycho-physical therapies, craftwork, and gardening.

In the 1960s and early 1970s, Findhorn was known as a "New Age centre" or a "centre of light" (Rigby and Turner 1972; Walker, 1994, 28ff.). More recently, "mystery school" (Walker 1994, 271ff.), "eco-village" (116–17), and "spiritual community" (74) have peppered colony discourse; the settlement now also describes itself as an "NGO [nongovernmental organization] associated with the Department of Public Information of the United Nations."[4] Clearly, future shifts in nomenclature cannot be discounted.

The kaleidoscope of self-representations found at Findhorn reflects the settlement's fluctuating "density" of institutionalization, which is in turn bound up with the brisk turnover of personnel at the settlement: "over half . . . have been there less than five years" (Metcalf 1993, 10). During the winter of 1996–97, for example, a particularly radical overhaul saw the en masse resignation of the Foundation management committee and a lengthy process of internal discussion on long-term structure and aims. Simultaneously another body, the Findhorn Bay Community Association, sprang up to speak for the interests of other alternative practitioners in the area.[5]

Findhorn in the 1990s is thus in a near-constant state of reflexive monitoring and organizational experiment. However, appraisal of the settlement's development over four decades only confirms this as the norm. The full history can be reconstructed elsewhere:[6] the gist follows. In 1962 Peter and Eileen Caddy, their three children, and their friend Dorothy Maclean—all recently unemployed—occupied a caravan on scrub land outside the peninsulate village of Findhorn, some twenty-five miles to the east of Inverness on the Moray Firth. They began a vegetable garden while they continued to explore their principal interests: the gathering and interpretation of information and "guidance" gleaned by telepathic, intuitional, and meditational practices, which they claimed to get both from other humans elsewhere on the planet and from superhuman, supernatural, and extraterrestrial sources. As the decade progressed and the myth of giant vegetables from the "Findhorn garden" circulated, a small community—mainly older followers of Spiritualism, Theosophy, and UFO lore—gathered around the three pioneers. At the beginning of the 1970s, their ranks swelled considerably with "hippie" recruits from the counterculture, including increasing numbers of Americans. An emphasis on educational provision and outreach in the pioneers' gnostic and esoteric 'syllabus' soon emerged, as did the provision of more secularly nuanced "human potential" systems and techniques for therapy and self-realization. With this ideological diversification came territorial expansion: in the later 1970s and 1980s, a second site was acquired, a variety of buildings bought or erected, and the total number of those involved—residents, ex-residents, friends, and associates in the neighborhood—grew to several hundred.

In the late 1990s, the colony[7] as a whole consisted of a number of buildings and grounds in and around the village of Findhorn and the nearby market town of Forres. There were two principal sites, some seven miles apart, known as "the Park" and "Cluny," respectively, and linked—with a few other properties owned by or affiliated with the foundation—by a daily minibus shuttle service.[8] The former is an abbreviation of "Findhorn Bay Caravan Park." Here the pioneers set up home in 1962, on a plot of land sandwiched between Findhorn Bay and RAF Kinloss, a busy airbase. It now contains a profusion of caravans, chalets and wooden houses. There is a sizeable community center and a large stone auditorium called the Universal Hall for conferences, meetings, and touring arts. The Phoenix Shop, a large whole and organic foodstore and bookshop, also serves the wider alternative community, as do the apothecary's homeopathic and herbal medicines. Communal meditation takes place in the "Sanctuary," a large wooden chalet, and in a semi-underground chamber, the "Nature Sanctuary." Ecological interests are evinced by some turf-roofing, experimental sewage treatment, a wind-powered turbine, and "Trees for Life," a charity regenerating native forest in Highland glens. There are cars and some bicycles, but people largely walk around the Park.

The second site, Cluny—short for "Cluny Hill Hotel"—was purchased in 1975. It consists of a large Victorian hotel building and grounds just outside Forres. The building has several floors and around two hundred rooms; its large formal spaces—ballroom, lounges—are now given over to relaxation and group-work. It is a busy building, not unlike a large but comfortable youth hostel and hosts the majority of Findhorn's visitors.

"AN ONGOING WORKSHOP"[9]

In the early 1990s, there were about one hundred and seventy "members"[10] at the community's core, including children and dependents, although the wider affiliated community probably numbered around four hundred. Almost two-thirds of the core residents were women, nearly three-quarters were aged between thirty and fifty, and a clear majority came from the United Kingdom, the United States, and Germany (Riddell 1991, 132).[11] A simple questionnaire that I circulated within the community clarifies this: My small sample reveals overwhelmingly early-to-late middle-aged respondents who recognized but generally rejected the "New Age" label, preferred "spirituality" to "religion," advocated and practiced alternative medicine and holistic healthcare, and were highly educated (nearly two-thirds had attended university).[12]

Findhorn then had a turnover of around one million pounds a year (Brierley and Walker 1995), most of which came from a year-round program of residential courses, conferences, and workshops in experimental spiritualities, healing prac-

tices, and ecological concerns. These are advertised in regular brochures distributed via an international mailing list of some twenty thousand individuals,
groups, and organizations. For example, over the winter of 1994–95, there were
conferences on "Process-Oriented Psychology" and "The Western Mysteries,"
and a three-month gardening course; weeklong courses included "Towards Inner
Peace and Planetary Wholeness" and "Celtic Creation." More recent conferences
include "Creating Sustainable Community" and "A Call to Peace," while recent
workshops feature "The Gay Man's Inner Journey," "Relationships as a Path of
Spiritual Growth," and "Shamanic Consciousness."[13]

Over five thousand individuals—mostly Euro-American, but also Japanese
—take a course each year. Riddell (1991, 112) summarizes their demographic
profile:

> Most are white and middle class . . . in various kinds of caring professions,
> already concerned with the environment and their own identity. Many will have
> explored some kind of therapy as a means of self-development. . . . There are
> more than average single and divorced people.

Metcalf (1993, 11) plausibly argues for a "dramatic shift" in visitor profile since
the 1970s: from an American to a European core and from the "alternative" to
the "mainstream" sector—he claims that two-thirds of contemporary guests now
pursue careers in the latter, half of these again being "business people." Furthermore, he suggests that a trend in the 1980s "of privatization and devolution" has
eroded the oft-perceived communality of Findhorn.[14] However, this perception
has been queried internally: "Findhorn . . . is often talked about as an intentional
community. It wasn't, it was an *accidental community*" (Buhler-McAllister 1995,
35; emphasis added). This is further support for "colony" or "settlement' as the
most apt description of Findhorn, since these terms accommodate the characteristic to-ing and fro-ing of seekers and the constantly shifting institutional forms,
characteristics homogenized and reified by the term "community." And as the
following account of "Experience Week" suggests, "community" is less a cause
than a by-product of Findhornian praxis: the real focus is the reflexivity and
regeneration of the individual seeker.

"EXPERIENCE WEEK": FINDHORN IN MINIATURE

Findhorn's mandatory vehicle of socialization for its international clientele is
"Experience Week," a weeklong introduction to community lifestyle that Riddell
(1991, 117) describes as "an experience of our life in microcosm." Since Experience Week has demonstrated consistency of form and content in recent
decades[15]—and this in a general climate of institutional flux—it serves as a reliable guide to certain norms and values operative at Findhorn (and, by associa-

tion, elsewhere in posttraditional spirituality). The following abbreviated account comes from my fieldwork notes and observations from one such week in 1995.[16]

My first contact with Findhorn was an envelope franked with the slogan "Expect a Miracle." Inside, I read that Experience Week encouraged individuals "to find personal expression in a group context":

> Work is an integral part of our life here through which many of our spiritual lessons are learnt. . . . The rest of the time is devoted to group activities, which aim to deepen your understanding of the Foundation, to encourage you to give and receive support in the ongoing process of spiritual growth, to bring forth your inner riches of love and truth as unique contributions to the world, and to honour the Divine in all life.[17]

It was clearly a serious undertaking. "Willingness to meet others with love and respect, to share yourself openly and to participate fully" was stipulated, and prospective participants had to submit a personal letter detailing their "spiritual background, if any" and explaining why they wished to come.

The process of composing a lengthy personal letter, and arranging travel[18] and (significant) expenses,[19] generated considerable expectancy in the weeks before the event. In fact, my journey (from central Scotland) was significantly simpler in cost and mileage than those of other members of my group, who came from England, Holland, Germany, the United States, Brazil, and Switzerland. We numbered fourteen, with a typical Findhornian profile: ten women, four men, all white Euro-Americans, and three-quarters in their thirties and forties. The first language of more than half of us was not English.

The week ran from Saturday to Friday, and the days were programmed with group sessions and work placements, so a good measure of concentration and stamina was required.

Saturday

> Saturday morning, Experience Week/I'm so nervous I can hardly speak/Arrive at Cluny Hill, half past ten/Almost turned and went home again.[20]

I arrived in Forres on a cold February morning and joined a handful of individuals in a plain white minibus in the station car park. One of them asked the driver about Findhorn as we set off, but he just said, "Wait and see." In the lea of the densely wooded Cluny Hill, we turned up a short drive—signposted "Private"—and emerged in front of Cluny's imposing bulk. The building sits on a rise overlooking a golf course. The reception area was busy: People came and went with luggage, greeting each other with smiles and hugs.

In the Beech Tree Room upstairs—a spacious bay-windowed apartment—it was darker and quieter. Popular music from the 1940s was playing; the atmosphere was demure yet relaxed. A bursar took outstanding monies and introduced our "focalisers"[21] for the week, Dagmar and Paul, respectively German and English, and both in their late thirties.

Dagmar gave us a timetable for the week and then led us on a brisk tour of Cluny's facilities. My notebook records: "Everything neat, precise, quite luscious." Most bedrooms were shared: I joined Conor, an Irishman now living in Kent, in a medium-sized room. On our beds, tucked into folded towels, were "blessings" cards—small, commercially produced mottoes—left by the housework team. On mine was printed, mysteriously, "Sisterhood." Conor and I chatted. When I explained my research interests, he said disapprovingly: "So you're not a heartfelt New Ager, then?"

We were just in time for the noon meditation. As mentioned, there are three sanctuaries[22] at Findhorn. The main Park Sanctuary is a wooden chalet with low ceiling, net curtains, and a weaving of a sunrise; there is also the more intimate Nature Sanctuary (described below). The Cluny Sanctuary, where we now headed, is an airy room with high bay windows and potted plants. A illuminated stained glass panel showing the roots and branches of a flourishing tree was fitted in the opposite wall. Outside the room, we followed etiquette and removed our shoes, leaving them alongside other neat pairs. Atmosphere and deportment around the sanctuary were markedly sober, even grave: I noticed that people now avoided body and eye contact where elsewhere they actively sought it.

Inside the sanctuary, about eighty chairs and a dozen cushions were arranged in a circle around a low table displaying a large candle set in an elaborate artificial flower arrangement. About two dozen people were already seated, mostly in the comfortable armless chairs; a few more trickled in. A volunteer switched on the red light outside the room to warn latecomers that the meditation had begun: No one should now enter or leave (without exceptional reason) to avoid disturbing the "energy." She then read a few words from a book of meditations by Eileen Caddy (1987) and struck a metal bowl with a stubby stick. Most meditators had closed eyes—one man wore a sleeping mask—and sat conventionally; others were cross-legged on their chairs; many had their hands in their laps with fingers cupped and palms uppermost. After twenty minutes, the bowl was struck to conclude the session. "How was the meditation for you?" asked Conor as we put on our shoes. His, he said, had been "powerful."

Communal meditation at Findhorn revolves around such sessions twice a day, in the morning and at noon. Abstract themes supply a focus—"love," "wisdom," and "healing," for example—and there are also sessions for devotional singing based on chants and rounds from the French ecumenical Christian community, Taize. There is also individual use of the sanctuaries: neat pairs of shoes were outside at most times of the day or evening.

After a vegetarian lunch in the palatial dining room, we gathered in the Beech Tree Room for our first group session. We sat on comfortable straight-backed chairs in a large circle. In the middle, on the floor, was a lit candle in an arrangement of dried leaves and pine cones. Our focalizers ran through the week's timetable and explained their role. "Remember," Paul said, "this place is about getting in touch with Spirit: the god within."

Now Dagmar and Paul introduced us to another Findhorn ritual: "attunement."[23] To "attune," we stood up, joined hands in a circle, and closed our eyes. The ritual requires a special way of connecting hands: The right hand is offered palm up, the left palm down (we fumbled self-consciously with this at first). Dagmar said, "Let us bless the week ahead and be open to all that it brings." After a pause for contemplation, she lightly squeezed her neighbors' hands and let go; this signal was passed on, the circle gradually dropping hands and opening eyes. Attunement was over. The group remained quiet and thoughtful, some smiling, others making gentle eye contact.

We were now ready for further instruction: "sharing." This is a style of communication in which individuals express themselves spontaneously, openly, and directly—"from the heart," as popular expression has it. But as Paul explained, sharing is not an emotional free-for-all: There were certain ground rules. First, we were to speak out of our own experience, from what we had "gone through" ourselves rather than from knowledge acquired "secondhand." Second, we were to speak in the first person only, an act known as making an "I" statement: Speculation and abstraction were out. Third, we should actively seek eye contact with whomever we were addressing. Fourth, listeners were not to interrupt when someone was "sharing" (unless, of course, that person was dissembling, in which case a challenge would be appropriate).

We now proceeded to introduce ourselves, drawing on our brief experience of focalizing, attuning and sharing as best we could. Nick, a computer programmer and regular Quaker attendee from Bristol, told us he'd known of Findhorn "for years . . . I knew I'd get here eventually!" Vicky from Manchester, a mother and a tentative pagan (she gave me a leaflet for the eco-pagan group "Dragon"), was keen to explore Findhorn's view of "Nature." Corinne, also a mother, used images from child-bearing as metaphors for her "journey"; born in America, living now in Switzerland, she described herself as a "world citizen." Kathy from Oregon, another programmer, was on an extended European tour and grappling with a floundering marriage. Veronique, a Swiss-born midwife in Berlin, had just ended a long-term partnership; like Kathy, she never fully lost a preoccupied mien. One interaction in particular underlined the new ethos. Conor was telling of how he had resigned from his job to travel on his savings—he described himself as "New Age and still searching"—but then became tongue-tied and agitated, whereupon Walter—a long-term Theosophist from Torquay—got to his feet, crossed the circle and said, "Come on, old son, stand up: you need a hug!" Thus two men—Walter in his late seventies, Conor some forty years his junior—who had only just met, embraced briefly and awkwardly in front of the group: the first of many such hugs.

And so it continued until all had spoken, whereupon we "tuned out"[24] and went to dinner. The scene was now set: Whatever else we did during the week, we met as a group every day, attuning, sharing, and generally following the hints and nudges of our focalizers. The intensity of this attitudinal transformation on the part of a number of hitherto strangers from all over the postindustrial world was summed up in Corinne's remark to me after dinner: "We're a family now." That same morning we had not even met.

Before bed, I spent half an hour in the sanctuary, alone, digesting events. My notebook reads: "I decide to go *deep within* and *listen*, rather than look to a lead from others in the group." Findhorn was casting its spell.

Sunday

Something inside me said, *Yeah—that's it*. It wasn't a voice, more a feeling, but I knew it was true. My mind said no, while my heart said yes (Tattersall 1996, 22).

At morning meditation, I recognized some of our group among the twenty or so present. (Although we participated most days, rarely was the sanctuary more than about half full). This morning a visualization exercise was read out by an Irish woman. We were to imagine clouds obscuring an intense source of light, but clouds without substance: They were soft and wet on our eyes as we moved into them, heading for the light beyond . . . then we were left to the morning silence. A thrush called; someone coughed; the candle flickered and recovered.

After sanctuary, we gathered in the old hotel ballroom to try out some "sacred dances"—folk dances, mostly from Eastern Europe—to the taped music of the Findhorn Sacred Dance Band. Once again we were encouraged not to flinch from eye contact or to "block the energy" in needless chatter. In the afternoon, we took a minibus to Findhorn village and visited the beach, where we milled around uncertainly, scanning the cold sea for dolphins, while Paul hunted for a pebble for group use. Then we drove the mile or so to the park, where an Australian resident took us for a guided tour.

The Park retains something of a "frontier" atmosphere: despite some new wooden houses, most accommodation remains chalets, caravans, and even whiskey barrels (a cluster of converted distillery casks, known as "Bag End" after the hero's home in *The Hobbit*). The overall impression is simultaneously countercultural and parochial. We visited the community center, the Universal Hall, and the Nature Sanctuary, all self-built. The last is a small oval-shaped chamber that our guide told us had been built to honor "the little people" (fairies). Inside, heating kept the room warm, comfortable, and womblike. We sat on cushions around the walls, a candle on the cleft stone centerpiece was lit, and Paul and Dagmar introduced a new exercise. First we attuned; then we each silently requested the "quality" we wished to receive from the week; finally we drew an "angel card,"[25] which represented the area we had to address, like it or not.

I requested "Confidence," but drew "Faith," which showed two angels in midair flight between trapeze swings. Kathy drew "Joy," and bitterly displayed this to us. Dagmar drew a card for the group as a whole: it was "Release." She nodded thoughtfully; Paul raised an eyebrow and smiled.

Back at Cluny, we gathered again after dinner. Paul added his pebble and the group's angel card to the candle arrangement in the center. Now we were to attune for work placements. Several of us—Anna and Vicky in particular—wanted to work in the famous Findhorn gardens. We were asked to meditate to discover which work department we felt "drawn to"—or as Tattersall (1996, 22) puts it: "[The focalizer] said we would feel something inside ourselves for the job that would be ours." A pragmatic combination of meditation and rationalization resolved a potential clash between organizational requirements and existential agendas.

Following half an hour of sharing, this group session concluded with a talk on the "Inner Life." "Frank is coming to share with you on spiritual practice," said Dagmar. Frank was an American in his late forties. Findhorn, he said, was "living Zen": "It's about being *here*, *now* rather than *there*, *then*." He spoke charismatically about his own "spiritual path," which had also taken in Psychosynthesis and Bhagwan Shree Rajneesh. Then he led a visualization exercise. For this we were asked to close our eyes and imagine ourselves in a cinema, viewing the "movie of your own life." The film begins to run backward: we watch our adulthood unravel into teenage years, and finally into childhood, finishing as discarnate spirits hovering above our mothers' wombs. We then reran the film to the present and imagined ourselves leaving our "movies" with fresh understanding of our life's purpose. Frank's mellifluous drone spun a web of drama and empowerment around the group.

Monday

Work is love in action (Findhorn saying).

On Monday we began work placements. Jutta—a young German—and I had attuned to the community center (or "CC") at the park, so we took the morning minibus from Cluny, arriving just in time for morning sanctuary.

Work began just after nine o'clock. We were six: Stella the CC focalizer, a Glaswegian with infectious humor and spontaneity; a studious American, Jane, who was a foundation student; Heidi from Switzerland, another student, but about to leave; an Austrian psychotherapist, Rudi, now experimenting with spiritual healing; and the Experience Week neophytes, Jutta and me. We sat around one of the dining tables to attune and share. "I'm feeling just great!" announced Stella, throwing out her arms and laughing. "Mmm," said Rudi, smiling and nodding slowly as he looked at each of us in turn: "Me, too—I'm feeling *good*." "I'm pretty good this morning but tired after a busy weekend," said Jane. Only Heidi stalled somewhat: "It's time for me to move on," she said, and shrugged. The others nodded soberly. But the general enthusiasm was contagious. I said I was glad to be at the park and among the wider community. Indeed, I was beginning to find the group sessions claustrophobic and slightly reminiscent of group therapy.

Our remit was to clean the entrance hall, toilets, and dining and lounge areas of the CC. We were to clean the furniture, maintain condiments and candles on the tables, and vacuum and mop the floors. I later discovered on the authority of Peter Caddy himself (1996, 328) that cleaning the CC was vital work—it provided

> a wonderful training ground for future leaders, for it was necessary to be very aware: to make sure that the tables were lined up, the salt and pepper pots were full, the window sills dusted, and that the tables were laid in time for each meal. It involved real discipline and attention to detail, and was where the founding principles of Findhorn could be put into practice—to love where you are, to love whom you're with, and to love what you're doing.

If the tasks were nevertheless menial, the atmosphere was pleasant—Rudi put orchestral music on—and the pace leisurely. "Those toilets look great!" called Jane to me as she passed with the vacuum cleaner. We had an extended tea break and were comfortably finished for noon sanctuary. We tuned out, Stella blessing the morning's work and enjoining us to "move on" to the rest of the day. After sanctuary, the CC filled up for lunch with about sixty people, most of them residents or foundation employees. Many lit candles at their tables. The atmosphere was busy and convivial.

Back at Cluny, a session of "trust" games and exercises was scheduled, led by two foundation staff: a young Italian, Dario, and an older German woman, Helge. "You're gonna enjoy this," said Dario, in heavily Americanized English, "I just *love* seeing groups open up in the games!" We began with a mirroring exercise. I paired up with Walter and, facing each other, we took turns to initiate movements—facial gestures, arm or torso movements—which the other copied as closely as possible. The aim was to reach a point where movement and response were so seamlessly integrated that an outsider—even ourselves—might not easily differentiate them. Next we played "cars and drivers": The "cars" closed their eyes and were steered by the "drivers," who "drove" them with hands on shoulders. I found Jutta's extravagant "driving" quite unnerving, and while I kept my eyes shut, I tensed my body. Afterward Jutta said, half-accusingly, half-jokingly: "You didn't trust me!" A tag game followed, where you could only escape being "it" by hugging somebody, triggering waves of adrenalin and gales of laughter. In a more intimate vein, we closed eyes and were paired with an anonymous partner. Taking their hands in ours, we were to express, through the activity of our fingers alone, certain moods and emotions stipulated by our instructors: for example, "sadness," "joy," or "liveliness."

The session promoted a spectrum of physical contact from the rumbustious to the sensual. Tears, laughter, and hugs spread among the group as we got into our new behavioral stride, encouraged by the pervasive Findhornian climate of physical contact and intense sharing.

That evening, a gardener talked to us about "Nature." We meditated to attune to the "nature spirits," and the gardener outlined her favorite practices, including meditating with the plants and dowsing for "earth energies." Some tentative discussion of nature spirits and Findhorn's "Pan energy" followed.

Tuesday

> Tuesday morning, with a Hoover in my hand/Cleaning out the dining room, beginning to understand/Tuning in, tuning out/Startin' to see what Findhorn is all about.[26]

In the morning I was back in the CC, one moment polishing table tops, the next discussing spiritual healing. These work placements gave us insight into the day-to-day life of the wider community, a factor also advantageous to Findhorn management, since without exception future employees must begin their careers in an Experience Week. Informal contacts suggested that the interpersonal intensity propagated in our group sessions remained high in the colony at large—certainly in comparison with "outside" norms—and was not simply an exaggerated distillate of Experience Week. Meanwhile, we were enjoined by Stella, our focalizer, simply to enjoy the work and see it as an end in itself. Hence buoyant conversation, jokes, and upbeat taped music were typical punctuations to otherwise undemanding, even dreary, tasks.

Back at Cluny, at 1:50 p.m. sharp—the week was sharply choreographed—we gathered outside for a group photograph. Next on the schedule was a "Nature Outing." We drove to a beauty spot on the Findhorn River known as "Randolph's Leap," attuned beside the swirling black water, and were invited by Dagmar simply to "*be* in nature." "*Feel* the energy, and see what happens," she suggested. Some wandered off in pairs; others, including me, dispersed alone. Apart from Vicky—whom I saw on a boulder beside the spate, swaying and chanting—Martine—whom I saw embracing a large Scots pine—and Sonja—whom I came upon in a sandy cove sadly prodding the water with a stick—I scarcely saw the others. It was cold; for a time I walked briskly, then squatted to watch the peaty spate.

The evening sharing was long and relaxed: My notebook records "much giggling, as well as from-the-heart accounts." But I also wrote: "When does it become 'easy', 'glib'? How, if at all, open would 'sharing' be to feelings of conflict and anger?" Nevertheless, the Findhorn experience could be seductive, for by the next page I had added: "The important work is to be in the moment. Perhaps it's the only work—that, and listening with an inner ear."

Christina, a single mother and overall focalizer for the park, joined us to describe management structures at Findhorn. To Corinne's complaint about the apparent lack of provision for children and families, Christina responded that the dynamic flux of the place "throws the spotlight on *you* to create the space *you* want." The suggestion was clear: What was missing was always rectifiable. And since "external events are really reflections of internal processes: the world, and everything in it, is a mirror of the self,"[27] then it was simply (and literally) down to us. Christina herself sought a "more feminine vision of leadership" to defuse polarities and embrace opposites. "There is no such thing as an enemy," she said, "only friends and potential friends." When Sonja described her guilt and paranoia as a Serb demonized by media coverage of the then-raging Balkan war, Christina embraced her warmly, declaring, "as a German, I know how this feels!"

That night Conor told me of an angel workshop he'd attended in France. "I definitely felt an energy," he said, "but it was very gentle, very subtle." He was both drawn to and cynical about Findhorn: Earlier in the evening I had joined a conversation between him and Kathy in which both were quietly casting a critical eye upon the settlement.

Wednesday

> Upon that Road one wanders not alone. There is no rush, no hurry. And yet there is no time to lose (Bailey 1967, 51).

After morning meditation, we gathered in Cluny's lounge. Sam, a New Zealander who described herself as a "modern gypsy," was to focalize a special group project: to spring-clean the room. We began, as usual, with attunement, Sam speaking of the need to approach the task as thoroughly as we would our "inner work."[28] I worked with Corinne and Sam, carrying chairs to the ballroom, where we painstakingly polished them. Sam was brisk and resolute: When I suggested we simply work outside the lounge to save time and energy, she said "No!"

In the afternoon we settled down to study a pamphlet by David Spangler, an American "New Age" activist—or "freelance mystic" (Spangler 1996, 46)—who shaped the community in the early 1970s (Sutcliffe 1998) and remains a regular visitor. *Cooperation with Spirit: Further Conversations with John* is a collection of communications Spangler claims to have received from "John," his "inner" guide. We read a paragraph each in turn. "Don't believe every word," Dagmar advised. "Just be open to what resonates with you."

Progress was slow: many of us struggled with Spangler's abstract language. Soon we stopped to share. Martine spoke of her sadness at living in Brazil in personal comfort but close to poverty and homelessness. She said, "I know it is their karma—they have chosen this purification—but to see little children starving, this makes me feel so unhappy." Some murmured agreement. But I declared myself skeptical of Spangler's "spiritual worlds" and reincarnation. The group listened impassively: Dagmar nodded thoughtfully. In my notebook I pondered how far "deviant" positions and real conflict could develop at Findhorn.[29]

Frank returned before supper to share a favorite passage from an Alice Bailey[30] book. "I've carried this around the globe with me," he said, brandishing a dog-eared paperback titled *Glamour: A World Problem*. Slowly and rhythmically he read out, and then interpreted, the "Six Rules of the Path," a Bunyan-esque allegory of the spiritual quest (a fragment appears as today's epigraph). This triggered an emotional response in Sonja about her Serbian identity: For the first—and last—time, a voice charged with real frustration and rage disturbed the equanimity of the Beech Tree Room.

Thursday

Thursday morning, at a quarter past three / I'm wide awake in the Sanctuary / Opening myself to the love and the light / Thanking God for steering me right.[31]

From my notebook: "Morning: work at Park. Conversation from Rudi about chakras and colour energy. I cleaned the toilets." The afternoon, however, was timetabled "Free." I browsed in the Phoenix Shop, which stocks an extensive selection of goods—books, magazines, postcards, tarot decks, jewellery, wind chimes, incense, music tapes and CDs, clothes, drums, candles, and whole and organic foods. Then I followed a path beyond the Bag End whiskey-barrel residences and beneath the blades of the wind turbine, over scrub and dunes to the long bare beach. In the lea of the dunes, I came across spiral mazes made of pebbles and driftwood, presumably by Findhornians. I trod the largest spiral into the center: It was just wide enough to accommodate one pair of feet.

That evening a former Buddhist nun and ex-resident spoke to us about "Personal and Planetary Transformation." Her point was simple: The latter would come only from the former.

Friday

We had naturally become as a family to each other in a mere seven days. However, in our final meeting we could feel our group's energy begin to dissipate. . . . The appropriate time to leave Findhorn had come (Tattersall 1996, 32).

On the minibus to the park for our last morning's work, I chatted with Martine. Experience Week had been her last port of call in a year of traveling, which also included four months on an Israeli kibbutz—"hard work," she said, "and fun, but not a very spiritual place, not like here."

On our chairs after lunch was the group photograph taken earlier in the week. Paul mentioned some ways of "keeping connected" to Findhorn: For example, we could meditate for twenty minutes at local noontime to "align with" sanctuary practice and so "create a network of light around the world."

Then we began our last session: "Completion." The pebble that Paul had selected last Sunday and that had nestled since beside the candle and group angel card in the center of our circle was to be the "talking stone." Whoever held it spoke, and when finished, passed it on to the person whom he or she sensed the pebble "wants to go to" next. "Say whatever you need to say to complete the week for you," explained Dagmar. Most took their time, weighing the pebble thoughtfully. Some remained shy or reserved; others tried to articulate difficult ideas and feelings; a few waxed lyrical. Conor described himself as a bird of passage: "Findhorn is a rock, and I'm perched on it for a while." Nick said gnomically, "I just want to say thank you," and quickly passed the stone on. I was last. I shared a photograph of my young son, to general amusement and cries of delight. Suddenly embarrassed, I averted my eyes. "Steve, look up!" prompted Dagmar. "See the pleasure on their faces!"

We finished by passing kisses on cheeks around the circle, and then we stood quietly together. "That's it," said Paul. "It's over!" Someone had a tape: The afternoon broke up amid lazy free-style dancing. By the following noon, we had gone our separate ways.

I returned home with a Findhorn candle and some books and—still in my participant-observer role—made a few attempts to "link up" with the noontime sanctuary meditation. Subsequent weeks brought a few communications from my fellow participants. Conor—who had stayed on for the three-month student program but soon left—wrote from Ireland: "Findhorn is great but it's not right for me at present." On a postcard of crowds swarming across the Berlin Wall, Veronique wrote: "I try to remember my angel and the angel of the group. I am feeling better at work; beside that, there has been no great miracle in my life." Vicky sent a birthday card with the pagan greeting "bright blessings." In the summer I received a circular letter from Sonja promoting a month of "meditation and prayers for Bosnia."[32] She wrote: "I have been so caught up in the process of 'recovering' from Findhorn. Time has come to go back there again."

Nearly two years later, Anna was one of the few participants to respond to my letter requesting reflections on the week. "What I learned from Findhorn is to be present in the moment," she wrote from the Netherlands. "Don't look too far ahead, because a lot of things come in another way than I expect."[33]

ANALYSIS

This ethnography of Experience Week—and the more general sketch of Findhorn contextualizing it—partly exemplifies two related theorizations: an "inward turn" (Needleman 1970, 13 ff.) in modern religion and "self-religiosity" (Heelas 1994).[34] That is, with the erosion of traditional sources of corporate authority (revealed text, priesthood, institutional calendar), religion becomes by default a self-sited, personally embodied, and internally authorized practice of strategically interacting individuals. To be sure, religion has always been this *in part*, but here it is *wholly* this.

An "inward turn" is clearly encouraged by the ground rules for Experience Week: speaking "from the heart," making "I" statements, seeking eye contact, not interrupting. By implication it is "personal space"—and especially the innermost reaches of this (those "within" the practitioner's self)—that is significant, not to say causative. Divinity is no longer "out there," so to speak, but "in here," seeking release: the god within "wants out." The influence on this immanentist theology of popular piety and "inspirational" literature (cf. Schneider and Dornbusch 1958) is clear, as is that of secular psychotherapy in the preoccupation with maximizing self-potential.

The cultivation of "interiority" and self-containment also has a more general strategic function: it cushions and nourishes the individual in a time of accelerating sociocultural change. A focused and relaxed self informed by "spirit" or "the god within" is in a strong position to handle both the stresses and the opportunities occasioned by that "pluralization of social lifeworlds" that Berger et al (1974, 62ff.) identified at the heart of modernity. A self "at ease" can better manage the contemporary flood of cultural pick-and-mix options and "off-the-peg" lifestyles in which "religion" itself is increasingly just one more ingredient. And if the choices alone of the modern individual are to make good the shortfall in meaning caused by the fragmentation of traditional religious authority, then it is all the more important that they be the *right* choices in any particular situation. To this end, individuals require competence in managing their "spirituality,"[35] by which is usually entailed a "holistic"[36] lifestyle, harmonizing and refining one's mind, health, and emotions and expressing them effectively in work and relationships. This is typically a microscale, highly localized phenomenon, since the spiritual dimension is a function of the "personal space" of the body: it is "anchored" within, embodied and expressed by, and enacted immediately around, the individual in the course of everyday life.[37] To this end, specific techniques—meditation, visualization, groupwork, reflective reading—and encouraging mottoes—"work is love in action," "be here now," "love where you are, love whom you're with, love what you're doing"—are incorporated into the daily round. Trial and error sampling is significant in determining what is appropriate. "Try it," suggests Findhorn founder Eileen Caddy (1992, 11) of the practice of "inner listening"; "it really does work." "Do something, anything, to deepen your relationship with the sacred," urges William Bloom (1993:18), a frequent visitor: "If you had an experience of the sacred and it was meaningful to you, why aren't you repeating it?" Wilson (1989, 66)—a keen promoter of Findhorn—puts it bluntly: "We should feel free to use any combination of techniques for change that seems right to us and gives us good results."

This is, then, a user-friendly, problem-solving, "domesticated" spirituality, the natural habitat of which is the everyday world of housework, jobs, leisure-

"Frances and the Fairies," July 1917, from Edward L. Gardner, *The Coming of the Fairies* (*reprinted with permission of the American Religion Collection*). The New Age interest in nature spirits evident in the early Findhorn Community has its roots in turn-of-the-century Theosophy and Spiritualism.

time pursuits, families, and relationships. Drawing upon the various idea systems, practical techniques, and social strategies on offer, the individual assembles a personal portfolio with which to gain purchase upon the exciting but increasingly decentered and de-differentiated culture now shaping this everyday reality. Portfolio components can either be acquired deliberately through specialist outlets (through a course like Experience Week at a resource center like Findhorn) or more diffusely and piecemeal, through international print, television, video, and computer media.

Those sufficiently receptive to such stimuli come gradually to think of themselves less as circumscribed "members" of, or "converts" to, demarcated religious organizations as first and foremost modern individuals in search of meaning yet skeptical of the revealed truths proferred by traditional and new religions alike. As individualists, or seekers, they strive to be less ensemble members than virtuoso soloists (to adapt Weber's musical metaphor), and they are hence more likely to heed gurus, counselors, workshop leaders, and fashionable paperbacks than to acknowledge the authority of ministers and Bibles or to respect the discipline of the congregation. As the ethnography above shows, this is not to say that ensemble work does not still happen: Groupwork, for example, is integral to both Experience Week and the general management structure of Findhorn and is arguably the linchpin of posttraditional spirituality as a social phenomenon. But the group is not the goal; creating a communal lifestyle is not an end in itself, as it is in some postsixties countercultures.[38] Indeed, just as individuals come and go at Findhorn, so do its various groups—whether for workshop, conference, management, or meditation—ceaselessly form, disband, and reconstitute (a central structural feature of posttraditional spirituality, as York [1995, 148] has already observed—"Both New Age and Neo-paganism are largely composed of short-lived groups"). As Findhornians themselves acknowledge, a "hothouse" effect is at work here (reflecting the contemporary pace of cultural change): Methods and tools are no sooner established than they are effectively superseded in anticipation of the next step on one's "spiritual path." The net effect is to intensify—or exaggerate—the current experience of the individual. Such a sense of a heightened—or feverish—present tense is suggested by Corinne's remark on the very first day of Experience Week: "We're a family now."

Hence, the authority of the group remains always contingent upon, and ultimately secondary to, that of its individual constituents. The group merely serves as a strategic device to gather, affirm, and sooner or later disseminate these individuals. And this returns us to the moot question of collective structure and identity at Findhorn with which this paper began. The evidence suggests that Buhler-McAllister (1995, 35) is indeed correct to consider Findhorn's "community" image misleading. Findhorn is surely better described as a "colony" or "training ground" (Walker, 1994, 17), terms that better express its aggregative yet internally differentiated, and ceaselessly reconstituting, ecology of religious individualists.

NOTES

1. Monographs/collections include Lewis and Melton (eds., 1992), Steyn (1994), York (1995), Heelas (1996), Harvey and Hardman (eds., 1996), Pearson et al. (eds., 1998), Sutcliffe and Bowman (eds., forthcoming).

2. Cf. Heelas (1996, 7): "Academics . . . simply do not know much, if anything, about the great majority of the thousands of different things which are going on." But see some chapters in the edited volumes listed in note 1.

3. Officially the "Findhorn Foundation and Community," a title differentiating the legal functions of the charitable body, the Findhorn Foundation (created in May 1972), and the wider colony of residents and affiliates (Metcalf 1993, 1; Walker 1994, 59, 71–8). But cf. Riddell (1991, 5): "For spiritual seekers, the Findhorn Foundation or the Findhorn Community is just 'Findhorn'" (after the eponymous nearby village). I mostly follow suit, although visitors should note that this effectively conflates "alternative" colony and rural village, fueling periodic tensions between them (Robinson 1995).

4. *Guest Programme*, October 1998 to April 1999, p. 3.

5. *Stewards of the Findhorn Foundation Network News* 10 (January 1997): 14. There are also some dissident voices locally: see York (1997) on a recent "expose" of Findhorn by disgruntled ex-participants.

6. In addition to cited texts, see Hawken (1990), Findhorn Community (1978), Maclean (1980), E. Caddy (1988), P. Caddy (1996), and Sutcliffe (1998).

7. This term illuminates Findhorn's resemblance to other modern utopian-countercultural settlements: Monte Verita at Ascona, Switzerland, between 1900 and 1920; Gurdjieff's "Institute for the Harmonious Development of Man" near Paris in the 1920s; and, in California, the prewar (Theosophical) Point Loma community and the postwar Esalen Institute.

8. Findhorn also has two "outposts" on the Scottish west coast: a crofthouse on the island of Iona and custodianship of Iona's neighboring island, Erraid.

9. Riddell 1991, p. 62. Cf. *Oxford English Dictionary*: "Workshop . . . a meeting for discussion, study, experiment, etc."

10. Categories of participation in and at Findhorn are similarly multiple and fluid: Buhler-McAllister (1995, 33), for example, distinguishes between "guest," "employee," "student," and "volunteer."

11. The involvement of Scots tends to be minimal, apart from a few early figures. Of two fieldwork visits I made, the "Experience Week" group (see below) contained only one participant resident in Scotland (myself) and no Scots by birth; and of an international conference group in April 1995, less than 10 percent lived in Scotland.

12. "Spirituality, Experience and the 'New Age'": questionnaire distributed in 1995 (37 responses). Cf. Rose's (1998, 11) demography of subscribers to *Kindred Spirit* magazine: "Almost without exception, participants are middle-class. . . . Almost three-quarters . . . are women. . . . Over half are middle-aged."

13. See *Guest Programmes*, October 1994–April 1995 and October 1998–April 1999.

14. For example, Rigby (1974) includes Findhorn in his seminal account of British communes.

15. Compare the accounts in Boice (1990, 60–77), Riddell (1991, 115–18), and Tattersall (1996, 11–32).

16. See also Sutcliffe (1995, 1998). All names and many personal details have been changed. My thanks to Findhorn and to my fellow participants for agreeing to my presence in the group as a participant-observer.

17. *Guest Programme*, October 1994–April 1995, p. 5.

18. "[Findhorn] is, by and large, dependent upon people travelling hundreds of miles to visit it" (Brierley and Walker 1995, 33).

19. In 1995, Experience Week cost between £225–335 according to means; in 1998, £295 (flat rate). There is also a bursary fund.

20. From the song "Experience Week," by folk/pop musician Mike Scott, in *One Earth* 17 (1995), p. 24).

21. The role of focalizer is ubiquitous at Findhorn. Riddell (1991, 97–8): "Focalisers have responsibility without authority over others in their working groups . . . connecting with, and making sure others connect with, an inner, spiritual significance of situations, so that things can happen 'from the inside out.'" On the (American) origins of "focalization," see Walker (1994, 136).

22. "Sanctuary" is a common term in Spiritualistic and contemplative circles. Harry Edwards established a "Spiritual Healing Sanctuary" in the late 1940s; Eileen Caddy's (1988, 27) first contact with the "god within" in the mid-1950s was in "a quiet sanctuary

for prayer and meditation"; and Williamson's (1990, 129) recent survey of Spiritualism notes the existence of "many healing sanctuaries in Britain."

23. Described by David Spangler as "the New Age method of prayer, of communication with vaster and freer levels of Life" (in Walker 1994, 174). On the origins of "attunement," see p. 136.

24. "At the end of the period of work, it is helpful if there is a completion or 'detuning'—a holding of hands, a 'thank you'" (William Bloom, Walker 1994, 170).

25. Like a "blessings" card, this displays an abstract word, but illustrated by a cartoon of angels.

26. See n. 20.

27. My gloss from field notes—but a common theme in "New Age" discourse; see Hanegraaff (1996, 229–45).

28. "Cleaning" is both practical activity and spiritual metaphor at Findhorn. One resident recalls her instructions on cleaning the Caddys' bungalow: "Don't leave even a speck of dust. It must be perfect . . . Only perfection is good enough for God" (in Caddy 1988, 2).

29. Our group was conformist: everyone attended all sessions; there was little challenge to the authority of our focalizers; and most of us worked diligently to adapt to our new environment. Skepticism, if any, was privately voiced, although criticism and "negative" feelings were not expressly forbidden. I would guess that our group's amenability is broadly typical of Experience Week culture, since several factors—considerable travel and expense, mythified expectations of Findhorn—combine to encourage "honeymoon" behavior. However, as and if neophytes penetrate deeper into colony life, they are likely to meet inevitable social issues of conflict, rights, and status already hinted at in my account (cf. Bruce 1998).

30. Alice Bailey, a former Theosophist, published in the interwar period many books that she claimed to receive telepathically from a Tibetan "Master," announcing an imminent "New Age." According to Walker (1994, 287), Bailey's influence upon Findhorn "should not be underestimated." On her influence on "New Age" discourse in general, see Sutcliffe (1998).

31. See n. 20.

32. Begun by William Bloom at "Alternatives," St. James Church, Piccadilly, London.

33. Personal communication dated 22 April 1997.

34. "A radical and constant movement inward, into the 'self'" (Needleman 1970, 13); "the ultimate source of existence is believed to lie within . . . in the realm of the true self [and] the natural at large" (Heelas 1994).

35. On this see Heelas (1996, 18–20), A. King (1996), U. King (1997) and Sutcliffe (1998, 240–61).

36. Cf. Beckford (1984), Hanegraaff (1996, 119–58).

37. Clearly, attending sanctuary—like collective worship anywhere else—routinizes charismatic expressions of this "spirituality"; but note my observation that sanctuary was rarely more than half full. Akhurst (1992, 113) confirms that this situation is the norm: "Guests told me they could see all the Experience Week in the Sanctuary morning and evening, but where were the members?" The implication is that longer-term participants come to resist the very routinization they must perforce commend to new recruits for a minimum collective structure to survive at all.

38. Cf. Rigby (1974), Pepper (1991), Lowe and Shaw (1993).

REFERENCES

Akhurst, R. *My Life and the Findhorn Community*. Falmouth: Honey Press, 1992.

Bailey, A. *Glamour: A World Problem*. London: Lucis Press, 1967 (first published 1950).

Beckford, J. "Holistic Imagery and Ethics in New Religious and Healing Movements." *Social Compass* 31, nos. 2–3, (1984): 259–72.

Berger, P., et al. *The Homeless Mind: Modernization and Consciousness*. Harmondsworth: Penguin, 1974.

Bloom, W. "Practical Spiritual Practice." *One Earth* 12 (1993): 18–21.

Boice, J. *At One with All Life: A Personal Journey in Gaian Communities*. Forres: Findhorn Press, 1990.

Brierley, J., and A. Walker. "Financing a Sustainable Dream." *One Earth* 18 (1995): 32–34.

Bruce, S. "Good Intentions and Bad Sociology: New Age Authenticity and Social Roles." *Journal of Contemporary Religion* 13, no. 1 (1998): 23–35.

Buhler-McAllister, J. "The State of the Foundation." *One Earth* 19 (1995): 32–36.

Caddy, E. *Opening Doors Within*. Forres: Findhorn Press, 1987.

———. *Flight into Freedom*. Shaftesbury: Element, 1988.

———. *God Spoke to Me*. Forres: Findhorn Press, 1992 (first published 1971).

Caddy, P. *In Perfect Timing: Memoirs of a Man for the New Millennium*. Forres: Findhorn Press, 1996.

Findhorn Community. *The Findhorn Garden*. London: Wildwood House, 1978 (first published 1975).

Hanegraaff, W. *New Age Religion and Western Culture*. Leiden: E. J. Brill, 1996.

Harvey, G., and C. Hardman, C. eds. *Paganism Today*. London: Thorsons, 1996.

Hawken, P. *The Magic of Findhorn*. London: Fontana, 1990 (first published 1975).

Heelas, P. "Self Religiosity." In M. Pye, ed. *Macmillan Dictionary of Religion*. London: Macmillan, 1994, p. 241.

———. *The New Age Movement: The Celebration of the Self and the Sacralization of Modernity*. Oxford: Blackwell, 1996.

King, A. "Spirituality: Transformation and Metamorphosis." *Religion* 26, no. 4 (1996): 343–51.

King, U. "Spirituality." In J. Hinnells, ed. *A New Handbook of Living Religions*. Oxford: Blackwell, 1997, pp. 667–81.

Lewis, J. and J. G. Melton, eds. *Perspectives on the New Age*. Albany, NY: SUNY Press, 1992.

Lowe, R., and W. Shaw. *Travellers: Voices of the New Age Nomads*. London: 4th Estate, 1993.

Maclean, D. *To Hear the Angels Sing*. Forres: Findhorn Press, 1980.

Metcalf, W. "Findhorn: the Routinization of Charisma." *Communal Societies* 13 (1993): 1–21.

Needleman, Jacob. *The New Religions*. Garden City, NY: Doubleday, 1970.

Pearson, J., et al., eds. *Nature Religion Today: Paganism in the Modern World*. Edinburgh: Edinburgh University Press.

Pepper, D. *Communes and the Green Vision: Counterculture, Lifestyle, and the New Age*. London: Merlin Press, 1991.

Riddell, C. *The Findhorn Community: Creating a Human Identity for the Twenty-First Century*. Forres: Findhorn Press, 1991.

Rigby, A. *Communes in Britain*. London: Routledge and Kegan Paul, 1974.

———. and B. Turner. "Findhorn Community, Centre of Light: A Sociological Study of New Forms of Religion." In M. Hill, ed. *A Sociological Yearbook of Religion in Britain*. London: SCM Press, 1972, pp. 72–86.

Robinson, R. "Love Thy Neighbour?" *One Earth* 19 (1995): 14–19.

Rose, S. "An Examination of the New Age Movement: Who Is Involved and What Constitutes Its Spirituality." *Journal of Contemporary Religion* 13, n. 1 (1998): 5–22.

Schneider, L., and S. Dornbusch. *Popular Religion: Inspirational Books in America*. Chicago: University of Chicago Press, 1958.

Spangler, D. *A Pilgrim in Aquarius*. Forres: Findhorn Press, 1996.

Steyn, C. *Worldviews in Transition: An Investigation into the New Age Movement in South Africa*. Pretoria: University of South Africa Press, 1994.

Sutcliffe, S. "The Authority of the Self in New Age Religiosity: The Example of the Findhorn Community." *Diskus* 3, no. 2 (1995): 23–42.

———. "Seekers, Networks, and 'New Age.'" *Scottish Journal of Religious Studies* 15, no. 2 (1997): 97–114.

———. "'New Age' in Britain: An Ethnographical and Historical Exploration." Unpublished Ph.D. thesis: Open University, 1998.

———, and M. Bowman, eds. *Beyond the New Age: Exploring Alternative Spirituality*. Edinburgh: Edinburgh University Press, forthcoming.

Tattersall, T. *Journey: An Adventure of Love and Healing*. Forres: Findhorn Press, 1996.

Walker, A., ed. *The Kingdom Within: A Guide to the Spiritual Work of the Findhorn Community*. Findhorn: Findhorn Press, 1994.

Williamson, L. *Mediums and Their Work*. London: Robert Hale, 1990.

Wilson, S. *A Guide to the New Age*. Newton Abbot: Wayseeker Books, 1989.

York, M. *The Emerging Network: A Sociology of the New Age and Neo-Pagan Movements*. Lanham, MD: Rowman and Littlefield, 1995.

———. "Review Article: Stephen J. Castro. 'Hypocrisy and Dissent within the Findhorn Foundation: Towards a Sociology of a New Age Community.'" *Journal of Contemporary Religion* 12, no. 2 (1997): 229–38.

7

ALL THAT GLITTERS
Crazy Wisdom and Entrepreneurialism in the Spiritual Schools of E. J. Gold

Susan J. Palmer

Eugene Jeffrey Gold, whose declared aim is "the education of the universe, one idiot at a time!" is the founder of the Institute for the Development of the Harmonious Human Being (IDHHB), the permanent and underground name of his organization based in Grass Valley, California. Most of his followers, however, initially encounter the master and his movement under different names and wearing a disguise, for since 1963 Gold has created, directed, and closed down a bewildering number of short-lived "spiritual schools." Rarely lasting longer than a year, these spiritual centers open up in different cities in the United States and Canada, where they disseminate freshly printed literature, hold classes—and then close abruptly, often without leaving a forwarding address. Techniques taught in these "schools" range from astronaut training, sufi storytelling, Hassidic dancing, Gurdjieff's Sacred Gymnastics, Ethiopian martial arts, Gestalt training, and biofeedback, to the Tibetan science of soul travel. Once a sufficient number of "students" are gathered and regularly attending classes, Gold will tour the centers across the United States and Canada, appearing one year in a turban and *dhoti* as "Pir al-Washi, the Sufi Master," then the following year in blackface as an Ethiopian warrior, and, more recently, sporting a fez and fake moustache as he lectured to "Work Groups" as the mysterious "Mr. G."

To describe Gold's movement as "experimental" and "eclectic" is a feeble understatement. To observe these characteristics in a new religion is, of course,

Written for this anthology. Unless otherwise noted, quotations are from the author's interviews.

nothing new—as Wallis (1984), Robbins and Bromley (1992), Ellwood (1973), Stone (1976), and others have explored and analyzed the eclectic, ephemeral and experimental aspects of new religious life. The IDHHB, however, provides a particularly exaggerated and striking example of these qualites. Its founder, moreover, appears to be deliberately planning each spiritual school with built-in obsolescence, so that his organization bears a closer resemblance to a street theater or a fly-by-night circus than to a well-established new religious movement (NRM) like the International Society for Krishna Consciousness (ISKCON) or the Church of Scientology. Gold's charismatic title has also undergone a series of transmutations: from "Mother Beast" to "Pir al-Washi," to "Just Jeff," to "Mr. G.," to the current, affectionate "E. J." This pattern is not so unusual if one examines the changing titles of Rajneesh (Gordon, 1987), of Werner Erhard (Stone, 1982) and of Da Free John (Feuerstein, 1991), but while the institutions of these founders are far from static, Gold exceeds them by a wide margin. The list of Gold's "spiritual schools" in table 1 will demonstrate the enormous range of his experimentation:

Table 1: Gold's "spiritual schools"

Name of Organization	Duration	Tradition/Theme
le Maison Rouge	1963–64	Gurdjieff, shamanism
Cowachin	1972	Gestalt Therapy
Le Jardin Electronique	1972	Biofeedback, sci-fi
Shakti! the Spiritual Science of DNA	1973–74	Bardos, genetics
Anonymous	1974	Survivalism, street theater, charity
Wud-Sha-Lo	1974	Ethiopian martial arts
Center for Conscious Birth	1975	Natural childbirth, Lamaze, shamanism
Bunraku Theatre	1976	Japanese puppet shows
Institute of Thanotology	1977	Tibetan Book of the Dead
Work Groups	1978	Gurdjieff
Fourth Way Schools	1979	Gurdjieff, sufism
The Gabriel Project	1984	Gourmet feasts, readings, theater

In attempting to explain Gold's peculiar brand of charisma in sociological terms, the most relevant framework (aside from Weber's familiar observations

[1946] on "ethical" vs. "exemplary" prophets), is found in Georg Feuerstein's recent book, *Holy Madness*. Feuerstein (1991) embarks on perhaps the first systematic study of spiritual masters whose teaching methods involve pranks, ordeals of terror, and ritual obscenity. He finds in the lives of these "crazy wisdom" gurus authentic "relics of an archaic spirituality," and he explains their controversial tactics as techniques designed to shock their disciples out of preconditioned responses and social conditioning. Gold himself acknowledges his affiliation with this particular *sadhana*, for he refers to his spiritual movement as "the heartless school of E. J. Gold," and his sudden outbursts of temper and off-color jokes are explained as "the way of *malamah*" or "the sufi way of blame." The absurd and outrageous ordeals that students undergo are spiritually validated by core group leaders as "the quick way of head bashing and ego-squashing" (Gold 1977). Many more colorful examples of "holy madness" might be found among the founders of new religious movements, but the career of Gold appears to be a particularly interesting case because his organization is the only example (to my knowledge) that clearly reflects and closely embodies the "crazy wisdom" pedagogy. Gold has apparently succeeded in institutionalizing the "holy madness" type of charisma that, more than any other type, is intrinsically opposed to, and resistant toward, the process of institutionalization and routinization (Weber 1946; Feuerstein 1991).

The purpose of this chapter is to unravel this enigma and to attempt to explain the modus operandi of Gold's personal and institutionalzed charisma in sociological terms. In order to do so, the IDHHB's social organization will be analyzed within the framework of Roy Wallis's cult/sect typology (1975). After demonstrating the ways in which Gold's movement resembles the *cult* type of NRM and yet, paradoxically, also resembles the *sect*, it will be argued that the unique syncretism of the two different types found in this NRM appears to serve two functions:

First, the short-lived "cults" are effective as a *marketing strategy*. The eclectic and ephemeral nature of the "school game" extends the IDHHB's outreach into the California "spiritual supermarket" (Greenfield 1973), attracting a wider range of inhabitants of the "cultic milieu" (Campbell 1972) than might be drawn to a narrower religious tradition.

Second, for the inner circle of disciples, the intensity of Gold's ordeals, unpredictable pranks, and harsh disciplinary tactics provide the necessary conditions in which to cultivate a personal sense of charisma. At this level, the IDHHB offers the satisfying commitment, doctrinal certainty, and elite community of a *sect*. The peculiar features of Gold's organization—its inefficient recruitment techniques, its ephemeral institutions, its massive drop-out rate—begin to make sense if we interpret the IDHHB as an *experimental teachers' training college* where "crazy wise" adepts may test their own leadership skills.

Very few studies of the charisma of new religious founders have, in their use of Weber's well-known model (1946), allowed room for the possibility that the leader might actually be genuinely interested in sharing his or her knowledge and authority with the disciples or in encouraging followers to graduate as spiritual masters in their own right. Stone (1982, 159), for example, creates the amusing term "pseudo charismatic redistribution" to explain one of Werner Erhard's craftier charisma-building processes: "[Erhard] attributes extraordinary powers to others, who in turn attribute even greater charisma to him. The effect was one of reciprocal reinforcement." Wallis (1982) analyzes the wildly erratic behavior of Moses David as "resistance"—a deliberate strategy to destabilize the Children of God movement, so as to undermine the institution-building efforts of COG local leaders and keep his own charisma untrammeled. Both accounts imply that successful leaders must, of necessity, selfishly hoard their store of charisma, and if their disciples persist in developing viable charismatic careers of their own, these must be truncated or aborted. In Gold's case, however, the evidence suggests that here is at least one spiritual leader who, in his "holy madness," has set out to create a viable "master class" for younger, budding "crazy wise" adepts. Some of these have graduated and moved on to found their own "crazy wisdom" schools, and many have remained on good terms with their former teacher, even collaborating occasionally in his latest projects.

While this is not the appropriate place to address the complex issue of the authenticity of a spiritual leader's particular *sadhana*, or to join in the debate concerning ethical questions raised by the controversial methods of "crazy wisdom," the author hopes that, through a phenomenological study of the IDHHB's history, sociological, and perhaps aesthetic, insights might be gained into the charm Gold's teaching holds for his disciples students and into the peculiar niche his movement has carved out in the Californian "cultic milieu" (Campbell 1972).

METHODOLOGY

The process of data collection was mainly confined to two participant observer periods. Initially, the group was investigated as part of an ongoing research project NRMs in Montreal at Concordia University (1973–1978), directed by Dr. Frederick Bird. Between April and December of 1973, this researcher enrolled as a student in one of Gold's groups, which bore the unlikely name of *Shakti! the Spiritual Science of DNA*. This involved regular attendance at the Wednesday evening "White Room Training" and spending every Sunday at the center practicing the "Nine Obligatory Movements" and keeping detailed field notes and conducting interviews (Palmer 1976). Further data were gathered by participating in the Chronic workshop, directed by Gold in New York City in August 1984 and by joining local study circle workshops in 1985: a "Sacred Dance" class and a "Mask of the Fool" workshop. Conversations with students, ex-students, and fans of Gold have also proved a useful source of information.

THE CHARISMA OF E. J. GOLD

Eugene Jeffrey Gold is an American Jew in his midfifties who grew up in New York City. His father was Horace L. Gold, the late founder/editor of *Galaxy* magazine, and the young Gold's imagination and religious sensibilities were nourished by his father's involvement in an esoteric spiritual group composed of science fiction writers, which included Isaac Asimov, Robert Heinlein, Philip Jose Farmer, L. Ron Hubbard, and Robert Silverberg. This group met every Sunday in a large water storage tank in Manhattan that had been converted by one of the writers into a self-regulating tropical forest—complete with plant, insect, and bird life and waterfalls. Horace Gold brought his son to these meetings, which were a forum for philosophical speculations and scientific extrapolations, where oriental meditation techniques and ESP training were tried out. Gold left home to attend the Otis Art Institute in Los Angeles where, in 1970, he helped create the original Earth Day. Since the early '60s, Gold has since been active in the West Coast Consciousness movement and has directed many Gestalt therapy groups and spiritual training workshops. He has made recordings of experimental music and, in recent years, has dedicated himself to his vocation as an artist, sculptor, and painter.

E. J. Gold is deceptively conventional in his appearance. He is well-fleshed, middle-aged, and of middle height, but he likes to wear scratchy woolen longjohns (with stripes, thereby suggesting the outlaw or jailbird) and keeps his head and eyebrows cleanshaven (the latter contributing to the bald intensity of his gaze). Disciples have reported conflicting first impressions: "He scared the shit out of me!"; "He was the greatest comedian I'd ever seen"; "He had the kindest, wisest eyes." He might be mistaken for a truck driver, a construction worker, or possibly a Hell's Angel. The stories of his conversion triumphs are testimonials to the power of his native charisma, which (reputedly) needs no props or "transcendance mechanisms" (Kanter 1972). A flyer distributed in the *Chronic* workshop in 1984 relates the tale of how Gold intercepted a stockbroker rushing to work one morning and simply asked, "Do you have the time?" That stockbroker never reached his office, nor even glanced at his watch, for he recognized the call to participate in the "Work" and followed his master to California. Gold's former wife, Cybele, offers a similar account of her first meeting with her future master while browsing through a perfume stall in a "hippie" crafts market. She had barely observed his disheveled appearance when he gazed into her eyes and said, "Well, ready to work this time round?" Her immediate reaction was, "Boy, am I ever!" (*Autobiography of a Sufi*, 1977: vii).

CHARACTERISTICS OF "CRAZY WISE" ADEPTS

Feuerstein (1991) describes the radical style of initiation into spiritual values of "crazy wise" adepts who seek to jolt their apprentices out of their cognitive boundaries by using trickery, clowning, obscenity, or threats, and they frequently employ the breaking of taboos associated with drugs, sex, and nudity. A uniquely American and secularized version of "holy madness" seems to surface among Orrin Klapp's five different kinds of American heroes. Klapp (1962) identifies the "Winner" (or smooth operator) and the "Splendid Performer" (which would correspond to the "crazy wise" characteristics of Trickster and Clown). Stone, in his study of Werner Erhard's image, adds the "Versatile Entrepreneur" (one who is successful in a wide field of endeavors) to Klapp's list of heroes. As the following examples demonstrate, Gold embodies these characteristics of the American folk hero, as do Erhard, and other "exemplary prophets" (Weber 1946) arising out of the Human Potential Movement.

THE "WINNER" OR CHARLATAN

Stone (1982) notes the appeal of the American mythic hero, the snake oil salesman, the brash and outrageous huckster whose behavior assaults the norms of genteel respectability. The 1960s witnessed a revival of interest in cynical heroes like the "con artist," the "smoothie," and "sharpie," according to Orrin Klapp (1964). Stone (1982) argues that contemporary Americans are inclined to trust the con artist hero, once he has been identified as such, if only because they can predict that his behavior will always be based on self-interest. Like Erhard (Stone 1982), Gold's "bad act" has turned away some potential followers, but it has intrigued others. One Montreal core group leader claimed that it was exactly this quality that initially drew him to Gold:

> A friend of mine was telling people he'd met a real teacher. I decided to check it out. Then I got the whole truckload dumped on my head. "Interesting!" I thought. "It's either true or else this guy al Washi has the most phenomenal way of dealing with people, or else he's the most incredible con man going." My initial reaction was either this is right on and there is nothing else to do, or else I'm being totally conned, and either way this is a good place to hang out because if I'm being conned I want to find out how, so it won't happen again, and if not there is nowhere else to be.

The theme of fakery and chicanery is rife in IDHHB literature. One poster, for example, blatantly advertised "Fake Sufi Dancing/Snake Fufi Dancing." The *Shakti Handbook* (1974) features a photograph of Gold and his wife posing in white robes and turbans at the entrance to a Disneyland cardboard mosque. The cover of *Autobiography of a Sufi* displays Gold sporting an obviously false wig and beard. In *The Seven Bodies of Man* (1989, iv), Gold tells us how he was engaged in a dinner conversation with a wealthy dowager who was about to write out a generous donation to the IDHHB. Gold, at that moment, impulsively bent forward, leering and drooling into her plate, and began spouting nonsense—causing his would-be benefactor to close her bank book and retreat in disgust. Paradoxically, this strategy is often successful as a "double bluff," attracting experienced seekers who have learned to be wary of the hustle of "fake" or incompetent gurus on the North American spiritual scene.

Gold plays the role of charlatan or quick-change artist in his public appearances. When this researcher attended an IDHHB "sufi dance," Gold bounded into the room, clad only in a loose *dhoti* and a turban decorated with a sequined dollar sign. When Gold visited the Montreal Shakti center in August 1973, he appeared for his lecture in an orange sari, his eyes ringed with kohl, and spoke for several minutes on *samadhi* with a thick Indian accent. Then he turned around, whipped off the sari, wiped his face clean, and donned a fez and mustache. Suddenly he was Mr. Gurdjiev, talking to the sophisticated Muscovites in his rustic Russian accent. Next, he proceeded to mime a Kentucky farmer humping his mule while declaring in a Southern drawl that *any* activity could become a path to spiritual awakening. He concluded this performance by asking his audience what criteria they would use to distinguish between a "real" and a "fake" master?

GOLD, THE JOKER

Gold once described himself as "a master of the anticlimactic punch line." A brilliant comic (his students claim he once worked professionally as a stand-up comedian in Hollywood nightclubs), he will eloquently build a suspenseful narrative only to conclude with a feeble, meaningless punch line. The puzzled silence that ensues is explained as "equivalent to a Zen koan." He maintains, however, that the purpose of his humor is to administer shocks to "wake up the machine." When a woman in the Chronic workshop complained, "I love your sense of humor, but when are you going to tell us something useful?" he explosively denounced her "ignorance" and reduced her to tears—but then kindly explained that through telling jokes he could "convey information more quickly."

THE VERSATILE ENTREPRENEUR

At the Chronic workshop in 1984, Gold told us the tale of how he went out and got his first job at fourteen. He walked into a large New York City department store and asked to speak to the manager, who assumed that he was offering his services as a delivery boy. "I'm not applying for a specific job," Gold said. "What I want is your permission to hang around for three days and observe how this store operates. Then, when I find a job that needs to be created I will apply for it." Sure enough, the young Gold drew up a proposal for a high-level managerial post and the manager, impressed by his initiative, awarded it to him. For Chronic participants, the moral of the tale was, "I'm not offering you a job, I'm encouraging you to create your own."

BREAKING TABOOS: THE SUFI "WAY OF BLAME"

One of the most baffling features of Gold's leadership is his sudden, shocking aberrations in behavior, which are referred to as "turn offs" and "gross outs" by his disciples. Gold's teaching method is rationalized by core group leaders as a test of loyalty: "The sufi way of *malamah* . . . which means the real master offers the student an excuse to leave, so he does something to destroy his own credentials, so that only the serious, discerning student will remain."

Feuerstein offers an alternative explanation—that the purpose of the "crazy wisdom" method of administering shocks is to awaken the disciples. Cybele Gold provides a striking example of this pedagogical method during her birthday party in the midsixties:

> Mr. Gold smilingly and gracefully cut a piece of cake for me, and suddenly smushed it in my face, inviting me afterward to do the same to him. . . . Pretty soon everyone was laughing and throwing cake around the room. "Remember this is food and food is sacred!" he shouted. . . . I said "Hey, I need to go and shower." So I went upstairs and turned on the water but before I could close the door or take off my clothes, Mr. Gold and a few of the older students ran in and grabbed me. . . . There we stood in our party clothes . . . in this very small shower stall with melted wet cake running down our socks and over our toes ("My Life with Mr. Gold," part 3, by Cybele Gold: no pagination).

A well-known spiritual therapist and colleague of Gold, Claudio Naranjo, describes a particularly outrageous terror tactic perpetrated by Gold on his unsuspecting followers:

> Let me tell, as an instance, how after a certain night of snowing, E. J. managed to convince everybody that they were not only snowed in, but (through simulated radio news to the effect that the orientation of the North Pole was rapidly changing) created a confusion to the effect that a new glaciation age was upon us. After some time of illusionism those present were convinced that they would never be able to get out of the house and that the best they could do was to prepare for death by lying down on the floor and listening to readings of the *American Book of the Dead*. And so they did, for days, I was told (*The Seven Bodies of Man*, E. J. Gold 1989, xv).

A similar event occurred at the "Christmas party" held at the Crestline Cal-ifornia headquarters in 1973. Visitors arriving were greeted by a "guard" dressed in a Nazi uniform carrying a toy machine gun who informed them that they were entering a Nazi concentration camp. Several students balked at this prospect and turned back home, but the three hundred–odd members who remained spent three days living in a crowded room, ate only lentils, peanut butter, and water; were deprived of adequate sleep; and were issued passes to go to the outhouses, escorted by the "guards." At the end of the third day, "Herr Commandant" Gold descended the spiral staircase to the bottom landing with his fellow "officers" (all wearing Nazi uniforms) and performed a slapstick comedy, which "broke up" the prisoners—until Gold announced it was *their* turn. Everyone had to stand up and entertain the company for five minutes. Then one hundred single dollar bills came floating down the staircase, and Gold announced it was time for a "beer bash," which reputedly turned into a "drunken orgy" (Palmer 1976, 17–19).

Paradoxically, Gold's students appear to derive a sense of security from the surrendering to the *insecurity* of their relationship with Gold. One woman who had lived in the Grass Valley community for five years commented: "Sometimes he will ask you to do something that is stupid, pointless—and then he will yell at you for being stupid enough to obey him. He'll say, 'Don't listen to me! What the Hell makes you think that *I* know what I'm doing!'"

THE HIERARCHY OF MEMBERS

Throughout its ephemeral experiments, the Institute for the Development of the Harmonious Human Being has retained its name and changed its location only once: from Crestline to Grass Valley, California, in the early eighties. Its mem-bership is composed of four levels: at the top of the pyramid is the founder E. J. Gold, but he sometimes shares his pedestal with colleagues. Between 1974 and 1980, he formed a charismatic duo with his (now-estranged) wife, Cybele, with whom he coauthored two books (Gold and Gold 1976; 1977). The editorial page of the *Shakti!* magazine, for example, lists "Babaji al-Washi and Mataji Kali-nanda" as "founders." Other spiritual teachers—distinguished mime artists, rabbis, sufi masters, and HPM therapists—collaborate on occasion with Gold and float in and out of his schools to lecture or conduct workshops. Former Gold disciples (Gestalt therapist "Sheikh Yassun Dede" of Vancouver and mime artist/puppeteer "Bob" in Winnipeg, for example) still consider Gold to be their "master," but they pursue independent careers, creating and directing their own spiritual schools. One noteworthy "crazy wise" graduate is "Rex" of the Hell's Angels, who met Gold in the early seventies:

> Rex was sitting in one of those all-night bikers bars in L.A., when E. J. walked in, sat down and started talking, got the gang's attention, and talked all night.

"Sufi Dancing" at the Abode of the Message, New Lebanon, New York. This former Shaker site has been communal from 1776 till today. (*Courtesy of Art Rosenblum*)

> The next morning a bunch of bikers rode up to Crestline to participate in the Work. Most of them dropped out, but [Rex] . . . well, he's greasy, fat and obscene, and *we* think he's pretty obnoxious . . . but E. J. considers him now a *master* in his own right.

Rex was a writer for *Penthouse* magazine and after meeting Gold continued to write the fake erotic testimonials for the *Forum* column, but he began to inject his pornographic stories with hidden "teachings" and "spiritual clues" in response to the advice of Gold, who claimed that *Penthouse* readers are really looking for spiritual not sexual highs—but they don't know it yet, because sex is the closest they've come to the "waking state." Rex works exclusively within biker gangs, seeking to transform them into "secret mystery schools."

The second level is formed by "Core Group," the circle of fifty-odd longterm disciples, family, and friends who live on or near the Gold estate in Grass Valley, California. Core Group members report that living with Gold involves intense spiritual training. These disciples compose, edit, and print IDHHB literature; rehearse the traveling puppet shows; and plan the ongoing experimental "schools." Annual workshops are held at the IDHHB (most recently the "Bardo Boot Camp"), and many of the Core Group leaders are beginning to form small spiritual groups of their own.

The third layer of the hierarchy is represented by local "study circle leaders"—who originally joined a local "school," survived its "debriefing," and accepted Gold's invitation to join in the "Work." Study circle leaders often move into the centers and live communally, following their sudden promotion to full-blown teachers and proselytizers in Gold's latest "school," where they are "put on the spot" and must learn to take risks in what turns into a crash course in "crazy wisdom." They must invent ordeals for their students and draw upon their own innate source of "holy madness." Many of these study circle leaders join the Grass Valley community on a temporary or permanent basis.

The bulk of membership is provided by the lowest stratum—the ephemeral "students" who sign up for one of the schools, become "sufis," "puppeteers," or "thanatologists" but rarely survive the "debriefings," the "gross outs," or the organization's subsequent metamorphosis into a new NRM. Intending to explore dimensions of sufism, sci-fi, mime, shamanism, gestalt, and so on, these students are puzzled by the scientific flavor and gnostic underpinnings of the literature. They are likely to be "turned off" by Gold's weird sense of humor and by the flimsy, "phony" quality of the institutions. When the "school" is debriefed after a few months or weeks, they are invited to join in the "Work." If they ask "What is the Work?" they are told, "When you are ready for the Work, you will know what the Work is." Very few respond to this challenge.

The attrition rate at this level is very high. In Montreal, for example, between 1973–1974, around three hundred young people drifted through the *Shakti!* training, but not one of them signed up for the freshly concocted *Wud Sha Lo* (Palmer 1976). Very little effort is made to retain these lower-level members, who are viewed as unwitting and expendable "guinea pigs," recruited for the benefit of Core Group and study circle leaders who need practice in honing their "crazy wisdom" teaching skills.

Gordon Melton's *Encyclopedia of American Religion* (1984) cites the IDHHB's 1988 membership figures, which claim 250 members in the twenty U.S. centers and fifty members in five Canadian centers. These figures fluctuate according to how successful the most recent "spiritual school" has been in its recruiting efforts. While no random membership survey has been conducted on the IDHHB, on the basis of participatant-observation in the 1973 *Shakti!* "white room training," and the 1984 Chronic workshop in New York City, a rough sketch of Gold's following might be attempted, as follows: Around 80 percent are U.S. citizens and the rest, Canadians and Europeans, and perhaps 40 percent of Gold disciples are Jews. Their ages range from twenty-five to forty, with a few older Jewish couples in their sixties.

The Core Group and study circle leaders might be described as experienced spiritual seekers, people who, by their own account, were disillusioned with the more "world-rejecting" NRMs (Wallis 1984) like the Divine Light Mission or dissatisfied with the commercialized, unwieldy institutions of more "world-affirming" NRMs like Scientology and Arica. While they appreciated the spiritual training offered in "world-rejecting" groups, they were too sophisticated to imbibe their totalistic worldviews and too individualistic to tolerate their authority patterns. As for the "world-affirming" groups, they found their teachings watered down and popularized and their clientele overcrowded and undiscriminating. IDHHB leaders tend to be well versed *before* encountering Gold's ideas in some of the more sophisticated and intellectual mystical literature available in the counterculture: with authors like Carlos Castaneda, Idries Shah, Herman Hesse, Sufi Sam, and P. D. Ouspensky, and sacred texts like the *Way of the Pilgrim*, the *Philokalia*, and the *Tibetan Book of the Dead*. Already familiar with the "crazy wisdom" aesthetic, they were attracted on first encountering the IDHHB by its aura of romance, mystery, and adventure, which Gold and his Core Group exude so potently.

RECRUITMENT STRATEGIES

One of the most puzzling aspects of Gold's operation is the apparent reckless waste of human resources and money. Much of their advertising is ineffective because their posters are so subtle that it is highly unlikely the public would recognize these as invitations to spiritual work. For those few who do respond, it can be very difficult to locate the centers or get permission to attend meetings. Once inside the door, the aspiring initiate is often put through daunting tests. One study circle leader described her initiation as follows:

> I first wandered into a second hand Science Fiction store called Cowachin, and I noticed the clerk was acting strange like a robot, repeating the phrases of his customers and moving in a jerky, mechanical fashion. My friend and I were amused, but as we left, he handed us a flyer advertising a "Sacred Dance" demonstration. We decided we had stumbled upon a secret Gurdjiev group after seeing the dance, which was like the Sacred Gymnastics. So, we called the bookstore several times, but they put us off for weeks. When Gary went to visit Cowachin, the young man behind the counter denied that there was anything spiritual going on. Meanwhile we saw all these cryptic posters showing a fat lady from the back sitting at a soda counter, labelled "Objective Thinking" with no explanation, just the phone number of the bookstore. Finally, after several weeks, they phoned and invited us to an evening meeting.

It appears obvious that the group's inaccessibility at certain phases and the obscure references used in their advertising would *limit* their appeal to a fairly sophisticated clientele. Only those who were familiar with *In Search of the Miraculous*, Castaneda's books, or the Nasruddin stories would be likely to persist. One member, steeped in the lore of Gurdjiev and Hesse, described herself as "mad with spiritual desire" when she first encountered Gold's movement:

> [I] felt very lost . . . I was reading a lot of Gurdjiev, but it made me feel a sort of calling to something inside me. I would meditate every morning before I went to work, but when I got back in the evening everything seemed meaningless and unreal. I would feel a pain in my chest as if something were tugging at me, and would get into my car and drive and drive. I was hoping to meet someone or see a sign, but all I saw were shopping centers, Howard Johnsons, parking lots.

This state of mind evidently rendered her receptive to the mystification and baffling ordeals presented by the IDHHB.

INTERPRETATION

Wallis argues that the *sect*, previously defined as a splinter movement from a church, can also evolve out of a *cult* type of religious organization. According to his redefinition of a *sect*, the latter is understood by its members to be *uniquely legitimate* as a means of access to truth or salvation, as opposed to the *cult*, which, like the denomination, is conceived by its members to be *pluralistically legitimate*—that is, but *one* of a variety of paths to salvation (Wallis 1975). The IDHHB, in a paradoxical fashion, appears to combine certain features of a cult with certain characteristics of a sect and might be analyzed as composed of constantly shifting, concentric *layers* of "cultlike" and "sectlike" communities. Gold appears to trigger these transformations and separate or combine these layers through what Weber (1936) termed *charismatic displays*. Some of Gold's displays (like his millenarian/survivalist prophecies) *enhance* his authority and intimidate students into withdrawing into the womblike world of the sect. Other displays (like his "debriefings," "turn offs," and "gross outs") appear to be deliberate attempts to *diminish* his authority and send students away.

The IDHHB is "cultlike" in that it has developed an eclectic synthesis of ideas and practices that are available in the prevailing "cultic milieu." It is "loosely organized, with no clear distinction between members, non-members, tolerant of other groups and beliefs, and often transitory" (Wallis 1975, 41). Gold appears to be on good terms with other religious leaders emerging out of the Human Potential Movement—leaders like Oscar Ichazo, Jose Silva, Claudio Naranjo, Werner Erhard, and Pir Valayat Khan—and freely draws upon their techniques and ideas. Gold's "schools" share many of the characteristics of weekend intensive therapies in the HPM, noted by Stone (1976), including multiple participation, eclecticism, and no expectation of organizational loyalty. Above all, Gold's organization, like the ideal-typical "cult," grants its members the freedom to determine what constitutes acceptable doctrine—that is, it operates on the basis of "epistemological individualism."

A deeper examination of the authority patterns and ideology of the IDDHB, however, suggests that it is really a sect masquerading or posing as a cult. First, the ideology only *seems* to change or fluctuate. Gold is actually expressing the same basic ideas over and over again in different languages. Underlying his eclectic forays into sufism, Tibetan Buddhism, Gurdjiev "ideas," and Christian/Jewish mysticism is the same concern, which might be characterized as a neo-Gnostic quest for knowledge, a search for the shaman's power of flight and control over the soul's destiny. Gold's cathartic ordeals to "awaken the machine" are not so very unlike Scientology's "process" of "erasing engrams" and ultimately unveiling the omniscient, omnipotent, immortal being L. Ron Hubbard identified as the "thetan." Gold's eschatology is expressed in its purest and most comprehensible form in the "Grapefruit Rap" audiotape, which is often played for students shortly before their school is "debriefed." In this lecture, Gold uses the metaphor of the grapefruit to explain how one can feed and strengthen the Essential Self through engaging in irritating work to "wake up the machine."

The IDHHB's highly controlled leapfrogging between religious traditions, each language highlighting a new facet of Gold's revealed Truth, serves to underscore the inadequacy of traditional attempts to encapsulate the sacred. For Gold students, these deceptive departures into ecumenism demonstrate the ineffable nature of spiritual life and the urgent necessity for firsthand experience. When Gold spreads the fan of his dazzling doctrinal kaleidoscope, rather than implying a message of epistemological pluralism, he is convincing his students that religious traditions offer no more than distorted glimpses of partial truths and that only a living enlightened master can provide the necessary stimulus for real spiritual growth. While Gold savors the wisdom of other traditions, he also pokes fun at their rules and taboos, and he mimics or mocks their holy men. This establishes his own credentials as a "real master." While Gold's illusory openness, pluralism, and cynicism is what might initially appeal to experienced and jaded seekers who have learned to be wary of authoritarianism, in the end, they must turn to him as the final repository of revealed Truth and submit to the extraordinary rigors of the "Work"—or leave.

The conviction members cherish—that they are part of an elite "mystery school"—reoccurs in their interviews and published testimonials. Cybele reports her experience of dancing in a circle with the IDHHB Core Group and suddenly feeling dizzy—then receiving a hallucination of Gold, his features transforming into those of Gurdjiev, the great Russian mystic—and realizing the true identity of the IDHHB dancers as Gurdjiev's reincarnated community at Fontainebleu ("My Life with Mr. Gold," part 1, n.d.).

Gold reveals his own sectarian stance in a dialogue with Claudio Naranjo concerning "the internal conflicts that have so far kept the human potential movement from realizing its own potential." Whereas Naranjo describes the HPM as "the democratization of psychotherapy," Gold insists that "for every one individual who goes through transformation, there are a thousand who just go through the motions . . . if you have the intensity, you don't need the belief system" (*Magical Blend* 29 (January 1991, 25). Thus, he upholds the notion of the elite, the elect or chosen few, characteristic of a sect (Wallis 1975, 42–43). In response to Naranjo's assertion that the "global predicament" requires that salvation should become the destiny of a greater number of human souls, Gold cuts in:

> *Gold*: Don't say it; the numbers are the same.
> *Naranjo*: There has to be a larger number for the. . . .
> *Gold*: No, it's the same number, and it always will be.

Wallis argues one of the main distinctions between a *cult* and a *sect* is that, as a result of its individualistic nature, the former maintains *weak* boundaries between its own ideology and competing ideologies in the cultic milieu. Hence, "members typically move between groups and belief systems" (Wallis 1975, 42). This does appear to be the case for the short-term students involved in the "schools." A careful scrutiny, however, of the long-term members' careers suggests that the IDHHB might, in fact, be described as a self-contained *replication* of the surrounding "cultic milieu." Gold's close disciples, experienced "seekers" and avid readers of the wide range of occult and mystical literature available to participants in the counterculture, have evidently found within the IDHHB a playing field for spiritual experimentation and innovation. They can sample California's abundant "spiritual supermarket" (Greenfield 1973) without even venturing outside the boundaries of the IDHHB. Their "conversion careers" are *speeded up* as they dress up as sufis one year, Hassidic dancers or Christian angels the next. Their energies are absorbed in role playing as they assume the doctrinal certainty of a "sufi" or "Franciscan" and set up new centers and proselytize. While superficially maintaining these public roles and sectarian stances, they are inwardly cultivating a detachment from all "religious trips" and are relativizing these competing authoritative claims. One *Shakti!* leader noted:

> I had just come out of the Divine Light Mission where we used to stand on the street and hand out literature. Now, after *Shakti!* came out, I found myself back on the street, wearing white robes and a turban, handing out this weird literature I didn't understand myself. A friend saw me and got really worried. He used to play bridge with my old husband. I tried to tell him it was a game, that I was only *playing* at being the brainwashed religious nut—I was now *watching myself* in this role—but he didn't understand. He kept saying, "I'm worried about you, L——, let's go for coffee and talk about it!"

TEACHERS' TRAINING IN CRAZY WISDOM

The unusual features of the IDHHB resemble some of the "major puzzles" that Wallis (1982, 106) confronted when studying the Children of God:

> The rapidity and extent of change, the willingness continually to . . . break down the institutional structures so laboriously created, and the frequent turnover in leadership; the constant ambiguity and contradiction as to approved belief and practice; the perpetual movement; the tensions between open and closed attitudes to membership . . . and between freedom and control, and finally, the relative indifference to prophetic failure.

Wallis's variation (1984) on Weber's theory of charisma suggests a promising framework for interpreting Gold's career. Wallis sees the divagations in Moses David's career, his abrupt volte-faces, his series of failed "world's ends," his doctrinal improvisations as explicable strategical responses to the perennial problem every charismatic leader confronts: that of "creeping institutionalization." By pruning his followers so that only the most loyal remain, by over-turning the institutions leaders have set up and depriving them of "tenure of office," Mo is able to keep his creativity unbridled and to remain the sole direct access to truth.

At the August 1984 Chronic workshop, Gold delivered a speech asserting that his aim was not to build a large corporation but to "keep the family business run-ning"—to show his friends how to "operate the corner store." His dearest wish, he claimed, was to "retire from the business," to "hand over the keys— both sets of keys." It became clear as a participant observer in *Shakti!* that the purpose of Gold's enterprise was *not* to build a large membership nor to make money. I was puzzled by what appeared to be his reckless inefficiency when I observed over the summer of 1973 how the core group managed to collect a group of twenty-odd students to enroll in the Wednesday night "White Room Training," how these stu-dents eagerly anticipated the visit of "Pir al-Washi," and how they responded to one of Gold's abusive tantrums in which he dismissed them as a "high school debating club"—a ritual "turn-off" that drove all but three students away. One leader noted in retrospect that this experience was for her "a real lesson. We worked *hard* to find those people—we had a nice little group going and he had to come along and ruin it! I really resented it, but now I appreciate that E. J. was giving me the opportunity to learn." This and other accounts seem to support my argument that the purpose of these experimental schools was to provide a chal-lenging learning environment for young spiritual teachers. Indeed, it appears that the most outrageous antics perpetrated by study circle leaders on their unsus-pecting students received the greatest approval from headquarters:

> All of a sudden we found ourselves distributing this weird Shakti literature. I hardly had time to study it myself before we were teaching it. I couldn't believe anyone would respond to this stuff. We'd put up posters announcing sufi story-telling evenings with the words "Objective thinking" and nothing but our address. No one would call, then suddenly a bunch of people would arrive out the blue and we'd have to scramble to set up a class. We kept calling Core Group and asking "what do we do next?" and they'd just say "Use your initia-tive, keep them working. You guys have no imagination." It seemed the more ridiculous things you could make people do, the more approval you got.

One ex-member described her first workshop as follows:

> I was shown into a room and told to sit there until my guru told me what to do. I kept waiting for someone to come and give me instructions. After a while I noticed all these lollipops—hanging from the plants, under the cushions, the curtains . . . I figured this was some kind of test, so I began to collect them and ate one—but I never found out if I'd passed the test or not. Next we were told to put on diapers, bonnets and knitted booties, and we played all afternoon in a huge playpen, saying "goo" and "gah," and building block castles, and drinking

out of oversize baby bottles. Later, when I got to know Lucille she told me she was in a panic because she'd received no instructions about this workshop, so she invented these exercises at the last minute.

Another informant recalled how she received a phone call at 4:00 a.m. inviting her to a cocktail party commencing in half an hour, and she scrambled to dress appropriately and found herself sipping cocktails and listening to jazz at the Shakti center by 5:00 a.m.

If the divagations in Gold's career are to be explained as another instance of "resistance" (Wallis 1982)—a strategy to avoid the rigidity, compartmentalization, and complacence that tend to "settle in" once a movement becomes large, successful, and institutionalized—surely the extraordinary degree and refinement of the IDHHB's planned instability is unnecessary and overdone. Gold's postmodernism, his sophisticated and self-conscious conceptual artistry—closer to the tradition of John Cage than to America's great New Religious founders like Mary Baker Eddy and Joseph Smith—"makes sense" as conceptual art and also as a new pedagogy, the endeavor to provide a stimulating learning environment, an exclusive academy for talented "interns" in the "crazy wisdom" tradition.

CULTIVATING ENTREPRENEURIALISM

The phoenixlike quality of Gold's schools, each one born out of ashes of the last, might be perceived as a dramatization of Gold's eschatology, in which death and rebirth play a prominent part. Disciples must get used to living "between lives" in the "transit state," so that their anonymous passage from mask to mask, their shamanic ability to transform into sufis, robots, or Japanese puppets, is understood as practice for future conscious rebirths. From a sociological perspective, the participation of IDHHB members in role-playing exercises and in creating and destroying institutions might be seen as a means of cultivating skills and attitudes to cope more efficiently with the pressures and precariousness of modern life, identified by neologisms like "role overload" (Glendon 1985), "future shock" (Toffler 1974), and "facework" (Goffman 1976). In this respect, Gold's movement accommodates our pluralistic, fragmented and rapidly changing society.

But Gold moves far beyond encouraging accommodating attitudes toward "mainstream culture" and the docile indifference this stance implies. Pervading IDHHB literature is a euphoric celebration of the American Way, a vision of U.S. urban life in its bustling, incongruous vulgarity, as a glamorous frontier and playground for spiritual hustlers and adventurers. Its patriotic message might be compared to the *Book of Mormon*, which informs us that the Lost Jews of the Old Testament are alive and well in the Americas and that Jesus appeared to us over here. Gold's books, particularly *The Avatar's Handbook* and *The American Book of the Dead*, preach a similar message of spiritual nativism and promise endless "journeys to the east" in suburban malls. They tell us you don't have to cross the Caucasus with Gurdjiev's White Russian refugees to find mystery and adventure: you don't need to travel to Turkey or to Persia to find secret sufi masters; you can stumble over them in Alex's Borscht Bowl in Manhattan, in Disneyland, or in small-town laundromats. Failing that, you can create your own postmodernist "mystery school" out of brash commercial symbols and American folk motifs.

Zarestky and Leone (1974) see NRMs as providing an important outlet for individual needs, community services, and the free enterprise that is part of the American heritage but is stifled by the large corporations and the universalistic norms of today's society. They see "cult conversion" as "a folk answer to a system that is over-diploma-ed, over-certified, too specialized . . . it is the last voice for de-centralization and the free enterprise system" (1974, xxxvi). The IDHHB stands out as an extreme expression of this entrepreneurial spirit.

REFERENCES

Campbell, Colin. 1972. "The Cult, the Cultic Milieu, and Secularization." *A Sociological Yearbook of Religion in Britain* 5: 119–36.

Ellwood, R. S. 1973. *Religious and Spiritual Groups in Modern America:* Englewood Cliffs, NJ: Prentice-Hall.

Feuerstein, Georg. 1991. *Holy Madness: The Shock Tactics of Crazy-Wise Adepts, Holy Fools, and Rascal Gurus.* New York: Paragon House.

Gold, Cybele, and E. J. Gold. 1976. *Beyond Sex.* Crestline, CA: And/Or Press.

———. 1977. *Joyous Childbirth: The Conscious Birth.* Crestline, CA: And/Or Press.

Gold, E. J. 1975 *Shakti: The Gestalt of Zap.* Crestline, CA: Core Group Publications.

———. 1974. *The Butterfly of Retribution.* Crestline, CA: Core Group Publications.

———. 1974. *You Look Somehow Familiar Forever.* Crestline, CA: Core Group Publications.

———. 1975. *American Book of the Dead.* San Francisco: And/Or Press.

———. 1975. *The Joy of Sacrifice: Secrets of the Sufi Way.* And/Or Press.

———. 1978. *Autobiography of a Sufi.* Nevada City, CA: And/Or Press.

———. 1977. *Applying the Science of Conscious Death, Rebirth, and Awakening: As Taught by E. J. Gold* (pamphlet).

———. 1977 and 1979. *Secret Talks with Mr. G.* Vols. 1 and 2. Nevada City, CA: IDHHB Inc.

———. 1990. *Pure Gesture: Macrodimensional Glimpses of Other Realities.* Nevada City, CA: Gateways Fine Art Series.

Kanter, Rosabeth Moss. 1972. *Commitment and Community: Communes and Utopias in Sociological Perspective.* Cambridge, MA: Harvard University Press.

Klapp, Orrin. 1962. *Heroes, Villains and Fools: The Changing American Character.* Englewood Cliffs, NJ: Prentice-Hall.

Stone, Donald. 1976. "The Human Potential Movement," pp. 93-115 in *The New Religious Consciousness,* ed. Robert Bellah and Charles Glock. Berkeley: University of California Press.

Stone, Donald. 1982. "The Charismatic Authority of Werner Erhard." In Roy Wallis, ed. *Millennialism and Charisma* Belfast: Queens University, pp. 141–75.

Wallis, Roy. 1975. "The Cult and Its Transformation," in *Sectarianism.* London: Owen.

Weber, Max. 1946. *Essays in Sociology* by H. Gerth and C. Wright Mills, eds. New York: Oxford University Press.

8

KASHI

A Meeting of East and West in a "New Age" Community

J. Gordon Melton

What is broadly termed the New Age movement manifests in many different forms, from environmental activism to the wearing of crystals believed to possess transformative powers. One item high on the New Age agenda is the call for the development of a new religion that can rise above the sectarian strife and obvious differences between religions and, without losing the special assets and contributions of the various world religious traditions, find common ground in a more universal realm. As a whole, attempts to produce such "universal" religions have merely produced new sects, usually advocating a theosophical-occult perspective.

During the 1970s, in central Florida, a different experiment in realizing such a universalized religious faith/practice emerged in the Kashi Church Foundation, a small community of some one hundred sixty individuals. It should be noted that Kashi has not developed as a part of the New Age movement and might resent any attempt to connect it with that movement, especially with some of its popular practices, such as channeling. However, Kashi developed out of the same milieu that produced the New Age movement and seems to have realized in practice exactly what the movement has set as its goal. For fifteen years, Kashi has demonstrated the workability of a universal "ecumenical" perspective in the life of an otherwise diverse faith community. As might be deduced, the life of such a community is not found in its agreement on beliefs but in its experience of unity in worship and daily life. Thus, an exploration of the community most appropri-

---

Written for this anthology.

ately begins in its activities rather than its tenets.

ENCOUNTERING KASHI

SRI GURU CHARANA SAROJA RAJA
NIJA MANU MUKURU SUDARI
BARANOAN RAGUBARA BIMALA JASU
JO DIAYAKU PHALA CHARI

About one hundred people were gathered at an outdoor shrine dedicated to Hanuman, a deity figure representing divine service, when they rose to begin singing the Hanuman Chalisa, a lengthy hymn composed by Tulsi Das, the celebrated Indian poet of the fifteenth century. The shrine is located, however, in rural Florida, not India, and the hymn is sung by a community of American devotees to a new (for Florida, at least) faith, which, while drawing heavily on Indian sources, has a decidedly interfaith character. At first appearance it seems Asian, but group members insist that it embodies a broad, tolerant approach to all expressions of faith, be they Christian, Buddhist, Hindu, Jewish, or Muslim. The community finds its common life of devotion in the guidance, teachings, and example of Ma Jaya Bhagavati, the founder/leader of the community, who established Kashi (now the Kashi Church Foundation) on the Sebastian River in the fall of 1976.

Before the chanting, which begins the regular evening gathering, the fire had been lit in the *dhuni*, a hearth that had been carefully and lovingly decorated several hours earlier. The signal for the chanting to begin is the appearance of a light across the small pond adjacent to the shrine, the signal that Ma, as the community's leader is respectfully and affectionately known, has begun the short trek to the shrine to begin an hour of *darshan*, during which time she shares her personal presence and insights with the gathered throng. As she makes her way around the water, accompanied by several of her close disciples, the chant continues in medieval Hindi:

SANKATA KATAY MITAY SABA PIRA
JO SUMIRAY HANUMATA BALABIRA

As it reaches the next verse (translated "Glory, glory, glory be to Hanuman"), the only visible reference point in the song for the uninitiated is reached as hands clap three times to emphasize "Jay, jay, jay."

JAY JAY JAY HANUMANA GOSAEE
KRIPA KARAHU GURUDEVA KINAEE

By this time, Ma has arrived, and, as the sound of the hymn fades, she is seated and ready to begin. She follows her usual practice, beginning with the very young. One by one she draws the nursery-age little ones to her. She is obviously enjoying her chance to hold each, however briefly, and to give each a favor or two, a piece of candy and/or a cookie. Everyone else delights in the Art Link-letter–like interaction with the unpredictable two-year-olds. The children set a positive, uplifting, even humorous beginning for the serious phase of the darshan, which is to follow.

Now, those who chance to be attending their first darshan really see Kashi's guru in action, and she begins to break their traditional images of a religious leader one by one. Dressed more for the weather (the temperature has dropped into the thirties), she has none of the appearance of a religious prima donna. Her accent is pure Brooklyn, not Indian. She has no pious platitudes to offer. She is direct and straightforward, never pulling her punches with either her admonitions or her words of genuine compassion. Her language is expressive, liberally sprinkled with profanities, which jar the attention of the uninitiated. As she speaks, she calls individuals before her. The interaction immediately crosses some boundaries. The local ministers in nearby churches might surely say she had stopped preaching and gone to meddling.

She answers questions that several people have written to her. She calls others who are making a transition through a crisis before her and in the same no-nonsense fashion tells them to get their act together. She shares a personal victory with one person. Overall, the message is not so much one of specific direction as it is an encouragement to take the context of love and service provided by Kashi and herself as additional strength to face problems, make necessary decisions, and become a person of integrity, love, and devotion. Her toughest words are for those who are trying to avoid facing unavoidable obstacles to their growth and maturity. Noticeably, the harshest statement is never left isolated but consistently tied to a reminder of the context of her continuing concern and caring for the individual. She has no power to control and direct, only to cajole and remind each person of the goal toward which they have chosen to go by their presence at Kashi.

The personal work finished for the evening, it is time for Ma to speak. Tonight she chooses not to address the group but to sing. It is a long devotional narrative, Ma's own composition, sung with great emotion, about the River Ganges. Again to the uninitiated it is simply a moving presentation, until one understands the context of the song as a remembrance of a previous incarnation in which she is with her husband-guru. After the song, darshan ends quickly. Ma steps to the fire and engages in *arti*, an offering of light, a traditional Indian devotional practice. As she departs around the pond to her dwelling, another *bhajan*, that is, devotional song, begins, and others continue the arti. The darshan ended, everyone goes home to one of the four main houses or several apartments on the Kashi grounds or to a private dwelling in the community nearby.

INVADED AND INVESTIGATED

I have chosen to begin this report of an investigation of the life of the Kashi, an ashram located in east central Florida, with a description of a darshan session because it best symbolizes in its foreign words, unfamiliar setting, and high-level strangeness in the midst of a conservative southern community, all the obstacles I encountered in attempting to assess this unique community. I was one of several specialists in the study of nonconventional religion in the West who, over the initial objections of the guru, was invited to evaluate Kashi. After a decade of cordial relations with the local community, the ashram had been attacked by the local media as a result of some members of the community opposing the expansion of the local airport. The local attacks on Kashi found their way to Miami and then to Chicago, where a leading anticult organization (without investigating the charges) had repeated all the accusations in their newsletter. Neither would probably have affected Kashi too much had not an unexpected traumatic event intruded.

Some seven years ago, a woman left her infant in the care of Ma. The mother disappeared and the child was raised with Ma's family as one of her own. Then suddenly, the mother reappeared and with the aid of the local sheriff seized custody of the child (later permanently awarded by the courts) and returned to Denver, where she now resided. The seizure of the child was done, to say the least, without finesse, and the court's seeming refusal to recognize any familial attachments between the child, Ma, and Kashi led some at Kashi to feel that Kashi might be vulnerable at other points. The leadership wanted some expert opinion about both their life and their risk-level. In light of my years of study of so-called cults, I was one of several people invited to evaluate Kashi.

I agreed to participate only if I could have complete access to the community—its records, its worship services, its people (including former members), the school and its children, and its leadership. All was made available as requested. In December 1989, I made a trip to Kashi for four days as part of a research team. During our stay, I interviewed a number of members both formally and informally, looked through the community's records, spoke with most of the leadership, and had several lengthy interviews with Ma Jaya Bhagavati, who overcame her initial concerns (about invasion of the privacy of the pastoral relationship she has with Kashi's members) and cooperated fully in the research efforts. We prepared and administered a questionnaire to all the adult members, along with more direct probings. Subsequently, a survey was conducted among former members. Then in January 1990, I returned to Kashi for several additional days of observation.

It had been my usual practice to enter into the process of assessing a community through its literature. Religious leaders tend to write treatises, scripture commentaries, or meditation manuals. Followers tend to record, transcribe, and publish their guru's speeches or at a minimum the accounts of their own experiences of transformation under their spiritual director's guidance. In the absence of literature, increasingly, there are cassette tapes. But at Kashi, published literature was woefully lacking. For more than a decade, Kashi had kept a low profile. Fortunately, there were a variety of records of the group's activities over the years, including transcripts of many darshan sessions. Most helpful, one of the leaders of the community, a former English professor, had been writing a history.[1] By the end of the week in Florida, I had enough data to finish the assessment.

While the submission of an initial report in January 1990 essentially ended the research on the community, I became intrigued with the group, which has, for new Eastern-based religious groups, an unusual commitment to social service. Thus in subsequent years I stayed in touch. I was able to visit Kashi on several occasions when business otherwise took me to Florida. More important, I have several times annually been able to visit with members during their regular visits to their West Coast center in Los Angeles, where they maintain a unique ministry to victims of AIDS. These visits have provided a means of verifying the observations made during the original visit to the Florida center in 1990. Also, by staying in touch over the years, I was able to continue a dialogue, especially with Thomas Byrom (who unfortunately passed away in October 1991), who patiently answered all my questions about the fine points of the group's belief structure and explained in detail how their practices flowed from their spiritual commitments.

BACKGROUND

What now exists as the Kashi Church Foundation emerged in the mid-1970s as a result of the intense religious experiences of one Joyce Green, then a housewife in Brooklyn, New York. Green was born in Brooklyn into a poor Jewish family, the youngest of four children. Her mother died when Joyce was thirteen, and Joyce spent much of her teen years on the streets. In 1955 she married an Italian Catholic and settled down to life as a wife and mother. Her life took a dramatic turn in December 1972. A person whom she recognized as Jesus Christ appeared to her. It was the first of four apparitions. The essence of these encounters was her experience of an overwhelming love coming from him. He also engaged her in several conversations in which he told her that she would find herself teaching, and she must "teach all ways, because all ways are Mine." He spoke also of his mother and about the meaning of humility, service, and suffering. When he departed the last time and did not return, she was left with a great sense of spiritual hunger.

The experiences of Jesus appearing left her, a Jewish housewife, with somewhat of an identity crisis, but nevertheless, she took her problem to a Jesuit seminary on Long Island. She found some empathetic responses from a few of the residents who were open to her story of an encounter with Jesus, and it was at the seminary that she began her teaching, in a somewhat informal setting.

In the spring of 1973, she had a second set of apparitions, this time from someone who called himself Nityananda (d. 1961). According to her own account of the period, at the time she had never heard of this former Indian teacher who had become so influential among Americans attracted to Hinduism.[2] Nityananda introduced himself as her teacher. He promised that if she listened to him and learned from him, Christ would return to her in a most unexpected way. He appeared to teach her every evening for almost a year. Nityananda's main teaching concerned what is termed *chidakash*, the state in which love and awareness are one.

Nityananda also called Green by the name of *Jaya* ("victory" or "glory" in Sanskrit), and, in addition, mentioned someone named Hilda. In the course of her activities, Green, who began to call herself Joya Santanya, was finally led to the center founded by Swami Rudrananda, the recently deceased disciple of Nityananda's who had brought his teachings to America. From there she was led to Hilda Charlton, a pioneering teacher of Eastern wisdom in the New York City metropolitan area. Charlton had spent many years in India and had returned after World War II to teach. Because she wrote little and traveled out of New York City infrequently, she was not as well known as some of those gurus who led the expansion of Eastern faiths in the 1970s.[3]

As Joya was discovering this new world, events at home took a different turn. On Good Friday 1974, while the housewife Joyce Green was making preparations for her Roman Catholic family, she began to bleed. The bleeding stopped on Saturday, but on Easter Sunday shortly before the family meal she began to bleed not only from her hands but her forehead. The stigmata, often associated with Christian holy people, became noticeable to all, producing some consternation among her pious Catholic relatives.

Then in July, after many months of regular instructions from Nityananda, she saw yet another person, this time an old man wearing a blanket. He introduced himself as simply her guru, but she recognized in his devotion to Christ the fulfillment of his promised return. Now, she felt, she had a constant inner companion with whom to share her love of Christ in all its singularity and intensity, such was the intensity of this person's devotion to Christ.

Meanwhile, Hilda Charlton was directing Joya into new avenues of experience. She catalyzed Joya's role as a teacher. Having sought out Charlton to become her student, she found herself quickly lifted up as an equal and a teacher in her own right. Charlton also introduced her to Richard Alpert. In the 1960s, Alpert had emerged beside his colleague Timothy Leary as a prophet of psychedelic drugs. Then, in the late '60s, he had left the drug scene and traveled to India, where he encountered and accepted one Neem Karoli Baba as his guru. Baba was near the end of his life on earth (he died in 1973). Though Joya had

Statue of Jesus on the grounds of the Kashi Church Foundation. (*Courtesy of Richard Rosenkrantz*)

never met Neem Karoli Baba physically in this life, she quickly recognized him as the person who had appeared to her and identified himself as her guru.[4]

Consequently, Joya and Alpert (now known as Baba Ram Dass) had an immediate and intense point of bonding. Ram Dass, the intellectual, was most impressed by the wisdom he found in this unlettered young woman, and he soon announced that his followers should look to her for spiritual guidance.[5] Those who found their way to Charlton's apartment where Joya usually held forth, most having already spent some time with the new wave of Eastern spirituality spreading across the West, either loved her or hated her. For some she was a refreshing voice of directness and clarity. But others were repulsed by her street language and her most ungurulike appearance. She had little use for the trappings of the average Eastern teacher. By the time of her break with Ram Dass (and with Charlton), those who did like her had founded some thirteen "houses," cooperative living facilities where they could have daily satsang (gatherings). Joya began to travel, lecture, and give retreats.[6]

In July 1976, along with a few of her closest students, Joya moved to Vero Beach, Florida, and in October 1976 they leased the first seven acres of what became the ashram. About this time she made her first West Coast tour. Life settled down into a routine. She lived in Florida and periodically visited the houses scattered across the country. All that changed in 1978. In the fall of that year, she became seriously ill. The illness lasted into the new year, and many believed that she might die. In response, most of the houses closed and the people moved to Florida. By the middle of the year, approximately eighty people had established their residence on or near the small parcel of land. Only slowly did Joya's health return.

Once settled, and as Joya's health improved, the new residents turned their attention to other concerns. Not satisfied with the quality of education in the local public school, they began their own school. In 1980 they purchased an additional thirty-five acres and began to erect the buildings for needed classrooms, residence space, and meeting rooms. They incorporated the Kashi Church Foundation. In July 1980, Ma married a Korean Tae Kwon Do master, Soo Se Cho. A short time later, using Cho's experience, and in need of creating jobs for a number of the new residents, members of the community began a company that manufactures martial arts equipment. The company was called Macho, a appropriate image for the company but in fact derived from the names of Ma and her new husband.[7]

During the next nine years, the community grew steadily. It now comprises approximately one hundred adults and sixty children who live either at the ashram or nearby. The children attend the Kashi school, which is completely staffed by the members. Many more have an affiliation to Kashi but continue to reside in other locations around the country. They often come to the ashram for special occasions. Outside of Florida, a small active community exists in the Los Angeles area. It has a significant outreach to the AIDS victims, and Ma and members of the ranch visit it for a long weekend once a quarter.

BELIEFS AND PRACTICE

Kashi is organized around the presence and teachings of Ma Jaya Bhagavati and as such is not a doctrinally oriented organization. It draws its existence out of the dynamics of interaction between *guru* (teacher) and *chela* (student). Those who operate out of a Western religious tradition, which generally gives doctrinal statements and affirmations of beliefs a central role in both the shaping of identity and the maintenance of boundaries, have some difficulty in approaching and comprehending religions in which beliefs are given secondary status.

To say that the group is not doctrinally oriented is not to say that it does not have a body of beliefs that are held in common, only that they are assigned a secondary status and are rarely used to define a member of the ashram. Also, rather than having a single scripture from which beliefs are derived, a number of sources have contributed to the building of Kashi's perspective. Of particular importance are the monistic philosophies of Nityananda (and the writings of two other significant Indian teachers, Shirdi Sai Baba and Ramana Maharshi, to whom Ma was introduced by Hilda Charlton) and especially the example and instruction of Neem Karoli Baba. Virtually all members of Kashi accept Baba as Satguru and acknowledge their affiliation with his lineage. Beside these sources, however, stand the more traditional sacred writings of the Bible, the Bhagavad Gita, the Ramayama, the Dhammapada, and the sacred poetry of such saints as Rumi, Kabir, and Ramprasad.[8] At the most basic level, ashram members assume the presence of God in everything and in each person. The object of their life together is to become aware of that presence in their daily life and to manifest that presence in a life of service.

The events that catalyzed the formation of Kashi began with the identification of Joya's guru, the one who had appeared to her at her home in July 1974, with Neem Karoli Baba. Baba had been a revered holy man in India. His early years were somewhat obscure. He had many names and had finally settled upon one that meant "a *sadhu* (mendicant) from Neem Karoli." He died in India in 1973. His followers were many, and the stories about him abundant. Some of his disciples saw him as an incarnation of Hanuman, the ideal servant of God in traditional Indian thought.[9] Hanuman's adventures are recounted in the Ramayama, a classic Hindu scripture. Others revered him as an incarnation of Padmasmablava, who first brought Buddhism to Tibet.[10]

Out of the relationship with the old man in the blanket who appeared to her, Joya came to believe that she had known him in a previous incarnation. When Neem Karoli Baba had been a young man, he had been known as Lakshman. Lakshman had taken a child bride (a common practice in India), and they lived happily together for a half century. Joya came to believe that she was that woman and that she had since been reincarnated as a Jewish housewife. Having grasped the import of that prior relationship, she was ready to begin her life of teaching in seriousness. She understood that Baba was her former husband and guru and that he represented to her an ideal of devotion and service to God. She also came to believe that the essence of Hanuman was the essence of Christ, and in sharing this belief with Neem Karoli Baba, she felt her original awakening to Christ deepened and fulfilled.

The perspective shared at Kashi most closely resembles a form of *Advaita Vedanta*, a Hindu perspective that attempts to overcome the dualisms of the common sense view of existence and present the truth of the essential oneness of inner and outer, human and divine. The perspective that all is one, an essential insight shared by various forms of mysticism East and West, leads both to an acceptance of and to an extreme relativizing of all particular religions and religious expressions. They are simply individual attempts to express the Truth of Oneness. Eventually all religious strivings lead to the same place. However, while in one sense religions are lesser phenomena, in another sense they are valuable tools that function as bridges in the self's awakening to reality. Thus at Kashi, all "Ways," all religions, are welcomed and find their expression in some manner.

Hindu lore pictures humans as possessed of a subtle body and energy system. An important aspect of that system are seven centers of psychic energy located along the spine, the *chakras*. The system is energized by *kundalini* or *shakti*, which is seen as rising up the spine to the crown or *sahasrara chakra*. The goal of yogic practice (kundalini yoga) is to rouse the latent kundalini (which is seen as sleeping at the lowest or *muladhara chakra*) and allow it to rise to the crown, where it merges with the Absolute. The sahasrara chakra is seen as the seat of self-realization, the contact point between human and divine, where the individual comes to know his or her identity (oneness) with the Absolute. Nityananda uses the image of a wave (the Self) coming to know the self's complete identity with the ocean.

In classic kundalini yoga, along with enlightenment, a concentration is placed upon the rising kundalini and the various manifestations that it produces—psychic phenomena and unusual states of consciousness. Swami Muktananda taught such a system. Nityananda (and Ma), however, concentrated upon the awareness that comes from self-realization. In the awakening of the divine energy and the realization of the oneness that is pictured as occurring at the sahasrara chakra, the individual consciousness is experienced as dissolving into (merging with) the divine consciousness. This moment of self-realization produces a state of all-encompassing loving consciousness. From living in this state of consciousness, a new awareness arises, chidakash. Nityananda's teachings centered upon an exposition of chidakash; that is, he spoke from the awareness he had obtained from living in the state of loving awareness. Chidakash is also spoken of as the state in which love and awareness are one. Kashi's members believe that Ma operates from a similar state of awareness and speaks and works from chidakash.

Another way of expressing the unitive awareness is with *svasthya*, a term prominent in the Ashtavakra Gita, which means, literally, resting in your own true nature. Svasthya is a state of loving awareness. Ma shares svasthya in *darshan* (a term that means "sharing the inner sight of God"), and she refers to the chela's being in the presence of a self-realized person (the guru) and sharing in his or her consciousness. Most members of Kashi report having had one or more particular moments when they have shared an intense experience of loving awareness that has arisen in a moment of special rapport with Ma and has become a key event in their ongoing relationship with her as guru and spiritual guide.[11]

The basic perspective adopted by Kashi is expressed in a cycle of worshipful activity. By the time the move was made to Florida, regular evening darshans had become common. In 1977, Ma and some of the group were in India for Durga Puja, a popular Indian festival centered upon the Mother Goddess under her various guises, especially as Durga. It became an annual festival at Kashi in 1978. Durga Puja is a ten-day observance each October. Also added to the annual calendar was Shiva Ratri (at the new moon in March); Ma's birthday (May 26); Guru Purnima, the day for honoring gurus held in July; and the Maha Samadhi (death) of Neem Karoli Baba, in September.

CHRISTIANITY AT KASHI

In the context of the American religious community, those elements of religious practice that Kashi has drawn from India attract attention by their uniqueness. However, from its beginning, Kashi has been inspired by Christianity at all levels of its life and work. This Christian inspiration runs far deeper than simply an attempt to accommodate to the surrounding dominant culture, though it does provide a base for initial interaction with the local religious community. The Christian orientation initially derives from the apparitions of Jesus Christ to Ma in December 1972. Those visitations initiated Ma's career and developed within her a devotion to Jesus, which, however unorthodox, is quite genuine. The initial apparitions were, of course, followed by the stigmata, which have appeared on several occasions.

The initial departure of Jesus after his four apparitions led to a great hunger in the then–Joyce Green for his return. That hunger was not satisfied until she encountered Neem Karoli Baba, who had experienced as she did an intense inner communion with Christ. He saw Christ as everyone's guru, and he often remarked, "He was crucified so that his spirit could spread throughout the world. He never died, He never died. He is the soul, living in the hearts of all." Thus, in accepting Neem Karoli Baba as her guru, Ma also added his unique Christian piety to her own.

As her relationship to Neem Karoli Baba and her devotion to his favorite deity, Hanuman, deepened, Ma found that, to her, the essence of what Baba called Hanuman and what she saw in the Christ was the same. Thus, her devotion to Hanuman was seen as another factor in her maturation as a Christian mystic as well. In reading the Christian mystics, she equated the experiences of someone such as a St. Theresa of Avila with similar experiences she was having through Baba.

A final element undergirds the Christian element at Kashi and tends to negate the tension that many might feel between the Eastern practices and Christianity. Advaita Vedanta, by relativizing all religions, sees each of the many different religious strivings as aimed at the same goal and hence ultimately equal. All paths that are inspired by love and are followed with a pure heart lead to God, the Absolute, self-realization. The following of a different path is more a matter of culture, tradition, and personal taste than of Truth. Thus, what has emerged at Kashi is a universal faith very much informed by Christian mysticism, symbols, and piety (though a form that is quite alienated from orthodox Christian faith). One is continually reminded of this Christian element in the several statues and numerous pictures of Christ and the Virgin Mary encountered throughout the ashram. Kashi's own path respects and honors all, since members believe that ultimately other paths, followed with sincerity and love, lead to the same goal.

Belief in the worth of all paths has been of particular comfort to a number of members of Kashi who have retained some attachment to the Christian church in which they were raised. Approximately 20 percent of the members are regular in their attendance of Sunday worship at one of the local Christian congregations. The celebration of Good Friday, Easter, and Christmas has become a standard part of the annual cycle of celebration for the entire community. Members have sought and found acceptance and become active in the local ecumenical association. Finally, the Christian orientation manifests in the importance given to service in the local community and beyond. Above and beyond their jobs and obligations to Kashi, members are expected to spend some time each month in a self-chosen effort assisting people in need.

While Christian practices and expressions are most evident to the outside observer, not to be missed are the welcome expressions of other religions. Judaism, Islam, Buddhism, and American Indian spirituality all find a place at Kashi. And around the lake that dominates the center of the ranch, shrines to Judaism and Buddhism have assumed their place beside those to Hinduism and Christianity.

ORGANIZATION

Kashi's reason for existence is to provide a community for those people who wish to relate to Ma Jaya Bhagavati as their spiritual guide or guru. She offers her guidance in darshans each evening and in a *puja* (worship) session each morning at 6:30. The darshans will usually last between one and two hours and feature both personal

Statue of Hanuman on the grounds of the Kashi Church Foundation. (*Courtesy of Richard Rosenkrantz*)

work (in which Ma will deal with individual concerns and questions) and talks by Ma. The puja began in recent months as community members asked to share the early morning worship conducted by Ma for many years. On any given day, depending upon work schedules and the weather, as many as half of the community will attend.

Ma is assisted in spiritual leadership by a small number of ordained ministers. The ministers are the ones who generally relate to the larger ecumenical religious community in the county, and some are active as lay people in nearby churches. Overlapping with the ministers are approximately forty monks, the most dedicated of the community who have been selected by Ma for special teaching. A monks-only darshan is held on Wednesday evenings. Among the monks (primarily the older ones) are ten *pujaris* who assume leadership roles in the major festivals, especially in the Durga Puja each October.

While Ma gives spiritual leadership, the church is organized as a corporation that is headed by a fifteen-member board of directors. The board, which meets monthly, is elected at the annual community meeting, and members serve two-year terms. The board has hired executives to manage the day-to-day affairs of the community and oversees the large staff, which works in the church office and the school.

Over the years, the board has led in the construction of the ashram, which began with two buildings in 1976. There are now four large houses, each of which includes some rooms used as residences and other for communal use (including a library, communal kitchen, and school rooms). Ma and her husband have a modest apartment in Kashi house. Their apartment opens onto an enclosed parklike area called the "Corral." The Corral is the location of several small temples dedicated to different deities. With the exception of the daylight hours several days each week when the area is reserved for Ma's use, it is open for members of the community who wish access to the temples or simply experience the beauty of the area. Once or twice a week, Ma conducts a yoga class for the children there. There is also a small studio where Ma paints. Her impressionistic paintings decorate most of the buildings on the property.

The overwhelming majority of Kashi members are college graduates, and many have graduate degrees. They had a primary concern for providing a solid education for their children and thus made the establishment of a school a top priority in 1979. The school now includes facilities to care for students from the age of six months through high school. As of 1979 there were seventy-eight students, of whom seventeen were from homes not associated with the community. (Those now attending the school include some from both ends of the educational spectrum, some very gifted children and a few problem children who were failing in the public school.) The school, though not accredited, is licensed by the state of Florida, and its program is directed to college attendance. Its graduates who have gone on to college have done well. In 1989 six were in college and all six were consistently on the dean's list.

On the spectrum of religious groups in America, on the issues of recruitment, Kashi would be identified with those groups that actively discourage high-pressure recruitment. Almost all of their members had previously been attracted to Eastern thought, and usually vegetarianism, and discovered Kashi as they moved around from one group to another looking for the right one. A high percentage of the group has been affiliated for more than five years. New people who wish to join, especially those who also want to move to Florida, go through a rather rigorous screening process. They must first visit for a short time on at least three occasions. They then have a personal interview with Ma. They must then agree to the basic rules: The diet is vegetarian, though fish and milk are consumed. No alcohol, tobacco, or narcotic drugs (except as prescribed for medical purposes) are allowed. Chastity is the norm, except for brief periods when a couple is attempting to have a child. (While adopting some of the disciplines of a monastic life, the ashram existence in by no means separatist. Televisions and newspapers abound and contacts with the outside world are many and varied.)

Having adopted ashram life and agreed to the basic rules, the individual must then make a commitment to a life of serious religious seeking. Finally, a weekly financial commitment is made. This money covers the person's room and board and the operation of the school and ashram. As of the end of 1989, the weekly assessment was $163. The assessment demands that all of the members be employed. While a few have jobs on the property (school, grounds, and office staff), most have jobs in the community. These jobs vary widely from skilled to semiskilled. Approximately twenty are employed by Macho Products.

INTERACTION WITH THE OUTSIDE WORLD

Since the 1990s, while not seeking any presence on the national level, Kashi has been quite active in interaction with its neighbors in the county where it resides. The majority who work away from the ashram hold a variety of jobs from domestics to nurses, business executives, and professionals. While a number of community members work for Macho Products, the business started by church members, Macho also employs a number of people not affiliated with Kashi and thus provides a setting for constant community interaction.

Each spring and fall, Kashi sponsors a community openhouse to allow neighbors, friends, and acquaintances to spend a day at the ashram, tour the grounds and school, and meet the members. In recent years, over five hundred people have attended.

Kashi calls its community service organization "Annadana." Through Annadana, members have been active participants in volunteer capacities with the county Meals on Wheels, the soup kitchen, the hospice, the crisis hotline, and the antidrug program. Many regularly visit in nursing homes and the local hospital. Each Christmas, they sponsor a Christmas tree sale.

The very visible action of Ma at the beginning of each darshan symbolizes a special ashram concern for children. That concern permeates the Kashi membership. It is most visible in the commitment to pro-life activity, the willingness to assist unwed mothers, and the opening the ashram to homeless children. Through the Christian Children's Fund, Kashi members support children in India. Kashi School has taken in several children who had experienced problems adjusting to the public school environment. The low student-teacher ratio has allowed for the personal attention that was necessary for meeting their particular needs.

Since the early 1990s, the social outreach of Kashi in response to the encouragement of its leader has been dramatic. A number of charitable enterprises have emerged, none more dramatic than the ministry to people with AIDS in Los Angeles. The AIDS ministry has been all the more noteworthy because of its willingness to encounter and its ability to be helpful to a group of the most personally alienated and socially isolated of AIDS victims.

CONCLUSION

While the New Age movement has become an international phenomenon of some major cultural import and even staged some massive interfaith New Age celebrations, it has largely failed to create the worshipful communities that demonstrate its universal spiritual ideals. Operating without particular reference to the movement, Kashi has, in effect, quietly developed the workable model of an ideal New Age religion. Kashi is not a perfect model, but it has seriously tackled the key problem of integrating its members' diverse religious allegiances into a common religious life of devotion and service that retains aspects of and honors all of the world's faiths. While keeping a low profile during its period of initial growth, it has refrained from separatism and demonstrated its willingness and ability to work with the larger religious community in its neighborhood. Rather than merely paying lip service to Jesus as another significant religious figure, it has encouraged and nurtured a form of Christian mystical piety that thrives within an interfaith context.

The New Age has emerged at a time when the great religious traditions of the world are no longer separated into closely knit geographical communities. Every community has become religiously diverse. On a theological level, such diversity calls each tradition into question. On a social level, some manner of peaceful interaction among differing religious communities has become a necessary element in its very survival. The New Age approach, borrowing heavily form Eastern and Western mystical spirituality, offers one possible (though by no means the only) solution to the problems created by religious pluralism.

In a relatively short period, "New Age" religion has established itself in the West. The movement is still relatively small, but it has attained a measurable presence. Its universal mystical approach to life has shown itself attractive to a wide variety of individuals. While fifteen years is hardly enough time to indicate whether it is the wave of the future or merely another religious perspective that will now offer itself on the menu of Western religious options, there is little doubt that a community like Kashi is more than just another item of social or religious exotica. In its life, it is dealing with one of the more vital problems confronting Western religion.

NOTES

1. Much of the story of the development of Kashi has been told in Thomas Byrom, "River Child: The Course of an Apprenticeship" (MS. loaned by the author, 1990), 265 pp.

2. Through the presence of his students, Nityananda has emerged as one of the more important Indian gurus in the West, though he never visited Europe or North America. His students, especially Swami Muktananda, brought his lineage and his teaching to the West, and Nityananda now claims a strong following. Nityananda did not write books, but his teachings were written down by early disciples and published in sev-

eral editions in his native language, Kanarese. The first English translation appeared as *Chidakash Geetha* (Mangalore, South Kanara, India: Anand Math Mannagudde, 1941). A second English edition (translation) appeared in 1963, and in 1981, one of Hilda Charlton's students, designated only as Dennis, brought out a new edition without the explanatory notes as *Chidakash Geetha: Greatness of the Soul* (South Kortright, NY: Eden Books, 1981). Most recently, M. U. Hatengdi of the Nityananda Institute headed by Swami Chetanananda, of Nityananda's lineage, has written a biography, *Nityananda: The Divine Presence* (Cambridge, MA: Rudra Press, 1984), and with Swami Chetanananda produced a new translation of the Geetha, which appeared as *Nitya Sutras* (Cambridge, MA: Rudra Press, 1985).

    3. Charlton taught a form of spirituality that tried to synthesize Eastern perspectives with the more mystical approaches to Western faiths. As such, she did not see herself as a Hindu but as decidedly interfaith. Shortly after her death in 1988, Golden Quest, an organization composed of some of Charlton's former students, began to publish collections of her talks. To date, four titles—*Master Hilarion, Skaanda, Saints Alive,* and the *New Sun*—have appeared, with others scheduled for publication in the near future. Biographical material can be found in "Hilda: A Celebration of Love," *New Sun* 2, no. 6 (June 1978): 20–29; and Ian Cohen, "New Age Notes," *New Frontier* 8, no. 3 (April 1988): 27, 41–43. The story of her relationship with Ram Dass and Joya Santanya is told in Stephen Diamond, "In the Garden of Forking Paths," *New Age* 2, no. 7 (December 1976): 30–36, 62–69.

    4. Ram Dass originally introduced the American public to Neem Karoli Baba through his early work, *Remember, Be Here Now* (San Cristobal, NM: Lama Foundation, 1971).

    5. In the months following the dissolution of the relationship between Baba Ram Dass and Joya Santanya, a number of articles appeared, almost all of which concentrated their analysis upon Ram Dass, already a national personality. He wrote his own account of the incident in "Egg on My Beard," *Yoga Journal* 11 (November 1976): 6–11. The most widely read account was by Colette Dowling, "Confessions of an American Guru," *New York Times Magazine* (December 4, 1974): 41–43, 136–49. A more sympathetic account, written by someone who witnessed the relationship but has remained a disciple of Joya is to be found in Bill Byrom, "Finding Joya," *Yoga Journal* (May/June 1978): 23–29, 54–55.

    6. During this period, one book was published of the collected sayings of Joya Santanya, *Sharing Moments* (n.p.: Orphalese Foundation, 1976).

    7. On Master Cho and Macho Products, see Ata Yesilyaprak, "Master of the Macho Touch," *TaeKwonDo* 8, no. 8 (July 1988): 30–35.

    8. This list should not be seen as necessarily exhaustive.

    9. Hanuman is generally pictured as a monkey, and as such his image is one of the most frequently encountered in India.

    10. The stories about Neem Karoli Baba were collected and published by Ram Dass in *Miracle of Love* (New York: E. P. Dutton, 1979). The volume is standard reading for Kashi members, and large pictures of Neem Karoli Baba vie for wall space at the ashram with the pictures painted by Ma.

    11. The experience is analogous to, but quite distinct from, the experience in kundalini yoga of *shaktipat*, in which the guru uses his or her power to awaken the kundalini and give the first experience of shakti to the chela. The sharing of the loving consciousness of svasthya or chidakash produces a mystical experience in the chela, but one distinct from the rush of power reported by those who have experienced shaktipat.

9

"OUR TERRESTRIAL JOURNEY IS COMING TO AN END"

The Last Voyage of the Solar Temple

Jean-François Mayer

We, Loyal Servants of the Rosy Cross, declare that, as we left one day, we will return stronger than ever . . . for the Rosy Cross is immortal . . . Like Her, we are of all time and no time.[1]

The mysterious circumstances surrounding the dramatic "transit" of fifty-three members of the Order of the Solar Temple (OTS, Ordre du Temple Solaire) in Switzerland and in Quebec in October 1994 have spawned an unprecedented wave of public speculation and conspiracy mongering. The subsequent death of sixteen people in France in December 1995 and of five more in Quebec in March 1997 have only added to these conspiratorial speculations. Ironically, Joseph Di Mambro, Luc Jouret, and those who, over the course of months, methodically prepared their own deaths and the deaths of dozens of others were quite concerned about the impact their departure would have on the public mind and spent many hours creating a kind of legend that would survive their earthly exit. Why else would they have felt the need to send manifestos justifying post mortem their decision not only to members of the order but also to television stations, newspapers, and some other correspondents (including the author of this article)? The Swiss investigators found a tape, dating probably from the spring of 1994, in which one can hear the core group discuss the "departure." There is a telling exchange between Joseph Di Mambro and Luc Jouret:

Translated by Elijah Siegler. From *Nova Religio: Journal of Alternative and Emergent Religions* 2, no. 2 (April 1999): 172–96. Copyright © 1999 by Seven Bridges Press. Reprinted by permission of University of California Press.

JDM: People have beaten us to the punch, you know.

LJ: Well, yeah. Waco beat us to the punch.

JDM: In my opinion, we should have gone six months before them . . . What we'll do will be even more spectacular. . . .[2]

"More spectacular": such are the words used by Joseph Di Mambro himself. A movement such as the Solar Temple cannot escape its media-saturated era. It worries about its public image until the very hour of the "crowning of the work," to use its own vocabulary. Many fringe movements tend to cultivate a very high estimation of their own importance, and the OTS was no exception. The core members of the group understood themselves as an elect people who had incarnated periodically on Earth since ancient times in order to fulfill a cosmic mission. They had gathered together for that purpose and were ready to sacrifice their lives for its sake. Especially toward the end, some internal texts disclose these grandiose perspectives:

> Do you understand what we represent? We are the promise that the R[osy] C[ross] made to the Immutable. We are the Star Seeds that guarantee the perennial existence of the universe, we are the hand of God that shapes creation. We are the Torch that Christ must bring to the Father to feed the Primordial Fire and to reanimate the forces of Life, which, without our contribution, would slowly but surely go out. We hold the key to the universe and must secure its Eternity.[3]

In reality, like so many other movements that see themselves on the cutting edge of cosmic progress and that assign to minor events in their own history a global significance, the Solar Temple was in fact a tiny (and actually declining) group whose claim to cosmic importance would have been viewed as dubious by most commentators. But through a sensational act of self-immolation that compelled the attention of both popular and academic observers, the leaders of the Solar Temple came close to creating a durable legend for their esoteric order.

Unfortunately for the order's leaders, documents exist that, when analyzed carefully, begin to deconstruct this legend. If everything had worked as Di Mambro planned, no trace would have remained. Nothing, not even the bodies themselves, would have been recovered: "We will not let our bodies dissolve according to nature's slow alchemy, because we don't want to run the risk that they become soiled by frantic lunatics."[4] The Solar Temple's thorough preparation for their mysterious exit, however, could not take into account certain technical problems: Some of the devices intended to start the fire did not function properly, which made it possible for the investigators to seize a large number of written documents (in part found on computers that survived the fires relatively unscathed) as well as videocassettes and audiocassettes belonging to the group's archives. It is upon these sources that this article is in large part based.[5]

JOSEPH DI MAMBRO, THE GOLDEN WAY FOUNDATION, AND THE NEO-TEMPLAR MOVEMENT

Joseph Di Mambro was born in Pont-Saint-Esprit, in the French department of Gard, August 19, 1924. At the age of sixteen, he began an apprenticeship as a watchmaker and jeweler and very soon became fascinated with esotericism. In January 1956, he joined the Ancient and Mystical Order Rosae Crucis (AMORC), to which he would belong until at least 1968. In the 1960s, he apparently established links with several persons who would later play a role in OTS history, including Jacques Breyer, the initiator of a "Templar resurgence" in France in 1952 to which several groups, including Di Mambro's OTS, trace part of their roots.

Several major points of doctrine, as well as an embryonic circle of disciples, began crystalizing during the 1960s. After visiting Israel and dealing with legal problems in Nîmes in 1971 related to swindling and writing bad checks, Di Mambro set himself up in Annemasse, near the Swiss border. In 1973, he became president of the Center for the Preparation of the New Age, which was presented as a "cultural center for relaxation" and a yoga school. The center became a full-time job by 1976. That same year, eight people (seven of whom resided at a common address) formed a building society and purchased a house named "The Pyramid" at Collonges-sous-Salève, close to Geneva. Of these eight people, four would lose their lives in October 1994. The building society in fact sheltered an esoteric activity: the consecration of the Temple of the Great White Universal Lodge, Pyramid Sub-Lodge, was celebrated on June 24, 1976. Internal documents show that, of the fifty-three believers who died in October 1994, at least twelve already belonged to the group by the end of 1977.

The next step commenced on July 12, 1978, with the creation of the Golden Way Foundation in Geneva. This foundation would remain at the very heart of activities undertaken by Di Mambro's various groups over the ensuing years. Thanks to substantial financial sacrifices made by several members, the foundation bought an attractive property in a suburb of Geneva that was the site of meetings open to nonmembers. The Golden Way Foundation was above all a front for a nucleus of people called simply the "Fraternity,"[6] who took part in esoteric rites in a communitarian setting. This communitarian ideal played a role in attracting people to the group and also led later to disappointments when the gap between the ideal and the reality of everyday life became untenable for certain members. People belonging to the "Fraternity" held all assets in common; along with them lived people belonging to what was called the "Community," who kept their income, paid a rent, and bought tickets for food and beverages. In the context of the 1970s, it was only one attempt among many others at developing an ideal communal life. Indeed, one member who joined at that time had lived in the New Age community of Findhorn, Scotland, and was hoping to find something similar in the Golden Way.

Excerpts from an account given at a 1994 OTS meeting provide us with retrospective (and no doubt idealized) glimpses into the experiences of the pioneer members of the brotherhood:

> Meeting at first in a house which they called "the Pyramid," where every evening was devoted to rituals and meditation, they later moved near Geneva, to a large property which was discovered to be an ancient Templar command post. . . . There, living in a perfect fraternity where all was equally shared—salaries were put into a common fund and everyone received in return an equal share—they devoted all their free time to the cause of spirituality. Daily ceremonies quickly became operational at the highest degree, even more so because hermeticists, alchemists, and spiritually elevated people joined in. The Masters of the beyond regularly manifested themselves, with a presence visible, audible, and olfactory.

The Golden Way Foundation had impressive headquarters, but in order to spread its ideas on a larger scale the group needed a communicator. Enter a Belgian homeopathic physician, Luc Jouret (born October 18, 1947), who was probably introduced to Di Mambro by one of the victims of October 1994. On May 30, 1982, Jouret and his then-wife[7] were "accepted in the Golden Way" and took the oath of "Knights of the Rosy Cross." Di Mambro confided to some members at the time that Jouret had charisma and, being a physician, would be taken seriously; therefore, he should be pushed into the limelight, while Di Mambro would remain discreetly backstage. From that moment on, Luc Jouret became the propagandist for the group. Beginning in 1983, he gave lectures in Switzerland, France, and Canada. Cultural clubs were created and, from 1984 to 1990, the organization operated as a tripartite structure involving (1) public lectures and seminars given by Jouret and a few others under the label of Amenta; (2) an exoteric structure, the Archedia Clubs, for those wishing to go further; and finally, for a limited number of candidates, (3) an initiatory order (organized as the esoteric counterpart of the clubs) called the "International Order of Chivalry, Solar Tradition."[8]

Obviously, the group hoped to attract a wider audience, and it thus prepared structures meant for a much larger movement than it ever became. The success of Luc Jouret, a gifted speaker who easily attracted hundreds to his lectures, could only add fuel to the fire of such hopes. That Jouret was able to draw such large audiences to his lectures is proof that the topics he was dealing with were of interest to at least a part of the cultic milieu of the time.[9] However, because of the seeker's mentality typical of the cultic milieu, most of those who came to Jouret's lectures did not want to commit themselves on a firm basis and, despite the lecturer's success, significant growth for the OTS in terms of committed membership never materialized.

The group's Templar activities[10] had their roots in a 1952 "resurgence" in which the French esoteric author Jacques Breyer (1922–1996) played a central role. While reluctant to take upon himself any administrative responsibility in those Templar circles that claimed some link with the "resurgence," Breyer enjoyed the role of an elder adviser to whom those groups turned at crucial times in order to ask his opinion. Di Mambro did so several times.

Although Di Mambro's OTS considered the 1952 resurgence as a "first impulse," the real resurgence began for them on March 21, 1981. On that day, "knights" met at the Golden Way Foundation headquarters "to renew their oath of allegiance to the Order of the Temple and to the XXIIIrd Occult Grand Master to come."[11] One of the goals of the meeting was to achieve "Templar unity," and for this purpose the heads of two neo-Templar orders had been invited—Jean-Louis Marsan, Grand Master of the OSTS (Ordre Souverain du Temple Solaire, that is, Sovereign Order of the Solar Temple), and Julien Origas (1920–1983), grand master of the ORT (Ordre Rénové du Temple, that is, Renewed Order of the Temple). Like Di Mambro, both Origas and Marsan had been connected with the resurgence initiated by Breyer. "Templar unity" was not achieved, but such meetings show that members of these neo-Templar groups were partly interacting in the same milieu, with each group maintaining its specific features. For instance, the ORT was originally sponsored by Raymond Bernard (born in 1923), head of AMORC for French-speaking countries, who functioned for a time as the secret grand master of the ORT.[12]

After the death of Julien Origas, Luc Jouret briefly took control of the ORT as Grand Master, but he immediately found himself confronted with opposition from Origas's wife and daughter. At the same time, some Canadians linked to the ORT expressed a strong interest in Jouret's message. During this period of crisis (March 1984), Jouret, Di Mambro, and a Canadian member went to consult Breyer. Breyer told them that he thought it possible to develop something out of the small Canadian nucleus through restructuring the local groups and transferring the center of the OTS's activities to Canada. Breyer's advice was connected to apocalyptic considerations typical of his way of thinking: the "age of plagues," needed to open people up spiritually, was about to come because of the earth's growing corruptions. The area around Toronto, Breyer claimed, would experience less upheaval during this time of troubles. In 1984, the Golden Way Foundation financed Joseph and Jocelyne Di Mambro's emigration to Canada; according to Breyer's advice, the Di Mambros first moved to Toronto. And Breyer himself, at a conclave of ORT officers during Easter 1984 in Geneva, informed the gathered people that the deposit was "to be transported to Canada" where a "Noah's ark" was to be built.[13]

From 1984 forward, the movement had two centers of activity—French-speaking Europe and Quebec. The presence in Canada was also meant to reach the English-speaking world, mainly the United States:

> The Executive Council of this New Order decided that, in line with the historic destiny of the Order of the Temple, the headquarters of the Order should be

located somewhere on the North American continent. The reason for this decision is simple. North America has become the source of most of the new impulses which determine the way life evolves on this planet. It is therefore fitting that the modern Knight Templar of the old continent should play his part in the Age of Aquarius by adding his inspiration to that which his counterparts in the New World will bring to the planet.[14]

However, despite the beginning of a translation project designed to make certain rules and ritual texts available to English-speaking audiences, the order never had more than a handful of isolated members in the United States. In January 1989, at the height of its development and before internal turmoil took its toll on membership, OTS had 442 members, of whom ninety were in Switzerland (monthly revenues: $12,600), 187 in France ($12,700), fifty-three in Martinique ($3,400), sixteen in the United States ($1,125), eighty-six in Canada ($7,000) and ten in Spain.

FROM SURVIVALISM TO SELF-DESTRUCTION

In addition to these revenues, several well-endowed members donated large sums that amounted to hundreds of thousands (and up to millions) of U.S. dollars over the years. These donors hoped that their generosity would permit the financing of "life centers" on farms acquired in Canada and in Cheiry, Switzerland, in 1990. But the group's leaders diverted part of these donations into other areas, including their own travel expenses and living costs for community members with no external means of support. The constant need for funds led to financial problems, which were perhaps not entirely unrelated to the events of 1994.

Beginning in the 1990s, several members began distancing themselves from the order. Important donors among these members wanted to recoup at least some of their money, and the group's revenues began to decline. Di Mambro had long pretended (since at least the late 1970s) to represent the "Mother Lodge" and to receive his orders from mysterious "Masters" in Zurich. The theme of "Unknown Superiors" is a commonplace of occult movements such as Rosicrucianism, Theosophy, and the I AM Activity.

However, around 1990, Di Mambro's son Elie (1969–1994) began seriously to doubt the existence of the "Masters" of Zurich and discovered that his father had practiced fakery to produce the illusion of spiritual phenomena during the ceremonies celebrated in the order's sanctuaries. These phenomena—which included apparitions of spiritual entities—had been a major reason why several members had accepted Di Mambro as what he claimed to be. Even today, several leading former members remain convinced that, notwithstanding occasional fakery, some of the phenomena were authentic. Elie spoke openly about what he had discovered, which led to the departure of fifteen members. In 1993, there was a wave of resignations of French members who saw that their donations ended up as home improvements for their leader's residence. In February 1994, two members from Geneva sent an open letter to announce their decision to leave the movement because "real fraternity [did] not exist in this structure, as extolled in the teachings." They were also worried about what happened to their contributions, observing the absence of the "life centers" that were supposed to be created.[15] And these were not the only examples of defections.

Throughout the years, according to explanations provided by former members, Di Mambro had grown more authoritarian. He no longer helped with the daily chores, as he had in the original community.[16] He wanted to gather bright people around him but probably was also afraid of potential competitors. There was never any attempt at a takeover, but there were rivalries among Di Mambro's underlings, and some people felt that he was playing a game of divide and rule while expecting unconditional obedience from all members.[17] When speaking to the police, a Canadian member who broke with the Solar Temple in 1993 summarized the feelings of many defectors: "I did not feel that the people were living what they preached. And I was tired of the infighting and never being able to find out what was going on, so I left."[18]

A report on the organization's situation in Europe written to Di Mambro on December 10, 1993, by a Swiss OTS officer reflects the growing dissent that was affecting the group at this time. The document also shows how a longtime follower who had developed serious doubts about Di Mambro's honesty nevertheless wanted to persevere in serving the ideal he had dedicated his life to for so many years. This loyalty had tragic consequences, as he was murdered in October 1994 as he was about to leave the farm where he lived with other members. The report states,

> Rumors about embezzlement and various [forms of] skullduggery are propagated by influential ex-members. Many members . . . have left or are leaving. They feel their ideals have been betrayed. . . . It is even said that you have fallen because of money and women, and you're no longer credible. This is very serious for the Order's mission. There are even more serious grumblings, and you know them. Here they are: everything that we saw and heard in certain places has been a trick. I have known this for some time. Tony [Dutoit][19] has been talking about this for years already. . . . I have always refused to pay attention to these rumors, but the evidence is growing, and questions are being asked. This calls into question many things I've seen, and messages. I would be really upset if I had to conclude that I had sincerely prostrated myself in front of an illusion!!! . . . There is enough stuff here to send less committed people packing. And all the resignations and departures of recent times just confirm it. I don't want to analyze the reasons that could lead to such trickery, which was motivated by good intentions no doubt, but which transgressed the rules of common sense, when we see the mess we're in now. It's also been said that Zurich has never existed, that it's pure fantasy . . . . As for myself, I believe in the cosmic

law. I believe in the message received 2000 years ago by which I aim to live. I believe in the life ethic which my parents taught me and which I aim to apply. I believe in a conscience which I aim to find within myself. If I go down this path, I cannot be wrong. And no rumor, true or false, could deter me from what I have to do. I will continue to work in the Order and for the mission as long as you need me and as long as I can do it.[20]

These controversies were not confined to the OTS sanctuaries. During the 1980s, the Solar Temple had more or less escaped anticult polemics. Jouret had two lines written about him in an entry on the ORT in a booklet put out by a French anticult group in 1984,[21] but in the 1987 edition, both he and the ORT were left unmentioned. Oddly enough, in the end critical coverage did not come from Europe or Canada but from the island of Martinique: on September 10, 1991, Lucien Zécler, president of the local branch of the Association for the Defense of Families and Individuals (ADFI), the leading anticult movement in France, sent a letter to several associations and centers in Quebec, asking for information on the OTS. The request followed the decision of several citizens of Martinique to sell their worldly goods, leave their families, and move to Canada to escape coming disasters. At the end of 1992, a former member of the OTS went to Martinique to publicly denounce the Solar Temple, which provoked local media coverage.

Not long after, Luc Jouret ran afoul of law enforcement officials in Quebec after he encouraged trusted members to buy guns illegally. The police were investigating anonymous threats from an unknown terrorist group at the time and, when tipped off by an informer about the attempt by an inexperienced OTS member to get three guns with silencers, began to watch several members of the group. The members were arrested in March 1993. The Canadian media reported the story and published extracts from police wiretaps revealing the homeopath's unusual interest in firearms. This gave the OTS more unwanted publicity and cooled the enthusiasm of several members, even though Jouret and two of his followers were given the relatively mild sentence of one year of unsupervised probation and a fine of one thousand Canadian dollars (to be paid to the Red Cross) for buying prohibited arms.

These problems, internal and external, are crucial in understanding the OTS's gradual distortion and disintegration. Di Mambro had gathered around him a group that lent an appearance of reality to the fictions he created. And now this imaginary universe began to come under critical scrutiny. The head of the Solar Temple apparently decided to respond by taking himself and his followers away from the scene altogether.

Throughout the 1980s, the Solar Temple's doctrine had grown increasingly apocalyptic. Even in his public meetings, Jouret frequently alluded to cataclysmic upheavals that threatened the planet with imminent destruction. The apocalyptic thinking of the Solar Temple had clear ecological connotations, and Jouret's lectures often described the earth as a holistic living entity who could no longer endure what humankind was inflicting on her.[22] The concern of the leaders for the environmental situation seems to have been a sincere one: Di Mambro kept several video recordings of TV reports about ecological problems; in his home, investigators also found a testament showing that Di Mambro and his wife had considered listing ecological organizations in their will.

The Solar Temple's message was survivalist as well. We have already seen that this had caused the group to establish a base in Canada, which was considered to be a safer place. In 1986, the temple published in Toronto two volumes under the title *Survivre à l'An 2000* (Survival beyond the Year 2000). The first volume was mostly doctrinal. The second dealt with the subject in a very practical way, establishing guidelines as to what provisions to store in order to survive a disaster that would destroy all essential technologies and what to do to survive atomic, bacteriological, or chemical warfare. In addition, it provided a detailed first aid manual. Nothing in these volumes would lead one to suspect suicidal tendencies; to the contrary, it seemed as if the adepts hoped to find themselves among those who survived the apocalypse unscathed.

How, then, can one explain the reversal that led a core of members to choose collective self-immolation? Besides survivalism, there were other latent themes, always on the same apocalyptic foundation, which had the potential to encourage somewhat different pursuits in the group.[23] In a certain way, the Solar Temple's goals were classically gnostic in that they ultimately aimed at "the release of the 'inner man' from the bonds of the world and his return to his native realm of light."[24] The manifesto-testaments sent just prior to the events of October 1994 echo such feelings: "We, Servants of the Rosy Cross, forcefully reaffirm that we are not of this world and we know perfectly well the coordinates of our Origins and our Future."[25] "Always belonging to the Reign of the Spirit, incarnating the subtle link between Creature and Creator, we rejoin our Home."[26] The most devoted Solar Temple adepts would push this reasoning to its extreme logical consequences.

According to several testimonies gathered by the investigators, the theme of "transit" began to be evoked by Di Mambro in 1990 or 1991. It meant a voluntary departure or a consent to bring the germ of life to another planet. It was necessary to be ready to leave at any time in response to the call. Di Mambro said he did not yet know what the mode of transit would be: he presented the metaphor of a passage across a mirror and evoked the possibility of the coming of a flying saucer to take faithful members to another world. On this last point, it is worth noting that, at some of Jouret's seminars that I attended in 1987, a comic strip called *Timeless Voyage* was on sale.[27] This strip tells the story of a group of UFO believers who, before the imminent "great mutation," are brought on board a "cosmic vessel" to "Vessel-Earth."[28] Solar Temple members were thus already familiar with this type of scenario well before 1990. An ex-member explained to the investigators that talks about transit never implied suicide but rather the idea of being saved from disasters. Perhaps the theme of "transit," rather than marking a break with survivalism, should be interpreted as a reorientation toward a survival in other dimensions following the irreversible worsening of the situation on this planet.[29]

If we believe their declarations to the police after the events of 1994, most of those members who had heard about the idea of "departure" or "transit" considered it as rather nebulous or interpreted it innocuously as a departure to other geographical locations (for example, leaving Geneva). When members wanted to know more, they sometimes received evasive answers:

> Transit was the return to the Father, the return to the Unity, after having left Earth. . . . Two or three years before October 1994, I discussed with —— what was meant by the concept. She told me that I shouldn't worry, that I wouldn't realize, that we would all leave together, as one. At the time, naively, I never thought that meant collective suicide.[30]

Some members had known a little more precisely how things would happen. One remembers that Di Mambro "started talking about transit to another world. He said that this would be accomplished by shift in consciousness and we wouldn't be aware of it."[31] But this operation presupposed a certain degree of preparation:

> [Di Mambro] explained to us that one day we'd all be called to a meeting at which a transit would be accomplished. It had to do with a mission, with a departure towards Jupiter. . . . He said to his listeners that they had to be on call twenty-four hours a day so as not to miss the departure and that once the order was given, we would have to move quickly.[32]

This helps to explain the speed with which some of the victims suddenly abandoned everything to head to their mysterious demise. But if this confirms the emergence of the idea of "transit" well before October 1994, it does not explain the reasoning that led Di Mambro toward this plan of action. Outside of possible explanations linked to Di Mambro's mental state, it seems likely that criticism by ex-members, episodic public exposure in Martinique and Quebec, and disappointed hopes for success led the Solar Temple's leadership to revise their view of the future. In addition, the wiretaps of Luc Jouret made by the police in Quebec during the 1993 investigation reveal that the charismatic physician was in a depressed mood, constantly complaining about feeling tired and expressing eagerness to leave the world. Still, no one factor is sufficient in and of itself, especially since the collective self-immolation involved not just one individual but the order's entire core group. We can not rule out the possibility that some elements in the decision still remain unknown to us.

The first known version of a text explaining "departure" had been written by February 1993. This coincides with the opening of the investigation into the group by Quebec police on February 2, 1993; since some sources suggest that Jouret may have gotten word of the investigation before the police interventions of March 8, 1993, we do not know with absolute certainty whether the text was written without knowledge of the investigation in progress.[33] At any rate, even if the problems in Martinique and in Quebec confirmed Di Mambro and his close associates in their plan to leave a world perceived as unjust and doomed, these events did not initiate the idea of departure: The attempt at buying guns indicates that the idea was already under consideration prior to these investigations.

PASSING THE TORCH

The fact that texts trying to explain and justify the "transit" (including two of the four which were sent to the media in October 1994) were written by 1993 reveals that a group of people methodically prepared for their deaths over a period of many months. To be ready for the passage to other spheres, the most dedicated members progressively severed all ties with the outside world. Messages received from other dimensions came to bolster them in their resolve to quit this planet. For example, a series of five messages collected under the title "The Polestar" and supposedly delivered by "the Lady of Heaven" were received between December 24, 1993, and January 17, 1994. The first message calls on the recipients to root out their "terrestrial attraction" and talks about Jupiter as their "Next Home." The second message exhorts them to "put [their] last things in order to leave Earth free and clear." The third message declares, "We want you free to rejoin us, without feeling constrained, without feeling pressure, but of your own free will," and warns, "If you do not try your hardest to escape the attraction of this Earth, woe is you!" The fourth message repeats, "It is now time to leave humanity to its deadly destiny, you are done with it. Don't look in the world for whomever or whatever to save. Close the door on humans." As for the fifth message, it announces in a solemn tone that "no Light will stay on Earth" and can be summed up by the sentence, "Retire, let go of this Earth without remorse."[34] It no doubt took a great deal of persuasion to convince a nucleus of members to accept such a radical step. Some documents reflect the hesitation that was probably expressed and the arguments used to reassure and maintain adherence to the plan. A few of these arguments were in keeping with classic themes of millenarian literature not otherwise found in the group's teachings:

> The idea of the passage from one world to another might worry some of you. I assure you that you are going towards a marvelous world which could not be, in any case, any worse than the one you are leaving. Know from now on that after the passage, you will have a body of glory but you will still be recognizable. You will no longer need to eat but if you want to eat, you will be able to do it without earning your bread with the sweat of your brow.
> Your eternal body will be subject neither to aging nor to pain nor to sickness.[35]

According to Solar Temple beliefs, the departure was only possible because on January 6, 1994, the mysterious "Elder Brothers of the Rosy Cross" "effected their Transit for an Elsewhere that only the initiates know and serve."[36] Taking off toward superior dimensions, the "Brothers" in some way carried Solar Temple members in their wake, allowing those who were worthy to ascend to a higher level. Significant allusions to this subject can be read in notes found on a diskette in one of the chalets in Salvan (Switzerland): "Take the place of the E[lder] B[rothers] on Venus, so that later on J[upiter?], we will be reunited. They will precede us, make room for us, show us the way and we will follow them." According to the declarations of a witness who later perished during the second "transit" in December 1995, Jouret, at a small gathering just before the events of October 1994, explained that if the leadership would cross a new step in effecting a passage from matter to essence, all the subsequent levels would automatically progress one degree.

Even within this perspective of escape from worldly catastrophes and transit to a better world, however, the order's leaders deemed it fitting to leave something behind for posterity. Only this desire to leave a legacy can explain why the leadership continued to be as active as ever while making preparations for its exit. The exact date of "departure" was probably decided on short notice: The outline of the internal monthly instructions meant for distribution to the members, which was found by police in the chalets in Salvan, continued until May 1995. These instructions were prepared by Jocelyne Di Mambro, who knew about the self-destruction project. If the day or the month had been set a long time in advance, she would certainly not have taken the time to prepare instructions for the period after the set date. The will to leave a legacy and a following behind after the "transit" also shows itself in the initiative of summer 1994 (and up to the eve of the events) to start up a new organization, the Rosicrucian Alliance (Alliance Rose-Croix, ARC).

Over the years, it appears that the group devoted a great deal of energy to organizing and reorganizing its various subsidiaries. As early as 1991, documents had suggested that the Templar Order should soon make room for "a new Rosicrucian Fraternity"; but there was resistance to this idea in some OTS sectors by believers who were attached to the Templar form. Although there is no real historical connection between the medieval Templar Order and Rosicrucian doctrines, the conjoining of the Temple and the Rosy Cross was nothing new, since such theories had originally appeared in Western occult circles during the eighteenth century.[37] According to the teachings of the Solar Temple, "the true Order of the Rosy Cross is . . . the Order of the Temple in its center. . . . More than an esoteric institution at the heart of the Order, it was and it is in truth its secret Church."[38]

At a first meeting in Avignon on July 9, 1994, ninety-five out of the one hundred eighteen people present responded positively to the proposition to create a new association. The ARC's constituent assembly, a purely administrative operation, met with a few people present in Montreux on August 13, 1994. Of the four committee members elected that day, two were found dead in October. The real launching of the ARC took place at a second meeting in Avignon on September 24, 1994, with the theme "The new mission of the Rosy Cross"; the invitation described the new order as "the natural successor to the OTS."[39] One hundred people were present, including eighty-eight dues-paying members plus some of Di Mambro's entourage. The documents revealed a desire to simplify the organizational structure. Participants had the feeling of a new beginning; the notebook of one of the participants had listed under September 24, "Meeting of the New Alliance in Avignon."

A PERSECUTION MANIA

Many of those present on September 24, 1994, were not aware that the hour of the "departure" was approaching. Joseph Di Mambro and those close to him were becoming more and more discouraged, as an audiocassette from spring 1994 in which several core members of the group discussed their "departure" demonstrates. Di Mambro is heard saying,

> We are rejected by the whole world. First by the people, the people can no longer withstand us. And our Earth, fortunately she rejects us. How would we leave [otherwise]? We also reject this planet. We wait for the day we can leave . . . life for me is intolerable, intolerable, I can't go on. So think about the dynamic that will get us to go elsewhere.

Compared with other controversial groups, the Solar Temple encountered very modest opposition; it would be excessive to use the term "persecution," despite what the group's spiritual testament would have us believe. In fact, Di Mambro's loss of a sense of reality made any opposition or criticism intolerable. The legal problems encountered by Jouret and others in Quebec in 1993 did nothing to assuage his growing sense of paranoia. After all, the press had reported that several members of the group had been subjected to official surveillance and wiretapping.[40] This led the core leadership to believe itself the object of omnipresent police control and the victim of traitors who had infiltrated the movement.

Jocelyne Di Mambro's difficulties in getting her passport renewed only exacerbated these suspicions. This and the fact that Di Mambro sent a posthumous letter to Charles Pasqua (then the French minister of the interior) gave rise to speculation concerning a mysterious political or criminal background for the OTS's leader. The explanation is simpler. Di Mambro had traveled several times to Australia, where he attempted to create a "life center." Suspicious international monetary transfers drew the attention of the Australian police: During the month of October 1993, Di Mambro received on three separate occasions $100,000 from Switzerland, money that was then deposited into bank accounts he had opened in Sydney. Canberra Interpol asked the French police for information regarding Di Mambro, who had no known resources. The French police squad in charge of financial improprieties wondered if it might be a case of illegal trafficking in foreign currency.

The French consulate in Montreal also became suspicious of the Di Mambros. In March 1994, the French Ministry of Foreign Affairs asked the Ministry of the Interior to advise whether it should extend Jocelyne Di Mambro's passport, as the family was unable to provide proof of their residence in Canada and had changed residence five times in five years. Even stranger, Joseph Di Mambro had obtained no fewer than five passports in seven years, and his visas showed he had made numerous short international trips, including several to Malaysia. By October 1994, the inquiry headed by the financial squad of the French judicial police was still ongoing. As for Jocelyne Di Mambro's passport, the French embassy in Ottawa finally renewed it, but only for three months, and this gave rise to a strange incident. Jocelyne Di Mambro hired a Montreal lawyer to defend her interests in the passport renewal affair. Through an unknown channel (perhaps simply the French consulate?), the lawyer heard about the investigation of his client and her husband and seems to have become reluctant to be associated with the couple and their possibly questionable business affairs. He wrote to Jocelyne Di Mambro on August 25, 1994, to explain to her that the affair had implications that were "political as much as they were legal," and the nonrenewal decision came from the French Ministry of the Interior and was linked "to a police investigation of a criminal matter." Even as he told his client that he would no longer be representing her interests, he advised her to "take very seriously the results of the investigation by the French authorities."[41]

In point of fact, during the investigations following the events of October 1994, nothing came to light confirming a surveillance of the group during this period.[42] Not only did the financial investigations squad of the French police likely have more urgent business to attend to, but the matter appears to have been related only to unexplained financial transfers by an individual French citizen and not by the leader of a small apocalyptic order. The police in Quebec ceased their surveillance of the Solar Temple after the incident with the illegal gun purchase in 1993, and the French Renseignements généraux (political police), which also keep an eye on religions and "cults," knew little about the Solar Temple. But one can imagine what the lawyer's statement could have meant for an increasingly paranoid leadership, which now believed that its worst suspicions were confirmed. It is significant that the document sent in October 1994 to Charles Pasqua (enclosed with the Di Mambro's passports) was written on a computer at Salvan on 30 August 1994—just after the Di Mambros received the letter from their Montreal lawyer. As minister of the interior, Pasqua was held personally responsible for the problems they encountered: "We accuse you of deliberately wanting to destroy our Order and having done so for reasons of state."[43] Such writings confirm the Di Mambros' growing persecution paranoia but lend no credibility to the theories linking the letter to Pasqua with mysterious underworld connections.

Another text found on Jocelyne Di Mambro's computer and written after a conversation with an unknown speaker adds further evidence of a growing sense of persecution:

> We don't know when they might close the trap on us . . . a few days? a few weeks?
>
> We are being followed and spied upon in our every move. All the cars are equipped with tracing and listening devices.
>
> All of their most sophisticated techniques are being used on us. While in the house, beware of surveillance cameras, lasers, and infra-red.
>
> Our file is the hottest on the planet, the most important of the last ten years, if not of the century.
>
> However that may be, as it turns out, the concentration of hate against us will give us enough energy to leave.[44]

The alleged surveillance was construed as one more proof that the group was really what it claimed to be, the vehicle of a mission of cosmic magnitude. The previous document also mentions two members (one of whom died in Switzerland and the other a year later in France) suspected of infiltrating the movement. Several texts written during that period warn against "traitors," and the group believed in the right of applying "justice and sentence" to those who showed disloyalty. In a videotape dated September 1994, Di Mambro explains that "justice and sentence" are the equivalent of "vengeance," but in an impersonal sense. In the spring 1994 audio track about the "departure," Di Mambro talks about those "who had committed themselves and then no longer wanted to remain involved. That changes nothing about their commitment. . . . You'll see, you'll see how things will go for them." The letter to Charles Pasqua is explicit:

> If we must apply our justice ourselves, it is because of the fact that yours is rotten and corrupt. . . . It behooves us, before we leave these stinking terrestrial planes, to reduce certain traitors to silence, which you and your agencies have directly or indirectly manipulated . . . to destroy our honor and our actions.[45]

While it cannot be doubted that the external opposition encountered by the Solar Temple strengthened the resolve of its leaders to depart for a higher plane of existence,[46] the root of Di Mambro's decision to launch the process that led to the "transit" is most closely connected to internal dissent (the theoretical idea of the possibility of having to "depart" having already been present longer in the ideology of the group, as we have seen). Di Mambro nourished a deep resentment toward critical members and former members, although these dissidents had kept their criticism within the confines of the group and had not gone public—except for the ex-member who spoke with the media in Martinique in December 1992 and who had repeated her accusations to the Canadian media in March 1993.[47] In the important tape recording (mentioned earlier) of a discussion within the core group in spring 1994, Di Mambro declared to his most trusted disciples:

> There are people who claim that I have taken everything for me. . . . what I have taken, I haven't taken it for me, since I leave everything behind. But I will leave nothing, I will leave ashes, I will leave nothing to the bastards who have betrayed us. The harm they have done to the Rosy Cross, that I cannot forgive; what they have done to me, it doesn't matter. But the harm they have done to the Rosy Cross, I won't forgive it. I cannot.[48]

Di Mambro still harbored feelings of betrayal and resentment during the final hours of his life. On October 3, 1994, when the "transit" had begun and a number of victims had in all likelihood already lost their lives, Di Mambro (or one of his assistants) wrote two drafts of letters to a general attorney that accused two former members of blackmailing him and of tarnishing the Temple's reputation.[49]

THE CREATION OF A LEGEND

As already asserted, however, it was not just a matter of "leaving" and punishing "traitors" but of accomplishing these ends in such a manner as to leave behind an enduring legend. The group was convinced that it belonged to "the pivotal elite" that "has been removed from the collective by superhuman effort." The temple "did not recognize" itself "as belonging to the human world, but to the race of Gods."[50] The leaders of the Solar Temple explained their actions in the texts sent to the media from a Geneva post office on October 5, 1994, and in three videocassettes that were shipped to a French OTS member by another trusted member at the same time. Two of these cassettes are titled "Testament of the Rosy Cross," and the third is titled "Joseph of Arimathea—Messages."

The lengthy recording of the "Testament of the Rosy Cross" opens with the symbol of ARC (a double-headed eagle behind a rose with a cross). On the screen a seated woman[51] appears who reads a text; in the background, a rose emerges from a misty landscape; as background music, the Grail theme from Richard Wagner's opera *Lohengrin* plays throughout the entire lecture.[52] The lengthy "testament" is read with a growing exultation; there are several mentions of "departure." This "Testament of the Rosy Cross" is most interesting because of its synthesis of Solar Temple beliefs on the eve of the group's self-immolation.

The testament first underlines man's mission as mediator between God and the Earth: "We are the focalization on which the Creator rests. . . . Today, we are in the final cycle of conscious creation; we must be able to control these bodies . . . and, with full maturity, to leave the mother [i.e., the Earth]. . . . We must not bring back consciousness to the state before the fall, but become aware of this state, enrich it with the painful experience of the fall and redeem our being, so that we could continue after the fall with a capital of enriched consciousness-energy-love." In this way, the spirit is able to follow its route across the sublimation of matter and, enriched by its experience in matter, "start up a superior cycle of evolution."[53]

According to the testament, 26,000 years ago the Blue Star (related to Sirius's energy) left on the earth "Sons of the One"; it appears in the sky every time its help is needed and responds to magnetization when humanity undergoes its crises of transmutation. The years 1950 to 1960 saw a growing change in the consciousness of human beings. Humanity is passing through periods of preparation called "tribulations," successive cycles of seven years that end in 1998. The circumstances of the "departure" are then explained:

> In the 1980s, the Sons of the One called the Blue Star. With man's consciousness still too fragmented, it was asked of the spiritual forces to intervene and to allot an additional period of time to move back the date, to slow down the irrevocable changes on Earth. . . . The Earth was given an additional seven years to prepare. . . . This delay acts like a rubber band which, when stretched to its limit, becomes unstable and too powerful. This limit has been reached. . . . and we still need more time. But this delay given to us has nonetheless allowed beings to hear the message, to prepare and to participate with full consciousness in this unique event which we call the passage. The passage, which is also the gathering of the Sons of the One. The Blue Star has come to magnetize the last workers and bring them back towards those of the first hour. The time of return is at hand and the astrological influences are affecting all the physical and non-physical planes. They work on the hearts and spirits of all those who accept their divine origin and are ready to play their part until the end. At the moment of passage, the Blue Star . . . will instantly transform in a flash the carriers of life and of the consciousness.
>
> The Star will unleash its influence on the earth, and there man, the unbeliever, remaining on Earth, will hope for death. The Blue Star will leave, he will feel abandoned and he will be right, but it will be too late. The radiant Star will be gone, bringing with it every chance at redemption. Yet, if man had wanted to remember, wanted to hear, wanted to see . . . Why did he not seize his last chance, brought by the Blue Star?[54]

The third cassette is a composite of four elements: three messages received from above by one of the members and a strange sequence that Di Mambro wanted to leave to posterity. In a room that looks like a church crypt, we see through a doorway, in front of a large pillar, people's profiles, one by one, whom it is not possible to identify because they are dressed in ample capuchin capes pulled around their faces. They process in a slow and untiring march, each holding in both hands a lit candle. This mysterious procession is commented on by the voice of Joseph Di Mambro and a member of the fraternity:

> *JDM*: Space is curved, time comes to an end . . . Our cycle is over, these images tell all.

F: On 6 January 1994, at 0h15m, the Elder Brothers of the Rosy Cross left their terrestrial planes, preceded by entities from the Great Pyramid who have gone back to their original planes. Programmed for all eternity, this unique event in history confirms the truth and the actualization of the prophecies that warned man that one day, because of [mankind's] disdain for the Word, the Gods would leave the earth. . . . A unique time is coming to an end as these knights, anonymous by choice, last carriers of the original fire, prepare in their turn to proceed, by their own means, with the liberation of the capital of energy-consciousness which the Rosy Cross bequeathed to them until the completion of the work.

JDM: The good-hearted man can live in this precise second . . . a sublime event: the passage of the cycle of Adamic man towards a new cycle of evolution, programmed on another earth, an earth prepared to receive the stored vibrations enriched by the authentic servants of the Rosy Cross.[55]

This solemn scene is meant to symbolize the final procession of the Knights of the Solar Temple, who are leaving this Earth: "Noble travelers, we are of no era, of no place."[56] If there were still a need to demonstrate that Di Mambro planned to create and leave behind a grand legend concerning his order's transit, this "choreography" offers persuasive evidence.

THE END OF THE SOLAR TEMPLE

On October 4, 1994, at 1:40 p.m. (Swiss time), Canadian police intervened at a fire in Morin Heights and discovered two adult corpses. On October 6, the corpses of two parents who, with their baby, had been savagely murdered were found hidden in a closet. It was later discovered that the murders had occurred on September 30 and that the perpetrators had subsequently flown back to Switzerland. Also on October 4, a little before midnight, residents of the small Swiss village of Cheiry noticed that a fire had started at the La Rochette farm in the heights around the village. On Wednesday, October 5, around 3 a.m., three chalets were in flames at another place in Switzerland, Granges-sur-Salvan. Twenty-three corpses were discovered at Cheiry, twenty-five at Salvan. In Cheiry, most of the victims had apparently been called to a meeting on Sunday and were probably already dead on Monday, October 3. A total of sixty-five bullets were found in their heads, and most of the victims had absorbed a strong soporific before being shot. No firearm had been used at Salvan, where only members of the core group lived; they had been injected with a poisonous substance provided by Jouret.

It has been clearly established that some of the fifty-three victims were murdered, while others submitted to execution voluntarily. However, even if their deaths were technically assassinations (bullets in the head), we will never know with absolute certainty how many victims volunteered for their "departure" or how many realized beforehand that the fabulous voyage to another planet they had been hoping for would take such brutal form. The fact that members who were fully cognizant of the macabre details of this "departure" and who were deeply affected by the loss of long-standing friends nevertheless decided, in December 1995, to themselves "leave" (again using firearms) in a clearing in French Vercors left many observers in such a state of incredulity that a number of journalists advanced the hypothesis of external intervention. But no such trace has been found (which would have been easy, since the area was snowy), and without ruling out the possibility that some victims did not fully consent or wanted to back out at the last minute, the deeds of these members are explicable without the intervention of a third party. It is true that several OTS survivors (including victims of the December 1995 "transit") were troubled over the methods used in October 1994. However, this discomfort did not stop a few of them from recognizing that they would have responded to the call if it had been addressed to them or indeed from feeling a little disappointed not to have been invited to participate.

Several testimonies collected by the Swiss police after the event of December 1995 show that a process of reinterpretation was quickly elaborated among the core of the surviving believers, leading to the conclusion that what happened was in fact positive and that those who departed had sacrificed to save the consciousness of the planet and to pave the way for others. In their eyes, the "departure" conjoined the horrible and the sublime in a strange harmony. They came to the decision to follow the same path, probably convinced that the first group was waiting for them. The death of five more persons in Quebec in March 1997 follows the same pattern, and the letter sent to the media by this handful of hard-liners articulates their doubts that there remain other people ready to follow the same path after them.[58]

Scholarly observers have advanced varied interpretations of the Solar Temple's saga.[59] Whatever the primary cause of the "transit," it was not a hasty decision, and the core group took time and care to legitimate ideologically the suicides and murders. This process probably also helped them reinforce each other in their choices, which had to be agreed upon collectively. Moreover, they likely celebrated ceremonies that ritualized their beliefs concerning the act they were about to commit near the time of the final departure. Texts detailing these ceremonies were discovered at Di Mambro's residence at Salvan. They strikingly illustrate the mind-set of the core group with regard to the coming transit:

> Brothers and Sisters of the First and of the Last Hour . . . Today . . . as we are gathered here in this Holy Place . . . The Great Terrestrial Cycle is closing in on itself. Alpha and Omega are fusing [to initiate] a new Creation. The Time of the Great Gathering is proclaiming the Departure of the Sons of Heaven.
>
> In the Name of a Will above mine . . . I am handing the seed of our Immortality and of our Transcendent Nature to the Infinite Worlds . . . At this Supreme

Moment . . . The ruby power of the Work should free itself and rejoin the Levels of the Future . . . So that, engendered by ourselves . . . Like the Phoenix . . . We might be reborn from our ashes. Through the Sword of Light . . . Raised toward the Levels Above, what is refined should depart from the world of density . . . And ascend toward its Point of Origin.

Our Terrestrial Journey is coming to an end . . . The Work is being completed. Everyone must return to their position on the Great Celestial Chessboard.[60]

We have to consider seriously the OTS's beliefs. Di Mambro acted at times like a common swindler, but he very likely remained convinced of his message and mission until the end. Certainly, internal dissent and outside criticism helped to convince hesitant members of the core group that radical methods were needed in order to leave Earth. But, although we will never know for sure, it seems doubtful that a lesser degree of public exposure would have prevented the "transit." Even if he was able to hide such feelings when it was needed, Di Mambro had reached the point that he could no longer accept questioning of or disagreement with his views. Convinced of its own superiority and insulated psychologically from countervailing perspectives, the leadership came to view any dissonant voice as unbearable.

Finally, the transit presented an attractive response to the movement's decline: The temple needed to be "redynamized" periodically. The transit also allowed the group to escape from perceived threats and offered a way to assert dramatically its claims before the entire world. Creators of their own legend, the core members of the Solar Temple considered themselves as an elect circle, heirs to an uncommon destiny who were invested with a cosmic task to fulfill. Believing that they would become gods, they followed the flute player in a dance of death and paid the ultimate price.

NOTES

1. Concluding text from two videocassettes titled "Testament of the Rosy Cross," sent from Geneva to a member of the OTS on October 5, 1994.

2. This quotation is excerpted from a tape transcript made for the use of the police investigation. All documents without specific indication of source belong to the material gathered by the police and kept either in Fribourg or in Martigny (Switzerland). These documents are not individually numbered, and they are not presently accessible to researchers; the author has been able to use them solely because of his participation in the official police investigation of the Solar Temple case. Regarding quotation from interrogations conducted by the police with witnesses, they can be included only if the anonymity of the individuals quoted remains fully protected. For this reason, it is not possible to provide references in the usual way.

3. Taken from a document dated May 28, 1994, found on one of the order's computers. Rituals celebrated toward the end, especially one called "The Return of the Fire,"

develop such ideas and show how the core members had the feeling of being in control of events when committing suicide and returning to their original home after having been enriched through their experiences.

4. "Transit to the Future," one of four texts delivered to several dozen recipients on October 5, 1994. All the (unpublished) internal documents of OTS quoted in these notes were written in French, but their titles are translated here into English.

5. An original, longer version of this study was published in French as *Les Mythes du Temple Solaire* (Geneva: Georg, 1996). A revised and updated Italian translation was published the following year as *Il Tempio Solare* (Leumann [Turin]: Editrice Elledici, 1997). There is also an updated and extended German version, *Der Sonnentempel: Die Tragödie einer Sekte* (Freiburg: Paulusverlag, 1998). The English version has been rewritten to a large extent and also contains several passages and quotations that are not found in the previous versions. The author thanks the three anonymous reviewers for their critical comments: he has tried to take several of their remarks into consideration. Comparisons with other cases of suicide or violent action by religious groups, however, will be kept for a future article. This one concentrates exclusively on the OTS case.

6. There were always people who belonged to the inner "Fraternity" around Di Mambro and never to OTS itself. Hence the use of "OTS" as a generic label can be misleading.

7. He divorced his first wife in January 1985, but she continued to follow the group and was found dead at Cheiry in October 1994.

8. Although it is used here generically for describing the group, the name "Order of the Solar Temple" was only one label among several and was not always in use between 1970 and 1994.

9. Some attendees with whom the author spoke did not like Jouret's apocalyptic leanings. He sometimes conveyed the ambiguous impression that he was possessed of both charm and fanaticism.

10. An overview of the various(and sometimes unconnected) movements with reference to the neo-Templar tradition is provided in the first part of an article by Massimo Introvigne, "Ordeal by Fire: The Tragedy of the Solar Temple," *Religion* 25 (1995): 267–83.

11. Gaetan Delaforge, *The Templar Tradition in the Age of Aquarius* (Putney, VT: Threshold Books, 1987), p. 136. "Gaetan Delaforge" is the pseudonym of a North American OTS member (who is still alive).

12. See Serge Caillet, *L'Ordre Rénové du Temple: Aux racines du Temple Solaire* (Paris: Dervy, 1997). There is no relation between the French citizen Raymond Bernard and his American homonym who wrote books on the "hollow earth" theory and other topics popular in some segments of the cultic milieu; according to information provided by Joscelyn Godwin, the (late) American Raymond Bernard's real name was Walter Siegmeister (Joscelyn Godwin, *Arktos: The Polar Myth in Science, Symbolism, and Nazi Survival* [London: Thames and Hudson, 1993], p. 122).

13. Tape of conclave of ORT officers, Easter 1984, Geneva, Switzerland, found in personal archives of Joseph Di Mambro.

14. Delaforge, *The Templar Tradition*, 138.

15. Open Letter, February 1994. See note 2.

16. However, there were several other members who remained totally devoted to Joseph Di Mambro, as their decision to follow him in death demonstrates. Regarding the question of the nature of Di Mambro's charisma, see Jean-François Mayer, "Les Cheva-

liers de l'Apocalypse: l'Ordre du Temple Solaire et ses adeptes," in *Sectes et Démocratie*, eds. Françoise Champion and Martine Cohen (Paris: Seuil, 1999), pp. 205–23. The article also examines the interaction between affiliations with the Solar Temple and previous backgrounds in the cultic milieu.

17. He justified this demand by claiming that he was only relaying the orders from the "Mother Lodge."

18. Interrogation of former member by Canadian police, December 28, 1994. See note 2.

19. Tony Dutoit, his wife, and their baby were the first victims of the carnage of 1994, savagely murdered in Morin Heights (Quebec).

20. Report to Joseph Di Mambro by OTS officer, Switzerland, December 10, 1993. See note 2.

21. *Les Sectes: que sont-elles? comment agissent-elles? comment s'en défendre? ce qu'il faut en savoir* (Paris: Centre de Documentation, d'Education et d'Action contre les Manipulations Mentales, 1984), p. 49. In 1987, during a discussion with the author, Jouret did not hide his irritation concerning those two lines.

22. For more details about the ecological concern behind the apocalpytic views of the Solar Temple, see Mayer, "Les Chevaliers de l'Apocalypse," pp. 211–14.

23. See also the interesting observations by Susan Palmer, "Purity and Danger in the Solar Temple," *Journal of Contemporary Religion* 11 (1996): 303–18.

24. Hans Jonas, *The Gnostic Religion* (Boston: Beacon Press, 1958), p. 67. "The reawakening of the gnostic conscience in a few human beings is considered as the sign that the diffuse parcels of light dispersed in the world will reunite and that apocalyptic events are imminent" (Massimo Introvigne, *Il ritorno dello gnosticismo* [Milan: SugarCo, 1993], pp. 15–16).

25. "To those who can still hear the voice of wisdom . . . we send this final message," Manifesto-testament of OTS, 1994, p. 2.

26. "Transit to the Future," Manifesto-testament of OTS, 1994, p. 5.

27. Appel Guery and Sergio Macedo, *Voyage intemporel* (Grenoble, France: Glénat, 1983). There exists an English translation, *Timeless Voyage* (Papeete, Tahiti: Transtar Pacific, 1987).

28. This is not merely a comic strip because it carries the message of a French UFO group that really exists.

29. "The current planetary situation is irreversibly escaping all human control . . . All creative and positive forces are strangled . . . we refuse to participate in the assassination of our carrier the Earth, we leave this world where our voices can no longer be heard" ("Transit to the Future"). "Once the time of the Great gathering will have come and the Sons of the One will withdraw, . . . the North and South Poles, deprived of their magnetic balance which had until now been kept by the conscious carriers, will give birth to cataclysms and final destruction. This is the Third secret of Our Lady of Fatima, which is revealed here" (from a document dated 28 April 1994 found on a computer in Salvan, Switzerland).

30. From interrogation of former OTS member by Swiss police, January 18, 1996. See note 2.

31. Ibid., January 22, 1996.

32. Ibid.

33. John R. Hall and Philip Schuyler, "The Mystical Apocalypse of the Solar Temple," in *Millenium, Messiahs, and Mayhem: Contemporary Apocalyptic Movements*, ed. Thomas Robbins and Susan J. Palmer (London: Routledge, 1997), p. 300.

34. "The Polestar," a series of five OTS messages found at Salvan, Switzerland, December 1993–January 1994. See note 2.

35. "Last Voyage," document found at Salvan, Switzerland, in 1993. See note 2.

36. Message dated 28 January 1994.

37. See René Le Forestier, *La Franc-Maçonnerie occultiste et templière aux XVIIIe et XIXe siècles*, 2d ed., 2 vols. (Paris: La Table d'Emeraude, 1987).

38. "Epistle/Archives ZZA-4," OTS teaching material sent to members, n.d. See note 2.

39. OTS invitation to meeting, September 24, 1994. See note 2.

40. This wiretapping was conducted over several weeks spanning February and March 1993.

41. Letter from Di Mambro's lawyer in Montreal, August 25, 1994. See note 2.

42. It should, however, be mentioned that the French embassy in Washington, D.C., sent a request to law enforcement agencies in Canada in early 1994 requesting information concerning possible involvement of Joseph Di Mambro in money laundering. It is not known whether active investigations were undertaken following this request.

43. Letter sent by Di Mambro to French Interior Minister Charles Pasqua in October 1994. See note 2.

44. Untitled document found on computer at Salvan, Switzerland. See note 2.

45. Letter sent by Di Mambro to French Interior Minister Charles Pasqua in October 1994. See note 2.

46. In a recent article, two American scholars have very pointedly observed that the "critical issue seems to concern whether the group's principals can legitimate to their followers the claim of persecution by apostates and other external opponents as the basis of their troubles." See John R. Hall and Philip Schuyler, "Apostasy, Apocalypse, and Religious Violence: An Exploratory Comparison of Peoples Temple, the Branch Davidians, and the Solar Temple," in *The Politics of Religious Apostasy: The Role of Apostates in the Transformation of Religious Movements*, ed. David G. Bromley (London: Praeger, 1998), p. 168.

47. In a few cases, dissidents were threatening to go public with their criticisms in an attempt to recoup financial contributions.

48. Transcript of tape, spring 1994. See note 2.

49. For unknown reasons, the letters were never completed or mailed.

50. From a document titled "Exit toward the light," end of 1993. See note 2.

51. The woman was one of Joseph Di Mambro's most convinced followers. In the spring 1994 audiocassette, already cited several times, this woman is shown as one of those most in favor of the idea of a "departure": "Yes, I have asked for that for a long time, I think I will have no regrets. . . . I think I will have no doubts or fears. . . . I am ready to leave."

52. Di Mambro enjoyed Wagner's music, which was often used in OTS ceremonies.

53. Excerpt from two videocassettes called "Testament of the Rosy Cross." See note 1.

54. Ibid.

55. Excerpt from third videocassette sent with "Testament of the Rosy Cross." See note 1.

56. Sometimes used by OTS members, this phrase is actually borrowed from the famous occultist and adventurer, Cagliostro, whose real name was Giuseppe Balsamo (1743–1795). Di Mambro considered himself a reincarnation of Cagliostro. The author wishes to thank Massimo Introvigne for bringing the original author of this phrase to his attention.

57. Internal documents show that the leadership was considering the possibility (and hoping) that other people would follow at a later stage. The manifesto "To those who can still hear the voice of wisdom" concludes with the following sentence: "From where we will be, we will always hold our arms toward those who will be worthy of joining us." It is difficult to establish accurately how far the media harassment and the wild theories spread about the group contributed to the resolve of surviving OTS members to "leave" in December 1995 and March 1997. The conclusions of the French investigation have not yet been made public at the time of the last revisions to this article (November 1998).

58. Letter sent March 21, 1997, to leading newspapers in Quebec, including *La Presse*, *Le Devoir*, and *Le Soleil*.

59. For an overview of the various interpretative categories, see Massimo Introvigne, *Les Veilleurs de l'Apocalypse: Millénarisme et nouvelles religions au seuil de l'an 2000* (Paris: Claire Vigne, 1996), pp. 223–45.

60. Ritual titled "The Return of the Fire," n.d., found at Salvan, Switzerland, with manuscript corrections. See note 2.

10

MARKETING LAZARIS
A Rational Choice Theory
of Channeling

Elijah Siegler

Using a few verifiable propositions, rational choice theory provides new models for explaining religious behavior and reevaluating religious history, American or otherwise. In a sentence, rational choice theory states that individuals act rationally, by weighing the costs and benefits of potential actions and choosing those actions that maximize their potential benefits. Religion is a commodity; it is "an object of choice and production."[1]

This chapter asks the question: What if a religious movement were to operate under the assumption that spirituality is a product and religion is a marketplace to such a self-conscious and self-reflexive degree that this movement would seem to have a knowledge of rational choice theory? How would that movement behave?

This is of course different from asking how a religion would act if it acted out the assumptions (religious pluralism, competing marketplace) behind rational choice theory. Certainly every rabbi, minister, and voodoo priestess in this country is aware of the fact that there are more religious choices out there than their own and that individuals can and do choose different religious options. Most religious organizations operate under the assumption, to some degree at least, that they are selling a brand name; Methodism wants to maintain a Methodist brand of Christianity, for example. But even the most laissez-faire religion will have some entrance requirement that distinguishes it from a commercial enterprise, be it acceptance of a credo, a core of shared experience, or a seriousness of purpose.

Written for this anthology.

But what if a religious organization's only mode of operation was selling a brand? What if it knew itself to be a producer offering certain compensations to consumers who will seek to maximize their benefits? A religious organization that did so might exhibit some of the following characteristics:

1. It would be adaptable, changing rapidly with the times, tailoring its approach to fit the current cultural style.

2. It would target a certain demographic cohort that would be most receptive to its message (niche marketing) but within that homogenous clientele, the message could be decoded in multiple ways; that is, each consumer could read very different meanings into the same religious products.

3. It would be "brand conscious," emphasizing loyalty to the religious product as distinct from the religious organization itself.

4. It would distribute rewards (compensators) at a rate individually tailored to each participant; whereas the commitment it asked would be standardized and easily procurable.

Such an organization does exist; it is called Concept:Synergy. And it offers a unique religious product, Lazaris (for the purposes of the paper, I will assume Lazaris to be a religion).[2] Lazaris is the name of a discorporate spirit channeled for the past twenty-three years by a man named Jach Pursel. Pursel and his associates run a successful business that markets Lazaris's wisdom in the form of tapes and seminars.[3]

By examining Lazaris through the lenses of history, ethnography and sociology, this paper will show how Lazaris, by self-consciously assuming spirituality to be a marketable product, represents an important emerging way of being religious in America. My interrogation of Lazaris includes a history of the organization, a reading of the meaning behind the content of his teachings (not of the teachings themselves, however), interviews with active participants in Lazaris, a cost-benefit analysis, and to begin, a visit to a typical Lazaris event.

AN EVENING WITH LAZARIS

On July 25, 1996, at a hotel in downtown San Francisco, I was one of approximately three hundred people attending an evening with Lazaris called the "Power of Our Chakras" held in the Emerald Room of the Holiday Inn. I was somewhat surprised by the disparate ages represented, with people who ranged from early twenties to late seventies. I was less surprised by the ethnic makeup, which seemed to be about 98 percent white.

The participants browsed the merchandise tables on the side of the room, sat down, talked. They wore a lot of purple, which would certainly be the official color of the New Age, if there were such a thing. Most of them had notebooks, and many of them had crystals or small cloth bags containing several crystals and gems, which they kept under their seats during the seminar.[3]

At 7:30 p.m., Jach Pursel, a portly man with white hair and beard, walked into the room and sat in a chair on a raised platform, flanked by two potted palms with a blackboard behind. He introduced himself, speaking, as he always does, in an engaging and unpretentious manner.

After a few more introductory notes, his eyes closed, his head bobbed down, and he went into trance. As this was happening, a large woman with long, curly hair stood and spoke. Mary Beth is the only paid staff member of Concept:Synergy (besides Jach) who travels to the seminars. She spoke for the benefit of newcomers and asked that they "stay seated until Jach is back in the room" after Lazaris left, so that Jach would not be disconcerted. She mentioned a new Lazaris book for sale and some upcoming August events. Then she moved to the back of the room.

Pursel, his eyes still closed, shook a few times, and Lazaris spoke out of Pursel's mouth. It was the first time I would share a room with a channeled entity. His accent was hard to place. It seemed vaguely Scottish, like a courtly Sean Connery. Lazaris spoke quickly, fluidly, without notes. His diction and rhetoric were slightly eccentric. He began each session with something like: "Well, yes, it is a pleasure to see you, yes, fine," and he used roundabout phrasings like "the month that is August" and "the one you call Jach," that seemed quasi-medieval in flavor.

Other distinctive speech patterns included verbal stutters, such as "all right" and "we suggest." And he always referred to himself as "we" because, as was explained in a note to the interview book:

> Lazaris says that each of us has many "selves," but that right now we are expe-
> riencing them "one at a time," and thus refer to ourselves as "I." Lazaris has
> many selves as well—many selves in many dimensions—but experiences them
> all simultaneously, and therefore refers to himself as "we." It is not the use of
> the "royal we," but rather Lazaris' experience of his own reality (vii).

He took twenty minutes to get into the subject at hand, by first reviewing some basic Lazaris concepts like "Will," "Choice," and "Artistry" (over the years of tapes and seminars, Lazaris and his audience have developed a large special-ized vocabulary, a jargon that can be rearranged as needed). He tied in some upcoming Lazaris events and current affairs. Then, he turned to the topic of the evening: chakras.

Lazaris described the seven chakras, common throughout New Age thought (as borrowed from Hinduism). He then described five more that lie outside the body. Lazaris constructed an elaborate metaphor of a chakra as a juke box or multidisc compact disc player (a metaphor based on a piece of consumer technology his listeners most likely possess). The audience wrote in its notebooks rapidly as Lazaris next talked about the twelve senses: the five everyone knows about and the seven that have been lost but are recoverable.

At 9:10 p.m., it was time for a break. Lazaris said, "Twenty minutes, twenty minutes, with love and peace." The channel bowed his head, shook a few times, opened his eyes, rubbed his face, and yawned. Jach Pursel was back in the room. New Age music played softly, as people stretched or left the room to buy coffee.

At 9:35, Pursel walked back into the room and immediately went back into trance. Lazaris led a guided meditation, backed with music that lasted about an hour. Lazaris's guided meditations are trips into the geography of the subconscious, where one meets archetypes, different selves, or even Lazaris himself.

The meditation began by asking each to picture himself or herself in a "safe place" and proceeding out from there, to a river, a path through the woods, a cave. The psychological or metaphysical goal that was the purpose of the workshop seemed meant to become an actual, physical goal in meditation. Thus, Lazaris instructed participants to visualize a sun dial, which then became an elevator. When people came out of the visualization, Lazaris explained that whatever the number the shadow on the dial pointed to was the chakra they needed to work with and whatever the level the sundial/elevator took each participant to was "the slot" that was blocked. The meditation ended, and Lazaris gave a few last words, exhorting participants to "play with the possible"—to accept his news that people have more than seven chakras. The evening ended at 11 p.m. Lazaris did not take questions.

ANALYZING THE EVENING

From the preceding description, a Lazaris seminar would seem to exhibit many of the characteristics associated with the New Age: an emphasis on self-improvement, combined with terminology borrowed from Asian traditions and references to pop culture and consumer technology that cater to the baby boomers who make up the bulk of the audience. In fact, in Lazaris seminars in general, the content of channeled information is usually quite similar from one occasion to the next and not all that different from the message of more fleshly New Age teachers. Common themes include universal interrelatedness, the existence of meta-empirical beings, the psychologization of religion, reincarnation, a certain vision of the past, a future brought on by conscious evolution and most important, the belief in conscious reality. These are some of the more important "Varieties of New Age Experience" that Dutch scholar Wouter Hanegraaff enumerates (pp. 113–361: see also Brown, p. 69).

Certainly, Lazaris, or at least what we know of him from a seminar, seems the perfect example of what Laurence Iannaccone calls religions that "will come to resemble highly specialized boutiques" (38). And at first glance, the audience at the evening could be characterized by Finke and Stark's definition: "casual dabblers in various pseudo-scientific activities and techniques promoted as New Age" (245).

To leave it at that generalization would be underestimating this fascinating phenomenon. By the ephemeral standards of the New Age movement, Lazaris has been channeling a long time (since 1974), and many members have been devotees for almost that long, demonstrating a high level of financial, practical, and spiritual commitment. According to anthropologist Michael Brown's recent examination of channeling, Lazaris is perhaps the most financially lucrative of any channel working today. Indeed, for every channel as successful as Jach Pursel, hundreds of channels barely "eke out more than a frugal living" (153).

How does the Lazaris organization do it if it offers only one of many channels, which is one of many New Age options? What is the secret of Lazaris's success? And how would answering these questions add to an understanding of channeling, the New Age, and indeed American religion and culture?

HISTORY OF A CHANNEL

John Willits Pursel was born in 1947. The Pursel family moved every two years or so as the father, a traveling salesman, was assigned different territory. John Pursel, called Jach,[5] had an average childhood, almost a boring one: "I didn't have abusive parents. I loved my childhood. I had an all-American, normal family," Pursel told a journalist (D'Antonio, p. 140). His family settled in Lansing, Michigan, where at fourteen, Jach met his first and only sweetheart, Penny Lake. They went off to the University of Michigan together and were married in their junior year. Although both dreamed of becoming lawyers, after graduation Jack took a nine-to-five job at an insurance agency, while Penny stayed home and read voraciously on Eastern religion, meditation, parapsychology, and Theosophy.

In 1972, Penny "dragged Jach along" to a class on Silva Mind Control, a meditative technique (D'Antonio, p. 142). On the evening of October 3, 1974, Jach fell asleep during his meditation. According to Penny, Jach began talking in another voice, as if an entity was talking through him. When asked his name, the entity replied "Lazaris." Jach was scared at first, but Penny was intrigued. Every evening she would talk to Lazaris through Jach, while Jach tried to ignore the ramifications of what was happening to him. As Jach tells it: "Every evening I would sit and close my eyes and take an 'after-dinner' nap. Every evening Peny [sic] would enthusiastically tell me all that had transpired. I listened. I smiled. I avoided."[6] Later, of course, Jach began to accept, and then welcome, these visits from a noncorporeal entity.

Jach became what is known as a full-trance, objective channel: "objective" in that Lazaris is not a part of Jach's consciousness; "full-trance" in that he is not conscious when Lazaris comes through. Lazaris describes himself, in a book of published interviews, as a formless noncorporeal entity, a "spark of conscious- ness" beyond our physical planes, beyond even mental and causal planes (23). Lazaris often explains himself by using the channel metaphor literally; Lazaris is no more "inside" Jach's body than Peter Jennings is "inside" your television set every night.

Soon after he began channeling Lazaris, Jach's insurance employers ordered him to transfer to Florida. There, Jach and Penny called a friend, a man named Michael Prestini, to help them further explore the phenomenon of Lazaris. Soon after, with Lazaris's approval, Penny divorced Jach and married Michael. After the divorce, Jach chose to remain celibate and unattached.

At the same time and for the same numerological reasons that prompted Jack to change his name to Jach, Penny changed hers to Peny and Michael his to Michaell. (Later, around 1987, Peny and Michaell Prestini, "for esoteric reasons" [Lazaris, p. 14], changed their name to Peny and Michaell North). The trio moved to Atlanta in the late 1970s. Jach continued to channel Lazaris for Peny and friends. Meanwhile, he was working as Richard Bach's private secretary, flying around the country with the popular author of *Jonathan Livingston Seagull*.

By the late 1970s, channelers were abundant throughout the country, espe- cially in California, where Lazaris's reputation as a high-level source of informa- tion slowly spread through word of mouth. Jach would appear on a local radio show, explain who he was and what he did, and announce a free open meeting the following evening, then go into trance so that Lazaris could answer questions.

In 1977, at one such open meeting, Jach announced that he would cease channeling Lazaris in one year. In Lazaris's place, the Synergy Foundation, a nonprofit organization founded by Jach, Peny, and Michaell—which Jach described as a "clearinghouse" for information and ideas—would propagate metaphysical techniques inspired by Lazaris.[7] For reasons as yet unknown to this author, Lazaris did not stop coming through Jach in 1978 as planned. Jach has been channeling Lazaris ever since. Lazaris has stated that he will come through right up until the channel's (Jach's) death. Lazaris will not come through another source, he states quite clearly. (This should avoid the problems encountered when Jane Roberts, who channeled the entity Seth, died in 1984, after which other people claimed to be channeling Seth.) Jach will live a long time, according to Lazaris.

The Synergy Foundation re-formed into Concept:Synergy, a for-profit cor- poration. In 1980 it relocated to Marin County, north of San Francisco. That year Lazaris gave a lecture called "Message to the California Consciousness" about how California and Californians would be on the cutting edge of change for the next decade.[8] In 1981, the group made a conscious effort to collect and retain control of the Lazaris "material." Lazaris would interface with small groups that would meet at Jach, Peny, and Michaell's house in Marin County or at small conference centers in one-day meetings known as "Sundays with Lazaris." Week-long sessions with Lazaris were also possible. One-on-one contact was relatively easy, although there was always a waiting list. People could have personal readings with Lazaris on a monthly basis. Lazaris also did "Life Readings" in which he told seekers of several of their more significant past lives.

Lazaris's popularity continued to grow through word of mouth. By the mid-1980s, the "New Age" had snowballed out of its regional enclaves and into the mainstream media. This coincided with a period of several years in which Lazaris had a higher profile in the public eye. In 1986, Concept:Synergy began to mass-market tapes and videos. Lazaris set up a regular touring schedule in Philadelphia, Los Angeles, and San Francisco and soon added other cities, with a repertoire of intensives of three or four days, two-day weekends, and evenings.

The Lazaris organization consciously chose greater public visibility to counteract what it saw as a "metaphysical circus"; to offer a stable option amid people getting on and off "a New Age bandwagon." Thus, Jach Pursel channeled Lazaris live on two daytime talk shows, Mike Douglas and Merv Griffin. Lazaris was mentioned in Shirley Maclaine's 1987 book, *It's All in the Playing*.[9] Lazaris gave interviews for New Age magazines. Sharon Gless, winning an Emmy award for best actress in a television drama for her portrayal of a tough woman detective in the TV police drama *Cagney & Lacey*, thanked Lazaris in her acceptance speech.

In the late 1980s, the organization moved to Beverly Hills. Jach, Michaell, and Peny moved their New Age art gallery to One Rodeo Drive at the corner of Wilshire Boulevard, one of the most exclusive business addresses in the world. This was just the latest manifestation of their other business interests. Their gallery, Isis Rising, sold paintings and objets d'art in the style known as "visionary art," a representational style that depicts crystals, pyramids, and rainbows. Although it was possible to buy Lazaris books and tapes at the Isis Rising gallery, it was not a "Lazaris center" to attract new members or to cater to old ones.

Lazaris saw 1989 as a key date: the end of what he called "the New Age Circus." His mainstream profile was at its highest. But at that time he chose, if not a withdrawing, certainly a leveling off. Concept:Synergy relied again on promotion through word of mouth. Then, in 1990 or 1991, the Lazaris triumvirate of Jach, Peny, and Michaell closed their Beverly Hills gallery and moved to Palm Beach, Florida, although they eventually reestablished a residence in Marin county. The 1990s saw more regular seminars offered, with routine visits to San Francisco and Los Angeles, Newark, Atlanta, and Orlando, where the organization relocated in 1996, while Philadelphia, Seattle, Vancouver, and other previous venues were bumped off schedule. In the summer of 2000, Jach announced he would be giving up traveling. The seminars would be held only in Orlando from then on.

DAILY OPERATION

Today, Lazaris's teachings are transmitted through limited phone time, a Web site, books, videos, and an ever-growing body of audiotapes. But these experiences cannot replace the experience of seeing Lazaris in the flesh, or rather, in Jach's flesh. Ways of doing this include the previously described evening, as well as two-day weekends and three- or four-day "intensives."

The intensive format follows the same combination of lecture and guided meditation but differs from the two-day weekend or the four-hour evening by the addition of two important features: "Magic Time," a kind of question-and-answer period with Lazaris, and the "Crystal Ceremony," the final event, where participants line up to receive a small crystal from Lazaris.

Lazaris still gives personal consultations (by telephone), but it is very hard to get an appointment. One must write to Concept:Synergy with a request, which is processed by Peny and Lazaris. (Jach goes into a trance to speak with Peny, every night, whether in person or on the phone.) One might be scheduled for a phone conversation every month, every other month, twice a year, or not at all. People who fifteen years ago could speak face to face with Lazaris, on any topic that crossed their mind, for an hour each month might now be limited to a half-hour on the phone once a year.

Lazaris's topics are arranged a year in advance. A Lazaris evening or intensive will fulfill expectations of the ticket buyers. They know Lazaris will always begin with a talk on a predetermined subject and follow that with a meditation.

CHANGING WITH THE TIMES

The history of the Lazaris organization reveals its malleability. The Lazaris phenomenon came out of the esoteric milieu of Peny's theosophical studies. Moreover, Lazaris's organizational and geographic changes seem to correlate with the pattern of the baby boomers: The 1970s was a decade of exploration, of building a "counterculture." The moment Synergy Foundation, a budding "cult movement," chose to become Concept:Synergy, a for-profit (and profitable) private corporation, was at the dawn of the 1980s, a decade known for its conspicuous consumption and display. At the same time, so the story goes, the "hippies" cut their hair and got jobs as computer consultants. Spiritually minded people suddenly had access to disposable income, and buying into Lazaris was one way to dispose of it. By 1989, however, the spotlight on the New Age had become too harsh, as popular culture satirized New Agers as politically conservative, inward-looking, and ungenerous.

By contrast, the 1990s seem to be a time of settling down, of "nesting" for both Lazaris and the aging baby boomers to whom he caters. The number of cities Lazaris visits has been standardized and cut back. Recently, after years of eschewing any sort of community building, Concept:Synergy is sponsoring a community of sorts, albeit on the Web. *The Lazaris Material*, a 1997 listing of all Lazaris tapes and books, beseeches us to "Please also join us on the World Wide Web at www.Lazaris.com. This thriving website is home to more than 60,000 messages from the vast *community* of people worldwide who are working with the Lazaris message" (italics added). This is perhaps the first time in any Lazaris literature that the word "community" has been used.

Privacy is an important development in later-period Lazaris. Membership lists are kept confidential. Communication with Concept:Synergy is through a toll-free telephone number, a post office box, or the Internet. Personal time with Lazaris is in a group setting in a generic hotel room or over the phone.

AN ABUNDANCE OF MEANINGS

Rational choice theory, according to Laurence Iannaccone, assumes two ways to deal with the problem of religious risk. One is by emphasizing congregational leadership and testimonial and thereby lessening the risk of religious fraud that comes from putting a lot of faith in one religious leader. The other is by diversifying the religious portfolio, whereby religious consumers might "hedge their religious bets by going to confession on Sunday, consulting a medium on Monday, and engaging in transcendental meditation on Wednesday" (Iannaccone, pp. 36–7). Portfolio diversification among "collective" religious groups that emphasize membership and sacrifice is not possible. On the other hand, in New Age religions, which often distribute rewards on a straight fee-for-service plan, this diversification is tolerated, even celebrated.

"Exclusivity and diversification do not mix" (24). But in Lazaris they can and do. Lazaris is more than just one among many New Age commodities: It is a clearinghouse or source of information about almost any New Age phenomenon. Continuing Iannaccone's stock market metaphor, if the New Age represents the portfolio diversification strategy of minimizing religious risk, then Lazaris can become a portfolio manager, both creating and integrating religious capital.

In one three-day seminar, for example, Lazaris referred to chakras, archetypes, alchemy, Einsteinian curved space, extraterrestrial life, past lives, Tarot, numerology, and much else. Lazaris places them all on a coherent meaning grid and also relates the concepts to current events. However, during "magic time," Lazaris mostly uses the language of self-help and psychology: childhood traumas, unresolved conflict with parents, guilt, and shame. This combination of references to "occult" practices, to the metaphysical significance of current events (a kind of millennialism), all with a therapeutic bent, is typical of New Age discourse.

What distinguishes Lazaris from other New Age commodities, like crystals, Tarot reading, or past-life regression? Lazaris's information is both specific and universal, both practical and profound. "Astrologers offer specific advice, but they do not reveal the meaning of the universe" (Stark and Bainbridge, p. 30). Lazaris does both.

The material channeled by Lazaris contains a super abundance of information— "compensators" to use the rational choice term—in the form of metaphysical formulae, meditation techniques, prophecies, psychic readings, and psychological axioms. Hundreds of Lazaris tapes are available on a multitude of topics. Consumers are encouraged to pick and choose what they need.

Indeed, the deliberate decoupling of the content and meaning of Lazaris is key to his appeal. According to Lazaris, when he speaks through Jach Pursel, every listener quite literally hears something different, thanks to Lazaris's metaphysical prowess. Interviews with several longtime Lazaris followers might seem to corroborate this story. Despite their similar backgrounds (white, educated, upper middle class, self-employed), and despite their participation in the same Lazaris events, each of the interviewees gleaned very different messages from the Lazaris material.

I conducted in-depth interviews with a number of what are often termed "Friends of Lazaris," all of whom were within twenty years of each other in age, all white, middle-class Californians. Yet each interview represented a subjective model of how Lazaris provides "compensators." For one man, Lazaris is a tool for personal enrichment: a way to learn about his past lives, a resource for self-discovery. For another, Lazaris is about creating abundance, material and spiritual, in his life. For a woman, Lazaris provides emotional and physical healing. For a fourth, herself a healer, Lazaris is a source of deep metaphysical knowledge and a way to recharge spiritual batteries. For one subject, Lazaris represents the spiritual sea change that is occurring simultaneously with personal and geographical changes (divorce, moving).

LAZARIS AS PRODUCT

Iannaccone proposes two solutions to the problem of consumer religious risk— one is congregational leadership and the other is portfolio diversification: a consumer choosing among many religious options. Certainly, this is the path taken by many New Age consumers and one encouraged by a tradition of combinativeness in metaphysical movements dating back at least to Madame Blavatsky.

Channeling offers a third solution, more radical in its implications: it separates the religious product from the producer. For most other religious movements, the product and the producer are the same: the Southern Baptist Church promotes the Southern Baptist faith. To use more economic terminology: The

Southern Baptists sell compensators under the Southern Baptist brand name (which includes many regional variations of Southern Baptists, of course).

If a religious consumer becomes disenchanted with the producer of a religion, whether it be the organization or the individual, said consumer will no longer subscribe to the religion. Take a man who regularly watches a Pentecostal television evangelist. The man reads the preacher's mailings, sends him money, and has been healed through his TV set. Now imagine a scandal in which the evangelist is revealed to be an adulterer and embezzler. In all likelihood, the man will take his religious business elsewhere.

Channeling is different. This time, imagine a woman, who while participating in a Lazaris seminar finds she dislikes the other participants. Furthermore, she disapproves of how Concept:Synergy is run and even has argued with Jach via e-mail. None of this should disrupt her relationship with Lazaris. As long as this woman accepts the basic truth claim that Lazaris is a separate consciousness, she can continue to buy the tapes and attend the seminars. Very little religious risk exists for either producer or consumer.

This radical separation of religious producer and product is one thing that makes channeling such an innovative socioreligious practice. Channeling is rarely considered innovation because it is often seen as a continuation or least a recurrence of age-old spiritual practices. Showing that this assessment is at least subject to debate requires an excursus into the history of channeling.

Channeling might be briefly defined as an individual's receiving or transmitting information through a consciousness not his or her own. Most writers about channeling make the assumption that because channeling exists now, it must have existed in the past under different names (see Klimo, pp. 76–113). So scholars enlist Greek oracles, Siberian shamans, American spiritualists, even Jesus and Mohammed as channels before the word existed. Hanegraaff argues that while this is a valid hypothesis, it is an unprovable one. He uses the term "articulated revelation" to encompass all aforementioned phenomena (24).

Modern-day channeling, in which the channeler can conjure and dismiss particular, personalized sources at will, as practiced by Pursel, J. Z. Knight, and less-renowned channelers described in Michael Brown's book, is a quite recent phenomenon. Gordon Melton dates the term "channeling" to the UFO contact movement of the 1940s and 1950s. If UFO cults conceived of channeling, the birth of the modern channeling movement must be when Jane Roberts began channeling Seth in 1963. Several of the interviewees for this paper had their first experience with channeling from reading *The Nature of Personal Reality* and other books written by Seth via Jane Roberts.

Channeling is not an age-old manifestation of primal religious impulses but a modern religious practice. Similarly, channeling is not marginal to the American religious experience but becoming more and more central. With that in mind, it should come as no surprise that channeling is a form of religious exchange equivalent to the capitalist mode of commercial exchange: The product does not represent the producer. The consumer of a McDonald's hamburger is not a member of a McDonald's community. His feelings toward the CEO of the McDonald's Corporation, the branch manager of his local franchise, or even the fry cook are irrelevant. It is the product—in this case a burger and fries—that is important. This is a quintessentially American way of doing business just as, I argue, Lazaris is a quintessentially American way of doing religion. I have shown how the Lazaris phenomenon caters to the individual. The other side of the equation is that organization and community are downplayed.

Access to Lazaris is maintained by Concept:Synergy. It is the corporation's job to intrude minimally on the Lazaris experience. Signing up for an intensive, for example, requires giving your credit card number, in a toll-free call lasting about thirty seconds. The mailing list, in the thousands, receives weekly communications from Concept:Synergy about upcoming events and new material.

Concept:Synergy is "well organized and well run," according to one interviewee. She appreciates the fact that the charge for a seminar can be paid over two credit card billing periods. It is possible to have disagreement with the organization and people within it and still be devoted to Lazaris.

It is more than possible to interface with Lazaris solely through tapes, books, and the Internet, never meeting another "friend of Lazaris" face to face. Even the meetings such as the evening described earlier, which might assemble several hundred participants, always emphasize Lazaris's relationship with each individual, not with the group as a whole. As a recent flier states, "Though we gather together, Lazaris will work with each of us personally as we learn to chart our uncharted and explore our unexplored."

Indeed, Concept:Synergy explicitly denies that any Lazaris community exists. The organization eschews even the most practical community devices. The Lazaris seminars do not include childcare, carpooling, or ride boards. After the seminar is over, people walk out of the hotel in a jubilant or introspective silence. The strategy is deliberate, and most people like it. One interviewee stressed that there was nothing to join or enroll in, no rituals to perform, nothing to worship, no way to serve Lazaris even if you wanted to (except by volunteering to take tickets at the seminars). These absences reinforce the optional quality of Lazaris. "You don't have to go" to the intensives; everyone winds up in the same place is Lazaris's message, according to one source.

BRAND LOYALTY

Continuing the capitalist analogy, instead of loyalty to an organization (which implies responsibilities, submission, guilt, and blind trust, all the negative associations accrued by traditional religion), Lazaris inculcates the more capitalist notion of loyalty to a brand.

The Lazaris organization, on the whole, keeps a stable clientele, and except for a few years in the 1980s when the organization ventured tentatively into mass media, knowledge about Lazaris spreads through word of mouth. My five interviewees became involved through business or social relationships and, with one exception, were already involved in the New Age.

But because Lazaris gains clients through small networks should not imply that Concept:Synergy is lax about its marketing. C:S keeps access to Lazaris under tight control. There is little written material—none is passed out at the seminars, and only a handful of books have been published by Concept: Synergy. This might be partly attributable to the postliteracy culture, a culture in which most people get their news from television and "read" their books on tape. If culture and education no longer depend on the written word, why should religion? But, of course, an oral culture also creates a more dependent, ongoing relationship with Lazaris—why spend five hundred dollars on a seminar if the same information were available in a ten-dollar paperback book?

Concept:Synergy does not encourage any unsupervised Lazaris groups; people rarely meet in each other's living rooms to discuss the positive impact Lazaris has played on their lives, for example, and if they do, the gathering has no official sanction. Also, Concept:Synergy bans other sources of information at the official Lazaris events. No advertisements or announcements are made, and only the Lazaris material and Isis Rising products are sold.

The Lazaris Web site (www.lazaris.com) has no links to other sites—that is, the Lazaris Web page will not lead you to any other Web pages of related interest. So Concept:Synergy does its best to seal off Lazaris from other influences as well as to keep Lazaris a private property. Indeed Lazaris is assigned copyrighted authorship by the Library of Congress (Brown, p. 161).

COMMITMENTS AND COMPENSATORS

A religious group that operates according to the principles of rational choice should be explicit about the compensators it provides and at what cost. Concept:Synergy published for the first time in 1997 a catalogue of all the Lazaris material. The titles and brief descriptions of the material, mostly audiotapes, take up thirty-nine pages. The variety is astounding. Most telling is the subject index that ends the booklet, which is quite simply a naked list of all the compensators Lazaris provides. Here is a list of the various mail-order how-to techniques Lazaris offers: avoiding Failure, overcoming Fear, expressing your Feelings, embracing Feminine Energy, granting Forgiveness, controlling Frustration, awakening the Future Self, and that's just the letter "F!" The index reminds one of nothing so much as the opening pages of a Gideon Bible: Both imply that their respective products offer remedies for all occasions.

Stark and Bainbridge define a "compensator" as "the belief that a reward will be obtained in the distant future or in some other context which cannot be immediately verified" (6). New religious phenomena, whether audience "cults," client "cults" or full-blown "cult" movements, must find novel ways not based on tradition or past record to dole out compensators. Stark and Bainbridge spend a lot of pages on compensators (deferred rewards) but nary a sentence about the different ways in which compensators are distributed. As I see it, a new religious movement has two choices, which I call gradual and sudden.

These two opposing strategies of new religious movements for delivering compensators I will term "compensation delivery systems" (CDS). The gradual CDS can be best described as religion as a multi-level-marketing (MLM) tactic—a term I take from the business world. Here compensators are awarded based on progression through the ranks. The organization is structured like a pyramid (hence pyramid scheme). A new member comes on as a consumer but quickly advances to being both a consumer and a seller. High compensators are promised in exchange for a minimum commitment—a small amount of money, a few hours of time. However, to rise higher and higher in these organizations, one must successfully recruit people to become lower initiates, as well as commit ever-increasing sums of time and money. Exemplars of new religious movements with a gradual CDS are Scientology and Erhard Seminar Training in its various manifestations. It should be noted that many well-established American companies work this way, too, including Arthur Murray dance studios and Amway. These companies sell not dance lessons or skin cream but themselves.

The other kind of CDS is sudden. The best example are the devotional cults from Asia (like those of Guru Maharaj Ji and Bhagwan Shree Rajneesh). Here compensators are abundant so long as one is on the good side of the guru, roshi, or other personal charismatic leader. Often these groups are in high tension with rest of society and require a high commitment—communal living, giving away personal property.

Most dedicated Lazaris followers (qualitatively speaking—I have only anecdotal data) came to Lazaris after having spent time in groups with either one of the two delivery systems—groups with gradual or sudden CDSs. How refreshing it must have been for them to find a spiritual movement that rejected both these options.

Concept:Synergy operates on a principle of straight fee-for-service compensators. Lazaris has no levels, no hierarchy, no schedule of advancement. Anyone is free to attend any seminar or sit close during "magic time." Any or all of the panoply of compensators Lazaris offers—the collected Lazaris material—is available at the push of a phone button or the click of a mouse. Lazaris uses compensators as a resource that allows people to take what they choose in whatever dosage they please. So if Lazaris functions neither as multilevel marketing commodity nor guru, how does the movement attract new participants while retaining old ones? What keeps people interested?

The "Lazaris experience" combines the excitement of hearing from a discorporate spirit with the predictability of knowing exactly when, where, and for how long he'll speak. Over the years, Lazaris has developed a specific vocabulary. Both the promotional flyers and his own speech are replete with key words and phrases like "resonance," "the Journey of Coming Home," "High Magic," "Higher Self," "Great Work," "Great Adventure," "Lemuria," and "Sirius."[10] This recombining of familiar terms in new ways allows a certain security for longtime friends of Lazaris, while setting up pleasurable expectations for upcoming events.

The Lazaris material is notable not only for its jargon but also for its intertextuality; advertisements frequently refer to previous seminars. Take, for example, the flyer for "The Mapmaker's Dream: Beyond Conscious Reality Creation":

> Some of us have laid a foundation (The Great Adventure Part I) and the groundwork is done (The Grand Adventure Part II). Some of us are only now beginning to explore what might lie beyond conscious reality creation. Because of who Lazaris is, there need be no prerequisites to our growing, changing and evolving. Because of the energy and force that Lazaris brings, there need be no prerequisite to these three days. Well-seasoned or just beginning we can step in.

A clever marketing technique: The appeal to regulars is that this workshop is the culmination of a series. Novices are appealed to with the promise of "no prerequisite."

This technique is a common trope in Lazaris material. The seminar on April 23, 1994, was about the "Sirius vortex," how it "opened our neurons and DNA flooded with Light and Information." Three years later "it is still impossible to imagine the planetary and global implications." And so in April 1997, another seminar revisits this vortex opening. Lazaris events are predicated on backsliding, on people forgetting the techniques they learned previously.

MONEY

The compensators Lazaris provides are appropriate for both novice and initiate. But what does the Lazaris organization ask in return? As we have already seen, no organizational loyalty, community fellowship, or doctrinal orthodoxy is expected or required. The answer is simple: money.

The Lazaris experience does not come cheap. An Evening with Lazaris, lasting about four hours, costs approximately $50. A two-day "Lazaris Weekend" is $300, and the "Intensives" range from $350 to $600. These events also have cancellation and transfer fees. Lazaris Tapes (usually a three-hour double cassette in a plastic case) go for $25 and videotapes for $60. A one-year subscription to the Lazaris Web page forum is $60.

The live events, where two or three hundred pay to sit in a hotel conference room that might cost only a few hundred dollars a day to rent, are high-profit generators. There is little overhead. Participants receive no worksheets, no coffee or snacks. There are no labor costs (the ticket takers and vendors are all volunteers) and since Jach stopped traveling, no longer any travel costs.

So how much do people spend on Lazaris? Someone who attended one Lazaris event a month and who bought most of the tapes as they came out could easily spend five or six thousand dollars a year, not including transportation or lodging. Is it worth it? Without a doubt, according to those who are satisfied.

But the money made by Lazaris is not merely justified or rationalized; it is celebrated. One of the first principles of Lazaris is that money is the easiest and most fun of all illusions to create. Lazaris often uses the metaphor of a children's tea party. Just as children never run out of imaginary tea, so, too, should "mapmakers and metaphysicians" never run out of playful money.

Using code words like "abundance" and "success," Concept:Synergy sells the promise of financial prosperity in its promotional literature. Here is a sampling of "prosperity thinking" quotations from one year of mailings, April 1996 to April 1997:

- "Manifest a vast array of success."
- "Reap the bounty and abundance."
- "The success can flow into our lives."
- From a flyer for a four-day intensive called "The Wonder of Celebration and Triumph: Having It All" comes this: "We will learn to embrace the magic to see how success, happiness and joy actually follow the force of celebration and triumph."
- From a flyer promoting a weekend intensive called "Prosperity and Abundance": "Opportunity and financial wherewithal too often lag behind our gracious generosity and our clear intent of creating and manifesting what we want . . . Welcome to a weekend just for us."

Concept:Synergy's genius for making money is neither hidden nor minimized. If Lazaris's techniques assure financial success, and if Jach, Peny, and Michaell are the most familiar with his techniques, then it follows logically that their own wealth is not merely accepted but celebrated as proof positive of Lazaris's credentials.

CONCLUSION

This paper applied rational choice theory to what some might see as one of the most "irrational" of contemporary religious experiences: Channeling Lazaris, by self-consciously assuming spirituality to be a marketable product, represents an important emerging way of being religious in America.

An examination of the history of Lazaris has shown the organization to be supremely adaptable, to have changed rapidly to fit current cultural style. The material channeled by Lazaris contains a superabundance of information—"compensators" to use the rational choice term—in the form of metaphysical formulae, meditation techniques, prophecies, psychic readings, psychological axioms. Hundreds of Lazaris tapes are available on a multitude of topics. Consumers are encouraged to pick and choose what they need.

Indeed, the deliberate decoupling of the content and meaning of Lazaris is key to his appeal. According to Lazaris, when he speaks through Jach Pursel, every listener quite literally hears something different, thanks to Lazaris's metaphysical prowess. Interviews with several longtime Lazaris followers corroborate this story. Despite their similar backgrounds (white, educated, upper middle class, self-employed) and participation in the same Lazaris events, each of the interviewees has gleaned quite different messages from the Lazaris material.

Unlike many new religious groups, Lazaris has no hierarchy, no levels of involvement. Anybody may attend any Lazaris event. But what does the Lazaris organization ask in return? As the paper has shown, no organizational loyalty or community fellowship is expected or required. The only commitment needed is money. This straight fee-for-service approach to religion has made Jach Pursel and his partners extremely wealthy. But the money made by Lazaris is not merely justified or rationalized; it is celebrated. One of the first principles of Lazaris is that money is the easiest and most fun of all illusions to create. All this should go to show that Lazaris, as one of the most powerful practitioners of channeling, embodies a style of religious experience deeply informed by American capitalism.

Rational choice helps us to understand Lazaris as more than a New Age "fringe" group with limited application to the study of American religion and culture as a whole. Insofar as rational choice is a valid tool for the study of religion, examining a phenomenon such as Lazaris, which so clearly incorporates rational choice into its own practice, may help us to understand the dynamics operative in other, more conventional, religions.

NOTES

1. Laurence Iannaccone, "Rational Choice: Framework for the Scientific Study of Religion," in Lawrence A. Yount, ed., *Rational Choice Theory and Assessment* (New York: Routledge, 1997).

2. Although legally Lazaris is not a religion and has no formal creed or membership requirement, its implicit threshold of belief provides comfort similar to any religion.

3. I use the term "Lazaris" to refer to both the formless channeled entity and the organization, participants, and general milieu that surround this entity. Concept:Synergy will refer to a specific organization.

4. A common New Age belief is that crystals focus and store energy.

5. Later, he changed the spelling to Jach (for numerological reasons), and that is how I have spelled it throughout.

6. This and other oral history can be found at "Some Time with Jach," Public Library, Lazaris Home Page, (www.lazaris.com).

7. This information was discovered in an amateur audiocassette recorded in Berkeley, CA, on August 8, 1977 and found in a private collection.

8. The same year as Marilyn Ferguson published the influential *Aquarian Conspiracy*.

9. In fact, channeler Kevin Ryerson is more prominent in all of Maclaine's books than is Lazaris. Ryerson played himself in the 1987 TV movie based on Maclaine's 1983 book *Out on a Limb*).

10. Many of these terms are found elsewhere in the New Age, with some dating back to Theosophy.

REFERENCES

Bainbridge, William Sims. *The Sociology of Religious Movements*. New York: Routledge, 1997.

Bjorling, Joel. *Channeling: A Bibliographic Exploration*. New York: Garland, 1992.

Brown, Michael. *The Channeling Zone*. Cambridge: Harvard University Press, 1997.

D'Antonio, Michael. *Heaven on Earth*. New York: Crown, 1992.

Evening with Lazaris. *The Power of Our Chakras: Removing Blockages to Our Success.* July 25, 1996, San Francisco, CA.

Ferguson, Marilyn. *The Aquarian Conspiracy*. Boston: Houghton Mifflin, 1980.

Hanegraaff, Wouter J. *New Age Religion and Western Culture*. New York: Brill, 1996.

Heelas, Paul. *The New Age Movement: The Celebration of the Self and the Sacralization of Modernity*. Cambridge: Blackwell Press, 1996.

Iannaccone, Laurence. "Rational Choice: Framework for the Scientific Study of Religion." In *Rational Choice Theory and Assessment*, edited by Lawrence A. Young. New York: Routledge, 1997.

Klimo, John. *Channeling*. New York: St. Martin's, 1987.

Lazaris Intensive. *The Alchemy of UltraConsciousness: To Create Wondrous Success and Beyond.* July 26–28, 1996, San Francisco.

Lazaris Material. Orlando, FL: Concept:Synergy, 1997.

Lewis, James R., and J. Gordon Melton, eds. *Perspectives on the New Age*. Albany, NY: SUNY Press, 1992.

Pursel, Jach [Lazaris]. *Lazaris Interviews*, 2 vols. Beverly Hills, CA: Concept:Synergy. 1988.

Stark, Rodney, and William Sims Bainbridge. *The Future of Religion: Secularization, Revival and Cult Formation*. Berkeley: University of California Press. 1985.

Stark, Rodney, and Roger Finke. *The Churching of America*. New Brunswick, NJ: Rutgers Press. 1994.

11

DAMANHUR
A Magical Community in Italy
Massimo Introvigne

amanhur is, arguably, the largest communal group in the world today or, at
least, the largest communal group in the "ancient wisdom" magical tradition. Although the movement has been in existence for some twenty years, it has
been the subject matter of very few scholarly studies. Apart from some unpublished papers read at sociological conferences, and from an entry in my own
1990 encyclopedic volume on "new magical movements," *Il cappello del mago*,[1]
I am aware of only two relevant sociological papers, written by Italian sociologists Luigi Berzano[2] and Maria Immacolata Macioti.[3] Although non-Italian
social scientists have occasionally visited Damanhur, the group has been mentioned outside of Italy only in papers by Isotta Poggi, an Italian-born assistant to
J. Gordon Melton at the Institute for the Study of American Religion, Santa Barbara, California.[4] On the other hand—in Italy and occasionally abroad[5]—
Damanhur has been featured in countless magazine articles, TV programs, and,
occasionally, pieces of anticult literature.[6] Damanhur itself has produced through
its publishing branch, Edizioni Horus, more than one hundred fifty books and
booklets, mostly authored by its founder, Oberto Airaudi.[7]

Press and TV interest increased enormously after 1992, when the huge
Underground Temple—successfully kept secret for fifteen years—was discov-
ered (following the indications of a disgruntled exmember) and seized by the
Italian authorities for having been built in breach of a number of zoning and tax

requirements. This paper will in brief place Damanhur within the alternative spirituality tradition of its Italian region, Piedmont (Piemonte); will detail its origins, history, and worldview; will explore the meaning of the Underground Temple; and will raise some sociological questions on the structure and future of the community and on its relationship with the New Age in Italy.

ALTERNATIVE SPIRITUALITY IN PIEDMONT

Damanhur is situated in Piedmont, less than thirty miles north of the city of Turin. Before 1861—when the Kingdom of Italy was established—Italy was divided into a number of small states. Piedmont and the island of Sardinia, together with some districts presently part of France, constituted the Kingdom of Sardinia, ruled by the House of Savoy. Although early Savoy rulers were rather conservative—and, in the eighteenth and early nineteenth centuries, hostile to the Enlightenment—things changed in the 1840s. For a number of reasons, Turin, a university city, became the home of the most progressive and liberal intellectual renewal in Italy; the renewal in turn gained leading politicians and the kings themselves. Under the leadership of Prime Minister Count Camillo di Cavour (1810–1861), the Kingdom of Sardinia eventually became the Kingdom of Italy under what Cavour called the "artichoke policy." Little by little, through war, international alliances, and negotiated settlements, the Kingdom of Sardinia added—one after the other—all the small Italian states to the crown of the Savoy family. By 1861 the Kingdom of Sardinia encompassed all of Italy, excluding Rome and the surrounding area, still ruled by the pope.

Rome was eventually invaded and made the capital of the Kingdom of Italy (established with this name in 1861) in the year 1870. Because the unification of Italy under the liberal House of Savoy was seen as a threat to the continuous existence of an independent state ruled by the pope in central Italy, and also because of the frankly anticlerical orientation of the Count of Cavour and other leading politicians in Piedmont, Savoy politics were actively opposed by the Vatican and by the Catholic Church, including that in Piedmont itself. This, in turn, only increased the anticlerical measures of the Count of Cavour and his associates; many leading Catholic clergymen in Piedmont suffered imprisonment and exile. Within the frame of this policy, Piedmontese governments were extremely tolerant—for the standards of their time—toward alternative spirituality, seen as another way to harass the largely predominant Catholic Church. Not only were American new religious movements such as Mormonism and, later, Seventh-Day Adventism allowed into Piedmont (while they were prevented from entering any other Italian state), but—although statutes against magic and witchcraft remained on the books—Turin also became a surprisingly tolerant city as far as the activities of occult and magical groups were concerned. As a result, not unexpectedly, occult leaders, spiritualist mediums, and practitioners of magnetism and mesmerism settled in Turin, after fleeing the more hostile conditions prevailing in other Italian states (and, occasionally, France, Austria, and Belgium). The capital of Piedmont became between 1850 and 1880 one of Europe's main centers for occultism and spiritualism. By 1890—twenty years after the Italian Army had conquered Rome—the political function of alternative spirituality in Turin had exhausted itself, and the prosecution of a number of spiritualist mediums and mesmerists in a celebrated trial marked the end of this occult spring.

The reason why Turin became the home of many occult and spiritualist groups, thus, has nothing to do with the alleged esoteric interests of the Savoy family (largely a legend) but should rather be explained by the political situation and the hostility between the governments of Piedmont and the Catholic Church during the process that eventually led to the unification of Italy. One of the results of the Savoy politics of tolerating a number of occult and spiritualist groups in Turin was the production of a propaganda literature, particularly in Rome and Naples, accusing the government of Piedmont of protecting "satanists." The label of "City of the Devil" for Turin was largely generated by this propaganda and has remained with the city ever since, although in the twentieth century the number of occult and spiritualist groups in Turin has not been exceptional, if compared with other large Italian and European towns.[8]

On the other hand, it is true that Turin's occult spring of 1850–1890 left a certain legacy. The Theosophical Society and the splinter United Lodge of Theosophists have been particularly active in Piedmont's capital. A succession of local independent groups in the Theosophical or "ancient wisdom" tradition have also been founded in Turin throughout the twentieth century. Finally, it should be mentioned that the existence from the times of Napoleon in Turin of what is now the largest Egyptian museum in the world is not without relation to the birth of a number of occult groups inspired by Egyptian rituals and religion.[9]

THE ORIGINS AND HISTORY OF DAMANHUR

Oberto Airaudi was born in Balangero in the Lanzo valleys north of Turin in 1950. A precocious young man, he published at age fifteen a book of poetry, and at age seventeen *Cronaca del Mio Suicidio* ("A Chronicle of My Suicide"), a rather morbid book where he announced in a literary form his "possible" suicide.[10] At the same time, Airaudi was fascinated by Turin's occult milieu. He visited a number of healers and "pranotherapists" (healers claiming to use the force of "prana" by raising their hands, and, occasionally, by physical manipulations) and learned the secrets of their profession, quite popular in Italy in the 1970s. Soon, Airaudi became a successful "pranotherapist" himself, with offices in a number of different small towns of Piedmont. He practiced also as a spiritualist

Oberto Airaudi (Falco), founder of Damanhur.
(*Courtesy of Damanhur*)

medium—and later coauthored a spiritualist manual[11]—and became familiar with Turin's theosophical subculture. In 1974 he had enough friends and clients to establish his own organization, the Horus Center, backed up by a School of Pranotherapy.

Almost immediately after the establishment of the Horus Center, Airaudi mentioned to the members that they should eventually organize to live communally. In 1975 steps were taken to rent (and subsequently to buy) a property in the valley called Valchiusella, between the villages of Baldissero Canavese and Vidracco. The valley is situated between Ivrea (one of Italy's "technocities" and the home of the computer company Olivetti) and Castellamonte (a town in Italy famous for the china industry). In 1976 a settlement was established under the name of an ancient Egyptian city, Damanhur, with two dozen pioneers.

Damanhur was officially inaugurated as a community in 1979. In 1981 the previous by-laws were modified into a "constitution," a move emphasizing that the community regarded itself as a "separated people" and even as "an independent state." The constitution was revised in 1984, 1986, and 1987, until—in 1989—it was reissued as the *Constitution of the Nation of Damanhur*. In fact, the definition of Damanhur as a "state" had been actively opposed by anticultists and some local authorities, and the 1989 text opted finally for the word "nation." At any rate, Damanhur has a "government" of its own and a currency, the credit ("credito"), the value of which, however, is based on the Italian lira and function of which is largely symbolic. From the very beginning, the "citizens" of Damanhur in part work in the community and in part have outside work but return to the community after their working day is finished. Although exceptions existed, a large majority of the original pioneers was composed of young adults who had finished high school. A few had college degrees, and a small group included skilled workers with no high school training.

Couples were admitted and children were raised in small units composed of a number of families. Very soon Damanhur had its own day-care center, preschool, and elementary school; an intermediate school, for children aged eleven to fourteen, was inaugurated in 1994. After a few conflicts, the autonomy of these schools was accepted by local authorities. Yearly examinations by school authorities of the nearby municipalities have confirmed that the educational standards of Damanhur schools are high, and the results scored by children are higher than average.

The growth of Damanhur has been continuous. There were two hundred "citizens" in 1985 and four hundred in 1994. Since, according to the constitution, a community could not exceed two hundred twenty members, Damanhur is now a "federation" of a number of different communities, all located in the Valchiusella Valley within a radius of twenty miles. The mother community has been renamed Damyl, and the daughter communities are called Rama Pan, Tentyris, and Vidracco Alta. In fact, there is a continuum of homes in the valley, each inhabited by ten to fifteen people, including children. Some services are centralized in Damyl, including the schools. Damyl also houses the "open temple," an impressive open structure with statues of Greek and Egyptian divinities, and a larger open area with symbols of different religious traditions. A market is held there every Sunday, when the community opens its gates to welcome tourists and visitors.

The products of the community are also sold through normal commercial channels (including international duty-free shops as far as Saudi Arabia and Abu Dhabi). Damanhur is reputed for its health food products, china, and jewelry. Paintings by community artists (including the founder, Oberto Airaudi) are also sold to the general public. More surprisingly, Damanhur has a high percentage of computers (one to every six "citizens"), and one of the community's resources is the sale of software. Although self-sufficiency is a stated goal, even today a percentage of "citizens" have outside jobs.

In addition to the four hundred "citizens" (all resident in the community homes), Damanhur is composed of some three hundred "associated members," who live in their own homes (the vast majority in the province of Turin), contribute economically to the community, and visit on weekends and when special celebrations are held. At least another one thousand people are regularly in touch with Damanhur and attend the courses of the Free University of Damanhur in Turin and elsewhere, but they do not contribute or tithe regularly and are not regarded as "members." The constitution suggests that "citizens" deed all their properties to the community, but in fact areas of private property have always been kept and the economic arrangements of Damanhur have passed through various phases.[12]

The organization of the family in Damanhur has attracted considerable Hostile interest. Couples may join the community and continue as such, although they should live communally with other families in one of the valley homes. On the other hand, many "citizens" who were unmarried when they joined Damanhur have entered into one of the community marriages, stipulated as a contract that provides for a "provisional" marriage for one, two, and three years. When the contract expires, the marriage can be renewed or dissolved. Sensationalist press reports have always equated the Damanhur system of marriage to free love. Damanhur's "citizens" counter that a significant percentage of the marriages are regularly renewed and that against the hypocrisy of the larger society—where marriages are theoretically "forever" but in many cases end in divorces—the possibility of checking periodically whether a real marriage still exists results in better couples and in fact contributes to the stability of the families. Children, at any rate, spend a significant portion of their time in the community schools and other communal activities.

As might be expected, conflicts and lurid, but often inaccurate, reports on the family arrangements of Damanhur have arisen in child custody cases when only one of the parents has left the community. Disgruntled ex-members have also informed the press of Damanhur's practice of "programming" the birth of each new child according both to the economical possibilities of each unit and to astrologically defined times. In many tabloid articles this has simply been reported as the couples of Damanhur "having sex only when Airaudi gives his permission," actually a caricature of Damanhur's "programmed births" project.

DAMANHUR'S WORLDVIEW

According to sociologist Luigi Berzano, Oberto Airaudi's worldview shows elements of four different religious traditions: Egyptian, Celtic (including Christian Celtic), occult-theosophical, and New Age. Although when asked, any "citizen" of Damanhur would insist that the community's worldview is absolutely new and original, in fact the influence of a larger theosophical and occult tradition is at times evident. Many ideas popular in the New Age movement have been incorporated within the community's literature, although—contrary to other New Age meccas in Europe—Damanhur is not vegetarian, and in fact its restaurant (open to the public) excels in the preparation of meat specialties. The list of wines is also rich in the tradition of Piedmont but unlike the case in many New Age vegetarian restaurants. Vegetarian meals are available, but Airaudi himself is not vegetarian and does not abstain from wine. All "citizens," according to the constitution, must abstain from tobacco and drugs, and this provision is strictly enforced. Although no worldview may be entirely new, it should also be recognized that elements of different origin have been integrated by Airaudi in a rather original synthesis.

Damanhur does not allow itself to be called polytheistic. "Only one God exists," members state, but it is impossible to contact him directly. God remains largely unknown and can be accessed only through *the gods,* the "Intermediate Deities."[13] Only nine "Primeval Deities" are self-generated; all the others have been created by humans, but, not unlike the Jungian archetypes, now have an existence of their own. Not to be confused with the "Intermediate Deities"—or "the gods"—are "Entities," which include angels, nature spirits, and demons. While today the entities are "subtler" than humans, the first human was a "Primeval Deity" who—according to a gnostic myth with a long history in the hermetic and esoteric tradition—was the victim of a fall and lapsed into the present union with the body.

Many deities and entities voluntarily followed humans into their exile and may now help us when we try to return to our original "subtler" state (according to a scheme the theosophical origin of which is apparent). Our return to the original condition may be made easier by different sciences, including modern physical science but also by magic, alchemy, and "selfic," the science studying the particular properties of spiral-like forms (called "self" in Damanhur). Through these techniques, the "citizens" of Damanhur also learn to recognize the "synchronic lines" that constitute the Earth's nerves, for the Earth—as in many occult and New Age traditions—is considered as a living being. The very site of Damanhur was selected because of the "synchronic lines" converging in the valley; knowing the "lines" is essential in order to communicate with distant places and even to program our future reincarnations.

Damanhur's cosmology includes the early generation of three "Mother worlds"—the world of human beings, the world of plants, and the world of nature spirits; they are not capable of communication between themselves but instead generate "Echo worlds" through which the "Mother worlds" become able to communicate. Each race has an "astral tank" (a concept similar to the "akashic memory" of the theosophical tradition). Human beings may get in touch, through particular techniques, with the human "race mind" (the "astral tank" of the human race), but they may also find very useful information in the "race minds" of animals. To this effect, each human being may enter into a special magical relation with an animal by assuming its name. In fact all the "citizens" of Damanhur are identified not by their original family names but by the names of animals. The founder is Hawk—an illusion to Horus—but one finds as well names such as Elephant, Kangaroo, and so on.

Because the number of "citizens" is now in excess of the animal names available—and also for magical reasons—each "citizen" is now identified by two names, the first of an animal and the second of a plant. Animal names also serve the obvious sociological purpose of marking the community's "otherness," a purpose also served by the custom of the "citizens" greeting each other (but not outsiders) with the words "with you" (*Con te*) rather than with the more usual "Good morning" or "Good evening."

Spiritualism, parapsychological experiments, and other classical techniques of the occult-esoteric milieu are still used in Damanhur, but increasingly important are the use of a distinctive esoteric language ("citizens" regard this as an ancient secret language rediscovered by Damanhur)—written both in Latin characters and in ideograms—and of musical themes and dance movements corresponding to this language. Rituals, including ritual dresses, have been devised by Oberto Airaudi in order to facilitate the reintegration of humans into their original exalted condition and at the same time the reintegration of Mother Earth (threatened by an ecological disaster). Although observers may note that Egyptian symbols are somewhat predominant, Airaudi insists that the Egyptian religion is not more important than other traditions in building Damanhur's new synthesis. Egypt, he mentioned in a recent interview with the author, has also been used as a convenient *external* symbolism, in order to hide more esoteric truths that Damanhur is not prepared to share with the outside world.

THE UNDERGROUND TEMPLE

Only in 1992—due to unpredictable external circumstances—did it became clear to outside observers that the main task for the "citizens" of Damanhur was not the building of a self-sufficient community nor the performance of certain rituals and dances in the Open Temple. The most important work was the building of the Underground Temple. The completion of this building is magically linked, in Damanhur's inner worldview, to the salvation of the whole planet Earth.

Damanhur has been a remarkably stable community, with the number of defections actually lower than in noncommunal new religious movements. Accordingly, lawsuits by former members, although not unknown, have not been a significant problem and have normally been settled. In 1991, however, Filippo Maria Cerutti—a former member of the "government" of Damanhur—left the community and sued Airaudi, asking for compensation for his former services and financial contributions; Cerutti, a rich man, had in fact never contributed all his fortune to the community. In this case, the counterevaluations by Cerutti and by Damanhur of what would be a fair settlement were so distant that an amicable solution proved impossible, and the case went to court (where it still is). Cerutti—who had been part of Damanhur's inner circle—threatened to expose the existence of the Underground Temple. When it became clear that no settlement was possible, Cerutti visited a district attorney, Bruno Tinti, telling him the amazing story of a huge temple located under a small mountain, with miles of galleries and rooms. Although initially skeptical, the judge ordered a raid. Following Cerutti's directions, agents of the tax police were able to uncover a large number of secret passages and technologically advanced devices hidden in the very heart of a small mountain that led, one after the other, to hidden rooms of almost incredible magnificence.

Building a temple, of course, is not a criminal offense in Italy, but Airaudi and Damanhur's "government" were accused of the breach of zoning regulations, statutes requiring building permissions, and tax laws. In 1993 the City of Vidracco, having jurisdiction over the Underground Temple, ordered its destruction. Due to the opposition of a considerable part of public opinion—including social scientists and the artistic community—the order has never been enforced, and it appears now very unlikely that it will be enforced in the future. An inspection by state engineers has ascertained that the underground works have not damaged the mountain but rather consolidated it. On the other hand, authorities in charge of the preservation of the cultural patrimony of Piedmont have decided that the temple is a significant work of art and should be preserved. Without entering into the legal technicalities, the temple does not at present seriously face the threat of destruction. There is, however, a possibility that it will be confiscated by the state and assigned to the City of Vidracco. It could subsequently rent it back to Damanhur for a fee, or, alternatively, impose its own policy of admitting tourists. At present tourists are not admitted, although they can visit an exhibit with facsimiles and models. Even this latter possibility is probably unlikely. What really hangs in the balance is whether Damanhur will be permitted to continue work on the temple, which is not finished. According to Airaudi, only 10 percent of the work, as originally planned, has been completed during the last sixteen years. Cerutti was sued before a criminal court by Damanhur for libel and slander, but he was found not guilty. The civil suit is still going on, although the latest news is that the evaluation of the amount due to Cerutti by a technical expert designated by the Turin court is not far from the offer made by Damanhur.

The Italian authorities in charge of the preservation of the works of art seem to have correctly assessed the artistic value of the Underground Temple. For the outside visitor, it is a breathtaking experience, offering—room after room— amazing and unexpected discoveries. The artworks (mainly stained glass windows, frescoes, and mosaics) are reminiscent of Byzantine, Egyptian, and Greek models but also of Liberty and Art Deco, all with these styles merged into a unique Damanhur perspective. The main rooms are the Water Room (dedicated to the Mother and the female principle, with a spectacular dolphin mosaic); the Earth Room, with eight huge columns and a bull mosaic, dedicated to the male principle; and the Glass Room, with the largest underground dome in the world, made of 60,000 small glass pieces, the site of Damanhur's most important rituals.

In addition to the three main rooms, there are apparently never-ending corridors, with stained glass windows, Egyptian-style frescoes, many secret passages (often unsuspected and astonishing), and smaller rooms for parapsychological and magical experiments. Particularly significant is the Room of the Spheres, where big glass spheres are each connected to the always-present "self" (i.e., a metal spiral). Through these spheres, the "citizens" of Damanhur may get in touch with the continents and direct their magical energy where it is most needed. All in all, it is impossible to describe the Underground Temple, called the Temple of Humankind (*Tempio dell'Uomo*), a term using gender-exclusive language, although women are prominent in the leadership of Damanhur. There are literally miles of corridors and thousands of statues, windows, and paintings. In fact, each member of the commu-

A cross section of the underground Temple of Humankind. (*Courtesy of Damanhur*)

nity makes with his or her own hands a statue symbolically representing his or her connection with the animal whose name each "citizen" has selected.

Entering the Underground Temple—an experience for the time being reserved to a small number of non-"citizens," including state and local officers, social scientists, and some journalists—is, as sociologist Maria Immacolata Macioti has written, "entering into a fairy tale."[14] Although rituals are performed in the temple, it is thought that the most important ritual has been—for the last sixteen years—the construction of the temple itself.

Most of the construction has been performed at night, and the need of preserving secrecy has not allowed the use of noisy modern technological devices. Probably the secret was doomed from the beginning: It was very unlikely that it could be kept forever, even if the number of "apostates" who defect from Damanhur is small. However, the very fact that a secret about so huge a project was effectively kept for a fifteen years by some five hundred people, with no hint reaching the anticultist activists or the press, is the real "miracle" of Damanhur. On the other hand, all the experience of Damanhur should be reevaluated, taking into account the temple. Like the early Mormons in Nauvoo, Illinois, the "citizens" of Damanhur regard building the temple as their most sacred duty, and all the other experiences, including the economic structure of the community, have the main aim of allowing them time enough for their building enterprise. For this reason, Airaudi regards it as extremely important that Damanhur be allowed to continue the construction. In his vision, construction should still go on for some decades as the most important spiritual activity of the "citizens." Although he admits that secret portions of the temple still exist, undisclosed to all outsiders, any visit will show that there are large rooms and corridors where work has been left unfinished, awaiting the developments of the legal case.

THE FUTURE OF DAMANHUR

It is not impossible that the unwanted disclosure of the Underground Temple in 1992 will start a new phase for Damanhur. It has already compelled the community to engage in a closer dialogue with local and national authorities and with the public at large. Cerutti's "revelations" have in fact made Damanhur a more important target for anticultists than it used to be. Even the Roman Catholic bishop of Ivrea, in whose diocesan territory Damanhur is located, Monsignor Luigi Bettazzi—who is controversial in Italy for his extremely liberal political views—has released a document emphasizing that no one could at the same time become a "citizen" of Damanhur and remain a Roman Catholic in good standing (a statement regarded as reasonable even by some Damanhur leaders). The bishop has also accused Damanhur of "immoral practices" and "brainwashing," without further specifications and apparently following the anticult literature on the subject.[15]

The birth of Damanhur could be described according to the well-known Stark-Bainbridge typology of audience cults, client cults, and cult movements.[16] Damanhur's experience shows that a leader and his or her followers can pass subsequently through the three stages. Damanhur started as an audience cult that included the readers of Airaudi's popular books. When Airaudi started a professional career as a "pranotherapist" and healer, his regular clients moved from the audience cult to the client cult stage. Finally, Airaudi was capable of organizing his clients into a movement, which eventually became communal.

The communal form of Damanhur, on the other hand, is not really typical of the Italian New Age movement. The New Age is—particularly in Italy—a network of independent and loosely structured groups.[17] Damanhur is anything but loosely structured. It claims to be a "nation" with a "government," a "constitution," and a well-established hierarchy. It was developed before New Age became a household name in Italy, although it subsequently incorporated some (but not all) of New Age's most popular ideas. It will probably survive what J. Gordon Melton has called "the demise of the New Age."[18] Structured and hierarchically organized movements such as Damanhur were not really part of the New Age network, although they found many of their followers within the New Age milieu.

In this respect, it would be interesting to compare Damanhur to another community in Piedmont, the Green Village (*Villaggio Verde*) of Cavallirio (Novara).[19] Although Damanhur and the Green Village have in common a theosophical reference, the Green Village is an "open" community where only a dozen people live but members of many different groups of the theosophical and New Age milieu gather, particularly on Sunday, to perform a variety of different activities. Damanhur, on the other hand, is not an "open" community. Although it welcomes visitors of different persuasions, in order to become a "citizen," one must share the rather precise worldview of Oberto Airaudi (although he insists that the worldview is evolving and would not use the word "religion").

Even the notion of "movement," or "new religious movement" fails to capture exactly what Damanhur is. Damanhur is, in fact, a community, and Oberto Airaudi insists that he has decided that it should *not* become a "movement." In discussing the matter with Airaudi, it becomes clear that what he does not like in the idea of "movement" is the geographical dispersion of the members in a large territory. He claims that all attempts to organize settlements too far from the original location of Damanhur have not been successful. Damanhur could still grow in the future, but Airaudi would prefer that all the settlements—part of what the constitution calls a "federation"—remain in the Valchiusella Valley or at least in the province of Turin. It is true that Damanhur emphasizes computing, and computer links could be easily established at larger distances. On the other hand, it is crucial for Airaudi that all "citizens" could meet regularly to share the life of the one and the same community (and—as we now know—attend the Underground Temple rituals and participate in its never-ending construction). This has made Damanhur a selective community with little interest in proselytism; all new "citizens" must pass through a probationary period before joining. The number of people who meet Damanhur through the lectures of Oberto Airaudi, his books, and visitation on Sunday as tourists results already in more applications to join than the community is prepared to accept. Groups of people who have visited Damanhur (coming as far as from Los Angeles, California) have been counseled to "do their own thing" and keep some sort of loose association without joining as "citizens" or "associates." In other words, building the community has been more important for Oberto Airaudi and his friends than taking a message to the outside world; this second aspect has not been completely neglected, thanks to the publishing house, the magazines, and the lectures. Building the Underground Temple and performing the rituals are more important than attracting new converts. This is probably also due to an esoteric and not-yet-fully-disclosed apocalyptic vision of the fate of planet Earth.

Oberto Airaudi did not turn fifty before the year 2000, and the group—despite being itself more than twenty years old—is still in an early and charismatic phase. Incidents such as the one involving the forced disclosure of the Underground Temple may accelerate the Weberian processes of routinization of the charisma and lead to new directions. It would become increasingly difficult for the community—particularly if it will continue to be successful—to avoid or prevent its own institutionalization as a movement.

NOTES

1. See my *Il cappello del mago, I nuovi movimenti magici dallo spiritismo al satanismo* (Milan: SugarCo, 1990), pp. 87–90.

2. Luigi Berzano, "Religione e autoperfezionamento," in Maria Immacolata Macioti, ed., *Maghi e magie nell'Italia di oggi* (Florence: Angelo Pontecorboli Editore, 1991), pp. 141–86; republished in an updated version as "Damanhur: Un monastero per famiglie nell'età dell'acquario," in L. Berzano, *Religiosità del nuovo areopago. Credenze e forme religiose nell'epoca postsecolare* (Milan: Franco Angeli, 1994), pp. 143–70.

3. Maria Immacolata Macioti, "Il tempio sotteraneo di Damanhur," *Ars Regio* 4, no. 19 (July–August 1994): 4–9.

4. See, for example, Isotta Poggi, "Alternative Spirituality in Italy," in James R. Lewis and J. Gordon Melton, eds. *Perspectives on the New Age* (Albany: State University of New York Press, 1992), pp. 271–86.

5. See, for example, the lengthy article by Javier Sierra, "El secreto de Damanhur," *Mas allá de la ciencia* 50 (April 1993): 38–51.

6. See for examples of anticult treatments of Damanhur, Pier Angelo Gramaglia, *La reincarnazione* (Casale Monferrato/Allessandria: Piemme, 1989), pp. 384–92, and Cecilia Gatto Trocchi, *Viaggio nella magia* (Rome/Bari: Laterza, 1993), pp. 59–72. For a criticism of the anticult book by Gatto Trocchi (an anthropologist), see my "A proposito di viaggi nella magia," *La Critica Sociologica* 106 (summer 1993): 127–343.

7. For a comprehensive bibliography of Damanhur's own writings, see Berzano, "Damanhur," pp. 166–70.

8. See, on this point, my "La citta delle meraviglie. Spiritualità alternative, nuove religioni e magia a Torino," *Ars Regia* 3, no. 12 (May–June 1993): 24–35, and *Indagine sul satanismo: Satanisti e anti-satanisti dal Seicetito ai nostri giorni* (Milan: Mondadori, 1994).

9. See, on this point, Alessandro Bongioanni and Riccardo Grazzi, *Torino, l'Egitto e l'Oriente fra storia e leggenda* (Turin: L'Angolo Manzoni Editrice, 1994). It is interesting to note that what is known to the Mormons as the Book of Abraham in the *Pearl of Great Price* was "translated" by the Mormon prophet Joseph Smith by interpreting papyri originally excavated in Egypt by the archaeologist Antonio Lebolo, a native of Castellamonte (near Turin, and in fact not far from present-day Damanhur), an associate of Turin's Egyptian Museum.

10. Oberto Airaudi, *Cronaca del Mio Suicidio* (Turin: CEI, 1968).

11. Oberto Airaudi and U. Montefameglio, *Lo Spiritismo* (Turin: MEB, 1979).

12. See Berzano, "Damanhur," pp. 146, 150.

13. See Gabbiano [Mauro Gagliard], ed., *La Via Horusiana. Il Libro. Princìpi e concetti fondamentali della scuola di pensoero di Damanhur,* 2d. ed. (Turin: Horus, 1988), pp. 104–10. Further information has been supplied in personal interviews by "citizens" and leaders of Damanhur, including Oberto Airaudi.

14. Macioti, "Il tempio sotterranco di Damanhur," p. 5.

15. Luigi Bettazzi, "Parliamo di Damanhur," *Il risveglio popolare* (22 October 1992): 3.

16. See Rodney Stark and William Sims Bainbridge, *The Future of Religion: Secularization, Revival, and Cult Formation* (Berkeley/London: University of California Press, 1985), pp. 26–30.

17. See my *Storia del New Age 1962–1992* (Piacenza: Cristianità, 1994).

18. See J. Gordon Melton, "The Future of the New Age," unpublished paper presented at the RENNORD 1994 conference, Greve, Denmark, August 1994.

19. See Isotta Poggi, "An Experimental Theosophical Community in Italy: The Green Village," *Theosophical History* 4, nos. 4–5 (October 1992–January 1993): 149–54.

12

BRITISH BUDDHISM AND THE NEW AGE

Denise Cush

INTRODUCTION

The relationship between Buddhism in Britain and the "New Age" movement became an issue of interest for the author during 1993–94. At several points in the year, the topic of the influence (often perceived as negative) of "New Age" on British Buddhism and on British perceptions of Buddhism was raised in different quarters. For example, a joke reached me from one Buddhist community in this country to the effect that the abbot of a certain British *vihara* had been elected on a "no-crystals ticket." There was concern among the community that Western Buddhism needed to strive for greater orthodoxy and scholarship, and there had been "too much truck with New Age trends like alternative therapies, astrology, etc."[1]

During consultations about the proposed model syllabi for religious education in schools, the advice from the Buddhist consultants included the recommendation to "beware the influence of Theosophy and New Age." Whereas in an earlier draft of my recent book on Buddhism for students (Cush 1994), I had (writing in the mid-1980s) identified communist and capitalist materialism as the two greatest threats to Buddhism, the publisher's reader of the draft identified as a greater and more insidious threat the facile universalism of New Age–type thinking. This antagonism toward New Age was something of a shock to me.

From *Journal of Contemporary Religion* 11, no. 2 (1996): 195–208. Copyright © 1996 by the *Journal of Contemporary Religion*. Reprinted by permission of the *Journal of Contemporary Religion*. http://www.tandf.co.uk/journals/carfax/13537903.htm/.

When I first studied British Buddhism in the mid-1970s, Buddhism and the New Age movement seemed to be close allies in the loose federation of ideas generally referred to in the 1960s and 1970s as the "counterculture" or "alternative society." For example, I made my first contacts with British Buddhists through a book called *Alternative England and Wales* (Saunders 1975), rather than the Buddhist Society Directory, where in the context of information on squatting, whole-food, alternative technology, drugs, and left-wing politics, under the heading of "Mystical," were listed thirty-six Buddhist groups, alongside Hindu-based new religious movements, Theosophy, occultists, pagans, druids, divination, Steiner, and various New Age groups. To give a further example of the flavor of the publication and the "counterculture" it represented, the only Muslims listed were Sufis, the only Jewish connections Kabalah, the only Christian groups were based on Teilhard de Chardin.

It is probably significant that the tradition I chose to concentrate on at that time was Tibetan Buddhism. Dharmachari Vishvapani (1994, 19) refers to a "New Age orientalism" that idealized Tibet and Tibetan Buddhism, and in making that particular choice I was simply reflecting the cultural preferences of that time and subculture. In the centers I visited in the 1970s, the clientele seemed to be mostly drawn from the "alternative" section of society.

In the mid-1980s, I revisited British Buddhism to write a book based on the lives of practicing Buddhists, this time from a wide range of traditions (Cush 1990). At this time New Age did not seem to be an issue. Several of my interviewees had first met Buddhism on the hippie trail to India and the East but had progressed into serious Buddhism. Some were too young to have been hippies, and the clientele at the centers I visited were far more respectable and mainstream than in the 1970s. Any shallow, fashionable interest in Buddhism was not from hippies rejecting the mainstream culture but from those attracted to Nichiren Buddhism for its promise of success in the mainstream world.

As of the 1990s, there seems to be a new interest in the sort of topics listed by *Alternative England and Wales* and the New Age is back on the agenda, for Buddhists as for others. This pattern of an initial closeness, followed by a period of separation, and then in the 1990s the two movements thrown together again by a renewed interest in the "alternative," was confirmed by Vishvapani[2] (1994, 10). I conducted a small survey of attitudes to the New Age movement among British Buddhists during 1994. The results were first presented as a paper at a conference at Leeds University, "Contemporary Buddhism: Text and Context," in April 1994, and in a similar paper given to the Network of Buddhist Organisations in September 1994. Partly as a result of my inquiries, Dharmachari Vishvapani of the Western Buddhist Order wrote a paper on "Buddhism and the New Age,"[3] and I was able to refer to this paper in the conference papers. Since then, Vishvapani has published a later version of his paper (Vishvapani 1994), in which he referred to the unpublished version of the present article.

WHAT IS NEW AGE,
AND WHAT IS BRITISH BUDDHISM?

At this point I need to define what I mean by New Age and by British Buddhism. This is not an easy task, as both are nebulous concepts. Accepting that these are both "just denominations, designations, conceptual terms, current appellations and mere names and that no such entities can be apprehended" (Conze 1959, 147), I shall use them as convenient labels as follows.

By "New Age," I mean a cluster of related ideas, teachings, and groups, not altogether coherent, most of which would identify with this title. As Vishvapani points out, "the indefinability of the New Age is at the heart of its nature" (Vishvapani 1994). The most helpful definitions I have come across are those by Michael York, who describes the New Age as "a mainstream adaptation of the 1960s counterculture" (York 1994, 14) and "one of the foremost religious expressions of postmodernity" (York 1994, 15). The central idea is that there has been or is about to be a "quantum leap in consciousness" (York 1994, 14), "a transformation in human consciousness that is cosmically significant" (Bloom 1991, xviii). A 1970s song proclaimed, "This world is waking up into a New Age revelation / our spirits are responding to the raising of vibrations."[4] This new higher consciousness brings with it new views of the human being, the divine, cosmology, ethics, religious practices, social organization, language, symbol, and communication, and a new relationship with tradition. These views can be summarized as follows:

1. The view of humanity is very exalted. There are no limits to human potential. Humans need to discover their inner spiritual selves and wider, deeper, higher forms of consciousness. The spiritual self does not die but lives on, usually by reincarnation. The New Age implies a new transpersonal and supraconscious psychology. New methods of psychotherapy are very important. It is an optimistic and evolutionary concept of humanity. It is very individualistic in that progress is made by self-effort, and the self is the ultimate arbiter of spiritual truth.

2. The concept of the divine is very much one of divine immanence. All living beings are divine, even nonliving matter. Just as the inner reality of the human being is spiritual, so is the inner reality of matter. On a lower level of divinity, many New Agers believe in many realms of being to include spirits, *devas,* angels, and extraterrestrials. Spiritual progress can lead to contact with such realms.

3. If the divine is immanent in the natural world, then the natural world itself is divine. There is a spiritual dimension to all life. The concept of the interdependence of all life is very strong. "Holistic" is the key word. The concept of the earth as a living organism, Gaia, is influential. New developments in

physics and biology are held to support New Age cosmology. There is a practical outcome in a concern for ecology and green issues. The interdependence
of all things also supports astrology.

4. The ethics of New Age as an individualistic movement are rather vague. The
   key words are "love," "peace," "light," "freedom." "Thou shalt not" is not the
   style. Yet positive ethical action can be seen in work for the improvement of
   life for humans and animals: concern for healing, for human and animal
   rights, for environmental issues, for social justice. New Agers are active in the
   hospice movement and new psychology.

   The view about money and possessions is ambiguous. There are those
   who believe in "owning nothing, caring for everything" (Parry 1991) and
   those who believe that money is part of empowerment. There are New Age
   travelers and New Age management consultants.

5. New Age rituals are rich and varied. Important areas are healing rituals; spiritual practices such as meditation; occult practices, such as magic, crystals,
   contacting spirits, and channeling messages from beyond; and divination
   (e.g., the I Ching). Many are drawn from existing traditions, but new traditions can also be invented. Festivals are important as expressing the joyous
   and optimistic views of the New Age.

6. Social organization is very loose. There may be influential teachers but no
   overall leaders or priests. The New Age movement is individualistic, but it is
   also about interdependence, so the characteristic social organization is that of
   the "invisible, leaderless network" (Stern 1993).

   This is identified by Michael York as what sociologists would call a SPIN
   organization (segmented polycentric integrated network; York 1994, 16).

   New Agers also experiment with new forms of social existence, such as
   communes and other communities. With regard to orientation toward the
   larger society, these range from the world-rejecting counterculture of the New
   Age travelers to the world-affirming New Age management consultants and
   psychotherapists. Both would be united in the goal of transforming the world.

7. Language and symbol are drawn from a rich variety of religious traditions and
   from psychotherapy, magic, and science. The latest advances in science and
   technology are seen as useful servants of New Age consciousness. Music and
   the creative arts are highly valued as means of expressing spiritual truth.

8. New Age has no fixed doctrines or dogmas. Each person has to find his or her
   own path. "There are a thousand different ways of exploring inner reality"
   (Bloom 1991, xvi). These results are a pluralist and eclectic view of tradi-

tional religions. They "accord equal devotion to the spiritual leaders of all races" (Bailey 1991). Diversity is valued: "honouring of all the esoteric religious traditions and of the mystic traditions of native peoples" (Bloom 1991, xvii). However, there is some picking and choosing (e.g., the stress on the esoteric and mystical strains of each tradition), which has led to the characterization of the New Age movement as a reflection of the market economy, commercialism, and the commodification of culture associated with a postmodern capitalism. Traditions are acquired, decontextualized, and used.

9. Having no fixed doctrines and valuing diversity, New Age is often accused of having no philosophical underpinning, of irrationality, of romanticism, and of woolly thinking. There are those who would deny this and outline a philosophical position and those who would glory in this accusation: They have transcended conventional rational straight-line thought.

British Buddhism is also, in the words of Phillip Mellor, "a deeply problematic category" (Mellor 1991). By "British Buddhism," I do not mean only those forms of Buddhism that consciously identify themselves as British or Western Buddhists but all the varieties of Buddhism that are present in the United Kingdom.

NEW AGE ATTITUDES TO BUDDHISM

Returning to the question of the relationship between New Age and Buddhism, it is easier to deal with New Age views of Buddhism than Buddhist views of the New Age.

As Buddhism is a spiritual tradition based on human potential rather than an external divinity, New Age is very positive about it. Particularly attractive is the emphasis on meditation. Buddhist speakers are included in New Age programs such as the "Alternatives" program at St. James Piccadilly.[5] *Alternative England* listed thirty-six Buddhist groups. William Bloom's anthology of New Age writings ends with a blessing for the planet based on the Brahma-*viharas*. New Age and alternative bookstores stock a good selection of books on Buddhist groups and articles about or by Buddhists, such as the article on Western Buddhism by Vishvapani of the Friends of the Western Buddhist Order (FWBO) in the spring of 1994 edition of *Kindred Spirit*.[6] Michael York includes both "Trungpa Rinpoche" and "Zen" in his spiritual division of New Age (his other categories being "occult" and "social") (York 1994, 15). Zen and Tibetan Buddhism do seem to be the most approved of, presumably the former for its naturalness and spontaneity and the latter for its variety of colorful rituals and meditations, and the esotericism of Tantra, as well as the romantic orientalism referred to above.

However, for the New Age movement, Buddhism is one of many equally valid paths, rather than *the* path, suitable for some, and its rich treasures can be mined to suit the individual making up his or her own pick-and-mix spiritual path.

BUDDHIST ATTITUDES TO THE NEW AGE MOVEMENT

The data upon which I am drawing here include books and articles, interviews and correspondence. The interviewees were a small sample, which cannot therefore claim to represent British Buddhism as a whole, but which serve to illustrate some of the variety of approaches to the New Age movement taken by British Buddhists. There are differences between Buddhist groups in the level of engagement with the question initially posed as "Buddhism and the New Age: Friends or Foes?" and in where groups would place themselves on the continuum of very negative to very positive views of the New Age.

There is also a noticeable pattern of changing attitudes over the last few decades, as referred to above and confirmed by Vishvapani. The pattern appears to be a close relationship in the 1960s through 1970s, followed by a conscious differentiation and disassociation in the 1980s, followed by a diversification of views and a new engagement in the 1990s. Some British Buddhists are stressing the need to reject New Age influence in favor of tradition and orthodoxy, whereas others feel that it is important to make links with New Age thinking to the benefit of both sides. The least engaged with the question were the Theravadins with origins in Theravadin countries. The typical response could be characterized as "What New Age?" "I know little about this," said one Sri Lankan correspondent. This is hardly surprising, as New Age is a product of the Western world, despite its use of Eastern terminology.

Interestingly, in the light of what prompted this investigation, my respondents from the Thai forest tradition now claimed not to be engaged with this question. The New Age movement was said to be "not much of a problem" and associated with the plethora of "views" that "have been with us in one form or another for thousands of years."

Another Theravada group, the House of Inner Tranquillity, which could be described as a modern Theravada group seeking to return to the purity of the Pali Canon, is definitely critical of New Age thinking. Alan James, in *Modern Buddhism* (James and James 1987), makes it quite clear that "the Buddha's teaching is not an alternative therapy." While he accepts that the alternative movement at least recognizes that materialism is not the answer, he describes the interest of New Age in Buddhism as "a superficial meeting of two cultures on the popular front: deep and subtle teachings are not fully understood and there is often serious misunderstanding and corruption of ancient truths" (James and James 1987, 8).

Therapists who use meditation techniques derived from Buddhism with the aim of improving this life are criticized: The only valid aim is that of eliminating ignorance and desire. My respondent from the group was mainly critical of New Age for its eclecticism. While accepting that there are many valid paths and that Buddhism is not the only one, he felt strongly that it is important to stick to one complete path to make spiritual progress. The confusion in people's minds between Buddhism and New Age was blamed on the 1960s, hippies, early British Buddhism trying to be populist, and on Trungpa Rinpoche: "Of course it's worse in the USA."

The most critical stance came from the Soka Gakkai International, which had an article in its monthly magazine, *UKE*, in November 1992 directly dealing with New Age teaching. Nichiren Buddhism is *not* one of many paths to self-awareness. It is "totally different from all the New age philosophies"; "This Buddhism is vastly superior, broader, deeper than any other teaching." The need to spread Buddhism *(kosen-rufu)* means that provisional and partial truths need to be swept away. Apparently, some members had been dabbling in New Age techniques: This was roundly condemned. It is wrong to diversify your energy into other practices; dabbling will hinder your path to happiness, good fortune, and enlightenment. Nichiren himself likened dabbling in different traditions to adultery. As for putting crystals on your *butsudan,* "to chant to crystals in the Butsudan is slandering the gohonzon" ("New Age Teaching" 1992).

The Soto Zen tradition based at Throstle Hole Priory did not see New Age as an issue. This tradition stresses quietly getting on with your own zazen practice, serene reflection. This is perhaps surprising, as in the public consciousness and from the New Age viewpoint, Zen is most often associated with alternative thinking and lifestyles. This was largely the more dramatic Rinzai Zen, which so appealed to the beatniks in the 1950s and the hippies in the 1960s and may be more relevant to the American situation. Even at the time, a distinction was made between "beat Zen" and the genuine article. The Western Ch'an group in this country reported that although some participants of their "Western Zen" retreats have "various New Age superstitions to examine,"[7] it is not really a problem, and these open retreats are carefully distinguished from the orthodox Chinese Ch'an retreats. Thus, there is both an openness to a New Age clientele with a careful distinction between beginners' interest and the genuine tradition and a criticism of the New Age. The real Ch'an is said to be "far from the idealisations and false comfort of New Age spirituality," and such movements are dismissed with "the multiple alternatives of this age of postmodern relativism all seem relatively cheap, sentimental or superstitious, lacking anchorage in a firm sea-bed" (Crook 1994). Some German members of the same tradition are worried that the Christian use of Zen techniques out of context is a symptom of New Age–type acquisition and degradation of tradition.

It was from a Tibetan Buddhist that I received a crystal mala and I expected more positive attitudes from Tibetan groups, not just because Tibetan Buddhism had been welcomed by the hippies in the 1960s and 1970s, but also because Tibetan Mahayana stresses skillful means and many different paths for different

Western Zen Buddhist students meditating. (*Courtesy of the Rochester Zen Center*)

sorts of people. In fact, I found a whole range of responses. Some did not engage with the question; others were critical. A respondent from the New Kadampa tradition criticized New Age for using techniques like meditation for the purpose of improving this life, for dabbling rather than following one path, and for techniques that are completely opposite to Buddhism, such as therapists who teach the need to express anger: "Finding your own path is not Buddhist."[8]

On the other hand, Lam Rim Bristol sponsors the "Centre for Whole Health," which includes courses on homeopathy, shiatsu, counseling, acupuncture, massage, psychotherapy, and osteopathy. The newsletter for the "Holy Island Project" (1993) contained a very positive article on New Age religion by Peter Russell, reprinted from *Resurgence* magazine, and presumably the editors approved of the claim that "we are entering the most turbulent, most exciting, most challenging, and most critical times in human history" (Russell 1993).

As a center for interreligious dialogue, as well as Tibetan monastic tradition, there was not much talk of the need to keep pure but shared interests in ecology, alternative therapies, and Celtic Christianity were welcomed. Lama Yeshe was very positive about interfaith activities. These can only dilute a tradition if there is lack of clarity and insecurity about your tradition. Tibetan Buddhism "has a strong tradition, which includes tolerance of other points of view." Interfaith activity "actually enriches your knowledge" (Lama Yeshe Losal 1993). Similarly, an FPMT (Federation for the Preservation of the Mahayana Tradition, a Gelugpa organization) center claimed that "Buddhists do not feel that other philosophies are dangerous" (excepting any that physically attack religion, such as communism in Tibet), and "different religions fit the different compatibilities and predispositions of different people" (Lama Yeshe Losal 1993). If a religion teaches morality and compassion, it should be considered good.

A similar positive yet not-uncritical approach was expressed by one member of the FPMT Gelugpa tradition. The very question "friends or foes" was rejected as a false polarization. Compassion means that one remains friends, but wisdom means that this is not uncritical. All practices need to be checked against a matrix of wisdom, compassion, and morality: "Every page of every sutra is emphasising the centrality of wisdom and compassion, which is why if you do not develop this matrix you risk ending up in a vajra hell." According to my interviewee, New Age can be incoherent and uncritical. It can be a form of "postmodern cultural imperialism" in its consumer attitude to traditions. However, New Agers could be "skilful partners in the continuing quest for wisdom." Buddhists may well have something to learn from them, for example, "New Age may show some Buddhists how arrogant they are." As for the possibility of a New Age dawning: "human knowledge progresses by leaps, it is possible." On astrology: "who knows what connections exist?" On taking ideas and practices from other traditions: If done with wisdom, compassion, and respect for the tradition, it may be enriching, but "you need an anchor tradition." [9]

Finally, from the Tibetans, a thought from the Dalai Lama. I do not have this firsthand, but in an article in *Inquiring Mind* journal, it is claimed that when asked whether he was part of the New Age, the Dalai Lama answered, "I hope so. We should all be happy to have a New Age" (Nisker 1993).

The most positive orientation toward New Age came from the "vipassana community" of which *Inquiring Mind* is the U.S.-based journal, and which is connected in the United Kingdom with the open, nonsectarian Buddhism of Gaia House and the Sharpham community in Devon (the latter claims to be Buddhist-based but not exclusively Buddhist). Gaia House offers talks and retreats drawing on all traditions of Buddhism psychology, ecology, and the arts, and the Sharpham community hosts not only Buddhist speakers but also Green spirituality, shamanism, Taoist yoga, and workshops that use the traditions of the Hopi Indians. The name Gaia House echoes both New Age ecology and the birthplace of the Buddha. As with New Agers, there is talk of a "network of international contacts of likeminded people." Spiritual books recommended include the Bhagavad Gita, the Gospels, and one by the popular New Age psychologist M. Scott Peck, as well as Buddhist sources. The Sharpham community farm is run on Steiner's principles of biodynamics. *Inquiring Mind* has included articles by spokespersons for the counterculture, such as Allen Ginsberg, John Cage, and Ram Dass, as well as interviews with the Dalai Lama. I particularly liked the

advertisements: As well as a variety of Buddhist retreat centers, there were advertisements for psychotherapists, Stephen Levine's conscious living and conscious
dying workshops, new designs in meditation stools, friendly dentists, meditative
investment advice, and my favorite: "sometimes even the Buddha mind needs to
talk to an attorney." However, this is an American publication and not without a
sense of humor. As Gaia House and the Sharpham community are based near the
New Age center of Totnes, this openness to the New Age is seen as Buddhism
speaking to the situation that people are actually in. It is not uncritical. New Age
was criticized by my respondents for woolly thinking, superficiality, excessive
positivity, and the facile acceptance that all paths are equal. However, although
some aspects of New Age do not stand up to rigorous inquiry, others perhaps do.
One teacher felt that the very concept "New Age" was something of a media
invention and preferred to talk of "the alternative movement" (Saunders 1975).
The relationship between Buddhism and the alternative movement should be one
of mutual learning: "The alternative movement has a lot to learn from Buddhism.
But Buddhism also has a lot to learn from the alternative movement, in areas such
as diet, healing, mind-body work, holistic education, community life and new
forms of language. Buddhism needs to change and adapt to the West."[10]

One speaker to be found on the Gaia House program is Ken Jones, who has
pioneered "engaged Buddhism" in Britain. Engaging with the pressing ecological
and social problems of our times, engaged Buddhism shares a lot of common
ground with the "social" wing of the New Age movement. However, although "at
first sight the New Age movement might appear to be the major contributor to a
spiritually informed green politics" (Jones 1993, 90), he is critical of many aspects
of New Age. It can be irrational, overoptimistic, trusting in unfolding evolution or
some miraculous divine intervention to solve our problems instead of serious hard
work. It does not tend to engage with the ecosocially exploitative and oppressive
institutions and structures and so is no real help to the poor and oppressed: "New
Age is cold comfort to someone in a Central American prison" (Simmonds 1990,
qtd. in Jones 1993, 93). In fact, its otherworldy orientation can leave people open
to exploitation. It tends to be a shallow amusement for the affluent, "an all-
singing, all-dancing, fast-food spirituality which is superficial, self-centred and
self indulgent" (Jones 1993, 95). It is a problem for Buddhism when it is confused
with New Age thinking, especially a hindrance to dialogue with radical movements, deeply committed to planetary survival and social justice, with a secular,
humanistic or Marxist background. "It can be something of an incubus for the
socially engaged Buddhist."[11] In spite of such criticism, the movement is not
written off altogether. At least New Age has "helped to popularise a paradigm
which challenges the assumptions of the scientific industrial culture."[12] New Age
is "a diverse and contradictory phenomenon . . . cannot at least part of the movement be weaned away from consumerism to the ancient spiritualities of self surrender . . . and become a resource for the radical green project?" (Jones 1993, 95)

The most thorough treatment of the New Age movement in relation to Buddhism was provided by the Friends of Western Buddhist Order (FWBO). This is probably not surprising. Started in 1967, the FWBO had the same potential clientele *as* the New Age movement and in its early years tended to be viewed as part of "a vague broadbased movement of people who were all going the same way" (Subhuti 1983). Writing in 1983, Subhuti talked of the need in the early years "to distinguish Buddhism from hippyism, from therapy, and from the great mass of confused views and opinions which people brought to it" (Subhuti 1983, 33). Yet, in the same book, he talks of "the Higher Evolution of the Individual" and admires Nietzsche and William Blake.

Dharmachari Vishvapani, not finding anything in print from the FWBO, kindly wrote me a seven-page article in response to my query. This has now been made available in a revised edition, where reference is made to the unpublished version of the present article as "Buddhism and the New Age" in the *Western Buddhist Review* (December 1994).

The earlier correspondence, as well as the later published version, proved to be an excellent treatment of New Age thinking, its relationship to Buddhism and to the FWBO in particular. Quotations are from the published version where appropriate.

According to Vishvapani, New Age is characterized by its indefinability, spiritual individualism, eclecticism, consumer mentality, decontextualization of tradition, apocalypticism, and philosophical immanence. The support of New Age for Buddhism is acknowledged, through New Age bookshops, magazines, and so on, but "Buddhism should beware of being added to the New Age soup, vegetarian or not" (Vishvapani 1994, 16).

Important differences are that "a Buddhist cannot agree that 'all religions are expressions of the same inner reality'" (Vishvapani 1994, 18). Buddhism is not an inner quest for experience but about rational inquiry, growth, work, and duty. It is not "an accessory to an other wise unchanged lifestyle."[13] New Age can often be a form of eternalism and spiritual materialism, both directly combated by Buddhism. There is an attempt to be positive: "Buddhists might see New Age as a kind of contemporary ethnic religion, which can coexist with Western Buddhism as tribal and national traditions co-exist with Eastern Buddhism" (Vishvapani 1994, 21).

With regard to the FWBO specifically, there have been changes in attitude to the New Age over the last two decades, mirroring what I found in my own research about British Buddhism as a whole. In the early days, FWBO was closely associated with the New Age movement. In the late 1970s until 1981, FWBO had a stall at the "Festival of Body Mind and Spirit." In the 1980s, FWBO distinguished itself from such events, feeling that "the Dharma is devalued by being sold in the spiritual supermarket" (Vishvapani, unpublished paper).

In the 1990s, with a confidence in the strength of its tradition, FWBO moved back "into contexts where the prevailing ethos is New Age" (Vishvapani, unpublished paper). There has been an FWBO presence at the Glastonbury Festival in the last few years (the 1993 poster advertised Buddhists along with stone circles, leylines, tipis, psychedelia, and juggling). A Dharmachari has given talks at the University of Avalon in Glastonbury. Retreats for New Age travelers are planned. However, FWBO centers do not have non-FWBO speakers; the status of "mitra" can only be given to those who have stopped shopping around and have committed themselves to the single path of FWBO; and basic meditation is taught separately from Buddhism. In the final analysis, "The Buddhist concern with Truth is fundamentally at odds with the eclecticism and relativism of the New Age and Buddhists have to make distinctions between teachings and traditions which the New Age is happy to mix together" (Vishvapani 1994, 17), and "A New Age Buddhism would be a *reductio ad absurdum* of Buddhist tradition; it would be a Buddhism constructed from Western fantasies of the East and post-Christian yearnings for salvation" (Vishvapani 1994, 21).

THE IMPORTANCE OF THEOSOPHY

The entanglement of British Buddhism and the New Age movement can be traced back not just to the counterculture of the 1960s but to the Theosophical movement of the nineteenth century. Theosophy, founded in 1875 by Madame Blavatsky and Colonel Olcott, is one of the most important ancestors of New Age thinking and one of the most important early sponsors of Buddhism in the West. Michael York asserts that "New Age has its roots in Theosophy and its synthesis of the notion of evolutionary progress with chiefly Hindu-Buddhist ideas" (York 1991, 1). The Theosophists claimed that their teachings were channeled from "Tibetan Mahatmas." Like the current New Age movement, Theosophists were eclectic, mixing what they called the "esoteric" traditions of the world religions, especially Hinduism and Buddhism, with spiritualism, occultism, and evolutionary science. The esoteric traditions of all world religions were held to teach the same inner essence, and individual souls would evolve into greater consciousness of the universal One through their incarnations. All these aspects are echoed in the New Age movement, and a direct link is provided by the writings of Alice Bailey, a Theosophist who founded an associated group called the Arcane School in 1923. She claimed to channel teachings from Djwhal Khul, a Tibetan teacher, and is credited with being the key inspiration for the New Age movement (Bloom 1991).

The Theosophical Society was also one of the first groups to take Buddhism seriously as a faith for Westerners. Their interest helped Buddhism in Sri Lanka withstand the Western imperialist and Christian attack. Colonel Olcott and Madame Blavatsky may well have been the first Westerners to take refuge in the precepts and thus formally become Buddhists in 1880. There are those who credit Colonel Olcott with the design of the Buddhist flag still used today. Many of the early pioneers of British Buddhism came from a Theosophical background.[14] The Buddhist Society of Great Britain started life in 1924 as a lodge of the Theosophical Society. Its famous president, Christmas Humphreys, wrote two of the most widely known paperbacks on Zen and on Buddhism in 1949 and 1951. Although these have been criticized for their Theosophical slant, especially the interpretation of "no-self" as Self with a capital S, they have been very influential in introducing Buddhism to the British public. Allan Bennett, the second British person to be ordained a Theravada Buddhist monk in 1902, came to Buddhism from a previous interest in magic and occultism (Snelling 1987, 227). Sangharakshita, the founder of the Western Buddhist Order, "was decisively influenced by Theosophy" in the quest that eventually led to Buddhism (Vishvapani 1994, 15). In the words of John Snelling, in spite of the distortions of Buddhism found in Theosophy, "to their lasting credit, the Theosophists prepared the way for Westerners to go deeper into the study of Buddhism" (Snelling 1987, 227).

SIMILARITIES AND DIFFERENCES

With their common ancestry in the Theosophical movement, it is not surprising that British Buddhism and the New Age movement are closely entangled. There are, indeed, many similarities, which is partly because Buddhism was one of the ingredients of the "New Age soup." As both the New Age movement and British Buddhism are labels covering a rich diversity of beliefs and practices, the following lists of similarities and differences are bound to be generalizations. Areas in which many Buddhists and many New Agers may share similar approaches include:

- A lack of dogmatism and a stress on the need for the individual to be his own authority.
- The locating of human problems and their solution in the consciousness.
- The use of meditation to alter and improve consciousness.
- The idea that religious traditions, teachings, practices, and conventions are a means to an end, a raft to be used, rather than sacred in themselves.
- The idea of a new form of community and life in community.
- An acceptance that other realms, spirits, and deities exist, but that they are not of central importance.
- A stress on human potential rather than on an external deity.
- The interdependence of all things leading to a concern for ecology.
- A belief in rebirth.
- A concern for animal rights, healthy dying, psychology, and world peace.
- An acceptance of astrology.

Major differences would seem to be that New Age lacks the rational analytical philosophy of Buddhism, is optimistic in seeing enlightenment as a natural evolution, and tends to stress the joy in life rather than suffering. Some Buddhism is eclectic, but even the eclectic forms stress the need to stick to one path. Tradition and orthodoxy are respected in Buddhism rather than just acquired. In many forms of Buddhism, great stress is placed on lineage and the importance of receiving teachings, initiations, ordination, and so forth, from an accredited teacher in direct personal transmission. Although some New Age teachers who have their own disciples exist, there is more of a stress on the need to "be our own teachers." The New Ager can simply buy from a bookstore advanced Tantric texts, access to which for a Tibetan Buddhist could only be gained by permission and initiation from a *lama*. Attitudes to sex can be more negative in Buddhism, and traditional Buddhism has a somewhat secondary place for women. Buddhism does not accept that all paths are equally valid or that a New Age is about to dawn. Most of all, the central Buddhist teachings of no-self and of emptiness are very different from much of the Self-based (whether with a little s or a big S) religion of the New Age movement.

CONCLUSIONS

The conclusions of my investigation are

1. That there is a close, entangled, and ambiguous relationship between British Buddhism and the New Age movement.

2. That a changing relationship can be seen over the last two decades, from a closeness to a conscious differentiation, followed by a diversification of approaches.

3. That different Buddhist groups and different individuals within groups have different orientations toward the New Age movement, ranging from extremely negative to quite positive.

4. That the close entanglement can be traced back, among other influences, to a common ancestry in Theosophy.

5. That there are both important similarities and important differences between British Buddhism and the New Age movement.

6. That the original question posed to interviewees and correspondents, "Friends or Foes?" although unearthing some useful information, was

actually wrongly put from the point of view of many British Buddhists and many New Agers. It is one of the false polarities (or "antithetical bondings" as Ken Jones puts it) that lead to conflict in our world. Wisdom and compassion combined lead to the position of "critical friend," which is a more appropriate Middle Way.

In the final analysis, from a Buddhist point of view, Buddhism can be open to New Age thinking insofar as it does not hinder its ability to lead beings to enlightenment.

In the words of the Buddha, whatever leads to spiritual progress, "to dispassion, detachment, decrease of materialism, simplicity, content, solitude, delight in good," "this is the Dharma . . . this is the master's message."[15]

7. That both New Age and some forms of Buddhism find a positive value in a diversity of paths. Not only is it a matter of different paths for the special needs of different people, but there is also a value for the whole community in preserving spiritual biodiversity. The value of such close encounters as that between British Buddhism and the New Age is that each can benefit from the critical friendship of the other. Some examples have been indicated by my respondents above. I would argue that the role of Buddhism as "critical friend" to the New Age movement and vice versa is better served by there being a diversity of perspectives, some more positive and some more negative, than by any attempt at a definitive statement.

Michael York suggests that for New Age to become a viable religious tradition, it needs to be grounded in either paganism or Christianity (York 1994, 21). The above discussion suggests that it could equally root itself in a Western form of nonsectarian Buddhism or Mahayana Buddhism. Vishvapani takes up this point and claims to see something of the sort already taking place in the United States, while being very wary of anything that might call itself "New Age Buddhism" (Vishvapani 1994, 21)

However, for good or ill, religious traditions today exist in interaction with one another, and we may well see some interesting developments from the meeting of New Age and Buddhism in Britain.

NOTES

1. Private communications.

2. This article was written partly in response to the unpublished version of this paper, which was delivered in April 1994.

3. Vishvapani, "Buddhism and the New Age," unpublished draft of Vishvapani (1994).

4. Steve Hillage, "Electrick Gypsies," on L. Virgin Records, 1976.
5. Alternatives St. James Church, 197 Piccadilly, London WIV 9RE.
6. *Kindred Spirit,* Foxhole, Dartington, Totnes, Devon.
7. Correspondence.
8. Correspondence.
9. Personal interview.
10. Correspondence.
11. Correspondence with Ken Jones.
12. Ibid.
13. Vishvapani, unpublished paper, cf. Vishvapani (1994, 18).
14. On the early history of Buddhism in Britain and the role of the Theosophical Society, see Humphreys (1968), Oliver (1979), and Snelling (1987).
15. *Vinaya* ii/10.

REFERENCES

Bailey, A. "The Way of the Disciple." In Bloom, p. 22.
Bloom, W., ed. *The New Age: An Anthology.* London: Channel 4 Publications, 1991.
Crook, J. "New Ch'an Forum." *Clevedon* 9 (winter 1994).
Cush, D. *Buddhists in Britain Today.* London: Hodder & Stoughton, 1990.
———. *Buddhism.* London: Hodder & Stoughton, 1994.
Humphreys, C. *60 Years of Buddhism in England.* London: Buddhist Society, 1968.
James, A., and J. James. *Modern Buddhism.* Box, Wiltshire: Aukana, 1987.
Jones, K. *Beyond Optimism: A Buddhist Political Ecology.* Oxford: Jon Carpenter, 1993.
Lama Yeshe Losal. "Lama Yeshe Interview." *Holy Island Project Newsletter* 19 (1993).
Mellor, P. "Protestant Buddhism? The Cultural Translation of Buddhism in England." *Religion* 21 (1991): 73–92.
"New Age Teaching." *UKE, United Kingdom Express,* magazine of SGI-UK, Maidenhead (November 1992): 32–33.
Nisker, W. "Welcome to the New Age." *Inquiring Mind* 10, no. 3 (1993): 43.
Oliver, I. *Buddhism in Britain.* London: Rider, 1979.
Parry, D. "Earthstewards." In Bloom, p. 221.
Russel, P. "New Age Religion." *Holy Island Project Newsletter* (1993): 22–23.
Saunders, N. *Alternative England and Wales.* London: Saunders, 1975.
Simmonds, J. L. *The Emerging New Age.* Santa Fe: Bear & Co., 1990, p. 216. Qtd. in K. Jones.
Snelling, J. *The Buddhist Handbook.* London: Rider, 1987.
Stern, D. "The New Age/Alternative Spirituality," in C. Erricker, ed. *Teaching World Religions.* London: Heinemann, 1993, p. 152.
Subhuti. *Buddhism for Today.* Salisbury: Element, 1983.
Conze, E., ed. *Buddhist Scriptures.* Harmondsworth: Penguin, 1959.
Vishvapani, D. "Buddhism and the New Age." *Western Buddhist Review* 1 (1994): 9–22
York, M. "The New Age and Neo-Pagan Movements." *Religion Today* 6, no. 2, 1991: 1–3.
———. "The New Age in Britain Today." *Religion Today* 9, no. 3 (1994): 14–21.

THE SUCCESS OF
A COURSE IN MIRACLES
IN THE WORLD OF
MATERIAL CULTURE

Kelly T. Pollock

When Helen Schucman first heard the words, "This is a course in miracles; please take notes," she could have had no way of knowing how many people would someday read those notes. Since that time in 1965 when a voice began to channel through Schucman, her shorthand notes, which were compiled by Schucman and her colleague as *A Course in Miracles (ACIM)*, have been the subject of hundreds of books, audiotapes, and Web pages. The theology espoused in *ACIM* has become the faith of thousands of people. Hundreds of thousands of copies of the text have been sold, and some spin-off texts have been even bigger sellers. In an age when new spiritual texts are being published daily, what has caused the phenomenal and long-lasting success of *ACIM*?

The answer to this question seems to lie in the ways in which *ACIM* combines different elements that meet the spiritual needs of today's society. Its popularity stems from the way in which it picks up on certain popular culture trends of spirituality. Although students of *ACIM* come from all backgrounds, the major demographic of students is that of the baby boomer generation. Their interest in *ACIM* can be explained by looking at the way in which *ACIM* taps into the major spiritual trends that Wade Clark Roof identifies in *A Generation of Seekers*.[1] These four patterns of change for the 1990s and beyond are the reemergence of spirituality, religious and cultural pluralism, multilayered belief and practice, and transformed selves. In his most recent book, *Spiritual Marketplace,* Roof explores the associations between popular material culture and popular religious

---

Written for this anthology.

culture.[2] Again, *ACIM* fits in with this trend to successful ends. Thus, the success of *ACIM* can be explained by the ways in which it picks up on the cultural trends that Roof identifies. Ultimately, it can be seen through *ACIM*'s success how *ACIM* is both the product of today's popular culture and an influence on that same culture.

In order to explore the ways in which *ACIM* is integrated into popular culture, it is useful to begin with a definition of popular culture. In *Virtual Faith*, Tom Beaudoin defines popular culture as "a shared set of cultural referents."[3] With this definition, Beaudoin uses the term "popular culture" to refer to everything from books and films to fashion and games. Catherine L. Albanese believes that deciding what is popular is easy: "It is what everybody (mostly) likes or has heard about, what people are doing, wearing, eating, feeling."[4] However, defining popular culture in an academic context is more difficult. For her purposes, she defines "popular" as "the product of mass culture especially as it is mediated by, in, and through print and electronic sources."[5] In his book *Selling God*, R. Laurence Moore looks at popular culture in terms of the market. He feels that popular culture is the market of cultural goods being expanded from the elite to ordinary people.[6] This definition is useful to this paper because Moore believes that religion has become a commodity in the popular culture marketplace, especially in the ways in which religion looks for ways to appeal to all consumers. Viewing *ACIM* as a commodity can help in determining the reasons behind its success. Synthesizing these different definitions of popular culture, for the purposes of this paper, popular culture will be defined as the products and commodities that are associated with the lives of ordinary people, especially in the realm of print and electronic media, specifically books, newsletters, and Web pages.

An analysis of the ways in which *ACIM* is a product of popular culture must begin with the background behind the movement. *ACIM* was first published in 1976, but its beginnings can be traced back into the 1960s. Helen Schucman, a professor of psychology at Columbia University, began to have "waking dreams" in which she would hear a voice. In October of 1965 this voice said to Schucman, "This is a course in miracles, please take notes."[7] For seven years, Schucman took shorthand notes when the voice spoke through her. She shared her experiences with her colleague Bill Thetford, who helped her with the arduous process of typing and editing the notes.[8] Schucman did not always agree with the voice, and she attempted to resist the channeling, a point that has lent the text greater authority to many. They say that if Schucman was resisting the voice, it could not be a matter of a text that she made up but must really be the voice of Jesus. This theme of resistance leading to greater authority of a religious leader or founder is also found in stories of female preachers. Elaine Lawless has studied the stories of women who are called to preach, and she concludes, "Because of the inherent dangers of pronouncing this belief [the call to preach], most of the stories have embedded in them a 'ritual disclaimer' of sorts—a message that either states clearly or translates to say, 'Look, I didn't ask for this. God called me. What could I do but obey? I tried to resist but you really ought not try to resist God.'"[9] This implication that the call was unwanted validates the women's legitimate calls to the pulpit because it is something decided by God. This same implication is true in Schucman's story. By denying that she wanted this channeling to happen, she is legitimizing the message she received.

What Schucman would eventually construct was a 1,249-page book in three parts. The first part is the text of the book, written in poetic language. The second part is titled "Workbook for Students." It contains 365 daily lessons for students of *ACIM* to follow in order to provide practical application for the lessons in the text. The third part is titled "Manual for Teachers." It provides a description of the function of a teacher and who can be a teacher within *ACIM*. It also provides a "Clarification of Terms" for the major concepts of *ACIM*. The Foundation for Inner Peace published *ACIM* in 1976.[10] It continued to publish *ACIM* until 1996, when the publishing rights to ACIM and its related spin-offs were sold to Penguin USA.[11]

The history and success of *ACIM* would be difficult to understand without an exploration of the people who have been involved with the movement from the beginning. *ACIM* would not have become what it is without the work of several people. The most important person in the entire movement is Schucman. When she agreed to write down the course she was "channeling," she made available to the masses a set of teachings that had previously been known only to her.[12] The events and circumstances of Schucman's life seem to have had a profound impact on her religious outlook and the eventual form of the course. Her father, Sigmund, had a Jewish father and a Lutheran mother, but he remained agnostic throughout much of his life.[13] Her mother's father was a Jewish rabbi, but Schucman's mother, Rose, apparently resented her Jewish roots. Rose was a spiritual seeker throughout much of her adult life. When Schucman was trying to battle a weight problem, Rose sent her to a Christian Science practitioner because she was studying Christian Science at the time. During another period of her life, Schucman's mother was very interested in Theosophy.

Theosophy seems to have been one of the major influences on what would become *ACIM*. Theosophy was a nineteenth-century metaphysical movement founded by Helena Blavatsky, Henry S. Olcott, and William Q. Judge. Students of Theosophy believed in a common set of "universal truths" found in the different religious traditions. The Theosophical Society provided "an institutional model for mixing Eastern and Western materials," which would become an important tenet of *ACIM*.[14] Although Schucman claims that she did not understand much of what her mother told her about Theosophy, it is certain that she did pick up some of it, which may have later influenced her during the writing of *A Course in Miracles*.[15] When Schucman's mother died, she was beginning to explore the Unity Church, which is now considered a form of New Age Christianity. Interestingly, the most common meeting place for *ACIM* study groups now is at Unity Churches.

At the time that she began scribing the course, Schucman considered herself to be an agnostic. She had given up on God after a botched gallbladder operation had left her in the hospital for four months. She had prayed to God to help her through the surgery, and when things went wrong, she blamed God. She turned to psychoanalysis instead of religion. This eventually led to her returning to school to earn her doctorate in psychology. Psychoanalysis plays a very large role in *A Course in Miracles*. Schucman also studied a great deal of philosophy, especially Plato, and loved logic and syllogisms. Syllogisms show up often in ACIM, perhaps due to Schucman's familiarity with them. Schucman remained an avowed agnostic, so much so that she tried to resist "the Voice" who was authoring the text and often disagreed with what she was scribing.

When Schucman was faced with the daunting responsibility of transcribing the course, she did not make the decision to take on the task alone. Her friend and boss, Bill Thetford, guided her through the process. Thetford's childhood was religiously devoid, as his parents had given up on religion after his two siblings died at young ages. Despite a childhood illness of his own, Thetford graduated from high school with honors and would eventually attend medical school. While attending medical school, he took a course on "client-centered psychotherapy," which led to the beginning of his interest and eventual career in psychiatry. Despite earlier resistance to an academic career, Thetford accepted a position at Columbia University, where he would meet Helen Schucman.[16]

When Schucman began to have a series of strange dreams, she shared them with Thetford, who was very interested in her visions and began to study psychic phenomena and Eastern and Western spirituality.[17] It was Thetford who suggested to Schucman that she begin to keep a journal of her visions.[18] This journal would eventually become *ACIM*. Each day, Schucman would meet with Thetford and read the shorthand notes that she had made while he typed them up.[19] At the beginning of Schucman's channeling, the voice would give her specific directions for how to handle her specific relationships, especially her relationship with Thetford. Their relationship was often strained to the point where the only time they got along was when discussing the course. These personal comments were later mostly edited out of the text, but there are occasional points where the text seems to be speaking personally to Schucman and Thetford.[20]

The next person to become significantly attached to the movement was Kenneth Wapnick. Wapnick was raised Jewish but considered himself to be an agnostic by high school. He eventually realized that he wanted to become a monk in Galilee and thus converted to Catholicism. After a few months at the monastery, Wapnick returned to the United States to "tie up loose ends." When he did so, he visited Schucman, whom he had met once before and demanded to be able to examine the book. After reading the course, Wapnick realized that his life's work would not be in a monastery but instead in helping to edit and teach the course.[21]

After Wapnick and his future wife, Gloria, met at an *ACIM* workshop, they dedicated their lives to teaching *ACIM*.[22] They created the Foundation for "A Course in Miracles" in 1982 and set up a retreat center in Roscoe, New York, in 1988. Wapnick sees this retreat center as a fulfillment of the vision that he and Schucman had. They had both seen the center as "a place where the person of Jesus and his message in the Course would be manifest."[23] The Wapnicks continue to run the retreat center and raise money through the sale of books and tapes.

Despite the enthusiasm and hard work of Schucman, Thetford, and Wapnick, the course might have remained relatively unknown if not for the efforts of Judith Skutch. Skutch had been studying holistic healing and running a "consciousness salon" from her house when a friend introduced her to Schucman and Thetford. Sensing that Schucman was hiding something, Skutch asked, "You hear an inner voice, don't you?"[24] Schucman and Thetford shared the entire story with Skutch, who hurried home to read the manuscript.

It was Skutch who finally began to distribute the course beyond the small circle of people who had been involved. In 1975, Skutch distributed three hundred photocopies of *ACIM*. Finally, in 1976, the group of four met and they consulted with the Voice, which urged them to publish the course. A wealthy Mexican industrialist who had studied the photocopy offered money to cover the cost of printing five thousand copies. Skutch and her husband, Bob, started the Foundation for Inner Peace, which was the original publisher of the course.[25]

While all of these people were vitally important in the publication of *ACIM*, one individual has done more to make *ACIM* the success it is than any other person. She was not part of the original group of people involved with the course, and she is not associated with any of the major organizations of *ACIM*. Her name is Marianne Williamson, and her contribution to the success of *ACIM* lies in the related books that she has written. Williamson has been one of *ACIM*'s biggest supporters and has single-handedly introduced a huge number of people to *ACIM* since she herself saw *ACIM* sitting on the Manhattan coffee table of a friend in 1977.[26] Williamson's first book, *A Return to Love*, was directly based on the principles of *ACIM*. Her big break came when Oprah Winfrey read the book and loved it. Oprah told viewers of her talk show, "I have never been as moved by a book as I have by Marianne Williamson's book," and said that she had experienced 157 miracles after reading the book.[27] Oprah bought one thousand copies of the book to distribute to the audience of her show.[28] Williamson appeared on Oprah's show, promoting the book, and the appearance propelled sales of *A Return to Love*, so that it eventually would stay on the best-seller list for thirty-nine weeks. A great majority of the people who read Williamson's book after her Oprah appearance had never heard of *ACIM* before reading *A Return to Love*, and while some never did open the actual text, many were moved by Williamson to read and follow the course.

Perhaps the biggest reason that Williamson has such a large appeal to masses of people is that she considers herself to be one of them. While *ACIM* itself speaks in lofty terms that people may have difficulty understanding, Williamson uses language that people will understand. "The majority of Williamson's followers . . . are glitzless baby boomers. Many are graduates of twelve-step programs—they are the addicted, or the obsessed and compulsive . . . Williamson considers herself one of them."[29] What makes people flock to Williamson is their identification with her life. Her past is out in the open and she admits that she tried everything before finding *ACIM* and starting the path to self-enlightenment. A former boyfriend explains Williamson's success as a knack in making "spiritual matters relevant to her own generation—something that young, liberal urban professionals can relate to."[30]

However, while Williamson has her many followers, she also has detractors who claim that she is not really a spiritual guru at all but rather a sham. One expert on new religious movements claims, "She's an expression of the entertainment industry-fueled by fame and the desire to be a star."[31] More disturbing perhaps are the insinuations by former associates and employees of Williamson that she is a cruel and egotistical person, even when it comes to her work. They cite her displays of temper and high-handed management in demonstrating how her personality may destroy the good of her message.[32] As can be seen with other people associated with the course, a greater study and understanding of the course is not necessarily followed by a greater application of course principles to daily life.

By looking at the history and background behind *ACIM* it is possible to see the ways in which *ACIM* may have been influenced by cultural trends. In particular, Schucman's writings were certainly influenced in some part by the spiritual quests of her mother and herself. A greater emphasis on spirituality and a rejection of mainstream institutionalized religions by society allowed room for their quests and may have thus had an influence on Schucman's scribings.

REEMERGENCE OF SPIRITUALITY

In *A Generation of Seekers,* Wade Clark Roof argues that spirituality, which had disappeared in the 1960s, reappeared in the 1990s as a "grass-roots movement." This spirituality is more diverse than it had previously been and reflects a much broader range of movements. Roof explains, "The diversity of spirituality reflects, of course, a consumer culture, but also a rich and empowering melding of traditions and existential concerns."[33] Roof sees this spirituality in contrast to institutionalized religions. The baby boomers' revolt against establishments extended into the spiritual realm, and baby boomers are more likely to express their spirituality outside of organized religions. *A Course in Miracles* plays into these fears of organized religion and has itself emerged as a spiritual movement.

Throughout the text of *ACIM*, formalized institutional religion and churches are rejected in favor of a more personalized spirituality. The greater course community has rejected the few churches that have been based on *ACIM*. One church in particular, the Endeavor Academy in Wisconsin, has been rejected to such an extent that it has been labeled a "cult" by much of the course community. According to D. Patrick Miller, "In the larger Course community Endeavor Academy is often described as a 'cult' that seriously misrepresents the Course teaching."[34] The idea that Endeavor Academy is a cult seems to stem from the fact that many people go there for courses and end up staying on there. Another reason behind this belief is that Endeavor Academy has a leader who is referred to as the Master Teacher. Although these claims that Endeavor is a cult may have some shaky basis on their own, it seems unlikely that many people outside the course community would label it as such on their own. The word "cult" is often used today to cast a negative light on a movement. Scholars today prefer to use the term "new religious movement." Thus, these claims that the Endeavor Academy is a cult seem to grow out of the fears that course students have of organized religion.

Because they fear institutional structure, many practitioners of the course participate in study groups. The study groups are generally very informal, but they allow *ACIM* students to meet with each other and provide some sense of community. Like Bible studies, these study groups aim at looking closely at the text for a better understanding. While study groups are not actually a form of worship, they are one of the few ways in which a great many course students meet in groups. Some groups even include collection baskets and music, in the spirit of a church service. According to some reports, there are at least nineteen hundred to over two thousand groups throughout the country. They meet in a variety of different places that are sympathetic to *ACIM*, such as Unity churches, bookstores, and people's homes.[35]

Rella Hawkins, who has led a study group from her house for years, explains that "most [students] come to study groups to advance their understanding of its concepts and to share in a sense of community with one another."[36] The idea of community is important to people who study the course, but it is not necessarily an *ACIM* concept. The course could be studied by an individual, although greater understanding seems to be reached by people who study in groups. It is impossible to count the number of course students that exist because of the possibility that people have picked up the book and begun studying without joining any groups.

ACIM plays nicely into the ways in which societal trends have adopted spirituality by providing a spiritual program without the confines of structured religious institutions. Because there is no institutionalism of *ACIM*, there is also a lot more freedom of expression within the community. There is a great variety of course students and a greater variety still in the ways in which they practice the course and what it means in their lives. Because they come from such diverse backgrounds, course students are naturally tolerant of each other and of other people.

RELIGIOUS AND CULTURAL PLURALISM

Although baby boomers may have experienced their parents' generation of religion as young children, for most of their lives they grew up with great tolerance. Before the baby boom generation, "mainline" religious traditions were the norm in American culture. In 1955, Will Herberg wrote, "Almost everybody in the United States today locates himself in one or another of these great religious communities [Protestantism, Catholicism, and Judaism]."[37] Statistically, the majority of Americans may still locate themselves within these traditions, but Americans have become more accepting of other traditions. As Roof notes, "Tolerance and respect for others are widely affirmed as basic values, to be honored in religious as well as other contexts."[38] In addition, Americans now see religion as something that one chooses on one's own, not something that is simply handed down by one's parents.

ACIM fits in very nicely with these ideas of tolerance and pluralism. Unlike many mainstream religions, *ACIM* does not have a missionary aspect. Students of *ACIM* believe, as the text states, that *ACIM* is required of all people.[39] However, the students also believe that everyone will find *ACIM* on their own. They are not required to spread the word to all people. Some course students believe, "We would eventually hear the Course in Miracles inside ourselves even if Helen Schucman hadn't channeled her version."[40] In fact, many students believe that people can find the truth without studying the course. They acknowledge that there are many paths to enlightenment, and *ACIM* is only one of them, though it might be seen as the most effective.

The students of *ACIM* obviously accept the idea that religion is something that one chooses for oneself. Because *ACIM* has only been around since the early 1970s, there are not yet families of *ACIM* students. There are very few examples of people who study *ACIM* and then teach it to their children. In part, this trend is due to the fact that many people do not discover *ACIM* and begin to study it until after they are through their child-rearing years. Unlike more mainstream religions, where people believe in the religion because their parents did, people become students of *ACIM* through spiritual journeys or through popular culture.

By looking at the spiritual journeys of some students, it is possible to see how little tradition or family religion have to do with their decisions to study *ACIM*. In the publication *One Light, Many Visions*, Jodie Krull explains the circumstances around her introduction to *ACIM*. For Krull, a series of events led to her association with *ACIM*. As she explains, "I have heard it said that there is no such thing as a coincidence. I'm beginning to believe that's true. The series of events that led me to study *A Course in Miracles* seems less like a coincidence, and more like an orchestrated plot."[41] Krull was in school at the time and very busy with student teaching. When she finally had some free time, she began to read Deepak Chopras's *The Seven Spiritual Laws of Success* and Marianne Williamson's *A*

Woman's Worth. She was surprised to find that both books quoted *A Course in Miracles*, a book that was previously unknown to her.

When Krull visited her local bookstore, she found numerous books about *ACIM* but not a copy of the text itself. She became discouraged and forgot about *ACIM*, but then she heard about the text again in a self-esteem class she had just begun to take. When she asked the teacher about it, he suggested that *ACIM* itself was too difficult to understand and that she should read Gerald Jampolsky's *Love Letting Go of Fear* instead. This time, in visiting the library, Krull did not find Jampolsky's book, but she did find both *ACIM* and Marianne Williamson's *A Return to Love*.

Since that time, Krull has continued to read portions of *ACIM* every day and follow the exercises for students. Krull's complicated path seems to resemble the paths of many other people. In Krull's case, she was not searching for spiritual enlightenment when she came across *ACIM*. Instead, *ACIM* infiltrated her life through several other sources, most notably the books of other authors. In her article, Krull questions, "How could there exist a book so important that there were so many others written about it, and I had lived unaware of its existence."[42]

In D. Patrick Miller's *The Complete Story of the Course*, several students of the course share their experiences. Among these experiences are diverse accounts of their introductions to *ACIM*. A detective on the Los Angeles police department who had stumbled through other spiritual paths finally found peace in *ACIM*. He remembers, "I was beginning to feel that I was no different from the people I was trying to put in prison."[43] He found *ACIM* in a bookstore and began to read it. He found peace when he realized that the course was saying that he truly was no different from the criminals he was trying to arrest.[44] Although this detective was just beginning the course and was unsure of its impact on his life, he seemed to feel that finding the course in the bookstore was something that was meant to be.

The feeling that finding the course was destined is a common theme in this type of story. Both Kenneth Wapnick and Judith Skutch expressed similar sentiments, as did Jodie Krull. Ann from Virginia expresses, "I was an atheist until about two and a half years ago, shortly before I stumbled across—or was led to—the Course."[45] Another student, Mike Gole, is an ordained minister who is pastor of an Assembly of God church in California. He also asserts that his introduction to the course was more than just coincidence: "Marianne Williamson's *A Return to Love* entered my life unwanted; one of my book club memberships sent it to me by mistake. It was one of those divine mistakes that play so subtly into nudging one's life path in a new direction."[46] Although Gole had difficulties harmonizing the Bible and the course, he believes that the philosophies espoused in the course should stand on their own merits.

MULTILAYERED BELIEF AND PRACTICE

Roof describes baby boomers as more accepting than earlier generation of mixing different religious traditions. He gives several examples of people who view themselves as belonging primarily to one religion but who incorporate philosophies from many different traditions into their faith. In addition, it can be seen in the heroes that people have, such as Martin Luther King Jr., and Mother Teresa, that they do not limit themselves to admiring people from their own tradition or cultural background. Roof sees this mixing of faiths as spiritually creative and rejuvenating. As he points out, "In other historical periods, deeply personal, syncretistic-style faiths have been a source of spiritual vitality and empowerment."[47] One important example of this blending in a previous historical era would be the Theosophical movement, which was an important background in *ACIM*.

ACIM has borrowed from so many different sources that many people do not know exactly how to classify *ACIM*. Although it is usually grouped with other New Age metaphysical texts, many people see connections between *ACIM* and other disciplines, such as Christianity, psychotherapy, and Eastern thought. At first glance, *ACIM* seems to have the greatest connection with Christianity. It seems so Christian, in fact, that many people have turned away from it at first because they believe that it is just another form of Christianity. However, as one examines *ACIM* more thoroughly, it becomes obvious that while *ACIM* uses similar terminology to Christianity, the concepts are used in very different ways. Kenneth Wapnick was one of the first people to become involved with the *ACIM* movement, and he has written several books about *ACIM*. One of these books is *Forgiveness and Jesus: The Meeting Place of "A Course in Miracles" and Christianity*. In this book, he discusses the different ways in which the two traditions use the same concepts.

The most important concept in common between *ACIM* and Christianity is Jesus. In the New Testament, Jesus is the most important character. He is the only Son of God and yet also God. One of the most difficult concepts of Christianity is the idea that Jesus was both divine and human at the same time. In *ACIM*, Jesus is still the Son of God and still divine, but the focus has shifted from Jesus to all of humanity. Jesus is no longer the only Son of God. Instead, all humanity is the Son of God collectively. With that, all humankind is also divine because the split between God and humans is imagined. *ACIM* teaches that in reality, people are part of God. What makes Jesus special is that he has figured out that humankind and God are not supposed to be separate. He has woken up from the nightmare of separation and is teaching everyone else to wake up. In this way, Jesus fulfills a similar role to that of a bodhisattva in Buddhism. As in Christianity, Jesus is a teacher. In Christianity, Jesus came to earth in part to teach humanity. In *ACIM*, Jesus came to earth in order to realize the separation. After death, Jesus spoke through Helen Schucman to teach humanity.

There is one group within the *ACIM* community who explicitly states that *ACIM* and Christianity can be used in conjunction with each other. The following statement comes from *Out of Time,* the journal of the Endeavor Academy in Wisconsin:

> To the question, "Can the scripture and catechism of Christ Jesus in His *Course in Miracles* be incorporated into the sermons and prayers of established Christian denominations and worldwide Christianity?" The answer is a resounding, "Yes!" Its simple message of personal salvation through the resurrection of Jesus and the practice of unconditional love and forgiveness is almost always readily acceptable.[48]

However, many within the ACIM community see Endeavor Academy as misinterpreting the *ACIM* beliefs, which may undermine some of their credibility.

Within the text of *ACIM*, there is no mention of how *ACIM* is meant to stand in relation to Christianity. However, Kenneth Wapnick has made it clear that while there may be some room for dialogue between Christianity and *ACIM*, the two are not meant to be complementary traditions or two separate manifestations of the same tradition, but rather they should stand separately as two distinct traditions. However, many students would argue with this assessment. In fact, some students of the course are Christian ministers, and many others continue to practice Christianity while studying the course.

For many people, *ACIM* does not resemble Christianity so much as it does psychotherapy. Many of the concepts in *ACIM* are borrowed from psychotherapy. Most important among these concepts is the idea of the ego. However, there are differences between the definitions of ego in *ACIM* and in psychotherapy. Freud defined the ego as the conscious self. This definition of ego is a good starting place for the way that ego is used in *ACIM*. The ego is still the conscious self, but it is also a greater controlling force. The idea behind *ACIM* is that the ego should be left behind. The goal is to let go of the ego and live through the Holy Spirit. In the "Clarification of Terms" section of *ACIM*'s Manual for Teachers, the ego is described as "nothingness, but in a form that seems like something" (2.2, p. 2). Students of *ACIM* believe that the entire world is an illusion and that the ego is the part of the illusion that we see as ourselves. Humans are actually part of God, so the individual ego cannot exist.

However, this definition of the ego makes it very difficult to understand how the ego is also a controlling force. For instance, chapter 15 says, "The ego, like the Holy Spirit, uses time to convince you of the inevitability of the goal and end of teaching" (15.1.2, p. 7). If the ego does not really exist, how can the ego use time to show anything? Later passages refer to the teachings of the ego but do not describe how it is that the ego can teach if it does not exist. Besides making understanding difficult, this seeming contradiction also makes it very difficult to study these teachings in comparison with psychotherapy. This twofold nature of the ego does not have a counterpart within the realm of psychotherapy. Thus, despite the use of similar terminology, *ACIM* and psychotherapy do not appear to be extremely similar.

Arnold Weiss investigates *ACIM* and tries to apply it to several categories such as religion and church, but the category he feels it most fitting is that of psychotherapy. While still maintaining that *ACIM* is a religion of sorts and does fit into the legal definition of religion, Weiss says, "It [*ACIM*] stands apart as a psychological system with a unique view of the individual as a mind dreaming this world of physical existence in a harmless dream from which it can awaken by forgiving itself and others for literally nothing but dreaming!"[49] However, many world religions could be classified as psychological or sociological systems that present unique worldviews. For instance, the idea in Hinduism that time is circular could also be considered a psychological system, but that does not preclude Hinduism from being a religion.

For Marianne Williamson, a student of the course, *ACIM* is the basis of her best-selling self-help books. Williamson's retelling of the principles in *ACIM* seems to be a distilled version. As one reporter remarks, "She falls back on language familiar to anyone who has read a self-help book. Much of her writing is intentionally easy to digest, if hyperbolic and given to psychobabble."[50] For her, the psychotherapeutic aspect of *ACIM* is brought to the forefront. It is also a different interpretation of that same aspect that is important to Williamson. While *ACIM* itself focuses on the nightmare of the separation of the ego and awakening that must take place, Williamson focuses on the love between God and humanity. Williamson believes that love will heal all problems. In *ACIM*, it is clear that there is a belief in self-healing. Nothing is physically sick because the physical does not really exist. If the physical is just a projection of the mental, it is possible to heal the physical by healing the mental. Williamson would most likely agree with this premise, but what she highlights is that we should all just relax and let love conquer all.

Williamson illustrates an interesting point about *ACIM*. Although the idea is to wake up from this dream we are having and realize that everything around us does not exist, the point is not to then decide that the world is not worth anything. On the contrary, *ACIM* advocates helping fellow people. Williamson says to love everyone, and *ACIM* would even say to be compassionate to all people. The idea that people should care about others instead of themselves may seem odd in the wake of the "Me" decade, but Roof would find this idea as fitting into a spiritual trend of the baby boomers.

TRANSFORMED SELVES

Roof points out that many people accuse baby boomers of a lack of commitment, but "boomers will commit themselves to religious activities and organizations, including traditional congregations, where they feel there is some authentic connection with their lives and experiences."[51] Thus, the problem is not that boomers will not make personal commitments but that they have problems finding things to which they can commit. Boomers give of themselves when it means that they get something in return, especially personal enhancement. The view of self has changed "toward a more psychological, more dynamic conception,"[52] and political activism has changed with it to a greater concern with the self.

Because *ACIM* is both a religion and a guide for life, for students to follow the course, they must incorporate the concepts of the text into their daily lives. One of the ways to do this is to follow the daily lessons in the workbook section of *ACIM*. The workbook was also written by Helen Schucman and is usually included with the text. These lessons start out simply. Lesson one states, "Nothing I see in this room [on this street, from this window, in this place] means anything."[53] Each day, there is a new mantra to repeat throughout the day, incorporating the concepts of the course. The aspects of *ACIM* that invade the daily life go beyond the workbook, however. As Cecile Holmes White explains, "The Course unites basic psychological concepts in a logical fashion that is applicable to daily life."[54]

A common theme in stories from course students is that their lives are dramatically changed when they begin to incorporate the course. One such story is that of Debra Balentine of Bellflower, California. She had such a deep fear of life that at twenty-five she would not leave her apartment by herself. She had tried everything when she finally turned to *ACIM*. It was with the course that she was finally able to resume a normal life. However, it was not so much the actual philosophy espoused in the course that saved her but rather the way in which she is able to use the course every day. As she explains, "Now whenever I'm afraid I ask the Holy Spirit to correct my thinking. I remind myself that the Love of God surrounds me and His power protects me, wherever I go He is with me, there is nothing to fear."[55] Clearly, her life was deeply changed after she began to study the course, and this change was lasting because the course offers help every day.

Don Fry of Houston shares a similar life-changing experience. Among his friends, he was known as someone who lost his cool quickly, and he would have flashes of anger when he yelled at his mother or be critical of someone. He often wondered whether he would be able to live what *ACIM* teaches. He started to make progress when he decided to make it a goal to be at peace at all times. He accomplished this goal of peace by incorporating *ACIM* into everything he did: "While at work, anytime I would feel tension starting or I would feel tightness in my stomach, I would stop whatever I was doing and ask the Holy Spirit to heal me and release me of my past learning."[56] Fry reports that he has had remarkable success with this process so that he is able to get along better with his family. After a wonderful Christmas visit at home, he reflected, "My life has become so wonderful and peaceful because of applying the principles of *A Course in Miracles*."[57]

These sentiments are not limited to extreme stories. Nearly every course student has a similar reaction. For instance, Laura York of Burbank, California, shares, "My life is totally different now than it was seven years ago, I have healthy relationships, my health has improved."[58] Judy Black of Portland, Oregon, concurs: "With constant attention to *A Course in Miracles,* my life has remarkably changed. . . . I know now that I can choose how I want to see the world."[59]

POPULAR CULTURE MARKETPLACE

Throughout his book *Spiritual Marketplace*, Roof discusses the ways in which religion and popular material culture intersect. Specifically, he deals with the ways in which religion is a marketplace and its goods are for sale. In saying this, Roof does not mean to judge what these religions are doing. As he says of religious leaders, "To speak of them as suppliers, or entrepreneurs, is not to reduce what they do to economics, and certainly not to imply that their motivation is mercenary; many church growth and megachurch consultants, avant-garde theologians, and spiritual leaders—perhaps most—are doing what they do with good intentions."[60] Whatever the intentions of *ACIM* students, they have certainly taken advantage of the entrepreneurial aspects of the movement. There is a great proliferation of *ACIM*-related materials for sale, and the business is so big that it has become the subject of great controversy.

One of the most fascinating merchandising aspects of *ACIM* is that books that have been written about *ACIM* are often more popular than is the course itself. As Leslie Knowlton points out, "Some spin-off books, such as Gerald Jampolsky's *Love Is Letting Go of Fear,* have sold far more copies than the course itself."[61] *ACIM* may have been born in the age of emerging popular culture, but the study and worship of *ACIM* was born in the age of self-help groups and constant popular culture references. There are books discussing the meaning of *ACIM*, the ways to use *ACIM* for success in life and at work, and what it means to practice *ACIM*. There is an endless list of the types of books and other related materials that are marketed. Even books that have a very small connection at best with *ACIM* are marketed as part of the *ACIM* bookshelf and are successful because of that. While books and tapes are the most popular objects in the *ACIM* maket, the list does not end there: "In addition to newsletters and magazines, there are lectures, retreats and weekly conferences around the nation, with the highest concentrations of activity on both coasts."[62]

All of these spin-off books and other items lead to certain tensions within the *ACIM* community. These tensions are related to the controversy surrounding the copyright of *ACIM*. The copyright originally belonged to Helen Schucman, who gave it to the Foundation for Inner peace, the original publishers of *ACIM*. Recently, the copyright was transferred to the Foundation for "A Course in Miracles" (FACIM), whose head is Kenneth Wapnick. Since the transfer of the copyright to the FACIM, several lawsuits have been brought by the FACIM against people it believes have abused the copyright of *ACIM*. There are several issues that make the copyright controversy so volatile. These issues include: the validity of the copyright, the type of enforcement that is necessary or proper, and the reasons behind the strict enforcement of the copyright.

Many people have recently questioned the validity of the copyright held by the FACIM. A recent attack on the FACIM argues that legal authorship requires "a contribution of original creative content" and "a *claim* to copyright *at the time* of writing."[63] As many people have pointed out, Helen Schucman did not claim to be the author of the course, and it was originally published anonymously. Thus, not only did she not claim originality, but she especially did not claim copyright at the time of writing. Because of this fact, many opponents of the copyright would like to say that the copyright itself is not valid and should be abolished. Not only did Schucman not claim authorship, but in fact she said, as did the text, that the author was Jesus. Because Jesus does not have a body, he cannot hold a copyright.

What further complicates this issue is that Kenneth Wapnick has made varying statements about the authorship of *ACIM*. At some points he has said that the author was clearly Jesus, but when arguing the copyright, Wapnick has claimed that the author was Schucman, as is claimed in the copyright. If the author is Jesus, there is a problem in determining how a divinely authored work can be copyrighted. However, legal scholar Jonathan Kirsch has argued that at least some of what the FACIM is doing is perfectly legal. Kirsch believes that any judge or jury would uphold the copyright based on Schucman's authorship because judges and juries will justify copyright by any human involvement. In this case, Schucman was definitely involved in the process of writing the text, and there is ample evidence in her own accounts and the writings of Wapnick. According to Kirsch, in order for *ACIM* to be considered a spiritually authored text, Schucman would have had to have gone into a trance and awoken with the text in front of her. By Schucman's own admission, the Holy Spirit "made use of her talents." Throughout *Absence from Felicity*, Wapnick describes how Schucman would argue with the voice and occasionally change the grammar in what she was writing.[64] Thus, according to the legal definition, the copyright for *ACIM* in Schucman's name would be valid. Even certain ancient spiritual texts, such as the Bible, are copyrighted in specific forms and translations, and this sets a precedent for cases such as the *ACIM*.

Even if the copyright is valid, however, there is still a question of whether the type of enforcement that the FACIM is doing is proper and legal. Doug Thompson, a course student with a background as a newspaper reporter, has set up a Web site to serve as a clearinghouse for information about the copyright debate. His reason for creating the Web site is that he feels that the FACIM has gone too far in its enforcement, and he wants the public to be able to keep tabs on the situation. As he explains the situation, "Early in 1999 the FACIM began a campaign of aggressive enforcement of copyright—even draconian enforcement according to some observers—which resulted in considerable outrage and opposition in the Course community worldwide."[65] Clearly, the ways in which the copyright is enforced have changed dramatically in recent times. Again, Jonathan Kirsch says that the FACIM is not doing anything beyond the law. Because they own the copyright, they have the right and responsibility to protect that copyright.

What are the reasons behind the strict enforcement policy that was instituted? According to D. Patrick Miller, course student and author of *The Complete Story of the Course,* the tighter policy resulted from a trend toward more and more books and articles using quotations from *ACIM* and the *ACIM* name to sell their products.[66] Judith Skutch Whitson and others associated with the FIP, the original holders of the copyright, have said that they were guided by the Holy Spirit to protect the copyright and that many students have expressed concern that the text is being used by people who should not be allowed to use the course for their own purposes.

However, other people have expressed the belief that the strict policy is in effect for one of two reasons: religious orthodoxy or monetary gain. Wapnick himself says that they do not have the purpose of preventing people from speaking about the course.[67] However, in an e-mail sent to a long list of people associated with the course, Doug Thompson points out that true scholarship requires access to the original sources and good critical articles always include quotations from the source, so scholarship may be hindered if people are not allowed to use the course. Several people have accused Wapnick of trying to be the pope of *ACIM*. They feel not only that he is being unreasonable in his enforcement of the copyright policy, but also that he is being selective in allowing only those books whose opinions and interpretations match his own to be published.

The other possible reason for the strict enforcement is that the FACIM wants to keep the profits of *ACIM*-related materials. The FACIM Web site lists over twenty books, fifty audiotapes, and ten videotapes of course-related material for sale. In the competition for sales of course materials, the FACIM has an unfair advantage if it can sue the authors and publishers of the other books. In addition, if the FACIM can keep the lawsuits going for the five years of their contract with Penguin Books, they will make 2.5 million dollars from the license with Penguin. If, in contrast, they are sued for having an invalid copyright and a jury finds that their copyright is invalid, they will lose that money.[68] Thus, money may be a very big factor in this copyright controversy.

CONCLUSION

A Course in Miracles is not easy-to-read pop psychology based on notions of feel-good mantras. In fact, *ACIM* is very difficult to understand and even harder to accept. Instead of a philosophy based on the idea that everyone is loving and good, *ACIM* is based on the philosophy that no one really exists. Instead of a simple self-help manual, *ACIM* is a 1,249-page tome with difficult language and confusing concepts. So why has it been so successful for so many years? The success of *ACIM* can be attributed to the way it taps into basic human spiritual needs. By asserting that we are all really just a part of God, *ACIM* provides a sense of belonging. It does not answer the question of why we are here, but rather it demonstrates why that is the wrong question to ask. We should instead be questioning why we stay here when we could wake up and be again a part of God.

However, the most basic and fulfilling message will still not be successful if people never hear it. In this regard, *ACIM* has benefited from latching onto certain cultural trends that have made its message heard throughout society. *ACIM* has been extremely successful in tapping into, and benefiting from, the cultural spiritual trends that Roof explores in his books, *A Generation of Seekers* and *Spiritual Marketplace*. The trends that he identifies are reemergence of spirituality, religious and cultural pluralism, multilayered belief and practice, transformed selves, and an integration of popular material culture and popular religious culture. Because *ACIM* has fit so neatly into these trends, it has had great success on the spiritual market. However, once the message of the text itself is heard, it is the strength and depth of the message, not just its trendiness, that ultimately determines its success. The form of *ACIM* has been influenced by popular culture. *ACIM*'s combination of elements of different traditions and rejection of traditional institutional religions are products of the culture in which it was conceived. However, *ACIM* itself also helps to shape the culture. From Marianne Williamson's books, lectures, and appearances on *The Oprah Winfrey Show* to the self-help books written by Gerald Jampolsky, the tenets of *ACIM* are being explored and exploited on the mass market. Not only the philosophies behind *ACIM* but also its very form have become the model of future popular culture.

There is a great need for further research on *ACIM*. Despite the great proliferation of popular material written on *ACIM*, there is an extreme lack of serious academic studies about this fascinating religious movement. The research that has been done has mostly focused on the lives and stories of the people involved with the writing, distributing, and studying of the course. There needs to be a greater emphasis on scholarly analysis of this movement, both of the text and its success in the spiritual marketplace. A greater understanding of *ACIM* in particular could lead to a greater understanding of the link between religion and popular culture in a more general sense.

NOTES

1. Wade Clark Roof, *A Generation of Seekers: The Spiritual Journeys of the Baby Boom Generation* (San Francisco: HarperSanFrancisco, 1993), pp. 242–50.

2. Wade Clark Roof, chap. 3 in *Spiritual Marketplace: Baby Boomers and the Remaking of American Religion* (Princeton, NJ: Princeton University Press, 1999).

3. Tom Beaudoin, *Virtual Faith: The Irreverent Spiritual Quest of Generation X* (San Francisco: Jossey-Bass Publishers, 1998), p. 22.

4. Catherine L. Albanese, "Religion and American Popular Culture: An Introductory Essay," *Journal of the American Academy of Religion* 64, no. 14 (winter 1996): 733.

5. Albanese, "Religion and American Popular Culture," 737.

6. For a more extended discussion of popular and commercial culture, see R. Laurence Moore, *Selling God: American Religion in the Marketplace of Culture* (New York: Oxford University Press, 1994), pp. 5–6.

7. D. Patrick Miller, *The Complete Story of the Course: The History, The People, and the Controversies behind "A Course in Miracles"* (Berkeley, CA: Fearless Books, 1998), p. 10.

8. No one knows exactly how much Thetford may have contributed of his own to the text, but he was very involved with the compilation process.

9. Elaine Lawless, *Handmaidens of the Lord: Pentecostal Women Preachers and Traditional Religion* (Philadelphia: University of Pennsylvania Press, 1988), p. 76.

10. The above history of ACIM comes from Miller, *The Complete Story of the Course*, pp. 10–29.

11. Phyllis Tickle, "Viking to Bring 'Course' to the Trade," *Publishers Weekly*, 243, no. 120 (4 March 1996): 18.

12. In the mid-1950s, as a result of sightings of Unidentified Flying Objects (UFOs), many theosophists believed that their masters were space commanders who were "transmitting" their messages through "channels," who were the human contacts. This was the origin of the term "channel," although the practice was not new. See Catherine Albanese, *America: Religion and Religions* (Belmont, CA: Wadsworth Publishing Company, 1999), p. 357 for more on this subject.

13. All details of Helen Schucman's family life come from Kenneth Wapnick, *Absence from Felicity: The Story of Helen Schucman and Her Scribing of* A Course in Miracles (Roscoe, NY: Foundation for "A Course in Miracles," 1991).

14. Albanese, *America: Religions and Religion*, p. 268.

15. For a more thorough explanation of the teachings of Theosophy, see Robert Ellwood, *Theosophy: A Modern Expression of the Wisdom of the Ages* (Wheaton, IL: Theosophical Publishing House, 1986).

16. Miller, *The Complete Story of the Course*, pp. 45–47.

17. Wapnick, *Absence from Felicity*, 114.

18. Ibid., p. 185.

19. Introduction to *ACIM*, p. viii.

20. Miller, *The Complete Story of the Course*, pp. 17–18.

21. Ibid., pp. 108–109.

22. Ibid., p. 111.

23. Appendix to Wapnick, *Absence from Felicity*.

24. Miller, *The Complete Story of the Course*, p. 25.

25. The history of Skutch's involvement comes from Miller, *The Complete Story of the Course*, pp. 25–28.

26. Martha Smilgis, "Mother Teresa for the '90s? Marianne Williamson is Hollywood's New Age Attraction, blending star-studded charity work with mind awareness," *Time,* 138, no. 4 (29 July 1991): 60.

27. Susan Schindehette, "The Divine Miss W," *People Weekly,* 37, no. 9 (9 March 1992): 35.

28. Terry Pristin, "The Power, The Glory, The Glitz: Marianne Williamson, An Ex-Nightclub Singer, has attracted many in Hollywood," *Los Angeles Times* (16 February 1992): 6.

29. Smilgis, "Mother Teresa for the '90s?" p. 60.

30. Schindehette, "The Divine Miss W," p. 38.

31. Smilgis, "Mother Teresa for the '90s?" p. 60.

32. Schindehette, "The Divine Miss W," p. 36.

33. Roof, *A Generation of Seekers,* p. 244.

34. Miller, *The Complete Story of the Course*, p. 66.

35. Leslie Knowlton, "Divine Lessons in Study of Miracles: Book Is a Source of Inspiration to Followers," *Los Angeles Times,* section E (18 April 1993): 1.

36. Shera Dalin, "Book Helps People Find Love, Forgiveness," *St. Louis Post-Dispatch* (9 January 1999): 31.

37. Will Herberg, *Protestant, Catholic, Jew: An Essay in American Religious Sociology* (Garden City, NY: Anchor Books, 1960), p. 46.

38. Roof, *A Generation of Seekers*, p. 245.

39. *ACIM*, Introduction.

40. Personal e-mail from the Holy Instant Church.

41. Jodie Krull, "How *A Course in Miracles* Found Me," *One Light, Many Visions Online,* www.olmv.com/course.htm [1 February 2000].

42. Krull.

43. Miller, *The Complete Story of the Course*, p. 190.

44. Ibid., p. 190.

45. Ibid., p. 194.

46. Ibid., p. 203.

47. Roof, *A Generation of Seekers,* p. 246.

48. "Opinion." *Out of Time* (Baraboo, WI: Endeavor Academy): 40–41.

49. Arnold S. Weiss, "A New Religious Movement and Spiritual Healing Psychology Based on *A Course in Miracles*," *Religion and the Social Order* 4 (1994): 214.

50. Lynda Gorov, "Faith: Marianne Williamson Is Full of It," *Mother Jones* 22, no. 6 (Nov.–Dec. 1997): 55.

51. Roof, *A Generation of Seekers,* p. 246.

52. Ibid.

53. *ACIM,* Workbook, p. 3.

54. Cecile Holmes White, "Her Crash 'Course in Miracles': God Is Love," *Houston Chronicle,* Lifestyle (16 February 1992): 1.

55. Debra Balentine, "Fear Doesn't Live Here Anymore," *Holy Encounter* (November/December 1992): 4.

56. Don Fry, "Healing in the Now," *Holy Encounter* (March/April 1993): 8.

57. Ibid.

58. Laura York, "Dear Beverly" Letter, *Holy Encounter* (November/December 1997): 8.

59. Judy Black, "Dear Beverly" Letter, *Holy Encounter* (March/April 1998): 8.

60. Roof, *Spiritual Marketplace*, pp. 109–10.

61. Knowlton, "Divine Lessons in Study of Miracles," p. 1.

62. Ibid.

63. Personal e-mail from Doug Thompson.

64. Wapnick, *Absence from Felicity*, pp. 255–56.

65. From Free CIM Web page: http://home.golden.net/~dthomp/ACIM/index.html.

66. Miller, *The Complete Story of the Course*, p. 59.

67. Kenneth Wapnick, Gloria Wapnick, Judith Skutch Whitson, and Robert Skutch, "*A Course in Miracles*: Clarification of Copyright Policy," *Lighthouse* 4, no. 2 (March 1993): 1.

68. Dan Thompson, "Analysis of the Copyright Question," *Free ACIM—The Course in Miracles Free Press,* http://home.golden.net/~dthomp/ACIM/analysis.html [2 March 2000].

REFERENCES

A Course in Miracles. New York: Viking Press, 1995.

Albanese, Catherine. *America: Religions and Religion.* Belmont, CA: Wadsworth Publishing Co., 1981.

———. "Religion and American Popular Culture: An Introductory Essay." *Journal of the American Academy of Religion* 64, no. 4 (winter 1996): 733–42.

Balentine, Debra. "Fear Doesn't Live Here Anymore." *Holy Encounter* (November/December 1992): 4.

Beaudoin, Tom. *Virtual Faith: The Irreverent Spiritual Quest of Generation X.* San Francisco: Jossey-Bass Publishers, 1998.

Black, Judy. "Dear Beverly" Letter. *Holy Encounter* (March/April 1998): 8.

Brown, Michael F. *The Channeling Zone: American Spirituality in an Anxious Age.* Cambridge, MA: Harvard University Press, 1997.

Dalin, Shera. "Book Helps People Find Love, Forgiveness." *St. Louis Post-Dispatch* (9 January 1999) 31.

Ellwood, Robert. *Theosophy: A Modern Expression of the Wisdom of the Ages.* Wheaton, IL: Theosophical Publishing House, 1986.

Fry, Don. "Healing in the Now." *Holy Encounter* (March/April 1993): 8.

Gorov, Lynda. "Faith: Marianne Williamson Is Full of It." *Mother Jones* 22, no. 6 (November/December 1997): 52–56.

Hanegraaff, Wouter J. *New Age Religion and Western Culture: Esotericism in the Mirror of Secular Thought.* New York: E. J. Brill, 1996.

Herberg, Will. *Protestant, Catholic, Jew: An Essay in American Religious Sociology.* Garden City, NY: Anchor Books, 1960.

Knowlton, Leslie. "Divine Lessons in Study of Miracles: Book is a Source of Inspiration to Followers." *Los Angeles Times,* Section E (18 April 1993): 1.

Krull, Jodie. "How *A Course in Miracles* Found Me." *One Light, Many Visions Online Publication,* http://www.olmv.com/course.htm [1 February 2000].

Lawless, Elaine. *Handmaidens of the Lord: Pentecostal Women Preachers and Traditional Religion.* Philadelphia: University of Pennsylvania Press, 1988.

Miller, D. Patrick. *Complete Story of the Course: The History, the People, and the Controversies behind a Course in Miracles.* New York: Dell Publishing, 1997.

Moore, R. Laurence. *Selling God: American Religion in the Marketplace of Culture.* New York: Oxford University Press, 1994.

"Opinion." *Out of Time.* Baraboo, WI: Endeavor Academy, n.d.

Pristin, Terry. "The Power, the Glory, the Glitz: Marianne Williamson, an Ex-Nightclub Singer, has attracted many in Hollywood with her blend of new-time religion and self-help—and alienated more than a few." *Los Angeles Times,* calendar section (16 February 1992): 6.

Roof, Wade Clark. *A Generation of Seekers: The Spiritual Journeys of the Baby Boom Generation.* San Francisco: HarperSanFrancisco, 1993.

———. *Spiritual Marketplace: Baby Boomers and the Remaking of American Religion.* Princeton, NJ: Princeton University Press, 1999.

Schindehette, Susan. "The Divine Miss W." *People Weekly* 37, no. 9 (9 March 1992): 35.

Smilgis, Martha. "Mother Theresa for the '90s? Marianne Williams is Hollywood's New Age Attraction." *Time* 138, no. 4 (July 29, 1991): 60.

Thompson, Doug. *Free ACIM—The Course in Miracles Free Press,* http://home.golden .net/~dthomp/ACIM/index.html [20 February 2000].

Tickle, Phyllis. "Viking to Bring 'Course' to the Trade." *Publishers Weekly* 243, no. 20 (March 4, 1996): 18.

Wapnick, Kenneth. *Absence from Felicity: The Story of Helen Schucman and Her Scribing of* A Course in Miracles. Roscoe, NY: Foundation for "A Course in Miracles," 1991.

———. *Forgiveness and Jesus: The Meeting Place of "A Course in Miracles" and Christianity.* Roscoe, NY: Foundation for "A Course in Miracles," 1994.

———, Gloria Wapnick, Judith Skutch Whitson, and Robert Skutch. "*A Course in Miracles*: Clarification of Copyright Policy." *Lighthouse* 4, no. 2 (March 1993): 1.

Weiss, Arnold S. "A New Religious Movement and Spiritual Healing Psychology Based on *A Course in Miracles.*" *Religion and the Social Order* 4 (1994): 197–215.

White, Cecile Holmes. "Her Crash 'Course in Miracles': God Is Love." *Houston Chronicle,* lifestyle (16 February 1992): 1.

Williamson, Marianne. *A Return to Love: Reflections on the Principles of "A Course in Miracles."* New York: HarperCollins Publishers, 1993.

York, Laura. "Dear Beverly" Letter. *Holy Encounter* (November/December 1997): 8.

14

THE AQUARIAN FOUNDATION

James A. Santucci

INTRODUCTION

In 1926, there appeared a small pamphlet titled "A Message from the Masters of The Wisdom in 1926" proclaiming that the Masters of the Wisdom[1] were about to initiate further work in the world. Such an assertion, especially for those sympathetic with the teachings of the Theosophical movement, was surely to have a profound impact. And indeed it did. Over the next seven years, from 1927 to 1933, the individual who wrote this provocative and encouraging "message," the inspirational yet diabolic Edward Arthur Wilson (1878–1934), would convert such a promising undertaking to one so "bizarre that it out rivalled in

This article originally appeared in *Communal Studies* 9 (1989): 39–41. Copyright © 1989 by the National Historic Communal Societies Association. Reprinted with permission by the Communal Studies Association. James A. Santucci is professor of comparative religion at California State University, Fullerton. This is a slightly revised version of a paper that originally appeared in an issue of *Communal Studies* (noted above). The author wishes to acknowledge the help and cooperation of the following: Grace F. Knoche, leader of the Theosophical Society (Pasadena); Kirby Van Mater, archivist of the Theosophical Society (Pasadena); John Van Mater, librarian of the Theosophical University Library (Pasadena); Ted G. Davy, editor of the *Canadian Theosophist;* J. Gordon Melton of the University of California, Santa Barbara; and Nicholas Campion of Bristol, England. In particular, the author wishes to acknowledge a special debt of gratitude to John Oliphant of Vancouver, B.C., and Hong Kong for spending so much time in answering my questions, sending invaluable primary material, and lending his unique expertise to this effort.

real life the wildest imaginings of an old-fashioned dime novel."[2] As sensational as the events were that led to the dissolution of the organization that Wilson founded to further the "work," (the Aquarian Foundation and its colony located at Cedar-by-the-Sea on Vancouver Island, British Columbia), there is a paucity of primary sources that would give a complete picture of both Wilson and the Aquarian Foundation. As usual, the media emphasized scandalous and criminal revelations that came out of court cases in 1928 and 1933 and in typical tabloid fashion sensationalized these revelations while at the same time either misrepresenting or ignoring the often remarkably articulate and appealing esoteric teachings. During this interval, headlines appeared in many papers in the United States and Canada dramatizing Wilson's often startling and disturbing conduct. Many reflect an irresponsible and flippant tone not in keeping with the supposed best traditions of journalism:

> Weird Occultism Exemplified in Amazing Colony at Cedar-by-the Sea
> B.C. Love Cult Rites Bared by Witness
> Osiris and Isis Met on Train Between Seattle and Chicago
> Black Magic, Gold and Guns Feature Strange Cult Case
> Cult Holds Members as Slaves on B.C. Island.

Nonetheless, enough information is available in extant publications of the Aquarian Foundation and in external sources to provide a sketch of its teachings and operation. In doing so, this paper will summarize the teachings of Edward Wilson and the foundation, outline what little information is known about him and why he was successful in attracting a large number of well-educated disciples with the means to carry out his plans for the foundation, provide a description of the colony in British Columbia, and outline the events that led to his downfall.

TEACHING

In *Foundation Letters and Teachings*, one of the few accessible works by Wilson (or as he was known to his followers, Brother XII), there is a significant extract that places the message of the author in perspective:

> You know that my Brother H.P.B. [Helena P. Blavatsky (1831–1891)] founded an *esoteric school* [the Esoteric Section of the Theosophical Society, founded on October 9, 1888], which was to have been the Chalice into which the Knowledge and Power of the Masters would have been poured. For reasons well known, that school was dissolved, and the present E. S. [Esoteric Section] is not its successor. In this present Work, . . . it is the purpose and intention of the Masters to restore that inner and sacred heart of Their Work. This Work is the real Esoteric heart of True Theosophy, *and much more*.[3]

It is obvious that Wilson's message was basically Theosophical in content; understandably, it was aimed at a Theosophical audience. Yet it went beyond the Theosophy of Blavatsky and her masters, and it was that part of the message that was so fascinating and indeed troubling to those who ruminated on his occult revelations. To put it in the simplest terms, Wilson combined the Theosophy of Helena Petrovna Blavatsky with the promise of a coming New Age, the Age of Aquarius. The millenarian flavor of the latter resembled somewhat the Second-Generation Theosophical (hereafter known as SGT: sometimes known—pejoratively—as Neo-Theosophical) teachings of the imminent incarnation of Krishnamurti.

A brief overview of Theosophy and certain events within the Theosophical Society (Adyar) is necessary if Wilson's teachings are to be understood. Theosophy, or "Divine Wisdom," according to Blavatsky and her followers, refers to the ultimate truth of the supreme, the cosmos, and humanity. It is a truth that in its pure form is *primordial*, in that it existed from the dawn of humanity, thus reflecting a perennialist[4] flavor; *esoteric*, since it is a form of thought that is characterized by the acknowledgment of analogy as a primary means of establishing truth,[5] by the acknowledgment that nature is alive,[6] by the acknowledgment that there is a reality beyond the material plane of which one can be conscious (the imaginal), and by the acknowledgment that a transmutation or second birth is attainable through initiation;[7] and *universal*, because all great minds throughout the world enunciated the same wisdom. In the Theosophical teachings of Blavatsky, the primordial teaching mentioned above assumes a more universal dimension by claiming that at least a portion of the truth or Divine Wisdom was "known in every ancient country having claim to civilization,"[8] not just the Abrahamic religions and pagan religions of the West. Furthermore, it was Blavatsky's contention that the wisdom could be partially recoverable from a "comparative study and analysis"[9] of selected philosophers (Pythagoras, Plato, Plotinus, Porphyry, Proclus, Patañjali, and Shankara) or schools of philosophies (the Greek mystery schools, neoplatonism, Vedanta, Taoism, Cabalism) and the sacred writings of the great historical religions (Christianity, Hinduism, Buddhism). A study of these philosophers, schools, and religions by Blavatsky, under the guidance of two masters of this ancient wisdom[10]—one usually identified by the initials K. H. (Koot Hoomi), the other by the initial M. (Morya)—led to the writing of her two great works, *Isis Unveiled* and *The Secret Doctrine,* works that partially revealed the ancient wisdom in a modern form.[11]

The "truth" that has been revealed in *The Secret Doctrine* [*SD*], the principal source of modern Theosophical doctrine,[12] and works based on its contents may be summarized in the following statements:

1. A single, supreme, eternal, immutable, unknown and unknowable, infinite principle or reality [*SD* 1:14];
2. The fundamental unity of all existence: no thing is apart from the infinite reality;[13]

3. The eternal, manifested universe and everything within it is subject to the "law of periodicity, of flux and reflux, ebb and flow": such is the doctrine of cycles [*SD* 1:17];

4. The evolution of nature—material and spiritual[14]—reflects progressive development and not merely repetitive action [*SD* 1:43, 277–78; 11: 653];

5. The evolution of the individual is not limited to one life but continues through innumerable lives made possible by the process of reincarnation, the entrance of self—the trinity of spirit, soul, and mind—into another (human) body;[15]

6. This evolution is brought about by the law of cause and effect—karma (good actions leading to good consequences, bad actions to bad consequences)—thus assigning full responsibility to the individual who performs the actions as well as providing the impetus to future births or incarnations;[16]

7. The structural framework of the universe, humanity included, is by nature septenary in composition [*SD* 2:605–41];[17]

8. The cyclic, evolving universe, including humanity, is also hierarchical in constitution, each component—for instance, the planets in our solar system—consisting of seven components or globes that represent varying levels of the material and spiritual spheres [*SD* 2:68ff., 434ff.];

9. Human evolution on the Earth is taking place within seven major groups called Root Races, each of which is divided into seven subraces. In our present state of evolution, we humans belong to the fifth subrace (the Anglo-Saxon) of the fifth Root Race (the Aryan) [*SD* 1:610; 2:1ff., 86ff., 300ff., 434ff., 688ff.];

10. The individual is in actuality the microcosm, a "miniature copy of the macrocosm" [*SD* 1:274], or to put it in terms of the Hermetic Axiom:

> As is the Inner, so is the Outer; as is the Great, so is the Small; as it is above, so it is below;
> there is but ONE LIFE AND LAW; and he that worketh it is ONE.
> Nothing is Inner, nothing is Outer;
> nothing is GREAT, nothing is Small;
> nothing is High, nothing is Low, in the Divine economy;[18]

11. The universe is guided and animated by a cosmic hierarchy of sentient beings, each having a specific mission [*SD* 1:274–77].

Although Blavatsky was certainly the most influential and most articulate interpreter of Theosophy, there was a subtle challenge to her position as protagonist of the Theosophical movement. The challenge came primarily from the two shining lights of the Adyar Theosophical Society during the first third of the twentieth century: Annie Besant (1847–1933), the president of the society from 1907 to her death in 1933, and Charles Webster Leadbeater (1854–1934), arguably the most influential Theosophical writer from the early years of the twentieth century to his death in 1934. The two were largely responsible for the introduction of new teachings that were often in total opposition to the Theosophy of Blavatsky and her masters. These teachings, which are today termed as second-generation teachings (SGT), were usually designated by their opponents as Neo-Theosophy,[19] less frequently Pseudo-Theosophy. The differences between Theosophy and Neo-Theosophy are too numerous to mention in the context of this paper,[20] but it is possible to capture the broad distinctions between the two:

Annie Besant, an influential Theosophist who led the Theosophical Society after H. P. Blavatsky's death. (*Reprinted with permission of the American Religion Collection*)

1. The introduction of Catholicism and its attendant sacraments into the Adyar Theosophical Society through the agency of the Liberal Catholic Church and the efforts of its presiding bishop, James Ingall Wedgwood (1883–1950), and his close associate, Charles Webster Leadbeater;
2. The claim, based on a psychic reading by Leadbeater in 1909, that a young Indian boy, Jiddu Krishnamurti (1896–1886), would serve as the vehicle of the world teacher, the Christ or Maitreya. With such a claim came the establishment shortly thereafter of an organization to promote this belief, the Order of the Star in the East;
3. Emphasis on the writings of Annie Besant and C. W. Leadbeater as the main purveyors of Theosophy to the almost total exclusion of the writings of H. P. Blavatsky;
4. More emphasis on the acquisition of and participation in psychic or occult powers rather than on the theoretical understanding of the occult.

Also, since charges of sexual impropriety were brought against two of the leading exponents of SGT, Leadbeater and Bishop Wedgwood (the latter also the acknowledged founder of the Liberal Catholic Church), many of their more vehement opponents associated immorality with SGT, since Leadbeater, and to a lesser extent Wedgwood, were continuously defended by Besant and others in the second-generation Theosophical wing of the Adyar Theosophical Society.

These teachings and the pretenses of their leaders were despised by Edward Wilson. He considered SGT (or, in his language, Neo-Theosophy) to be a "poisonous corruption of the earlier teachings [the teachings of Blavatsky] and the introduction of disharmony, error, lies and confusion."[21] It is not surprising, therefore, that Wilson considered himself allied with the "Back to Blavatsky" movement,[22] a group composed of theosophists within the Adyar Society as well as other Theosophical associations who looked to the writings of Blavatsky and the masters as the source of genuine Theosophy.[23] Not surprisingly, Wilson specifically addressed this group: "If you would be true to Theosophy, you cannot go 'back to Blavatsky,' you must go *forward* to Blavatsky. . . . [O]ur Brother H. P. B. is not behind you, buried in the 'eighties' where you would enshrine her."[24]

Wilson's support of the "conservative" wing of the Theosophical movement helped attract a number of Theosophists of this persuasion to his message. It was, however, the novel millenarian aspect of his teaching that was to be especially attractive to those who were open to Wilson's message. This and the personality of Wilson himself, who devised a means of marketing the "truth" in such a way that there could be no doubt that the events foretold, on the one hand, would actually come about and that such events, on the other hand, were in no way contradictory or demeaning to the teachings of Blavatsky and her masters on the other.

The mid-1920s were a time when many within the Theosophical movement perceived the leaders of the Theosophical Society (Adyar) and their Neo-Theosophical teachings as totally opposed to genuine Theosophy. Wilson thus struck a chord when he wrote in an early article, "The Shadow,"[25] that Blavatsky's message of the ideal of universal brotherhood, first raised in 1875,[26] had been rejected. According to Wilson, this rejection was confirmed by a number of incidents that had taken place in the recent past, among which were crime waves, child murders, suicides, cases of "possession," growing class hatreds, multiplying instruments of death and destruction, World War I, the "capitalistic war in South Africa, and the atrocities in the Belgian Congo."[27]

The rejection of Blavatsky's call to universal brotherhood was interpreted by Wilson in a typically millenarian fashion: Imminent destruction of the present age and civilization and the uprising of a New Age, in this case the Aquarian Age. The timing of such an event revolved around three dates: 1875, 1925, and 1975. The year 1875 referred to the message of brotherhood given to the world by Blavatsky, the messenger and disciple of the Masters of the Wisdom. That having failed, the Masters of the Great White Lodge decided to renew the call to brotherhood and to begin work toward this goal. The beginnings of this work took place in 1925, with Wilson receiving information and instructions for the preparation of the work ahead from his master, a member of the Great White Lodge.[28]

By 1975, the new teacher and the new truth were supposed to appear. At this time, spiritually advanced egos, the grandchildren of those living in the mid-1920s, trained in "just Principles and in true Ideals" by those in the Aquarian Foundation, would be the "Rulers and Governors" ushering in an era of righteous governments.[29]

THE AQUARIAN FOUNDATION AND ITS COLONY

The beginning of the foundation was outlined in a letter (dated July 17, 1926) from Wilson to the editor of the *O. E. Library Critic,* Henry N. Stokes, one of the more vociferous exponents of the "Back to Blavatsky" movement: "Although Master gave me personally an outline of the way He intends the Work to develop on outer planes, no name or designation was mentioned until three weeks ago [the end of June 1926]—this has now been given to me, and it will be known as The Aquarian Foundation (I received my first instructions early in February, 1926)."

This is consistent with his remarks in "Letter IX" in the *Foundation Letters and Teachings* (p. 45), in which he mentions the visitation from his master in February giving the plans for the "work" to be commenced and Wilson's role, and who from this time on served as the personal disciple (or "chela") of the master. On May 15, Wilson was given further instructions to organize the master's work in England. If we accept Wilson's account, it appears that the foundation was conceived between February and May 1926 and that it was given the designation "Aquarian Foundation" by the master himself in June of that year. The foundation was given legal status when it was incorporated in Canada (May 16, 1927) and granted a charter by the British Columbia government under the Societies Act.[30]

The principles and objectives of the foundation appear on the back cover of the official organ, the *Chalice*. They are

1. RIGHTEOUSNESS (right action) in all the relationships of life,
2. ALTRUISM and the dis-interested impersonal service of Humanity as a whole,
3. DISCRIMINATION which includes the industry and patience required to examine motives, policies and actions for ourselves,
4. SERVICE: not the clap-trap variety now so widely advertised, by the solemn dedication of one's whole life to the true interests of the individual, the family, the nation, and the Race.

Since these principles reflect the ideals of a number of movements, in particular the Theosophical movement, they cannot be considered novel but rather were meant to enhance what Wilson considered to be themes emphasized in Blavatsky's writings. In other words, they served to reiterate in a more forceful way original Theosophical teachings *and* virtues that would naturally serve as the modus vivendi in this present period of transition. In addition to these principles, however, certain actions and associations were to be avoided at all costs. They suggest at least the immediate causes of the evils that were rampant in the world in this present age: evils that would be wiped out in the coming Aquarian Age. Thus, the four "things to which we are unalterably opposed" exhibit Wilson's own unusual explanation of causes for the continuing suffering in the world:

1. The furtherance of selfish personal or party interests at the expense of others.
2. Corrupt Governmental and legislative actions, oppressive financial policies and combines, market "rigging," corners and Trusts. Also secret control of the Press, the suppression of truth and the deliberate creation of those sentiments, views and ideas generally known as "public opinion."
3. Those open or secret activities calculated to undermine and overthrow *good* government, amongst which are certain brands of Communism, Bolshevism, and anarchistic tendencies and practices. We are opposed to all those movements which work openly or secretly for disorder, chaos and destruction.
4. We are equally opposed to those factions which seek to preserve class privileges or unfair methods and advantages at the expense of progress and the general good. Especially and particularly are we against those who oppose freedom of thought and the right of private judgement, that they may perpetuate superstition and credulity to their own advantage. We stand for *"no bargains between Church and State."*

This last position created considerable controversy in Theosophical circles in Canada. In a rambling article ["Canada's Peril," the *Chalice* (February 1928)] designed to awaken paranoiac and jingoistic tendencies in Canada and the United States, Wilson, signing himself "Watchman," asserted that the Roman Catholic Church was seeking complete domination of North America through a series of machinations by its hierarchy. Wilson's insistence that Canada was in imminent danger of internal convulsions initiated by the church led the general-secretary of the Theosophical Society in Canada, A. E. S. Smythe ["Blind Leaders of the Blind," the *Canadian Theosophist* (April 1928): 57?ff.], to oppose vehemently such claims with the view of protecting the Theosophical Society from a leader who prophesied that "the Society will suffer some appalling fate" if its members did not pledge themselves to the leader of the Aquarian Foundation. Smythe's criticism led to a blistering response from Wilson in the June 1928 issue of the *Chalice* (pp. 27–35), charging Smythe with a choice number of infamies and slurs, including his being "a self-convicted traitor to the principles he is supposed to represent," a "hate-inspired misanthrope, an ancient and envenomed 'leader,'" a "brazen and cowardly calumniator [who] would make our Order the scapegoat of his own misdeeds," and "a pusillanimous mother of empty words, a traitor with a foot in both camps ready to kowtow to the Roman Catholic power enthroned in Eastern Canada." If anything, a comparison of the foundation's four principles cited above with Wilson's vehement defense certainly would cause many neutral observers to question his true intentions and bona fides. To take one example, the editor of the *O. E. Library Critic* (18, no. 3:9) concluded "either that his claim to communion with the White Lodge is a delusion . . . or that the Members of that Lodge of Masters have been singularly unfortunate in their choice of a Messenger."

In all likelihood, however, controversies such as the above were diversionary to a minority of the members of the foundation and the Theosophical Society. The special work of the Aquarian Foundation was to prepare for the coming New Age, a notion uppermost in the minds of all the members of the foundation and a great many within the Adyar Theosophical Society. Such a teaching was closely connected with the Theosophical notion of the progressive development or evolution of humanity, the latter explained in terms of the seven Root Races and seven subraces. The New Age was not for the old humanity, those belonging to the fifth subrace of the fifth Root Race; most in fact would be dead by the time the New Age arrived. Humanity instead would advance under the "law of cyclic periodicity" in the form of the appearance of advanced egos incarnating as the new sixth subrace, the subrace that would realize brotherhood on the institutional level, a level beyond the mental or intellectual level, the only level that the fifth subrace was capable of achieving. It was the Aquarian Foundation that had to prepare for this new spiritual impulse by replicating the methods and organization of the Great White Lodge.[31] The lodge itself, according to Wilson, is made up of twelve groups corresponding in nature to the twelve astrological houses. Of these twelve, the foundation reflected the Ninth and Twelfth Houses: The Ninth House concerned with the Higher Mind, the Twelfth concerned with the unseen spiritual powers and karmic accounts or consequences. Thus, all within the foundation belonged to a "mental and spiritual aristocracy" leading the world to a higher spirituality.[32]

A few months prior to the incorporation of the Aquarian Foundation, a community or colony was conceived, with eventual establishment on a waterfront property located in Cedar-by-the Sea on Vancouver Island.[33] There were a number of reasons why such a center was required: the first and foremost being that it would serve as the cradle of the new sixth subrace.[34] The other reasons given were

1. To serve as a retreat or place of residence for foundation members;
2. To serve as a training ground for those selected for work of "Restoration," that is, the coming New Age;
3. To provide an environment wherein one might live in accordance with the principles of the New Age;
4. To provide training of "certain great Souls," that is, the children who would inherit the coming Age;

5. To be a center from which the ancient Mysteries would be propagated;
6. To provide a pattern for the new social order based upon truth.[35]

Why the foundation and its colony were headquartered at Cedar-by-the Sea (Cedar District), which was situated a few miles south of Nanaimo, reflects to a surprising degree second-generation Theosophical speculation. In this regard, Annie Besant, the president of the Adyar Theosophical Society, often referred to California as the site for the coming sixth subrace, and indeed Wilson himself strongly hinted at the outset that it was to be the "heart and centre of 6th sub-race civilization."[36] The final decision for the site, however, came from Manu,[37] who revealed to Wilson while in a meditative trance that the location would be southern British Columbia, a locale familiar to Wilson, since he lived in Victoria prior to 1914.[38] According to one source, a map was given him by the masters that showed the exact spot of the headquarters or Center Building.[39] Most probably, it was an Admiralty chart of British Columbia's west coast.[40]

The land chosen for the colony was idyllic. When Wilson arrived in Cedar from Southampton, England,[41] he soon met one of his most avid followers, a Vancouver lawyer named Edward Lucas, who advised Wilson to incorporate the Aquarian Foundation.[42] Following a trip to California to meet admirers, he returned to Vancouver and with a number of followers who had recently arrived from England[43] soon located the site of the colony, 126 acres of groves and forest area facing the Strait of Georgia. A view of the islands composing the DeCourcy Group, opposite Cedar, provided a lovely vista as well as the outlines of Gabriola, Valdes, and Galiano Islands beyond.[44] Following the purchase of the land in May 1927, tents were put up on the property for the permanent residents, followed by the construction of a number of houses for the Barleys, Wilson, and Phillip Fisher, a son of a Birmingham manufacturer and avid supporter of Wilson.[45] By the summer of 1927, the first annual general meeting was held on July 25, 1927, at the colony,[46] which gave Wilson the opportunity to expand upon the teachings about the groups within the Great White Lodge.

The reaction of the local inhabitants was obviously one of surprise at this sudden influx, but because the residents and visitors—mainly Americans, with a sprinkling of British subjects—were persons of means who spent large sums either for accommodations or to hire local craftsmen, carpenters, and artisans to build permanent residences at the colony, the locals did not display hostility to or excessive curiosity about their presence, perhaps also owing to the fact that many did not understand the nature and purpose of the foundation. An example of this ignorance is reflected in a newspaper interview of a local inhabitant who was of the opinion "that they had something to do with fish," obviously confusing aquarium with Aquarius.[47]

By October 1928, one visiting reporter, B. A. McKelvie, noted that all but two of the "eight or ten homes" built by this time were rather on the expensive side, costing from $8,000 to $15,000 each. An administration building (the Center Building), actually a large house, was also built by this time,[48] as well as the "House of Mystery," where Wilson alone could enter for the purpose of communing with the Masters on the Higher Planes.[49]

The number of permanent residents was not very large but all were well educated and wealthy. Those who were permitted to buy land and erect homes in order to be near their leader needed to surrender all their personal possessions to prove their dedication. They included Maurice and Alice von Platen, a wealthy California couple; James Janney Lippincott, a draftsman from Los Angeles;[50] George P. Hobart, a former druggist and advertising man from Hamilton, Ontario, and his wife; Coulson Turnbull, a prominent astrologer; Robert England, a man in his thirties who was a detective with the William S. Burns Agency and a security agent with the U.S. government;[51] Alfred Barley, a retired chemist and subeditor of *Modern Astrology* from 1903 to 1917, and his wife, Annie, a retired teacher for the London County Council and secretary of the Astrological Institute: in all about twelve original members who accompanied Wilson or who lived at the colony at its inception.[52]

As soon as the colony was established, announcements were sent to the followers of Wilson, who now numbered between fifteen hundred and two thousand, divided into one hundred twenty-five groups throughout the United States, Britain, Canada, and as far as South Africa and New Zealand,[53] to announce plans to build the City of Refuge at Cedar.[54] In response, money came pouring in. One lawyer in Topeka, Kansas, for instance, wired $10,000.[55] The Barleys also contributed over $12,000 for this purpose.[56]

Instead of building the city, however, this money, with the added sum of $25,000 collected from a rich widow from Asheville, North Carolina, Mary Connally,[57] allowed Wilson to purchase four hundred acres of land on Valdes Island in order to establish a new settlement called the "Mandieh Settlement."[58] The settlement's purpose, according to Wilson, was to serve as the site of an "Ashrama" or a "school for occult training"; its unstated purpose, however, was perhaps to get away from the discord that arose after the arrival of a woman who was to be his live-in companion, Myrtle Baumgartner, the wife of a wealthy physician from Clifton Springs, New York. Baumgartner, or "the Magdalene from Chicago," as she was called by some at the community, was declared by Wilson to be Isis in a lifetime 26,000 years previous. He also asserted that he, as the reincarnation of Osiris, and Isis would become parents of the World Teacher, the reincarnation of Horus. At the new settlement, the teacher would be raised by the parents, Wilson and this young woman whom he had met on a train trip from Seattle to Chicago in 1928.[59] Only a few of his most loyal followers were allowed to reside at Mandieh, with the condition that they give their unfledged loyalty. One rule that all were to abide by was "mind your own business," a condition designed to keep each disciple totally dependent on Wilson and isolated from the other members of the community. This dependence and isolation were attempted at Cedar as well, by his planting suspicions in each new candidate about the other residents in the colony. Another important requirement was the surrender of all worldly wealth, the same regulation that residents at Cedar were required to obey.[60] The purchase of the Valdes property with foundation funds led to discord and a court case in late 1928. Robert England, the secretary of the foundation, and the plaintiffs in the case, Maurice von Platen, Robert de Luce, and Edward Alexander Lucas, all governors of the foundation, charged that Wilson misappropriated funds given him by Mary Connally in August 1928. Instead of the total sum of $23,000 being deposited in the foundation coffers, England charged that $13,000 was used for the establishment of the Mandieh Settlement, considered to be a private venture and not part of foundation oversight. Though the by-laws of the foundation provided for seven governors to oversee its business, broad discretionary powers were given to Wilson, who was also president for life of the foundation.[61] Perhaps Wilson saw nothing wrong in doing this, but the plaintiffs and others in the foundation were clearly upset by Wilson's claim of being the Egyptian god Osiris and his plan to procreate the World Teacher with a woman not his wife, the above-mentioned Myrtle Baumgartner.[62]

Countercharges were then made by Wilson against England, charging him with the embezzlement of $2,800. The outcome of the case was that charges were dropped after Connally, in a dramatic appearance, came to his defense, stating that the money was a personal gift to Wilson to be used at his discretion. Furthermore, England's disappearance caused the magistrate to cancel plans to commit both Wilson and England to stand trial.[63]

After the court proceedings, the disaffected leaders of the foundation left and Wilson set about building up a new group of supporters. One of his wealthier patrons, Roger Painter, a millionaire wholesale poultry farmer from Florida,[64] was invited to live at the colony together with his wife. This he did after giving up his business and turning over $90,000 to Wilson upon arrival. Also from Florida came Bruce Crawford and wife, proprietors of a cleaning and dyeing business in Lakeland, Florida,[65] and generous contributors, who turned over their remaining $8,000 in cash upon arrival. Mary Connally remained in Victoria for the winter after her court appearance and again returned to live at Cedar in April 1929. She continued to contribute large sums to the foundation, the amount itemized being at least $40,000.[66]

The court actions did not weaken the dedication of those loyal followers of Wilson and his teachings. Money continued to pour in from the outside, and membership seemed stable. Furthermore, his taste for land acquisition did not stop with Valdes Island. With Mrs. Connally's money, he purchased three islands in the DeCourcy Group, a group of islands between Cedar and Valdes Island, for the sum of $10,000. On two of the islands, a new City of Refuge was planned; to this end, houses were constructed, a storehouse was built and provisioned, and a schoolhouse was built for the children who would later reside in the colony.[67]

For all this activity, however, the situation at the colony did change. Although Wilson and the foundation survived the insurrection, many talented individuals left, among them Will Levington Comfort, a well-known novelist and short story writer, with many works published in the *Saturday Evening Post*. He edited the Aquarian Foundation magazine, the *Glass Hive,* from April 1927 to his departure in 1928.[68] The birth of the World Teacher in which Wilson placed so much stock went awry. Baumgartner suffered a mental collapse brought on by her failure to give birth to "Horus," most likely due to a miscarriage and mistreatment from Wilson.[69] Apparently, Wilson blamed the misfortune on his followers, for in his judgment they lacked sincerity. Because of this failing, they had to submit to penance, the severity of which his followers would soon discover to their regret. Thus began a series of events that were most bizarre to those observing the activities of Wilson and his new companion, Mabel Skottowe.

In mid-1929, Skottowe (née Mabel Rowbotham; sometimes spelled Rowbottom) arrived at Cedar to become the "secretary"-companion of Wilson. How he came to meet her is not known, but she became the agent in carrying out Wilson's verdict placed on his "insincere" followers. Possessing a ferocious temper, she both verbally abused the women in the community with a tongue sharp enough to make even the most insensitive brute blush and physically abused them if they did not comply with her commands. One example of her cruelty involved a seventy-six-year-old retired schoolteacher named Sarah Tuckett, who was driven to attempted suicide from the repeated beatings and overwork imposed upon her. Another example involved the above-mentioned Connally, one of Wilson's most avid supporters. After losing a lawsuit in Washington, D.C., in December 1929, rendering her almost penniless, she was removed from her house by a group of followers on Wilson and Skottowe's orders and taken to a beach on Valdes Island. There she was ordered to dwell in a small house that was almost uninhabitable and forced to perform physical labor that must have been torturous for her. To be sure that she followed these instructions, Leona Painter, the wife of Robert Painter, was given instructions by Skottowe to live with her to be sure that Connally did what she was told.[70]

These conditions continued down to 1933 except for a respite of eleven months, when Wilson and Skottowe, now known as Amiel and Zura de Valdes (also known as Madame Zee), sailed for England after appointing Alfred Barley as business agent to oversee the colony. When they returned, the abuse against the residents at the colony was resumed. They continued to submit, but as Wilson and Madame Zee became more and more strident and impossible in their demands, dissent apparently emerged among some of the residents. As a result, twelve of the alleged dissenters were banished by Wilson, including Mary Connally, the Barleys, and the Painters. Because of their destitute situation, the Barleys and Mrs. Connally were compelled to initiate a legal action in the spring of 1933 in order to regain the money that they donated to the Aquarian Foundation.

It did not take long for the court to decide in favor of the plaintiffs. In the case of *Connally v. de Valdes*, Connally was awarded $37,600 less $10,000 for the value of the DeCourcy Island awarded to her as well as the four hundred acres on Valdes Island. Alfred Barley was awarded $14,232 and the legal title to the community land at Cedar.[71]

Wilson responded with an act of vengeance that surprised even his detractors. Deserting the colony after destroying much of the furniture, buildings, equipment, and the yacht, the *Lady Royal*, he and Madame Zee left on their yacht, the *Khuenathen*, for points unknown with a huge sum of money collected over the previous six years. The amount was not known, but apparently most of it was in the form of gold pieces stored in forty-three quart jars as well as in Canadian one- and two-dollar bills.[72] With the flight of the couple and the court decision in favor of the plaintiffs, the Aquarian Foundation was disbanded. Connally remained on Valdes Island with a caretaker, Sam Greenall, for a number of years after. In 1941, she left the area for good to return to North Carolina to reside in a nursing home. After her departure, Greenall searched the property on Valdes Island and uncovered a concrete vault, its sole contents a roll of tar paper with a message written on it in Wilson's hand. It was a message that reflected nothing of his original ideal of brotherly love; rather, it more than likely reflected his true character. The message read, "For fools and traitors, nothing!"[73]

EDWARD ARTHUR WILSON

It should not be surprising that very little is known of Edward Arthur Wilson prior to 1926, for the less the world knows of a leader's private or early life, the easier it is for the leader—religious or otherwise—and his followers to mythicize his life. Regarded in this manner, Wilson was not much different from a Cagliostro or Blavatsky, a Pythagorus or Paracelsus. He was, at least to his followers, a magus or modern-day shaman. Like other magi, we find reference to a number of traits that Wilson and others like him possessed or manifested: access to supernormal helpers or the Masters of the Wisdom, the direct experience of truth or wisdom through an "ecstatic experience," the use of or belief in the efficacy of magic or occult power, a long period of wandering culminating in an initiatory experience. Sometimes, as in the case of Wilson, there is an importance placed on the establishment of a sacred center serving at once as a ghetto and a Mecca: a place of separation from the evils of the outer world but at the same time serving as a place of pilgrimage to acquire the wisdom.[74] The fact that Wilson assuredly displayed the charisma of a magus will help explain the hold that he had on his followers, no matter how preposterous his teachings seemed to those not under his power.

Edward Arthur Wilson was born in Birmingham, England, on July 25,

1878.[75] Although he claimed that his mother was an Indian or Kashmiri princess and his father an Anglican missionary,[76] a claim that is not unique in the annals of the Theosophical movement because of the highly charged spiritual atmosphere of India and Tibet as fonts of the ancient wisdom, he was actually born to Irvingites or members of the Catholic Apostolic Church, a Christian sect founded by Edward Irving (1792–1834) that conformed more to the Pentecostal form of Christianity, which recognizes the speaking in tongues, prophecies, and healings. It also recognized a Second Advent or Second Coming of Jesus, to which preparation for this event required the restoration of a proper ministry (based on Eph. 4:11–14) for this Second Coming. As a result, twelve apostles, called by God, govern the church and not authorities ordained by men. In this regard, six apostles were identified during Irving's lifetime, six after his death.[77] It appears that Wilson regarded the Catholic Apostolic Church as preparation for the work of the Theosophical Society fifty years later.

Aside from this, we know nothing about his early life until 1910 or thereabouts. At that time, he appears in Victoria, British Columbia, working first as a driver of a delivery wagon and then as an express clerk who handled the Wells Fargo account in the Dominion Express office on Government Street. His departure from the company in 1914 came after his request for a pay increase nearly matching that of the president of the Canadian Pacific Railway was refused.[78]

While in Victoria, he spent much of his leisure time sailing the Strait of Georgia and the Juan De Fuca Strait, which helps explain his subsequent involvement in the merchant marine—either British or American—from 1914 to 1918 and, still later, his interest in sailing and skippering yachts after the formation of the Aquarian Foundation. The only solid evidence, and the evidence is meager, concerning his involvement with the merchant marine is a series of addresses listed on his membership record at the American headquarters of the Theosophical Society in Wheaton, Illinois: Ocean Beach, California, as of May 16, 1915; to S. R. Maxwell and Co., Papeete, Tahiti, via San Francisco a year later (June 9, 1916); and 1615 3rd Street, San Diego, the following year (April 1917). These addresses question the notion that he sailed on the Atlantic in the merchant marine.[79]

Besides his love of the sea, he also was deeply interested in occultism. If O'Hagan's account is accurate, his landlady, Peggy Reynolds, claims to have seen publications of the Theosophical Society and notes on astrology scattered about in his boarding house room in Victoria.[80] Such an interest explains his membership in the Theosophical Society from January 6, 1913, to June 30, 1918.[81] Judging from his writings, Wilson was well informed in Theosophical teachings and kept up with the affairs of the society even after he was no longer a member.

The only autobiographical account of the period prior to 1924 that is still available appears in his "Letter IX: Preparations for the Work" (dated July 1926) in his *Foundation Letters and Teachings* (pp. 43–46). In it, he reveals to his disciples the events that led him to his present status as personal chela, or disciple, to a Master of the Wisdom. Having undergone an initiation in 1912 called the Ceremony of Dedication, which gave him the understanding that he had a special mission, he claimed to have traveled to all parts of the world and to have undergone repeated testing in preparation for the work to be done. Then, in October 1924, while in the south of France, he underwent a second initiation or Ceremony of Dedication in which he went through a series of experiences over a three- or four-day period that connected the work he performed in the past with the work he was to undertake in the present. Almost a year later, in September 1925, while in Italy, he was given material by a master to write *The Three Truths,* which was completed in early 1926. Wilson remarked that during the course of the writing, his subtle body was transported to the master so that the master could dictate some of the passages. In fact, he claimed that the third part of the book was dictated in this way.

It was only on February 13, 1926, that plans for Wilson's present work were given in full by the master. At this time, he was chosen personal chela to the master, serving as his messenger. About this time, he began to call himself Brother XII, being the only earthly brother in the council of what had been the Eleven Masters of the Wisdom.[82] About this time, correspondence apparently was also conducted, judging from the first six letters in his *Foundation Letters,* which were dated from February to April of 1926 and sent from Italy. Who the recipients were, however, is not clear, since few, if any, knew of Wilson at this time.

From Italy, he departed on May 20, 1926, for Southampton, England, where he publicized the master's message in two articles written in a prominent English journal, the *Occult Review,*[83] titled "The Shadow" (the May issue) and "The Tocsin" (the July issue) under the name "E. A. Chaylor."[84] "A Message from the Masters of the Wisdom in 1926" was also published around this time. The teaching was also spread in a number of addresses to local Theosophists in a small hall rented by him for that purpose.[85] Thus begins the story of the Aquarian Foundation. The promise of a colony in which brotherhood was uppermost was quickly brought to fruition. Wilson's unquestioned success, however, was undermined in 1928 with the legal action taken by a group of disgruntled officers in the foundation. From 1929 on, Wilson became more and more involved with self-aggrandizement and acts of cruelty toward his followers until legal actions destroyed his hold on the persons he and Madame Zee caused so much suffering.

What became of Wilson and Madame Zee is not certain. One plausible account accepts the story that Wilson, under the name of Julian Churton Skottowe, died in Neuchatel, Switzerland, on November 7, 1934. It was only in 1939 that a London solicitor's notice of the intended settlement of his estate was announced. The amount left was surprisingly small, barely enough to cover the costs of the legal fees. If Wilson supposedly absconded with a large amount of gold and currency, it was not evident in the final accounting. Perhaps Mabel Skottowe took the bulk of the money, but her trail disappears in Switzerland.

CONCLUSION

The Aquarian Foundation was an organization based on the millenarian vision of Edward Arthur Wilson also known as Brother XII, Amiel de Valdes, and Julian Churton Skottowe. Although considered by most observers as a complete fraud who duped many who should have known better, Wilson had the requisite knowledge (a Theosophical substructure and astrological superstructure), the ability to communicate that knowledge, and the charisma to create an effective and sustaining messianic myth to retain his disciples. Unfortunately, the community established at Cedar-by-the-Sea on Vancouver Island was never allowed to develop to the degree promised by Wilson. The fault for this failure lay solely with Wilson, who, for reasons of greed and power, strayed from his original program of salvation. Despite this fact, the control that he had over his followers, many if not most well into middle age and wealthy, was quite remarkable. Even through the most trying of times—during the last two or three years of the foundation's existence when Wilson subjected his followers to physical torment, tyranny, and virtual slavery—most remained loyal to him because of the force of his personality and the attractiveness of the ideals of the foundation. These ideals of brotherly love and the promise of residing in a place of refuge from the iniquities of the world were very appealing indeed. As early as 1928, when he was challenged for his actions surrounding the purchase of land on Valdes Island and his liaison with Baumgartner, many could not reconcile the drastic change in the Brother XII who announced the masters' call to brotherhood. Their rationalization was that he was no longer the same individual who first inspired his followers but rather a black familiar who took possession of Wilson's body when he attempted the sixth initiation to attain spiritual perfection.[86] This explains Connally's statement, before leaving Valdes in 1941, to the caretaker, Greenall: "For the old Brother, I'd give that much money again, if I had it to give."[87]

The quality of Wilson's personality—the messenger announcing the call to brotherhood and the fiery, immature, and sometimes mean-minded personality— were certainly present prior to 1928. One example of this latter characteristic appears in an account of the late Buddhist jurist and member of the Buddhist Lodge of London, Christmas Humphreys: "[Wilson] wished to join the Buddhist Lodge as Brother XII. Then I pointed out that we could not have people joining anonymously, though he could call himself what he liked when he had joined. He replied like a small school-boy in a huff."[88]

It is clear that Wilson's tirade against Smythe and his subsequent actions against his dissenters originated from a facet of his personality that he chose not to reveal until such time that his position as absolute leader was consolidated. What he did reveal to his would-be followers in the early days was a persona of considerable charm and an intellect that was quite stimulating. An early acquaintance of Wilson's, Walter Miles, described him as "one of the most fascinating personalities and conversationalists I ever met."[89] Furthermore, there was his magnetic appeal, as evidenced by an observation by the Vancouver barrister Edward Lucas that Wilson had "hypnotic dark eyes that did strange things to you."[90] This combination is conducive to a cult figure who apparently placed his own importance and self-interest above that of the welfare of the community. Indeed, this was the true cause of the failure of the community, for the common-weal was actually discouraged by Wilson. The purpose of communal societies in the broadest sense is to create an atmosphere of mutual support for its members: physical as well as psychic. Such was the purpose of the City of Refuge, a city as we have seen that was never built. When all is said and done, the account of the Aquarian Foundation and E. A. Wilson gives further evidence of the power that myths of the New Age have over the minds of men and women of whatever culture, age, and level of education. The failure of a millenarian message to come to fruition does not necessarily cause disillusionment; it more likely will lead to rationalization for the failure—witness Wilson's own explanation of Blavatsky's role as a messenger who called for universal brotherhood and its subsequent rejection—and a future teacher's claim to revive the message at a more appropriate time. In the words of Alexander Pope: "Hope springs eternal in the human breast:/Man never is, but always to be, blest" ("Essay on Man," Epistle I, line 95).

NOTES

1. Men who are highly evolved morally, intellectually, and spiritually and who belong to a brotherhood (the Great White Lodge, as it is sometimes called) preserving the Wisdom of the Ages and guiding the evolution of humanity. See H. P. Blavatsky, "The Theosophical Masters," *Theosophical Articles by H. P. Blavatsky,* vol. 1 (Los Angeles: Theosophy Co., 1981), p. 302; Bruce F. Campbell, *Ancient Wisdom Revived: A History of the Theosophical Movement* (Berkeley: University of California Press, 1980), 53 ff.

2. "Finis Written to Long Search for Man of Mystery," *Daily Colonist* (Victoria, B.C.), 16 July 1939: 12.

3. Brother XII, "Letter XV: True Theosophy" [November 1926], *Foundation Letters and Teachings* (Akron, OH: Sun Publishing Co., 1927), p. 69.

4. The *philosophia perennis,* a term used during the Renaissance, most notably in the title of Agostino Steuco's (1497–1548) tome, expressed the idea that a universal philosophical tradition existed prior to the pagan and Abrahamic religions. Many of the teachings are discoverable through these later religions. Since the latter portion of the nineteenth century, perennialism or traditionalism has taken on more of an ideological flavor. This also comprises a component of esotericism as defined by Antoine Faivre. See note 7 for source.

5. This makes it possible to propose that there is a viable correspondence between the microcosm of the individual and the macrocosm of the universe.

6. In other words, nature is possessed of hidden interconnective forces that can be manipulated by magicians.

7. I chose only those characteristics that are especially pertinent to Wilson's teachings. For further information on the components of esotericism, see Antoine Faivre, *Access to Western Esotericism* (Albany, NY: State University of New York Press, 1994), pp. 12–15.

8. H. P. Blavatsky, "What Is Theosophy?" in *H. P. Blavatsky: Collected Writings,* vol. 2: 1879–1880, comp. Boris De Zirkoff (Wheaton, IL: Theosophical Publishing House, 1967), p. 89.

9. James A. Santucci, *Theosophy and the Theosophical Society* (London: Theosophical History Centre, 1985), p. 1.

10. See note 1 and H. P. Blavatsky, "The Theosophical Mahatmas," *Theosophical Articles by H. P. Blavatsky,* 1:301–307.

The connection of Theosophy with the masters is stated in clear terms by Annie Besant in her address to the Theosophical Congress held at the Parliament of Religions in Chicago, aptly titled "Theosophy Is a System of Truths Discoverable and Verifiable by Perfected Men."

These truths [are] preserved in their purity by the great brotherhood, given out from time to time as the evolution of man permits the giving; so that we are able to trace in all the religions the source whence they flow, the identical teaching that underlies them [*The Theosophical Congress Held by the Theosophical Society at the Parliament of Religions, World's Fair of 1893, at Chicago, IL, September 15, 16, 17: Report on Proceedings and Documents* (New York: American section headquarters, 1893), p. 24].

11. Charles D. Ryan, *What Is Theosophy?* (San Diego: Point Loma Publications, 1975), p. 3. The following quotation from *The Secret Doctrine* is pertinent:

The Secret Doctrine is the accumulated Wisdom of the Ages, and its cosmogony alone is the most stupendous and elaborate system . . . . It is useless to say that the system in question [of ancient cosmogony] is no fancy of one or several isolated individuals. That it is the uninterrupted record covering thousands of generations of Seers whose respective experiences were made to test and to verify the traditions passed orally by one early race to another, of the teachings of higher and exalted beings [Masters], who watched over the childhood of Humanity . . . . No vision of one adept was accepted till it was checked and confirmed by the visions—so obtained as to stand as independent evidence—of other adepts, and by centuries of experiences [1:272–73 of the edition cited in note 8].

12. H. P. Blavatsky, *The Secret Doctrine,* 2 vols. in 1 (Los Angeles: Theosophy Company, 1974). This is a facsimile of the original 1888 edition.

13. Robert Bowen, "*The Secret Doctrine* and Its Study," in Ianthe H. Hoskins, ed., *Foundations of Esoteric Philosophy* (London: Theosophical Publishing House, 1980), pp. 17, 64.

14. William Q. Judge, *The Ocean of Theosophy* (1893; reprint, Los Angeles: Theosophy Company, 1915), p. 61.

15. Ibid., pp. 60 ff.

16. Ibid., pp. 89–90: "Karma produces the manifestation of it [the cause] in the body, brain, and mind furnished by reincarnation." For a general overview of karma and reincarnation as it is taught in Blavatsky's writings, see Ronald Neufeldt, "In Search of Utopia: Karma and Rebirth in the Theosophical Movement," in Ronald W. Neufeldt, ed., *Karma and Rebirth: Post Classical Developments* (Albany: State University of New York Press, 1986), pp. 233–55.

17. In *Isis Unveiled* 1:508 [Los Angeles: Theosophy Company, 1982 (photographic facsimile reproduction of the original 1877 edition)], Blavatsky observes that "[e]verything in this world is a trinity completed by the quaternary, and every element is divisible on this same principle."

18. Bowen, *"The Secret Doctrine* and Its Study," pp. 18, 65–66. This is probably based in part on the Emerald Tablet, one of the seminal Hermetic texts.

19. The label was most likely coined in 1914 by F. T. Brooks, author of *Neo-Theosophy Exposed* and *The Theosophical Society and Its Esoteric Bogeydom*. The designation second-generation Theosophy is employed in this paper as already noted.

20. An extensive overview is given in the unpublished booklet, *Theosophy or Neo-Theosophy* by Margaret Thomas, a member of the Theosophical Society in Scotland, Wales, and England. The booklet first appeared around 1925.

21. "Letter XVIII: Those Who Oppose" [June 1927], *Foundation Letters and Teachings*, p. 96. See also his article "Things We Ought to Know," *Foundation Letters and Teachings*, p. 139 ff. On p. 146, he writes: "The Society has been irreparably discredited through its self-appointed leaders depending upon the mediumistic pronouncements of certain psychics, one of whom has been described as "standing upon the threshold of divinity" [i.e., C. W. Leadbeater].

22. A phrase coined by Henry N. Stokes in his periodical, the *O. E. Library Critic* (November 14, 1917). The *Critic* was perhaps the foremost Back-to-Blavatsky periodical between 1918 and 1940.

23. "Letter XIV: Forward to Blavatsky" [October 1926], in *Foundation Letters and Teachings*, pp. 67–68.

24. Ibid., p. 67.

25. Reprinted in *Foundation Letters and Teachings*, pp. 151 ff.

26. This date is not entirely accurate. The first mention of a brotherhood of humanity as an object of the Theosophical Society appears in an informational circular dated May 3, 1878. The original 1875 objects of the society were "to collect and diffuse a knowledge of the laws which govern the universe." This is contained in the "By-Laws" of the Theosophical Society (October 30, 1875).

27. "The Shadow," pp. 151, 154. Elsewhere ("Letter III: The Vital Necessity" [April 1926], *Foundation Letters*, pp. 18–19), he writes that prior to the commencement of the new cycle in 1975, a flood of evil would be manifested on the physical ("national wars, anarchy, bloodshed, and Bolshevism"), mental ("the thoughts and inventions of men will be placed at the service of demons and will be used for the wholesale destruction of humanity"), and psychical levels, the last being even more terrible than the preceding two. Wilson compared it to the end of the Atlantean epoch, for all the evil forces of the lower astral planes would be unleashed, engulfing the world in "a tidal-wave of horror as no living generation has seen."

28. "Letter IX: Preparations for the Work" [dated July 1926], *Foundation Letters*, p. 44.

29. "Letter XVII: Great Britain's Place in the Plan and Aquarian Characteristics" [November 1926], *Foundation Letters*, p. 86; "Letter I: The Purpose and the Plan" [February 1926], *Foundation Letters*, p. 10; "Letter IX," *Foundation Letters*; "Letter III: The Vital Necessity," *Foundation Letters*, p. 18. See also "A Message from the Masters of the Wisdom in 1926," in *Foundation Letters*, pp. 2–3.

30. "Dissolution of Island Cult Urged," *Daily Province* (Vancouver, B.C.), 29 October 1928: 1, 17; Gwen Cash, "Bridey Murphy Case Recalls Brother XII," *Daily Colonist* (Victoria, B.C.), 26 February 1956. I thank Mr. John Oliphant for providing me with this latter article.

31. "Letter XVI: A Talk about Group-Work" [March 1927], *Foundation Letters*, pp. 74–75. See also "Letter VI: The Deep Significance of the Message" [dated April 1926], *Foundation Letters*, p. 32.

32. "Letter XVI," *Foundation Letters*, pp. 76–77, 79. On the inside cover of the *Chalice*, a more complete explanation is given regarding the nature of the work of the foundation. The Ninth House "is concerned with the Higher Mind, with those spiritual and aspirational powers in man which are distinct from the ordinary activities of the lower mind." The Twelfth House "represents those Unseen Spiritual powers and influences which work below the surface in all affairs of men, and shows that this is a work to be accomplished in the adjustment of accounts which we term Karmic, and through which nations as well as individuals must work out the present consequences of past actions,— it is 'the writing on the wall.'" The Third House is also mentioned as "the outward and visible expression of the Ninth; it represents the channels of communication and that the present Work will be accomplished largely through literary effort; also that much of the Higher Teaching will be made available in this way."

33. John Oliphant, "The Teachings of Brother Twelve," *Theosophical History* 4, nos. 6–7 (April–July 1993): 200. Further information is found in Oliphant's *Brother Twelve: The Incredible Story of Canada's False Prophet* (Toronto, Ontario: McClelland & Stewart Inc., 1991), pp. 44–62. The land, 126 acres in all, was bought for $20 an acre (p. 55).

34. "Cult's Revolt Eye-Opener to Old Nanaimo" [the title of a newspaper article taken from the files of Henry N. Stokes. There is no reference to the paper in which the article appears, but it would seem that it is the *Daily Province* (Vancouver, B.C.), since the author of the story is B. A. McKelvie. The date of the paper is most probably October 29, 1928].

35. *Unsigned Letters from an Elder Brother,* 2nd. ed. (Montreal: Aura Press, 1979), pp. 213–14 [first published in 1930 by L. N. Fowler & Co., London].

36. "Letter XII: Europe and the United States" [September 1926], *Foundation Letters*, p. 60. The *O. E. Library Critic* (18, no. 5:9; 19, no. 2:8, respectively) pointed out the similarity between Annie Besant's colony in Ojai, California, and Brother XII's (Wilson's) on Vancouver Island:

Mrs. Annie Besant has started to establish a colony at Ojai, 'the Happy Valley Foundation,' the object of which she has stated to be to form 'a cradle for the new sixth race.'

Mrs. Besant informs us that the Manu has told her that the starting point of the sixth race is to be in Southern California at her Happy Valley Foundation at Ojai. "Not so," says Brother XII of the Aquarian Foundation. The Manu has told me that the cradle of the sixth race is to be in British Columbia.

37. A Manu, a regent of a planetary system, refers to one of the more highly advanced beings who direct the evolution of a new race type. He is also called a Watcher, that is, a watcher of the life-waves or collective hosts of monads or incarnating "spirits" or the essence of an entity. The somewhat complicated explanation in Theosophy revolves around the law of periodicity or that of cyclic motion. The universe is explained as a period of activity or manifestation, called Manvantara ("between the Manus") and a period of rest or dissolution (Pralaya). A period of manifestation lasts a Day of Brahma, or 4,320,000,000 years. This is the period of a Kalpa or a planetary Manvantara. During this period, fourteen Manus appear: seven of which are Root-Manus, seven Seed-Manus. The Root-Manus appear at the beginning of evolution, the Seed-Manus at the close of evolution. These latter supply the seeds for human races in the coming period of evolution. The term "evolution" here refers to a Round, a term referring to a passage or circuit through the seven Globes of a planetary chain [each planet, including Earth, is a living evolving being existing in a septenary makeup, the seven Globes] by a monad or incarnating spirit. At present we are in the Vaivasvata Manvantara, since the seventh Manu, Vaivasvata Manu, is presiding. Most likely, it is this Manu that Wilson had in mind.

See *The Secret Doctrine*, pp. 1: 48, 36S ff.; 2: 69, 308–11; Annie Besant, *The Ancient Wisdom* (Adyar: Theosophical Publishing House, 1939), p. 361; Geoffrey A. Barborka, *Glossary of Sanskrit Terms* (San Diego: Point Loma Publications, Inc., 1972), p. 44.

38. "Cult's Revolt Eye-Opener to Old Nanaimo"; Pierre Berton, *My Country: The Remarkable Past* (Toronto: McClelland and Stewart Limited, 1976): pp. 104–105; "Finis Written to Long Search for Man of Mystery."

39. Oliphant, *Brother Twelve*, pp. 57–59; "Finis Written to Long Search for Man of Mystery."

40. Berton, *My Country*, p. 105.

41. Before arriving in Cedar-by-the-Sea, Wilson spoke to a number of Theosophical lodges in eastern Canada, including the Ottawa Lodge, the Toronto Lodge, and lodges in Hamilton, London, and Windsor (Oliphant, *Brother Twelve*, pp. 39–43; "The Teachings of Brother XII": 200). From eastern Canada, following successful speaking engagements, capturing "much of the Canadian membership of the Theosophical Society for the Aquarian Foundation," he then traveled by train to British Columbia.

42. Oliphant, *Brother Twelve*, p. 45. The four objects of the foundation were

1. To give teaching and instructions to its members upon philosophical and occult subjects, and upon all matters concerning their physical, mental, and spiritual welfare; and to print and publish such books, magazines, or documents as may be necessary for that purpose.
2. To form and operate one or more central communities to be conducted upon mutually beneficent and fraternal principles, and to provide for the education of its members and their children in accordance with the general principles herein laid down.
3. To provide for the pursuance and carrying out of such actions and policies as may be deemed advisable for the welfare of the society and its members.

4. To cooperate directly or indirectly with all other societies, orders, or organizations which are activated by the same principles of Truth, Justice, Brotherhood, and mutual service; to the end that all may share in that greater strength and solidarity which is the outcome of unity of effort and purpose (ibid.).

43. These included Wilson's wife, Elma; Alfred and Annie Barley; Frederick Pope; and Sidney Sprey-Smith (Oliphant, *Brother Twelve*, pp. 36–37). See note 52 for information on the Barleys. Frederick Pope was a young man about whom not much is known; Sprey-Smith was a retired British army captain (Oliphant, pp. 37, 53–54).

44. "Weird Occultism Exemplified in Amazing Colony at Cedar-by-Sea," *Sunday Province* (Vancouver, B.C.), 28 October 1928: 1, 34.

45. Oliphant, *Brother Twelve*, pp. 56, 59.

46. Ibid., pp. 50–56, 66, and "The Teachings of Brother XII": pp. 201–202. Those in attendance were the seven governors of the foundation. See note 61.

47. "Cult's Revolt Eye-Opener to Old Nanaimo."

48. "Weird Occultism Exemplified in Amazing Colony at Cedar-by-Sea."

49. "Finis Written to Long Search for Man of Mystery"; "Amazing Disclosures Made in Action against Cult Leader," *Daily Colonist* (Vancouver, B.C.), 27 April 1933 [a clipping found in the files of H. N. Stokes. No pages are recorded, but most probably the story was found on p. 2 and continued to the next page]; Berton, *My Country*, p. 109.

50. Lippincott was not a member of the publishing family as formally reported in the earlier version of this paper and in the definitive biography of Wilson, John Oliphant's *Brother Twelve*, p. 90. This information comes from a telephone conversation on March 17, 2002. Oliphant also related to me that Lippincott was a frequent visitor to the headquarters of the Rosicrucian Fellowship and a friend of the widow of Max Heindel, the founder.

51. Oliphant, *Brother Twelve*, p. 89.

52. "Vancouver Island Colony in Trouble," *Mail and Empire* (Toronto), 29 October 1928. Both Mr. and Mrs. Barley were members of the inner circle of the Theosophist astrologer Alan Leo, one of the most influential astrologers since 1800 and indeed the father of modern astrology. Leo published his own journal, *Modern Astrology*. I thank Nicholas Campion (letter dated September 22, 1987) and John Oliphant (letter dated July 30, 1987) for this information. Barley is the author of the *Rationale of Astrology,* an "old Leo manual" (*O. E. Library Critic* 17, no. 11: 16).

Coulson Turnbull, PhD, is the author of *The Divine Language of Celestial Correspondences, The Life and Mystical Teachings of Giordano Bruno, The Rising Zodiacal Sign, The Solar Logos,* and *The Astrologer's Guide,* all published by the Gnostic Press (Santa Cruz, CA).

53. A group consisted of ten members each, so the membership could not have been more than two thousand. See Oliphant, *Brother Twelve*, p. 62. Further information is located in "Finis Written to Long Search for Man of Mystery"; "Osiris and Isis Met on Train Between Seattle and Chicago," *The Daily Province* (Vancouver, B.C.), 31 October 1928; *O. E. Library Critic* 18 no. 5: 8.

54. *Unsigned Letters from an Elder Brother,* pp. 70–71.

55. Berton, *My Country*, p. 107; "Finis Written to Long Search for Man of Mystery."

John Oliphant is of the opinion that the lawyer was Oliver G. Hess of Carthage, Missouri, a Civil War veteran, who endowed the Aquarian Foundation with a trust fund of $20,000. His name is mentioned in "Man from Carthage, Mo., Helped Reincarnated B.C. Egyptian God," *Sunday Province,* 4 November 1928: 1, 2.

56. "Failure of Brother XII to Start City of Refuge Cause of Court Action," *Daily Colonist* (Vancouver, B.C.), 6 November 1932.

57. Mary W. T. Connally was to play a central role in the downfall of Wilson and his companion, Mabel Scottowe (née Rowbotham or Rowbottom), when she initiated court action against the couple, now known as Amiel de Valdes and Zura de Valdes on April 2, 1933. The case was brought before the Supreme Court of British Columbia at the courthouse in Nanaimo.

58. "Weird Occultism Exemplified in Amazing Colony at Cedar-by-Sea."

59. Ibid. A letter written by Myrtle Baumgartner, dated September 13, 1928, discovered by John Oliphant after the publication of his book, *Brother Twelve,* and mentioned in his article, "The Teachings of Brother XII," raises doubts concerning this supposedly chance meeting on the train for the first time. The letter, presumably written to her husband, Dr. Edwin A. Baumgartner (the letter was addressed to "Ed"), reveals that Myrtle had dreams since her early childhood that she would meet a man who would be her spiritual companion:

> The proof that we really touch supernat. things in our night consciousness did not come to me from reading it in a book. It came to my [*sic*] from my own life experience. From earliest childhood I have had great and magnificent dreams which made lasting impressions. One of the earliest in this connection came while I was in St. Louis. I dreamed that I was crossing a long difficult, exposed bridge. At the end of the bridge a man stood and I knew he was waiting for me.

In 1922, she experienced a "long and wonderful Egyptian dream" with the "same man" appearing in it:

> I knew that I never *really* loved anyone but *him,*—but it never ocurred [*sic*] to me that he was on earth in physical embodiment. . . . Then in 1926 came the great experience,—a great dedication to the service of humanity, taken also in my night consciousness. This great service was a joint service which I undertook with this Beloved One with whom I had been in contact for years. Even yet though I did not know he was in physical embodiment; I thought he was on another plane, and that when the time came for my work to commence on the physical plane, he would direct and inspire it from a higher plane.

The following passage suggests that Baumgartner knew of the Aquarian Foundation before the fateful train journey:

> As the Aquarian Foundation grew I gradually began to recognize those with whom I worked at night and knew beyond a doubt that here I belonged. Even yet it did not dawn on me that this very dear and close one was on the physical plane. I gladly and willingly pledged myself to the work of the A.F., —I believe

in it; I know it is good. . . . When the opportunity came to me to take a trip to the headquarters of the A.F. I came because I knew that I would meet here those people whom I knew so well on inner planes. . . .

Now for the great experience. Upon my arrival at the A.F. headquarters, I was met at the boat by Coulson Turnbull,—and an hour or so later ushered into an office where. . . I saw walking to meet me This One—I gasped and the expression on his face was of as intense a surprise. It was reunion. . . .

The episode of the chance meeting in a train, first introduced by Robert England in court proceedings held on October 30, 1928, may never have happened if the above letter is any indication of the truth.

60. "Amazing Disclosures Made in Action Against Cult Leader"; "Vancouver Island Colony in Trouble."

61. The governors were Wilson; Lucas, a Vancouver barrister; von Platen; De Luce; Coulson Turnbull; P. F. Fisher; and J. S. Benner of Akron, Ohio. Benner was secretary-general of the foundation for the eastern United States. He was also the head of Sun Publishing Company, which distributed and printed much of Wilson's writings. See "Osiris and Isis Met on Train Between Seattle and Chicago"; "Dramatic Surprise at Aquarian Hearing"; *Daily Province*, 2 November 1928.

62. Wilson denied that the Osiris-Isis story was the invention of the secretary of the foundation, Robert England. In a letter (dated January 2, 1929) to the editor of the *O. E. Library Critic* (18, no. 10: 9–10), Wilson writes that:

Osiris-Isis are not personal god and goddess but *living principles in Nature*. . . . The principles are exemplified (or incarnated if you will) in every human being, one or the other being predominant in each individual case. The 'divine child' Horus was the realization of these truths in the reasoning mind, corresponding to the birth of the Christos in esoteric christianity.

63. "Woman's Evidence Favors Brother XI [*sic*]," *Toronto Mail and Empire*, 1 November 1928; "Dramatic Surprise at Aquarian Hearing," p. 32; "Finis Written to Long Search for Man of Mystery."

64. "Alfred Barley, Plaintiff, and Amiel de Valdes and Zura de Valdes, Defendants." Court proceedings held in the Supreme Court of British Columbia, Holden at Nanaimo, B.C. (April 3, 1933).

65. "Mary W. T. Connally, Plaintiff, and Amiel de Valdes and Zura de Valdes, Defendants." Court proceedings held in the Supreme Court of British Columbia, Holden at Nanaimo, B.C. (April 2, 1933).

66. This is based on the accounting of the April 2, 1933, Supreme Court proceedings. This does not necessarily represent the total figure, for Connally does mention other expenses that she had accept, such as watching over Baumgartner after medical and mental problems surfaced in 1929. The estimates in the popular press were therefore much higher: $250,000 in "Finis Written to Long Search for Man of Mystery"; Berton, pp. 111–12. The figure of $250,000 is Oliphant's estimate. In the article, "Amazing Disclosures," a high figure of $520,000 is mentioned, whereas in "Cult Holds Members as Slaves on B.C. Island," *Seattle Post-Intelligencer,* 28 April 1933, a low figure of $50,000 is given.

67. The schoolhouse was to be the site where the future "Rulers and Governors" would be trained "in just Principles and true Ideals" ("A Message from the Masters of the Wisdom," *Foundation Letters*, p. 3).

The souls that would incarnate in the children were said to be derived from two sources: (1) those whose last birth was prior to the Christian era and (2) those whose bodies perished during World War I, thus balancing the account of their respective national karmas ("Message," p. 3).

In this context, Wilson writes (*O. E. Library Critic*, p. 10):

> We have a small school for the training *of a few*. . . . We have reason to believe that many advanced souls will be born into the world in the near future—some are already born and are now children of eight or nine or ten years of age. They are of the new type, spiritually and psychologically and our hope is to give them such training as is fitted to them. These children are (and will be) born to parents who are already serving this Cause.

Yet, according to Berton (pp. 111–12), the schoolhouse was never used for its intended purpose because most of the inhabitants were beyond childbearing age.

68. Information on Comfort (1978–1932) is available in Mary Adams Stearns, "An American Mystic: Will Levington Comfort and His Work," *National Magazine* (July 1913): 605–608; and J. Berg Esenwein, "Will Levington Comfort: The Man and His Books," *Book News Monthly* (December 1912): 234–38. Comfort's novels include *Routledge Rides Alone*, *She Buildeth Her House*, and *Fate Knocks at the Door*.

69. The mistreatment is mentioned in the testimony of Annie Barley in the April 2, 1933, Supreme Court proceedings. Howard O'Hagan, "The Weird and Savage Cult of Brother 12," *MacLean's Magazine* (23 April 1960): 39. According to O'Hagan, Baumgartner was sent east to a mental hospital. See also "Cult Holds Members as Slaves on B.C. Island," pp. 1–2; "Amazing Disclosures"; Sydney Blake, "Connally vs. de Valdes," *The Lawyer* 311 (September 1939): 13.

70. "Amazing Disclosures"; Berton, *My Country*, pp. 114–16; Blake, "Connally vs. de Valdes," p. 13; "Amazing Disclosures Made in Action against Cult Leader"; "Black Magic, Gold and Guns Feature Strange Cult Case," *Daily Colonist*, 28 April 1933: 1, 2. According to the testimony of Leona Painter in the April 2, 1933, Supreme Court proceedings, Wilson received $10,000 from Mary Connally to buy the DeCourcy Group of islands, and he in turn promised Connally a house next to his. But Wilson wanted to renege on the agreement and so attacked her character and trustworthiness. This was the beginning of a sustained bad treatment bordering on torture for Connally.

71. Oliphant, *Brother Twelve*, p. 333; Berton, *My Country*, p. 120; "Finis Written to Long Search for Man of Mystery"; "Failure of Brother XII to Start City of Refuge Cause of Court Action."

72. Blake, "Connally vs. de Valdes," p. 13; O'Hagan, "The Weird and Savage Cult," p. 39; "Finis Written to Long Search for Man of Mystery."

73. Oliphant, *Brother Twelve*, p. 348; O'Hagan, "The Weird and Savage Cult," p. 39; Berton, *My Country*, pp. 120–21; Blake, "Connally vs. de Valdes," p. 13.

74. Robert S. Ellwood and Harry B. Partin, Religious and Spiritual Groups in Modern America, 2nd ed. (Englewood Cliffs, NJ: Prentice Hall, 1988), pp. 14–16, 38–40.

75. This appears in John Oliphant's *Brother Twelve: The Incredible Story of Canada's False Prophet*, pp. 17, 359. The year is also confirmed by Wilson himself, who writes in his "Greetings," in Brother XII, *Foundation Letters and Teachings* (Akron, OH: Sun Publishing Co., 1927):

> And now this body!
> Seven times seven years I have trained it, taught it,
> Urged it to effort, tried it to the limit of its strength,
> Knowledge I gave it—a little at a time,
> And as the brain could bear it.

Wilson's age is given "Seven times seven years": forty-nine years minus 1927, the date of the publication of this poem, or 1878.

76. Oliphant, *Brother Twelve*, p. 18; Berton, *My Country*, p. 101; Gwen Cash, "Bridey Murphy Case Recalls Brother XII," *Daily Colonist* (Victoria, B.C.), 26 February 1956. I thank John Oliphant for providing me with the latter article.

77. "Irvingites," *Catholic Encyclopedia*, http://www.newadvent.org/cathen/08174a .htm. It is curious that the number twelve plays such an important role in the Aquarian Foundation. It is very likely that Wilson or Brother XII was influenced by Catholic Apostolic Church's emphasis on the twelve apostles. Regardless, on the cover of the *Chalice* appears the Aquarian explanation of the number twelve, written in italics as *XII*:

> The Roman numerals [III, IX, XII] indicate the nature of the Work, for it is associated astrologically with the Third, the Ninth, and the Twelfth Houses. . . . The Twelfth House represents those Unseen Spiritual powers and influences which work below the surface in all affairs of men and shows that this is a work to be accomplished in the adjustment of accounts which we term Karmic, and through which nations as well as individuals must work out the present consequences of past actions,—it is "the writing on the wall."

78. "Finis Written to Long Search for Man of Mystery"; Berton, *My Country*, p. 101; O'Hagan, "The Weird and Savage Cult of Brother 12," p. 22. The date of Wilson's early arrival in Victoria is uncertain. In "Finis," the implication is that he was already there in the late 1890s. Berton claims that 1905 is the more likely date, while O'Hagan gives 1912 as the year he joined the express company.

79. I wish to thank the former national president of the Theosophical Society in America, Dora Kunz, for allowing me to examine Wilson's membership record. O'Hagan mentions that Wilson sailed in the British merchant marine on the Atlantic (p. 22).

80. O'Hagan, 22; Berton, *My Country*, p. 101.

81. See note 66.

82. Berton, *My Country*, p. 103.

83. Both articles are reprinted in Foundation Letters, pp. 151 ff., 157 ff. The *Occult Review* has been described "as the best general occult periodical in the English language" by H.N. Stokes (*O.E. Library Critic* 17, no. 12: 13).

84. O'Hagan, "The Weird and Savage Cult of Brother 12," p. 34.

85. Berton, *My Country*, p. 120; Blake, "Connally vs. de Valdes," p. 13.

86. "Weird Occultism Exemplified in Amazing Colony at Cedar-by-Sea," p. 34.

87. O'Hagan, "The Weird and Savage Cult of Brother 12," p. 39.

88. "The Sappers and Miners," *Canadian Theosophist* 7, no. 12 (15 February 1927): 263.

89. Cash, "Bridey Murphy Case Recalls Brother XII."

90. Ibid.

15
THE "I AM" ACTIVITY
J. Gordon Melton

In 1929, while walking the slopes of Mount Shasta in northern California, Guy W. Ballard ostensibly met an extraordinary gentleman. The man claimed to be an ascended master by the name of Saint Germain. He had picked Ballard to be his messenger and the messenger of his colleagues, who together made up the Great White Brotherhood, a group of evolved souls who at a spiritual level collectively guided the destiny of the world. Ballard's account of his experiences with Saint Germain and the messages he received from him over the next few years were compiled in a set of volumes first published in the mid-1930s. These volumes detailed the basic teachings and describe the basic practices of what became known as the "I AM" Religious Activity.[1] The knowledgeable outsider, one who is generally aware of the larger metaphysical culture, will immediately perceive substantial roots of the "I AM" in that larger culture.

Two practices dominated the life of the "I AM" Religious Activity: the reception of messages from the ascended masters and decreeing. The former suggests the "I AM" Religious Activity's roots in Theosophy and the latter in New Thought. In the 1880s, Helena P. Blavatsky, one of the founders of the Theosophical Society, claimed to be in contact with an unusual group of people. These

Written for this anthology. This survey was developed from the extensive collection of documents in the files of the Institute for the Study of American Religion, now on deposit in the American Religions Collection at the Library of the University of California, Santa Barbara. No attempt has been made to minutely document every item cited.

individuals were not spirits in the classical sense of Spiritualism, nor did they reside in Summerland, the Spiritualist heavenly afterlife. Rather, they claimed to be somewhat ordinary individuals who had, through completing a number of incarnations on Earth (and other planets), evolved to the point that they now held positions in the spiritual hierarchy that ruled the cosmos. The hierarchy had a particular interest in evolving human life, Earth being the home to innumerable embodied spirit entities who were on a path back to godhood.

In her writings, particularly *The Secret Doctrine*, Blavatsky presented the teachings of the masters as they had communicated them to her.[2] Following her death, another one of the founders of the Theosophical Society, William Q. Judge, claimed also to be in contact with the masters. Judge, a lawyer, had remained in America when Blavatsky and Henry Steel Olcott, the third founder, had moved to India. Judge's claimed contacts were immediately questioned by European Theosophists, many of whom rejected them, and the controversy festered during Judge's few remaining years.

While dominating the society in North America, Judge was little known abroad at the time of Blavatsky's death. Blavatsky turned over the Esoteric Section, the independent fraternity of Theosophical elites, to Annie Besant and William Judge, her most promising students. Through the 1890s, Judge and Besant engaged in a power struggle within the society, which led in 1895 to the American section's withdrawal from the international Theosophical Society. Judge died the next year and passed his mantle to his most promising student, Katherine Tingley. Besant and Tingley were both strong, extraordinary leaders, but neither was in contact with the masters.

Besant's confidant, Charles W. Leadbeater, purported to possess clairvoyant powers with which he saw numerous things, from the past lives of the leaders of the society to the colorful shape of thought forms, but he was not a messenger of the masters. Eventually he gave the international Society its program for the early twentieth century when he picked out a young boy, Jiddu Krishnamurti, as the vehicle of the coming world messenger. Krishnamurti's voice, which emerged after World War I, replaced the longing for immediate contacts with the masters for many, but when Krishnamurti resigned his role as the world teacher in 1929, the society was cut off.

Like the American branch since Judge's death, the Adyar branch (as the international society is generally known from the location of its headquarters in Adyar, Madras, India) has generally avoided any claims to immediate, direct ongoing contact with the Masters. Only the messages received by Blavatsky and the few lesser messages received by Olcott and Judge are considered valid. As early as 1920, Alice A. Bailey challenged Blavatsky's exclusive position as amanuensis of the masters. She had been receiving messages from one of them, Djwal Khul. Popularly known as the Tibetan, he began to dictate messages to her around World War I, and she published the first volume of his messages in 1920.

That same year, Alice and her husband, Foster, were dismissed from the society and they, in turn, founded a competing organization, the Arcane School.

Guy Ballard's contact with Saint Germain in 1929 placed him in the same role claimed by Madame Blavatsky. Upon his return to Chicago, he began to deliver dictated messages to a small group who met in his southside home. From that time forward he regularly dictated messages from Saint Germain, Jesus, and those personages described by Blavatsky as the lords of the seven rays—those masters most immediately concerned with the course of human evolution. Ballard also identified a number of the members of the spiritual hierarchy from whom he dictated messages. Several of these were especially related to the United States. Ballard was intensely patriotic and through the messages of such masters as lady liberty, the master who inspired her representation as the Statue of Liberty, he passed a noticeable patriotic stance to the "I AM" movement. July 4 remains an important national gathering day for members of the "I AM" and those groups which derive from it.

Though Ballard's wife, Edna W. Ballard, and their son, Donald, were also designated as messengers of the ascended masters, in fact, through the 1930s, Guy Ballard was the only person who received dictated messages. These were published in the magazine of the Saint Germain Foundation, and many were later compiled in the several volumes of the Saint Germain series. They provided immediate regular guidance from the masters. Donald never received dictations from the masters. Guy Ballard died in December 1939, and for many years Edna did not receive messages. As in the Theosophical Society, that void created a crisis among some members.

"I AM" AND NEW THOUGHT

While the "I AM" roots in Theosophy are well known, its heralding in New Thought has been little considered, primarily because of the lack of historical work on New Thought. However, many of the unique teachings and practices of the "I AM" were originally taught by Emma Curtis Hopkins, the founder of New Thought, and her student Annie Rix Militz. Hopkins, the editor of the *Christian Science Journal*, broke with Mary Baker Eddy in 1885 and moved to Chicago as an independent Christian Science teacher. In 1886, she opened a center and began to train practitioners and other teachers. Over the next decade, she taught almost all the people who were to become the founders of the major New Thought groups—Divine Science, the Unity School of Christianity, and the Home of Truth.

From Christian Science, Hopkins inherited the use of affirmations, a form of prayer in which the petitioner makes a positive statement about a desired condition as if that condition already exists. Thus a person experiencing symptoms of illness might affirm, "I have the energy of God, in whose presence illness cannot exist, flowing through my body." One who makes affirmations understands that in the spiritual world only perfection exists. He or she attempts to change the self's self-perception—believed to be the ultimate cause of all negativities in an individual's life—in such a way that spiritual reality can be actualized in the visible world.

However, Hopkins took the process one step further and began to decree. Decreeing is a form of affirmative prayer in which one seems to demand of the cosmic powers that certain conditions (all for the good) prevail. In the 1890s, Hopkins made a first mention of decreeing. In a speech recalling a period of unrest through which her organization had recently passed, she celebrated the ending of the chaos. She noted that in 1887, at the time of the dedication of a new center, she had "decreed certain good things to come to pass."[3] The good things arrived but not without the group's first overcoming a number of obstacles.

In connection with her decreeing, Hopkins and her students also used the term "I AM" in the peculiar manner later to be identified with the "I AM" movement. Her teachings concerning the "I AM" are most clearly laid out in her little pamphlet *The Radiant "I AM."*[4] One of her students, Thomas J. Shelton, expanded on her ideas in his book of *"I AM" Sermons.*[5]

The idea of the "I AM" was based upon a variety of biblical passages. Hopkins related it to Jesus' prayer in John 10 in which he affirmed "I and the Father are one" and prayed that his disciples "may be one with me as I am one with thee." Throughout the Gospel of John, Jesus makes a number of statements about himself that begin with the words "I am," phrases that have been traditionally popular subjects for sermons by Christian ministers. Ultimately, however, the "I AM" position rests upon Exodus 3:14, when in reply to Moses' inquiry Yahweh reveals himself as the self-existing One: "And God said unto Moses, I AM THAT I AM; and he said, Thus shalt thou say unto the children of Israel, I AM hath sent me unto you" (King James Version). "I AM" is a name/designation of God. Thus, merely making a simple statement about the self (for example, "I am a good person"), one also says the name of God. Members of the "I AM" view the pronouncing of that name as making an identification of the conscious self with God as represented in one's higher self, or "I AM Presence." Used as part of a decree, the divine part of the self, the "I AM Presence," is called to the fore as the active agent on the spiritual plane.

Hopkins passed her teachings to Annie Rix Militz, who, just before the turn of the century, founded her Home of Truth center in Los Angeles and used it as a base from which other Homes of Truth were soon established along the West Coast. In her *Primary Lessons in Christian Living,*[6] Militz echoes her teacher by affirming that man is the expression of God's own being, the "I AM" of God. The true selfhood of man, the "I AM" of God, is the Christ within us all. All healing, all prosperity, all happiness hinge on the single metaphysical point: affirming the "I AM" Christ-self as the only *true* self.

In her last years, Militz went beyond her teacher and began to devote considerable time to speculation on the goal of human life and the afterlife. At this time she was obviously disturbed by the emergence of reincarnation as a powerful idea competing with more traditional Christian notions of resurrection. Reincarnation was a strong belief of Militz's colleague, Charles Fillmore of the Unity School, with which Militz had closely cooperated through the years. However, she rejected the emphasis on reincarnation. Reincarnation occurs, but it is to be surpassed. The real goal for a human being is ascension.

Militz noted that embodiment in flesh, incarnation, is for a very limited purpose of experiencing embodied life. The higher self, the "I AM" self, never incarnates, only that part of the self which is a reflection of the I AM. There is no need for the individual to reincarnate, and humans should orient their lives around the real goal of Ascension, the goal illustrated by Jesus in his ascension (Acts 1:9–10). As she noted, "That the same consciousness and power of translation has come to others besides Jesus should be evidence that his ascension was not an exclusive miracle for him alone, but an attainment open to all and a prize to be sought by the faithful, for the advancement of the race and to add another stone to the causeway that unites the upper and lower worlds."[7]

ENTER GUY BALLARD

In 1930, six years after the death of Annie Rix Militz in Los Angeles, Guy W. Ballard was hiking through the forests on the slopes of Mount Shasta. He had heard reports of the strange occult events that had been reported to have occurred either near or on this most impressive of mountains. One day while hiking, he ran into a person whom he first mistook for another hiker. However, the person turned out to be no less than the Ascended Master Saint Germain, famous in occult circles as one of the great practitioners. Saint Germain had lived an earlier embodiment in the eighteenth century, during which time he acquired his reputation as an alchemist and a man of mystery. He caught the thirsty Ballard's attention by offering him a creamy liquid that had an unusual and refreshing effect on him. He was later told that the liquid was from the "Universal Supply."

Saint Germain's more important task was to recruit Ballard as the messenger of the ascended masters. He had searched unsuccessfully for several centuries to find someone in human embodiment to release the instructions of the great law of life to humanity. He wanted to initiate the Seventh Golden Age, the permanent "I AM" age of eternal perfection on this earth. Having been unable to find a messenger in Europe, Saint Germain had come to America. His search had led him to Mount Shasta and the encounter with Ballard.

Ballard accepted the task assigned him by Saint Germain, who in turn began to introduce him to the new world of metaphysical reality. Ballard began to write down his experiences and at the same time penned lengthy letters to his wife, Edna, then back at their home in Chicago, relating his awakening.[8] Saint Germain later also designated Edna and the Ballards' son, Donald, as messengers.

Ballard returned to Chicago in 1931 to launch the "I AM" Religious Activity. In 1932, the Saint Germain Press and the Saint Germain Foundation were incorporated. A small group of people began to meet in the Ballards' home, and Ballard began the dictations during which the ascended masters, primarily Saint Germain and Jesus, spoke through him. In 1934, *Unveiled Mysteries*, the first of the basic library of "I AM" books, was published. It described his initial experiences with Saint Germain. A sequel, *The Magic Presence*, continued the story. A magazine, the *"Voice of the I AM,"* provided an outreach to a larger audience.

The practice of the "I AM" Religious Activity was spelled out in the *"I AM" Adorations and Affirmations* (1935) and *"I AM" Songs* (1938). The former contained texts of the decrees and affirmations to be used by "I AM" students. The basic teachings were defined in *The "I AM" Discourses* (1936). *Unveiled Mysteries*, *The Magic Presence*, and *The "I AM" Discourses* remain the basic reading material of the "I AM" student.[9]

BASIC BELIEFS AND PRACTICES

The Great White Brotherhood, the spiritual hierarchy, that group of beings who constitute the spiritual cosmos have been referred to in occult texts for generations. The contact begun with the ascended masters through Guy Ballard, however, led to the releasing of what the "I AM" Religious Activity believed to be a threefold truth not previously known outside the masters' secret retreat centers. This truth includes:

1. Knowledge of the individualized presence of God, which is known as the "Mighty I AM Presence," God in action;

2. The use of the violet consuming flame of divine love; and

3. The Ascended Masters' use of God's creative name, "I AM."

While parts of this message have been circulating in metaphysical circles for several decades, Ballard was the first to bring them together into a unique system.

The activity affirms the reality of one God who is omnipresent, omniscient, and omnipotent and who rules all creation. As the life of the universe, God permeates all things and is individualized for dynamic action. From the "I AM" perspective, light is the dominant form taken by divine realities. At the heart of our universe, the great central sun, the source of God's power and authority, emanates forth as the "Mighty I AM Presence." As that presence goes forth and is individualized, creation is brought into existence. Each individual begins as a spark from the divine flame. The "I AM Presence" is the light in the electron and the cells of the body; it is the light in the mind and heart. However, the misuse of the divine energy over the centuries has resulted in the present condition of humanity, manifest in discord, hate, impurities, and death, which hide the perfection, harmony, love, purity, and life that is God and his "I AM Presence."

As the individualized "I AM Presence," God is the master within each person, the Christ Self. God is also individualized within each of the members of the hierarchy who govern the cosmos, this planet, and solar system. Members of the hierarchy are known as the ascended masters of love, light, and perfection. They are the guardians of humanity and have worked through the centuries from the invisible, as well as from the physical, to awaken, bless, enlighten, and lift humankind out of the self-created situation in which it now finds itself. Once like other humans, they have, through a series of reembodiments, overcome the present condition and, by attuning themselves to the "I AM Presence," ascended into the light. To follow their path is the goal of each person.

One of the ascended masters is the Master Jesus. Through his ministry and ascension, he released the Christ light, the "Mighty I AM Presence," to move the Earth forward out of darkness and hate into the light of divine love. A picture of the Master Jesus, next to that of Saint Germain, adorns the platform of every "I AM" sanctuary. The activity's emphasis on Jesus' work and teaching leads the members to affirm themselves as members of a Christian religion.

The activity also teaches that each ascended master radiates a certain color, an aspect of the divine light representative of a specific divine quality. "Clean, clear, bright colors," said Edna Ballard, "are rivers of blessing from the realms of light, the source of all perfection." However, members generally refrain from wearing red or black or having objects of these colors in their immediate environment. Black is indicative of hate, death, and destruction. Red is associated with anger, irritation, and impurity. When impurity is removed from red, for example, it will be transformed instantly into gold.

Within the "I AM" Activity, contact with the ascended masters and cooperation with their work is a central goal of each individual's life. According to present "I AM" teachings, the ascended masters regularly communicated with the "I AM" membership through their authorized messengers, the Ballards. Those communications were delivered before gatherings of members, published in the monthly periodical, and the more prominent ones collected and reprinted in the textbooks. (In all, over three thousand dictations from the masters were received during the Ballards' lifetime.) In these dictations, the masters offered a total program of guidance for both individual development and effective action in the world.

Each individual person in his or her fullness is pictured in the chart of the

"Mighty I AM Presence," which also is to be found on the platform of "I AM" sanctuaries. The individual is shown possessing a "Mighty I AM Presence," a higher self, which is the focus of the light and power of God within the self. The "I AM" is the designation of God's creative word or power in action in everyone. It is pictured as a being of light surrounded by a rainbow of lights, above each person and connected to each conscious self by a thread of luminosity. The purpose of the "I AM" Activity is to release the "I AM" power within and to make it available for the student to use, in cooperation with the ascended masters, in the elimination of evil and for the advent of freedom and justice in the world.

Each person is also shown surrounded by a violet flame, a cylinder of light created by the "I AM Presence." It is released to function whenever the individual calls forth his or her "I AM Presence" to consume discord and impurity in the world.

The most definitive activities for "I AM" members, by which they seek to attune themselves to their "I AM Presence" and thus align themselves to the path of the Ascended Masters, are (1) quiet contemplation and (2) the repetition of affirmations and decrees. Affirmations are sentences that affirm the individual's attunement to God and the blessing due to the person as a result of that attunement. A decree is a fiat spoken from the standpoint of the higher self, the "Mighty I AM Presence," and may be, depending on the occasion, peaceful, calming, or powerful in content and/or enunciation. The repetition of decrees is devotional activity, and all decrees are given in the name of God, the "Beloved Mighty I AM Presence," and in the name of the Ascended Master Jesus the Christ. Decrees are repeated daily for the release of the violet consuming flame and the dissipation of discord in the individual's environment. One typical decree, repeated in a strong commanding voice, might be:

> In the Name of God, the "Beloved Mighty I AM Presence," and in the Name of the Beloved Ascended Jesus Christ, "I AM" the Strength, the Courage, the Power to move forward steadily through all experiences, whatever they may be, by the glorious Presence with "I AM." "I AM" the Commanding Presence, the Exhaustless Energy, the Divine Wisdom, causing every desire to be fulfilled. The "Presence which I AM!" remains untouched by disturbing outer conditions. Serene, I fold my wings and abide in the Perfect Action of the Divine Law and Justice of my Being, commanding all things within my radiance to appear in Perfect Divine Order!

Students are taught basic decrees from the beginning of their work in the movement, and booklets of decrees for every occasion have been published.

Freedom was a persistent theme in the teaching of the ascended masters, who assigned America a special role in the unfolding plan for the coming Golden Age. As a result, the activity and its members have become known for their patriotism and love of country. American flags are prominently displayed at all "I AM" centers, and patriotic literature is integral to all their teaching activity.

THE PROGRESS OF A MOVEMENT

By the end of 1939, as the world was plunging into war, the "I AM" movement had experienced a highly successful five years under the leadership of Guy and Edna Ballard. It had become a national movement with sanctuaries established in most of the major cities. In spite of a few detractors, the future looked bright. Then, beginning in December 1939, the movement entered a period of turmoil from which it would recover only in the 1950s. The problems began when Guy Ballard died, to the surprise of most members of the movement. Many believed that he would never die bodily, and his death set off an internal doctrinal controversy over the nature of his ascension, which the movement affirmed had actually occurred.

Ballard's death, however, gave an opening to the movement's dissidents, who had found a leader in the person of Gerald B. Bryan. Bryan had written a set of booklets attacking the Ballards and the "I AM" teachings. These were gathered into a single volume, *Psychic Dictatorship in America* (1940), an especially effective title given the rise of Hitler and Mussolini. He organized media opposition and motivated some former students, who filed lawsuits against the Saint Germain Foundation. Finally, the state's attorney in Los Angeles stepped in and charged the movement with mail fraud. The substance of the case involved the argument that the beliefs of the group were so unbelievable that the Ballards and other leaders of the movement could not possibly believe them. Therefore they must be insincere and the movement a fraud. Though the great majority of the Ballards' students supported the Ballards, Edna and Donald and a number of others who worked in the Chicago headquarters were convicted. As a result, the movement's right to use the mail was revoked, and the convicted leaders faced jail terms.

The convictions were appealed, and over the next few years a lengthy process of review ensued. In the process the Supreme Court ruled twice, and the opinions stated in *Ballard v. United States* have become some of the most quoted in church-state legal opinions. While some of the ultimate decisions were made on legal technicalities, along the way the court ruled on the very significant matter of putting the teachings of a defendant's religion on trial. The legal proceeding finally ended in 1946 when, after a second overturn of the conviction by the court, the case was dropped. Meanwhile, with the first conviction, the foundation's right to use the U.S. mail had been revoked, and the Supreme Court's ruling did not automatically return that right. Gaining access to the mail required a lengthy appeal process, which took a decade to plod its way through the system. Finally, in 1954, that privilege was returned. Meanwhile, the movement had spent large sums of money to use an alternate carrier, the Railway Express, to distribute its material, especially the regular monthly issues of the *Voice of the "I AM."* The last step, the return of tax-exempt status, took place in 1957.

Following the 1946 ruling, even as the remaining mail and tax issues were being cleared up, the movement began to rebuild. A twelve-story office building in Chicago's Loop, purchased in 1948, and a resort/retreat center near Mount Shasta, California, were the primary symbols of that new life. However, no sooner had attacks from the outside slowed than controversy arose within the movement that would lead to the founding of a number of splinter groups and eventually to the foundation of the Church Universal and Triumphant. Both the "I AM" activity and its splinters would in turn influence other groups and contribute to the emerging New Age movement.

NOTES

1. The "I AM" Religious Activity was given corporate form as the Saint Germain Foundation. Related corporations, such as the Saint Germain Press, carried out specific missions for the foundation.

2. Blavatsky, of course, ran into a furious controversy over the masters when she was charged with fraud in attempting to demonstrate the extraordinary powers the masters possessed.

3. *Christian Science* [Chicago] 2, no. 7 (March 1890): 230.

4. Putnam, CT: Emma Curtis Hopkins Publications, n.d.

5. Denver, CO: "The Christian," 1900.

6. Annie Rix Militz, *Primary Lessons in Christian Living and Healing* (New York: The Absolute Press, 1904).

7. Annie Rix Militz, "Translation Not Reincarnation." *Master Mind*. Reprinted in J. Gordon Melton, ed., *New Thought: A Reader* (Santa Barbara, CA: Institute for the Study of American Religion, 1990), pp. 211–15.

8. In his letters, Ballard also mentioned that at the same time he was reading Baird T. Spaulding's *Life and Teaching of the Masters of the Far East* (Los Angeles: DeVorss & Co., 1924), whose teachings have often been compared with those later presented by Ballard.

9. All the basic "I AM" books were published by the Saint Germain Press in Chicago under Ballard's pseudonym, Godfré Ray King.

16
CHILDREN OF THE CHURCH UNIVERSAL AND TRIUMPHANT

Gary Shepherd and Lawrence Lilliston

PROLOGUE

Our first direct perceptions of anyone representing the Church Universal and Triumphant were provided by a national television broadcast of the *Jane Whitney Show* in early May 1993, just a few days after the tragic Branch Davidian conflagration in Waco, Texas. The luridly presented theme for this talk-show program was: "Is David Koresh in Your Own Backyard?" The organizational candidate designated as a possible affirmative answer to this question was the Church Universal and Triumphant. Members representing the Church[1] as a legitimate religious entity were a middle-aged mother of four children, LaVerne Macchio—who had been kidnapped a year previously in an unsuccessful attempt to "deprogram" her—and Murray Steinman, Church news director and media liaison. Their counterparts were two former Church members (one of whom was a direct participant in the Macchio kidnapping case), and they argued that the Church was a dangerous "cult" that merited suppression. Macchio's account of her ordeal and religious convictions struck us as both poignant and convincing. The majority of the studio audience, however, appeared to favor the need-to-repress-cult thesis and, ignoring the welling tears in Macchio's eyes, reserved its loudest applause for guest "cult experts," who characterized people like Macchio as "brainwashed."

A little less than two months later, we found ourselves directly interviewing

Written for this anthology.

Macchio, Steinman, and scores of other members of the Church Universal and Triumphant in their own backyard at Church headquarters on the Royal Teton Ranch in Corwin Springs, Montana. The general context for these interviews was the Church's yearly international conference, which is attended by several thousand members (and other interested parties) who come from most states in the union and from many foreign countries. Outside of popular media accounts that we were able to locate through hasty library forays, we were not particularly well versed in the theology, social structure, or history of the Church prior to our arrival. This resulted in our spending a good deal of the relatively short time we were in Montana (three weeks) simply becoming oriented about the basics of belief and practice in this complex socioreligious system.

While we were becoming generally educated about this system, we did try to develop a particular focus on issues related to socialization and education of the Church's young people. The arrival of a second generation in new religious movements is always pivotal for understanding the process by which these movements may become organizationally transformed. In addition to this more abstract sociological interest, there is also, in modern countries, intense popular and legal concern about the well-being of children who are raised in groups that outsiders perceive as religiously and socially deviant. It is widely believed by the general public that adult members of new religious movements—"cults"—are "brain-washed" into joining these groups in the first place. What about the children of these people: Are they "brainwashed," too? Are they being coerced in a fashion that exceeds normal parental constraints? Are they being abused?

In this chapter, we will address these kinds of questions about young people in the Church Universal and Triumphant (rather than issues of theology, conversion/defection experiences of adults, the Church's legal problems, etc.) What we have to say will almost always be more specific and descriptive than general and analytical because of the limitations of our preliminary observational experiences and open-ended interviews. We are not prepared, for instance, on the basis of our current data, to develop rigorous models of child-rearing practices and consequences among Church members. But we are able to describe, in broad strokes, several important educational and child-rearing attitudes and practices that are both advocated by the Church and prevalent among parents and teachers. We are also able to identify certain problem areas in the relationships between adults and young people as the Church struggles to adapt its organizational and spiritual goals to the needs of families. And we are largely able to dispel myths and rumors that Church children may be systematically abused—mentally or physically—as a result of established programs and policies. Our discussion of the children of the Church will be preceded by a general overview of the Church's history and ideas.

HISTORY AND BELIEFS

The Church Universal and Triumphant (CUT) is a second-generation splinter of the "I AM" Religious Activity, a popularized form of Theosophy, founded by Guy Warren Ballard and his wife, Edna W. Ballard. Mark L. Prophet had been active in two earlier "I AM" splinter groups, the Bridge to Freedom (now the New Age Church of Truth) and the Lighthouse of Freedom. He eventually founded his own group, the Summit Lighthouse, in Washington, D.C., in 1958. In the Theosophical tradition, the spiritual evolution of the planet is conceived of as being in the hands of a group of divinely illumined beings—Jesus, Gautama Buddha, and other advanced souls. In the tradition of earlier theosophical leaders, Prophet viewed himself as serving as the mouthpiece for

Mark Prophet, founder of the Church Universal and Triumphant. (*Courtesy of the Summit Lighthouse*)

these ascended masters. Elizabeth Clare Wulf joined the group in 1961, eventually marrying Mark Prophet. Over the course of their marriage, Elizabeth Prophet also became a messenger. After her husband's death in 1973, Elizabeth took over his roles as the primary mouthpiece for the masters and as leader of the organization.

The headquarters of Summit Lighthouse moved to Colorado Springs in 1966. In 1974, the Church Universal and Triumphant was incorporated, taking over ministerial and liturgical activities from Summit Lighthouse, which remained the publishing wing of the organization. During the seventies, the work of CUT expanded tremendously. After several moves within southern California, Church headquarters was finally established on the Royal Teton Ranch in Montana, just north of Yellowstone Park, in 1986. The Church also established an intentional community of several thousand people in the surrounding area.

The core beliefs of Church Universal and Triumphant are held in common with other branches of the Theosophical tradition. These include the notion of ascended masters guiding the spiritual evolution of the planet and certain basic ideas from the South Asian tradition, such as the belief in reincarnation and karma. The Church views itself as part of the larger Judeo-Christian tradition, although traditional Christians would not thus classify it.

When "cults" became a public issue in the mid-1970s, Church Universal and Triumphant was not particularly prominent. The group remained a relatively minor player in the cult wars until the move to Montana. As should have been anticipated, the intrusion of a large number of exotic outsiders into a predominantly rural area evoked curiosity and antagonism.

Much of the Church's subsequent negative media coverage derived from incidents clustered around its extensive fallout shelters and its preparations for the possibility of a nuclear attack against the United States. At one point in the construction, for instance, fuel stored in several underground tanks ruptured and spilled gas and diesel oil into the water table. Also, in 1990 members from around the world gathered in Montana because of the predicted possibility of an atomic holocaust. This story made the front page of the *New York Times* on December 15, 1990, resulting in a flood of reporters from around the world eager for sensationalist stories about a "doomsday cult."

Also, in 1989 two Church members—one of whom was Elizabeth Prophet's third husband— attempted to acquire otherwise legal weapons in a nonpublic, illegal manner for storage in underground shelters, providing more fuel for the organization's negative public image as a survivalist group. The motivation for this ill-considered act was to avoid the negative media exposure that would have resulted if members had purchased guns in Montana. The plan, however, backfired and resulted in a public relations disaster. This and other incidents were the basis for later accusations that Church Universal and Triumphant was a potential Waco.

In the mid-nineties and early twenty-first century, the Church began to face a very different set of challenges. The Church entered a period of organizational crisis, brought on, in part, by a deterioration in Elizabeth Clare Prophet's health. By the late nineties, she was effectively out of the picture. The post-Prophet era has been characterized by tensions between factions within the organization and a decline in the numbers of active participants in North America. There has, however, been an expansion of Church membership in Russia, Brazil, and certain African nations.

OBSERVATIONS

Church Membership Distinctions

One structural feature of the Church Universal and Triumphant that makes generalizations about child-rearing and educational practices difficult is a distinction between different levels of membership. Thousands of people who affiliate themselves with the Church in some way do not live in Montana. Some may simply receive regular mailings of Church literature (e.g., *Pearls of Wisdom*) or occasionally attend local study centers. Others may have committed themselves to an intermediate member status as "Keepers of the Flame" and more actively identify with and practice Church teachings. In either case, these are people who live in cities and towns all over the world, hold regular jobs, send their children to public schools, and so on. Full members are designated "communicants," but even they may choose to live in a secular setting outside of Montana.

Royal Teton Ranch in Montana is both headquarters for the Church and, according to Church teachings, a specifically sacred geographical location. But not even all Montana Church members actually live in the ranch community. Many, both Keepers of the Flame and communicants, live in nearby small towns such as Gardiner and Livingston; some live even further away in cities like Bozeman and Billings. Finally, can a distinction be made even among members who do live somewhere on the approximately 25,000 acres of Church property: Some live in privately constructed homes or double-wide mobile homes on large-acreage plots within the confines of formally platted subdivisions. The others live in more tightly clustered regular-sized mobile homes that are located adjacent to central Church offices and working facilities in at least three different locations. These last identified members are not only almost all communicants (or members of communicant families) but are also officially designated as "staff"—people who have made full-time commitments to working for the Church and fulfilling a variety of organizational roles (and spiritual requirements). Staff (and their children) number only about eight hundred people.

It is not possible, then, to characterize the Church as a homogeneous, monolithic community/organization that collectively experiences the same environmental pressures, problems, and needs. More specifically, with regard to the focus of this chapter, it is also not possible to make many Church-wide generalizations about the socialization practices and experiences of all member parents and their children. As we elaborate our observations about young people, we will try to be mindful of variations in setting and background characteristics of different member categories.

A Sampling of Outsider Attitudes

Outsiders are not typically as mindful of these distinctions. It is instructive to begin our discussion of Church children with views about them derived from local nonmembers who have varying degrees of contact with the Church. Our sources for these views include four area clergymen: a Baptist pastor, a Methodist minister, a Catholic priest, and a Mormon branch president. We also interviewed the local public school district superintendent. Finally, we interviewed two married couples who are longtime area residents and are literally neighbors who live adjacent to Church operations in different ranch locations. In accordance with theories of social distance, it is not surprising to find a positive relationship between degree of actual contact with Church members and their children and favorable or unfavorable attitudes toward them.

The Baptist pastor was a relative newcomer on the scene, having arrived in Montana only six months prior to our interview. He had never visited the Church ranch and its operational facilities (which are generally open to the public), nor had he had any discussions with Church members. Yet he was a font of rumors and opinions, most of them negative in the extreme. He had heard that those Church kids who attended local public schools were "listless," probably from a combination of their [vegetarian] diet and brainwashing: "When mom and dad are zombies, the kids will be the same way." They "keep separate from the other kids, are not as likely to enter into social circles." At the same time, he worried about the potential baneful influence these children might exert over his own daughter through her contacts with them in school. A Church girl had, in fact, invited his daughter to an overnight party (her parents lived in town rather than at the ranch). But he was too concerned to permit it: "The Devil doesn't always appear as he is; he may transform himself into an angel of light."

The Methodist minister had been in the area for about ten years, and although he had never visited the ranch or any other Church facilities, he'd had occasional contacts with Church members and their children, mostly through school-sponsored activities. His son played on an athletic team with a Church boy, and there were no problems. He was reluctant to offer judgments about the children per se but was critical of parents and Church policies affecting children. He found parents who attended community meetings to be overly defensive, even when he felt that other parents were trying to be accommodating. He had the impression that many Church parents were single mothers and that this created an unstable situation for their children. And he was indignant about his perception that the Church used the public schools as a "dumping ground for their problem kids." Still, once in the schools, he admitted that Church students appeared to display "no obvious dysfunctioning" and were "integrated quite easily."

The Catholic priest had served many years as a parish priest and assistant director of the parish school. He had engaged in several adversarial contacts with Church officials in years past and has ongoing contacts with Church parents and children who live in town and become involved with the parish school. At one time, as many as a dozen Church children were enrolled as students in the parish school; currently there are only five or six. His concern about Church children peaked three years previously during the "shelter cycle" time when the Church was intensively preparing for a possible worldwide nuclear war. Children were coming to class "dead tired" from staying up all night to help move supplies into fallout shelters. Some of the younger children seemed especially upset about the prospect of having to live underground for an indeterminate time and having to ward off outside enemies who would try to invade their shelters.

These kinds of fears (and accompanying talk about "Us" versus "Them") appear to have faded away during the last few years. Currently he perceives the Church children who attend the parish school as being "accepted, extremely intelligent, and well cared for." He does suspect that children of staff may be "nutritionally deprived" because of their presumed vegetarian diet, and he cites as an example a thirteen-year-old boy consuming inordinate numbers of hamburgers at a parish picnic.

The Mormon branch president is also the Forest Service district ranger and has had a number of contacts with Church officials (whom he describes as "amenable") concerning a variety of property and natural resource issues. His basic attitude toward the Church members is "let 'em be," as long as they are exercising their legal rights. He noted that several Mormon young people had developed friendships in the public schools with Church kids and that there had been home stay-over exchanges. He's not concerned about the possibility of Mormon young people falling prey to "brainwashing" influences; he's heard comments in the past about Mormons "being a cult," too. He knows that Church children attending the public schools are perceived as "different," less outgoing, and that they are subjected to teasing from the other kids. But he doesn't believe that they are any "different" than other children would be coming out of a highly insulated social environment into a skeptical (sometimes hostile) public setting.

The outsider who is perhaps most closely in touch with Church young people is the public school district superintendent. He has good working relationships with several Church officials and appreciates the extent to which Church parents seem concerned and involved with school programs. On the whole, parents are not inclined to complain or agitate but rather ask questions about policies in a positive way. As for the children, he believes that they run the gamut of ability and social behavior. His policy is to be as evenhanded as possible with Church students; they are not even officially identified on school records as coming from the Church. He acknowledges that other children soon enough discover on their own who their Church classmates are and that informal peer group teasing and heckling occur. He was consternated the previous year when, just before the opening of school in the fall, forty "out-of-district" Church children unexpectedly sought to be enrolled. This created a number of last-minute problems (e.g., adjustments of busing schedules, class sizes, etc.). A Church official told him, "We can't control everything," but the superintendent believes that it won't happen again: "Typically, when problems are brought to their attention, they deal with it and the problem dissolves." In general, he has sympathy for the difficulties associated with trying to run a small private school, as the Church is trying to do (he was once a director of a Catholic parochial school system). It's not uncommon for private schools to "dump" into the public schools students who don't measure up, he said. And it's also not unusual in this area, which supports a very mobile, transient population, for children from other backgrounds to be moving in and out of the school system (e.g., children of parents who are Yellowstone Park employees, miners, horn hunters, etc.).

The above informants have varying degrees of contact with Church members, particularly in the outlying towns, but none of them has regular contact with the Church on its own ground. The Church does have nonmember neighbors whose homes are enveloped by Church properties and activities, however, and we were curious to discover their impressions. One older couple, who have been residents in the area for over fifty years, live adjacent to the member-operated ranch kitchen and post office/convenience store at Corwin Springs. (Both of these facilities, in fact, used to be owned and operated by this couple.) Church young people are frequently around and lend assistance in a variety of chores both inside and outside of their home. The wife characterizes the children as "polite and neat." They come by the house to sing Christmas carols in December and leave a basket of flowers at the door on the first day of May. When she was in the hospital a while back, "I got a bunch of letters from [Church] first graders that were written better than what third or fourth graders could do." It "tickled us pink" when a number of Church children made the honor roll at the public school.

A second older couple live in a farm house (in which the husband was born and raised and has lived all his life) that is located across the road from a Church office complex and a Church family's private home. This couple has business dealings with the Church over water use and property that they rent to the Church. They also have occasional neighborly visits with Church people, some of whom they have come to know and like well. They have been invited to Church picnics and weddings. The member family across the road has four young children who "come over to visit us all the time. They're well-behaved, sharp kids."

We don't pretend that the impressions we have gleaned from our tiny sample of outsiders are representative of public opinion in the larger community. But they do offer a range of attitudes and beliefs about Church young people that is useful to keep in mind as we summarize some of our own direct impressions below. It does seem clear that for Montana residents living in this region who have had little or no sustained contact with the Church community as a whole (the vast majority of the region's residents), the Church and its members are viewed with alarm, hostility, and prejudice. We saw bumper stickers on local residents' cars and trucks with the letters "CUT" encircled and a line drawn through the middle. Local papers overflow with negative stories. One sixteen-year-old member told us that the news she reads in papers and sees on TV about the Church "is sickening; it really bothers me that the community is portrayed in ways that are not true." This complaint was echoed by many parents, who reported that their children were upset about being tagged as members of a "dangerous cult." One father related his personal feelings about having to conduct business in a nearby town: "You're an alien there. It feels like racism." When their son played on a Little League baseball team, people would ask where he was from. When told, "They would go, 'Ohhhhh . . .'; it was a real turnoff."

This sense of being a beleaguered and persecuted (but righteous) minority group can root itself deeply in the emergent self-conceptions of young people.

We found it revealing, for instance, to ask teenagers what were their favorite works of fiction when they had free time for reading. One older teen unhesitatingly put the Leon Uris novels *Exodus* and *Mila 18* at the top of her list, saying that she likes anything about the Jewish Holocaust, especially how groups survived in the Warsaw Ghetto underground because "it's so inspirational how they kept their faith." In a similar vein, a younger teen identified Lloyd C. Douglas's *The Robe* as her all-time favorite book. When we asked this same young woman to mention some of the people she most admired, she included Catherine the Great ("who carried on a tradition and was a strong woman leader") and Socrates ("who was ridiculed for his beliefs"). When asked about contemporary heroes, she singled out Oliver North (because "he stood up to Congress and a corrupt government; he tried to do some good and was willing to stand on his own").

Child Care and Youth Programs at the Conference

Our first opportunity to directly observe Church young people occurred in an atypical setting, namely, the yearly international conference that convenes in a magnificent alpine valley ("the Heart") encircled by craggy, snow-capped peaks. Thousands of people from all over the world with all levels of membership and religious commitment were in attendance. For the most part, we were unable to distinguish member status of conference attendees but have to assume that the bulk of our observations about child socialization during the conference involved nonstaff, and probably even non-Montana, children. Excepting preschoolers, young people were allowed to attend various adult conference sessions and workshops if they chose, but as a rule the assumption seemed to be that they would not so choose, and a multitude of alternative activities were organized for them instead.

These arrangements were truly impressive. A veritable village of large, heavy-duty army surplus tents was created for child day care and youth activities. These tents were arranged according to different age and interest levels; for example, infants, toddlers, preschoolers, elementary children, and teens; each group had its own designated tent areas and adult-supervised activities. Each tent was equipped with a fire extinguisher, a phone, first-aid kits, and large "heat tubes" that conducted forced warm air from externally generated sources (even in July, at an altitude of 6,400 feet, Montana temperatures can routinely dip into the thirties). Some of the tents were also supplied with television monitors so that the adult caregivers and supervisors, if not the children, could occasionally tune in to closed-cable broadcasting of main conference proceedings.

Tents for the younger ones replicated the appearance and functioning of well-provided nursery schools, with a plethora of toys, games, books, tables, art supplies, snack items, posted activity schedules, nap cots, and neatly lined-up hooks and shelves for stashing clothing articles. Tents for older youth were set up for more specialized activities, such as crafts, first aid, games, and religious instruction. Swings, sand boxes, jungle gyms, and other play equipment were set up outside younger ones' areas. Older youth could participate in a variety of outdoor activities, including soccer, volleyball, archery, hiking, and fishing. Specific activities were categorized under four general headings, and each category was allocated a two-hour time block during the day. According to adult supervisors, the order of popularity of these activity categories was sports first, crafts second, survival skills third, and "spiritual" last. Teacher-student ratios for these different kinds of activities were posted and carefully adhered to; for example, for field sports, the ratio was ten youngsters to one teacher; for hikes the ratio was three to one; and, for classroom situations, it was five to one.

Adult supervisors of the younger children (mostly female) were virtually all Montessori-trained teachers. (See emphasis in the Church on the Montessori method, discussed in more detail below.) They were caring, competent, and professional in their dealings with the children in their care. We observed no instance of children clinging to their parents when being dropped off nor any other expressions of reluctance on the part of children about being left in the child-care area. The second author picked up and held many of these children and found them to be relaxed and accepting, qualities not found among children who are abused or who have reasons to be fearful of adults.

Male teachers and supervisors were more visible in the areas set up for older children and teens but were no more authoritarian in their interaction style than their female counterparts. For instance, we observed one male teacher (a former GM engineer from Dearborn, Michigan) discipline a group of seven- to eleven-year-olds (mixed gender) for throwing sand. Not all the children were guilty, but all were collectively punished with a five-minute "time-out" and made to sit quietly together in a line on a log. There was no yelling, blaming, or physical handling involved in this episode. The supervisor later informed us that in instances of more severe rule violations, children would simply be dismissed from that day's activities and sent back to their parents.

The teen activity area was less obviously controlled by tight rules and scheduling; in the manner of most teens everywhere in the Western world, these young people seemed much less susceptible to regimentation and direct supervision by adults. Not that we observed dramatic expressions of rebellion and alienation, just typical teenage social behavior in large group settings. Clothing favored by Church young people was standard youth fare: jeans, cutoffs, baseball caps, and so on, with a lot of sports logos on sweatshirts, T-shirts, and jackets (e.g., of the Chicago Bulls, the Oakland Raiders, the Minnesota Twins, etc.). Indoor competitive games (Ping-Pong, skittles, goalie) flourished during rainy weather periods and aroused occasional heated arguments over points. But direct accusations of cheating were never made nor were criticisms of partners in team contests. We observed no real displays of temper or poor sportsmanship in general when games were lost, and the strongest language we heard was "Crud!" and "Dang it!"

Occasional mild forms of deviance could be observed. On one occasion outside the game tent, we overheard one twelve-year-old boy exclaim to another: "There's that smoking dude!" and they both rushed over to ask an older teenager if he had his cigarettes. Later in the day, four young teenage boys and four teenage girls were sitting around a fire getting acquainted. The content of the conversation tended toward the sarcastic and the forbidden. For instance, several mocking comments were made about health food menus: "Vegetarian burritos, so appetizing and delicious, too!" A few minutes later, two of the boys began regaling their newfound friends with the gruesome details of horror movies they had seen.

Our conference observations were technically superficial but they did suggest major disconfirmations of general stereotypes about the socialization experiences and characteristics of children and young people in the Church Universal and Triumphant. Most of the parents and teachers we had thus far been able to observe seemed to be quiet, laid-back types who were gentle with children (and each other). Young people of all ages gave the appearance of being well cared for and perfectly normal. On average they seemed better behaved than most groups of young people that one could imagine in a similar setting. Although we observed no instances of major misbehavior, it was still somehow reassuring to note the occasional deviation from idealized expectations to reassure us that these were, after all, pretty regular kids who were not so stifled that they could not give some expression to impulses disapproved of by adults. We were curious to see how these initial impressions would hold up when we had a chance, after the conference ended, to focus more specifically on children who grow up in staff households.

Formal Education in the Church System

We began with two areas of interest: the general patterns of parenting and other socialization experiences that young people are subjected to as members of the Church community at large and the more formal schooling and educational experiences of Church young people. Here, we will begin by first outlining what we learned about issues related to formal education.

The Church operates its own private school system on the ranch and had enrolled approximately two hundred K–12 students during the preceding year. As we have previously noted, a number of Church children wind up attending either public or private schools in nearby communities. Since regular school was out for the summer, we had to rely heavily on interviews with teachers, students, and parents for much of our information rather than on our own direct observations of classroom activities. However, nursery and day-care programs for infants and children up to the age of ten are available year-round to staff parents, and we were able to spend considerable time in these settings. We were also able to attend children's Sunday school classes that proved useful in affording additional insights about the education of Church youth.

The Church has ardently embraced the Montessori approach to early childhood education, preschool through grade four. Maria Montessori, in fact, has been elevated to the status of an ascended master in Church teachings. (One of Montessori's earliest and most devoted disciples, Elisabeth Caspari, is still living, at an agile-minded age of ninety-four, and is in residence in one of the Church subdivisions. She continues to be involved in teaching activities, especially music, and is widely revered and regarded as the community grandmother.) The Church is sanctioned to operate its own Montessori training program; the majority of Church preschool and elementary school teachers are, in fact, certified through this program.

Montessori methods are supplemented by other contemporary early-education philosophies and techniques that stress cognitive learning and precocious acquisition of reading skills, especially those of Glenn Doman (e.g., rapid but repeated presentations of picture and word cards to very young children; physical devices to stimulate early purposive body movements, such as crawling, etc.). Finally, the school staff includes at least one certified special education teacher who is skilled in administering and interpreting a battery of standardized intellectual, physical, behavioral, and learning disability tests.

The preschool day-care units we visited on the ranch were housed in long, mobile trailers and were extremely well equipped and organized. Children were categorized into four different age groups (i.e., infants, 16 months–2 years, 2–3 years, and 3–6 years), and each group was placed in a separate facility. The interior rooms of the trailers were immaculately clean, brightly decorated, and crammed with age-specific toys and teaching/learning devices. In keeping with the philosophies of both Montessori and Doman, emphasis was placed on sensory and experiential materials. The teacher-child ratio varied from unit to unit but in general was quite small (supplemented by older children serving as teacher aides). Teachers and their aides were all female.

Religious objects (statues of Buddha or the Virgin Mary, pictures of Jesus or El Morya, etc.) were present in most of the rooms (along with little American flags). Religious subjects were integrated into various learning activities (e.g., references to elemental spirit beings, the ascended masters, etc.). Every trailer was equipped with a small, standard Church Universal and Triumphant altar, which features a pictorial chart of the "Real Self" flanked by pictures of Jesus on the left and Saint Germain on the right.

Older elementary-age children (up to fourth-grade level) in attendance at the summer day-care program were exposed to a more diverse array of educational, religious, recreational, and work activities. The group we observed the most comprised six boys and seven girls, all between the ages of seven and ten. They were supervised by two teachers, a married couple. A typical day began with a morning devotional period of approximately forty-five minutes. Usually there would be a series of diverse prayer activities, including standard Protestant-style invocations, Catholic rosary prayers, and the Church's version of the Lord's Prayer (the "I AM" Lord's Prayer). Bible readings were also common, as were recitations of the Pledge of Allegiance and the American's Creed and singing of both religious and patriotic songs. "Decreeing" (the Church's distinctive form of affirmative chanting) appeared to be the religious activity accorded the greatest importance during the devotional period since it was the only constant over several days, and teachers were more likely to reproach children for missing decrees due to tardiness than for missing other activities.

The children were then bused (singing and decreeing en route) to some Church facility where they would spend approximately one hour participating in an organized work project. For instance, the girls might spend time in the ranch bakery helping to make "seitan" (a ubiquitous wheat-based food that serves in many Church members' diets as a meat-protein substitute). The boys might be assigned to outside cleanup tasks, such as weeding or painting. In general, the girls seemed better workers, more industrious and careful than the boys.

Recreation followed work. Somewhat warmer weather had finally arrived, and this permitted outdoor swimming on the days we observed. Rules were firmly established: No hitting while swimming; no splashing or water fights; if bumped, don't yell; no gum chewing. The children were energetic in their play; the boys, especially, were boisterous and, in spite of the rules, verged on being unruly. The teachers exercised great patience and remained generally unflappable in resolving minor conflicts and infractions. One teacher was heard to sardonically comment, "Sometimes I wish they were brainwashed robots!"

An hour was set aside for lunch, sack lunches provided, and children were allowed free-time play when they had finished eating. After lunch, the children spent an hour engaged in Kumon math drills and phonetics (outdoors, weather permitting). The day was typically concluded with a final recreational activity, such as kickball or fishing. Again, the children would be noticeable for their high spirits, but we did not observe many instances of spontaneous helping behavior or cooperation in their play.

The majority of students who enroll in the Church's private school system during the regular school year attend either the Thomas More School (grades K–6) or the Henry Wadsworth Longfellow Academy (grades 7–12). Both programs are housed in North Glastonbury, one of the Church's platted subdivisions that is located approximately twenty miles from the ranch headquarters. The principal of both schools is a graduate of the University of California, Santa Cruz, in literature and the humanities and is an impressively bright, articulate, and dedicated woman. She sees her schools as both providing a rigorous academic environment and reinforcing basic values, both civil and spiritual.

She acknowledges (with regret) that many Church parents cannot afford tuition fees (around $2,000 a year) to send their children to school here and that high academic and conduct requirements also exclude other potential students.

These students, as previously indicated (and discussed in more detail below), are then forced to enroll either in outside public schools or less costly and demanding parochial schools. All the junior high and high school teachers have college degrees. All but two of the elementary grade teachers have degrees, and these two are both Montessori certified and both close to completing their degree programs at Montana State University.

The schools are not accredited by the state, not for academic deficiencies (she claims that they easily surpass state scholastic standards, which we verified from other sources) but because of inadequate physical facilities. Severe space restrictions, for example, force them to seat as many as twenty-three students in a room designed to accommodate only eight. However, lack of accreditation has not hampered their older students from being admitted into either colleges and universities or exclusive private prep schools in other parts of the country. Students begin PSAT testing as early as the ninth grade and typically score satisfactory to very high on their final SAT and GED tests. Currently nine of their high school students have been accepted as transfers to East Coast prep schools, and they have previously graduated a number of students directly into a number of prestigious colleges and universities.

Rules at the schools are strict, and their violation may lead to expulsion. It goes without saying that drugs, alcohol, and sexual activity are forbidden. A general honor code prevails that targets cheating, lying, and stealing. In addition, the schools also enforce Church policies that prohibit listening (or dancing) to rock music, early dating, swearing, or consumption of candy or other sugar-laced foods. Elementary-grade children wear uniforms, which the principal would like to extend to the upper grades as well. She would also like to rule against students' watching TV during the week. (Significant parent and student resistance to these last two restrictions render them unlikely to be implemented.)

As with the Montessori program, religious education and practice are incorporated into the curriculum. A major building in the school system is actually the Glastonbury chapel, in which subdivision residents conduct early morning, evening, and weekend religious services. And so students are surrounded by the visible symbols of their faith. However, compulsory, supervised decreeing sessions were recently dropped from the school day when older students complained and voted against mandatory decreeing. The curriculum has always included a comparative religious studies component in which students read about and discuss the basic tenets of Hinduism, Buddhism, Islam, Judaism, Christianity, and even agnosticism.

The single most disruptive force underlying student problems in the Church schools, according to the principal, is divorce of parents. She estimates that divorce among parents throughout the Church community is at least as high as the national average, perhaps as high as 50 percent. Some of the children in the schools have gone through two or three different stepfathers with visible negative impact. Typically, it is the mother who retains custody of the children, and in the principal's experience, it is generally the sons of single mothers who become problem cases in the school. She and her staff provide some counseling for students experiencing personal difficulties, but she also makes referrals to licensed therapists (of whom there are several, some with advanced degrees, on the Church staff). She believes that girls, especially between the ages of eleven and fourteen, are more likely to benefit from this counseling but that boys typically do not benefit from counseling until later in their teens.

We talked to several teenagers who had attended the Church schools for varying lengths of time and with varying degrees of success. One mature and musically talented sixteen-year-old girl had just recently been accepted as a transfer student from Longfellow Academy to Berkshire School, a college prep school in Massachusetts; we asked her to reflect on some of her experiences in the Church school system. She was born into "the teachings" and had lived in Montana since 1982. She believed that the Church academic program is accelerated a year ahead of the public schools, based on her acceptance at Berkshire and her comparative experiences with non-Church students while attending Montana State–sponsored educational activities. She does well on standardized tests and loves to read, especially historical novels, which she consumes "by the dozen." She expressed great admiration for the school principal, who "has such staying power and cares so much, trying to keep the school together and dealing with certain obnoxious kids." She thinks that some of the "obnoxious" students are those whose parents bring them here to live after they have already become accustomed to attending public schools, and they are resentful at having to leave their old friends. "But for those who are born here, this is their life and home."

She affirmed the school's receptivity to a certain amount of student and parental input, citing the change in decreeing requirements as an example. Elizabeth Clare Prophet visits the schools, she said, and has private sessions with the students in which they are supposed to express their concerns regarding rules, unfair teaching practices, and so on. She doesn't think that students always fully speak their minds on these occasions but states that "Mother is open and knows how to talk to kids" (since she has raised four of her own).

Among her several anxieties about attending Berkshire in the fall were the fears that she wouldn't fit in and that she might be teased. Her parents had admonished her to stay away from alcohol, drugs, and the wrong crowd. It helped to know that several of her good friends would also be attending other prep schools in the same general vicinity (her best friend, for instance, had been accepted to Groton), but mostly she would be on her own for the first time and "just have to use my own good judgment." In some ways, her school experiences had not prepared her for going outside. For instance, she had never been on a date with a boy. She had received some general counseling at school about boy-girl relationships, including some role-playing sessions about how to handle certain situations that might come up. But these hypothetical experiences did not inspire confidence now in her actual ability to interact appropriately with members of the opposite sex. Last year, a few teens "got interested in each other," which subsequently got them into trouble with teachers, who "kept tabs on them to make sure they were kept apart." She loves to dance, but only ballroom dancing is allowed, and in fact she has danced only with her father and other adults on Church-sponsored occasions.

Church Children Attending Public Schools

Emblematic of a different kind of educational experience was another young woman who had attended the Church school the first two years her family lived in Montana. Then, as a ninth grader, she transferred to a public high school in one of the neighboring towns, where she completed the final four years of her secondary education. Classes at the Church school were demanding and the rules were strict (more so then, she thinks, than currently). At that time, the school was just starting up and many of the students were trying to make adjustments from the previous schools they had attended. Only a relatively small proportion of the kids then, she said, were "totally straight" about observing all the rules. For instance, a number of her friends would buy Walkman cassette players and pass around "underground" tapes of forbidden rock music. She didn't obtain a Walkman herself, but she did pretend occasionally to be sick so she could stay home and listen to rock on her family's stereo. Sometimes the "neat kids," according to peer assessment, were the rebellious ones. She remembers, for instance, being intrigued by a girl who bleached her hair, wore several earrings "bigger than quarters" and had an attitude: "I'm here; you can like me or not."

When she entered the public schools, she found that she and her other Church friends who also transferred were a year ahead in standard subjects like algebra. While she didn't pretend to be an outstanding student (she continued having some difficulty in science and math), she observed that many of the public school students did not read very well or very much. She contrasted this to her own delight in reading (she checks out books "ten at a time" from the library) and the emphasis that the Church school had placed on vocabulary and exposure to more advanced literature, such as classical Greek plays.

The social transition was much more difficult than the academic, and she would come home crying almost every day for a year. The public school students were "real negative towards the Church"; they would call her and the other Church transfers "gurus" and generally mock them about their beliefs. In defense some of the Church students would covertly hide their religious identity or overtly deny being members or even adopt the mores of their public-school peers. When the big Yellowstone fire threatened Church land in 1988, she and other Church students went up for several days to help "pray the fire away."

Upon return to the high school, the nonmember students teased them unmercifully and called them "spiritual firefighters." The teachers, she said, seemed mostly fair. Once, however, one teacher did "go around the room asking kids to say what their religion was," and she got "booed" when it came her turn. She had only one non-Church friend during her years at the high school, a Hare Krishna girl; she was never invited to any parties or other social events outside of school.

She and her Church peers did participate in some extracurricular school activities, such as speech and debate, choir, and athletics. During her senior year, she wanted to attend the homecoming dance. Her mother was opposed, but she went to Elizabeth Clare Prophet for advice: Yes, she should go. She was a senior and "should be a shining example." She wondered how she could be a "shining example," since she didn't know how to dance, but she was just excited about the prospect of dressing up and being there. Other Church girls also went, accompanied by some of their mothers, including her own. A general let-down ensued. She felt ambivalent about the loud rock music being played and the kind of dancing that was mostly occurring, especially with the mothers present. No one asked her to dance, and all the Church girls "huddled together in a mass."[2]

General Parenting and Socialization Issues

Although the *very earliest* members were older people with families, the Church Universal and Triumphant (originally known as the Summit Lighthouse) did not, as it began to expand, attract proportionately large numbers of converts with already established families. Nor did this movement initially emphasize in its teachings and organizational thrust the specific needs of families and the problems associated with child rearing. Many of the earlier members joined the Church as young adults who were engaged in a personal quest for spiritual meaning through ascetic and mystical processes. In the words of one early devotee (now on staff, married, and a father of four): "In the beginning, this was primarily a singles community of monks and nuns." The gradual accretion of marital relationships and children, however, forced increasing recognition of a host of family issues, particularly after the Church moved its headquarters from Malibu, California, to Montana in 1986.

A number of structural problems have made the transition to family concerns rather difficult for the Church, especially for staff and members living at or near Church headquarters (versus the majority of Church affiliates who are dispersed in secular communities around the world). One is the intense commitment expected of staff in both the fulfillment of their organizational jobs (often multiple) and the continuation of their higher-level spiritual quests. These are commitments that, when faithfully performed, consume an enormous amount of time and energy and make child rearing more problematic. Some informants also mentioned the disparity of child-rearing standards among members hailing from dif-

Elizabeth Clare Prophet in December 1993.
(Courtesy of Kali Productions)

ferent cultural traditions. Another problem is the level of opposition encountered in surrounding communities. At the very least, to the degree that Church young people come into contact with outsiders, it constitutes a kind of "countercultural" allure that parents may find particularly hard to contend with. This conflict is exacerbated when newly arrived parents bring with them older children who may resent being uprooted from familiar environments in the secular world.

Financial concerns pose an especially vexing problem for most members in Montana. Staff members are offered free housing and meals on the ranch, but most are paid only nominally for their work, and many take on evening and/or part-time jobs outside of the Church to scrape together more income. This subtracts even more time and energy from direct family involvements. (A number of nonstaff members who move into nearby communities also experience great financial anxiety due to lack of employment opportunities.) Personal austerity is prized as a virtue by many Church members, especially singles. But family obligations markedly intrude upon this ideal, especially among people who are above average in educational attainment and who tend to entertain high expectations for their children's own educational development.

Given the complexity, diversity, and structural pressures operating in this environment, we were not surprised to encounter people, both youngsters and adults, who expressed varying levels of concern about the growing-up experiences imposed upon young people in the Church. At the same time we were also informed of (and noted on our own) many positive characteristics of youth socialization, some of which we have already alluded to. In our discussion here, we will first summarize some of the specific problem areas brought to our attention, with a primary focus on older children and teens. We will then address several positive programmatic responses of the Church in attempting to deal with some of these problems.

Episodes of juvenile delinquency have occasionally flared up on the ranch. According to a member who is a former big-city police officer and now serves as an informal liaison between the county sheriff and some of the outlying

Church subdivisions, the delinquent acts typically involve only a few young people and are on a relatively small scale: vandalism, "joyriding," shoplifting, and such. ("They don't have any idea what 'bad' really is up here.") She strongly advocates turning the kids over to local authorities when actual crimes are committed and has been strongly criticized by some parents for so doing. She says that a few parents are very defensive and don't usually do anything to correct their kids when problems are brought to their attention. Reasons advanced for this neglect are poor parenting skills, single-parent homes, and a failure on the part of a few non-American citizens to take seriously American laws.

As far as we could see, the vast majority of deviance on the part of Church young people, when it does occur, does not involve breaking civil laws but rather resisting certain Church beliefs and rules. A repeated theme in this regard is the Church's prohibition against musical forms that feature a heavy beat (including some jazz and country-western, but most emphatically, rock and roll). Several teenagers admitted to us that they surreptitiously listen to rock and other popular music, some with considerable feelings of guilt conflicting with the thrill of the forbidden. Others experienced little if any ambivalence about the music per se, enjoyed it, and felt no actual harm to themselves from listening to it. All of them agreed that this is perhaps the single most onerous restriction placed upon them and the one most widely flouted.

Another source of tension for older teens on the ranch is the Church's restrictive policy regarding boy-girl relationships. As already mentioned, many Church young people, especially those "born into the teachings" and the children of staff, have never been on a date with a member of the opposite sex. Indeed, it is only within the last year that young people over fourteen were officially allowed to "go out" (parental permission must be obtained first). Some of the young people we talked to had not taken advantage of this relaxed policy, either because they felt residual awkwardness or because they claimed that no acceptable age partners were available: "I've gone to some mixed boy-girl activities, chaperoned by adults, off the ranch [e.g., bowling, movies]. The guys were younger and as obnoxious as my own brother." One young woman who was home for the summer from her freshman year at a Midwestern college said that she gets nervous around boys and turned down a request at school to go on a date. According to our informants, several girls over the years have gotten pregnant "off the ranch" immediately after they "dropped out of the teachings" and began associating with outsider boys.

There does seem to be a paucity of older teens on the ranch and environs compared to younger children. In part, this may be due simply to the demographics of younger families. But in part, it is also the case, as we were informed by both young people and adults alike, that many older teens do leave the Church community. One young woman in her late teens reported that of ten friends she originally started with on the ranch, only one was still around by that summer.

Some depart, as we have seen, because their parents send them away to school. Others find paying jobs in the neighboring towns on weekends, after school, and during vacations. Older teens often wind up leaving and living with the divorced parent who may also be religiously estranged from the Church. The chance to get away from an insular community with restrictive rules and to "experiment without pressure to conform," as one young person put it, may appeal to some. One teenager told us that younger children on the ranch tend to be "oohed over and interacted with a lot by adults, but the teens are ignored." The adults seem "to be afraid of them," don't know how to handle them, are overly critical, and "don't think you can be a good chela" [spiritual student and devotee of a guru]. Another teen admitted that she doesn't talk frequently with her parents about many issues because "everybody's so busy," and "in my dad's family, you solved your own problems."

As an essentially theocratic society, the Church can enunciate and impose radical new programs of great scope that are widely complied with by faithful followers. Some of these programs may have significant socialization implications for children and young people. One such program was the construction of fallout shelters on the ranch during the late 1980s, culminating in the "shelter cycle" period of spring 1990, when intensive preparations were made for nuclear war in an atmosphere of expectation that such a war might be about to commence. This was a seminal experience for the Church in many ways; here we wish only to suggest some of its impact on the young. This impact was at least threefold: First, a number of children and teens were precipitously moved from all around the world into the Montana environment by parents who were anxious to secure a haven for their family's safety. Some of these families departed disillusioned and in debt when war did not occur, but some remained and have struggled to achieve viable economic well-being in the area. Second, these events aroused international media coverage and dramatically heightened local suspicions and antagonism. Church children attending public and parochial schools were subjected to even more ridicule and ostracism. Third, actual experiences associated with the shelter cycle traumatized a number of children, made others cynical, and for some offered lessons in cooperation and community responsibility.

One young woman we talked to was sixteen years old and in eleventh grade at a public high school in 1990. She said she lost her shyness after going through the "drills." She worked night shifts helping to get things ready for the main staff shelter and was placed in charge of a radiation door for her unit. These preliminaries seemed fun and exciting. It was "like a war zone, with bright lights and people wearing camouflage and helmets." Trial-run alarms were given without prior warning on different occasions. By the last time it had ceased being fun. Staff entered their assigned shelter areas and strapped themselves into bunks to prevent the possibility of being tossed by shock waves and earth tremors. Church leaders radioed each shelter subunit, and it all sounded very serious. "It was so

The heart of the inner retreat near the Church Universal and Triumphant's controversial fallout shelters. (*Courtesy of Kali Productions*)

scary" at this point that she thought it was "really going to happen. You could hear praying up and down the halls and a lady crying." She thought she would never see her outside friends and relatives again. People were "hugging, kissing, and crying with relief the next morning." Some kissed the ground when they left the shelter. A young man who was also a teen at the time (and is now a graduate student in computer science at Duke University) recounted similar experiences to us. On the one hand, young people helped out substantially and were integrated into the whole process. On the other hand, there was confusion and a letdown for everyone, including the kids: "What did it all mean? Why are we here?"

Church Responses to Parenting and Socialization Needs

A number of significant changes in Church policies and orientations appear to have emerged since the grim times of the shelter-cycle period. Those most affecting young people include an increasing emphasis on development of parenting skills, more released time for staff with children, establishment of ties to national youth programs, the possibility of revamping the Church's own internal youth apprenticeship program, and the expanding role and influence of staff psychologists and therapists.

Elizabeth Clare Prophet had, in response to concerns expressed by staff psychologists, recently become a particularly forceful advocate of adult member participation in standard, formal programs (such as STEP and STET) that are designed to improve effective parenting skills. Parenting workshops are now regularly held at the Ranch, and we talked to many parents who participated in them and seemed to be taking the lessons to heart. (One wry commentary was noted in the form of a *Calvin and Hobbes* cartoon pinned to the cafeteria bulletin board at ranch headquarters: "What assurance do I have that your parenting isn't screwing me up?") A related emphasis on discovering and responding to "the inner child" has also become pervasive (although for many this may dovetail more with personal searches for spiritualized self-insights than with concrete child-rearing practices). Several staff parents also expressed relief that the Church has finally implemented their requests for more released time to be with children during the working day, pointing to this previous lack as one of the contributing factors in staff burnout and parent-child alienation. Staff members can also take weekends off from work and two weeks for vacation; more vacation days can be saved by working on weekends.

We were mildly surprised to discover that the Church operates a nationally sanctioned Boy Scout program and also offers programs for Explorers and Brownies. (Unfortunately, some local Scout groups in the surrounding communities have thus far refused to participate in Church-sponsored Scouting events on the ranch.) The Church has also begun actively participating in such youth antidrug programs as QUEST. For years the Church has run an apprenticeship program for children of staff in which young people are assigned work tasks in various adult occupational areas. For instance, one girl we talked to had assisted in the graphics department in publications, a second did filing in a slide library, and a third put in time at the ranch cafeteria and learned how to prepare macrobiotic meals. The normal expectation in these jobs is eight hours of work a week during the school year and twenty hours a week during vacation periods. Apparently this program has failed to generate much enthusiasm among teens. Although one girl described her job as a technical aide in planning and engineering as "neat," many find their particular assignments tedious and, above all, financially unrewarding—they are not paid. (This reaction does not seem very different from that of adolescents found everywhere who chafe at having to carry out unredeemed family chores.) To avoid this community obligation in the summer, some teens cajole their parents into farming them out to relatives or subscribing them into various summer camps.

Perhaps the single most unexpected general attitude we encountered among many adults we talked to was their professed openness about exposing children to a diversity of religious views (if not secular activities) and respect for free choice in making confessions of religious faith. One young married woman from out of state who attended the conference assured us that she and her husband would "not force religion" on their children. She knew about "the problems with the kids of staff" but then dismissed these problems as "just them feeling their oats the same as any other kids." Another nonstaff conference visitor stressed the concept of free will, which parents "must allow their children to express." She cited Elizabeth Clare Prophet as an example with her own family: "Her oldest daughter was disaffected [until recently], but this is typical of most families—you can't force anyone."

Several staff parents expressed similar views. One mother asserted that her "kids are not weird; we're trying to give them a normal life." She and her husband allow their children to engage in a variety of "outside" activities, such as Little League baseball for their son. A father told us that he and his wife were "equipping our children to make their own choices. Our parents didn't tell us what to do; we want the same for our own kids." Elaborating on this same theme, yet another mother, who has already "lost" one teenage daughter in a custody settlement with her ex-husband, knows that "kids have to make choices. We did, when we were kids. They're better off than us with our drugs and smoking; they can step off from a better foundation. You just have to have faith that they're going to be all right."

A few parents even expressed willingness to relinquish Church commitments in favor of their children's perceived welfare. One single mother told us that "nothing is more important to me than my children; not beliefs, Church, anything." Although she didn't think it likely, she vowed that "if the government ever attacked us [as in the Waco siege], I would be out of here in a minute." A disgruntled father was considering leaving the community because he wanted a different lifestyle for his family: "I want my daughter to be able to use all colors and not be told that red and black are bad, to be able to watch TV and have my daughter taught about dinosaurs and liberal ideas."

EPILOGUE

We noted that many of the parents who spoke to us were not just expressing a willingness to be flexible about their children's religious choices; they seemed philosophically resigned to the strong possibility that their older sons and daughters would, in fact, eventually drop out of the Church. All our sources—adult and youth, staff and nonstaff—suggested to us that this tends to be empirically the case: Relatively few young people beyond high school age have elected to join staff or remain otherwise within the Montana Church community. This doesn't necessarily mean, of course, that these young people become literal religious defectors. Operating in the Church environment, as we have seen, is a host of pragmatic forces that combine to push the young away from the community. When this happens, they may continue to associate with Church study centers in other cities around the country where they are, for instance, attending school or finding employment.

But our sense is that many of these young men and women do markedly decrease their religious commitments and identity. Many of them are the children of well-educated parents who entertain ambitions for the advanced technical training of their offspring. These are children whose cognitive and intellectual growth has been made an object of paramount concern but who have seemingly not been provided with commensurate socioemotional experiences of the sort that bind people to primary groups.

If this is true, it poses a potentially serious problem for the long-term stability and success of the Church. Unlike certain other new religious movements, the Church Universal and Triumphant does not emphasize a strategy of rigorous recruitment. People are typically attracted to and join the Church on the basis of preformulated interests in esoteric religious subjects that are further stimulated when they happen across some of the voluminous literature produced by the Church. Should this predisposed audience begin to shrink, there may not remain enough internal generational growth to counter the loss.

Of course it may be the case that the Church, as an international spiritual movement with an emphasis on acquiring mystical knowledge and personal spiritual fulfillment in one's own locale, can continue functioning very well with only a relatively small number of dedicated adult staff members who cycle in and out of Church headquarters as they are financially and otherwise able to do so. But to secure the ideal of a concrete, family-based religious community that will guide the world into a New Age, requires, we believe, that the Church discover structural mechanisms that will increase the longterm loyalty of its children.

NOTES

1. In this chapter, we have often chosen to use "Church" with a capital "C" to stand in for the longer title, Church Universal and Triumphant. It would be even more economical, of course, to simply use the initials, "CUT," which is in fact widely done. However, the CUT designation has been employed so frequently in a derogatory context by local Montana critics and opponents that it has acquired a pejorative connotation for many Church members.

2. It should be noted that not all public school experiences have been this negative. For example, the son of a Church member was a member of the football team at a nearby public high school and homecoming king as well.

CHRISTIANITY AND THE NEW AGE

17

A CHRISTIAN RESPONSE TO THE NEW AGE

John A. Saliba

The emergence and success of the New Age movement (NAM) in the last decade have generated a lot of discussion among Christians of all denominations. Because the New Age worldview seems to permeate all aspects of culture, it has raised many theological and pastoral issues which must be addressed. There is no doubt that Christians should be legitimately concerned about the influence it might have on their faith and morals.

The Christian response to the NAM is especially difficult because it is by no means easy to specify what the New Age is all about. Descriptions of the New Age by adherents[1] and scholars[2] alike tend to be idealistic, highlighting its more acceptable ideological aspects. But when one looks into its specific beliefs and practices, one is overwhelmed by the diversity and complexity of its theological views and ritual practices.[3] And because the New Age is characterized by a lack of a central organization or specific creed, a rather diffuse leadership, and different types and degrees of involvement and commitment, a uniform Christian reply to the NAM as a whole may not even be feasible. Unfortunately, Christian replies to the NAM have often been determined by the consideration of some of its more negative features that are assumed to be typical of its ideology and ritual.

One of the main reasons why the NAM has encountered so much opposition is not only because it proposes an alternative religious worldview that cannot be

From *The Way: Review of Contemporary Christian Spirituality* 33, no. 3 (July 1993): 222–32. Copyright © 1993 by *The Way*. Reprinted by kind permission of *The Way*, a journal of contemporary spirituality published by the British Jesuits.

easily reconciled with Christianity, but also because it endorses a reinterpretation of several major Christian themes, such as the nature of Jesus Christ and his place in the history of religions. Moreover, many New Age writers tend to depict Christianity as a spiritually bankrupt and intolerant religion that is more interested in safeguarding doctrine than catering to the real needs of the people.[4] Such attacks are bound to elicit both apologetic arguments in defense of traditional faith and reciprocal charges against the New Age itself.

CHRISTIAN FUNDAMENTALIST RESPONSE TO THE NEW AGE

The initial and most vociferous rebuttals of the NAM have come from fundamentalist or evangelical Christians[5] who have interpreted its popular appeal and success as a significant threat to the survival of Christianity. Two broad approaches to the New Age can be detected among these Christians. The first, spearheaded by Constance Cumbey's[6] and David Hunt's[7] virulent denunciations of the movement, can be described more accurately as a hysterical tirade against all New Age ideas and activities, irrespective of their worth.

Cumbey assures her readers that the NAM is not only a serious deviation from orthodoxy but also a demonic conspiracy aimed at destroying Christianity itself. She lumps the movement with Nazism and secular humanism and condemns it as the antithesis of Christian belief and morality. Apparently oblivious to such pitfalls as historical anachronism, she subsumes under the New Age everything she disagrees with, including the ecumenical movement, holistic health centers, humanistic psychology, and the Montessori schools.

This approach has become typical of many Christian arguments against the New Age. Additional and unsubstantiated charges are brought forth in support of the theory that the New Age is a demonic conspiracy to destroy Christianity by infiltrating all aspects of human life, be they political, educational, or religious. Christians themselves are being subtly inundated with New Age ideas. The leaders of the movement are sometimes judged to be self-consciously in league with Satan.[8] Some writers[9] hold that New Agers are "immoral" because of their belief in reincarnation, which is wrongly linked with witchcraft. Others[10] go as far as to accuse New Agers of performing bloody human sacrifices.

The second fundamentalist technique to counteract the teachings of the NAM concentrates on the theology of the movement and endeavors to evaluate it in the light of biblical teachings. This strategy is also apologetic, but it refrains from making preposterous accusations against the New Age. It strives for a more balanced and fair evaluation of the movement. Douglas Grootius,[11] a leading representative of this approach, spends some time analyzing New Age theology and concludes that it is characterized by a monistic worldview that is in sharp contrast with orthodox Christianity. By postulating that the movement has sociological roots in the counterculture of the 1960s and 1970s, he de-emphasizes the theory that it is a satanic plot to overthrow Christianity. And by remarking that the NAM does offer hope in a hopeless world, he indirectly suggests that it has some beneficial features that may account for its popularity and success.

Other writers[12] continue the traditional fundamentalist approach to contrast the teachings of the NAM with those of the Bible and discover, to nobody's surprise, that the movement's religious ideology deviates from biblical texts. And while the tendency remains to condemn the movement lock, stock, and barrel, some[13] have admitted, however, that it has focused our attention on a number of issues that Christians have lost sight of or misunderstood. Most fundamentalist writings on the NAM spur Christians to counteract its activities belligerently, although a few have advised Christians to be more prudent and less confrontational.[14]

The fundamentalist assault on the New Age contains some valuable critique of the New Age.[15] But this critique is frequently overshadowed both by the polemical tone of its writings and by poor scholarship. Unfortunately, to many fundamentalist writers, the New Age has become a convenient label for what they have judged to be not only unorthodox but also inherently evil. Christian apologists often portray little understanding of the causes of the movement and show even less talent for discriminating between its laudable and faddish elements. They are reluctant to recognize that the movement has positive features and that discrimination between, for instance, its desire to preserve the environment and its magical rituals is necessary. Moreover, their emotional outbursts and angry recriminations have little pastoral value. Their persistent and repetitive outcries are not likely to convince New Agers to return to their previous religious affiliations or to help Christians in their task of making their faith relevant in the fast-changing socioeconomic conditions of the end of the second millennium.

MAINLINE PROTESTANT RESPONSES

The mainline Protestant Christian reaction to the NAM has also been preoccupied with its teachings. Like the fundamentalist perspective, it has drawn attention to the gnostic elements of the movement and stressed their incompatibility with traditional Christian doctrine. Mainline Protestant writers, however, tend to ignore or reject the satanic conspiracy theory. Their responses are geared to make Christians reflect theologically on, rather than react emotionally against, the presence and influence of New Age ideas and practices. They further see some benefits stemming from the movement.

Richard Thompson, reflecting a United Methodist Church perspective, acknowledges that the New Age preaches hope in confusing times and that it has "come rushing in to fill the void left by the decline of Christianity and secular humanism."[16] He berates its evolutionary credo and is more concerned with pointing out how it radically differs from Christianity. He never specifies what answers a committed Christian can give to the movement, though it is apparent that he leans toward confrontation.

More thoughtful evaluations of the New Age, however, have led several commentators to abandon the idea that it epitomizes the antithesis of Christianity. Philip Almond,[17] for example, writing in an Anglican magazine, states that the movement is a revival of the Western esoteric tradition which has sometimes existed in creative tension with orthodox Christianity. The New Age's concern for the environment is based not only on its pantheistic slant, but also on a millenarian vision of a world in which all living creatures exist in perfect harmony.[18] When seen as "a reaction to the technological rationalism and materialism of late twentieth century culture," and as a religious movement that "re-establishes the connection between the mundane and the transcendent,"[19] the New Age has something to teach those Christians who have been swept away by the secularization process in Western culture.

One of the most elaborate and comprehensive Christian attempts to deal with the New Age is that of Ted Peters, who teaches at the Lutheran School of Theology in Berkeley, California. Peters suggests that four propositions or theses should guide Christians in their encounter with the NAM. He asserts that 1) "modest dabbling in New Age spirituality is probably harmless; it may even be helpful"; 2) "the New Age vision is a noble and edifying one"; 3) "pastors, theologians and church leaders should take the New Age movement seriously"; and 4) "the gnostic monism at the heart of the New Age teaching is dangerous because it leads to naiveté and to a denial of God's grace."[20]

Ted Peters's treatment attempts a balanced assessment which, while recognizing the New Age's merits, pays attention to those teachings that make it a distinct religion. His approach is more ecumenical. Though still worried about doctrinal matters, it avoids hysterical outcries and fearful condemnations. Besides recognizing what is good in the movement, it looks for areas where Christians can learn from, and cooperate with, those involved in the New Age.

CATHOLIC RESPONSES

The Catholic answer to the New Age has been varied and contradictory. Some Catholic writers have, in fact, embraced the method and tone of Christian fundamentalists who repudiate anything connected with the NAM and who find little or nothing in it that can benefit Christian theology and/or spirituality. Rejecting in spirit, if not in word, an ecumenical perspective, they envisage the New Age largely as a threat to orthodoxy and orthopraxis.

Among the most comprehensive Catholic conservative assessments of the

NAM is that of Ralph Rath.[21] He starts by providing a broad picture of the various elements that compose the New Age scene. He then detects the inroads the movement has made in the fields of cults, religion, education, politics, science, health, business, and entertainment. Finally, he outlines a Christian rebuttal that is aimed largely at those New Age doctrines that are in conflict with Christianity.

Rath is one of the few commentators on the New Age who refers to interreligious dialogue. Yet he exhibits little understanding of the requirements of dialogue and even less appreciation of the fact that dialogue is basically a relationship between individuals who have embarked on a religious quest. At one point he states that "the New Age is based on deception. This is certainly allied to the satanic."[22] Such statements reiterate the familiar anticult rhetoric that indiscriminately lumps together all non-Christian groups (such as transcendental meditation, yoga, contemporary paganism, and satanic cults). They are definitely not conducive to dialogue. Rath, moreover, fails to find any points of contact between the New Age and Christianity. In his final two chapters on basic Christian teachings and evangelization, he relies completely on fundamentalist literature. Although he correctly draws attention to the fact that the New Age religion differs from Christianity in doctrine, he overstresses the pantheistic element in the former and fails to make any reference to Christian teachings on the indwelling of the Holy Spirit and divinization. And he omits any reference to the rich tradition of Christian mysticism. Apparently unaware of the changing cultural and religious worldview of the late twentieth century, his response to the New Age is bound to be unconstructive and ineffective and is likely to achieve nothing but to buttress the convictions of those who already share his opinions.

A similar, though much more personal, approach to the New Age is that of Mitch Pacwa[23] who appears to have embarked, for a while at least, on a conversion career[24] from involvement in drugs, to astrology, the Enneagram, and other New Age fads. His final conversion to the charismatic movement led him to realize that all his previous experiments were completely opposed to Christian doctrine. While some of Pacwa's critical remarks, for example, those on astrology, Jungian psychology, and Matthew Fox's creation spirituality, are valid, they are deficient for the precise reason that they make no mention of their attractive features that can be reconciled with Christian doctrine. He does not follow the official procedures of dialogue that the Catholic Church has adopted since Vatican II. The way he deals with Jung is typical of the method that builds walls of separation rather than bridges to understanding. Pacwa rightly reminds his readers of Jung's personal antipathy to Christianity and mythological interpretation of the major Christian articles of faith. He then adds: "My problems with Jung do not necessarily stem from the psychological insights he offers. In the hands of a professional, these can be useful for personal growth."[25] Surely, this is the very area that requires further study and development.[26] It is Jung's original psychological insights, his appreciation of spiritual matters, and his sensitivity toward the individual's religious quest that account to a large extent for the revival of interest in his works.

Both Pacwa and Rath, together with the majority of Catholic writers on the NAM, explicitly reject the satanic conspiracy theory, even though a few indirectly seem to admit that satanic influence is present. They are convinced that the movement is the antithesis of Christian belief with few, if any, redeeming qualities. Their approach revolves around the identification of false doctrine conceived as a list of static propositional truth statements. These authors tend to evaluate New Age teachings in the light of conservative Catholic theology. They write as if theological development has already come to an end. They consequently make little attempt to discover and build on common ground.

In contrast to Rath's and Pacwa's somewhat superficial handling of, and response to, the New Age, David Toolan's erudite and highly sophisticated analysis[27] is in a class by itself. Toolan, like Pacwa, was personally involved in the New Age scene but on a deeper and more intellectual level. He considers the quest for meaning and healing, which are central to New Age consciousness, as being rooted in both Eastern and Western contemplative and mystical traditions. He therefore sees a continuity between Christian thought and some philosophical and theological trends in the New Age. Uniting modern developments in philosophy, psychology, physics, and cosmology, Toolan looks toward future developments in Christian theology that would incorporate the best elements of the New Age.[28] He faults the New Age for its idealism and self-centeredness and accuses the movement of having a "claustrophobic, inbred quality characteristic of sects concerned only with saving club-members' own skins."[29] In agreement with many Christian and non-Christian critics, he dismisses the crystal-gazers and psychic channellers as "the lunatic fringe."[30]

Writing for a much more general audience than Toolan, George Maloney[31] adopts an ecumenical perspective to the influx of New Age ideas. Like Toolan, he is willing to learn from the NAM. He accepts some basic insights from Jungian psychology on which, he believes, a Christian spirituality can be built. Rather than advocating a total rejection of the New Age, he looks for areas in the movement that can be positively related to the Christian tradition. He thinks that the New Age's holistic vision of the universe and the role of humanity in it can be harmonized with Christian thought. Moreover, certain elements of the New Age, like the stress on good nutrition, the avoidance of drugs, and the respect for the environment, can all be grounded in Christian theology. He berates the New Age's view of Jesus and its pantheistic theology. But he points out that several aspects of New Age theology are redirecting Christians to traditional theological themes that have been neglected. New Age theology points to the Christian doctrines of Christ the "logos" and the immanence of God. The New Age is fulfilling an important function: it is helping Christians rediscover the richness of their tradition.

The most comprehensive official response to the NAM is probably Cardinal Godfried Danneels's pastoral letter on new religious movements, a letter that includes a large section on the New Age, which is called a "new religion."[32] While criticizing the New Age for its egocentric worldview and its syncretism, the pastoral letter does not link it with satanism and much less with a satanic conspiracy. It admits that

> the New Age also offers good things: a sense of universal brotherhood, peace and harmony, raising people's awareness, a commitment to bettering the world, a general mobilization of energies for the sake of good, etc. Nor are all the techniques they advocate bad: yoga and relaxation can have many good effects.[33]

The letter's tone suggests that the New Age gives alternative answers to humankind's religious quest. It hints that there are several points of contact, such as mysticism, between the New Age and Christianity. It concedes that the New Age criticism of Christianity may not be completely unfounded.[34] Its stress, however, is still on those doctrinal issues that make the New Age incompatible with Christianity. And it offers little speculation on what the New Age can contribute to Christian theology and spirituality.

A similar approach is taken by Archbishop Edward A. McCarthy of Miami. In a pastoral instruction titled "The New Age Movement," he asserts that "many of the elements of the New Age Movement are altogether incompatible with Christianity."[35] But he then explicitly recognizes many of the movement's positive features and observes "that actually the Catholic Church offers many of the answers which New Agers are seeking."[36] The New Age's reaction to scientific rationalism, its integration of matter and spirit, and its stress on mystical experiences are solidly based in the Church's tradition. Spiritual seekers need not look outside the Church in their quest for peace, harmony, and union with God.

TOWARD A CHRISTIAN RESPONSE TO THE NEW AGE

An effective and relevant response to the New Age must be compatible with the principles of interreligious dialogue. Dialogue, while admitting that there are doctrinal and moral differences between diverse faith perspectives, seeks understanding and cooperation and avoids confrontations and harangues.

Whether the current apologetic attacks against the NAM have a measurable impact on its popularity is debatable. The refutation of its philosophical and theological premises and the ridiculing of its magical beliefs (like those concerning the healing powers of crystals) and practices (like channeling) probably have little effect on those already committed to them. Livid condemnation of New Age ideas, blanket accusations of satanic involvement, and emotional tirades against its ritual practices are more likely to reinforce New Agers' dislike of and attacks on Chris-

Some New Age groups adopt Christian beliefs. Rev. Patricia Talis in front of the emblem of the New Age Bible and Philosophy Center, a winged cross. (*Courtesy of Heline Corinne Books*)

tianity.[37] The reasons why the popularity of the New Age has already peaked and might also be waning is due more to the problems endemic to the movement itself than to outside factors.[38] There is no doubt, however, that even if the NAM will not survive, it has already left its mark on contemporary religion and culture. Thus, for example, Jungian psychology and holistic health, both of which are an integral part of New Age, have been incorporated in retreat programs and have influenced many Christians seeking growth in their spiritual lives.

A Christian evaluation of the New Age must be guided both by understanding and discernment. The following guidelines should contribute to a better assessment of New Age ideas and practices:

1. Critique of NAM must rely on informed sources and must be conducted in an academic manner. The need to clarify, explain, and defend, when necessary, Christian doctrine must be attended to. But the Church's pastoral ministry must devise more positive ways of relating to and influencing those individuals attracted to the New Age.

2. Refutation of New Agers' arguments that certain beliefs (such as reincarnation) are compatible with Christianity has its proper place. It is also

important, however, to point out that many New Age ideas are hardly alien to Christian theology.[39]

3. General condemnations of the New Age as a whole should be avoided and its good features recognized.

4. Stress must be placed on those elements of the New Age that can be harmonized with Christian doctrine and spirituality. For instance, in spite of the theological problems inherent in Matthew Fox's creation-centered spirituality, there are some elements in this spirituality that can be based on a Christian theology of creation.[40]

5. Efforts must be made to imbue some New Age practices with the Christian spirit. Thus, for example, the environmental movement to preserve the earth need not be based on a pantheistic viewpoint. It could easily be founded on traditional Christian theology.

6. It should be recognized that the Church is in constant need of renewal and that the New Age may be pointing to those areas where reform and renewal are most required. "Spiritual innovation," writes William Dinges,[41] "is more often than not an indictment of organized religion and its failure to respond in creative and dynamic ways to new cultural trends." Official Catholic reactions to the new religious movements have admitted that more can be done for the pastoral needs of the faithful.[42]

THE NEW AGE AS A "SIGN OF THE TIMES"

In conclusion, the advent of the New Age can be seen as a mixed blessing for Christians who are called upon to respond in faith to the presence of new religions at the beginning of the twentieth-first century. While the New Age may be drawing away from traditional faith many who have embarked on a personal religious quest, it might also be doing a service to Christianity by encouraging Christians to delve deeper in their religious tradition and rediscover its treasures.

Rather than being an indication of satanic conniving or an omen of impending apocalyptic doom, the New Age, like all new religious movements,[43] is "a sign of the times," calling Christians to self-examination and reform in the light of the Gospel.[44] The New Age religion presents an excellent opportunity for the Christian Church to better understand and execute its mission, to adapt and react more meaningfully to the changing needs and conditions of the modern age, to express its teachings clearly to an ecumenical audience, and to reform and renew itself in the spirit of the Gospel.

NOTES

1. David Spangler, *The New Age* (Issaquah, WA: Morningtown Press, 1988), p. 3.

2. J. Gordon Melton, *New Age Encyclopedia* (Detroit: Garland, 1990), p. xiii.

3. For an insider's view of the many practices that can be included under the New Age, one can consult *The New Age Catalogue: Access to Information and Sources*, by the editors of *Body, Mind, and Spirit* (New York: Doubleday, 1988); the *New Age Sourcebook*, by the editors of the *New Age Journal* (Brighton, MA: Rising Star Associates, 1991); and Marcia Gervase Ingenito, ed., *National New Age Yellow Pages* 2nd. ed. (Fullerton, California: Highgate House, 1988). For a scholarly description, see J. Gordon Melton, *The New Age Almanac* (Detroit: Gale Research, 1991).

4. See, for instance, Shirley MacLaine, *Out on a Limb* (New York: Bantam, 1983), pp. 50–51, who gives a rather mild criticism of Christianity.

5. For surveys of the Christian fundamentalist approach to the New Age movement, see James R. Lewis, "The New Age Movement: A Bibliography of Conservative Christian Literature" (Santa Barbara: Santa Barbara Center for Humanistic Studies, 1989), and Irving Hexham, "The Evangelical Response to the New Age," in James R. Lewis and J. Gordon Melton, eds., *Perspectives on the New Age* (Albany: State University of New York Press, 1992), pp. 152–63.

6. *The Hidden Dangers of the Rainbow: The New Age and the Coming Age of Barbarism* (Shreveport, LA: Huntington House, 1983).

7. *Prosperity and the Coming Holocaust: The New Age Movement in Prophecy* (Eugene, OR: Harvest House, 1983).

8. Texe Marrs, *Dark Secrets of the New Age: Satan's Plan for a One World Religion* (Westchester, IL: Lion Publishing, 1986).

9. See, for example, Dave Hunt and T. A. MacMahon, *The Seduction of Christianity: Spiritual Discernment in the Last Days* (Eugene, OR: Harvest House, 1985), p. 213.

10. Such as Paul de Parrie and Mary Pride, *Unholy Sacrifices of the New Age* (Westchester, IL: Crossway Books, 1988).

11. *Unmasking the New Age* (Downers Grove, IL: InterVarsity Press, 1986).

12. For example, Russell Chandler, *Understanding the New Age* (Dallas: Word Publishing, 1988).

13. See Karen Hoyt, ed. *The New Age Rage: A Probing Analysis of the Newest Religious Craze* (Old Tappan, NJ: Fleming H. Revell Co., 1987), p. 12.

14. Consult, for instance, Walter Martin, *The New Age Cult*, (Minneapolis: Bethany House), pp. 97 ff.

15. Cf., for example, Hexham, "Evangelical Response," pp. 157–58.

16. "A Look at the New Age Movement," *Military Chaplains' Review* (fall 1989), p. 20.

17. "Towards an Understanding of the New Age," *St. Mark's Review* 144 (summer 1991), pp. 2–5.

18. Ibid., p. 3.

19. Ibid., p. 5.

20. *The Cosmic Self* (San Francisco: Harper, 1991), pp. 194 ff.

21. *The New Age: A Christian Critique* (South Bend, Indiana: Greenlawn Press, 1990).

22. Ibid., p. 273.

23. *Catholics and the New Age* (Ann Arbor, MI: Servant Publications, 1992).

24. See, for instance, James Richardson, "Conversion Careers," *Society* 17, no. 3 (1980), pp. 47–50.

25. Pacwa, *Catholics and the New Age*, p. 68.

26. Toward the end of his book, Pacwa (p. 198) counsels Catholics to "look for good in their [i.e., New Agers'] ideas and relate it to the truth that God has already revealed." He disappoints his readers, however, by not following his own advice.

27. *Facing West from California's Shores: A Jesuit's Journey into New Age Consciousness* (New York: Crossroad, 1987).

28. In a similar approach, Bede Griffiths outlines some of the positive impact the New Age can have on both Christian theology and practice. See his *A New Vision of Reality: Western Science, Eastern Mysticism and Christian Faith* (Springfield, IL: Templegate Publishers, 1989).

29. "Harmonic Convergences and All That: New Age Spirituality," *Way* 32, no. 1 (1992), p. 42.

30. Ibid., p. 35.

31. *Mysticism and the New Age: Christic Consciousness in the New Creation* (New York: Alba House, 1991).

32. An English translation of this section on the New Age appeared under the title "Christ or Aquarius?" *Catholic International* 2, no. 3 (May 1991), pp. 480–88.

33. Ibid., p. 485.

34. Ibid., p. 483.

35. *Catholic International* 3, no. 7 (1–14 April 1992), p. 335.

36. Ibid.

37. Paul McGuire, *Evangelizing the New Age* (Ann Arbor, MI: Servant Publications, 1989), p. 66.

38. J. Gordon Melton, "Introductory Essay: An Overview of the New Age Movement," in *New Age Encyclopedia* (Detroit: Gale Research, 1991), pp. xxx–xxxi.

39. Consult, for example, Paul Collins, "What's New about the New Age?" *St. Mark's Review* 144 (summer 1991), p. 14.

40. See the whole issue of the *Way* 29, no. 1 (1989), which is dedicated to "creation-centered spirituality."

41. "Aquarian Spirituality: The New Age Movement in America," *Catholic World* (May/June 1989), p. 141.

42. Cf. my essay "Vatican Response to the New Religious Movements," *Theological Studies* 53, no. 1 (1992), pp. 3–39.

43. This view was expressed by Cardinal Ernesto Corripio Ahumada in his report to the 1991 Consistory of Cardinals. Cf. *Catholic International* 2, no. 13 (1–14 July 1991), p. 618.

44. The phrase "sign of the times" occurs near the beginning of *Gaudium et Spes*, Vatican II's "Pastoral Constitution on the Church in the Modern World." See Walter M. Abbott, ed., *The Documents of Vatican II* (London: Geoffrey Chapman, 1966), p. 201.

18
CHRIST CONSCIOUSNESS AND THE COSMIC CHRIST

Gillian Paschkes-Bell

New Agers are often—even typically—in reaction against Christianity. They react against the patriarchal and hierarchical nature of the Church, against abuses perpetrated through the Church, and against the exclusivity claims that Jesus was the only Son of God and that only those who believe in him shall be saved. It must be acknowledged that there are church-going Christians who share all or some of these views. In the same way, it should be acknowledged that there are New Agers in reaction against the term "New Age" due to its association, in its eclecticism, with beliefs or practices that they do not share. But with these qualifications the opening statement remains true, and the term "New Agers" will be used for ease of reference.[1] Among New Agers, and despite the reaction against Christianity, there are those who aspire to a form of consciousness known as Christ consciousness.

What is Christ consciousness? At its most general, the term may be understood as referring to a Divine consciousness, that is, a form of consciousness that transcends the personality self and is directed toward the unfolding of the Divine will, which is endlessly creative and characterized by love. So Christ consciousness transcends any specific religious creed. This chapter gives exposure to a view of the Christ that underpins this concept, and shows it in relation to the concept of the Cosmic Christ, developed from within the Christian tradition.

In a book published in the late 1970s, David Spangler wrote about his inter-

---

Written for this anthology.

pretation of the work of the Christ.[2] His view, expounded in *Reflections on the Christ*, was that the "Christ pattern" is universal: "Each one of us is intimately concerned with the unfoldment and development of that pattern which for centuries has been called the Christ pattern. This is true wherever an individual may be upon the Earth, whatever creed or religion he is involved in, whatever nationality . . . he belongs to."[3]

The Christ pattern is understood by Spangler as being essentially "educative," in the following sense: "The Christ is that force which has as its mission the nourishment and the cultivation of divine life throughout creation. It has as its task . . . continually being one step in advance of evolving life, always drawing out of that life the next manifestation of perfection. The Christ is the manifestation of the totality of the universe."[4]

A further characteristic of the Christ pattern is obedience to the Divine will. This is seen by Spangler as reaching its completion in the Gethsemane experience, when Jesus asks if "this cup" can be taken from him, "Yet not my will, Father, but thine be done."[5]

Although Spangler sees the Christ pattern as universal, he understands it as entering the conscious awareness of humanity through a historical progression starting with the Buddha. The Buddha was "the first one of humanity to fully awaken to the level of the cosmic Christ."[6] Spangler sees the Buddha's work as an upward movement, enabling humanity to awaken to the Christ pattern. He sees the work of Jesus of Nazareth as a downward movement that impregnates the very fabric of the Earth with the Christ pattern. But it is important to note that Spangler does not specifically associate this Christ pattern with Jesus except in the sense that Jesus performed the task of bringing it into the world. In Spangler's view, Jesus had first to awaken to the Christ pattern just as the Buddha did. Then,

> [w]hen he became awakened there was sufficient power generated within the race itself to lift that awakened state still further. It made it possible for him then to become the Anointed One,[7] for there to be in this case the reverse action of what happened with Buddha, a downward pull in which the Christ, or this cosmic force literally entered the vehicles of Jesus and took them over, and used those vehicles as a means of making a very important link with the Earth. . . . By being anointed with this cosmic power he became its incarnation. . . . It was this anointing of Jesus that was the actual birth of the Christ on Earth.[8]

The effect on the Earth of this anointing could occur because every level of existence on the planet is recapitulated in a human being:

> What was occurring is that one of the patterns that the Christ came to do through the instrumentality of Jesus' consciousness was to literally impregnate the etheric structure of the Earth, and to incarnate not only through a physical body of a human being, but through what a human being is. A human being has links with every kingdom on the Earth. A human being is partially mineral, partially

vegetable, partially animal, partially devic,[9] partially elemental.[10] There is no kingdom on the Earth that does not have its correspondence within man."[11]

This "impregnation" was not just into the human, and thence, by implication, the universe but also into the depths of negativity to which humanity can fall. In the Gethsemane experience, when Jesus manifested the Christ pattern of obedience to the Divine will, he did so in the face of fear, experienced within his own person, and subsequently within the actions of those who crucified him. Spangler comments that "there have been many people throughout history who have gone to apparent death and laughed in the faces of the people who were torturing them. So it is a little strange to conceive of this man who was enlightened and illumined by a cosmic consciousness, who himself saw through the illusion of death, suddenly becoming afraid. Unless we can go deeper into that pattern and see what was really occurring."[12]

Spangler sees the entry of the Christ pattern into the structures of the Earth as salvific. Such salvation is different in character from the interpretation that focuses on guaranteeing the individual believer a place in heaven. It is seen as having the potential to affect every level of existence.

What is striking about Spangler's account is that in the instances cited he takes themes that find expression within the Christian tradition and presents them to a New Age audience using terminology and concepts that resonate for that audience. So, the concept of the Christ pattern preexisting the birth of Jesus is expressed in the opening of John's Gospel, "In the beginning was the Word." The idea that it is educative, in the sense of being one step ahead of evolving life, links with the association that has been made within the Christian tradition between the preexistent Word of John's Gospel and the creative function of wisdom described in the Book of Proverbs.[13] The idea that salvation has to do with the whole of creation also finds biblical expression, notably in the passage from Paul's letter to the Romans in which he describes how the whole creation is eagerly—and painfully—awaiting liberation.[14]

This view of the Christ corresponds with the view presented by Matthew Fox in *The Coming of the Cosmic Christ*. Fox critiques the Christian tradition from within, citing evidence from the Bible and from major figures within Christianity to support his view that any narrowing down of the Christian religion to a focus on the human individual is a deep impoverishment of a tradition that, he seeks to demonstrate, contains a much wider, cosmological purview: "All the early hymns to the Cosmic Christ composed by first-century Christians celebrate the power of Jesus Christ over thrones, dominations, and angels. . . . In the modern era, however, the Enlightenment's encroachment on religion has resulted in Christians throwing out all cosmology, all angels (which represent cosmology in the Gospels), all mention of the Cosmic Christ."[15]

Fox believes that the task for our time is the 'quest for the Cosmic Christ':

The movement from the Enlightenment's quest for the historical Jesus to today's quest for the Cosmic Christ names the paradigm shift that religion and theology presently need to undergo. One cannot explore the meaning and power of the Cosmic Christ without a living cosmology, a living mysticism, and the spiritual discipline of art as meditation. *The holy trinity of science (knowledge of creation), mysticism (experiential union with creation and its unnameable mysteries), and art (expression of our awe at creation) is what constitutes a living theology.*[16] . . . To move from a 'personal Savior' Christianity—which is what an anthropocentric and antimystical Christianity gives us—to a 'Cosmic Christ' Christianity calls for *metanoia*, a change of perspective by all those who do theology and by those schools which claim to teach theology.[17]

Fox's and Spangler's interpretations of the work of Christ converge in this respect: that both see the Christ as a power that acts in relation to the universe as a whole, not just in relation to humanity or to individual Christians. This implies a form of salvation that is concerned with all things in the unfolding universe, shifting the focus away from the afterlife of individual souls.

The traditional Christian view of life after death is one of the aspects of the Western tradition that has not been incorporated into New Age thinking. New Agers tend to think in terms of reincarnation. Each lifetime is an opportunity to progress deeper into Divinity as a result of the experience of different states— whether joyful or painful is ultimately immaterial. Within such a view there is no need of a personal savior to rescue the individual from hell and provide a gateway to heaven. Yet in the course of an interview with a woman who in her own thinking spanned Christian and New Age thought, I encountered an ingenious idea. This woman wondered if there might be a choice between the slow road of journeying into Divinity through the accumulation of lifetimes of experience and the fast route of attaching oneself, in a single leap of faith, to one who has already done the whole journey. If, through the consciousness of Jesus, the Cosmic Christ has been brought into the fabric of the universe so that it is latent in all things, so the consciousness of an individual might attach to the Cosmic Christ, enabling the individual to share in the Christ on a level of being that transcends the personality self but also affects the personality self. Working in either direction, from Jesus to the cosmos or from the individual toward the Christ, the active and instrumental aspect of consciousness is the will—that is, Jesus' will to do the work of the "One who sent him," or the individual's will to become one with the Christ.

Matthew Fox sees the Second Coming promised in the Christian tradition in terms of "the Healing of Mother Earth and the Birth of a Global Renaissance."[18] David Spangler suggests that the work of Christ provides the potential to take humanity—and by implication the whole planet—to a new level through the emergence of individuals and communities that manifest the Christ pattern intentionally and sees in this the promised Second Coming. The term "the Cosmic Christ" proclaims a creative power that transcends the human, while the term "Christ consciousness" expresses human participation in that power.

NOTES

1. In this paper, the term "New Ager" will be used to denote persons on a conscious spiritual path followed outside a traditional religious system although it may incorporate elements of such systems.

2. Spangler was resident at the Findhorn Foundation in the late 1970s, and *Reflections on the Christ* was addressed initially to that spiritual community before being disseminated to a wider audience. He uses the terms "Christ pattern" and "cosmic Christ" to denote a nonmaterial form that exists prior to human consciousness of it. The term "Christ consciousness" may be held to refer to human awareness of this pattern and is a necessary precursor to the manifestation of the pattern in psychological and material terms.

3. *Reflections on the Christ*, p. 1. (Page numbers refer to the 1977 edition.)

4. Ibid., p. 4.

5. Matt. 26:39, 42; Mark 14:36; Luke 22:42.

6. *Reflections on the Christ*, p. 6. In *The Unknown Christ of Hinduism*, Panikkar sees evidence of the creative function of the Christ in Isvara, a personification within Hinduism denoting how Brahman, understood as transcendent and unrelated to the world, is also the world's cause. (*Unknown Christ*, p 158)

7. Spangler points out that this is the meaning of the Greek term "Christos."

8. That is, the birth of Jesus in Bethlehem was not the birth of the Christ. *Reflections on the Christ*, p. 6.

9. Angelic.

10. Faery.

11. *Reflections on the Christ*, p. 8.

12. Ibid.

13. Prov. 8:22 ff. The Greek term "logos," used at the opening of John's Gospel and translated there as "Word," can also be translated as "Wisdom," seen in Proverbs as a created entity that also has a creative function. From within the Christian tradition, Tielhard de Chardin is particularly associated with developing an evolutionary understanding of creation and relating this to the Christ.

14. Rom. 8:19 ff.

15. *The Coming of the Cosmic Christ*, p. 1.

16. Ibid., p. 78.

17. Ibid., p. 79.

18. Ex heading, part 5, *The Coming of the Cosmic Christ*.

REFERENCES

Fox, Matthew. *The Coming of the Cosmic Christ*. San Francisco: HarperSanFrancisco, 1988.

Griffiths, Bede. *The Marriage of East and West*. London: Collins, 1982.

Panikkar, Raymundo. *The Unknown Christ of Hinduism*. London: Darton, Longman and Todd, 1964.

Spangler, David. *Reflections on the Christ*. Forres, Scotland: Findhorn Press, 1977–78.

19

THE CHRISTAQUARIANS?

A Sociology of Christians in the New Age

Daren Kemp

Is there a movement of New Age Christians that we might call the Christaquarian movement after the astrological Age of Aquarius? A number of scholars have identified a New Age fringe of Christianity (e.g., Jorgensen 1982, 387; Heelas 1996, 163 ff.; D'Andrea 1997). But is this milieu sufficiently cohesive and self-conscious, such that we might describe it as a movement?

While the term "Christian" may be sufficiently understood, there have been a number of attempts at defining "New Age" (e.g., York 1995; Hanegraaff 1996). My preference is for a family resemblance or polythetic mode of definition. Scholars who have used such a definition of New Age include Prince (1992) (cf. Prince and Riches 2000), Barker (1992, 189), and Hanegraaff (1996, 14). Building on the work of Wittgenstein (1953) and Needham (1975), this mode of definition does not require a predefined list of characteristics in order to classify an item, but is flexible in its criteria. The core family members against which I define New Age are David Spangler, David Icke, aromatherapy, and the Mind Body Spirit Festival in London.

Discussions of the New Age movement to date have concentrated on traditional church-sect models and have not explored in any detail the insights of new social movement theory. This is despite the fact that Bochinger (1995/1994), Introvigne (2000/1994), Sutcliffe (1998), and Wood (1999) all deny that New

This paper is a précis of the author's doctoral thesis, Kemp 2000. Grants were obtained toward this research from King's College London Theological Trust and St. Olave's and St. Saviour's Grammar School Foundation.

Age qualifies as a movement. Accordingly, it would be expedient to explore such theorists as Touraine (1981), Melucci (1989), Scott (1990), and Tarrow (1994), among others. To be particularly noted in Scott's definition of a social movement is the requirement for self-perception of common identity. Without an emic understanding of themselves as a movement, a collective of actors cannot be regarded as such.

The methodology used to explore these notions is mixed. First, the literature of three Christaquarian groups, plus one control group (an Anglican evangelical church), was studied (see Kemp 2000). Second, participant observation was conducted at each of the groups. Third, semistructured interviews were conducted with members and leaders of these groups. Finally, a postal questionnaire survey of over seven hundred people belonging to these groups was conducted. The survey was piloted in a telephone interview program, and response rates of up to nearly 60 percent were achieved.

Although no other scholar has yet considered Christians in the New Age as a distinct religious movement that may be named Christaquarianism, a number of texts do discuss the crossover between Christianity and the New Age. Not only is this more restricted field of Christaquarians less widely discussed than the New Age in general, but most of the available texts are of a confessional nature.

From a conservative/evangelical bias, we have Barton Dean English's thesis, "The Challenge of the New Age to Christian Theology and Life" (1994); Alan Roxburgh's "On Being the Church in a New Age" (1991); and "An Examination and Evaluation of the New Age Christology of David Spangler" (1986) by Ron Rhodes. From a positive bias, Thomas Legere is a Catholic priest who wrote "A Popular Book: Christianity for a New Age" (1993).

The main exception to this rule of bias is John Saliba's excellent study, *Christian Responses to the New Age Movement* (1999). The book is clearly structured, with an opening attempt at definition of the New Age followed by three chapter-length discussions of various Christian responses: evangelical/fundamentalist, Protestant and Orthodox, and Catholic.

There have been a number of studies of the New Age movement in general, including Wood (1999), Sutcliffe (1998), Rose (1996), Heelas (1996), Hanegraaff (1996), Greer (1994), Introvigne (2000/1994), Bochinger (1995/1994), Lewis and Melton (1992), York (1995), and Melton et al (1990, 1991). For a detailed review, see Kemp (2000). Overall, while literature on New Age in general is growing, there is need for a more-detailed and less-biased study of Christians in the New Age. The four UK groups selected as case studies for such an inquiry are described in the paragraphs below.

St. James' Piccadilly is a large Anglican church in the center of London, where Rev. Donald Reeves was rector from 1980 to 1998. The church is well known, especially among Christaquarians and evangelicals, for its welcoming of New Age speakers. St. James' might almost be said to be the Canterbury of

Christaquarianism, in that it is a place for spiritual pilgrimage and viewed as a center of New Age Christianity in Britain. Nearly two-thirds of CANA respondents and half of the *Omega News* respondents (the two other Christaquarian groups studied for this project, with members across the United Kingdom) have been to St. James' Piccadilly and this is probably true of most other Christian New Agers. A memorial service held (like those of many other illustrious people) for Sir George Trevelyan, the New Age leader, conducted by Rev. Donald Reeves at St. James' during the course of my research, was an occasion for the reunion of many Christian New Agers and also New Agers who were not Christian but wanted to mark Trevelyan's death (*Positive News* 10, no. 32, [June 1996]). According to internal figures ("Parish Profile" 1998), the average congregation at the main service on a Sunday is 177, while special services and festivals attract over 500 people.

The New Age project of St. James' is Alternatives, a weekly lecture series held at the church on Monday nights that invites New Age and pagan speakers. Entrance is by a midpriced ticket, and the church is usually quite full, with around three hundred people; a press release dated October 1998 claims the Alternatives program attracts over fifteen thousand people every year. Alternatives developed out of a group known as Turning Points (formed in the late 1970s by Sabine Kurjo and Malcolm Stern) and was run from 1988 by Dr. William Bloom, his partner Sabrina Dearborn, and Malcolm Stern. Dr. Bloom is heavily involved with the Findhorn Foundation, and although he still occasionally attends Alternatives and gives lectures and his name and biography sometimes appear on the fliers, he has little day-to-day involvement with the organization. Some members of the church congregation are highly critical of Dr. Bloom and the "parallel church" that they claim he developed at St. James' in Alternatives, while Dr. Bloom denies that Alternatives was ever a "satellite" under his leadership. The churchwarden emphasizes that the audience at these New Age events is different from the audience on a Sunday morning, just as these are both different from the audiences at the concerts and the Blake Society events held at the church, for example.

Factor analysis of the regularity of attendance at church services and length of adoption of New Age ideas or practices[1] reveals an interesting relationship. Of those respondents who attend the church once a week or more often, 18 percent had adopted New Age tendencies for five years or more. Of those respondents who attend the church once every few weeks, 42 percent had adopted New Age tendencies for five years or more. Of those respondents who attend the church less frequently, 60 percent had adopted New Age tendencies for five years or more. Conversely, the three groupings of churchgoers reported increasing denial of New Age tendencies the more frequently they attended the church. The graph on page 326 illustrates this and strongly suggests that the core congregation at St. James' tends to be less New Age than those who do not attend as regularly. My interpretation of the statistics and fieldwork at St. James' suggests that it be considered as a response to the conditions of postmodern or late modern society (see Kemp 2001).

Fig. I. Regularity of attendance and adoption of New Age ideas and practices

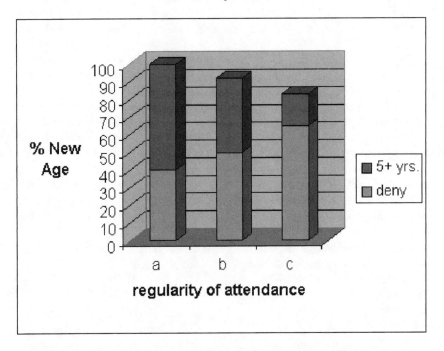

The second Christaquarian group studied, Christians Awakening to a New Awareness (known to its members as "CANA," as in the wedding of John 2, and originally called Christians Awakening to a New Age), is a network of nearly one hundred fifty people, drawn initially from a larger organization of about two hundred people known as the Bridge Trust. CANA formally separated (amicably) from Bridge Trust in spring 2000.

In 1999, CANA produced "A Paper for Dialogue" outlining its beliefs. This was to be used in round-table discussions with like-minded groups. Table 1 (CANA 1999, 2–6) gives some examples of the beliefs listed, together with the familiar traditional beliefs printed alongside them, as in the paper.[2]

Table 1. Some expressions of Christian belief

	Familiar Traditional	Contemporary Alternatives
1.	God has given us a full and final revelation of himself, to be guarded against corruption.	Humanity is still evolving, so our understanding of God is always in the process of developing.
12.	God is the all-powerful, all-knowing Lord of all creation; the loving Father who sent his Son to reveal the mysteries of Divine Grace.	God is the Divine presence in, and creative energy of, this world whom we discover through our relationships with people, things, events, and concepts.
19.	Jesus equals God, a Divine Being who took on human nature.	Jesus, in his humanity, does not equal God but is a human being who is transparent to the Divine. God was as fully present and active in Jesus as is possible in human form.
25.	Redemption is an act of rescue by an external, Divine agent.	Redemption is the transformation process by which the life-giving Spirit within us moves us from human-centeredness to Divine-centeredness.
28.	Sin is an offense against God.	Sin is a failure to grow in wholeness, within ourselves, with others, and in relation to the whole of creation. It is to ignore the Divine within us.
34.	Christianity alone holds the true revelation and key to salvation. All other religions are false or inadequate.	Christianity is the religion in which the role of Christ is most clearly under-stood. Other religions have different perspectives on the One Truth. Each is a path to ultimate union with God for their followers.
41.	Matters of the spirit are more sacred, of greater significance and value than matters of the flesh and the material and must be given greater reverence, respect, and care.	Spirit and matter are equally sacred. Therefore, we must revere, respect, and care not only for the spirit but also for the temple of the spirit—the human body, the body corporate, the planet and its biosphere, and the whole of material creation.

It will be seen that many of these beliefs and practices directly confront conventional Christian understandings, although all of them are also to be found in the writings of other contemporary Christian theologians. What makes members of CANA unusual Christians is that they also practice a large number of New Age techniques and teachings,[3] such as yoga, aromatherapy, and tarot cards. Leon Festinger et al. (1956; cf. Festinger 1957) famously studied an example of "cognitive dissonance," or conflicting beliefs, in their study of a millenarian flying-saucer group whose prophecies were not realized on the predicted date. The group was said to have responded to the uncomfortable mental situation by preaching their doctrine more forcefully, and this may be applicable also to New Age Christians.

The third Christaquarian group in this study, the Omega Order, is a small residential community of New Age Christians living in a converted manor house near Bristol, England. There is a structural hierarchy in place. Canon Peter Spink, the founder, is accorded most respect and heads his written communications "From the Prior," although this title is not generally used in the community. Since Canon Spink's conversion to Roman Catholicism, a Roman Catholic chaplain, Rev. Richard McKay, has been appointed to the house. Rev. Jim Hill, who has now left the order, was also highly respected by residents for his wide knowledge on religious—and other—matters. James Fahey takes responsibility for much of the day-to-day affairs of the community and also conducts retreats.

Below this tier of authority are the "Companions" of the Order. These are full-time residents who have been accorded a special status. To qualify for Companionship, applicants have usually been residents for at least a year. Then, they must lead the worship for several services. Finally, they may be asked if they want to become a Companion. In October 1996, when the main session of field-work was conducted, there were nine Companions out of a total of sixteen residents. The remainder have no special name and are referred to by the office secretary as "long-term residents" to distinguish them from occasional visitors.

There is a routine of daily offices at the community that are attended usually by from a third to half of the residents. Offices are currently held at 8 a.m., noon, 6 p.m., and 7:15 p.m. and are part of the daily routine, along with the communal meals. The liturgy is printed for the congregation on cards and is quite traditionally Anglo-Catholic, with some innovative meditative additions, such as the Omega Invocation (*The Omega Offices* 1994, 14):

> May the Light that shows the Way illuminate the mind,
> May the Love that knows the Truth unfold within the heart,
> May the Power that gives true Life arise within the soul,
> Let Light and Love and Power raise all in Christ to God.
> Amen.

Based on John 14:6, this replaced the invocation previously used by the order written by Alice Bailey and promoted by Lucis Trust. A bell is rung to indicate the beginning and end of silent meditations. Many chants are also used, including some from Taizé.

Apart from those of Canon Spink, the spiritual teachings and disciplines that have had most influence on *Omega News* readers are Christianity (cited by almost half the respondents in my survey), Buddhism, prayer, meditation, the mystics of the church, and those of G. I. Gurdjieff. Spiritual writers that have had an important influence include the authors of Bible, Alice Bailey, Paul Brunton, Fritjof Capra, Anthony de Mello, Matthew Fox, Bede Griffiths, Teilhard de Chardin, Joel Goldsmith, G. I. Gurdjieff, F. C. Happold, Martin Israel, John of the Cross, C. G. Jung, William Johnston, Krisnamurti, C. S. Lewis, John Main, Thomas Merton, Maurice Nicole, Henri Nouwen, P. D. Ouspensky, John Robinson, Sai Baba, Rudolf Steiner, George Trevelyan, Evelyn Underhill, Leslie Weatherhead, Ken Wilber, and Laurens van der Post—who all received six or more citations by the one hundred ninety respondents. After Peter Spink, Bede Griffiths, and Teilhard de Chardin were the most popular writers, with thirty-two and twenty-seven citations, respectively. To judge by this question, *Omega News* readers are more well-read in spirituality than members of St. James' Church or CANA.

It may be seen that there is what English-Lueck (1990) calls a "legitimating tradition" for New Age Christians. This tradition includes the Essenes, the Gnostics, Neoplatonists, Christian Qabbalah, the Rhineland Mystics, the Celtic tradition, Jacob Boehme, Emanuel Swedenborg, William Blake, Theosophy, Anthroposophy, the Arcane School, Christian Science, New Thought, Carl Jung, Edgar Cayce, Dion Fortune, and Pierre Teilhard de Chardin. It is not suggested that these thinkers and movements have ever formed a cohesive unity but rather that Christaquarians may use them as a legitimating tradition or frame. Further, it is not suggested that a legitimating tradition gives Christaquarians an objective claim to Truth; merely, the sociological observation is made that this tradition is available for use by the subjects of this study.

Any statistical survey must have a control group before the results can be properly analyzed. This is the major drawback with Stuart Rose's otherwise admirable survey of readers of *Kindred Spirit* (1996), a popular UK New Age magazine, as, until this project repeated some of his questions, it could not be seen how typical or atypical his results were. For this study, in addition to using Rose's results as a control group on the New Age side of Christaquarianism, a control group was selected on the Christian side: an Anglican evangelical church. The benefice in question splits its congregation between two churches, SS. Peter and Paul, Cudham, and St. Mary's, Downe. This is a rural area on the edges of greater London, England, with the vicarage located in Cudham, the larger congregation. In all, one hundred fourteen questionnaires were sent out to members of the two electoral rolls, and fifty-three were returned, a return rate of 46 percent.

The vicar, Rev. Tim Hatwell, defines the New Age (1) by its pantheism, including "those who are Green"; (2) by its moral monism, "there is no concept of evil, no concept of sin"; and (3) by its "anything goes" approach, "if it works." Examples he gives of New Age are White Eagle Lodge, Transcendental Medita-

The former headquarters building of the Universal Church of the Master located in Santa Clara, CA, one of the early New Thought denominations. (*Courtesy of the Universal Church of the Master*)

tion, crystals, astrology, and Tarot cards. However, he has never had a serious discussion with New Agers about their beliefs, and these ideas are mainly garnered from Christian writings, including *What Is the New Age* (Cole et al. 1990) and a booklet by Philip Seddon (1990). Rev. Hatwell speaks of "grey areas such as acupuncture and reflexology or even aromatherapy," for which he is unsure of the correct Christian approach. In general, though, he thinks a Christian should be open in friendship to New Agers and engage in dialogue with them.

Those of the congregation who were interviewed had generally not themselves read evangelical critiques of the New Age movement but were aware of the major themes. Douglas R. Groothuis's series on New Age (1986; 1988; 1990) is one of the most popular in evangelical circles. New Agers, whom he often refers to as "the One for all," are presented in Table 2 as being distinguishable by their beliefs (Groothuis 1986, 167).

It was assumed at the beginning of fieldwork for this study that New Age is at the opposite end of the spectrum from evangelical Christianity. However, a number of commentators have detected similarities between New Age and evangelical Christianity. These include Spangler (1984, 19–20), Thompson (1997, 208–212), Albanese (1988), Lucas (1992), and Steyn (1994, 7, 50, 166, 312).

Table 2. New Age and Evangelical beliefs according to Groothuis

	New Age	Christian
1. Metaphysics	God is the world, pantheism	Creator/creation distinction
	God is impersonal/amoral	God is personal/moral
	All is spirit/consciousness, monistic	Creation of God upheld by God, interconnected but not monistic
2. Epistemology	Man is all things, truth within	Truth revealed in the Bible
3. Ethics	Autonomous and situational (relative)	Based on the revelation of God's will, absolute
4. Nature of Humans	Spiritual being, a sleeping God	Made in the image of God, now fallen
5. Human problem	Ignorance of true potential	Sin—rebellion against God and his law
6. Answer to Human Problems	Change of consciousness	Faith in and obedience to Christ
7. History	Cyclical	Linear and providential
8. Death	Illusion, entrance to next life (reincarnation)	Entrance to either eternal heaven or hell
9. View of Religion	All point to the One syncretism)	Not all from God, teach different things
10. View of Jesus Christ	One of many avatars...	The unique God-Man, only Lord and Savior

Personal transformation is central to both evangelicalism and New Age, whether being born again or coming to enlightenment. Transformation centers on experience, either speaking in tongues and being slain by the Spirit or through altered states of consciousness. Another central experience is healing through the laying on of hands—the power coming through Christ or the auric fields. Both evangelical Christianity and New Age are ontologically positive—God is seen to embrace matter either through the doctrines of creation science or application of quantum physics. Both have a spiritual democracy with the traditional priesthood of believers or the idea that everyone is God. The sacred is continually present in the everyday lives of evangelicals and New Agers, who live in Christ or live as God. Both value the community. The attitude to the outside world in both is to transform it, either building God's kingdom or preparing for the New Age. Both share a similar attitude to money evinced in prosperity consciousness. The attitude to the future is also similar, both showing varying shades of millennialism. The form of worship among evangelicals and New Agers is also similar. For example, evangelical choruses are similar to New Age chants, and Taizé chants are used in both contexts. Prayer or meditation is often a group exercise in both congregations. Evangelicals cut across traditional institutional divides among the churches; New Agers are similarly outside of traditional institutions. Both have significant origins in the late-nineteenth century. The typical member of both is a middle-class, middle-aged woman.

The most surprising result of the interview program is the discovery that *all three* leaders of the Christaquarian groups studied had had an evangelical conversion experience in their youth. Both Janice Dolley (founder of CANA) and Rev. Donald Reeves had been converted by Billy Graham, the American evangelist, and Canon Peter Spink also had a conversion experience in his teens. Two other clergy at the Omega Order had had similar experiences. All had later repudiated this experience, expressing much dissatisfaction with the evangelical tradition, mainly due to its "dogmatism" and over-reliance on an authoritarian approach to the Bible.

The significance of this double conversion to and from evangelical Christianity is difficult to evaluate. It may well be that many leaders of religious groups today had similar experiences in their youth—similar to the "baby boomer" spirituality suggested by Roof (1993). In the absence of a wider survey, it cannot be determined whether it is common for leaders of religious groups to have had an evangelical conversion experience. It is suggested, however, that it is highly significant, because of the similarities in the style of religion as outlined above.

This project considered the hypothesis that there is a Christaquarian movement. Funding was not sufficient to conduct a worldwide survey of contemporary Christianity, and it was hoped that selected case studies would answer the question. A brief indication of the breadth of the phenomenon may, however, be given. Examples of positive Christian responses to the New Age movement include the channeled text *A Course in Miracles*, neognostic groups, Creation Spirituality, the Quaker Universalists, retreat centers, New Age Catholics, and New Age psychological theorists. Catholic Christaquarians include Paulo Coelho, John Main, Bede Griffiths, Thomas Merton, Laurence Freeman, and Anthony de Mello. For a more detailed survey, see Kemp (2000).

The official responses of the main Christian denominations to the New Age movement include the Irish Theological Commission's *A New Age of the Spirit? A Catholic Response to the New Age Phenomenon* (1994); *The Search for Faith,* a report published by the Anglican Church House in November 1996; and the Methodist Faith and Order Committee's *Report to Conference* (1994). There have also been a number of independent Christian outreach groups to the New Age.

Steven Sutcliffe concludes his thesis (1998) with the case that the so-called New Age movement itself is no more than a "collectivity" of individual seekers that happen to use the New Age emblem. The argument is that because it has "no essential purpose or goal," the collectivity cannot be classed as a movement. York (1995, 324 ff.), following Ferguson (1980, 235–36), suggested that New Age is best depicted as a meta-network, or a SPIN of SPINs—a SPIN is a segmented, polycentric, integrated network. Christaquarianism has not yet developed into a SPIN, however, since the network has not "integrated" its polycentric nodes. It is perhaps better depicted by Campbell's (1972) notion of a dispersed "cultic milieu," although this model does not do justice to the pockets of cohesively organized Christaquarian groups such as CANA and the Omega Order. What sociological model are we to use for Christaquarianism, then?

It is suggested that for the cultic milieu to succeed, it must enter the mainstream culture. The definition of "success" in new religious movements has been examined by Peter Clarke (1996): Christianity was "unsuccessful" for the first fifty years; groups that promote celibacy, such as the Shakers and Brahma Kumaris, do not intend to "succeed" in physical terms. A successful new socioreligious movement (NSRM)[4] popularizes its worldview in the wider culture. Churches and sects popularize their worldviews by institutionalization; NSRMs reach out, without institutionalization, through networks or associations. These different methods of entering the mainstream culture are pictured in Table 3.

Table 3. Development of NRMs

Traditional model	Alternative model
Cult	NRM
Sect	NSRM—an association of NRMs
Church	Mainstream assimilation

There is some overlap between the New Age Christian groups studied. Most dramatically, 50 percent of Omega respondents and 64 percent of CANA respondents have visited St. James' Church. A number of individuals were identified during the fieldwork who are members of two and sometimes all three of the New Age Christian groups studied. However, these were a tiny minority. Far more important is the fact that the leaders of the groups studied are part of a dense social network. However, there is little institutional linkage among the various groups. For example, although Rev. Adrian Smith is a member of CANA, a cofounder of Christian TM, and a visitor to the Omega Order, these remain entirely distinct organizations.

So, may we conclude that there is a *movement* of Christaquarians? Many of the characteristics necessary for this conclusion are present among the groups considered. There is a viable legitimating historical tradition; a sizeable body of critical literature, both emic and etic; and a marked similarity of sociological characteristics that was revealed in the statistical surveys. It is even easier to fit these factors into the "movement" label if we are to use the family resemblance model of categorization, for this allows us to emphasize the differences as well as the acknowledged similarities between the various groups.

But there is one vital characteristic missing from the groups considered: nobody calls himself a Christaquarian. If we take Wouter Hanegraaff's characterization of the New Age movement as the cultic milieu having become conscious of itself (Hanegraaff 1996, 17) and apply it to Christaquarianism, this should be represented as the New Age fringe of Christianity becoming conscious of itself as a movement. But although there is a sizeable New Age fringe within Christianity, and a hostile consciousness of it from the evangelicals and other critics within the churches, Christaquarians are not yet conscious of themselves as a movement. For this reason, the hypothesis was rejected—for the time being.

NOTES

1. As set out in Rose (1996) and further discussed in Kemp 2003.
2. The paper is further discussed in Smith 2002.
3. See note 2.
4. See Kemp 2001 for further discussion of this notion.

REFERENCES

Albanese, Catherine. 1988. "Religion and the American Experience: A Century After." *Church History* 57: 337–51.

Barker, Eileen. 1992. *New Religious Movements: A Practical Introduction*. London: HMSO.

Bochinger, Christoph. 1995/1994. *"New Age" und moderne Religion: Religioswissenschaftliche Analysen*, rev. ed. Gutersloh: Chr Kaiser.

Campbell, Colin. 1972. "The Cult, the Cultic Milieu, and Secularization." In Michael Hill, ed. *A Sociological Yearbook of Religion in Britain*, vol. 5. London: SCM, pp. 119–36.

CANA. 1999. "Exploring Ways Forward for Christianity into the Twenty-First Century: A Paper for Dialogue." Oxford: CANA.

Clarke, Peter B. 1996. "Why NRMs Succeed or Fail," paper delivered at the King's College social sciences and anthropology postgraduate seminar, 12 December, London.

Cole, Michael, et al. 1990. *What Is the New Age?* London: Hodder and Stroughton.

D'Andrea, Anthony. 1997. "O Self Perfeito e a Nova Era: Individualism e Reflexividade em Religiosidades Pos-Tradicionais." Master's thesis (2nd version), Rio de Janeiro.

English, Barton D. 1994. "The Challenge of the New Age to Christian Theology and Life." Ph.D. diss., Edinburgh.

English-Lueck, June Anne. 1990. *Health in the New Age: A Study in California Holistic Practices*. Albuquerque: University of New Mexico.

Faith and Order Committee. 1994. "The New Age Movement: Report to Conference 1994." Peterborough: Methodist Publishing House.

Ferguson, Marilyn. 1980. *The Aquarian Conspiracy*. London: Paladin.

Festinger, Leon. 1957. *A Theory of Cognitive Dissonance*. London: Tavistock Publications.

Festinger, Leon, Henry W. Riecken, and Stanley Schachter. 1956. *When Prophecy Fails*. New York: Harper & Row.

Greer, Paul. 1994. "The Spiritual Dynamics of the New Age Movement." Ph.D. diss., Stirling Open University.

Groothuis, Douglas R. 1986. *Unmasking the New Age*. Leicester: Inter-Varsity Press.

———. 1988. *Confronting the New Age*. Leicester: Inter-Varsity Press.

———. 1990. *Revealing the New Age Jesus*. Leicester: Inter-Varsity Press.

Hanegraaff, Wouter J. 1996. *New Age Religion and Western Culture*. Leiden: Brill.

Heelas, Paul. 1996. *The New Age Movement: The Celebration of the Self and the Sacralization of Modernity*. Oxford: Blackwell.

Introvigne, Massimo. 2000. *New Age and Next Age*. Cassale Monferrato: Piemme. (1st ed. pub. as *Storia del New Age 1962–1992*, 1994.)

Irish Theological Commission. 1994. *A New Age of the Spirit? A Catholic Response to the New Age Phenomenon*. Dublin: Veritas.

Jorgensen, Danny L. 1982. "The Esoteric Community: An Ethnographic Investigation of the Cultic Milieu." *Urban Life* 10, no. 4: 383–407.

Kemp, Daren. 2000. "The Christaquarians? A Sociology of Christians in the New Age." Ph.D. diss., King's College London.

———. 2001. "Christaquarianism: A New Socio-Religious Movement of Postmodern Society?" *Implicit Religion* 4, no. 1: 27–40.

———. 2003. *New Age: A Guide*. Edinburgh: Edinburgh University Press.

Legere, Thomas E. 1993. "A Popular Book: Christianity for a New Age." Ph.D. diss., Union Institute Graduate School.

Lewis, James R., and J. Gordon Melton, eds. 1992. *Perspectives on the New Age*. New York: State University of New York Press.

Lucas, Philip. 1992. "The New Age Movement and the Pentecostal/Charismatic Revival: Distinct Yet Parallel Phases of a Fourth Great Awakening?" In James R. Lewis and J. Gordon Melton, eds., *Perspectives on the New Age*. New York: State University of New York Press, pp. 189–212.

Melton, J. Gordon, et al. 1990. *New Age Encyclopedia*. New York: Garland Publishing.

———. 1991. *New Age Almanac*. Detroit: Visible Ink Press.

Melucci, Alberto et al. 1989. *Nomads of the Present*. London: Hutchinson.

Mission Theological Advisory Group. 1996. *The Search for Faith and the Witness of the Church*. London: Church House.

Needham, R. 1975. "Polythetic Classification: Convergence and Consequences." *Man* 10: 349–69.

Omega Trust. 1994. *The Omega Offices*, 5th ed. Winford: Omega Publications.

Prince, Ruth. 1992. "An Anthropology of the 'New Age' with Special Reference to Glastonbury Somerset." M.Phil. thesis, St. Andrews.

Prince, Ruth, and David Riches. 2000. *The New Age in Glastonbury: The Construction of Religious Movements.* New York and Oxford: Berghahn Books.

Rhodes, Ron. 1986. An Examination and Evaluation of the New Age Christology of David Spangler. Th.D. diss., Dallas Theological Seminary.

Roof, Wade Clark, et al. 1993. *A Generation of Seekers: The Spiritual Journeys of the Baby Boom Generation.* San Francisco: HarperSanFrancisco.

Rose, Stuart. 1996. Transforming the World: An Examination of the Roles Played by Spirituality and Healing in the New Age Movement: "The Aquarian Conspirators Revisited." Ph.D. diss., Lancaster.

Roxburgh, Alan J. 1991. "On Being the Church in a New Age." D.Min. diss., Northern Seminary (Toronto).

Saliba, John A. 1999. *Christian Responses to the New Age Movement: A Critical Assessment.* London: Geoffrey Chapman.

Scott, Alan. 1990. *Ideology and the New Social Movements.* London: Routledge.

Seddon, Philip. 1990. *The New Age: An Assessment.* Nottingham: Grove Books.

Smith, Adrian B. 2002. *A New Framework for Christian Belief.* New Alresford, UK: John Hunt.

Spangler, David. 1984. *Emergence. The Rebirth of the Sacred.* New York: Dell.

Steyn, Chrissie. 1994. *Worldviews in Transition: An Investigation of the New Age Movement in South Africa.* Pretoria: University of South Africa.

Sutcliffe, Steven. 1998. "'New Age' in Britain: An Ethnographical and Historical Exploration." Ph.D. diss., Stirling Open University.

Tarrow, Sidney. 1994. *Power in Movement: Social Movements and Contentious Politics.* Cambridge: Cambridge University Press.

Thompson, Damian. 1997. *The End of Time: Faith and Fear in the Shadow of the Millennium* (expanded ed.). London: Minerva.

The Voice and the Eye: An Analysis of Social Movements. Cambridge: Cambridge University Press.

Wittgenstein, Ludwig. 1953. *Philosophical Investigations,* trans. G. E. M. Anscombe. Oxford: Blackwell.

Wood, Matthew. 1999. "Spirit Possession in a Contemporary British Religious Network: A Critique of New Age Movement Studies through the Sociology of Power." Ph.D. diss., Nottingham.

York, Michael. 1995. *The Emerging Network: A Sociology of the New Age and Neo-Pagan Movements.* Lanham, MD: Rowman & Littlefield.

SPIRITUAL COMMODIFICATION AND ETHICAL ISSUES

HEALING IN THE SPIRITUAL MARKETPLACE

Consumers, Courses, and Credentialism

Marion Bowman

One striking feature of late twentieth-century spirituality is the perception of the need for healing. It seems that for many people nowadays, healing is the new soteriology. As scholars such as Albanese (1992) and McGuire (1988, 1993) have indicated, the emphasis in many quarters has shifted from such questions as "What can I do to be saved?" or "What can I do to save the world?" to "What can I do to be healed?" or "How can I heal the world?" These questions come with multiple-choice answers.

We find in Britain (as elsewhere) a huge variety of meanings of healing and proposed means of achieving healing (see Bowman 2000). In this paper, I will briefly review some of the trends that are contributing to the present focus on healing and the place of healing in the spiritual marketplace before looking at the industry that is emerging in Britain as a result of this need for healing and some of the spiritual and financial ideas underpinning it.

HEALING AND THE SPIRITUAL MARKETPLACE

The complexities of the term "New Age" have been addressed by scholars elsewhere, most notably for the present purposes York (1995, 1997), Rose (1996),

From *Social Compass* 46, no. 2 (1999): 181–89. Copyright © 1999 by the International Society for the Sociology of Religion. Reprinted by permission of the International Society for the Sociology of Religion.

and Van Hove (1999). Let me therefore briefly state what I mean when I use "New Age" in this article and how I see its relationship to the spiritual market-place and the new healing industry.

I am cautious about using the label "New Age" too broadly or indiscrimi-nately. However, there are those who articulate a belief in their participation in, or helping to usher in, or the expected arrival of a New Age. How this New Age is to be brought about (paradigm shift, astrological movement), when it will commence (if it has not already done so), what it will be like, and so on all remain subject to debate.

Nevertheless, certain packages of ideas have become increasingly common both within and outside specifically New Age circles, such as the importance of the individual spiritual quest, interconnectedness, synchronicity (or "meaningful coincidence"/Jung's "*sinnvolle koinzidenz*"), a particular understanding of rein-carnation, the notion that spirituality and money need not be mutually exclusive, and, most significant in this context, the need for healing.

Particular stress has been laid on the role of the individual, the focus on self, and the importance accorded to individual perception and experience in the con-temporary spiritual milieu. While this is indeed a striking and important feature, speaking from the viewpoint of a religious studies scholar with a particular interest in vernacular religion, I would counsel caution in overstating the novelty of this phenomenon. There has always been an extent to which personal reli-giosity has been a very individual collage of beliefs and practices drawn from both official and vernacular traditions, influenced largely by personal experience and perceptions of efficacy (Bowman 1992). Individuals within what might be thought of as fairly monolithic religious traditions have woven very idiosyncratic fabrics of belief. Scholars have tended, for the most part, to ignore this. Within Christianity, for example, many have specifically believed in the importance of the individual's response to the divine (whether external or within), the indi-vidual's own understanding of scripture and contemporary events, and the authentic and authenticating nature of individual experience. The charge that self-religion is essentially selfish religion is an oversimplification that tends to overlook the fact that much religious activity is essentially about looking after the spiritual well-being of the individual self or soul; even the goal of realization that there is no soul or self is essentially an individual spiritual quest.

The big differences nowadays can be seen in individuals' freedom to talk openly about their beliefs, the perception that there is not one version of "Truth," the notion of serial spirituality or "singular, serial and multiple seeking strate-gies" (Sutcliffe 1997, 106), and the range and availability of materials for the individual collage.

The term "spiritual supermarket" has often been used in a derogatory fashion to describe both New Age and late-twentieth-century spirituality gener-ally. However, I have long regarded this as an accurate, value-free characterization of the contemporary situation in which many people are experiencing greater religious consumer choice than ever before due to globalized spiritual commodification. In terms of abundance, accessibility, and availability, this is a comparatively new phenomenon. The spiritual marketplace (Van Hove 1999) is therefore a concept that is helpful and appropriate.

Turning to the place of healing in the spiritual marketplace, although boundary drawing is rather difficult in this situation, I am concentrating here on holistic healing: that which considers body, mind, and spirit as one package. The relationship of New Age and healing was both discussed in, and summed up by the title of, Stuart Rose's article "Healing and the New Age: It's Not What You Do But Why You Do It" (2000). In this sector, a number of different roles might be involved—the individual seeking healing, the individual offering healing, the spiritual seeker—but they are by no means mutually exclusive. While holistic healing takes myriad forms, the packages of ideas outlined above—the individual quest, interconnectedness, synchronicity, reincarnation, spiritual materialism, the need for healing—frequently supply the common currency underlying the superficial diversity.

In the world of holistic healing, there is no single paradigm of illness, healing, and cure; both clients and practitioners constantly negotiate what is meant by such terms. This is not an entirely new situation. In eighteenth-century Britain, for example, there was a variety of paradigms or models of illness and therefore of cure. Many views of health and illness were what we would now describe as holistic. They were much concerned with balance, whether that meant the balance of the humors or whatever was considered the vital force, which might be blood, semen, or some less tangible substance. Disease as imbalance meant that there was an element of personal responsibility in maintaining the healthy balance, relating it to all aspects of life. The part could not be treated without addressing the whole. Illness was also frequently considered to contain a message; it was often seen to have a religious meaning, whether as a punishment, a warning, an ennobling experience, or a test of faith. It might be potentially damning, but it might equally be positive and potentially redemptive, a timely reminder of appropriate behavior. Illness therefore had to be considered on both the physical and metaphysical plane. (It is also worth noting that many historians locate the beginnings of "consumer society" in Georgian England, and medical historian Roy Porter has described this period as "an age of golden opportunity for cultivating the business side of medicine" [1986, 21]).

While medical pluralism has of course continued in a variety of forms, through religious healing, homeopathy, herbalism, patent medicines, and folk practices, from the latter part of the nineteenth century and much of the twentieth century, what came to be considered "orthodox" medicine revolved around the allopathic approach and the primacy of the germ theory. In this model, illness is seen as the indiscriminate invasion of the individual's body by germs from outside, with medicine's job being to repel or kill the invaders; alternatively, illness is seen as a breakdown in the body's mechanism or a part failure, which can be repaired or replaced. In this model of physical illness, disease is random, an alien entity that "afflicts our 'body'—which is not quite the same as our selves" (Porter 1987, 25). Just as illness is external to us, we have come to rely on an outside agent, from the medical profession, to cure us; we are passive recipients of both disease and cure. Illness has lost its "meaning."

It is therefore significant that we are now seeing a large-scale reemergence of holistic ideas about health and illness, about the importance of balance, about the vital force at the base of health. What is happening in relation to healing reflects a number of social and religious trends, some of which have already been touched upon. It has, for example, been claimed that many are adopting postmaterial values that emphasize self-expression and quality of life, rather than simply economic and physical security, and involve a new attitude to self that takes responsibility in areas of life previously left to professionals, such as clergy or doctors. Meanwhile, the fragmentation of society experienced at the personal level might be seen to contribute to a stress on the need for wholeness and reconstruction.

Much contemporary religiosity, as I have mentioned, has been characterized as "the spiritual supermarket" or "pick and mix spirituality." This characterization would certainly fit aspects of holistic healing. The individual can choose one form of healing, or put together a package, from a huge reservoir of alternatives, according to personal choice.

Again, we do well to remember that this is not an entirely new phenomenon. Healing has often been related to religion and complementary resources used at times of need: "One woman told me that her mother used to treat sties by crossing them with her wedding ring (an established folk religious cure), crossing them with her picture of St Gerard (of whom she was particularly fond), and bathing them with boracic acid (a widely recognised folk remedy)" (Bowman 1992, 16).

Nevertheless, the perceptions of available resources for healing and what needs to be healed have changed. In the present climate of enhanced consumer choice of healing predicated on a variety of worldviews, I consider it both useful and legitimate to regard holistic healing as a form of nonaligned spirituality, "believing without belonging" (Davie 1994).

Disease is coming to be seen not simply as a powerful message for the individual but for the universe; the need for healing is being perceived at both the individual and global levels. As a leaflet advertising healing Reiki puts it, "Today, there is a growing awareness that each individual bears responsibility for their own health and ultimately the fate of the planet." The publicity for a workshop on crystals claims, "Crystals are remarkable tools for healing, personal development and planetary transformation." Sir George Trevelyan, often described as the father of New Age in Britain, commented, "Holistic includes holiness and wholeness. Healing is the restoring of harmony to the living whole" (*The New Age*, TV program on channel 4, 1991). A key concept in such healing rhetoric is interconnectedness. Individuals may embark upon their own spiritual quest or ostensibly seek healing for themselves, but it is ultimately seen as part of a larger whole.

HEALING AND THE SPIRITUAL SERVICE INDUSTRY

What it is that we and the world need to be healed of, what constitutes healing, how it is to be achieved, and the source of healing are matters for constant exploration and negotiation.

Healing can be a do-it-yourself project, embarked upon through reading within the vast range of publications on the subject. Increasingly, adult and continuing education in Britain includes study relating to therapies of various sorts. The program for the University of Bath's community courses, for example, always features (in addition to old favorites such as art, music, literature, history and languages) courses under the title "Personal Skills," which include aromatherapy, Alexander technique, shiatsu, yoga, and reflexology. Throughout Britain there are innumerable healing workshops and/or holistic healers to choose from (Bowman 2000). In Bath the local Further Education College offers a holistic therapy course designed, as the course literature explains, "to appeal to the mature student." It includes modules in aromatherapy, reflexology, advanced massage techniques, and "investigative study in iridology, homeopathy, shiatsu-do, and Tai-chi."

The dazzling range of consumer choice in the spiritual and therapeutic marketplace provides a host of job opportunities. Nowadays in management development (an area much influenced either overtly or covertly by New Age ideas), there are no problems, only opportunities. So what might be perceived as a problem—the need for healing—presents opportunities both for the individuals who aspire to take control of this situation, to exercise their spiritual and financial autonomy to commission healing, and for the healers, who aspire to help while simultaneously making a living. Many holistic healers are female, frequently in their thirties or older, "caring" and "spiritual" people, whose background, education, circumstances, or youthful inclinations denied them a profession, medical or otherwise, but for whom holistic healing provides hitherto unrecognized career opportunities.

For many what starts as a personal interest or spiritual quest comes to take the form of a sort of postindustrial home industry. One Bath therapist, who in the past spent time in both Buddhist and Sufi communities, is a now yoga teacher in a variety of venues and in her home provides aromatherapy, relaxation, massage therapy, yoga therapy, and stress management. She wishes to train as an interfaith minister. She is very much concerned with body, mind, and spirit—ministering to physical and metaphysical needs—but rejects the title "healer" as she sees herself merely as a facilitator, not the source of healing. The multiskill approach of this woman, like so many of the new breed of healers, might be seen to reflect the "bricolage" approach of much contemporary religiosity, constantly seeking new approaches and insights, both for her own benefit and that of her clients.

While many see the growth in holistic healing as being in tune with spiritual trends, it is not unrelated to other economic trends. In Britain, for the moment at least, National Health services are free, but holistic healing always involves charges. However, contemporary holistic healers see themselves as offering a service that should be valued in both personal and financial terms. Very much in the spirit of the New Age soteriological entrepreneur, it is thought that one can be spiritual and make money, that cash is cool, not cold. While on one level the holistic healer is trying to contribute to the paradigm shift, she or he tends to be very much in the business of consumer choice and customer care. Holistic healing is entirely client-centered, and in that respect no different from "conventional" private medicine, which thrives on dissatisfaction with the existing system, the desire for privileged access, and individual attention, where the "specialist" has time to listen. The spiritual service industry of which holistic healing is a part, alongside New Age bed and breakfast (Bowman 1993, 49–54), inspirational publishing, and so on, is very much in the "small business" ethos of the Thatcher era—although probably neither Thatcherites nor healers would be entirely happy with that thought.

The need for healing that gives rise to the healing business in turn leads to the business of training healers. One concern raised in some quarters in relation to the explosion of alternative therapies is that of training and credentials. Very much in the New Age spirit of having to "walk your talk," what some therapists and counselors stress to their prospective clients is personal experience: One Bath healer's literature stresses that he has trained in psychosynthesis and has more than twenty-five years' experience of spiritual and personal development. On the other hand, a core process psychotherapist stresses her membership in the Association of Accredited Psychospiritual Psychotherapists and her inclusion on the UK Register of Psychotherapists.

There is undoubtedly a growth in credentialism in the holistic healing sector as in society generally. This was brought home to me by a student in Bath Spa University College's new religions course who commented, "It's a funny thing. Have you noticed that loads of these New Age characters seem to have letters after their name?" Professionalization is often seen in connection with the "angels in pinstripes" aspect of New Age, one Bath example being that of Anne Hassett the clairvoyant who became Acushla the psychic consultant. It is perhaps not surprising that some feel the need for diplomas and letters after their name, to assist their career and establish their credibility.

Yoga class at Florida State University gym, circa 1973. (*Author's collection*)

For the prospective healer, or practitioner who wishes to add to her or his skills, the British School of Yoga (BSY, established 1946) now offers home study courses in herbalism, aromatherapy, reflexology, acupressure and acupuncture, color therapy, and homeopathy. The New Age Foundation (a recently established division of the BSY) offers, through correspondence courses, diplomas in applied astrology, crystal healing, dream analysis, pendulum dowsing and radiesthesia, and tasseography (teacup reading). Successful candidates in such courses will receive the appropriate diploma and be entitled to term themselves an adept in mantic arts of the New Age Foundation (AMNAF); those completing two courses become a master in mantic arts (MMNAF), while "success in three courses confers the qualification of fellow in mantic arts (FMNAF)." Associated Stress Consultants, another branch of the BSY, offers the professional stress consultant's course and the professional relaxation therapist's course, both correspondence courses of eight lessons and two cassettes, both leading to a diploma and the letters MASC after one's name.

As the BSY and NAF course literature explains, diplomas in applied astrology will "take you to the level of the average Astrological Counsellor," tasseography "can be used for personal interest or to further your development as a New Age Counsellor"; and dream analysis is described as "almost essential for any prospective New Age Counsellor." The creation or molding of the role of the "New Age

Counsellor" here is particularly interesting. BSY's advertisement in *Kindred Spirit* 40 (autumn 1997) appears under the banner "Start Your Own Health Business" (p. 63). Indeed, a brief look at the advertisements in that "10 Year Anniversary Issue" of "The UK's Leading Guide for Body, Mind and Spirit" demonstrates vividly the elements of variety, professionalization, credentialism, and multiskilling in the holistic healing sector. There appear advertisements for such varied institutions as the College of Past Life Healing (p. 74), the School of Channelling (p. 67), the English Huber School of Astrological Counselling (p. 64), and the School of Insight and Intuition (p. 47). The College of Past Life Regression Studies offers individual therapy, self-development courses, and a diploma for therapists (p. 74), while the Hygeia College of Colour Therapy offers "Professional Training with Diploma" (p. 74). The advertisement for the International College of Crystal Healing urges, "Train for a Professional Qualification with ICCH" (p. 72), not to be confused with the International Association of Crystal Healing Therapists' offer of "a Professional and Comprehensive Crystal Therapists' Training Course" (p. 55) or the "Crystal Healers' Certificate Courses" offered by another source (p. 72). An advertisement for a Louise L. Hay (author of *You Can Heal Your Life*) teacher-training course to be held in California offers the opportunity to "Transform Your Life *And* Be Certified To Lead Courses!" (p. 66). It is claimed that "body electronics," offered as part of "Graham Stroud's Bodymind Processing" ("Enlightened Body—Enlightened Mind"), "has developed from alternative healing methods, scientific research and shamanistic and spiritual teachings" (p. 55). A shamanic healing and soul retrieval practitioners course is described as "an advanced ongoing training course designed for holistic practitioners who are interested in incorporating classic shamanic healing methods into their existing practice" (p. 72). Moreover, there is a brief advertisement for a " 'Promote Yourself' Marketing Workshop for Holistic Therapists" (p. 68), while Manna Management promotes a one-day seminar on "The Business of Healing" (p. 68). As Manna Management's advertising copy points out, "The fine balance between the spirituality of healing and managing a commercial business is often a dilemma." The day is to offer guidance on *spirituality versus commercialism* ("How to gain the best of both worlds"), *going it alone*, and *balancing creativity with commerce*, and is described as "a 'must' for anybody wishing to develop themselves further" (p. 68).

These advertisements, along with the previous examples, tell us much about healing in the spiritual marketplace. There are books and courses that cater for the individual who becomes involved in healing therapies and techniques for her or his own interest and development. Once involved in holistic healing on a do-it-yourself or client basis, some feel moved to become providers or practitioners themselves. However, it is noticeable that many in the new healing industry feel the need for constant accumulation of new skills; they, too, continue to develop personally and professionally, as part of their spiritual quest, rejecting a single path or narrow specialism.

As I have already indicated, I regard holistic healing as a form of nonaligned spirituality that demonstrates a number of characteristics of late-twentieth-century religiosity. Among these is the motif of the individual quest, on the part of both the client and the holistic healer, and a particular attitude to money. Spiritual progress has a price, however it is measured; the idea that profit and spirituality cannot converge is rejected. Nevertheless, it is worth noting that while New Age management consultants can make hundreds (indeed thousands) of pounds a day, healers are often more of a cottage industry with comparatively modest profits. Whether this reflects the type of person drawn to healing, market forces, or the fact that so many healers are women would be a fruitful area for further study.

Within the late-twentieth-century spiritual marketplace, holistic healing is perceived as a valuable commodity, both in its provision of healing and as an aid to self-development. Through healing, a variety of worldviews may be explored and experiences and insights gained, often predicated on ideas such as the individual quest, interconnectedness, reincarnation, synchronicity/meaningful coincidence, and a positive view of "spiritual materialism." Furthermore, it has given rise to a spiritual service industry developing in parallel to the service industry/small-business ethos of mainstream society, including a tendency toward credentialism.

The perceived need for healing and the new healing industry thus spawned are fascinating and significant aspects of late-twentieth-century spirituality. Consumer choice has progressed from the "corner shop" of resources previously available to the healing "hypermarket," which is now such an important part of the spiritual marketplace.

REFERENCES

Albanese, C. L. 1992. "The Magical Staff: Quantum Healing in the New Age." In J. R. Lewis and J. G. Melton, eds. *Perspectives on the New Age*. Albany: State University of New York Press.

Bowman, M. 1992. *Phenomenology, Fieldwork, and Folk Religion*. Cardiff, Wales: BASR Occasional Papers, no. 6.

———. 1993. "Drawn to Glastonbury." In I. Reader and T. Walter, eds. *Pilgrimage in Popular Culture*. Basingstoke, UK: Macmillan.

———. 2000. "The Need for Healing: A Bath Case Study." In M. Bowman, ed. *Healing and Religion*. Enfield Lock, UK: Hisarlik Press, pp. 95–107.

Davie, G. 1994. *Religion in Britain Since 1945*. Oxford: Blackwell.

McGuire, M. 1988. *Ritual Healing in Suburban America*. New Brunswick and London: Rutgers University Press.

———. 1993. "Health and Spirituality as Contemporary Concerns." In *Annals of the American Academy of Political and Social Sciences*, p. 527.

Porter, R. 1986. "Before the Fringe: Quack Medicine in Georgian England," *History Today* 36 (November): 16–22.

————. 1987. *Disease, Medicine and Society in England, 1550–1860*. Basingstoke, UK: Macmillan.

Rose, S. 1996. "Transforming the World: An Examination of the Roles Played by Spirituality and Healing in the New Age Movement," Ph.D. diss., Lancaster University.

Rose, S. 2000. "Healing in the New Age: It's Not What You Do But Why You Do It." In M. Bowman, ed. *Healing and Religion*. Enfield Lock, UK: Hisarlik Press, pp. 69–80.

Sutcliffe, S. 1997. "Seekers, Networks, and 'New Age,'" *Scottish Journal of Religious Studies* 18, no. 2:97–114.

Van Hove, H. 1999. "L'emergence d'un 'marche spirtuel.'" *Social Compass* 46, no. 2: 161–72.

York, M. 1995. *The Emerging Network : A Sociology of the New Age and Neo-pagan Movements*. Lanham, MD: Rowman & Littlefield.

————. 1997. "New Age and the Late Twentieth Century." *Journal of Contemporary Religion* 12, no. 3:401–19.

21
APPROPRIATING THE DIDGERIDOO AND THE SWEAT LODGE
New Age Baddies and Indigenous Victims?
Christina Welch

INTRODUCTION

Cultural appropriation can be defined as when "Members of one culture take the cultural practices of another as if their own, or as if the right of possession should not be questioned or contested" (Hart 1997, 138). The politics of appropriation are perhaps nowhere more fraught than in regard to the New Age and New Age Pagan[1] appropriation of indigenous sacred traditions.

Both New Ageism and New Age Paganism are contemporary religiosities that emphasize personal transformation and healing. Further, in a reaction to the Western nature/technology dichotomy, they tend toward a discovery of the sacred in everyday life. Their desire to (re-)spiritualize is often achieved using the appropriated sacred traditions of indigenous cultures, in particular those of American Indian and Aboriginal Australian peoples. In the eyes of New Agers and New Age Pagans, these other cultures are seen as emphasizing elements missing from contemporary Western society, notably environmental friendliness, a tribal/community ethic, and a lack of technologization and industrialization; attributes that combine to form a Golden Age Arcadian fantasy of indigenous life. However, viewing indigenous peoples through Rousseau-tinted glasses and attempting to emulate their lifeways has led New Agers and New Age Pagans to

From *Journal of Contemporary Religion* 17, no. 1 (2002): 21–38. Copyright © 2002 by the *Journal of Contemporary Religion*. Reprinted with permission of the *Journal of Contemporary Religion*. http://www.tandf.co.uk/journals/carfax/13537903.html.

be perceived of "inherently exploitative . . . rip-off" merchants engaged in the "hyper-spiritualization" of indigenous sacred traditions (Neuenfeldt 1998, 74). Indeed, typically those engaged in cultural appropriation are dichotomized into "'bad' New Age[rs versus] 'good' Aboriginal victims" (Rowse in Grossman and Cuthbert 1998, 772). But are New Agers and New Age Pagans the bad guys of appropriation? Is such an accusation really justified?

Sociologist Brian Fay argues that human history is a bazaar, a "crossroads in which . . . skills and resources are traded, stolen, improved upon [and] passed along to others" (1996, 231). Certainly cultures are not static and enclosed entities, but dynamic and interactive. Yet the West's history of colonialism must not be overlooked in any discussion regarding appropriation, particularly since, although allegedly "post-colonial" (Grimes 1996, 433), the West continues to represent and legitimize the representation of other's culture and identity. With this as a background, I focus my analysis of the legitimacy of the West's utilization of knowledge and resources on two sacred traditions that are commonly appropriated by New Agers and New Age Pagans: the Aboriginal Australian didgeridoo, a sacred instrument, and the American Indian sweat lodge, a sacred ritual.

EARTHING THE DEBATE

The didgeridoo is the popularist name for an Australian termite–hollowed tree limb that produces earthy drones when air is blown through it. Today the instrument stands as an icon of Australian culture and a symbol of Pan-Aboriginality. Yet, until relatively recently, the didgeridoo was local only to certain areas of the continent, including northeast Arnhem Land, where to the resident people of the Yolngu community, it is known the *Yidaki*.

In its traditional Yolngu context, the didgeridoo is both a sacred and a not-so-sacred instrument, as indigenous cultures generally do not operate under the rigid sacred/profane divide that is common to Christianity and Western philosophy. Thus, in Yolngu culture the instrument has a special or set-aside use for ceremony, where one didgeridoo alone sets the rhythm to songs that, with the accompaniment of clapsticks, dancers, and singers, honors, brings to life, and reinforces the power of the ancestral Dreaming that is being sung into existence (Knopoff 1997, 41–42). Dreaming Law, the land-based and localized ceremonies performed by particular individuals and/or groups of individuals based upon birth heritage, seeks to unify that which the West understands as the past, present, and future (Swain 1995, 19–25).

For the Yolngu, the instrument is typically used in men's secret and sacred ceremonies, such as circumcision and initiation, or in the male preserve of mortuary ritual. However, in nonceremonial informal contexts, didgeridoos are available for women and children to use for their own enjoyment and as tools to provide a continuing link with the clan's public history (Knopoff 1997, 42; Magowen 1997, 165; Yunupingu 1997, viii). The didgeridoo therefore is an integral part of the sociocultural and musical practice of the Yolngu people, traditionally functioning to affirm sociality within the group and reconfirm relationships with Dreaming ancestors, regardless of its male-only ceremonial usage.

However, as the use of the didgeridoo has spread beyond its native context, prominence has been given to its connections with private male knowledge. Ethnomusicologist Linda Barwick argues that this overt sensitivity to gender differentiation has connections with the reclamation of identity in the wake of colonialism (1997, 89). Certainly the tolerance shown to female players by northern Aboriginals, whose language and culture have been less threatened by European invasion and settlement than other areas, opposes the stricter taboos of the south, whose experience of cultural loss and dispossession undoubtedly affords a desire to protect what remains of any Aboriginal way of life (Barwick 1997, 89).

With the didgeridoo then functioning traditionally, as well as providing a symbol for contemporary Aboriginal Australians wishing to construct an Aboriginal identity despite the historic and current lack of a distinct and single Aboriginal culture, it is perhaps unsurprising that the instrument now also functions as a Pan-Aboriginal connection to the land, a Pan-Aboriginal tool for accessing the Dreaming. Recent Aboriginal understandings of the land are perhaps best exemplified by Mandawuy Yunupingu, lead vocalist of Yothu Yindi, an internationally celebrated Yolngu rock group. He states of the didgeridoo, "Cherish the sound, for it is the sound of Mother Earth" (Yunupingu 1997, viii), and it is this perception of the instrument that has found resonance with many New Agers and New Age Pagans. For them, the didgeridoo's connections with the sacred, the land as Mother Earth, Dreaming spirit-ancestors, and indigeneity fulfills romantic yearnings for a pretechnological and pre-industrial, even precolonial, lifestyle.

In many ways, the same Byronic fulfillment could be applied to the New Age and New Age Pagan understandings of American Indian culture, where the concepts of universal sacrality and Mother Earth are also prominent. Certainly, the writings of persons perceived as authoritative in New Age understanding, talk of the earth in such terms, Wallace Black Elk (1991) and Wa'Na'Nee'Che (1996), for example. Yet traditionally many of the American Indian nations had not one but several Earth-based goddesses, a fact that these works seem to ignore. However, in a similar vein to modern Aboriginal Australians, contemporary American Indians have embraced Mother Earth as a Pan-American Indian icon, with the concept of the sweat lodge actualizing her womb.

Like the Australian instrument, this American Indian ritual goes by different local names, but unlike the didgeridoo, some variety of sweat lodge has existed virtually everywhere in North America and also in many other parts of the world. The benefits of such baths extend beyond those of personal hygiene to encompass social factors. Yet despite this or, as Joseph Bruchac argues, more possibly because of it, Christian colonizing nations forbade sweat lodges (1993, 25). Indeed, it was not until the 1930s that the United States federal government repealed the act that since 1873 had banned sweat lodges as religious ceremonies. Yet clandestine sweat lodges survived and some nations, such as the Lakota (popularly Sioux), have been able to revive this tradition (Bruchac 1993, 26–27).

For the Lakota, like other American Indian nations, the sweat lodge, or *intipi*, has much significance. Gifted to the people as a rite by White Buffalo Calf Woman, the lodge is used as a spiritual and/or physical reviver. Supervised and led by a sacred person of either sex, the lodge, which is traditionally single sex only, generally accommodates five or six persons. Purified by tobacco and sage, the lodge is the universe in microcosm, with each part of the construct having some sacred and cosmological significance (Powers 1977, 89). Yet the lodge is only a lodge, and thus sacred, when in use. Therefore, by having a special or set-aside status in a society where all is conceived of as sacred, the American Indian sweat lodge is like the didgeridoo in its ceremonial context.

Similarly, both didgeridoo and sweat lodge ceremonies have particular songs and words that are used during the ritual and function as sacred lore. While for Aboriginal Australians this lore is handed down orally/aurally over the generations, for American Indians it is generally exclusive to each medicine man or woman, coming to him or her through the years in visions from personal spirits, often in an ordinarily incomprehensible language (Powers 1986, 7, 25). Unlike the didgeridoo, however, the sweat lodge can and does function as a sacred rite alone or as a preliminary to other sacred rituals such as vision quest, and despite its contemporary Pan-American Indian construct, local differences still occur, such as the Oglala *Yuwipi* ceremony (Powers 1982).

The diversity of detail and personal practices in the sweat lodge tradition are in many ways consistent with the New Age tendency toward an individualized spirituality. This, when combined with the New Age perceived connections with Mother Earth, has allowed the American Indian sweat lodge, like the Aboriginal Australian didgeridoo, to function as a link between indigenous peoples and Westerners searching for a Golden Age lifestyle. Both traditions have been adopted and adapted by New Agers and New Age Pagans, often without addressing the controversies that rage when members of the originating peoples contest the appropriation of sacred traditions and sacred knowledge.

ALTERNATIVE ABORIGINALITY

To be able to comprehend the New Age and New Age Pagan understandings of indigenous traditions and their appropriation of such, it is necessary to examine the sources of information available. A look around any typical High Street bookshop will show that access to material written by indigenous peoples is limited. Writings about indigenous spirituality, which are generally confined to the Mind, Body, and Spirit shelves, are more often than not by Western-and/or New Age–oriented authors, anthropologists, and other academics. Similarly, Western conceptions of the didgeridoo are mostly confined to Western interpretation.

The increased awareness of world music has to some extent allowed indigenous recording artists the opportunity to gain success, but the need to fit into a Western commercial niche somewhat limits these opportunities. Hence the appeal of the Aboriginal group Yothu Yindi, which specifically gears its sound to a more Western ear.[2] In addition, festivals such as Glastonbury, and in particular WOMAD (the World of Music, Arts and Dance), have added to the appeal of the didgeridoo. With Aboriginal artists Yothu Yindi providing links with Mother Earth, and Kev Carmody (1997) supplying a political background to the instrument, it is perhaps unsurprising that the didgeridoo now has a countercultural, ecospiritual charm. This may be best expressed by didgeridoo players Justin Timson and Bart, whom I met at the 1999 Glastonbury festival.

Bart, who holds "Aboriginal philosophy in very high regard," advised me to read the highly controversial publication by the Western author Marlo Morgan, *Mutant Message Down Under*, to learn about Aboriginal Australian culture. He informed me that, through his understanding of the channeling of energy and the resonance of matter, playing the didgeridoo connects him to, and helps him heal, the earth. Told by David Blanazi, an Aboriginal elder, that "anyone could play the didj," he felt that the instrument functioned as a "great advert for Aboriginal culture [as] their more simple pure values" were being used by Westerners to help heal "our out of control society" (Bart 1999).

Unlike Bart, Justin Timson, who manufactures his Sacred Elder didgeridoos for sale at festivals and on the Internet, has traveled in northern Australia and was taught to play the didgeridoo by Aboriginal Australians. He admits to learning much of his cultural knowledge from the Internet but, by "confirming the content with other sites," ensures its authenticity as best he can (Timson 1999). Timson has seen firsthand the problems that Aboriginal people face: alcoholism, living rough, racial harassment in urban areas, and the loss of traditional ways. Yet it must be noted that none of this makes it onto his Web site, which arguably continues to perpetuate the stereotypical perception of a tribal people in touch with their environment (Timson).

It would seem then that despite an increase in the familiarity of the didgeridoo, there has not necessarily been a corresponding increase in the understanding of the culture that underpins it. Indeed it could be argued that there is a tendency for didgeridoo players like Bart and Timson to insist upon an insight into or a connection with Aboriginal culture that they do not fully comprehend or possibly, due to marketing reasons, do not wish to expound. While academic Sam Gill defends the right for people "to be inspired by and influenced by other traditions" he adds that "to do so superficially and to claim special knowledge of the source tradition is to engage in what can only be termed domination and conquest" (1988, 77).

While outside its Aboriginal context the didgeridoo can act as a tool for self-growth and increased groundedness, when misleading and/or potentially disrespectful information is sent into the public domain by persons indicating notions of authenticity, questions regarding the appropriateness of such arises.

This issue is perhaps most evident from the controversy surrounding Marlo Morgan's best-selling novel, which has been described as popularizing "racialized [and] disparaging views of Aborigines as Primitive, Other-Worldly and unable to compete in the 'modern world'" (Neuenfeldt 1998, 89).

So passionate is the feeling in regard to this work that Robert Eggington, a Noongar man and chairman of the Dumbartung Aboriginal Corporation, has demanded an apology from, and actively campaigned against, Morgan for her derogatory representation of Aboriginal Australians (Mulcock 1997). Yet such tales told as fact are not limited to Aboriginal culture. Anglo-American author Lynne Andrews has been accused of perpetuating the myth that American Indian peoples have been waiting for the right white person to whom to entrust their cultural values before modernity, which has brought them to the brink of extinction, completes its task and the world loses their precious knowledge forever (Miskimmin 1996, 207).

Nor indeed is such an understanding confined to novelists. Earth-mysteries writer Paul Devereux (1992, 1–2) and environmentalist Maurice Strong (qtd. in Milton 1998, 87) are among those who view indigenous peoples as superior to the West environmentally and spiritually. But such a conception has huge repercussions in how the West comprehends indigeneity. First, appropriating indigenous intellectual and cultural property is validated by the West's perceived need to save such valuable information for posterity, for so important for the planet are these pieces of very sacred knowledge that indigenous peoples "simply cannot be allowed to hold them in secret" (Brown 1994, 12). Further, urbanized indigenous peoples are often seen as having "developed into inferior and less authentic selves" (Lattas in Grossman and Cuthbert 1998, 871), while those with problems such as alcoholism and drug addiction are seen as unable to handle white civilization (Rose 1997). Such views are not only often inaccurate but tend to trap indigenous peoples within a false and static culture. Not only are they denied any change from the West's comprehension of what indigenous people should be, but their worldviews are defined for them.

A further problem emerges from Pia Altieri's (2000) argument that for some indigenous peoples, a copy is understood as the real thing, and as such any replication is perceived of as authentic. With settlers in Australia replicating, and thus legitimizing, Aboriginal identification with the land in order to authorize their own claims to Australia as a homeland (Marcus 1997, 29), Aboriginal Australians continue to function for the benefit of the West, and thus in many ways continue to be a colonized people. In addition, Patricia Sherwood argues that using the didgeridoo as "a bridge to bring whites back to the land, themselves and each other" allows it to literally function as an instrument of expiation absolving "new users of many of the sins of Western society" (1997, 150). Certainly this concept would fit with native wanna-bes yearning for a precolonial ideal, but it is one that I doubt many New Agers and New Age Pagans would openly adhere to.

Allied to the issue of potentially derogatory portrayals and inaccurate information of indigenous peoples is the problem of secret or restricted knowledge. Nowhere is this more open to misapplication than via the Internet. Concern has been expressed by Peter Danaja, an Arnhem Land representative, regarding the online publication of secret knowledge traditionally available only to the initiated during the *Djungguwan* ceremony (Tomita 1999), a ceremony that enhances the fertility of the land and the people (Neuenfeldt 1998, 76). Danaja requested that, in respect for the culture, the offending details be removed from Ed Drury's *Myths and Legends* site. Noting that such details were provided to anthropologists by Aborigines and are openly available in print, Drury replied that the request was tantamount to censorship, but he would "cut out the so called 'secret words' . . . and post a disclaimer about the rest" (Tomita 1999). Despite his being contacted with regard to furthering discussions about indigenous information available to nonindigenous peoples, Danaja has not taken a further role. Arguably this calls into question the agency of indigenous peoples who choose to take a role in the dissemination of cultural material to the West.

Certainly it should be noted that while many Aboriginal women are now prohibited from playing the didgeridoo in any context, the commerciality of the instrument seems to legitimize the overlooking of gender taboos. In Alice Springs and similar outback tourist destinations, Australian Aboriginal women make, play, and sell the didgeridoo to visitors and manufacture instruments for the export market (Neuenfeldt 1997, 109–12). Thus, while intercultural appropriation of knowledge, traditions and rituals undoubtedly poses the main threat to the heritage of indigenous peoples, intracultural appropriation has significantly altered traditional understandings of the didgeridoo.

It would seem then that New Age and New Age Pagan communities are fed a diet of nonnative Aboriginal information, which feeds their romanticized notions of Aboriginal life, combined with ambiguous information from Aboriginals themselves. Illusions to the underlying spirituality of all matter is used to justify the appropriation of their sacred knowledge and their perceived connections to the land as Mother Earth. The didgeridoo then functions as a tool for New Agers and New Age Pagans to access precious and ancient Aboriginal Australian knowledge and as a Pan-Australian symbol of Aboriginality, of belonging to Australia.

WHITE SHAMANS AND PLASTIC MEDICINE MEN

If the didgeridoo functions as a symbol of Aboriginality for Aboriginal and white Australians as well as acting as a tool for New Agers to access Aboriginal Australian spirituality and fuel romanticized notions of Earth-connectedness, does the sweat lodge tradition function similarly for American Indian spirituality?

Certainly there are similarities between the two indigenous cultures: Both are ex-colonies; both peoples are romantically portrayed by the West as inherently connected to the land as Mother Earth, despite traditions to the contrary; and both are also perceived by the West in Pan-indigenous terms, despite a traditional and contemporary lack of such a notion by the peoples themselves. In addition, authors and artists from both cultures are subject to the commercial restrictions of Western publishing houses.

The unequal balance of power in publishing has several effects. First, there is a tendency for Westerners when confronted with restrictions regarding secret knowledge to "cry censorship" (Hladki 1994, 104) rather than to respect the secrecy and sacrality of information—note that Drury removed only part of the offending Aboriginal Australian ceremony. Further, there is the issue of presenting indigenous peoples in a particular light; currently, the romantic myth of indigeneity is in fashion. This is propagated by a combination of "informal, imaginative and anecdotal" New Age work and the writings of academics who are engaged in the more "archival-based pursuit of knowledge" (Smith 1999, 20). However, this Rousseau-inspired perception of indigenous peoples is problematic because, as American Indian academic Vine Deloria notes, "Every significant [American Indian] leader of the previous century was eventually done in by his own people" (1977, 592), and indeed far from the noble savage image, many Indian tribes were "intolerant, patriarchal, hierarchical and warlike" (Marshall 1992, 148). In addition, archaeologist Julio Betancourt claims that evidence exists to suggest that intensive deforestation was the cause for the demise of the twelfth-century New Mexico farming community, the Anazasi (Malone 1992).

Whether it is true or not, a refusal to accept a darker side of American Indian life is something that is not indicative only of those engaged in New Age spirituality. American Indian Margo Thunderbird insists that Euro-immigrants "killed in battle or assassinated . . . the best of our leaders" (Churchill 1994, 216). It is arguable that appropriators who accept Thunderbird's argument can trap themselves in a complex web of "post"-colonial guilt, taking on an indigenous identity in order to reject the past and present flaws of Western society (Piggott in Bowman 1996, 243). Thus, wanna-bes emulate either because of their own, albeit misleading, perceptions of American Indians as romantic noble savages or because their forebears were, and their peers continue to be, exploitative ignoble savages.

It is notable that much of the literature on the market is written by nonindigenous authors and Westernized Native Americans such as Sun Bear and

Wallace Black Elk, who are considered by traditional American Indians to be inauthentic American Indians or "plastic medicine men" (Churchill 1992, 220). The tendency to portray American Indians as dancing through the summer rather than working their gardens has affected many young Indians who are learning traditional ways from such works instead of from traditional tribal elders. An example here is the plastic medicine man and author Wa'Na'Nee'Che, who has a tendency to gear sweat lodges to Western standards. In conversation he informed me that as the lodge is the womb of Mother Earth, the experience should only be a pleasant one. There was no indication of the intensity of heat in traditional sweat lodges, nor that the ceremony had or has national variations (Wa'Na'Nee'Che 1999). It would seem then that "academia and its by-products" continue to make American Indians victims of a "conceptual prison" (Deloria 1969, 85–87, 93) that categorizes indigenous peoples, their worldviews, and cultural practices only in Western imperialist terms.

The issue of plastic medicine men is a contentious one, as many of the American Indians on the New Age ritual circuit "honestly believe that the world will be a better place if people adopt key principles of [American] Indian spirituality" (Brown 1994, 16). John Two Birds, for instance, asserts that a vision told him not only to spread American Indian spirituality to the Western world and thus reawaken "tribal memor[ies]," but that his people would discredit him for doing such "salvational" work (Two Birds 1999). Whether this is a marketing ploy is difficult to say. The *Chovihano* Patrick Jasper Lee, a Romany gypsy shaman, says much the same of his calling to teach the Romany way to non-Romanies (Lee 1999). Certainly a rejection by one's own people can be seen to add notions of authenticity and desirability in the Christian-dominated West.

Such is the contention regarding the passing on of sacred knowledge by non-native peoples and those conceived of as plastic medicine men that in 1994 a declaration of war was made by the Lakota nation "against exploiters of Lakota spirituality." This declaration of zero tolerance, which undoubtedly inspired Eggington's 1995 proclamation against Marlo Morgan, was issued by Lakota, Dakota, and Nakota nations against "non-Indian . . . commercial profiteers" and charlatans and calls for an end to the exploitation and misrepresentation of "sacred traditions and spiritual practices" (Churchill 1994, 273–77). As "Indians don't sell their spirituality to anybody, for any price" (McCloud in Churchill 1992, 218), Sun Bear, Black Elk, and their ilk, who would "sell their mother if they thought it would turn a quick buck," are deemed not to be authentic (Churchill 1992, 218). Certainly Deloria agrees that the born-again missionary mindedness of intercultural conversion by those who instruct nonnatives in native ways is "contrary to every known tenet of any tribal tradition" (Deloria in Hernandez-Avila 1997, 346). Yet he has praised Black Elk for his "ethical teachings" (Porterfield 1990, 161). Thus, it would appear that not every American Indian is totally against the dissemination of indigenous practices. This is unsurprising considering that American Indians are not a homogeneous group with a unified perspective, just as the radical environmentalist group Earth First! is testament to the fact that not every appropriating group is guilty of disrespectful exploitation (Taylor 1997, 204).

There is evidence, however, of prophecies that foretold the need for Westerners to understand the ways of the American Indian, but it should be noted that those who spoke, and still speak, of such prophecies were and are generally those involved in the instruction of nonnatives. Sun Bear, for instance, taught that Western wanna-bes would need to join with "native peoples . . . to avert the destruction of the Earth." Further, he believed that reconciliation and renewal were possible only through the learning of the "sacred [red] path" (Johnson). As his teachings generally reach their audience through the New Age movement, it is perhaps predictable that many New Agers and New Age Pagans understand their appropriated practices as permissible. However, in her critique of white shamanism, Wendy Rose notes that Sun Bear, although Cherokee by blood, "never participated in bona fide native activities" (1992, 414). But where does this leave New Age and New Age Pagan appropriators, when their desire for indigenous information is met only by the works of natives such as Sun Bear and Wallace Black Elk, novelists such as Marlo Morgan and Lynne Andrews, and writers such as Paul Devereux?

The genuine need felt by some people for an alterNative way of living, more in-touch with nature and one's spiritual self, is ironically one that will be satisfied one way or another in a society that promotes the fast-living, quick-fix ethic and is in touch with the consumers' desires. However, what the New Age reader wants, what is palatable to the spiritual seeker, is not necessarily something that the traditional indigenous writer can provide. As William Powers notes, only when Westernized natives, such as Black Elk, speak do Westerners listen. In a society that allows Indians to be Indians because it dictates notions of authentic indigeneity, the "literary imperialism and literary compromise" that restricts both indigenous and nonindigenous authors further reinforces the romanticization and objectification of indigenous peoples (Powers 1990, 149–50).

This attitude can be exemplified by Timothy Frekes's impassioned introduction to Wa'Na'Nee'Che's *Principles of Native American Spirituality*, an introductory guide to native lifeways containing rituals to practice at home. What inspired Frekes's interest in American Indian culture was a poster depicting a "solitary and noble Native American looking wistfully at never-ending, empty, open plains" and the famous Cree-attributed statement, "Only when the last tree has been cut down, only after the last river has been polluted, only after the last fish has been caught, only then will you find that money cannot be eaten" (Wa'Na'Nee'Che and Freke 1996, xv).

This sentimental understanding of American Indian life is not only factually incorrect—the stuff of many Hollywood films—but it continues to trap contemporary native peoples in the Western mold of authentic indigeneity as defined by the Western media. In addition, by portraying American Indian life as fixed and frozen, the ongoing dynamic process of living is denied contemporary native peoples (Coombe 1997, 89), and they become subject to a future based on Western idealized nostalgia, which does little more than show that wanna-bes are sincere in their dissatisfaction with contemporary Western culture (Root 1997, 230). Interestingly, the ethically oriented magazine *New Internationalist* has successfully returned to using the Cree-attributed statement after a ten-year break to increase circulation and sales (York 2000).

A benefit that stems from the availability of writing about indigenous peoples and their lifeways arises for those seeking to return to forgotten ways. The Coquille nation has recovered lost traditions through accessing anthropological texts (Macnaughtan 1995), while for the Mi'kmaq nation, the powerful and beneficial effects of traditional rituals such as the sweat lodge are increasingly used to aid and support individuals in their fight against alcoholism, drug addiction, and family violence (Anderson, Crellin, and Misel 2000, 247–47). Yet ironically, many of the contemporary social problems that indigenous peoples are facing, such as unemployment, poverty, and homelessness, all arguably Western imports and/or products of "politically oppressive [colonial] regimes" (Smith 1999, 4, 146), are confronted using somewhat Westernized interpretations of traditional rituals. With "tradition" having been Westernized, the issues of decolonialization and a postcolonial West are surely problematic.

Considering the West's history, then, the appropriation of indigenous sacred traditions by New Age and New Age Pagan wanna-bes seems to have colonialist overtones. Yet, as previously noted, such an accusation should be tempered against the prevalence of intracultural appropriation and indigenous agency.

IN"DIDG"ENOUS ACTION

In examining the issue of indigenous agency in the dissemination of sacred knowledge and traditions and of indigenous understandings of appropriation, the question of respect is of prime concern. With an increase in Western curiosity for indigenous culture has come an increase in inaccurate information. Fiction writing in particular has provided a medium where profit-making rather than a true reflection of culture has surfaced. The work of Marlo Morgan, while lauded by the Wurundjeri elder Burnam Burnam as portraying Aboriginal Australians as "the regal and majestic people that we are" (Hume 2000, 134), has caused a storm in other quarters.[3] Thus, the issue of indigenous agency in regard to New Age and New Age Pagan understandings of indigenous culture needs to be addressed.

In reference to the didgeridoo and Aboriginal Australian culture, Yunupingu, lead vocalist of Yothu Yindi, emphasizes the healing aspect of the instrument, suggesting that the "peaceful vibrations" that penetrate one's mind lead to "inner spiritual oneness" (1997, viii). Indeed, his Web site deals specifically with the ability of the didgeridoo to act as a medium of reconciliation, in this case literally healing cultural differences. However, one must recognize that implicit in Yunupingu's understanding is the notion of respect. As he respects his traditions, he expects those who appropriate them to do likewise. Considering himself disconnected from the "ancestral spirit-related symbolic association of ceremonial performance," he continues to adhere to traditional understandings of Aboriginal culture; while sound engineers are consulted regarding the pitch of the instrument, the permission of clan elders is gained prior to using ceremonial headdresses during stage performances (Knopoff 1997, 50–53). By recognizing the continuing vitality of traditional lifeways in accommodating contemporary material, he believes that his didgeridoo playing does not interfere with Dreaming and that he is bringing important values into the Western marketplace.

Furthermore, in regard to respect, anthropologist David H. Turner writes of an Aboriginal man, Gula, who "knows secrets" of other lands, their people, and Dreaming. As he is forbidden to teach unowned knowledge, when he dies, such knowledge dies with him. His owned songs he has passed onto his eldest daughter, and despite traditional prohibitions it is her intention that when Gula dies, she will sing at his funeral. If she is unchallenged, a new tradition will be established, exemplifying the centrality of change in traditional life (1997, 234). Both here and with Yunupingu's use of the didgeridoo, the respectful nature of appropriation, of challenge and change to traditional life is explicit, as is the respect shown for the refusal to break traditional prohibitions on the dissemination of secret knowledge.

Respect is something often missing from New Age understandings of appropriation, as the following example shows. During a Reconciliation Circle at the 1995 Woodford-Maleny Folk Festival in Queensland, Australia, an Aboriginal woman spoke of her experiences as one of the stolen generation. After speaking she was confronted by a New Ager with the following grievance: "I came here to learn about your culture and to share in your culture [not] to be lectured at and made to feel bad about what happened in the past" (qtd. in Grossman and Cuthbert 1998, 779).

In reply Walbira Gindin, an Aboriginal activist, informed all present that: "You may think our culture is pretty, but you can't have our culture without our politics— and our politics ain't always pretty" (qtd. in Grossman and Cuthbert 1998, 780).

For many indigenous peoples, Western appropriation of traditional culture continues to be understood as a continuation of colonialism. This is due to the lack of Western appreciation of the political understandings that accompany and reinforce indigenous belief systems. Indeed, with the ownership and usage of objects and rituals so intrinsic to traditional systems, the issue of protocol by those outside the system is one that is close to the hearts of many indigenous people.

Arguably the lack of context in regard to the appropriation of indigenous sacred traditions by New Agers and New Age Pagans can be considered ironic. Not only are traditional rituals generally performed for the benefit of the community, reinforcing social cohesion and honoring ancestors and so forth, but, as Carol Lee Sanchez asserts, pedagogical issues such as wastefulness, violence, and hunting to near extinction are transmitted through the generations via the oral/aural tradition of native myths and legends (1993, 216). Yet in their search for Arcadia, these stories that pass on social and environmental teachings are ignored in favor of appealing but decontextualized rituals that are employed only to heal the self. What is of particular concern here is, as previously noted, that the decontextualized knowledge is then reattributed to indigenous culture, becoming normative in the process.

Yet, as plastic medicine men demonstrate, it is not only New Age and New Age Pagans that decontextualize indigenous sacred traditions. The agency of indigenous peoples in the dissemination of their culture must not be overlooked. Lynne Hume writes of two Australian Aboriginals who offer New Age workshops, David Mowaljarlai, a Ngarinyin elder from western Australia, who offers to share "the wisdom of an elder . . . to bring forth and nourish the potent, creative core of the masculine spirit," and Tjanara Goreng-Goreng, a traditional healer dancer, who offers Reiki and aromatherapy as well as uses "chakras" and "channelling" to draw "people closer to the essential force of [Dreaming] energy" (2000, 131–32). The sharing of knowledge with nonindigenous people is an activity not without controversy; while some approve, others do not. However, the differences in opinion highlight the fact that indigenous people are not a homogeneous group with a unified response to appropriative practices. This is perhaps most evident with regard to the American Indian tradition. While elder Lewis Sawaquat sees no difficulty in the imparting of sacred knowledge to those willing to listen and learn (Sawaquat in Cruden 1995, 38–39), the traditionalist Ward Churchill is fervently opposed to such activity.

However, the argument that native knowledge should be available only to and through native peoples raises concerns regarding wisdom in the blood and the role of academics teaching indigenous spirituality. Whether nonnatives should teach indigenous traditions is a hotly debated subject, particularly in regard to American Indian studies. Tensions include the political correctness of white academics, who have made capital on the basis of the colonial activities surrounding indigenous peoples' "captured heritage" (Macnaughtan 1995), continuing their control of knowledge that potentially violates the "emotional commitment and experiences of a specific group of people" (Deloria in Gill 1994). But does ethnicity provide an acceptable teaching qualification? Enforcing such may lead to accusations of elitist censorship and carrying "cultural and philosophical relativism to . . . untenable extreme[s]" (Cajete). In addition, as indigenous peoples are underrepresented in academia, such a stance would prove problematic (Rowanien 1996, 424).

Allied to this debate is that of access to indigenous information via the Internet. As shown previously, this medium has opened up the risk of sacred and secret knowledge being accessible to traditionally unauthorized others. But regardless of whom information is accessible to, the aptness of certain information is problematic. Issues such as whether the Coquille nation's Five-Generation Trickster myth should be accessible outside winter, the traditional time for its telling, poses dilemmas in a global context.

A benefit to the availability of online indigenous knowledge provided by native peoples is that Internet publication can give those indigenous peoples who have lost their traditions the opportunity of revival through the use of appropriate and sensitive intracultural appropriation (Macnaughtan 1995). Also, in providing the wider community with an opportunity to gain a greater understanding of contemporary indigenous lifeways, indigenous peoples gain agency in the dissemination of such information to the West. However, many indigenous people would rather Westerners "explore[d] their own spiritual heritage" (Taylor 1997, 190) and although studies suggest that American Indians "use Internet resources . . . intensively," the fear of colonial appropriation will undoubtedly limit the opportunities that this "revolutionary approach to disseminating cultural materials" presents (Macnaughtan 1995). So where does this leave the New Age and New Age Pagan appropriator?

If, as traditionalists believe, plastic medicine men and their rituals adapted for the cash-friendly New Age circuit are testimony to the lack of authentic indigeneity in the Western marketplace, then what is inappropriate about New Agers and New Age Pagans using these Westernized representations of indigenous sacred traditions? Are they not simply being "inspired by and influenced by other traditions" (Gill 1988, 77)?

On the other hand, should not New Agers and New Age Pagans look to their own heritage rather than someone else's, due to indigenous peoples' perceived connections between cultural appropriation and colonialism? As a respect for the political issues that affect indigenous peoples seems paramount for respectful and reciprocal relationships to take place between them and wanna-be natives, should appropriators not heed the following heartfelt message? "If people are genuinely interested in honoring [indigenous peoples, they] should remember that an honor isn't born when it parts the honorer's lips, it is born when it is accepted in the honoree's ear" (Morris in Churchill 1994, 65).

CONCLUSION

Appropriation of indigenous sacred traditions by New Agers and New Age Pagans is typically perceived as exemplifying the dichotomy of cultural trade on the one hand and a continuance of colonial theft on the other. In the context of the West's colonialist practices, the use of indigenous rituals and knowledge for the spiritual growth of Western individuals seems to leave indigenous peoples as victims of colonialism and New Agers and New Age Pagans as colonialist criminals.

This intercultural appropriation is generally lacking in respect and tends to fix indigenous peoples in Western understandings of indigeneity, thereby denying them the dynamism of cultural growth. Timson's understanding of Aboriginality is an example here. In contrast, intracultural appropriation does not bind the endowing culture within a static representation, and thus affirms cultural change. This is perhaps most evident in the case of the revived sweat lodge traditions where, despite similarities between nations, local differences exist. The irony is that the revived but somewhat Westernerized sweat lodge is being used to assist indigenous peoples in combating the effects of Western capitalism and in (re-)developing their own identities in the wake of colonialism. With the effects of colonialism present even in the process of decolonization, and with indigenous peoples still subject to colonial attitudes that ensure they remain prisoners of a Western-constructed past, one must question whether postcolonialism will ever be a reality.

However, the victim/criminal dichotomy can be countered. The agency of indigenous peoples refutes, to some extent, indigenous victimhood. Conversely, New Agers and New Age Pagans can be seen, to some extent, as the victims rather than the criminals of a colonialization process in which novelists, the media, and academia have the power to legitimize the representation of the indigenous Other in Western terms.

The material about indigenous peoples and their lifeways that is available for Western consumption suggests that the works of fiction writers such as Morgan and Andrews, along with the perceptions of musicians such as Timson, correlate strongly with understandings of nonfiction authors such as Devereux. Commerical interests are paramount here, and authenticity, even if only by association, sells. Yet indigenous people such as Wa'Na'Nee'Che' and Black Elk, Mowaljarla and Goreng, along with those engaged in the tourist trade at Alice Springs, can similarly be seen to advocate a somewhat materialistic and consumeristic position. But in a world ruled by capitalist market forces (including the commodification of the Western desire for anything that has Rousseauesque connotations), it would seem madness for indigenous peoples not to exploit a resource that would undoubtedly otherwise be exploited by the West anyway. At least they can do it on their own terms!

It seems that anything with a precolonial connection enhances Western understandings of earth-connectedness and nobility of spirit. The didgeridoo allows for connections with the land as Mother Earth, and the sweat lodge functions as a representation of her womb. Even though she is a modern and undoubtedly Western concept, Mother Earth now serves as a Pan-indigenous icon and as a symbol of a mythic precolonial Golden Age for dispossessed and dissatisfied Westerners and indigenous peoples alike.

Ironically for the appropraitors, the decontextualization of indigenous tradi-tions by Western representation marginalizes, at best, the more noble, social, and ethical aspects of indigenous life. These teachings that are transmitted orally/aurally contain lessons learned from the past. However, the simple fact that such teachings are not available in instant byte-sized and easily understood chunks indicates that they are unlikely to be heeded by those involved in a movement that is in many ways concerned with immediacy and simplistic interpretation. The do-it-yourself spirituality manual of Wa'Na'Nee'Che' provides evidence of this.

New Age and New Age Pagan appropriators might be victims of the capi-talist and colonialist West, but such wanna-bes can be seen to sustain Western capitalism and colonialism through their unquestioning acceptance of material that reinforces their romantic and putative precolonial yearnings. Further, their lack of active political involvement in the plight of indigenous peoples adds weight to an accusation of a naive and unintentional colonialism. Yet this does not excuse their practices if they are the hyperspiritualizing, inherently exploita-tive rip-off merchants that they are often accused of being.

Unquestionably, New Agers and New Age Pagans can be seen to hyperspiri-tualize. While the didgeridoo is only special in a ceremonial context for the Yolgnu and many other Aboriginal Australians, it has notions of permanent spe-cialness for many Western appropriators. Further, this ceremonial context is a local and socially enhancing one and as such conflicts with the Western under-standings of the instrument as a tool for personal growth, individual healing, and global planetary connectedness. Similarly, the sweat lodge when used in the New Age context has overtones of planetary healing with an individualistic bias, rather than emphasizing the localized tribal sociality of its Native American source.

As for the accusation of being inherently exploitative rip-off merchants, many New Agers and New Age Pagans engaged in appropriation practices sincerely believe that what they do is not exploitative. After all, their perception is reinforced by an abundance of lectures, workshops, books, and magazines, many by indige-nous peoples and Westerners with some form of authenticity and/or authority. Cer-tainly academia profits from the promulgation of representing Others in Western terms and is thus culpable of the continuation of colonialist practices. So, too, are those like Morgan and Andrews and to some extent Timson. These global authors deliberately misuse understandings of indigenous peoples and their lifeways for personal financial gain. Thus, it is academia and Western authors who can be labeled in such derogatory terms. For they leave at their creative mercy not only indigenous peoples but New Age and New Age Pagan appropriators.

The Internet proves a double-edged sword against such exploitation and misrepresentation. Although it provides access to inaccurate and/or inappropriate information, it also allows indigenous peoples the freedom to bypass the con-straints of Western publishing houses and represent themselves in their own terms. This allows people to go directly to the source for information and be acquainted with the respectful, appropriate, and reciprocal ways of entering into a genuine relationship with indigenous peoples.

New Age and New Age Pagan appropriators are not unequivocally "the bad guys." In unquestioningly accepting material that seeks to feed their romantic conceptions of indigeneity, some simply possess a naivete in regard to their colonialist practices. Similarly, indigenous peoples are not unambiguously victims. This colonialist presentation is refuted by indigenous agency in the dynamic of cultural growth.

NOTES

1. Here I refer to contemporary Pagans of a New Age persuasion, not Neo-Pagans in general.

2. While it could be argued that the group has an element of choice in regard to its chosen musical style, this choice is somewhat limited. Yothu Yindi expresses itself publicly through a Western genre partly because Yolngu tradition in regard to the didgeridoo emphasizes ceremonial (sacred and solo) playing; sound and repertoire are therefore limited. Also, in order to reach as wide an audience as possible with its message of reconciliation and healing, it recognizes that Westernized music is a more appropriate format.

3. Burnam Burnam subsequently retracted his endorsement of *Mutant Message Down Under*. However, Marlo Morgan has dedicated her latest work, *Mutant Message from Forever*, to him.

REFERENCES

Altieri, Pia. "Knowledge, Negotiation, and NAGPRA: Re-Conceptualizing Repatriation Discource(s)." In Peter Edge and Graham Harvey eds. *Law and Religion in Contemporary Society*. Aldershot, UK: Ashgate, 2000, pp. 129–49.

Anderson, Raoul R., John K. Crellin, and Joe Misel. "Spirituality, Values, and Boundaries in the Revitilization of a Mi'kmaq Community." In Graham Harvey, ed. *Indigenous Religions: A Companion*. London: Cassell, 2000, pp. 243–54.

Andrews, Lynne V. *Medicine Woman*. San Francisco: HarperSanFrancisco, 1983.

———. *Crystal Woman: The Sisters of the Dreamtime*. New York: Warner Books, 1988.

Bart. Personal communication, 1999.

Barwick, Linda. "Gender 'Taboos' and Didgeridoos." In Karl Neuenfeldt, ed. *The Didgeridoo: From Arnhem Land to Internet*. Sydney: John Libbey & Co. Ltd., 1997, 89–98.

Black Elk, Wallace, and Williams S. Lyon. *Black Elk: The Sacred Ways of the Lakota*. New York: HarperSanFrancisco, 1991.

Bowman, Marion. "Cardiac Celts." In Graham Harvey and Charlotte Holman, eds. *Paganism Today: Wiccans, Druids, the Goddess, and Ancient Earth Traditions for the Twenty-First Century*. London: Thorsons, 1996, 212–51.

Brown, Michael F. "Who Owns What Spirits Share? Reflections on Commodification and Intellectual Property in New Age America." *Polar* 17, no. 2 (1994): 7–17.

Bruchac, Joseph. *The Native American Sweat Lodge: History and Legends*. California: Crossing Press, 1993.

Cajete, Gregory. "Response: American Indian Religious Traditions and the Academic Study of Religion: A Response to Sam Gill." Undated. http://shemesh.scholar.emory.edu:6336/dynaweb/JAAR/JAAR_65.1@GenericBookView?DwebQuery=appropriation

Carmody, Kev (with Karl Neuenfeldt). "Ancient Voice-Contemporary Expression: The Didgeridoo (Yidaki) and the Promotion of Aboriginal Rights." In Karl Neuenfeldt, ed. *The Didgeridoo: From Arnhem Land to Internet*. Sydney: John Libbey & Co. Ltd., 1997, pp. 11–19.

Churchill, Ward (with M. Annette Jaimes). *Fantasies of the Master Race: Literature, Cinema, and the Colonization of American Indians*. Monroe, ME: Common Courage Press, 1992.

———. *Indians Are Us? Culture and Genocide in Native North America*. Monroe, ME: Common Courage Press, 1994.

Coombe, Rosemary J. "The Properties and the Possession of Identity: Postcolonial Struggle and the Legal Imagination." In Bruce Ziff and Pratima V. Rao, eds. *Borrowed Power: Essays on Cultural Appropriation*. New Brunswick, NJ: Rutgers University Press, 1997, pp. 74–96.

Cruden, Loren. *Coyote's Council Fire: Contemporary Shamans on Race, Gender, and Community*. Rochester, VT: Destiny Books, 1995.

Deloria, Vine, Jr. *Custer Died for Your Sins*. Norman: University of Oklahoma Press, 1969.

———. "We Talk, You Listen." In Frederick Turner, ed. *The Portable North American Reader*. London: Penguin Books, 1977, pp. 887–96.

Devereux, Paul. *Symbolic Landscapes: The Dreamtime Earth and Avebury's Open Secrets*. Somerset: Gothic Images Publications, 1992.

Drury, Ed. "Myths and Legends." 1999. http://www.mills.edu/LIFE/CCM/DIDGERIDOO/intro_didj/thread.html

Fay, Brian. *Contemporary Philosophy of Social Science: A Multi-Cultural Approach*. Oxford: Blackwell, 1996.

Gill, Sam. "The Power of Story." *American Indian Culture and Research Journal* 12, no. 3 (1988): 69–84.

Grimes, Ronald L. "Teaching Native American Religions." 1994. http://thor.anatomy.su.oz.au/danny/anthropology/anthro-1/archieve/august-1994/00.18.html

———. "This May Be a Feud, But It Is Not a War: An Electronic, Interdisciplinary Dialogue on Teaching Native Religions." *American Indian Quarterly* 20, no. 3 (1996): 433–50.

Grossman, Michele, and Denise Cuthbert. "Forgetting Redfern: Aboriginality in the New Age." *Meanjin* 4 (1998): 771–88.

Hart, Jonathan. "Translating and Resisting Empire: Cultural Appropriation and Postcolonial Studies." In *Borrowed Power*, pp. 137–68.

Hernandez-Avila, Ines. "Mediations of the Spirit: Native American Religious Traditions and the Ethics of Representation." *American Indian Quarterly* 20, no. 3 (1997): 329–52.

Hladki, Jane. "Problematizing the Issue of Cultural Appropriation." *Alternative Routes* 11 (1994): 95–119.

Hume, Lynne. "The Dreaming in Contemporary Aboriginal Australia." In Graham Harvey, ed. *Indigenous Religions: A Companion*. London: Cassell, 2000, pp. 125–38.

Johnson, Willard. "Contemporary Native American Prophesy in Historical Perspective." Undated. http://shemesh.scholar.emory.edu:6336/dynaweb/JAAR/JAAR_64.3/@ GenericBookView?DwebQuery=appropriation

Knopoff, Steve. "Accompanying the Song: Determinants of Didgeridoo Style in Traditional and Popular Yolngu Song." In Karl Neuenfeldt, ed. *The Didgeridoo: From Arnhem Land to Internet*. Sydney: John Libbey & Co. Ltd., 1997, pp. 39–67.

Lee, Patrick "Jasper." Untitled presentation at the Shamanism Today Conference, Milton Keynes, 18 September 1999.

Macnaughtan, Don. "Remembering the Rhinoceros: The Coquille Indian Tribe Establishes a Unique Tribal Research Library on the Southern Oregon Coast." 1995. http://www.olaweb.org/quarterly/quar1-2/macnaughtan.shtml#4

Magowan, Fiona. "Out of Time, Out of Place: A Comparison of Applications of the Didgeridoo in Aboriginal Australia, Great Britain and Ireland." In Karl Neuenfeldt, ed. *The Didgeridoo: From Arnhem Land to Internet*. Sydney: John Libbey & Co. Ltd., 1997, pp. 161–83.

Malone, David, writer and prod. "In Search of the Noble Savage." *Horizon* BBC 2, 27 January 1992.

Marcus, Julie. "The Journey Out to the Centre: The Cultural Appropriation of Ayers Rock." In Gillian Cowlinshaw and Barry Morris, eds. *Race Matters: Indigenous Australians and "Our" Society*. Canberra: Aboriginal Studies Press, 1997, pp. 29–51.

Marshall, Peter. *Nature's Web: Rethinking Our Place on Earth*. London: Cassell, 1992.

Milton, Kay. "Nature and the Environment in Indigenous and Traditional Cultures." In David E. Cooper and Joy A. Palmer, eds. *Spirit of the Environment: Religion, Value, and Environmental Concern*. London: Routledge, 1998, pp. 86–99.

Miskimmin, Susanne. "The New Age Movement's Appropriation of Native Spirituality: Some Political Implications for the Algonquian Nation." *Papers of the Algonquian Conference* 27 (1996): 205–11.

Morgan, Marlo. *Mutant Message Down Under*. New York: HarperCollins, 1994.

———. *Mutant Message from Forever*. New York: Harper Perrenial, 1999.

Mulcock, Jane. "Searching for our Indigenous Selves: Creating New Meaning Out of 'Old Cultures.'" Unpublished conference paper, 1997.

———. Personal communication, 2000.

Neuenfeldt, Karl. " "The Quest for a "Magical Island": The Convergence of the Didgeridoo, Aboriginal Culture, Healing and Cultural Politics in New Age Discourse." *Social Analysis* 42, no. 2 (1998): 73–102.

———. "The Didgeridoo in the Desert: The Social Relations of an Ethnographic Object Entangled in Culture and Commerce." In Karl Neuenfeldt, ed. *The Didgeridoo: From Arnhem Land to Internet*. Sydney: John Libbey and Co. Ltd., 1997, pp. 107–22.

Porterfield, Amanda. "American Indian Spirituality as a Countercultural Movement." In Christopher Vecsey, ed. *Religion in Native North America*. Moscow, ID: University of Idaho Press, 1990, pp. 152–64.

Powers, William K. *Oglala Religion*. London: University of Nebraska Press, 1977.

———. *Sacred Language: The Nature of Supernatural Discourse in Lakota*. Norman: University of Oklahoma Press, 1986.

———. "When Black Elk Speaks, Everybody Listens." In Christopher Vecsey, ed. *Religion in Native North America*. Moscow, ID: University of Idaho Press, 1990, pp. 136–51.

———. *Yuwipi: Vision and Experience in Oglala Ritual*. London: University of Nebraska Press, 1982.

Root, Deborah. "White Indians: Appropriation and the Politics of Display." In Bruce Ziff and Pratima V. Rao, eds. *Borrowed Power: Essays on Cultural Appropriation*. New Jersey: Rutgers University Press, 1997, pp. 225–33.

Rose, Deborah Bird. "Australia Felix Rules OK!" In Gillian Cowlinshaw and Barry Morris, eds. *Race Matters: Indigenous Australians and "Our" Society*. Canberra: Aboriginal Studies Press, 1997, pp. 121–37.

Rose, Wendy. "The Great Pretenders: Further Reflections on Whiteshamanism." In M. Annette Jaimes, ed. *The State of Native America: Genocide, Colonization, and Resistance*. Boston: South End Press, 1992, pp. 403–21.

Ronwanien, Christopher: Te Jocks. "Spirituality for Sale: Sacred Knowledge in the Consumer Age." *American Indian Quarterly* 20, no. 3, 1996: 415–31.

Sanchez, Carol Lee. "Animal, Vegetable, and Mineral." In Carol J. Adams, ed. *Ecofeminism and the Sacred*. New York: Continuum, 1993, 207–28.

Sherwood, Patricia. "The Didgeridoo and Alternative Lifestylers' Reconstruction of Social Reality." In Karl Neuenfeldt, ed. *The Didgeridoo: From Arnhem Land to Internet*. Sydney: John Libbey & Co. Ltd., 1997, pp. 139–53.

Smith, Linda Tuhiwai. *Decolonizing Methodologies: Research and Indigenous People*. London: Zed Books Ltd. and Dunedin, NZ: Otago Press, 1999.

Swain, Tony. "Australia." In Tony Swain and Gary Trompf, eds. *The Religions of Oceania*. London: Routledge, 1995, pp. 19-118.

Taylor, Bron. "Earthen Spirituality or Cultural Genocide? Radical Environmentalism's Appropriation of Native American Spirituality." *Religion* 27, 1997, pp. 183–15.

Timson, Justin. Personal Communication, 2000.

———. "About the Didjeridoo." Undated. http://www.bigwig.net/didgeridoos/Intro.htm

Tomita, Toyoji. Untitled site, 1999. http://www.mills.edu/LIFE/CCM/DIDGERIDOO/intro _didj/ thread.html

Turner, David H. *Afterlife before Genesis, An Introduction: Accessing the Eternal through Australian Aboriginal Music*. New York: Lang, 1997.

Two Birds, John. *Healing the Sacred Hoop and Avoiding Armageddon in the New Millennium*. Lecture, Brighton, 22 September 1999.

Wa'Na'Nee'Che' [Dennis Renault] and Timothy Freke. *Native American Spirituality*. London: Thorsons, 1996.

Wa'Na'Nee'Che. Bush Farm Powwow. Salisbury. 10 July 1999.

York, Michael (of New Internationalists Advertising Department). Personal conversation, 2000.

Yunupingu, Mandawuy. "Yidaki: A Forward." In Karl Neuenfeldt, ed. *The Didgeridoo: From Arnhem Land to Internet*. Sydney: John Libbey & Co. Ltd., 1997, pp. vii–viii.

———. "Reconciling with Aboriginality and Culture." Undated. http://www.yothuyindi .com/mand2.html

22

NEW AGE COMMODIFICATION AND APPROPRIATION OF SPIRITUALITY

Michael York

In the field of sociology—more specifically, the sociology of religion, the question of secularization is one of the more nuanced and complex issues the discipline must face conceptually. What do we mean by the "decline of religion" and how would we measure it? Though it *seems* apparent that secularization has been more pronounced in the twentieth and early twenty-first century than during any previous period of recorded history, putting a sociological "handle" to this likelihood has proven a daunting and elusive task. Even when we understand the process to involve a decline in the prestige and power of religious teachers, the electronic media industry of today has often extended their reach and appeal on unprecedented levels—such as we see, for example, with televangelism.

In general, the processes taken as signs of secularization include the ending of state support for religious organizations, the elimination of religious teaching in public schools, no longer employing religious tests for public officials, and the ending of legislative protection for religious doctrine or other state-sponsored controls designed to safeguard religion. In a secularized democracy in which religious dogmas and ethical notions have lost their dominance, there is more scope for individual dissent and change. India, Great Britain, and the United States are examples of "secular" states, but, this being said, there is a wide variation among these polities in terms of separation of church and state, summary as well as religious belief and participation.

Written for this anthology.

Perhaps more meaningfully, secularization can also refer to a pervasive decline of *interest* in religious traditions. Respect for religious institutions, as a consequence, is found to diminish throughout the general public. More concretely, established religious bodies no longer draw the same numbers of practicing supporters. Attendance and membership figures grow less and less. Contemporary secularization is seen, therefore, as a combined product of scientific/ humanistic rational thought and socialistic/communistic political theory. Religion comes to represent superstitious interference or a popular opiate or both.

In its fullest sense, secularization should indicate the cessation of all interest in religious perspective, practice, and institutionalized features. But while there appears to be little if any evidence that Western society has reached this stage, there does appear to be in the West a detectable and growing dissatisfaction with *traditional* forms of religion. Consequently, for secularization to be meaningful in sociological terms, we are best to follow Bryan Wilson's understanding of the notion as essentially the contemporary "process by which religious thinking, practice and institutions lose significance, and become marginal to the operation of the social system" in which they are found (1988, 954). In Wilson's perspective, the spiritual pluralism of the modern/postmodern era is itself a *consequence* of secularization. If traditional religiosity had formerly been central to society's decision making and general functioning, its secular loss of prestige, power, and influence opens the gates, if not floodgates, to private, marginal, and even deviant but certainly newer forms of religion beyond the originally established and popularly endorsed religio-social confines. Religious expression, therefore, becomes freed from the rule of conformity—especially in a condition when the status quo no longer remains fixed but itself has become something fluid. The accelerated technological, economic, and demographic changes underway in the millennium transition of the West make any present condition or state of affairs radically ephemeral and elusive. In the advent of what is often hailed as globalization, this means institutional and social change in the West has immediate worldwide implications as well—ones that possibly if not probably affect virtually everyone everywhere on the planet today.

Globalization, however, often appears to be simply another name for a new breed of American imperialism. The perpetual American championing of capitalist and individual freedom becomes pitted against the sanctity of "weaker" but autonomous systems or traditions. In today's world in which the entire international arena becomes a competitive marketplace, it is those with the greater financial (including military) clout who become the winners. In the relentless, market-fueled drive to reduce as much as possible to the same—whether the same range of goods, the same currency of exchange, or the same architectural "look"—it appears to be increasingly within the multifaceted diversity of religion that variety has its greatest chance of surviving. However, religion itself often becomes simply one more commodity and one more "tool" within the overall process of globalized homogeneity. If it can be argued that the evangelical missionizing drives behind Buddhism, Christianity, and Islam have already contributed to a process of universal sameness, some of our newer religions are no less immune to this same tendency. Among these is the New Age movement. While its missionizing efforts toward converting or "saving" the world may or may not place it into the same league as Christianity, it is certainly of equal stature when it comes to appropriation of indigenous and competing institutions. In other words, the issue of what it *gives* is one thing; the issue of what it *takes* is the other.

New Age itself is a difficult phenomenon to describe, let alone appraise. It has been summarized as "a blend of pagan religions, Eastern philosophies, and occult-psychic phenomena" (York 1995, 34). William Sims Bainbridge finds, for instance, that the "forms of religious movement most closely associated with the New Age are occult, neopagan, and Asian" (1997, 386). A key entry into understanding the complexities of the New Age movement is to be located in why some people (sociologists, scholars of religion, Christian apologists) include contemporary Western paganism as part of the New Age, whereas other people (other sociologists—myself included—historians, participants) consider New Age and Neo-Paganism distinctly separate.

At best, the New Age movement comprises a disparate and loosely coordinated confederation of contrasting beliefs, techniques, and practices. There is no central authority capable of speaking for the movement as a whole or of supplying membership registrars or even of ascertaining who and who is not a New Ager. New Age is largely a perpetually shifting and ad hoc alliance of exegetical individuals and groups, audience gatherings, client services, and various new religious movements that range between the cultic, sectarian, and denominational. Despite the often vehement distancing from and denial of the New Age by most contemporary Western pagans, Paul Heelas (1996) would also include witches, Wiccans, Druids, shamans, and other modern-day pagans within New Age identity. On the other hand, Vivianne Crowley (1989, 1996) expressed the general trend within contemporary paganism when she rereleased her 1989 bestseller *Wicca: The Old Religion in the New Age* seven years later as *Wicca: The Old Religion in the New Millennium*.

Heelas classifies both New Age and Neo-Paganism under the general rubric of "self-religions"—presumably to distinguish them from "God-religions" and to express what they have in common. But Heelas is never clear over what he means by "self." At times, the self is simply the ego of individual consciousness, but on other occasions—and more frequently—the self-referent is an indication of what New Age generally calls the "Higher Self." Whatever the Higher Self might be, it is not the ego-self with which the individual usually identifies, and Heelas has simply substituted one unclear metaphysical concept (namely, "God") with another (namely, the "Self").

From the start, it should be pointed out that the respective vocabularies of the two movements, though they may have points of overlap or similarities, are not the same. Neo-Paganism, contemporary Western paganism, and the various reconstructed ethnic paganisms (Druidry, Northern, Celtic, Hellenic, Egyptian, etc.) do not generally speak in terms of a "Higher Self" or of "a(n imminent) quantum leap in collective consciousness," that is, the coming Age of Aquarius. The New Age movement has essentially recast Joachim de Flores's twelfth-century "Three Ages of History" theory into astrological terminology (Melton, Clark, and Kelly 1990, 29 ff.). As Aidan Kelly explains, in this epochal frame-work, the Old Testament "Age of the Father" becomes identified as the Age of Aries. The New Testament "Age of the Son" then corresponds with the Age of Pisces, which de Flores understood as embodied in the Roman Catholic Church. However, the ensuing eon, the "Age of the Holy Spirit," is to be as different from the current "Age of the Son" as this last is from the "Age of the Father," which preceded it. Consequently, the "Age of the Holy Spirit" is recognized as the Aquarian New Age of great and millennial changes. If Jesus Christ represented the pivotal spiritual figure of the Age of Pisces, according to the New Age Church Universal and Triumphant, the Comte de Saint-Germain is to be the equivalent for the Age of Aquarius. On the other hand, with its essential distance from Christian terminology and astrological reinterpretation of the ages of his-tory, contemporary paganism does not entertain the notions of either literal apoc-alypticism or metaphorical millenarianism.

Part of the confusion between the two movements may stem from the inclu-sion of prominent Wiccan-activist Miriam Simos, or Starhawk, among the fac-ulty of Matthew Fox's Institute in Culture and Creation Spirituality (founded in Chicago in 1978) after it was reestablished in Oakland, California, at the Holy Names College in 1983. Most importantly, vis-à-vis mainstream and dominant Christianity, New Age and Neo-Paganism are natural allies. Much of the current confusion between the two orientations, in fact, is most likely a result of this alliance by default, which pits both traditions into the position of "outsider here-sies" from the perspective of the canonical spirituality of the Judeo-Christian West. But if the two movements are natural partners, their respective theologies and consequent practices are radically distinguishable.

Paganism itself subscribes to an immanent understanding of the godhead that allows—or even centralizes—the natural world as manifest sacrality. New Age, on the other hand, descends from a competing theological perspective, namely, a Gnostic/Theosophical tradition that views nature as an obscuring obstacle to hidden spiritual truth. The physical world becomes, accordingly, either an illusion or at least something of secondary and lesser importance. From a strictly socio-logical perspective, New Age and Neo-Paganism are simply rival theologies—each part of long-standing and legitimate spiritual traditions. However, in the emergent-twentieth-century notion that the individual alone is the locus for selec-tivity and determination of belief—a notion that may be a concomitant to the process of secularization itself, the antiauthoritarian impulse that increasingly denies that one can be told what to believe also denies that one can be told, at least spiritually, what not to take. Apart from the vexing question of whether new religious movements are themselves testimonies to secularization or, instead, represent an unexpected reversal of secularization, the increasing privatization of religion is intimately tied to the ethical question of spiritual appropriation.

If "self-religion" means personal exegesis and selection by the individual, the general rubric is applicable to trends in the late modern/early postmodern transition that encompass much more than simply New Age and Neo-Pagan religiosities. At its worst extreme, we find something like the World Church of the Creator, which encouraged twenty-one-year-old Benjamin Smith in 1999 and not far from Chicago to "appropriate" the integrity and/or lives of people who belonged to what Smith considered the "mud races." While this heinous act may represent an extreme illustration of nonaccountability and (someone's) individual freedom to decide what is right and wrong, it betokens the lack of moral guidelines consequent or at least possible when the permission to make such decisions shifts from traditional authority to the individual alone. This lack of moral consensus and legitimating sanction appears to be a direct result of the secular diminishment of religion's former role in traditional society.

Besides its narcissism, or perhaps even linked to it, one of the more controversial aspects of New Age concerns its commodification of religion and the freedom to appropriate spiritual ideas and practices from other traditions. The New Age is modeled on, and an outgrowth of, liberal Western capitalism. It is part of the same "cultural logic of late capitalism" that asserts the right to free and unrestricted global trade. As an aggregation or congeries of client services and competing audience cults, New Age is part of what is described as the "religious consumer supermarket"—one that thrives on competition and the offering of various spiritual commodities. Rather than a rejection of free-market principles, New Age endorses a spiritualized counterpart of capitalism—one that seeks ever-extended markets, new sources of marketable goods, and expanding profits. In that the profit motive of New Age is fully financial, if not also oriented toward greater spiritual well-being, it represents a modern continuation of Calvinistic principles that exalt material success as a sign, reflection, or consequence of one's spiritual state of grace.

But New Age liberalism falls into the same trap as political Anglo-American liberalisms of equal dignity in which supposedly neutral principles based on the denial of difference are really to be seen as reflections of hegemonic culture. As Charles Taylor (1994, 44) sees it, the very idea of "liberalism may be a kind of pragmatic contradiction, a particularity masquerading as the universal." "Procedural liberalism" finds human dignity in autonomy rather than with any particular view of what constitutes the good life. This popular view of "the human agent as primarily a subject of self-determining or self-expressive choice"

(Taylor 1994, 57) provides the New Age with its bedrock idea of human potential and its corresponding belief that one can create his or her own universe.

New Age solipsism, coupled with its advocacy of free-market principles, opens the world's spiritual arena as an opportunity for spiritual exploitation and even capitalistic imperialism. Not only does it encourage a paradoxical homogenizing to the cultural standards of North Atlantic civilization, but also it carries an implicit judgment of inferior status for nonhegemonic cultures. New Age upholds the idea that all past and present spiritual legacies are no longer private property but belong now, in the New Age of Aquarius, to the public domain. This idea easily translates into the rationale and justification for appropriating whatever third-world institution has appeal to the individual religious consumer, along with the "freedom," then, to market what one allocates to others.

The conflict involved with this belief in an unaccountable and free accessibility to the world's spiritual traditions and the countervailing insistence on cultural ownership by minority ethnicities became disturbingly clear to me during the 1993 Parliament of the World's Religions in Chicago. Despite the Amerindian pivotal role in launching and sustaining the success of the Parliament, in private Native Americans were debating a Lakota-sponsored "Declaration of War," which included among its targeted enemies "New Age profiteers and Neo-Paganists" [sic.] From the position as an "endangered species" on the verge of extinction, the loss of cultural artifacts, private practices, and the use of traditional sites or their own sweat lodges is viewed as the final loss of American Indian identity. The growth of popular forms of Neo-shamanism in the West was cited in particular as a "cultural theft" on the part of the Euro-American hegemony. Other disciplines usurped by New Age include Hawaiian Kahuna magic, Australian Aborigine dreamworking, South American Amerindian *ayahuasca* and San Pedro ceremony, Hindu Ayurveda and yoga, and Chinese Feng Shui, Qi Gong, and Tai Chi.

Consequently, in many cases the spiritual appropriation of nativistic practice and belief follows the same dynamic as, for instance, the steady elimination of the Brazilian rainforest or the ocean's whale population. Species become endangered and eventually extinct as a result of free-market operations and expansion. In a multicultural world, a procedural liberalism that adopts no particular substantive view about the ends of life may not recognize or even misrecognize particularity of religion and culture. The erosion of ethnic dignity and identity might be an inevitable aspect of historical and cultural change, on the one hand, or a catastrophic diminishment of human legacy on the other. In many cases, it is a complicit or even active disseminatory role of the original bearers themselves that has encouraged religio-cultural exportation. The Tibetans have consciously marketed Vajrayana Buddhism to the West and have recognized *tulku*-incarnation among Euro-Americans. Hindu swamis and gurus, Chinese martial art masters, and Japanese shidoin aikido teachers consistently promote their respective practices throughout a spiritually hungry West. Even the American Indian community appears split over the issue of keeping its traditions to itself or initiating Westerners into them. If there is an ethical question concerning spiritual appropriation, those who feel that their ways and identities are being appropriated are quite often actively part of the dissemination process.

There may, in the end, be no final answer to the dilemma between universal rights and particular identity. In defense of New Age, it could be pointed out that all religions appropriate from each other. Roman paganism, through its *interpretatio romana*, incorporated Celto-Gaulic deities; Hinduism included Gautama Buddha as an avatar of Vishnu; Christianity acquired pagan sanctuaries and festivals for its own; Islam seized the Kaaba and the site of the Jewish Temple in Jerusalem. Interreligious exchange may, in fact, be seen as an inevitable norm. As a rule, contemporary Western paganism does not appropriate from living cultures in the same willy-nilly and profit-motive manner as does New Age. Basically, if New Age is grabbing sacred truths from other cultures, its ultimate fruition might lie in reclaiming, like Neo-Paganism, sacred truths from the past—in other words, sacred truths that are no longer claimed as privately owned.

The real opposition of our day is perhaps not one between religion and science but rather one between religion and commercialism. If the modern commodification of religion is to be superseded, what is required might be a postmodern resanctification of the market. The prospect of "the sacred in the secular," that is, finding religious dimensions in the world beyond religion, could raise the postmodern challenge of resacralizing commerce.

REFERENCES

Bainbridge, William Sims. 1997. *The Sociology of Religious Movements*. New York/London: Routledge.

Crowley, Vivianne. 1989. *Wicca: The Old Religion in the New Age*, Wellingborough, England: Aquarian Press. Reprinted in 1966 as *Wicca: The Old Religion in the New Millennium* by Thorsons/Harper Collins.

Heelas, Paul. 1996. *The New Age Movement: The Celebration of the Self and the Sacralization of Modernity*. Oxford: 1996.

Melton, J. Gordon, Jerome Clark, and Aidan A. Kelly. 1990. *New Age Encyclopedia*. Detroit: Gale Research.

Taylor, Charles. 1994. "The Politics of Recognition," in *Multiculturalism* (originally published in 1992 as *Multiculturalism and "The Politics of Recognition"*), Amy Gutmann ed. Princeton, NJ: Princeton University Press.

Wilson, Bryan R. 1988. "'Secularisation': Religion in the Modern World." In *The World's Religions*, ed. Stewart Sutherland, Leslie Houlden, Peter Clarke, and Friedhelm Hardy. London: Routledge, pp. 953–66.

York, Michael. 1995. *The Emerging Network: A Sociology of the New Age and Neo-Pagan Movements*. Lanham, MD: Rowman & Littlefield.

23
NEW AGE OR HOW TO COMMUNE?

Anna E. Kubiak

I would like to ask the simple question: Are there communities in the New Age? The question is important in the context of many accusations of sects on the part of the Catholic Church in Poland. The answer is not univocal, as New Age is not homogeneous. So there are different answers and examples. By the notion of New Age culture—in other words, Aquarian culture—I understand (for the purpose of a preliminary demarcation of the field) an umbrella term covering different contemporary cultural phenomena. These include alternative therapies and psychotherapies, parapsychology, astrology and other oracular practices, practicing in nondenominational ways the religious-philosophical traditions of the West (theosophy, anthroposophy, the teachings of Gurdjief), Native American cultures, the East (Taoism, Buddhism, Sufism, yoga, teachings of Sai Baba), shamanism, channeling, and many others. In contrast to the first-sight phenomena is the field called New Age. However, their interconnectedness is manifested during "Mind Body Spirit" festivals (named "esoteric" in Poland), in special journals, in works by New Age authors (e.g., M. Ferguson, D. Spangler), in a network of face-to-face contacts, and in a "family resemblance" (Barker 1992, 189).

New Age culture distinguishes itself from new religious movements by an openness to all religions and by tolerance, a lack of proselytism, and practicing different traditions at the same time, rather short-time groups (with longer cooperation between some members), an emphasis on individual choices and styles of

Written for this anthology. This work was supported by the Research Support Scheme of the Open Society Support Foundation, grant no. 1150/1998.

living, and many, but not absolute, authorities. First of all, the most popular social forms in New Age circles are foundations, associations, clubs, therapy rooms, and schools. They work around two aims: to educate about different New Age subjects (to organize courses, workshops, and lectures) and to meet clients (to assess their needs and propose therapy). There is a constant flux of "students" and clients in New Age centers, often keeping in touch for some time. They are usually not oriented in one direction (one subject or therapy); thus they exchange their knowledge and experience. The whole New Age culture can be seen as a network rather than a community or communities. Along the network, there is a constant commotion of people who learn, experience, buy things, heal themselves, and look for something else. The form of the association, foundation, therapy room, or institute looks rather like *gesellschaft* not *gemeinschaft* mode: there is a secretary, and to meet someone, you must make an appointment. The best way is by telephone. "Time is money," so people do not have much time for you. A session usually lasts an hour or less. It may last longer if it is something special; for example, a numerological horoscope takes about three hours. So it is client-oriented communication, or consumer oriented, and does not reflect community.

This is the important change, in comparison with the seventies, when people would meet informally, often in their homes, and talk for hours. Sometimes, it is even more difficult, for the meeting place only exists during the organized gatherings, workshops, and lectures, subsisting in the interim in a virtual, disembodied association or club. During the Internet revolution, there is a growing tendency to commune virtually, and community often means belonging "in mind" but not inhabiting the same place. People commune with their foreign colleagues in the branch and feel closer to them than to their neighbors.

I see two predilections in these social forms that currently reflect more universal tendencies. One is breaking into smaller groups as larger communities are too tight for individuals, their ambitions, and their visions. Very often, in the seventies, it was the Psychotronic Society (or Dowsing Society) that concentrated people around one leader. Now, in the new century, there are many family groups (as Bauman has written), in which a couple represent the institute, esoteric shop, or workshop-therapy room. On the other side, there is a tendency to unify, to make federations and societies that would unite smaller societies around one branch, whether it is bioenergotherapy, Reiki, or Neuro-Linguistic Programming (NLP). But again, it is not community. It is a higher level *gesellschaft* structure, which serves to control the circles, practices, and certificates. It also serves to exchange ideas and to publish the results together, as well as to organize conferences, all forms in which people act as individuals or anonymously but do not commune.

The most popular social form in New Age circles is contract groups, which take part in self-development seminars. They create temporary communities, which may last three days, one or two weeks, or several years. The experience of community is seen as very important and is the subject itself. Some institutes organize "opening-workshops," which serve to develop deeper communication in the group. Encouraged by the trainers, participants share emotional stories of life; experience the physicality of diverse situations, such as hugs, dancing, bodywork, and massage; and create an atmosphere of closeness, safety, and openness. In the frame of the structure of *gesellschaft* (the contract, paying, and planned program), very often a *gemeinschaft* climate is created, which is temporary and lasts only during the course.

The atmosphere of the community is guided. For example, an advertisement for the NLP program says that the participant should bring loose clothing and a good sense of humor. This climate is often contrasted with the outside world and its role-playing ethos. In the following, Sutcliffe describes this "sharing" during a workshop at the Findhorn Foundation. Although speaking "from the heart,"

> it is carefully structured form with highly normative expectations. Our focalizers specified three ground rules for "sharing." Firstly, we were to speak out of our own experience; secondly, we were to speak in the first person only, which was known as making an "I" statement; lastly, we were not to interrupt— whether to agree, dispute or offer advice—when someone was speaking appropriately. A rare exception to the last rule could be a focalizer's challenge, on the basis of the second rule, to a contribution deemed to be overly discursive or abstract in content. Typically the challenge would take the form of the gentle question: "Is that an 'I' statement you are making?" (Sutcliffe 1995)

But again, it is not a classic *gemeinschaft* or community (in the Victor Turner sense). Haga Manabu describes the differences between *gemeinschaft* and seminar relationship: "The first involves the fact that the self-development seminars comprise a kind of service-industry 'communication space' artificially created on a contractual basis between the seminar organization and the individual trainees. Thus the trainees are complete strangers until the start of the basic seminar, and any relationships that emerge are, in general, limited to the period defined by the contract." But she concludes: "[T]he seminars have managed to create a communication space in which the healing atmosphere of the *gemeinschaft* type relationship coexists with the individual freedom of the *gesellschaft*-type relationship" (Manabu 1995, 295–99).

Another form is meeting groups. For example, once a month there are meetings of clubs and societies, which are organized around a lecture, a person who wants to share an experience, or someone from abroad who is skilled in New Age activity. The specifics of meeting groups is that in every meeting there is a different composition of participants. Despite the presence of new people, there is a core group of people who often take part in the meetings. The character of intimacy is kept, for people use their first names and the main holidays are usually celebrated together. For example, there is a New Year meeting of the Transpersonal Society in Steiner's kindergarten. The invitation is given by "shoe post," and those who know about the meeting invite other people who have concordant interests. There is an ornamental gate made of soft transparent tapestry and a colorful altar with many candles decorated with the saying: "Homo holos. When I become the whole My world becomes the whole and sacred. Not the imitation of life, but the initiation into real life." The minimal rent is collected from the participants.

The meeting begins with Kajah and Bregovic music and people arriving and talking, some of them dancing together with the main organizer, Tanna Jakubowicz, the president of the Transpersonal Society. Then, there is a sort of ceremony, taken from shamanistic ritual, according to Tanna. Each person takes the feather (signifying "the speaker"), presents himself or herself, and eventually, the workshops. Since there are about sixty people, it takes time. There are men and women, with an average age of about thirty-five. There are representatives of Subud, Tibetan, and Zen Buddhism; therapists; teachers; artists; students of psychology; people from Warsaw; and even some from abroad. Then, participants exchange small gifts and afterward share a light meal consisting of the various foods (salads, fruits, sandwiches) donated. Two concerts follow, including one in which a man plays a Hindu harmonium and sings in Lithuanian, English, and Russian. Then, musicians from Wolimierz in southern Poland, sing simple songs (hey-a-ho) and play different ethnic instruments.

Due to the approaching Christmas holiday, another meeting takes place in the school. The organizer is the bioenergotherapy society "I AM." The main participants are bioenergotherapists and people learning massage and Tai Chi. They are mostly women, with an average age of thirty-five to forty. There are representatives of Zen Buddhism, the Hare Krishna Movement, shamanistic paths, therapists, teachers, university workers, and students. The invitation is given in the same "shoe post" way. There are several people taking the floor. Then, people start to eat and talk individually. Everyone contributes the food.

Another social form in New Age circles is a kind of self-help group, which is similar to meeting groups but smaller and concentrated around one issue. There is less flexibility for the participants. There is, for example, the Successful People Club, organized by one man who learned "the success courses" in Canada. Once a week, approximately twelve people gather in a local cultural place, called, in Poland, "the house of culture." Here in Oliborz, it is named "The Club under a Pear Tree." The patrons resemble a "lonely hearts club" of retired employees. The average age is about fifty-five to sixty. There is a regular program. The meeting starts with prepared speeches (the topic is open). The speeches are reviewed, but people always emphasize the positive values and talents of the speaker. Then, everybody has one minute to speak about the success of the previous week. Next, the members make short speeches (the subject is given just before they begin). In this way, they exercise their imaginations and at the same time experience public speaking and applause. A characteristic of these different group meetings is that there are three features in the contents that are most important: education, play, and the sacred. Education is in the form of a lecture, taking part in the play actively, or taking part in the course, which usually consists in lecture plus exercises. It is comparable to a kind of university of the third age because of the average age of participants. There are people who want to learn something different than what they learned in school, and there are numerous engineers and technicians who are eager for a more humanistic, philosophic, psychological perspective. They are also looking for something helpful in life—knowledge about health, healthy lifestyles, and the psychological instruments (such as ideas and practices) to help one live a happier life. They are at an age at which life seems to decline, and they have reached their peak in their jobs and family life. But during New Age education, they learn that they are still creators of their destiny, discover and learn fascinating things, and sometimes meet new partners and friends who share their interests. This education includes a therapeutic attitude toward life that is reflected in the language. All New Age branches are treated not as historical knowledge but as methods to change one's life, to make it happier or at least more interesting.

Play is part of the education, as well as spiritual practice. Sometimes there is dancing and sometimes singing together. In the exercises, the role of humor is important. During the course of POP (process-oriented psychology), I observed how encouragement to laugh and play opens possibilities to act in new ways, overcome shyness, and fight doubts and prejudice. Because of the general attitude, there is a tendency to look for pretexts to laugh. Some meetings directly touch the spirituality, but many of them only marginally and only in this broad sense, which Paul Heelas (1996) calls self-spirituality. So it is the sphere of sacredness, which means seeking a broader perspective of life and the cosmos, examining values, and looking for methods of growth. These values, which are articulated in the New Age, are global, and here is the most visible effect of globalization: The values are universal, which is the effect of detraditionalization (Heelas, Lash, Morris 1996). The values transcend cultural diversity and touch the universal human conditions of health, nature, happiness, good relations with others, peacefulness, and contact with spiritual sources. These values, as the source of meaning in life, are the global representation of the domesticated sacred.

Luckmann calls it "shrinking transcendence." From the global perspective, because of its universal level, it is globalized transcendence. Or because of its contents (care of the body, health, relationships with family and friends), it is paradoxically (but only in Western metaphysics) incarnated transcendence. If they have their hierophants (in the Eliade sense), there are domestic altars putting together deities from different religions.

New Age rituals have their global level; prayers, visualizations and meditations do not have the specifics of any culture. They are inspired by many but are simplified. They start with reflection on family and friends but often finish in the broadest context: Earth and the cosmos. The practice is done for the benefit of the closest people and for all. It does not have parish, denomination, or national limits. The domesticated global rituals include making a circle, sharing, visualization, singing mantras, and attunement and are not attached to any particular tradition. For example, the everyday ritual in the Findhorn Foundation is attunement: "The aim of attunement is to gather and then focus group concentration and intention before a specific task, period of work, meeting or other event" (Sutcliffe 1995).

Another ritual is sharing, which usually opens and closes the meetings. What is shrinking is the sacred discourse. It is the narrative expressed as icon, or painting, or an emotional saying such as, "it was a powerful experience." And because every experience is individual, it is difficult to describe.

There is the dream of community. In these words about community and individuality, a New Age participant says, "There isn't a place for the commonality. I would like to create the space for people who come together because of a common idea. It will be a community of independent individuals. It will not be one organism and will have no leader. But there must be a common goal. It is the idea that this work (workshops) is their life path, the way of spiritual development. It must be individual effort but going beyond the narrow, egoistic interest. Emphasizing the differences is nonproductive. The development of the human being happens through return to unity. The space where people can meet is the space of love and good intentions. It is not a sect; there is no doctrine. The idea is to keep this place alive." So far, it is only an idea.

The visions of catastrophe, which for the first time in history are global, including images of nuclear war, ecological disaster, and extraterrestrial contact, create the need for planetary community. But planetary community is, for now, a bit abstract. Perhaps after ten years, because of the Internet, which seems to have revolutionized life, this abstraction will evolve into something tangible. The New Age workshops teach how to commune as the individual ability to create good relations. It seems that this disposition to commune may be an important ability in the age of globalization. However, New Age circles do not encourage optimism, rather, New Age associations are dispersed and quite self-critical. This is the effect of commercialization. Whether it is dowsing, bioenergotherapy, numerology, or astrology, each claims to have the best product while negating the efficacy of the others. In some circles, the concept, "to commune" means only to communicate effectively, and it again reflects marketing. The idea of community as a representation of New Age circles in the context of anti-Christian conspiracy sounds only as a church's whisper.

REFERENCES

Barker, Eileen. *New Religious Movements: A Practical Introduction*. London: HMSO, 1992.

Heelas, Paul. *The New Age Movement: The Celebration of the Self and the Sacralization of Modernity*. Oxford: Blackwell, 1996.

———, Scott Lash, and Paul Morris, eds. *Detraditionalization: Critical Reflections on Authority and Identity*. Oxford: Blackwell, 1996.

Manabu, Haga. "Self-Development Seminars in Japan." *Japanese Journal of Religious Studies* 22 (1995): 3–4.

Sutcliffe, Steve. "The Authority of the Self in New Age Religiosity: The Example of the Findhorn Community." *Discus* 3, no. 22 (1995).

24
THE NEW AGE
A Sociological Assessment
Michael Hill

Novelty is a central motif in the culture of consumerism—with which, as will be shown later, many contemporary religious movements have a strong affinity, but it is a motif that requires close scrutiny. It will be argued here that the "New" Age has a long historical pedigree and that its appearance was pre-dicted in remarkable detail by sociologists almost one hundred years ago.[1] While some of the features of movements located in the diffuse New Age network have a highly contemporary content and immediacy, these should properly be seen as reworkings of established cultural themes rather than as cultural inventions.

An example of this process can be found in the way that cultic groups "mys-tify" areas of uncertainty or incomplete knowledge: In the 1950s, outer space was just such an area, and there was a period of florescence in UFO and cosmic cults. By the early 1960s, outer space had been partly demystified, and the exploration of "inner space" became a major preoccupation of new religious movements; indeed, it will be argued that this remains a preoccupation of the contemporary New Age.

Historical antecedents of the New Age can be traced through the develop-ment of individualism in Western thought and especially its religious variants. It is beyond the scope of this chapter to trace the broader context of this develop-ment but a key aspect of it—and therefore a plausible reference point for the present argument—can be located in the Protestant Reformation. In both Calvinism, with its "unprecedented inner loneliness of the single individual," and

From *Australian Religion Studies Review* 6, no. 2 (1993): 6–12. Copyright © 1993 by the Australian Religion Studies Association. Reprinted by permission of the Australian Religion Studies Association.

Lutheranism, where the believer "feels himself to be a vessel of the Holy Spirit," there are unmistakable pointers to the emergence of the individualized style of religiosity found in the cultic milieu of the New Age. In the absence of structure or of clearly defined ideological boundaries, the social context of individualized religiosity depends on its adherents experiencing parallel emotions: instead of constituting a community of worshipers, they are—to use the kind of technical analogy which is often adopted by such movements—"in phase."

That such developments were well established by the turn of the present century can be seen in the work of two exceptionally prescient sociologists, Emile Durkheim and Ernst Troeltsch. Throughout his career, Durkheim was preoccupied with the question of social solidarity and the means by which it could be maintained in modern complex societies. His treatment of this theme involves an analysis of, and predictions about, religion in complex societies. The problem for Durkheim was that, while in traditional societies—characterized by a low level of division of labor—the basis of social solidarity could be found in moral consensus (or a strong collective conscience), in highly differentiated contemporary societies the same degree of moral consensus is not because social solidarity is based more on the mutual interdependence between people brought about by the division of labor. Implied in this account is the shrinkage of that part of the collective conscience maintained by religion and the reorientation of the latter in an increasingly secular, human-oriented direction. The social significance of religion would weaken, and there would be a decrease in the number of beliefs that were strong enough, and held on a sufficiently collective basis, to take on a religious character.

A theme which would take on a more central role in shared values was the way in which the individual was regarded. Hence, a supreme value would be placed on the rights and dignity of the individual and, being socially shared, this would assume a religious form, so that there would emerge a "cult of humanity."

The following is his account—first presented in 1897—of how this will occur, and is therefore his prediction of the form religion will take in complex societies:

> As societies become larger and more densely populated, they become more complex, labour is differentiated, individual differences multiply and one can foresee the moment when there will be nothing in common between all the members of the same human group except that they are all human beings. In these conditions, it is inevitable that collective feeling will attach itself very strongly to the single aim that it shares and to which it attributes by that very fact an incomparable value. Since the individual human being is the only entity which appeals without exception to all hearts, since its exaltation is the only goal which can be collectively pursued, it cannot but acquire an exceptional importance in all eyes. It thus rises far above all human objectives and takes on a religious character.

In arguing that humanity itself would come to be seen as sacred, there are obvious links with emphases in Protestant theology: "This is why man has become a god for man, and it is why he can no longer turn to other gods without being untrue to himself. And just as each of us embodies something of humanity, so each individual mind has within it something of the divine, and thereby finds itself marked by a characteristic which renders it sacred and inviolable to others."[2]

There are more detailed observations in Durkheim's prediction that offer insights on New Age religiosity. His statement that the "cult of humanity" will appeal in particular to those who are aware of having "nothing in common," which can be interpreted to refer to those who occupy specialist roles in the occupational structure and who lack primary group membership as a source of identity describes the environment of the skilled and the mobile who have been the main consumers of New Age religiosity. He also thought there would be a variety of groups within the overall "cult of humanity," appealing to specific social constituencies through the special emphasis of their beliefs but united in their elevation of human personality to an absolute goal. Contemporary scientific ideas, rather than being rejected, would be incorporated in the belief systems of such groups, though possibly in a transmuted form. Again, the presence in the New Age network of groups emphasizing therapy and self-transformation through esoteric techniques would appear to confirm his prediction.

An almost identical prediction about the future of religion was made in 1911 quite independently by Ernst Troeltsch. His church-sect dichotomy is well known, but he also developed the concept of an emergent form of religiosity in Western societies to which he gave the label "mysticism." Like Durkheim, he predicts a religious form characterized by individualism and combining religious ideas, often drawn from non-Christian religions—with modern scientific thought, albeit in a flexible, free-floating way. Adherents to mystical forms of religion, he suggests, have little desire for organized fellowship and place more emphasis on the importance of freedom for the interchange of ideas. He continues:

> Gradually, in the modern world of educated people, the third type has come to predominate. This means, then, that all that is left is voluntary association with like-minded people, which is equally remote from Church and Sect. . . . It is neither Church nor Sect, and has neither the concrete sanctity of the institution nor the radical connection with the Bible. Combining Christian ideas with a wealth of modern views, deducing social institutions, not from the Fall but from a process of natural development, it has not the fixed limit for concessions and the social power which the Church possesses, but it also does not possess the radicalism and the exclusiveness with which the sect can set aside the State and economics, art and science.[3]

Troeltsch uses virtually the same words as Durkheim when he argues that in this form of religion, "The isolated individual, and psychological abstraction and analysis become everything."

In view of the emphasis among New Age groups on the discovery and enhancement of the self, there is much resonance in Troeltsch's suggestion that self-perfection and self-deification are the ethical absolutes which emerge from modern individualism: When these are coupled with a strong emphasis on toler- ance, these goals are highly congruent with the pluralist environment of a modern, complex society. Pluralism can also be related to syncretism—another feature of the New Age movement—since consumers of mystical religion "mix and match" their beliefs from a variety of sources, both secular and spiritual, the latter also involving non-Christian sources of beliefs. Finally, Troeltsch saw the appeal which Romanticism—both because of its idealization of the individual and its pantheistic notion of an all-pervasive spiritual quality within the world— might have for liberal, educated Protestants (and we might indicate, for partici- pants in the New Age). The end product is "simply a parallelism of religious per- sonalities. . . . This is the secret religion of the educated classes."

Troeltsch's concept of mysticism was adapted by Howard Becker, who used the term "cult" to depict the end point of Christian individualism (note that his use of the term should be strictly distinguished from its current media usage). Becker drew attention to the way in which the "I" became the center of the believer's cosmos, and he thought that only a highly atomistic and secular social order could give rise to the cultic form of religion. In view of some of the more recent manifestations of New Age esoterica, it is interesting to note that even in the 1930s Becker could refer to a variety of "pseudo-Hinduisms" associated with "Swamis and Yogis who con- sent, for a consideration, to carry their messages to the materialistic Western World."

Based on the work of Durkheim and Troeltsch, and incorporating the more recent evaluations of Frances Westley and Colin Campbell, I would suggest the following inventory as a way of typifying the characteristic features of New Age religion:

1. It is *individualistic*. In a society with an increasing division of labor there is a demand for beliefs and lifestyles which permit individual choice and expression. There is considerable variety in religion of this sort, but a second feature provides its common thread:

2. It emphasizes an *idealized human personality*. The ideal personality takes on a sacred quality as adherents pursue the goal of self-perfection and a realization of their human potential. This will not lead to mere egoism, however, since an awareness of others in pursuit of similar goals will lead to a third feature:

3. It maintains a degree of *tolerance*. Though different elements in this humanized religion appeal to different social constituencies, with a pre- vailing emphasis on occupational specialists lacking intense primary group membership, there is a free exchange of ideas and a relativistic acceptance of alternative views and versions (though the precariousness of such groups may well undermine their capacity for tolerance). As a result:

4. It is *syncretistic*. A range of ideas from the beliefs of different world religions, philosophies, and esoteric and scientific traditions is shaped into a relatively plastic amalgam by adherents and adepts. As well as an emphasis on idealized human personality, this set of ideas has in common a fifth feature:

5. It is *monistic*. Humanized religion rejects the dichotomy of body and mind, matter and spirit in favor of a worldview which sees spiritual power as diffuse and all-pervasive. In therapeutic groups, the conception of the human being in relation to the natural environment is holistic. From this follows an important feature of the ritual of humanized religion:

6. It emphasizes a process whereby individuals are *"morally remade" or empowered*. Though ritual may be minimal in this associational milieu—sometimes involving only a guru/practitioner-client relationship—when it does exist, it dramatizes the release of inner power from a newly enabled personality.

With specific reference to the New Age, Campbell's claim that such groups operate within a "cultic milieu" is valuable. Networking and the interchange of ideas are prominent features of the New Age, and there is a large range of alternative networks which advertise and service consumer needs. In Britain there is the Holistic Network (a division of Earth Enterprises Ltd.) and publications such as *The Rainbow Ark*—which published "The Networker's Diary" in issue number 4—and *Glastonbury Communicator.* New Zealand has its Rainbow Network ("Your health and New Age network"), which offers a similar smorgasbord to that of its British counterparts. Even though New Age practitioners may have a competitive, market-oriented approach, they show an awareness of complementary groups and therapies and eschew the ideological closure and monopolistic conception of membership which is more typical of sectarian groups.

This results in part from the perception they have of their adherents or clients less as "members" than as "seekers." The term "seekership" has been employed by several sociologists to highlight the self-conception of many of the adherents of groups in the cultic milieu as serial consumers of new ideas, constantly looking for a truth or truths that will meet their own personalized situations. An important aspect of this is the emphasis placed on geographical mobility. In Britain, for instance, there is now a sizable army of "travelers"—estimated at over fifteen thousand—whose lives are constructed around journeys and gatherings, often at places of symbolic significance to the New Age such as Glastonbury. The historical parallel of pilgrimage is not very remote from the contemporary pursuit, and the notion of sites of intense spirituality links the New Age with prominent locations of mainstream Christianity. After two decades of agonized debate about their relevance to the contemporary world, Anglican cathedrals in Britain are now attracting revived attendance because they provide extraordinary settings for experiences which people find lacking in parish churches.

But "seekership" includes other forms of mobility. One of the most remarkable phenomena of the post-1960s period—and one which the New Age has intensively canvassed—is the issue of labile identity. The idea that identities can be—perhaps even should be—continuously reshaped and rediscovered has spawned a veritable industry of therapies and self-transformation techniques. One source of this particular quest lies in the humanistic psychology of the 1960s Human Potential movement, and it has been constantly repackaged—often with the input of Eastern religious ideas—to provide a protean resource for identity-management. Therapy books are to the twentieth century what etiquette books were to the nineteenth. One of the principal themes of New Age culture is how to access spontaneity, and it is plausible to suggest that the techniques offered by various groups have special resonance for those involved in what Hochschild calls "emotional labour." In response to the experience of personal authenticity in a work environment dominated by the management and commercialization of human feeling, solutions are sought in the therapeutic context of techniques such as Alexander, biorhythms, channelling, crystals, rebirthing, and tai chi. In the United States, where many of these techniques originate or are at least first successfully marketed, the rewriting of identity has grown to epidemic proportions, and for those who are dissatisfied with one, a diversity can be offered. Aldridge-Morris has commented on the "dramatic incidence of multiple personality syndrome in the United States relative to its virtual absence elsewhere in the world."[4] Given the capacity of psychological styles to be disseminated rapidly, this disparity may not long continue.

One very prominent facet of the New Age is a form of ethnic seekership which can best be labeled noble savagery. In several Western countries, there is a search for "roots" among educated and affluent sections of the population which doubtless reflects a wider sense of anomie in a period of economic and social dislocation: and in Durkheim's sense, this would indeed typify mobile individuals lacking strong primary group membership. Thus in Britain the "re-invention of the Celt," as folklorist Marion Bowman calls it, has provided a mythical model of spiritually immanent, ecologically sound religion which attracts a significant tourist trade to the western fringes of Britain. Glastonbury may well be a magnet for down-at-heel (or more likely, tire) New Age "travelers," but it has an extensive commercial network as well, where well-heeled American and British tourists can purchase relics of their true spiritual home. As Bowman has pointed out, in Glastonbury two trees constitute a "Druid Grove"! In North America itself, New Agers also have recourse to indigenous Indian spirit guides through whom spiritual power may be channeled. In New Zealand, there has been a resurgence of interest in Maori spirituality, though this has probably had greater influence on sections of the mainstream churches than on the New Age network.

These remarks introduce the final section of this chapter because they refer to New Age consumerism, which is seen as embodying three aspects. The first concerns Colin Campbell's argument in *The Romantic Ethic and the Spirit of Modern Consumerism*. Much simplified, his thesis is that mature capitalism requires for its maintenance a consumer ethic through which wants are converted into needs and consumers are persuaded through advertising that consumer items or services are essential to their lifestyles. While the austere and ascetic work ethic of the early Calvinists may have been a necessary factor in the generation of entrepreneurial capitalism, it is no longer required for its maintenance, as Weber himself noticed. In its place has been inserted an ethic which Campbell traces back to its origins in Lutheran pietism and its wider social dissemination through the Romantic movement. This is the ethic which emphasizes the enhancement and embellishment of the self and which thus creates a sense of constant dissatisfaction, introducing an expanding cycle of consumption. There is a strong affinity with some sections of the New Age movement here, because those groups offering self-transformative and therapeutic insights offer the opportunity constantly to rewrite one's personality in conformity with the latest gnostic style.

A second interpretation of the part played by consumerism among New Age movements is provided by Reg Bibby, who sees new religious movements as providing supplements for science. It will be recalled that both Durkheim and Troeltsch were discussing groups which operate on the boundaries of, and which incorporate transmuted versions of, science. Bibby terms this milieu the area of "a-science" and suggests that "a-science" explanations are drawn upon either because scientific explanations are unavailable or because the questions asked are not amenable to scientific answers. Because there is a potential for people to supplement science, a market for a-science is created. Arguing that such a-science products are an integral component of modern consumerism, he suggests that "a-science advocates who can make and create consumer demand, as well as publicise and deliver their products stand to know market gains."[5]

Finally, Paul Heelas offers an analysis of the New Age which brings us full circle, centering on the Durkheimian theme of "the sacralization of the self."[4] He perceptively traces the transformation of "self religions" from the drop-out culture of the 1960s to the more materially attuned New Age movement of the 1990s. The following passage encapsulates the process admirably:

> Of particular note, whereas hippies steered well clear of the capitalist mainstream, many "Naps" (New Age professionals) have acquired beliefs—of a kind not found in the counterculture—which enable them to believe that self religiosity can be practised in the world of business. Findhorn, the well-known commune in the northeast of Scotland began life with a strong countercultural orientation but is now involved in management and business activities. Some

Findhornians work as "angels in pinstripes" in Hampstead. Self-sacralization, it seems, can be pursued in an experiential setting far removed from that provided by rural tranquillity.[6]

The New Age has in fact penetrated the capitalist mainstream, offering packages of transformational techniques and stimulating a considerable literature: researchers in the field of contemporary religion could profitably spend some time browsing in the Australian Institute of Management bookshop. In addition to companies like Cunard and Pacific Bell, which have sent their executives on training courses based on the teaching of Erhard and Gurdjieff, one of the major multinational financial companies to be influenced by New Age was the Bank of Credit and Commerce International.

Heelas draws attention to the resonance between New Age capitalism and the Western ideology of perfectibility. This has a considerable history in the American tradition of positive thinking, but in many Western societies, there is an increasing emphasis on spiritual, psychological, and material progress, and these are ideals which New Age enterprises stress. Within this market, "designer" religion (I prefer to think of it as "deli" religion, in contrast to the more limited fare of parish/corner "dairy" religion) is likely to prosper. "So long as the consumer ethic retains its hold, it will seem that the ultimate act of consumption is to 'consume' all that could possibly lie within whilst obtaining all that lies without."[7]

NOTES

1. This chapter reviews and extends the material in Michael Hill, "New Zealand's Cultic Milieu: Individualism and the Logic of Consumerism," in B. Wilson, ed., *Religion: Contemporary Issues: The All Souls Seminars in the Sociology of Religion* (London: Bellew Publishing, 1992); and "Ennobled Savages: New Zealand's Manipulationist Milieu," in E. Barker, J. A. Beckford, and K. Dobbelaere, eds., *Secularization, Rationalism, and Sectarianism: Essays in Honour of Bryan R. Wilson* (Oxford: Clarendon Press, 1993).

2. E. Durkheim, *Le Suicide—Étude de Sociologie*, new ed. (Paris: Presses Universitaires de France, 1960), p. 382 (my translation).

3. E. Troeltsch, *The Social Teaching of the Christian Churches*, 2 vols., trans. O. Wyon (London: Allen and Unwin, 1931), p. 381.

4. Ray Aldridge-Morris, *Multiple Personality* (Hove: Lawrence Erlbaum Associates, 1989), p. 108.

5. Reg Bibby and H. R. Weaver, "Cult Consumption in Canada: A Further Critique of Stark and Bainbridge," *Sociological Analysis* 46 (1985): 451

6. Paul Heelas, "The Sacralization of the Self and New Age Capitalism," in N. Abercrombie and A. Warde, eds., *Social Change in Contemporary Britain* (Cambridge: Polity Press, 1992), pp. 139–66. The quotations are from p. 152 and p. 161.

7. Ibid., p. 161.

25
THE WEB OF NEW AGE SPIRITUALITIES

Dominic Corrywright

All testing, all confirmation and disconfirmation of a hypothesis takes place already within a system. . . . The system is not so much the point of departure, as the element in which arguments have their life.—Ludwig Wittgenstein

Believing, with Max Weber, that man is an animal suspended in webs of significance he himself has spun, I take culture to be those webs, and the analysis of it to be therefore not an experimental science in search of law but an interpretive one in search of meaning.—Clifford Geertz

We believe that God is speaking in this moment. The divine language may not be the language of our traditions and assumptions, but a new language altogether.—Marilyn Ferguson

THE LANGUAGE OF THE WEB

The models that we bring to our experience prefigure how we experience the world. This basic tenet has profound implications for the researcher. An explicitly empirical piece of research requires considerable sensitivity in the light of such an observation. The most extreme example of researchers paying heed to this continuous quandary (if by "extreme" we mean time, energy, and financial resources) can be found in particle physics research. George Johnson expresses the essence of the problem in this way:

> As we go from electrons to positrons to neutrinos to quarks, and from gas-filled discharge tubes to cloud chambers to accelerators shooting beams at detectors so elaborate that they are among the most complex, delicate devices ever made—it becomes harder to be sure that experimenters are simply observing what the theorists predict. There is a wide gulf between the beholder and the beheld, consisting not only of millions of dollars worth of detecting equipment but of the complex of theories with which the experiment is designed, its results interpreted. (Johnson 1995, 55)

At the quantum level of research there are peculiar problems, which require a "complex of theories." But even at the macro level of human experience and interaction, there are specific problems of interpretation, which require sets of theories to comprehend them. Underlying the scientific project that led to particle physics is the epistemological assumption of a directly observable world and that the universe is comprehensible to the human mind. The research, in this area of science at least, has refracted back onto its theoretical presuppositions, to question the interpretative role of the observer. Johnson expresses this questioning of presumptions by focusing on the observers' a priori belief that the universe has a symmetry: "Compelled by our faith in the brain's ability to see the core of creation, are we simply filling in the fractures of our imperfect theories? Are quarks and dark matter discoveries or are they inventions, artefacts of the brain's hunger for symmetry?" (Johnson 1995, 24).

Research into the new and fluid set of phenomena of the New Age spiritualities must equally be sensible of "artefacts" of the mind that impose order on the data. Both conscious assumptions, in the form of typologies, and unconscious predilections, such as the search for order and structure, require cautious appraisal. Those aspects of belief and practice that are amenable to quantifiable analysis, which fit easily into structural analysis, should also be considered carefully for the crucial element of change that militates against the reified world of absolute depictions. Given these criteria of caution, the researcher is left with only the ability to make statements of limited applicability or continually to qualify specific comments. Such a study, it would appear, will result in a survey of individualized instances and meaningless generalizations. Every attempt at clarity will die Anthony Flew's "death of a thousand qualifications" (1955, 107) or emerge in a highly relativized manner, scarcely different from a solipsist expression of the world.

These, at least, are the criticisms to which the nuanced method I am defining should respond. But the response is already included in the method: by accurately reflecting the ideas of those within the New Age, and by representing these ideas within the broader epistemological context of a critique of existing epistemology, it becomes possible to usefully assert certain "facts" about the New Age spiritualities. These facts are indeed temporally located, but they are no less valuable than other facts, contingent as all facts are upon the language of historical and cultural specificity. It is simply that these facts emerge in a different language game. The relationship between facts and language, and how they change, requires a brief excursion into Wittgenstein's linguistic analysis.

Wittgenstein asserted that the rules of the language game need not be explicitly learned: "The propositions describing the world-picture might be part of a kind of mythology. And their role is like that of rules of a game: and the game can be learned purely practically, without learning any specific rules" (1969, 95).

But his description here applies to a "common" language.[1] The rules for an unusual or new language have to be specifically described. There is not an "accustomed context" that "allows what is meant to come through clearly" (Wittgenstein 1969, 237). The onus in bringing forth a new language is to provide transparent presuppositions. The difficulty is to expose the complex system that underlies a "world-picture" and to explain the relationship between facts and the determinants for establishing them as facts.[2]

This very issue of the relationship between facts, language, the world, and our experience of it is at the heart of many of the claims in the broad spectrum of New Age spiritualities. Much of our experience, it is claimed, is mediated and limited by the functions of our language and the past construction of our knowledge. The overarching paradigm of positivist science has, from the position of the New Age spiritualities, foreclosed many areas of possible human experience, from past lives to past civilizations, from extrasensory to extraterrestrial. The paradigm shift proposed in the vision and language of New Age spiritualities is of knowledge and experience that extend beyond the narrow parameters of this scientific paradigm.

That language and knowledge can change is not such a revolutionary claim, though sometimes the claims themselves, especially certain millennialist predictions regarding extraterrestrial visitations, may indeed appear revolutionary. The challenge presented by much of the thinking within the New Age spiritualities amounts to a shift in language games. For those posing this challenge to scientific epistemology, the core theme is that we are in the process of a Kuhnian cultural and epistemic paradigm shift. Many of the concepts of spiritual growth, of transformation, current within the greater part of New Age spiritualities demand conceptual shifts and new language games.

The new language game proposed here is a new model for understanding the ideas and social interactions of those within the New Age spiritualities. It is a model that seeks to reflect the plurality and eclectic nature of New Age spiritualities, at the same time as highlighting the specificities of New Age religiosity. For one of the shortcomings of those sociologists situating and modeling the New Age as an NRM is that it does not function like a traditional religion such as Christianity. (That "traditional" religions transgress the fragile boundaries of the concept of "religion" is another issue.) David Spangler has given an apt metaphor by which the New Age can be distinguished from traditional religions. He compares Christianity to a cathedral whose architecture is "unified in the person of Jesus Christ"; while the New Age "is more like a flea market or county fair . . . [with] . . . jesters and jugglers, magicians and shamans, healers and mystics, and the inevitable hucksters eager for a quick sale before packing up and moving on." The error committed by many commentators, according to Spangler, "has been to isolate one or two tents and to deal with them as if they were cathedrals covering the whole fair." The fair, he says, "is a place whose architecture is horizontal rather than vertical" (1993, 80).

This spatial metaphor is a useful entry point for a discussion of models and typologies that may accurately describe the relations and functions of New Age spiritualities. The core theme of the framework I will outline is interconnections. The pathways of these interconnections form the weblike structure that composes the shape of the model. To extend Spangler's metaphor, we need to imagine the movements of those visiting the fair during the course of a day. Each person would leave a different trail of footprints from one tent to another. It is our task to reveal the nature of that pathway, to measure the consequences and meanings of the connections made at the fair. The tents, which incorporate certain specific traditions, are vital to our study, but they are the nodes, the points of linkage between the pathways—and in this fair, even the tents are not static. It is possible, and indeed useful, to do ethnographic studies of individual tents, for example, channeling (Riordan 1992) or the Osho movement (1997, 1999),[3] but such methods will not illuminate the whole. To view the whole, albeit a vision of a shifting pattern, requires a different vantage point that in turn incites the mapping of a new model.

THE WEB MODEL

Features of the Model

Methodology and phenomena are intertwined: as the former "discovers" the latter, so the latter defines the former. This sympathetic connection is a necessary presupposition if we are accurately to define the field of New Age spiritualities. The model of the web emerges in this interaction of theory and praxis as a means of explaining the complex phenomena that amount to the New Age spiritualities. The web is the interface linking methodology, model and phenomena. It has roots in diverse fields from systems theory to transpersonal psychology. In outlining these roots I will define the key features of the model.

The notion of the web has considerable currency, especially in information technology and the resources of the World Wide Web. It is significant as a para-digmatic model for living systems (Capra 1996; Anderson and Hopkins 1992, 226).[4] At the same time, the idea of the web has been explicitly applied to methodology in the study of religions, as in Rita Gross's construction of a femi-nist hermeneutic that is a "seamless harmonious web" (1993, 315). The idea of a web of interconnecting approaches is also *implicit* in a number of approaches, such as Helen Thorne's "synthesis of methods," which links multiple social research methods between a bipolar schema of knowledge and self-reflection (2000, 47–49); Lene Sjørup's "holistic" and "spiral" epistemology (1998, 129); and the model of the "segmented polycentric integrated network" developed by Luther Gerlach and Virginia Hine (1970, xii, 33–34—see below).

One of the factors influencing this perspective of applying interconnecting methods is the reaction against the limits of unitary linear approaches: Gross takes a stand against the predominant linear phenomenological approach in the history of religions (such as that outlined by Cox 1992, 24–40); Thorne critiques positivist and interpretative research methods as too linear and "essentially com-partmentalised"; while Sjørup suggests such approaches not only limit possible knowledge but may be intrinsic to the degradation of the planet:

> Clearly, a holistic epistemology cannot make an aeroplane fly. But it could pre-vent ecological catastrophes. If we want to search for new knowledge a spiral epistemology may be very useful. . . . One epistemology cannot be said to be the 'better'. However, the logical, linear epistemology is the dominant paradigm today. It limits the knowledge we can obtain, barring us from perceiving what we already know (1998, 129).

The reaction to the limitations of linear methodologies is then a preliminary feature of the methodology of the web, albeit a definition of what it is not. The assumption is that there are complex and ever-changing aspects to the phe-nomena studied that can only be described with an equally complex hermeneutic responsive to this shifting morphology. It is, in some ways, analogous to Der-rida's notion of "traces," which combines the historical circumstances of phe-nomena with the specificities of their present existence at the same time as inter-weaving the perspective, or traces, of the scholar's own particularities. Thus, while text, language, and argument necessitate a beginning and proceed *as if* developing a linear progression, it is possible to presume that any beginning emerges in a wider context of many possible beginnings.

The image of the web allows such a presumption: there is no necessary single point of entry. Methodologically the web describes the scholar's use of a multiplicity of methods to define phenomena. It is practicable to outline a single method as a means of study, such as the questionnaire, while recollecting that its application is an abstraction from many concurrent methods or approaches to the phenomena. The web of methods informs and is informed by a single abstracted method. Phenomenologically the image of the web means it is viable to consider a phenomenon in this abstracted sense also. However, without reference to the wider phenomena that constitute the context of singular practices and traditions, such descriptions are fictional or partial abstractions. One might adopt the epithet "context is all" in the descriptive methodology of the web.

Another feature of web theory (as I define it) is that it grows out of systems theory. A general systems theory was developed by Ludwig von Bertalanffy in 1968[5] to describe the basic relationships and principles of living systems. The core rubric for systems thinking is that it focuses on modes of organization, interrelation, and relationship rather than an atomistic view of intrinsic properties. Philosophically the theory has similarities to Alfred North Whitehead's "process" philosophy and bears some resemblance to Wittgenstein's analysis of language where "meaning is use," that is, concepts are defined by their context. So, for Bertalanffy, living systems are defined by their patterns of organization. It is, from a systems point of view, fallacious to reduce holistic systems to their parts in order to discover how the system operates.

Another key proponent of systems thinking is Ervin Laszlo, who has built upon Bertalanffy's biological systems theory to consider how the theory applies to culture. Laszlo has called for new scientific laws that deal with "integrated wholes," basing this claim on the principle that "holistic characteristics" of groups or wholes are irreducible and cannot be found in the separate categorization of their components (1972b, 11, 29). The most important aspects of organisms from a systems approach are not their reducible mechanistic functions, but their qualities to organize themselves as wholes. The qualities of self-organization are the themes that structure the systems worldview. Essentially they comprise four related ideas. The first is the idea of "homeostasis," which originally referred to the regulative mechanisms of warm-blooded animals but in its wider application refers to the mechanisms that regulate species in the biosphere. The second idea is "phylogenesis," which refers to species evolution rather than individual evolution. From a cultural perspective, phylogenesis stresses an anthropocentric vision. The third idea is "openness," which specifically refers to the dynamic functions of a system necessary to maintain a steady state. Finally, the idea of hierarchy posits a network system whereby "systemic units collaborate with units of their own level and form superunits, and these, in collaboration, with their own kind, form still higher level units" (Laszlo 1972, 73). Application of systems theory to the wider context of human society and beyond to the whole biosphere encourages a new ethic from Laszlo:

> It allows us to understand that man is one species of system in a complex and embracing hierarchy of nature, and at the same time it tells us that all systems have value and intrinsic worth. . . . Seeing himself as a connecting link in a complex natural hierarchy cancels man's anthropocentrism, but seeing the hierarchy itself as an expression of self-ordering and self-creating nature bolsters his self-esteem and encourages his humanism (1972, 118).

It is a vision at once resonant with a late-Victorian sense of man's responsibility (normative masculine gender pronoun included) and in sympathy with the more contemporary ethical standpoints of ecological awareness or even the 1993 World Parliament of Religions' "Declaration Toward a Global Ethic" (cf. Kung and Kuschel 1993). There are, however, certain elements within the criteria of systems thinking that resemble those I have elucidated regarding the web—most significantly, the ideas of interrelationship and dynamism with the emphasis on holistic characteristics.

Capra's Theory of the Web

Systems theory has progressed since Laszlo's definition of a "natural philosophy" and now more directly embraces both scientific and cultural worldviews, especially in the work of Fritjof Capra. I am greatly indebted to Capra's specific creation and explication of the web as a model for living systems in *The Web of Life* (1996) and "The Web Page" in *Resurgence* (1997–99). Capra has taken up Laszlo's broader concerns with the environment and human culture and society.[6] The focus of Capra's notion of the web does, however, differ from the systems of Laszlo through the rejection of hierarchical models because they are representative of "patriarchal society" (1996, 10). In fact, Capra defines a new paradigm shift in culture and society "from structure to process" (1992, xii), which amounts to a "shift in social organisation from hierarchies to networks" (1996, 10).

From an empirical perspective this excessively general claim of a paradigm shift is open to considerable counterargument and examples—hierarchies quite obviously function in many areas of society today. Contrary examples can equally be found to undermine his corollary statement of the "shift from objective science to 'epistemic' science" (1992, xiii). A basic knowledge of the way we teach science in our schools would show that the notion of objective science is a live and functioning paradigm. Nevertheless, Capra is correct in asserting the increasing influence of network models in science and the broader perspective of contemporary culture. It is worth citing Capra's explanation of how networks function at some length in order to clarify the fundamental features of the image of interaction and interdependence:

> The view of living systems as networks provides a novel perspective on the so-called 'hierarchies' of nature. Since living systems at all levels are networks, we must visualise the web of life as living systems (networks) interacting in network fashion with other systems (networks). For example, we can picture an ecosystem schematically as a network with a few nodes. Each node represents an organism, which means that each node, when magnified, appears itself as a network. Each node in the new network may represent an organ, which in turn will appear as a network when magnified and so on.
> In other words, the web of life consists of networks within networks. At

each scale, under close scrutiny, the nodes of the network reveal themselves as smaller networks. We tend to arrange these systems, all nesting within larger systems, in a hierarchical scheme by placing the larger systems above the smaller in pyramid fashion. But this is a human projection. In nature, there is no 'above', nor 'below', and there are no hierarchies. There are only networks nesting within other networks (1996, 35).

We thus have an image markedly similar to Spangler's horizontal fair. In terms of the phenomena of New Age spiritualities, there is no hierarchy of organization, unless the observer specifically adopts one, such as the statistical significance of certain New Age groupings (some tents/networks *are* bigger than others). It is simply the case that there are manifold networks operating within the larger network that I have defined as New Age spiritualities. But Capra should go further, because even the creation of networks is part of a human construction that, from a postmodern perspective, can be conceived as "at best no more than a temporarily useful fiction masking chaos" (Tarnas 1991, 401). The web is a means of organizing the chaos of overlapping institutions and practices that are the network of New Age spiritualities.

Within Capra's definition of ever-magnifiable networks is the notion of holography. The holographic model of the world is another significant idea in the realm of New Age thinking (Ferguson 1980, 177–87; Wilber 1982; Hanegraaff 1996, 139–51). It emerged from the field of neuroscience when Karl Pribram suggested in 1966 that the explanation for the continuation of memory, despite damage to major cognitive areas of the brain, was that memory is encoded in an "engram" not locally but distributed across the whole brain. Holography provides the explanation because a hologram can be entirely reconstructed from any single particle, even if the "whole" is broken. Capra's network model resembles this theory in that however much a network may be disassembled, its structural and constitutive units are always to be found in a network pattern.

Where Capra diverges from a strictly holographic model is that the hologram is still composed of discrete units or particles, and Capra seeks to divest his theory of the objective existence of particles—"what we call a part is merely a pattern in an inseparable web of relationships" (1992, 83). Furthermore, the holograph is static, while Capra's networks are essentially dynamic. The position he assumes is close to that of the nonrealist in that our theories of the world are not representational, they do not simply reflect an external reality. He is, however, careful not to enmesh himself in the more radical subjectivist position that there is *only* our description of the world and no *real* world to describe. The basis for Capra's nuanced position is the theory of networks where "things do not have intrinsic properties. All the properties flow from their relationships" (1992, 84). There is an a priori assumption of "things" to have "relationships," but these things can only be described, accurately, in terms of their relationships. This aspect of Capra's theory rests on the biologic-epistemic model of cognition developed by Humberto Maturana and Francisco Varela (1987).

In *The Tree of Knowledge*, Maturana and Varela set themselves the objective of outlining "a theory of knowledge . . . to show how knowing generates the explanation of knowing," which is quite different from "the phenomenon of explaining and the phenomenon explained belong[ing] to different domains" (1987, 239). They explicitly seek a via media "eschewing the extremes of representationalism (objectivism) and solipsism (idealism)" by constructing their theory on the principle that "human cognition as effective action pertains to the biological domain, but it is always lived in a cultural tradition" (241, 244). They conclude that the "knowledge of knowledge compels" toward ethical considerations. For if this knowledge is biological and cultural, every expression of it emerges from a "network of interactions" with the world and the human community. Thus, the "social imperative for a human-centred ethics" arises out of the understanding of the network relationships whereby "every human act has an ethical meaning because it is an act of constitution of the human world" (1987, 239–50).

Again we can recognize in this model of human interaction and knowledge certain themes that helpfully inform the web theory. The logical link between the phenomenon of explaining and the phenomena of the explained adds emphasis to the tenet (established in chapter 1) that "there must be some compatibility between the method of study and the phenomenon studied." Equally the observation that humans make meanings in a "network of interactions" seems further to establish the features of networks as the key to unlocking the nature of the many spiritualities developing in the New Age "fair." At the same time, the ethical imperative this self-reflective knowledge entails may partly explain the social and political activism espoused by many within the New Age spiritualities.

Transpersonal Models and the Web

Beyond Capra's networks and often incorporating holonomic or holographic theories of reality, the field of transpersonal psychology has useful insights to add to the web model. The sympathy many transpersonal psychologists feel for the holographic theory lies in a specific feature of the model that gives an explanation for transcendental or trans-human experience. The explanation lies with the corollary notion Pribram developed to the idea of a holographic memory, that the universe may also be holographic. Human perceptions of other worldly knowledge, even Jungian archetypes, occur according to this theory, because of the concordance of the holographic mind with the holographic universe. There is a connection with a "frequency realm" or "holographic blur," which allows transpersonal experience.

Not all advocates of transpersonal models of the human psyche concur with the "holographic paradigm." Ken Wilber is at pains to dissociate the holographic model of perception from what he considers to be the "eternal ground" of human experience that is beyond any structure, including that of the holographic frequency realm. Wilber considers the holographic model a useful metaphor for a pantheist expression of the world, where each aspect of the world contains the whole. Indeed, in this sense one might consider the holographic idea as parallel to Indra's many-jewelled net or even the dharma realm of the *Avatamsaka sutra*. "They perceive that the many fields and assemblies and the beings and the aeons are all reflected in each particle of dust" (Williams 1989, 124). Wilber, however, acerbically notes that this "timeless zone" of the holograph can be recorded like a tape by optical holography machines, "which has little to do with a metaphysical . . . eternity . . . break the tape recorder . . . and there goes your eternity. An eternity dependent for its existence on a temporal structure, tape or brain, is a strange eternity" (1982, 252–53).

Nevertheless, with or without the holographic model, transpersonal psychology and transpersonal ecology work under a paradigm of the human psyche that has a similar morphology to that of the web. The essence of this view is that the individual human psyche is situated in an intricate network of connections beyond the human self. (Warwick Fox correctly defines *trans-* in the context of transpersonal psychology as "beyond" rather than "across" [1990, 198].) Stanislav Grof suggests a "cartography of the unconscious" that includes not only the individual biographical but also the perinatal and transpersonal dimensions. Perinatal, for Grof, refers to biological birth and prebirth experiences. He uses transpersonal to refer to other experiences beyond the temporal embodied self, which include "peak experiences" and past-life experiences (in conversation with Russell Di Carlo 1996, 119–20.) Some transpersonal psychologists, such as Abraham Maslow who has studied "peak experiences" (1987), have focused on one specific aspect of the transpersonal element of the human psyche much as some scholars have made ethnographic studies of individual practices among the New Age spiritualities. Other transpersonal psychologists, such as Roberto Assagioli (1988), have further refined the notion of the unconscious mind established first by Freud, followed by Jung, as including more distinct and definable elements in the forms of "the superconscious and the spiritual Self" (1988, 23).

The key to each of these developments on the psychological model of the individual psyche developed by Freud is that there are complex interconnections and patterns of relationship, which determine the characteristics of the psyche. Any approach to understanding the whole psyche from this perspective therefore requires recognition of the wider pattern of relationships. Analysis of the discrete individual biography is analogous to describing one sector of the web. It would be equally possible to analyze another sector, such as peak experiences, but it would only provide one particular view of the whole human being. To arrive at a holistic description requires a web model and methodology.

Certain transpersonal theorists, such as Wilber, have sought to retain a hierarchical model of evolution, including the evolution of human consciousness, as
the fundamental structure of the interconnections and patterns defining transpersonal psychology. Yet it is possible to consider these patterns without hierarchy.
In fact, according to Warwick Fox, Wilber's hierarchical assumptions are
indicative of his anthropocentric worldview. Fox's critique brings transpersonal
theorising closer to the radically nonhierarchical and multiple entry points of
web methodology.

The central thesis of Fox's *Toward a Transpersonal Ecology* (1990) is that a
qualified expression of transpersonal theory under the rubric of Arne Naess's
"philosophical sense of deep ecology" provides a nonanthropocentric, nonhierarchical model for psychology that is ethically committed. He defines "transpersonal ecology" as "the idea of the this-worldly realisation of as expansive a sense
of self as possible" (1990, 204). He is thus less interested in the transcendental
impetus that was formative in the creation of transpersonal psychology (in the
work of Assagioli, Grof, and Maslow) but retains a wider notion of identity
incorporating the complex connections of interdependence. Fox cites Frances
Vaughan's description of the self in this context:

> Conceptualising the self as an ecosystem existing within a larger ecosystem can
> therefore facilitate the shift from thinking of the self as a separate, independent
> entity to recognising its complete interdependence in the totality. . . . [This]
> view of the self challenges the assumption that we exist only as alienated, iso-
> lated individuals in a hostile, or at best, indifferent environment (quoted in Fox
> 1990, 203).

In terms of the idea of self, what is offered here significantly opposes the narcis-
sistic conception of self provided by Paul Heelas's notion of Selfreligions (1982,
1984, 1988, 1996). But with reference to the category of New Age spiritualities,
we are again presented with the necessity of considering groups and individuals
in terms of the wider web of interconnections rather than as isolable units with
discrete boundaries.

"Family Resemblances" and SPINS

Wittgenstein coined the idea of "family resemblances" to characterize the relationships between ostensibly differing organizations. He used the example of
games whereby, for example, the key principles structuring chess and football
are quite different, yet both come within the field of games and the concept of
"game." In religious studies, the idea of family resemblances has been adopted
by Ninian Smart to support the functional meaning of the idea of religions: where
it is possible to conceive of two distinct and disparate belief systems, such as
Marxism and Taoism, yet relate them through other contiguous traditions that

share resemblances with both (1986, 46–47). The same idea has been used by Eileen Barker (1989, 189) to describe the New Age movement, and it also occurs in a footnote in Wouter Hanegraaff's work (1996, 14). It is applicable to the web as another typology that conceives a maximum differentiation of phenomena at the same time as allowing multiple approaches to study the phenomena.

In the notion of family resemblances, there is an implicit assumption of shared characteristics. The criteria governing the essentials of family characteristics are, however, by no means absolute. Hanegraaff, for example, isolates four "major trends of New Age religion": channeling, healing and personal growth, New Age science, and Neo-Paganism. These categories, he seeks to persuade, share sufficient essential characteristics to constitute the central components of New Age religion. The considerable omissions of Eastern religious traditions, for example, undermine his typology. Equally, many spokespersons of Neo-Pagan movements are unhappy about being classified as a part of the New Age.[7] Some scholars, notably Michael York, have sought to outline the many similarities and convergences of the basic beliefs between New Age and Neo-Pagan movements, while recognizing significant differences of worldview (York 1995, 144–77).

These problems of self-description and classification are overcome, in part, by the notion of a web of *relationships* rather than an assumption of similarity or identity of beliefs. In this way the family resemblances may be conceived not as essentially issues of religious *belief* but the functions of *interaction*, which may include religious beliefs as one form of these interactions. In other words, while the practices and beliefs of the New Age spiritualities are undoubtedly significant, the underlying familial resemblances are to be found in the *modes of connection* between individuals, organizations, and the wider network. The genealogy of the family resides more in the form than the content.

It is thus apposite to relate the notion of family resemblances to Luther Gerlach and Virginia Hine's concept of "segmented polycentric integrated networks." Three years of research into the dynamics of the Pentecostal and Black Power movements provided the research basis for Gerlach and Hine's model. The central features of the model they developed relate to the structural composition of the movement and are defined such that "an organisation can be characterised as a network—decentralised, segmentary, and reticulate." These features are elaborated to describe the essential structure of such movements: "decentralisation has to do with the decision-making, regulatory functions of the movement," which is not "acephalous" with a unitary hierarchy but "polycephalous"; "segmentation has to do with the social structure—the composition of parts that make up the movement as a whole"; "reticulation has to do with the way these parts are tied together into a network" (1970, 34–35). They note that "according to Webster something that is reticulate is weblike, resembling a network—with crossing and inter-crossing lines" (1970, 55). This model clearly has similarities to the web model articulated in this chapter, especially in terms of methodology.

Webs as "Thick Descriptions"

The problem of defining the web as at once multivalent and radically flattened, in order to avoid hierarchical presuppositions, is that as an image it appears to be two-dimensional. I have established a methodological presupposition that the phenomena included under the rubric New Age spiritualities function socially and conceptually like a web, a web that may be defined as a reticulated family that is (to appropriate Freud's dictum of human sexuality) "polymorphous perverse" in its interconnections. But the metaphor could become too flattened as representing merely the structural formation of New Age spiritualities and thus lose the dynamism and life that is an essential component of the contemporary existence of the manifold spiritualities. Indeed, without reference to the wider context, which includes historical influences, the effects of other religious traditions as well as individual biographies, the web is lifeless. A more accurate model, at least as a functional image of the New Age spiritualities, is the three-dimensional geodesic design of the carbon atom Buckminsterfullerene. The shape of this carbon atom is often likened to a segmentary football, whereby the electrons are reticulated from the center of the atom yet interconnect with each other. There is thus an extended web of connections around the central node. At least with such a metaphor, there is a sense of depth to both phenomena and methodology.

The notion of depth is a vital component of web methodology. If the heuristic framework of the web is to succeed in its object, to describe accurately and representatively the New Age spiritualities, the description must amount to more than a simple listing of network connections. There are many sources for this type of description, for example, Campbell and Brennan's "dictionary of New Age ideas, people places and terms" (1994); Brady and Considine's listing of "psychotherapy, alternative health and spiritual centres," (1990); or more local, frequent publications such as, in the UK, *The Spark* (a quarterly free newspaper composed largely of local listings of events and centers for alternative health and spirituality) and *South West Connection* (a quarterly magazine composed largely of local listings, which, in its own words, is a "guide to personal development and natural therapies"). The web should elicit "thicker" descriptions.

In this context, Clifford Geertz's essay on *Thick Description: Toward an Interpretive Theory of Culture* (1973) offers perspectives on methodology that provide the ground for such a thick, deeper analysis. He asserts that "cultural analysis is intrinsically incomplete" (29), a statement that is congruent with my claim of the "limited applicability," contingency, and temporal location of any "facts" I may assert regarding the New Age spiritualities. Nevertheless, it is incumbent upon the scholar to attempt to "construct a reading of" the phenomena while recognizing that this is a reading, an imposition of form on the phenomena. For, as Geertz explains, "What the ethnographer is in fact faced with . . . is a multiplicity of complex conceptual structures, many of them superimposed upon or knotted into one another, which are at once strange, irregular, and inexplicit, and which he must contrive somehow first to grasp and then to render" (1973, 10).

Geertz reiterates the necessity of using the voices of those who are being described. The great problem is "An explosion of debate as to whether particular analyses (which come in the form of taxonomies, paradigms, tables, trees and other ingenuities) reflect what the natives "really" think or are merely clever simulations, logically equivalent but substantively different, of what they think" (1973, 11).

The consequence of this problem is the necessity of developing a method that overcomes, at least in part, unrepresentative "clever simulations." The objection that the impossibility of arriving at a final, objective, *entirely* representative description therefore entails all descriptions are subjective expressions is, as Geertz points out, "like saying that as a perfectly aseptic environment is impossible, one might as well conduct surgery in a sewer" (1973, 30). The key is to develop a methodology and a method that is a plausible depiction of the self-expression of the "natives."

Yet the web is simply a metaphor. The polymethodic approaches of the scholar of religion could be accounted for by another image perhaps, and the multiplicity of the phenomena has been portrayed in many ways in postmodern analyses of culture. Nevertheless, any theoretical framework is equally as historically situated as the ostensible object of its study. The web emerges in contemporary culture as an image of interconnection, as a model of the "situatedness" or contextual nature of knowledge. The web also has a role as a model for living systems as an alternative to the linear positivistic schema that resonate in evolutionary principles and ideas of progress that yet pervade the epistemologies of modernity. Finally, it can be seen to be congruent as a methodological principle with a model of the phenomena of the New Age spiritualities. It is not logically necessary for methodology and model to resemble one another so long as the scholar is transparent in the presentation of a thesis where the epistemological assumptions of scholar and phenomena are significantly different. However, if a key aim is to represent the views of a culture or movement it is necessary to develop a more ethnomethodological standpoint and to use models acceptable both to outsider scholars and insider practitioners. From this perspective, it is possible to provide a thick description of what the "natives" really think.

NOTES

1. The notion of a common language is a very loaded concept. One can speak of languages like discourses, with different rules dependent upon different circumstances and indeed different speakers of a language. This issue has again been highlighted by feminist critics of the patriarchal functions of language; cf. Adrienne Rich's collection of poems *The Dream of a Common Language*, 1978.

2. In his response to G. E. Moore's "defence of common sense," Wittgenstein effectively undermines the criteria for the assertion of a basic set of facts that we know through common sense. He states "whether a proposition can turn out false after all depends on what I make count as determinants for that proposition" (1969, 5).

3. Elizabeth Puttick's research deals with women in NRMs, but her experience and empirical research focuses on the Osho movement—see Puttick 1997, 4–5.

4. Anderson and Hopkins's reference to Chief Seattle's 1852 response to the United States government inquiry regarding acquisition of Indian territory (which marked the end of the "permanent" frontier) has significant resonances for New Age spiritualities' conception of the self immersed in, Arne Naess's notion of, "deep ecology." Seattle's letter is quoted in full in Campbell (1988, 34–35). It has also spawned many creative endeavors, including the following poem by Ted Perry:

> This we know
> All things are connected
> Like the blood which unites one family
> Whatever befalls the earth
> Befalls the sons and daughters of the earth.
> Man did not weave the web of life,
> He is merely a strand in it
> Whatever he does to the web, He does to himself
>
> (quoted in Capra 1996, inside cover).

5. Capra notes that Bertalanffy is "commonly credited with the first formulation of a comprehensive theoretical framework," but in fact a similar theory called "tektology" had been developed by the Russian scientist Alexander Bogdanov "twenty or thirty years before" (1996, 43).

6. Capra outlined his concept of society in conversation with David Steindl-Rast and Thomas Matus, using the notion of paradigms, but it is apt to apply this vision to his understanding of how society functions as a network: "A social paradigm, for me, is a constellation of concepts, values, perceptions and practices, shared by a community that forms a particular vision of reality that is the basis of the way the community organises itself" (1992, 34).

7. See Harvey's excoriating criticisms of New Age (1997, 219–20).

REFERENCES

Anderson, Sherilyn, and Patricia Hopkins. 1991. *The Feminine Face of God: The Unfolding of the Sacred in Women*, London, Bantam Books.

Assagioli, Roberto. 1988 (trans. 1991). *Transpersonal Development: The Dimension Beyond Psychosynthesis*. London: Crucible.

Barker, Eileen. 1989. *New Religious Movements: A Practical Introduction*. London: HMSO.

Brady, Kate, and Mike Considine. 1990. *Holistic London*. London: Brainwave.

Brown, Susan Love. 1992. "Baby Boomers, American Character, and the New Age: A Synthesis." In James Lewis and J. Gordon Melton, eds. *Perspectives on the New Age*. New York: State University of New York Press, pp. 87–96.

Campbell, Eileen and Brennan, J. H. 1994. *Body, Mind and Spirit: A Dictionary of New Age Ideas, People, Places and Terms,* Boston, Mass., Charles E. Tuttle Company Inc.

Campbell, Joseph, with Bill Moyers. 1988. *The Power of Myth.* London: Doubleday.

Capra, Fritjof, David Steindl-Rast, and Thomas Matus. 1992. *Belonging to the Universe: New Thinking About God and Nature.* London: Penguin.

Capra, Fritjof. 1996. *The Web of Life: A New Synthesis of Mind and Matter.* London: Flamingo HarperCollins.

———. 1997–99. "The Web Page." *Resurgence* 184: 12–13; 185: 24–25; 186: 46–47; 188: 48–49; 192: 52–53.

Considine, Mike. and Andrew Ferguson. 1994. *The Holistic Marketing Directory.* London: Brainwave.

Corrywright, Dominic. 2001. "Praxis Prior to Doctrine: New Models of Relationship in Contemporary Spirituality." In U. King, ed. *Spirituality and Society in the New Millennium.* Brighton: Sussex Academic Press, pp. 192–205.

Cox, James. 1992. *Expressing the Sacred: An Introduction to the Phenomenology of Religion.* Harare: University of Zimbabwe Publications.

Di Carlo, Russell. 1996. *Towards a New World View: Conversations at the Leading Edge.* Edinburgh: Floris Books.

Ferguson, Duncan, ed. 1993. *New Age Spirituality: An Assessment.* Louisville, KY: Westminster/John Knox Press.

Ferguson, Marilyn. 1980 (updated 1987). *The Aquarian Conspiracy: Personal and Social Transformation in Our Time.* New York: Tarcher/Putnam.

Fox, Warwick. 1990. *Toward a Transpersonal Ecology: Developing New Foundations for Environmentalism.* London:Shambhala.

Geertz, Clifford. 1973 (Fontana, 1993). *The Interpretation of Cultures: Selected Essays.* London: Fontana Press.

Gerlach, Luther P., Virginia H. Hine. 1970. *People, Power, Change Movements of Social Transformation.* Indianapolis: Bobbs-Merrill Company.

Grof, Stanislav, and Christina Grof. 1991. *The Stormy Search for the Self.* London: Mandala.

Gross, Rita. 1993. *Buddhism After Patriarchy: A Feminist History, Analysis, and Reconstruction of Buddhism.* Albany: State University of New York Press.

Hanegraaff, Wouter. 1996. *New Age Religion and Western Culture: Esotericism in the Mirror of Secular Thought.* Leiden: E. J. Brill.

Harvey, Graham. 1997. *Listening People, Speaking Earth: Contemporary Paganism.* London: Hurst and Company.

Heelas, Paul. 1982. "Californian Self-Religions and Socialising the Subjective." In E. Barker, ed. *New Religious Movements: A Perspective for Understanding Society.* New York: Edwin Mellen Press, pp. 69–85.

———. 1984. "Self-Religions in Britain." *Religion Today* 1, no. 1: 4–5.

———. 1988. "Western Europe: Self-Religions." In S. Sutherland and P. Clark, eds. *The Study of Religions, Traditional and New Religions.* London: Routledge, pp. 167–73.

———. 1996. *The New Age Movement: The Celebration of the Self and the Sacralisation of Modernity.* London: Blackwell.

Johnson, George. 1995. *Fire in the Mind: Science, Faith, and the Search for Order.* New York: Knopf.

Kuhn, Thomas. 1962 (2d ed., 1970). *The Structure of Scientific Revolutions,* International Encyclopedia of Unified Science, vol. 2, no. 2. Chicago: University of Chicago Press.

Kung, Hans, and Karl-Josef Kuschel, eds. 1993. *A Global Ethic: The Declaration of the Parliament of the World's Religions,* trans. John Bowden. London: SCM Press Ltd.

Laszlo, Ervin. 1972a. *Introduction to Systems Philosophy: Toward a New Paradigm of Contemporary Thought.* London: Gordon and Breach.

——. 1972b. *The Systems View of the World: The Natural Philosophy of the New Developments in the Sciences.* Oxford: Basil Blackwell.

Lewis, J., and J. Gordon Melton, eds. 1992. *Perspectives on the New Age.* Albany: State University of New York Press.

Maslow, Abraham. 1987. *Religion, Values and Peak-Experiences.* London: Penguin.

Maturana, Humberto, and Francisco Varela. 1987. *The Tree of Knowledge: The Biological Roots of Human Understanding.* London: Shambhala.

Puttick, Elizabeth. 1997. *Women in New Religions.* London: Macmillan.

——. 1999. "Women in New Religious Movements." In B. Wilson and J. Cresswell, eds. *New Religious Movements: Challenge and Response.* London: Routledge, pp. 143–62.

Rich, Adrienne. 1978. *The Dream of a Common Language: Poems 1974–1977,* New York: W. W. Norton.

Riordan, Suzanne. 1992. "Channeling: A New Revelation?" In James R. Lewis and J. Gordon Melton, eds. *Perspectives on the New Age.* Albany: State University of New York Press, pp. 105–26.

Sjørup, Lene. 1998. *Oneness: A Theology of Women's Religious Experience.* Leuven: Peeters.

Smart, Ninian. 1986. *Concept and Empathy: Essays in the Study of Religion.* D. Wiebe, ed. London: Macmillan.

——. 1989. *The World's Religions: Old Traditions and Modern Transformations.* Cambridge: Cambridge University Press.

Spangler, David. 1976 (2d ed. 1977). *Revelation: The Birth of A New Age.* Forres, Scotland: Findhorn Foundation.

——. 1993. "The New Age: The Movement Toward the Divine." In D. Ferguson, ed. *New Age Spirituality: An Assessment.* Louisville, KY: Westminster/John Knox Press, pp. 79–105.

Sutcliffe, Steven, and Marion Bowman, eds. 2000. *Beyond New Age: Exploring Alternative Spirituality.* Edinburgh: Edinburgh University Press.

Tarnas, Richard. 1991. *The Passion of the Western Mind.* London: Pimlico, Random House.

Thorne, Helen. 2000. *Journey to Priesthood: An In-Depth Study of the First Women Priests in the Church of England.* Centre for Comparative Studies in Religion and Gender, Bristol: University of Bristol.

Wilber, Ken, ed. 1982. *The Holographic Paradigm and Other Paradoxes: Exploring the Leading Edge of Science.* London: Shambhala.

Williams, Paul, trans. 1989. *Mahayana Buddhism: The Doctrinal Foundations.* London: Routledge.

Wittgenstein, Ludwig. 1969. *On Certainty.* G. E. M. Anscombe and G. H. von Wright, eds. Trans. G. E. M. Anscombe and Denis Paul. Oxford: Basil Blackwell.

York, Michael. 1995. *The Emerging Network: A Sociology of the New Age and Neo-Pagan Movements*. Maryland: Rowman & Littlefield.

———. 1997. "New Age and the Late Twentieth Century." *Journal of Contemporary Religion* 12, no. 3: 401–19.

UNPUBLISHED PAPERS AND MONOGRAPHS

Corrywright, Dominic. 2001. *Theoretical and Empirical Investigations into New Age Spiritualities*. Ph.D. diss. University of Bristol.

Friends helping friends. 2000. 1st ed. Blackheath, London.

Greer, Paul B. 1994. *The Spiritual Dynamics of the New Age Movement*. Ph.D. diss. University of Stirling.

Sjöo, Monica. 1998. *New Age Channelings: Who or What is Being Channeled?* Bristol: Channelings, Green Leaf Bookshop.

26

CONTRADICTIONS OF THE NEW AGE

Olav Hammer

In 1996, Ma Oftedal, a priest in what was then the state-run Church of Sweden, published a book on her spiritual experiences.[1] To the surprise of many readers, Oftedal did not report visions of Christ or any of the other experiences that one might have expected of a member of the clergy. No, her book described some highly unorthodox events. She had been channeling messages from a spiritual entity called Orion. She told of participating in shamanic rituals. She informed her readers that she had been experimenting with what she took to be crystal energies. Scandal erupted. Predictably, the church threatened to suspend her from her position. Perhaps less predictably, Oftedal met with a considerable popular sympathy. In the conflict between the church and its dissenting representative, Oftedal was perceived by many as an underdog fighting a heroic struggle for a living spirituality against a sclerotic and hierarchical organization.

Studies that show what people in contemporary society actually believe in are rather scarce. It is considerably easier to find books that explain the details of various theological positions devised by and believed in by a minority of religiously inclined intellectuals. The story of Ma Oftedal, however, highlights a profound split between the official theologies of the various Christian churches and the more or less post-Christian ideas and rituals that resonate with many people. Some idea of that split is found in opinion polls. Although the results of such polls should perhaps be taken with a grain of salt, the figures do speak of a cultural shift.

Written for this anthology.

In several Western countries, alternative beliefs seem to be strong indeed. In the United States, half of the population or more believes in extrasensory perception or ESP.[2] Between one-third and one-half of Americans believe in unidentified flying objects (UFOs). Somewhat fewer people believe that aliens have landed on Earth. Approximately one-third believe in astrology. There are British figures that point at a similar prevalence of folk beliefs. Thus, 61 percent believe in the paranormal and some forty percent believe in faith healing.[3] Even in the Scandinavian countries, some of the most unchurched and ostensibly secularized nations in the Western world, such ideas are widespread. In a poll among Danes, 65 percent professed belief in clairvoyance, 57 percent in telepathy, and 36 percent in astrology.[4]

Scholars who have studied modern religious movements have generally been concerned with cults, sects, and denominations—organized bodies of believers led by a spiritual hierarchy. The loosely adopted ideas that are documented in polls reflect a very different kind of religiosity, a current of folk belief that sociologist Colin Campbell gave the name *cultic milieu*.[5] The cultic milieu consists of individuals who, for instance, believe in UFOs but do not choose to associate with a UFO cult.

The cultic milieu can embrace unrelated or even mutually contradictory beliefs and practices. Nevertheless, the elements of the cultic milieu share certain important sociological characteristics. Thus, the belief in divination, crystal healing, astrology, or channeled messages from various disembodied spirit entities constitutes what might be called rejected knowledge. These are ideas that flourish in a society whose institutions take little notice of them or even attempt to suppress them. For instance, the art of reading tarot cards is not taught in publicly funded schools, nor is it applied in health care, enlisted in the process of corporate decision-making, or invoked in judiciary procedures. Those who wish to defend the value of divination through tarot reading often do so in defiance of the mainstream worldview. Believers may be tempted to explain their position as the result of having reached further along the path of spiritual evolution than more skeptically inclined people.

People in a minority position tend to seek each other's company and support. This can lead to mutual sympathy between the various individuals and loose-knit groups that defend the beliefs prevalent in the cultic milieu. They find common interests, and gradually a social network is built up. Within that network, some individuals will have a firmer commitment to the various alternative practices and a stronger entrepreneurial spirit. Those with sufficient interest, time, and skill may take a leading role within the network. They will explain their ideas in courses, books, or lectures and can rise to become the dominant spokespersons for these unorthodox views. Theirs is the crucial task of transforming the vague and fragmented folk beliefs of the cultic milieu into a reasonably coherent worldview. The ensuing genre of popular writing has codified the set of practices and beliefs that are generally labeled "New Age."

As all writers do, New Age authors wish to convince their readership of the value of their messages. If New Age beliefs and practices are, from the point of view of much of the intellectual elite, rejected knowledge, why should readers adopt them? The spokespersons of the New Age present a number of characteristic arguments in favor of their views.

First, the New Age holds out the promise of holism. New Age writers will point at what they perceive to be a spiritual crisis in the modern West. This cultural malaise is caused by a lack of insight, faults in our thinking that make us believe that we are separated from each other and from nature and that the spiritual and the material are radically separate. New Age rituals of healing attempt to heal the rift between body, mind, and spirit. New Age science would similarly close the gap between science and faith. Several New Age writers have understood the scientific revolution and the Enlightenment in largely negative terms, as a fall into a materialistic illusion. Authors like Fritjof Capra have made claims to the effect that the latest developments in physics bear a striking resemblance to the statements of Oriental mystics and sages.[6] New Age holism is thus said to heal the ills of modernity by returning to an age-old wisdom.

A second theme is that of religious universalism. New Age writers embrace diversity. If a spiritual practice or belief is useful, why not adopt it? India and Native Americas, Tibet and the Celts, aboriginal Australia and ancient Egypt—anything and everything is grist for the New Age mill. The approach typical of most mainstream religious options is rejected: why opt for a single Scripture when there is inspiration to be found in any one of many dozens of competing sacred texts?

The freedom to choose among many religious options also implies a considerable degree of individualism. The third theme of New Age literature is therefore the promise of a mode of spirituality that is democratic, free, and unrestrained by church authorities. The individualistic creed of the New Age has given personal experience a rhetorical ethos of particular strength. The rituals and doctrines described by New Age authors should, it is sometimes claimed, only be accepted if they correspond to the spiritual insights of the reader.

These three features often seem to boil down to a kind of culture critique. The spiritual poverty that many people experience in present-day society will be overcome once an individual is spiritually transformed through the adoption of New Age values.

So much for the promises made by New Age authors. The question remains: do New Age beliefs hold out on their promises? To what extent do New Age spokespersons promote a way of thinking and of acting that really is holistic, universalistic, individualistic, and experience-based, one that ultimately constitutes a true alternative to the reigning values of the modern West?

HOLISM

The holism professed in much of New Age literature supposedly remedies the many splits of modern life: between creator and creation, between us humans and the planet we live on, between mind and body, between spirit and matter. Traditional Christianity, in this view, emphasizes the difference between the transcendent creator God and us, and focuses on our inferiority. Materialistic science, on the other hand, is atomistic in its approach, reducing everything to blind matter.

Holism may be a convenient term to label the rejection of contemporary mainstream values but is too indistinct a concept to form the basis for a common worldview. As a simple analogy shows, holism can be constructed on the most diverse underlying premises. Even such an utterly nonreligious philosophy as Marxism is in a sense holistic, since it sees the human condition as inextricably interconnected with the physical, social, and economic constraints of the environment. At the same time, this form of holism is built on a materialistic ontology. New Agers base their holism on a worldview that is very different.

A common creed in New Age literature is that any situation in which we find ourselves is the effect of our way of thinking. In the early 1970s, the American medium Jane Roberts began publishing books said to be channeled from the spiritual entity Seth. According to the Seth books, we literally create our own reality by means of our thoughts, attitudes, and beliefs. Everything we experience is a projection of our own inner world. Negative thoughts engender negative conditions in life. Once we realize this, we can begin to create the world we like:

> If you are in poor health, you can remedy it. If your personal relationships are unsatisfactory, you can change them for the better. If you are in poverty, you can find yourself surrounded by abundance. . . . The world as you know it is a picture of your expectations. The world as the race of man knows it is the realization en masse of your individual expectations.[7]

Similar ideas have reached a mass audience through one of the modern classics of the New Age movement, *A Course in Miracles*.[8] Compared with the Seth material, the idealism of *A Course in Miracles* is even more pronounced. Not only is the basic "stuff" of the cosmos immaterial—the *Course* also builds on the emphatic denial of the existence of anything else than God and love.

Literally everything we perceive in our familiar, everyday world is illusory. We believe that we live in a world in which people are separate from each other and in which suffering, sorrow and enmity abound. In reality, none of this truly exists; the entire world as we perceive it is a gigantic projection of our fear-ridden egos. We are thus responsible for the world, since we have created it ourselves:

> I am responsible for what I see.
> I choose the feelings I experience, and decide upon the goal I would achieve.
> And everything that seems to happen to me
> I ask for, and receive as I have asked.[9]

Thus, all the evil and suffering that we believe ourselves to be witnessing is, in fact, the outcome of our own fear and guilt. When we seem to fall ill or suffer the effects of old age, this is merely the result of our own mind projecting its attacks on the body. More surprisingly, perhaps, even seemingly positive features of the world of ordinary perception, such as many close personal relationships, friendships, and loves, are said to prevent us from arriving at the state in which we realize that God and love are all there is. Personal relationships are yet another way of projecting onto others what we believe is lacking in ourselves. Such relationships, just like sin and suffering, are therefore part of the illusion that the ego makes us live in.

Books like the *Seth* series or *A Course in Miracles* hardly promote a holistic outlook by any reasonable interpretation of the term. Behind the professed holism there is a strong strand of metaphysical idealism. This underlying belief has roots in much older forms of Western esoteric religiosity and has been an integral part of the New Age ever since its inception.[10]

UNIVERSALISM

New Age writers can claim that their ideas are basically identical to the spiritual insights of Hindu sages, Native American shamans, Japanese healers, Egyptian priests, or Celtic druids. Commonly, these various traditions are claimed to be various manifestations of a common underlying essence. This essence, sometimes referred to as the perennial philosophy, is seen by many New Agers as the core of their own beliefs.

Problems arise, however, whenever a New Age writer attempts to delineate precisely which doctrinal elements and rituals belong to this common spiritual heritage. Religions from around the world appear to offer the most diverse theories on topics such as the nature of the divine, the causes of evil, the reason for the existence of suffering, and life after death. Typical strategies have evolved to mask the differences. By claiming that all traditions are basically more or less divergent versions of the truths offered in their own New Age texts, contemporary spiritual entrepreneurs construct what is effectively a sectarian universalism.

A typical example concerns the belief in reincarnation. The term itself is quite vague and implies little more than the notion that it is our destiny after death to be reborn. Reincarnation beliefs are common throughout the world, a fact that a universalist might well find inspiring. The details, however, vary drastically depending on the specific religious context. In certain forms of reincarnation belief, a moral law determines which body we will be reborn into. In others, the process lacks ethical implications. In some belief systems, we can only be reborn as humans. In others, we can become animals or superhuman entities of various kinds. And most embarrassing for a true universalist, many religions, especially the three Abrahamitic faiths, base their views on life after death on other principles than reincarnation.

The specific reincarnation beliefs that one finds in popular New Age books are quintessential products of a Western religious imagination. As befits a theory of reincarnation in a society permeated with the idea of progress, the chain of successive lives that we pass through represents a ladder of spiritual evolution. The fundamentally optimistic outlook on life that dominates much of the New Age implies seeing reincarnation as a succession of opportunities to learn, experience life to the fullest, and fulfill our potential. By contrast, most orthodox forms of Hindu beliefs have no concept of progress and present reincarnation as an endless, nightmarish series of ups and downs. Rarely, if ever, does New Age literature concern itself with the incompatibility of Eastern and Western beliefs.

That the Abrahamitic faiths generally do not embrace reincarnation is readily explained away. First, it is noted that there are forms of Judaism as well as Islam that do accept reincarnation. The fact that these currents from an historical point of view represent unorthodox minority views is apparently not perceived as problematic. Second, the lack of reincarnation beliefs in Christianity has given rise to a modern legend.[11] Theosophical writers in the late nineteenth century explained that early Christianity had indeed accepted the doctrine of rebirth and that the church father Origen was a reincarnationist. The leading authorities of the church, however, decided to suppress this belief. In the second council at Constantinople, Origen was declared a heretic and reincarnation was banned from Christian orthodoxy. New Agers have adopted this theosophical version of history and seem generally unaware of the fact that more mainstream understandings of the development of early Christian doctrine are entirely at odds with this view.

The fact that New Age reincarnationism is a quintessentially modern view vastly different from for example, Hindu or Buddhist beliefs, is hardly surprising. Every religious system is a unique socio-historical constellation of elements, one that furthermore is constantly changing, adding new doctrines and rituals as well as shedding old ones. A truly universalist creed is a contradiction in terms. Universalism needs to exclude those elements that do not fit the preconceptions of what the core of human religion should be like in order to protect an illusion of coherence between faiths.

Religious universalism also carries with it another problem. The peoples from whom one borrows doctrines and rituals can become aware of the fact that their traditions are being appropriated and may resent this fact. The resistance against New Age reinterpretations has been especially vocal from various indigenous peoples. Spokespersons from a number of Native American communities, Australian aborigines, Saami people of Lapland, and others have protested vehemently against New Agers constructing their own versions of their religions. The modern Western reinterpretations are often seen as commercialized pastiches of the original worldviews.

The relation between various indigenous groups and New Age appropriations of their traditions becomes even more intricate in those cases where modern reinterpretations have been created by individuals who themselves are Native Americans, Australian aborigines, or Saami.[12] Elders within their respective ethnic groups can accuse these religious entrepreneurs of being motivated by commercial interests or of betraying the spiritual traditions of their own people.

The late twentieth century was a period of widespread tribalization. Consisting of ethnic groups whose members had been largely integrated into mainstream, white society discovered its roots and began defining itself as descendants of various indigenous peoples. Other groups, fighting a struggle for land rights and autonomy, had strong political motives for emphasizing their ethnic separateness. Although the languages, customs, and beliefs of some of these Native American or Australian peoples had become practically defunct, attempts were made to reconstruct their cultures. Scholars pointed out that some of these attempts seemed to invent indigenous traditions by projecting Western fantasy images onto the remaining vestiges of native cultures. The same radical reinterpretations that created New Age versions of tribal traditions seemed to be used by the ethnic groups to project positive images of themselves.

Spokespersons from numerous indigenous communities reacted by effectively branding critical scholars as agents of repression. Quite a few acrimonious battles have ensued over the legitimate interpretation of indigenous history. Thus Sam Gill, a scholar with an outstanding record of research in Native American religions, was fiercely attacked for a book that attempted to demonstrate that the image of the Indian venerating Mother Earth was largely a Western invention.[13]

INDIVIDUALISM

New Age beliefs are intended to promote holism. At the same time, the supposedly holistic doctrines and practices of the New Age worldview are used by most New Agers as a set of individual building blocks that can be accepted or discarded in piecemeal fashion. What persuades individual New Agers to adopt any given element? Is it their unconstrained individual choice?

The elements of the cultic milieu have characteristically short life cycles. Any specific building block of the New Age can be fashionable for a few years, only to be superseded by yet another trend. During the 1970s, there was a widespread belief in the imminent spiritual evolutionary leap of mankind, a belief connected with the astrological concept of the Aquarian Age. A couple of decades later, it is difficult to find anybody who is firmly committed to this vision.[14] In the 1970s, the values that were stressed in much of the literature were countercultural. Influential writers such as Pierre Teilhard de Chardin, C. G. Jung, and Abraham Maslow wrote about themes such as the spiritual maturity and evolution of the individual and of humankind as a whole. In the 1990s, the aim of much of New Age literature would appear to be to affirm the values of mainstream society. Widely read authors such as Shakti Gawain, Louise Hay, and Deepak Chopra present methods of attaining health, wealth, and personal happiness.[15] A romantic dream has largely been replaced by a neo-liberal utopia.

Such trends that persuade hundreds of thousands of people to adopt certain practices or espouse given beliefs contradict the picture of the New Age as a truly individualistic phenomenon. The amount of collective behavior is surely no less in the cultic milieu than in, for example, the fashion industry. The individual choices of millions of individuals lead them to buy essentially the same products.

What factors influence people to streamline their behaviors? The creation of new trends in the religious marketplace is especially linked to the production and distribution of books. Key players, such as publishers and trendsetting media personalities, are crucial to this process. The importance of individuals who host popular talk shows can hardly be overestimated. Books endorsed on, *The Oprah Winfrey Show* have a substantially better chance of becoming best-sellers in America. Agents see the commercial potential of marketing these books overseas. Sales campaigns then focus on those particular books rather than on the dozens of other volumes on similar subjects that happen to be published at the same time. The net result is that an appearance on American prime-time television can significantly boost sales figures even in countries where these talk shows are practically unknown to the general public.

The wide distribution of specific texts can profoundly influence the cultic milieu. A major role of canonical literature in any religious community is to allow readers to express the vicissitudes of their own lives in the terminology and concepts of the sacred books. Literary merit, depth of ideas, logical coherence, and other values that outsiders to the community may look for in a text are largely irrelevant to those who use the canonical texts in this way. For New Agers, the latest best-sellers by Shirley MacLaine, Jerry Jampolsky, James Redfield, Brian L. Weiss, or Deepak Chopra can serve such a function. By reaching millions of people, they contribute significantly to the construction of a collective identity.

Others will regard their circle of friends as the reference group that gives legitimacy to various practices and beliefs. In her book *Out on a Limb*, Shirley MacLaine describes her journey from being a skeptical onlooker to a convinced New Ager. The practices and doctrines she comes to accept are, of course, those made available to her by people in her social network. Nevertheless, MacLaine considers herself a person who has "never been much for doing anything communally"[16] and calls her participation in rituals constructed by other people and her gradual adoption of preexisting religious options a "quest for my self."[17]

The New Age literature tells us that we have a quasi-divine core, a spiritual self filled with untapped wisdom and potential. Truth lies within us. No guru needs to tell us how we should act and what we should believe in. Nevertheless, the same texts can then proceed to inform their readers in painstaking detail of the knowledge that they are deemed to already possess. The democratic ideal of the New Age is contradicted by the emergence of a tradition with canons of behavior and belief and with the concomitant possibility of gaining expert status at interpreting that tradition.[18]

Every sector of the New Age has its own more or less flexible rules governing correct praxis and orthodox doctrine. Astrological signs can be interpreted in many ways, but the allowable modes of interpretation are constrained by the rules of the astrological community. In theory, nothing would prevent the author of a textbook on astrology from going against the current and asserting that Leos are meek and Pisces assertive. Nevertheless, such statements would no doubt be branded as erroneous. Since numerous tests have shown beyond reasonable doubt that there is no empirical correlation between astrological signs and character traits, any critique from within the astrological community itself against such divergent views is necessarily directed against deviations from an established tradition.

The contradictions between the professed value of an individual quest and the existence of a canon are especially apparent in the attitude of the New Age toward religious experience. The often quite negative assessment of conventional religions—especially Christianity—tends to focus on the image of a patriarchal, hierarchical organization with rigid dogmas. This image of Christianity is rhetorically contrasted with the perceived freedom of New Agers to explore their own spirituality. Thus, in a way paralleled by few other modes of religiosity, New Age texts affirm that we all have the ability to receive prophetic messages through channeling. There are even do-it-yourself manuals teaching this rather arcane skill, for example, *Opening to Channel* by Sanaya Roman and Duane Packer. [19] Nevertheless, only a small minority of those individuals who claim to have this ability have succeeded in reaching an audience wider than the nearest circle of friends.

A perusal of the channeled literature reveals variations on a few common themes. For a number of reasons, these texts claim, we have forgotten our true identities. We are not the limited beings that everyday experience tells us that we are. In reality, we are sparks of the divine. Perhaps it is fear that has blocked us from realizing our true nature. Or perhaps it is the dominance of a monolithic religion, the materialistic culture we live in, or the limitations of rationality. We create the world we live in. Our inner states are reflected in the outer world. Since we have forgotten our true natures, we create a flawed reality. However, we have incarnated again and again, have learned our spiritual lessons, and are now ready for a great spiritual leap. To help us, a variety of spiritually advanced beings, such as angels, spirits or extraterrestrials, are ready to come to our aid. There are now ways for us to shift our perception in order to become aware of what magnificent beings we actually are.

The relative homogeneity of the messages received by New Age channelers

The Zodiac. (*Dover*)

is apparent when contrasted with the very different prophetic writings produced in other religious contexts, such as Theosophy or Mormonism. How can a large number of texts composed by many different individuals be based on such a uniform set of ideas? Modes of social pressure invisible to the New Age spokespersons themselves would seem to provide a parsimonious account of the phenomenon. A small number of channeled texts have become central components of the New Age. These books have attained the status of standards of reference. A new revealed message will be produced by a person who is already steeped in this common New Age culture and will only be accepted by its readers to the extent that it is sufficiently coherent with earlier messages.

CULTURE CRITIQUE

In his survey of New Age texts, Wouter Hanegraaff notes that the literature in its entirety sees its own form of "spirituality" as an alternative to the worldviews of mainstream society.[20] The very term New Age places this form of religiosity in opposition to the ëold age' values represented by the two main foes, institutionalized Christianity and materialism. It is often left vaguely sketched what these new and positive values will be. The uniting link is not so much the new values that one struggles *for* as the old values one struggles *against*.

For a mode of religiosity that survives on quasi-Darwinist principles, a critique of the prevailing cultural norms is problematic. The available customer base for the ideas that float around within the cultic milieu is predominantly composed of modern Westerners. In fact, surveys tend to show that New Agers are mainly well-educated, middle-class individuals.[21] In order to attract readers, New Age writers will thus need to express their culture critique in a way that nevertheless appeals to the culturally defined demands of a distinctly modern, urban audience.

It should therefore come as no surprise that some of the most successful attempts to define what this new spirituality is supposed to achieve present the results of spiritual advancement as personal success in a variety of areas. In his book *The Seven Spiritual Laws of Success*, best-selling author Deepak Chopra explains that we can change our circumstances by altering our way of thinking. Among the effects of a new, spiritualized mind-set, one finds not only good health, energy, enthusiasm for life, fulfilling relationships, creative freedom, emotional and psychological stability, a sense of well-being, and peace of mind but also the ability to "create unlimited wealth with effortless ease and to experience success in every endeavor."[22] The ultimate goal of the spiritual quest would seem to be to succeed in capitalist society.

Segments of New Age literature nonetheless remain committed to a critique of contemporary culture. To what extent might such a critique have any effect in the real world?

Parallels with other new religious movements give some indication of what is needed to achieve one's aims. What differentiates large, economically and politically successful bodies such as the Church of Jesus Christ of Latter-day Saints (that is, the Mormons) from their weaker competitors? The Mormons have an efficient and strictly organized missionary activity.[23] They have built up a bureaucratic power structure, and have, through the custom of tithing, established a powerful economic base. In communities where Mormons constitute a significant segment of the population, they exert considerable influence on business and politics.

The New Age presents a striking contrast. Despite its implicit emergent canon, it is embodied in the practices and beliefs of a large number of individual people without a common institutional affiliation. From a sociological point of view, it might be more appropriate to classify the New Age as a form of vague collective behavior than as a movement.[24] Even if New Age spokespersons should evolve a more distinct social or political agenda, their prospects of actually implementing their proposed goals would seem to be limited.

WHENCE THE CONTRADICTIONS OF THE NEW AGE?

New Age literature is filled with empirical claims: astrology is a key to character and destiny, therapeutic touch cures illness, dowsing can detect hidden energies. Skeptics present their reasons for regarding such claims as flatly contradicted by robust research. As this article has shown, there are also inherent contradictions in the broader aims of the New Age movement.

If the universalism of the New Age is insular, if its antiauthoritarianism is contradicted by the authoritarian voices of its founding texts, if so many of its claims are ultimately based on a subjective intuition that disregards critical rationality, why does the New Age hold such an appeal for millions of often quite well-educated people?

Its appeal, it would at times seem, lies less in the ideas of the New Age literature itself than in the way it defines its foes. Much of the New Age is a revolt against rationalism, even against modernity itself. Skeptics point to the fact that much New Age material flies in the face of contemporary scientific knowledge. What the skeptic perhaps misses is that this is precisely one of the appeals of the New Age message.

Why should New Agers want to revolt against science and critical rationality? A suggestive parallel is afforded by a study of the intellectual development of young women.[25] Many of the women had been plagued by the typical self-doubts of youth, had found it difficult during their school days to assert their own wishes and opinions and to see themselves as competent and intelligent individuals. Quite a few had resolved their doubts by quietly revolting against authority. They redefined the nature of knowledge. Previously, knowledge had been defined as passively assimilating the claims coming from parents, teachers and other adults. Knowledge gradually came to be understood as an inner, subjective or intuitive faculty. Almost half of the women in the study had at some time in their lives adopted a largely subjective epistemology.

Adopting a subjective view of knowledge has both advantages and disadvantages. It gave the women of the study the strength to assert themselves as individuals. At the same time, subjectivism entails a risk of marginalization by reinforcing culturally constructed stereotypes of women as being less logical than men. A subjectivist stance, if carried to extremes, also risks excluding women from careers in, for example, the sciences. Subjectivism, implying that an opinion that is deeply held needs no support from empirical evidence, rationality, or established knowledge, goes counter to the most elementary principles of higher education. Some of the women of the study went as far as adopting the view that rationality is a gender-specific male discourse.

There are obvious similarities between the women who identified strongly with a subjective view of knowledge and the supporters of New Age thinking. Science, abstraction, and critical rationality are in both groups seen as something profoundly alien. In their attempts to reject the perceived dogmatism of external authorities, both groups risk constructing an equally dogmatic position, in which science, logic, and rationalism are forcefully rejected for a priori reasons.

However, the story does not end there. A study of American college students suggests that there is a step beyond subjectivism.[26] A period of passive acceptance of authorities was frequently followed by an extreme subjectivism. However, for many college students this was a passing stage. They gradually arrived at a synthesis in which subjectivity and critical analysis could coexist. Personal areas of life were judged according to emotional or subjective criteria, whereas empirical matters were not.

In order to enable students to arrive at such a position, it would seem important to stress the difference between accepting a set of facts and assimilating the method of critical rationality needed to judge the veracity of facts. Research conducted as far back as the turn of the twentieth century has shown that intellectual aptitude in one area does not increase other intellectual skills.[27] Specifically, critical thinking does not just seep in as facts are assimilated but needs to be specifically taught.[28]

THE NEW AGE AND OTHER RELIGIONS

How should the many inconsistencies of the New Age be judged? Are they the result of an irrationality inherent in the spokespersons of the New Age? I would like to suggest a quite different interpretation. On this view, the contradictions of the New Age literature are an outcome of the fact that it is written by entrepreneurs from within the cultic milieu.

Once committed New Agers have established themselves as astrologers or healers, for example, they will typically work as self-employed practitioners rather than as members of a tightly knit professional corps. Their interests may be quite idiosyncratic, and their interpretation of doctrines and rituals will have a marked tendency toward individual variation. The diversity of opinion within the New Age is the direct result of the fragmented character of the cultic milieu.

Religions might be classified along a continuum, from centralized to socially peripheral. Peripheral religions have little or no support from official bodies, have few full-time officials, and are therefore not transmitted through generally recognized channels of learning. Within such centralized religions as many mainstream Christian denominations, it takes years of training, including courses in the history of Christianity and the historical-critical study of the Bible, to enter the clergy. New

Age spokespersons, by contrast, tend to be self-taught or may have pursued specialized courses at private institutions that do not generally foster historical, scientific, or philosophical awareness. The contradictions and incoherences of much New Age literature are therefore not checked by any counteracting forces.

Skeptical literature generally attempts to debunk the empirical claims of the New Age literature. The present article, although also written in a critical vein, has attempted a somewhat different mode of approach. Individual New Age writers can contradict themselves and each other, and can grossly misrepresent historical and scientific facts. The New Age as a whole lacks the structures necessary to detect and remedy such inconsistencies. No religion is based on logic and adherence to what is empirically verifiable; two basic elements of any faith are the willing suspension of disbelief and sheer habit. Incoherence is inevitable in any religion, no matter how elaborately theologized. However, the New Age generally lacks support from intellectuals. Whereas a number of other creeds have been defended by the ablest minds of each generation, the New Age remains a bare-bones rendition of religiosity.

Religion can be understood as a set of discourses and practices that "invest specific human preferences with transcendent status by misrepresenting them as revealed truths, primordial traditions, divine commandments and so forth."[29] Other faiths have simply had a considerably greater success at convincing large audiences that their discourses and practices are consistent worldviews grounded in ancient traditions and transcendent truths. For those of us who believe that religious worldviews are built on nothing more substantial than the predilections of certain individuals or social groups, the very fragmentation and incoherence of the New Age milieu is one of its most redeeming features. Unlike powerful and institutionalized religions, the New Age is likely to have a relatively limited effect on society as a whole. Whereas Christian creationists have the resources to wage a concerted war against the teaching of evolutionism, even the most committed New Agers will most probably never have the political clout to force schools to give classes on the occult energies of crystals.

NOTES

1. Oftedal 1996.

2. All figures concerning folk beliefs in America are taken from a summary of numerous polls, presented on the National Science Foundation Web site, www.nsf.gov/sbe/srs/seind00/access/c8/c8r.htm#spar98. The site was active in November 2001.

3. According to a *Daily Mail* poll from 1998 quoted in Harthill 2001, p. 264.

4. The poll was conducted in 1992; the figures were quoted in Denmark's leading daily newspaper *Berlingske Tidende*, April 1, 2000, under the title *Må kraften være med dig*.

5. The term originated in a seminal article by sociologist Colin Campbell, cf. Campbell 1972.

6. See e.g., Capra 1976 and 1982.

7. Roberts 1974: xviii ff.

8. *A Course in Miracles* is a channeled text dating back to the early to mid-seventies. According to the founding legend, the message of this book was received from an inner voice speaking to a research psychologist at Columbia University, Helen Schucman.

9. *A Course in Miracles, Volume I: Text*, p. 418.

10. Ultimately, the New Age belief that our consciousness creates the circumstances that we live in is a modern reflex of the much older belief in the power of our imaginative faculties. Images held in the mind, it was widely understood throughout the Middle Ages and the Renaissance, could either be projected onto others and used to influence them or could affect the person holding them. This latter concept was inter alia used to give a seemingly rational explanation of the then-current lore that fetuses were affected by the sense impressions received by pregnant women See Faivre 2000 for a brief overview of the concept of *imaginatio*.

11. Hanegraaff 1998, 321–22, briefly surveys the occurrences of this legend in New Age literature.

12. One of the most influential of these was Sun Bear (1929–1992), a man of Ojibwa descent who created a set of pan-Indian rituals that catered to the interests of whites.

13. Gill 1987.

14. Melton 1995.

15. Heelas 1996, 126.

16. MacLaine 1986, 143.

17. MacLaine 1986, 5.

18. See Culver and Ianna 1988 for a review of such studies.

19. Roman and Packer 1987.

20. Hanegraaff 1998, 515–17.

21. For a brief discussion, see Bruce 1996, 217–19.

22. Chopra 1996, 1–2.

23. On the succesful history of Mormonism, see Arrington and Bitton 1992; specifically on LDS recruitment and mission strategies, see e.g., Stark and Bainbridge 1985, 316–20.

24. Bainbridge 1997, 369.

25. Belenky et al. 1986.

26. Perry 1970.

27. Thorndike and Woodworth 1901.

28. Research to this effect is summarized in Nisbett and Ross 1980, 176–79.

29. Lincoln 2000, 416.

REFERENCES

Arrington, Leonard J., and Davis Bitton. 1992. *The Mormon Experience: A History of the Latter-Day Saints*. 2d ed. Urbana: University of Illinois Press.

Bainbridge, William. 1997. *The Sociology of Religious Movements*. London: Routledge.

Belenky, Mary F., et al. 1986. *Women's Ways of Knowing*. New York: Basic Books.

Bruce, Steve. 1996. *Religion in the Modern World: From Cathedrals to Cults*. New York: Oxford University Press.

Campbell, Colin. 1972. "The cult, the cultic milieu and secularization." In *A Sociological Yearbook of Religion in Britain* 5, pp. 119–36.

Capra, Fritjof. 1976. *The Tao of Physics: An Exploration of the Parallels Between Modern Physics and Eastern Mysticism*. London: Fontana/Collins.

———. 1982. *The Turning Point: Science, Society, and the Rising Culture*. New York: Simon and Schuster.

Chopra, Deepak. 1994. *The Seven Spiritual Laws of Success*. San Rafael, CA: Amber-Allen Publishing.

A Course in Miracles. 1985 (1st ed. 1975). Harmondsworth, UK: Arkana.

Culver, Roger B., and Philip A. Ianna. 1988. *Astrology, True or False?: A Scientific Evaluation*. Amherst, NY: Prometheus Books.

Faivre, Antoine. 2000. "*Vis Imaginativa* (A Study of Some Aspects of the Magical Imagination and its Mythical Foundations)," in *Theosophy, Imagination, Tradition: Studies in Western Esotericism*. Albany: State University of New York Press, pp. 99–136.

Gill, Sam D. 1987. *Mother Earth: An American Story*. Chicago: University of Chicago Press.

Hanegraaff, Wouter. 1998. *New Age Religion and Western Culture: Esotericism in the Mirror of Secular Thought*. Albany: State University of New York Press.

Harthill, Rosemary. 2001. "Mind, Body, Spirit—The New Millennial Age?" In Ursula King, ed. *Spirituality and Society in the New Millennium*. Brighton: Sussex Academic Press, pp. 261–74.

Heelas, Paul. 1996. *The New Age Movement: The Celebration of the Self and the Sacralization of Modernity*. Oxford: Blackwell.

Lincoln, Bruce. 2000. "Culture." In Willi Braun and Russell T. McCutcheon, eds. *Guide to the Study of Religion*. London and New York: Cassell, pp. 409–22.

MacLaine, Shirley. 1986. *Out on a Limb*. Toronto: Bantam.

Melton, Gordon J. 1995. "Whither the New Age?" In Timothy Miller, ed. *America's Alternative Religions*. New York: State University of New York Press.

Nisbett, Richard, and Lee Ross. 1980. *Human Inference: Strategies and Shortcomings of Social Judgment*. Englewood Cliffs, NJ: Prentice-Hall.

Oftedal, Ma. 1996. *Doxa—till hela härligheten*. Stockholm: Sellin & Partner.

Perry, W. G. 1970. *Forms of Intellectual and Ethical Development in the College Years*. New York: Holt, Rhinehart & Winston.

Roberts, Jane. 1974. *The Nature of Personal Reality*. San Rafael, CA: Amber-Allen

Roman, Sanaya, and Duane Packer. 1987. *Opening to Channel: How to Connect with Your Guide*. Tiburon, CA: H. J. Kramer.

Stark, Rodney, and William Bainbridge. 1985. *The Future of Religion*. Berkeley: University of California Press.

Thorndike, E. L. and R. R. Woodworth. 1901. "The influence of improvement in one mental function upon the efficiency of other functions," *Psychological Review* 8: 247–61.

27

DIVERSITY IN ALTERNATIVE SPIRITUALITIES
Keeping New Age at Bay

Adam Possamaï

In the early stages of my doctoral research, I discovered that the term "New Age" was highly problematic. On the first day "prospecting" for voluntary participants, a shop owner (of what I would have called a New Age shop) told me explicitly that he had nothing to do with New Age and that if I wanted some help, I should go to the Theosophical Society. What is more confusing is that for my honors thesis (Possamaï 1994), I interviewed members of this society who claimed that they had no connection with New Age. On top of this, during my first interviews, I realized that participants were negatively disposed to the term New Age. In 1996–1997, I interviewed thirty-five people who would "commonly" be described as New Agers. However, 71 percent of the participants negatively criticized New Age, and 9 percent, even if positive toward it, did not consider themselves as New Agers. Some negative comments were:

> It's like a train labelled New Age and everybody's jumping on it. And it started off very good, a very good term. But now there's a lot of people out trying to make big money on it for all the wrong reasons.

> And the other thing I find most irritating about the New Age movement is how gullible people are.

From *Australian Religion Studies Review* 12, no. 2 (1999): 111–24. Copyright © 1999 by the Australian Religion Studies Association. Reprinted by permission of the Australian Religion Studies Association. The author would like to thank Rowan Ireland for his helpful comments and suggestions.

> So I guess I'm a bit of a, you know I'm not your typical New Age, totally immersed in it sort of person. . . . I mean my personal feeling is that I like to keep my feet on the ground a bit. . . .

The term not only lacks a clear denotation in the academic literature and among the likes of the New Age spokespersons listed by York (1995, 48–88),[2] but creates problems when used in the field. Indeed, as Lewis realises:

> For any one researching the New Age movement, the reflections found in "Is "New Age" Dead?" raise several important issues. In the first place, because individuals, institutions, and periodicals who formerly referred to themselves as "New Age" no longer identify themselves as such, studies built around a distinction between New Age and non-New-Age become more complex. (Lewis in Lewis et al. 1992: 2)

I would argue that the word New Age is dead but not what it signifies. But what does it signify? One movement (e.g. Heelas 1996; Haneggraff 1996); a dual movement New Age and neo-paganism (e.g. York 1995); or a diversity of sub-movements? This article will argue that what is referred as New Age (and commonly used as a meronymy) covers a diversity of spiritualities: neo-paganism, what I call Aquarian perennism and presentist perennism. All these diverse spiritualities are elements of what I call perennism, i.e. a syncretic spirituality which interprets the world as monistic (the cosmos is perceived as having its elements deeply interrelated), whose teleology for its actors is the Integral Self (actors work on themselves for personal growth), and whose soteriology is sought through gnosis (the way to develop oneself is through a pursuit of knowledge).

This article is now introducing these three spiritualities.

AQUARIAN PERENNISM

Astrology has many branches and schools with a wide variety of astrological theories. One of them (which deals with nations and people) is called mundane astrology by Cavendish (1972), or religious astrology by Le Cour (1995). Just as a chart can be drawn for an individual, so too for a society. Following Le Cour, some modern astrologers claim that the sun changes its zodiacal sign every 2160 years, according to the astrological law of the precession of equinoxes. This migration into another zodiac is supposed to create important modifications on earth; and just such a profound alteration is about to happen in the third millennium. The sun is leaving the zodiac of Pisces and will gradually enter the zodiac of Aquarius, affecting the behavior and attitudes of every living creature. This is referred as the coming of the Age of Aquarius.

Because of the sun's appearance during the vernal equinox in the zodiac of

Aquarius, humankind will be influenced in attitude and behavior under the Aquarian "totem." Aquarians in astrology are, in astrology's own positive interpretation, brilliant and inventive and also persistent and determined. They are greatly concerned to help others, pouring themselves out on the world. It is therefore deduced from this identity that the paradigmatic characteristics of the world in the Aquarian Age will be orderliness, constructiveness, and intelligence. This belief in a positive change underlined a progressionist vision that was developed within the confines of the Theosophical Society in the 1930s. This society is a cult movement (in the sense used by Stark and Bainbridge 1985, 29–30), started in 1875 and valorized the coming of a golden age in the very far future, much later than the coming of the Age of Aquarius. During the 1930s, through some cultural transaction between members of the Theosophical Society and astrologers, an offshoot occurred and innovated the idea of the Age of Aquarius (for more details, see Possamaï 1998). However, this Aquarian eschaton is not followed by every perennist. Thus, the perennists valorizing this coming will be conflated under the term Aquarian perennists.

Aquarian perennist work for the coming of the Age of Aquarius. They are not involved in political or social action, but they believe that in order to change the world into a better one, they first have to transform themselves. As the insider Trevelyan (1984, 160) states, "change man and you change society. Try to change society without the inner change in man, and confusion will be the sole result." There is the belief that people have to work spiritually on themselves for the Age of Aquarius not only just to dawn but to happen in earnest.

The extension of this belief in individual work to the collective is found in the notion of the "critical mass."

> According to the critical mass theory, if enough people believe strongly in something, suddenly the idea will become true for everyone. This theory assumes that a reciprocity exists between one's individual consciousness and the collective or higher consciousness. . . . if a number of people—enough people to form a critical mass—concentrate on something, we may pass a threshold. Passing this threshold will have a spiritual and then a social impact on the whole world. (Peters 1991, 77).

For Aquarian perennists waiting for the coming of the Age of Aquarius in the very near future (around 2000 CE),[2] it is important to ensure that the dawning will have full effect. There will be a burst of new energies but for the planet to receive and deploy the energies in earnest, it is important to prepare the "recipients" through work toward the critical mass. For those who believe that the Age of Aquarius will come too late for them to live it, work on critical mass can fast forward the advent of the age (an idea already used in its original version by Le Cour [1995]). For those Aquarian perennists, it is important to change themselves quickly, and this, in turn, can transform the human consciousness within a single generation. As my informant Marilyn declares, "one of the principles around at the moment, the way we will save this planet and humanity is a thing called critical mass, which you've probably heard of, with the 100 monkey story. . . . And the principle is that when any one or small group of a species gets an awareness, at a certain point in their numbers, . . . it will suddenly become available to all the rest. Without them knowing it. And they will suddenly all start doing it."

Roger said, "If enough people are aligning spiritually, it will cause an effect, a resonance. A resonant effect, yes. And that's what happens. The more and more people. . . ."

In my sample, 17 percent of participants were concerned about the return of Christ. This Christ of Second Coming is not considered the Son of God but rather a form of energy that will be spread among everyone (or the elect) on earth. For others, this new energy will be embodied in a person who is called Maitreya. Even in my small sample, there are various interpretations of the Aquarian parousia, and more might be expected in a larger sample. However, all these believers equated this return with the Age of Aquarius and critical mass. Except for one, all view this coming positively. It is also striking to note that 46 percent of those who believe in the Age of Aquarius and critical mass also believe in the Second Coming of the Christ.

NEO-PAGANISM

Many Aquarian perennists do not consider themselves Neo-Pagan, and likewise, not all Neo-Pagan groups identify with what is called New Age. Neo-Pagans are mainly interested in practicing religions of the pre-Christian era, whether as a survival or a revival. These neo-tribes—in Maffesoli's (1988) understanding—are mainly focused on the atavistic pagan religions and are generally not interested in post-pagan religions (with the possible exception of Hinduism). Whereas Aquarian Perennism is self-styled as an *awakening* in the future, Neo-Paganism thinks of itself more as a *reawakening* of riches of the rituals and beliefs of the past (York 1995). Indeed, Neo-Pagans believe they are practicing an ancient folk religion and focus on the past; the past, however, is not romanticized but serves mainly as a source of inspiration to be selectively drawn on.[3] Furthermore, they are not particularly interested in a New Age in the future (Aidan Kelly in Lewis and Melton 1992, 138).

> In general, Neo-paganism may be summed up as comprising an animistic, panthe-istic, and pluralistic religious orientation that is non-doctrinaire but employs tra-ditional pagan metaphors (myths, foci, and rituals) or modern reconstructions of them as a means of celebrating a this-worldly emphasis either on a solitary basis or with others of a like mind. It stresses self-responsibility, self-development, indi-vidual exegesis, and full freedom of self-determination, the experience of ritual

and ecstasy, and an ecological preoccupation with the well-being of the planet regarded as a living entity. The interconnectedness of all life forms and the habitat is a central belief. Other concerns include tolerance, respect for diversity, healing, and the use of non-malevolent forms of "magic." Its ethics are pragmatic and grounded in the concept of honor (York 1995, 136).

None of the Neo-Pagans I interviewed believed in the critical mass or in the Age of Aquarius. Betty does not think that "the world is going to change. I certainly don't think it's going to change just because of anything in 200 or 300 years." In majority, they all envision social change but only for the Neo-Pagan community. Fully understanding that there will be hostility to their aim and rituals, they try to bring alive a Neo-Pagan lifestyle for themselves and sympathizers. The focus is therefore not on a global change as it is for believers in the Age of Aquarius but more a local communal one. As Jennifer expressed her goals and hopes: "I'm still a member of the women's spiritual community and I'm very committed to it, and I want to live in a women's spiritual community ultimately. That's how I want to live, in a community with women. On a spiritual path. . . . I would love to do it now but it takes a lot of work and it's just not happening. And we're meeting regularly and trying to make it happen. I've been trying to make it happen for years."

Betty also wants to live in a Neo-Pagan community, but she admits that it is going to be difficult to attain her goal: "I don't think there's enough community any more. I like the sense of community. That you're trying to build. I mean I don't think it's going to succeed completely because not everyone wants to be Wiccan [synonymous with Neo-Pagan]. And I don't think it's going to succeed because there are too many people."

I have found that the points made by York (1995) and presented in Table 1 clarify the distinctions between Aquarian perennism (what he calls New Age) and neo-paganism. The number in brackets refers to the page number of York (1995):

Table 1: Aquarian Perennism versus Neo-Paganism

Aquarian perennism	Neo-Paganism
1. "Pursues a transcendent metaphysical reality" (2)	"Seeks an immanent locus of deity" (2)
2. "Innovation—Awakening" (2).	"Links to the past—Re-Awakening" (2)
3. "Global transformation" and a "new planetary culture" (162–63)	No search for global transformation per se (162–63)
4. ———	More community oriented (162–63)
5. ———	Nature-based religion (200)
6. ———	Goddess worship (200)
7. ———	Ceremony and rituals (230)

In table 1, points 1, 2, and 3 on the Aquarian perennist side refer to the Age of Aquarius and its expected global transformation; on the Neo-Pagan side, as seen by my participants, these points refer to the desire of establishing a Neo-Pagan community. Points 5, 6, and 7 refer to a set of words that Neo-Pagans use and that were presented by my informants. However, an important remark has to be made about the goddess worship (point 6). The goddess (the personification of nature) is used as a metaphor of nature. "She is in the world, of the world, the very being of the world" (Luhrmann 1994, 49). She represents, in other words, monism. Thus Neo-Pagans distinguish themselves from other perennist subgroups by using the term Goddess as a powerful metaphor for monism.

If Aquarian perennism comes from the Theosophical Society's stream of thought, Neo-Paganism must also be located in relation to modern occultism. By modern occultism I refer to the movement created by Eliphas Lévi, the pseudonym of Alphonse-Louis Constant (1810–1875), who fought against materialism in France and named it Occultism. He was also a romantic, a communist, and a one-time Catholic priest. After the eighteenth century, the study of the Kabala was losing its vitality outside the Jewish community. Eliphas Lévi reintroduced this mysticism to his contemporaries. If the Theosophical Society was mainly based on Westernized Eastern doctrines, Occultism was strongly influenced by the Kabala. Another important figure of early Occultism is Papus, the nom de plume of Gérard Encausse (1865–1916). This movement attracted people of apparently diverse personalities who did not condemn scientific progress or modernity but who integrated science in their teachings against materialism. They planned to elucidate all the mysteries lying in the esoteric traditions and wanted to unveil all the secrets. Many new initiatory orders were created from this movement, for example, the Golden Dawn by Samuel Mathers, an order strictly for men.

Among contemporary Neo-Pagans, cabbalistic magic, high magic, and occultism often appear together with Neo-Paganism. This association has caused dissension: however, the link with occultism has always been there (Hume 1995, 6). T. M. Luhrmann (1994, 41–44) traces the roots of Neo-Paganism in the Hermetic Order of the Golden Dawn, an initiatory society founded in 1887. This group belonged to what I understand as Occultism. The Hermetic Order fragmented and one of the new groups, formed in 1922 by Dion Fortune,[4] was called the Society of the Inner Light. This society influenced new groups coming out of the Occultist stream, but they were not yet identifiably Neo-Pagan. Luhrmann (1993, 1994) calls the groups influenced by Dion Fortune the Western Mysteries groups, and they see themselves as the continuation of the mystery traditions of the West, for example, Eleusis, Mithraism, and Druidism. According to Luhrmann, the groups demand far more intellectual engagement than witchcraft (which "comes from the guts and loins," see below) does. The practitioners of Western Mysteries are grouped in fraternities or lodges, tend to be Christian, and often work on cabbalistic principles. They appear to be a contemporary form of modern Occultism.

Further fragmentations of Occultism, from the 1940s, saw the emergence of exactly the sort of Neo-Paganism under investigation. Gerald Gardner, who had met Aleister Crowley (from two occultist groups: the Golden Dawn and the O.T.O.), published fictitious ethnography of contemporary witches mainly in the late 1940s and the 1950s. He claimed to have been initiated and had revitalized Witchcraft (i.e., Neo-Paganism) in the Western world. For Gardner, witches had ancient knowledge and powers handed down through generations. This invention of tradition was claimed to be a revival of ancient nature religions. Witchcraft was organized in covens run by women called "high priestesses" who presided over rites of initiation for new members of the coven.[5]

Inside the Neo-Pagan movement, which for Lynne Hume (1995) addresses the modern concerns of ecology and feminism, there is also the Feminist Spirituality Movement (also called Feminist witchcraft and Female Divinity by Wendy Griffin [1995]). Its adherents and interpreters may be witches and/or goddess worshipers. This movement focuses on women's nature and women's experiences of the sacred. It characterizes dominant forms of organization of society as phallocracy and urges other modes be adopted. These Neo-Pagans mainly look for models in societies where interrelatedness is interpreted as being the primary value, as supposed of Palaeolithic and Neolithic societies. For example, Eisler (1990) uses Cretia[6] (before the Aryan invention that has, according to her, slain the people worshiping the goddesses peacefully) as the epitome of a perfect society, which she calls a gylany.[7] But eyes are not turned exclusively to the past: the movement also searches for a new model of society that remedies the supposed spiritual lack of Western society in indigenous cultures (e.g., Green 192, 237).

There is the assumption that the emergence of the feminine principle—the Goddess—will foster an alternative kind of political system, particularly if global emphasis is on interconnectedness rather than on hierarchy; indeed, for Rebecca Gordon (1995) there can be "inextricable links between politics and spirituality, particularly feminist politics." If Neo-Paganism celebrates the god (the male embodiment of monism, also called the Horned god) and the goddess, feminist spirituality focuses its ritual exclusively on the goddess, and the only participants are women. The Feminist Spirituality Movement covers many groups with different ideals, and not all of them consist of homosexuals and radicalist separatists. However, the Feminist Spirituality Movement has its counterpart, the Radical Faerie Movement (Rodgers 1995), which is a distinctly gay spirituality.

All of these varieties of Neo-Pagan spirituality,[8] we have seen, have at least genealogical links to modern occultism. It is this lineage and its effects on belief and practice that further distinguish Neo-Pagans from Aquarian perennists.

PRESENTIST PERENNISM

At issue among perennists is orientation to history. As we have seen, Aquarian perennists orientate themselves to the future,[9] while Neo-Pagans orientate themselves to the past. In this section still, a third subperennist type will be introduced, that of presentist perennism. This is the perennist group that has no concern with the past, no vision of a succession of age: it is perennism that focuses exclusively on the present.

Several of my informants were anxious to dissociate themselves from Aquarian history at least. Harry is one of them: "The Age of Aquarius, . . . it seems to be some kind of technical term to explain an astrological period. I don't know enough about astrology. There seems to be a fair amount of dispute and discussion amongst the astrologers as to exactly when it's going to happen. . . . I believe in symbols. I believe in metaphors. I believe in metaphors and metaphysics is what I believe in. I don't believe in facts. I don't believe in history. I don't believe in those things."

Sarah finds a certain arrogance in Aquarian history. I asked her what she thought about the Age of Aquarius and she answered:

> *Sarah*: I think it's arrogant to think that things get better as we go along and progress. We don't progress. It's cyclic. . . . I think we're all heading for another kind of spiritual time. But we could lose it and we probably will. Things seem to be cyclic. You get so far and then you go back and as I said there's nothing we've got that I don't think that people have had before at certain times and in different cultures. Egyptian culture, Mao culture. It may be expressed in different ways, maybe not. I don't know, is there a word for being time centric?

> *Interviewer*: Time centric?

> *Sarah*: Rather than ego centric. Yeah well I think we do. . . . Well you know how you can be ethnocentric and think that your culture's got it the best? . . . Yeah we can suffer from being time centric, but I don't know if there's a word for it.

Sue is an astrologer and uses astrology among other means as a psychological tool to understand herself, to reach self-knowledge. Since she has mastered this discipline, she has started to do meditation. She teaches astrology and also draws charts. Often, people ask her about their future: "I've often found it difficult to understand people who are obsessed with knowing their future. Because surely, I mean you've got to live in the present. This is what I try to do with meditation."

Later in the interview, knowing I was interviewing a professional astrologer, I asked her about the Age of Aquarius, and she explained what it was about. But at a certain stage in the interview, I asked her if this change would be better for her. Her answer made it clear that she is not an Aquarian of the kind described in the section above: "I don't know. I haven't thought about that much actually. I mean I think that's probably what New Ageism is all about. You know, en masse. I'm very non-global in the way I think often."

Harry, Sarah, and Sue, skeptical of historical knowledge, despairing of historical progress or critical of orientation to the future, all live mainly in the present. They provide us with a key to understanding presentist perennism as outlined below.

Some of my interviewees express interest in Aquarian perennism, Neo-Paganism, or feminist spirituality, but they do not expect the whole world to change as they follow their interests. At most, they hope for small changes in local places. They do not think of bringing a past world into the present. They are mainly concerned with developing their divine spark but often in an altruistic way, helping others, hoping to build a better world without transforming it radically as opposed to the critical mass supported by Aquarian perennists. Further, two understandings of the concept of critical mass were discovered in my field work, and in this lays a factor of differentiation between Aquarian perennists and presentist perennists. The term critical mass includes two major variations that are not noted in the literature; while they both aim for change, their methods for, and conceptions of change, differ: one method is based on meditation and aims at a change in consciousness and spirit, the other one is based on social action and aims at a change in the social paradigm.

1. The work for a Critical Mass by Meditation (CMM) refers to the belief that externally supplied energy may be harnessed by a certain mass of people meditating, or being transformed into integral selves, and this will change the world as explained above.

2. The work for Critical Mass through Social Networking (CMSN) does not refer to an unconscious shift brought by meditation but more to a paradigmatic shift in social life. It follows the description by Marilyn Ferguson (1981) of the Aquarian Conspiracy; it is a qualitative change in everyday life. This can happen by a networking of many networks aimed at social transformation. It is called a conspiracy by Ferguson, and it is for her a revolution of a new style. It aims at changing the consciousness of a critical number of people to provoke a renewal of the society as a whole. However, the changes have first to happen inside individuals, which, in turn will operate change in a larger scale. The aim is to provoke a "paradigm shift" in social structures and practices in the sense used by Thomas Kuhn. The interviewee Julia presents her view of critical mass brought by social action:

Western culture's becoming more and more alienated from a spiritual approach and a caring approach. But on the other hand you've got all these small community groups springing up all over the place that are quite strong and quite active and quite committed. And they're a substitute in a sense for what we lack in the Western culture at large. And I think those small community groups or spiritual groups or whatever they are, are really having a huge effect on people's lives, because without them we'd all be stranded. . . . Just general community groups where people will get together and try and work on a certain problem. Like the Save the Albert Park Group. Or there's a group that I belong to . . . ; and we talk about different social issues and things that are of a concern to people. Like the closing of Fairlea Prison. The exploitation of animals to make drugs. So it's a sharing of knowledge and it's happening on a small scale in a sense. You know we're not using the World Wide Web. We're talking to each other. And I'll talk to you and you'll go and talk to someone else and so on and so forth. I think that that sort of knowledge is not even really recognised largely in mainstream culture, but I think it's critical. It's a critical way of exchanging knowledge, and I think it's a lot more influential than we would think it is on the surface. Just handing someone a brochure about someone. It's like that concept, I don't know who coined it now, but a butterfly flaps its wings in Guatemala or somewhere. . . . And there's a tidal wave in Tokyo or something. And I think there's some truth to that. Just on a community level. You just spread the word. . . .

CMA refers to an action in the "collective unconscious" (to use Jung). It works on universal energies coming from above, which, if well channeled and tamed, will speed up the coming of the Age of Aquarius and render it fully effective. On the other hand, CMSN works through building on social change under way in everyday life, especially in a variety of social movements. It operates by the increment of small actions. Work in and on one's community affects other communities, and from this, a snowball effect (or a butterfly effect) takes shape little by little. In my sample, Aquarian perennists were all found to favor CMA and almost half of the presentist perennists CMSN.

Even if presentist perennists see cycles in history, they focus on the present, trying not to be "time centric." In some ways, they are like the Neo-Pagans who are also concerned with the local, and in a sense, they concentrate their ritual activity on the present. But Neo-Pagans still valorize history (or "invented" history). This is where they differ from presentist perennists.

A dichotomy raised by Gilbert Durand (1996, 166) and inspired by Paracelsus (an esotericist) can shed some light on these presentist perennists. Time is multiple and can be classified under two forms, the objective time (*Wachsendzeit*) and the subjective time (*Krafzeit*). The *Wachsendzeit* is the time followed by clocks, astronomy, and meteorology. This time is universal in a mechanical world and can be measured objectively, whereas the *Krafzeit* is locally placed in every human being. It is the destiny of each one of us, and it is for some the time fixed by God (or Goddess). Further philosophical discussion of this distinction is not the objective of this section. However, the dichotomy helps us distinguish presentist perennists from Aquarian perennists and Neo-Pagans. Aquarian perennists and Neo-Pagans, by positively valorizing the future or the past, include in their *Zeitgeist* an objective universal time. However, presentist perennists deal with the time of their destiny, their subjective time, their *Krafzeit* and do not feel a strong concern about universal time. For some of my informants (48 percent), there is no use in speculating about the past or the future but only on their subjective time, now.

This notion of subjective time (or eternity) is not new in itself. It even goes back to Plotinus, for whom time represented a prison for human beings (P. Davies 1995, 24). It is time as experienced by mystics in their peak experiences and is also described by Eliade (1959) as the myth of "eternal return," a transcending time that surpasses birth and death. However, these are expressions of subjective time in which the subject escapes the everyday mundanity. For presentist perennists, subjective time is inner-worldly and lends significance to the everyday. In this sense, presentist perennism is a very new development in perennism (in Western societies) in the sense that thos following the former appropriate a "divine" time in their everyday life and try to live it.

THE PERENNIST TRIAD

The Theosophical Society has engendered Aquarian perennism, while Occultism has inspired Neo-Paganism. These two perennist groups were formed in the 1930s and 1940s: they were not an outgrowth of the 1960s counterculture movements.

Presentist perennists are not connected to a specific esoteric movement but, I argue, have grown out of a cultural shift in industrial societies. Postindustrial societies (including their counterculture movements) are defined partly in terms of deep cultural changes occurring within them. These include declining belief in the idea of progress, radical individualism, and fluidity of movement between subcultures. Presentist perennism, even though it borrows eclectically from earlier esotericism, is to be understood as an expression, in the field of spirituality of emergent postindustrial or postmodern culture.

Jameson's (1984) observation about the postmodern world, that "we now inhabit the synchronic rather than the diachronic," helps establish the point about the ethos of postmodernity. Bauman's (1997, 89) notion that to live in a postmodern time is to live in a continuous present (a present severed from history) lends further authority to the argument about the characteristics of postmodernity. Maffesoli (1996, 59) characterizes postmodernity in terms of its ethic of the instant and even describes (ibid., 100–101) the postmodern focus on the present as intemporal time, an *illus tempus*. This appears to be very close indeed to subjective time experienced by presentist perennists.

They are perhaps other perennist spiritualities. The Rainbow Warriors described by Buenfil (1991) may represent another type. These warriors mix beliefs in the coming of the Age of Aquarius with Neo-Pagan perspectives and focus more on a deep ecological spirituality. Their Age of Aquarius is the "eco-topia millennium." Is this a spirituality blending the ideal-types of Aquarian perennism and Neo-Paganism? Or is it a new type of spirituality more focused on ecology than any of the other types? In this article I can only raise the questions and concentrate on the three ideal-types of perennism found in my sample. Their characteristics are summarized in Table 2.

Table 2:
Summary of the differences among perennist subtypes

	Aquarian perennism	Neo-Paganism	Presentist perennism
Eschatology	Age of Aquarius and critical mass by meditation (CMM)(universal)	Re-enactment of pagan lifestyle (local)	None.
Perception of time	objective	objective	subjective
Specificities	Some wait for the Aquarian parousia.	Focus on rituals, ceremonies and Goddess.	Some work on a Critical Mass through Social Networking (CMSN).
In connection to modernity (on the level of their cosmological discourses)	Modern (valorization of progress, e.g., the Age of Aquarius)	antimodern (valorization of pre-Christian values)	postmodern (valorization of presentist values)

NOTES

1. York (1995) has analyzed the spokespersons of NAS in a descriptive way and discusses the fact that some of these people tend to eschew the designation "New Age" (49). It is not my intention to summarize the works by Ram Dass, Edgar Gayce, Ruth Montgomery, Shirley MacLaine, etc.; for such an analysis, see York (1995).

2. There is a debate on the exact date for the coming of the Age of Aquarius: between the 1960s and 2160.

3. For a detailed account of the use of history as a source of inspiration, see Badone (1991), Bowman (1993), Harrow (1994), and Luhrmann (1994, 252–53). And as one of my participants, Judith, declared about the past: "I'm very much about utilising the best of everything. I believe we live in this society and there's no point in actually trying to recreate something that in all honesty never did really exist. It's an idealised image of something that we see as simple in the past. Well it's no more simple."

4. Her real name was Violet Mary Firth (1891–1946) and her motto was *Dio No Fortuna*, "God, not fortune" (Riffard 1990, 878).

5. However, among the Western Mysteries and Witchcraft groups, Luhrmann (1994) identifies also ad hoc ritual groups and "non-initiated" paganism. Ad hoc ritual magic groups (ibid., 74–81) comprise those who have discovered one another in networks and have devised their own rituals. These groups are not of the Western Mysteries lineage, and they do not call themselves witches. "Non-initiated" paganism (ibid., 82–91) is a term used by Luhrmann to include the meetings and rituals that she attended, which were open to uninitiated members. The point of these gatherings was to understand and to develop paganism. "Non-initiated" paganism appears to be mainly a networking form of Neo-Paganism.

6. This vision is romanticized if the myth of the Minotaur is taken into considera-tion. Each year, young people were sacrificed to the Minotaur until Theseus arrived. As for democracy in Athens, Gylany was for Cretians and not for slaves and foreigners.

7. A term created by Eisler (1990, 105) to express a society in which women and men are equal, in which there is a link and not a rank among people.

8. For an extended list of Neo-Pagan subgroups, see Hume (1997, 52–55).

9. They also deconstruct history in terms of Zodiacal ages (see Possamaï 1998).

REFERENCES

Badone, Ellen. 1991. "Ethnography, Fiction, and the Meanings of the Past in Brittany." *American Ethnologist* 10, no. 3: 518–45.

Bauman, Zygmunt. 1997. *Postmodernity and its Discontents*. Cambridge: Polity Press.

Bowman, Marion. 1993. "Reinventing the Celts." *Religion* 23: 147–56.

Buenfil, Alberto Ruz. 1991). *Rainbow Nation Without Borders. Toward an Ecotopian Mil-lennium*. Santa Fe, NM: Bear & Company.

Cavendish, Richard. 1977. *The Black Arts*. Picador Edition, London.

Davies, Paul. 1995. *About Time. Einstein's Unfinished Revolution*. England and Australia: Penguin Books.

Durand, Gilbert. 1996. *Science de l'homme et tradition. "Le nouvel esprit anthro-pologique."* Paris: Albin Michel.

Eisler, Riane. 1993. *The Chalice and the Blade*. London: Pandora (Harper Collins).

Eliade, Mircea. 1959. *Cosmos and History. The Myth of the Eternal Return*. New York: Harper & Row.

Ferguson, Marilyn. 1981. *Les enfants du Verseau: pour un nouveau paradigme*. Paris: Calmann-Lévy.

Gordon, Rebecca. 1995. "Earthstar Magic: A Feminist Theoretical Perspective on the Way of the Witches and the Path to the Goddess." *Social Alternatives* 14, no. 4: 9–11.

Green, Martin. 1992. *Prophets of a New Age. The Politics of Hope from the Eighteenth Through the Twenty-First Centuries*. New York: Macmillan.

Griffin, Wendy. 1995. "The Embodied Goddess: Feminist Witchcraft and Female Divinity." *Sociology of Religion* 56, no. 1: 35–48.

Hanegraaff, Wouter J. 1996. *New Age Religion and Western Culture. Esoterism in the Mirror of Secular Thought*. New York: E. J. Brill.

Harrow, Judy. 1994. "The Contemporary Neo-Pagan Revival." *Syzygy: Journal of Alternative Religion and Culture* 3, nos. 1 and 4.

Heelas, Paul. 1996. *The New Age Movement*. Oxford: Blackwell.

Hume, Lynne. 1995. "Guest Editor's Introduction: Modern Pagans in Australia." *Social Alternatives* 14, no. 4: 5–8.

Hume, Lynne. 1997. *Witchcraft and Paganism in Australia*. Melbourne: Melbourne University Press.

Jameson, Fredric. 1984. "Postmodernism, or the Cultural Logic of Late Capitalism." *New Left Review* 146: 53–92.

Le Cour, Paul. 1995. *L'ère du Verseau. Le Secret du Zodiaque et le Proche Avenir de L'humanité*. Paris: Editions Dervy.

Lewis, James R., et al. 1992. *Perspectives on the New Age*. New York: State University of New York Press.

Luhrmann, Tanya M. 1994. *Persuasions of the Witch's Craft. Ritual Magic in Contemporary England*. London: Picador.

Maffesoli, Michel. 1988. *Le temps des tribus. Le déclin de l'individualisme dans les sociétés de masse*. Paris: Méridiens Klincksieck.

———. 1996. *La contemplation du monde. Figures de style communautaire*. Editions Grasset & Fasquelles, Réédition Le Livre de Poche Biblio.

Peters, Ted. 1991. *The Cosmic Self*. San Francisco: Harper Collins.

Possamaï, A. M. 1994. *La Société Théosophique et son processus de diffusion dans le religieux post-moderne*. Honors thesis, Université Catholique de Louvain, Louvain-La-Neuve, Belgium.

———. 1998. "The Aquarian Utopia of New Age." *Beyond The Divide* 3, forthcoming.

Riffard, Pierre A. 1990. *L'ésotérisme*. Paris: Editions Robert Laffont.

Rodgers, Bill. 1995. "The Radical Faerie Movement: A Queer Spirit Pathway." *Social Alternatives* 14, no. 4: 34–37.

Trevelyan, George. 1984. *A Vision of the Aquarian Age. The Emerging Spiritual World View*. Walpole, NH: Stillpoint.

Stark, R., and W. S. Bainbridge. 1985. *The Future of Religion. Secularization, Revival and Cult Formation*. Berkeley: University of California Press.

York, Michael. 1995. *The Emerging Network. A Sociology of the New Age and Neo-Pagan Movements*. Maryland: Rowman & Littlefield.

PART TWO

THEOSOPHY

I

THEOSOPHICAL
TEACHINGS AS TO
NATURE AND MAN

H. P. Blavatsky

THE UNITY OF ALL IN ALL

ENQUIRER. Having told me what God, the Soul, and Man are not, in your views, can you inform me what they are, according to your teachings?

THEOSOPHIST. In their origin and in eternity the three, like the universe and all therein, are one with the absolute Unity, the unknowable deific essence I spoke about some time back. We believe in no creation, but in the periodical and consecutive appearances of the universe from the subjective on to the objective plane of being, at regular intervals of time, covering periods of immense duration.

ENQUIRER. Can you elaborate the subject?

THEOSOPHIST. Take as a first comparison and a help toward a more correct conception, the solar year, and as a second, the two halves of that year, producing each a day and a night of six months' duration at the North Pole. Now imagine, if you can, instead of a Solar year of 365 days, Eternity. Let the sun represent the universe, and the polar days and nights of six months each—days and nights lasting each 182 trillions and quadrillions of years, instead of 182 days each. As the sun arises every morning on our objective horizon out of its (to us) subjec-

From H. P. Blavatsky, *The Key to Theosophy* (New York: W. Q. Judge, 1889), section 6.

tive and antipodal space, so does the Universe emerge periodically on the plane of objectivity, issuing from that of subjectivity—the antipodes of the former. This is the "Cycle of Life." And as the sun disappears from our horizon, so does the Universe disappear at regular periods, when the "Universal night" sets in. The Hindus call such alternations the "Days and Nights of Brahma," or the time of Manvantara and that of Pralaya (dissolution). The Westerns may call them Universal Days and Nights if they prefer. During the latter (the nights) All is in All; every atom is resolved into one Homogeneity.

EVOLUTION AND ILLUSION

ENQUIRER. But who is it that creates each time the Universe?

THEOSOPHIST. No one creates it. Science would call the process evolution; the pre-Christian philosophers and the Orientalists called it emanation: we, Occultists and Theosophists, see in it the only universal and eternal reality casting a periodical reflection of itself on the infinite Spatial depths. This reflection, which you regard as the objective material universe, we consider as a temporary illusion and nothing else. That alone which is eternal is real.

ENQUIRER. At that rate, you and I are also illusions.

THEOSOPHIST. As flitting personalities, today one person, tomorrow another—we are. Would you call the sudden flashes of the Aurora borealis, the Northern lights, a "reality," though it is as real as can be while you look at it? Certainly not; it is the cause that produces it, if permanent and eternal, which is the only reality, while the other is but a passing illusion.

ENQUIRER. All this does not explain to me how this illusion called the universe originates; how the conscious to be proceeds to manifest itself from the unconsciousness that is.

THEOSOPHIST. It is unconsciousness only to our finite consciousness. Verily may we paraphrase verse five, in the first chapter of St. John, and say "and (Absolute) light (which is darkness) shineth in darkness (which is illusionary material light); and the darkness comprehendeth it not." This absolute light is also absolute and immutable law. Whether by radiation or emanation—we need not quarrel over terms—the universe passes out of its homogeneous subjectivity on to the first plane of manifestation, of which planes there are seven, we are taught. With each plane it becomes more dense and material until it reaches this, our plane, on which the only world approximately known and understood in its physical composition by Science, is the planetary or Solar system—one sui generis, we are told.

ENQUIRER. What do you mean by sui generis?

THEOSOPHIST. I mean that, though the fundamental law and the universal working of laws of Nature are uniform, still our Solar system (like every other such system in the millions of others in Cosmos) and even our Earth, has its own program of manifestations differing from the respective programs of all others. We speak of the inhabitants of other planets and imagine that if they are men, i.e., thinking entities, they must be as we are. The fancy of poets and painters and sculptors never fails to represent even the angels as a beautiful copy of man—plus wings. We say that all this is an error and a delusion; because, if on this little earth alone one finds such a diversity in its flora, fauna, and mankind—from the seaweed to the cedar of Lebanon, from the jellyfish to the elephant, from the Bushman and negro to the Apollo Belvedere—alter the conditions cosmic and planetary, and there must be as a result quite a different flora, fauna, and mankind. The same laws will fashion quite a different set of things and beings even on this our plane, including in it all our planets. How much more different then must be external nature in other Solar systems, and how foolish is it to judge of other stars and worlds and human beings by our own, as physical science does!

ENQUIRER. But what are your data for this assertion?

THEOSOPHIST. What science in general will never accept as proof—the cumulative testimony of an endless series of Seers who have testified to this fact. Their spiritual visions, real explorations by, and through, physical and spiritual senses untrammeled by blind flesh, were systematically checked and compared one with the other, and their nature sifted. All that was not corroborated by unanimous and collective experience was rejected, while that only was recorded as established truth which, in various ages, under different climes, and throughout an untold series of incessant observations, was found to agree and receive constantly further corroboration. The methods used by our scholars and students of the psycho-spiritual sciences do not differ from those of students of the natural and physical sciences, as you may see. Only our fields of research are on two different planes, and our instruments are made by no human hands, for which reason perchance they are only the more reliable. The retorts, accumulators, and microscopes of the chemist and naturalist may get out of order; the telescope and the astronomer's horological instruments may get spoiled; our recording instruments are beyond the influence of weather or the elements.

ENQUIRER. And therefore you have implicit faith in them?

THEOSOPHIST. Faith is a word not to be found in theosophical dictionaries: we say knowledge based on observation and experience. There is this difference, however, that while the observation and experience of physical science lead the Scientists to about as many "working" hypotheses as there are minds to evolve them, our knowledge consents to add to its lore only those facts which have become undeniable and which are fully and absolutely demonstrated. We have no two beliefs or hypotheses on the same subject.

ENQUIRER. Is it on such data that you came to accept the strange theories we find in Esoteric Buddhism?

THEOSOPHIST. Just so. These theories may be slightly incorrect in their minor details, and even faulty in their exposition by lay students; they are facts in nature, nevertheless, and come nearer the truth than any scientific hypothesis.

ON THE SEPTENARY CONSTITUTION OF OUR PLANET

ENQUIRER. I understand that you describe our earth as forming part of a chain of earths?

THEOSOPHIST. We do. But the other six "earths" or globes are not on the same plane of objectivity as our earth is; therefore we cannot see them.

ENQUIRER. Is that on account of the great distance?

THEOSOPHIST. Not at all, for we see with our naked eye planets and even stars at immeasurably greater distances; but it is owing to those six globes being outside our physical means of perception, or plane of being. It is not only that their material density, weight, or fabric are entirely different from those of our earth and the other known planets, but they are (to us) on an entirely different layer of space, so to speak, a layer not to be perceived or felt by our physical senses. And when I say "layer," please do not allow your fancy to suggest to you layers like strata or beds laid one over the other, for this would only lead to another absurd misconception. What I mean by "layer" is that plane of infinite space which by its nature cannot fall under our ordinary waking perceptions, whether mental or physical, but which exists in nature outside of our normal mentality or consciousness, outside of our three-dimensional space, and outside of our division of time. Each of the seven fundamental planes (or layers) in space—of course as a whole, as the pure space of Locke's definition, not as our finite space—has its own objectivity and subjectivity, its own space and time, its own consciousness and set of senses. But all this will be hardly comprehensible to one trained in the modern ways of thought.

H. P. Blavatsky and Col. Henry S. Olcott, founders of the Theosophical Society. (*Reprinted with permission of the American Religion Collection*)

ENQUIRER. What do you mean by a different set of senses? Is there anything on our human plane that you could bring as an illustration of what you say, just to give a clearer idea of what you may mean by this variety of senses, spaces, and respective perceptions?

THEOSOPHIST. None; except, perhaps, that which for Science would be rather a handy peg on which to hang a counterargument. We have a different set of senses in dream-life, have we not? We feel, talk, hear, see, taste, and function in general on a different plane; the change of state of our consciousness being evidenced by the fact that a series of acts and events embracing years, as we think, pass ideally through our mind in one instant. Well, that extreme rapidity of our mental operations in dreams and the perfect naturalness, for the time being, of all the other functions, show us that we are on quite another plane. Our philosophy teaches us that as there are seven fundamental forces in nature, and seven planes of being, so there are seven states of consciousness in which man can live, think, remember, and have his being. To enumerate these here is impossible, and for this one has to turn to the study of Eastern metaphysics. But in these two states—the waking and the dreaming—every ordinary mortal, from a learned philosopher down to a poor untutored savage, has a good proof that such states differ.

ENQUIRER. You do not accept, then, the well-known explanations of biology and physiology to account for the dream state?

THEOSOPHIST. We do not. We reject even the hypotheses of your psychologists, preferring the teachings of Eastern Wisdom. Believing in seven planes of Kosmic being and states of Consciousness, with regard to the Universe or the Macrocosm, we stop at the fourth plane, finding it impossible to go with any degree of certainty beyond. But with respect to the Microcosm, or man, we speculate freely on his seven states and principles.

ENQUIRER. How do you explain these?

THEOSOPHIST. We find, first of all, two distinct beings in man; the spiritual and the physical, the man who thinks, and the man who records as much of these thoughts as he is able to assimilate. Therefore we divide him into two distinct natures; the upper or the spiritual being, composed of three "principles" or aspects; and the lower or the physical quaternary, composed of four—in all seven.

THE SEPTENARY NATURE OF MAN.

ENQUIRER. Is it what we call Spirit and Soul and the man of flesh?

THEOSOPHIST. It is not. That is the old Platonic division. Plato was an Initiate and therefore could not go into forbidden details; but he who is acquainted with the archaic doctrine finds the seven in Plato's various combinations of Soul and Spirit. He regarded man as constituted of two parts—one eternal, formed of the same essence as the Absoluteness, the other mortal and corruptible, deriving its constituent parts from the minor "created" Gods. Man is composed, he shows, of (1) a mortal body, (2) an immortal principle, and (3) a "separate mortal kind of Soul." It is that which we respectively call the physical man, the Spiritual Soul or Spirit, and the animal Soul (the *Nous* and *psuche*). This is the division adopted by Paul, another Initiate, who maintains that there is a psychical body which is sown in the corruptible (astral soul or body) and a spiritual body that is raised in incorruptible substance. Even James (3:15) corroborates the same by saying that the "wisdom" (of our lower soul) descendeth not from the above but is terrestrial ("psychical," "demoniacal," vide Greek text), while the other is heavenly wisdom. Now so plain is it that Plato and even Pythagoras, while speaking but of three "principles," give them seven separate functions, in their various combinations, that if we contrast our teachings this will become quite plain. Let us take a cursory view of these seven aspects by drawing two tables.

THEOSOPHICAL DIVISION

SANSCRIT TERMS	EXOTERIC MEANING	EXPLANATORY
LOWER QUATERNARY		
(a) Rupa, or Sthula-Sarira	Physical body	Is the vehicle of all the other "principles" during life functions
(b) Prana	Life, or Vital principle	Necessary only to a, c, d, and the of the lower Manas, which embrace all those limited to the (physical) brain
(c) Linga Sharira	Astral body	The Double, the phantom body
(d) Kama rupa	The seat of animal desires and passions	This is the center of the animal man, where lies the line of demarcation which separates the mortal man from the immortal entity.
THE UPPER IMPERISHABLE TRIAD		
(e) Manas—a dual principle in its functions	Mind, Intelligence: which is the higher human mind, whose light, or radiation links the MONAD, for the lifetime, to the mortal man	The future state and the Karmic destiny of man depend on whether Manas gravitates more downward to Karma rupa, the seat of the animal passions, or upwards to Buddhi, the Spiritual Ego. In the latter case, the higher consciousness of the individual Spiritual aspirations of mind (Manas), assimilating Buddhi, are absorbed by it and form the Ego, which goes into Devachanic bliss.*
(f) Buddhi	The Spiritual Soul	The vehicle of pure universal spirit
(g) Atma	Spirit	One with the Absolute, as its radiation

*In Mr. Sinnett's "Esoteric Buddhism" (d), (e), and (f) are respectively called the Animal, the Human, and the Spiritual Souls, which answers as well. Though the principles in Esoteric Buddhism are numbered, this is, strictly speaking, useless. The dual Monad alone (Atma-Buddhi) is susceptible of being thought of as the two highest numbers (the sixth and seventh). As to all others, since that "principle" only which is predominant in man has to be considered as the first and foremost, no numeration is possible as a general rule. In some men it is the higher Intelligence (Manas or the fifth) which dominates the rest; in others the Animal Soul (Kama-rupa) that reigns supreme, exhibiting the most bestial instincts, etc.

Now what does Plato teach? He speaks of the interior man as constituted of two parts—one immutable and always the same, formed of the same substance as Deity, and the other mortal and corruptible. These "two parts" are found in our upper Triad and the lower Quaternary (vide Table). He explains that when the Soul, *psuche*, "allies herself to the *Nous* (divine spirit or substance),[2] she does everything aright and felicitously"; but the case is otherwise when she attaches herself to *Anoia*, (folly, or the irrational animal Soul). Here, then, we have Manas (or the Soul in general) in its two aspects: when attaching itself to *Anoia* (our Kama rupa, or the "Animal Soul" in "Esoteric Buddhism"), it runs toward entire annihilation, as far as the personal Ego is concerned; when allying itself to the *Nous* (Atma-Buddhi), it merges into the immortal, imperishable Ego, and then its spiritual consciousness of the personal that was becomes immortal.

THE DISTINCTION BETWEEN SOUL AND SPIRIT

ENQUIRER. Do you really teach, as you are accused of doing by some Spiritualists and French Spiritists, the annihilation of every personality?

THEOSOPHIST. We do not. But as this question of the duality—the individuality of the Divine Ego and the personality of the human animal—involves that of the possibility of the real immortal Ego appearing in Seance rooms as a "materialized spirit," which we deny as already explained, our opponents have started the nonsensical charge.

ENQUIRER. You have just spoken of *psuche* running toward its entire annihilation if it attaches itself to *Anoia*. What did Plato, and do you, mean by this?

THEOSOPHIST. The entire annihilation of the personal consciousness, as an exceptional and rare case, I think. The general and almost invariable rule is the merging of the personal into the individual or immortal consciousness of the Ego, a transformation or a divine transfiguration, and the entire annihilation only of the lower quaternary. Would you expect the man of flesh, or the temporary personality, his shadow, the "astral," his animal instincts and even physical life, to survive with the "spiritual Ego" and become sempiternal? Naturally all this ceases to exist, either at, or soon after, corporeal death. It becomes in time entirely disintegrated and disappears from view, being annihilated as a whole.

ENQUIRER. Then you also reject resurrection in the flesh?

THEOSOPHIST. Most decidedly we do! Why should we, who believe in the archaic esoteric philosophy of the Ancients, accept the unphilosophical speculations of the later Christian theology, borrowed from the Egyptian and Greek exoteric Systems of the Gnostics?

ENQUIRER. The Egyptians revered Nature-Spirits and deified even onions: your Hindus are idolaters, to this day; the Zoroastrians worshiped, and do still worship, the Sun; and the best Greek philosophers were either dreamers or materialists—witness Plato and Democritus. How can you compare!

THEOSOPHIST. It may be so in your modern Christian and even Scientific catechism; it is not so for unbiased minds. The Egyptians revered the "One-Only-One" as Nout; and it is from this word that Anaxagoras got his denomination *Nous*, or as he calls it, *Nous autokrates*, "the Mind or Spirit Self-potent," the *archetes kinedeos*, the leading motor, or primum-mobile of all. With him the *Nous* was God, and the *logos* was man, his emanation. The *Nous* is the spirit (whether in Kosmos or in man), and the *logos*, whether Universe or astral body, the emanation of the former, the physical body being merely the animal. Our external powers perceive phenomena; our *Nous* alone is able to recognize their *noumena*. It is the *logos* alone, or the *noumenon*, that survives, because it is immortal in its very nature and essence, and the *logos* in man is the Eternal Ego, that which reincarnates and lasts forever. But how can the evanescent or external shadow, the temporary clothing of that divine Emanation which returns to the source whence it proceeded, be that which is raised in incorruptibility?

ENQUIRER. Still you can hardly escape the charge of having invented a new division of man's spiritual and psychic constituents, for no philosopher speaks of them, though you believe that Plato does.

THEOSOPHIST. And I support the view. Besides Plato, there is Pythagoras, who also followed the same idea.[3] He described the Soul as a self-moving Unit (monad) composed of three elements, the *Nous* (Spirit), the *phren* (mind), and the *thumos* (life, breath, or the Nephesh of the Kabalists), which three correspond to our "Atma-Buddhi," (higher Spirit-Soul), to Manas (the Ego), and to Kama-rupa in conjunction with the lower reflection of Manas. That which the Ancient Greek philosophers termed Soul, in general, we call Spirit, or Spiritual Soul, Buddhi, as the vehicle of Atma (the *Agathon*, or Plato's Supreme Deity). The fact that Pythagoras and others state that *phren* and *thumos* are shared by us with the brutes proves that in this case the lower Manasic reflection (instinct) and Kama-rupa (animal living passions) are meant. And as Socrates and Plato accepted the clue and followed it, if to these five, namely, *Agathon* (Deity or Atma), *Psuche* (Soul in its collective sense), *Nous* (Spirit or Mind), *Phren* (physical mind), and *Thumos* (Kama-rupa or passions), we add the *eidolon* of the Mysteries, the shadowy form or the human double, and the physical body, it will be easy to demonstrate that the ideas of both Pythagoras and Plato were identical with ours. Even the Egyptians held to the Septenary division. In its exit, they taught, the Soul (Ego) had to pass through its seven chambers, or principles, those it left behind, and those it took along with itself. The only difference is that, ever bearing in mind the penalty of revealing Mystery-doctrines, which was death, they gave out the teaching in a broad outline, while we elaborate it and explain it in its details. But though we do give out to the world as much as is lawful, even in our doctrine more than one important detail is withheld, which those who study the esoteric philosophy and are pledged to silence, are alone entitled to know.

THE GREEK TEACHINGS

ENQUIRER. We have magnificent Greek and Latin, Sanskrit and Hebrew scholars. How is it that we find nothing in their translations that would afford us a clue to what you say?

THEOSOPHIST. Because your translators, their great learning notwithstanding, have made of the philosophers, the Greeks especially, misty instead of mystic writers. Take as an instance Plutarch and read what he says of "the principles" of man. That which he describes was accepted literally and attributed to metaphysical superstition and ignorance. Let me give you an illustration in point: "Man," says Plutarch, "is compound; and they are mistaken who think him to be compounded of two parts only. For they imagine that the understanding (brain, intellect) is a part of the soul (the upper Triad), but they err in this no less than those who make the soul to be a part of the body, i.e., those who make of the Triad part of the corruptible mortal quaternary. For the understanding (*nous*) as far exceeds the soul, as the soul is better and diviner than the body. Now this composition of the soul (*psuche*) with the understanding (*nous*) makes reason; and with the body (or *thumos*, the animal soul) passion; of which the one is the beginning or principle of pleasure and pain, and the other of virtue and vice. Of these three parts conjoined and compacted together, the earth has given the body, the moon the soul, and the sun the understanding to the generation of man."

This last sentence is purely allegorical and will be comprehended only by those who are versed in the esoteric science of correspondences and know which planet is related to every principle. Plutarch divides the latter into three groups and makes of the body a compound of physical frame, astral shadow, and breath, or the triple lower part, which "from earth was taken and to earth returns"; of the middle principle and the instinctual soul, the second part, derived from and through and ever influenced by the moon,[4] and only of the higher part or the Spiritual Soul, with the Atmic and Manasic elements in it does he make a direct emanation of the Sun, who stands here for Agathon the Supreme Deity. This is proven by what he says further as follows: "Now of the deaths we die, the one makes man two of three and the other one of (out of) two. The former is in the region and jurisdiction of Demeter, whence the name given to the Mysteries, *telein*, resembled that given to death, *teleutan*. The Athenians also heretofore called the deceased sacred to Demeter. As for the other death, it is in the moon or region of Persephone."

Here you have our doctrine, which shows man a septenary during life; a quintile just after death, in Kamaloka; and a threefold Ego, Spirit-Soul, and consciousness in Devachan. This separation, first in "the Meadows of Hades," as Plutarch calls the Kamaloka, then in Devachan, was part and parcel of the performances during the sacred Mysteries, when the candidates for initiation enacted the whole drama of death and the resurrection as a glorified spirit, by which name we mean Consciousness. This is what Plutarch means when he says:

> And as with the one, the terrestrial, so with the other celestial Hermes doth dwell. This suddenly and with violence plucks the soul from the body; but Proserpina mildly and in a long time disjoins the understanding from the soul.[5] For this reason she is called Monogenes, only begotten, or rather begetting one alone; for the better part of man becomes alone when it is separated by her. Now both the one and the other happens thus according to nature. It is ordained by Fate (Fatum or Karma) that every soul, whether with or without understanding (mind), when gone out of the body, should wander for a time, though not all for the same, in the region lying between the earth and moon (Kamaloka).[6] For those that have been unjust and dissolute suffer then the punishment due to their offenses, but the good and virtuous are there detained till they are purified, and have, by expiation, purged out of them all the infections they might have contracted from the contagion of the body, as if from foul health, living in the mildest part of the air, called the Meadows of Hades, where they must remain for a certain prefixed and appointed time. And then, as if they were returning from a wandering pilgrimage or long exile into their country, they have a taste of joy, such as they principally receive who are initiated into Sacred Mysteries, mixed with trouble, admiration, and each one's proper and peculiar hope.

This is Nirvanic bliss, and no Theosophist could describe in plainer though esoteric language the mental joys of Devachan, where every man has his paradise around him, erected by his consciousness. But you must beware of the general error into which too many even of our Theosophists fall. Do not imagine that because man is called septenary, then quintuple and a triad, he is a compound of seven, five, or three entities, or, as well expressed by a Theosophical writer, of skins to be peeled off like the skins of an onion. The "principles," as already said, save the body, the life, and the astral *eidolon*, all of which disperse at death, are simply aspects and states of consciousness. There is but one real man, enduring through the cycle of life and immortal in essence, if not in form, and this is Manas, the Mind-man or embodied Consciousness. The objection made by the materialists, who deny the possibility of mind and consciousness acting without matter is worthless in our case. We do not deny the soundness of their argument, but we simply ask our opponents, "Are you acquainted with all the states of matter, you who knew hitherto but of three? And how do you know whether that which we refer to as Absolute Consciousness or Deity for ever invisible and unknowable, be not that which, though it eludes forever our human finite conception, is still universal Spirit-matter or matter-Spirit in its absolute infinitude?" It is then one of the lowest, and in its manvantaric manifestations fractioned-aspects of this Spirit-matter, which is the conscious Ego that creates its own paradise, a fool's paradise, it may be, still a state of bliss.

ENQUIRER. But what is Devachan?

THEOSOPHIST. The "land of gods" literally; a condition, a state of mental bliss. Philosophically a mental condition analogous to, but far more vivid and real than, the most vivid dream. It is the state after death of most mortals.

NOTES

1. Paul calls Plato's *Nous* "Spirit," but as this spirit is "substance," then, of course, Buddhi and not Atma is meant, as the latter cannot philosophically be called "substance" under any circumstance. We include Atma among the human "principles" in order not to create additional confusion. In reality it is no "human" but the universal absolute principle of which Buddhi, the Soul-Spirit, is the carrier.

2. "Plato and Pythagoras," says Plutarch, "distribute the soul into two parts, the rational (noetic) and irrational (*agnoia*); that that part of the soul of man which is rational is eternal; for though it be not God, yet it is the product of an eternal deity, but that part of the soul which is divested of reason (*agnoia*) dies." The modern term *Agnostic* comes from *Agnosis*, a cognate word. We wonder why Mr. Huxley, the author of the word, should have connected his great intellect with "the soul divested of reason" which dies? Is it the exaggerated humility of the modern materialist?

3. The Kabalists who know the relation of Jehovah, the life and children-giver, to the Moon, and the influence of the latter on generation, will again see the point as much as some astrologers will.

4. Proserpina, or Persephone, stands here for postmortem Karma, which is said to regulate the separation of the lower from the higher "principles": the Soul, as Nephesh, the breath of animal life, which remains for a time in Kamaloka, from the higher compound Ego, which goes into the state of Devachan, or bliss.

5. Until the separation of the higher, spiritual "principle" takes place from the lower ones, which remain in the Kamaloka until disintegrated.

2

THE "THEOSOPHICAL MAHATMAS"

H. P. Blavatsky

ARE THEY "SPIRITS OF LIGHT"
OR "GOBLINS DAMN'D"?

ENQUIRER. Who are they, finally, those whom you call your "Masters"? Some say they are "Spirits," or some other kind of supernatural beings, while others call them "myths."

THEOSOPHIST. They are neither. I once heard one outsider say to another that they were a sort of male mermaids, whatever such a creature may be. But if you listen to what people say, you will never have a true conception of them. In the first place they are living men, born as we are born and doomed to die like every other mortal.

ENQUIRER. Yes, but it is rumored that some of them are a thousand years old. Is this true?

THEOSOPHIST. As true as the miraculous growth of hair on the head of Meredith's Shagpat. Truly, like the "Identical," no Theosophical shaving has hitherto been able to crop it. The more we deny them, the more we try to set people right, the more absurd do the inventions become. I have heard of Methuselah being 969

From H. P. Blavatsky, *The Key to Theosophy* (New York: W. Q. Judge, 1889), section 14.

years old, but, not being forced to believe in it, have laughed at the statement, for which I was forthwith regarded by many as a blasphemous heretic.

ENQUIRER. Seriously, though, do they outlive the ordinary age of men?

THEOSOPHIST. What do you call the ordinary age? I remember reading in the *Lancet* of a Mexican who was almost 190 years old, but I have never heard of mortal man, layman or Adept, who could live even half the years allotted to Methuselah. Some Adepts do exceed, by a good deal, what you would call the ordinary age, yet there is nothing miraculous in it, and very few of them care to live very long.

ENQUIRER. But what does the word "Mahatma" really mean?

THEOSOPHIST. Simply a "great soul," great through moral elevation and intellectual attainment. If the title of great is given to a drunken soldier like Alexander, why should we not call those "Great" who have achieved far greater conquests in Nature's secrets than Alexander ever did on the field of battle? Besides, the term is an Indian and a very old word.

ENQUIRER. And why do you call them "Masters"?

THEOSOPHIST. We call them "Masters" because they are our teachers and because from them we have derived all the Theosophical truths, however inadequately some of us may have expressed, and others understood, them. They are men of great learning, whom we term Initiates, and still greater holiness of life. They are not ascetics in the ordinary sense, though they certainly remain apart from the turmoil and strife of your Western world.

ENQUIRER. But is it not selfish thus to isolate themselves?

THEOSOPHIST. Where is the selfishness? Does not the fate of the Theosophical Society sufficiently prove that the world is neither ready to recognize them nor to profit by their teaching? Of what use would Professor Clerk Maxwell have been to instruct a class of little boys in their multiplication-table? Besides, they isolate themselves only from the West. In their own country they go about as publicly as other people do.

ENQUIRER. Don't you ascribe to them supernatural powers?

THEOSOPHIST. We believe in nothing supernatural, as I have told you already. Had Edison lived and invented his phonograph two hundred years ago, he would most probably have been burned along with it, and the whole attributed to the devil. The powers which they exercise are simply the development of potencies lying latent in every man and woman and the existence of which even official science begins to recognize.

ENQUIRER. Is it true that these men inspire some of your writers, and that many, if not all, of your Theosophical works were written under their dictation?

THEOSOPHIST. Some have. There are passages entirely dictated by them and verbatim, but in most cases they only inspire the ideas and leave the literary form to the writers.

ENQUIRER. But this in itself is miraculous, is, in fact, a miracle. How can they do it?

THEOSOPHIST. My dear Sir, you are laboring under a great mistake, and it is science itself that will refute your arguments at no distant day. Why should it be a "miracle," as you call it? A miracle is supposed to mean some operation which is supernatural, whereas there is really nothing above or beyond *Nature* and Nature's laws. Among the many forms of the "miracle" which have come under modern scientific recognition, there is Hypnotism, and one phase of its power is known as "Suggestion," a form of thought transference, which has been successfully used in combating particular physical diseases, etc. The time is not far distant when the World of Science will be forced to acknowledge that there exists as much interaction between one mind and another, no matter at what distance, as between one body and another in closest contact. When two minds are sympathetically related, and the instruments through which they function are tuned to respond magnetically and electrically to one another, there is nothing which will prevent the transmission of thoughts from one to the other, at will; for since the mind is not of a tangible nature, that distance can divide it from the subject of its contemplation, it follows that the only difference that can exist between two minds is a difference of *State*. So if this latter hindrance is overcome, where is the "miracle" of thought transference, at whatever distance?

ENQUIRER. But you will admit that Hypnotism does nothing so miraculous or wonderful as that?

THEOSOPHIST. On the contrary, it is a well-established fact that a Hypnotist can affect the brain of his subject so far as to produce an expression of his own thoughts, and even his words, through the organism of his subject, and although the phenomena attaching to this method of actual thought transference are as yet few in number, no one, I presume, will undertake to say how far their action may extend in the future, when the laws that govern their production are more scientifically established. And so, if such results can be produced by the knowledge of the mere rudiments of Hypnotism, what can prevent the Adept in Psychic and Spiritual powers from producing results which, with your present limited knowledge of their laws, you are inclined to call "miraculous"?

ENQUIRER. Then why do not our physicians experiment and try if they could not do as much?[1]

THEOSOPHIST. Because, first of all, they are not Adepts with a thorough understanding of the secrets and laws of psychic and spiritual realms, but materialists, afraid to step outside the narrow groove of matter; and, second, because they must fail at present, and indeed until they are brought to acknowledge that such powers are attainable.

ENQUIRER. And could they be taught?

THEOSOPHIST. Not unless they were first of all prepared, by having the materialistic dross they have accumulated in their brains swept away to the very last atom.

ENQUIRER. This is very interesting. Tell me, have the Adepts thus inspired or dictated to many of your Theosophists?

THEOSOPHIST. No, on the contrary, to very few. Such operations require special conditions. An unscrupulous but skilled Adept of the Black Brotherhood ("Brothers of the Shadow," and Dugpas, we call them) has far fewer difficulties to labor under. For, having no laws of the Spiritual kind to trammel his actions, such a Dugpa "sorcerer" will most unceremoniously obtain control over any mind and subject it entirely to his evil powers. But our Masters will never do that. They have no right, except by falling into Black Magic, to obtain full mastery over anyone's immortal Ego and can therefore act only on the physical and psychic nature of the subject, leaving thereby the free will of the latter wholly undisturbed. Hence, unless a person has been brought into psychic relationship with the Masters, and is assisted by virtue of his full faith in, and devotion to, his Teachers, the latter, whenever transmitting their thoughts to one with whom these conditions are not fulfilled, experience great difficulties in penetrating into the cloudy chaos of that person's sphere. But this is no place to treat of a subject of this nature. Suffice it to say, that if the power exists, then there are Intelligences (embodied or disembodied) which guide this power, and living conscious instruments through whom it is transmitted and by whom it is received. We have only to beware of Black Magic.

ENQUIRER. But what do you really mean by "Black Magic"?

THEOSOPHIST. Simply abuse of psychic powers or of any secret of nature; the fact of applying to selfish and sinful ends the powers of Occultism. A hypnotizer, who, taking advantage of his powers of "suggestion," forces a subject to steal or murder would be called a black magician by us. The famous "rejuvenating system" of Dr. Brown-Sequard of Paris through a loathsome animal injection into human blood—a discovery all the medical papers of Europe are now discussing—if true, is unconscious Black Magic.

ENQUIRER. But this is medieval belief in witchcraft and sorcery! Even Law itself has ceased to believe in such things?

THEOSOPHIST. So much the worse for law, as it has been led, through such a lack of discrimination, into committing more than one judiciary mistake and crime. It is the term alone that frightens you with its "superstitious" ring in it. Would not law punish an abuse of hypnotic powers, as I just mentioned? Nay, it has so punished it already in France and Germany; yet it would indignantly deny that it applied punishment to a crime of evident sorcery. You cannot believe in the efficacy and reality of the powers of suggestion by physicians and mesmerizers (or hypnotizers) and then refuse to believe in the same powers when used for evil motives. And if you do, then you believe in Sorcery. You cannot believe in good and disbelieve in evil, accept genuine money and refuse to credit such a thing as false coin. Nothing can exist without its contrast, and no day, no light, no good could have any representation as such in your consciousness, were there no night, darkness, or evil to offset and contrast them.

ENQUIRER. Indeed, I have known men, who, while thoroughly believing in that which you call great psychic, or magic powers, laughed at the very mention of Witchcraft and Sorcery.

THEOSOPHIST. What does it prove? Simply that they are illogical. So much the worse for them, again. And we, knowing as we do of the existence of good and holy Adepts, believe as thoroughly in the existence of bad and unholy Adepts, or—Dugpas.

ENQUIRER. But if the Masters exist, why don't they come out before all men and refute once for all the many charges which are made against Mme. Blavatsky and the Society?

THEOSOPHIST. What charges?

ENQUIRER. That they do not exist and that she has invented them. That they are men of straw, "Mahatmas of muslin and bladders." Does not all this injure her reputation?

THEOSOPHIST. In what way can such an accusation injure her in reality? Did she ever make money on their presumed existence, or derive benefit, or fame, therefrom? I answer that she has gained only insults, abuse, and calumnies, which would have been very painful had she not learned long ago to remain perfectly indifferent to such false charges. For what does it amount to, after all? Why, to an implied compliment, which, if the fools, her accusers, were not carried away by their blind hatred, they would have thought twice before uttering. To say that she has invented the Masters comes to this: She must have invented every bit of philosophy that has ever been given out in Theosophical literature. She must be the author of the letters from which "Esoteric Buddhism" was written; the sole inventor of every tenet found in the "Secret Doctrine," which, if the world were just, would be recognized as supplying many of the missing links of science, as will be discovered a hundred years hence. By saying what they do, they are also giving her the credit of being far cleverer than the hundreds of men (many very clever and not a few scientific men) who believe in what she says—inasmuch as she must have fooled them all! If they speak the truth, then she must be several Mahatmas rolled into one like a nest of Chinese boxes; since among the so-called "Mahatma letters" are many in totally different and distinct styles, all of which her accusers declare that she has written.

ENQUIRER. It is just what they say. But is it not very painful to her to be publicly denounced as "the most accomplished impostor of the age, whose name deserves to pass to posterity," as is done in the Report of the "Society for Psychical Research"?

THEOSOPHIST. It might be painful if it were true or came from people less rabidly materialistic and prejudiced. As it is, personally she treats the whole matter with contempt, while the Mahatmas simply laugh at it. In truth, it is the greatest compliment that could be paid to her. I say so again.

ENQUIRER. But her enemies claim to have proved their case.

THEOSOPHIST. Aye, it is easy enough to make such a claim when you have constituted yourself judge, jury, and prosecuting counsel at once, as they did. But who, except their direct followers and our enemies, believe in it?

ENQUIRER. But they sent a representative to India to investigate the matter, didn't they?

THEOSOPHIST. They did, and their final conclusion rests entirely on the unchecked statements and unverified assertions of this young gentleman. A lawyer who read through his report told a friend of mine that in all his experience he had never seen "such a ridiculous and self-condemnatory document." It was found to be full of suppositions and "working hypotheses" which mutually destroyed each other. Is this a serious charge?

ENQUIRER. Yet it has done the Society great harm. Why, then, did she not vindicate her own character, at least, before a Court of Law?

THEOSOPHIST. First, because as a Theosophist, it is her duty to leave unheeded all personal insults. Second, because neither the Society nor Mme. Blavatsky had any money to waste over such a lawsuit. And last, because it would have been ridiculous for both to be untrue to their principles because of an attack made on them by a flock of stupid old British wethers, who had been led to butt at them by an overfrolicksome lambkin from Australia.

ENQUIRER. This is complimentary. But do you not think that it would have done real good to the cause of Theosophy, if she had authoritatively disproved the whole thing once for all?

THEOSOPHIST. Perhaps. But do you believe that any English jury or judge would have ever admitted the reality of psychic phenomena, even if entirely unprejudiced beforehand? And when you remember that they would have been set against us already by the "Russian Spy" scare, the charge of Atheism and infidelity, and all the other calumnies that have been circulated against us, you cannot fail to see that such an attempt to obtain justice in a Court of Law would have been worse than fruitless! All this the Psychic Researchers knew well, and they took a base and mean advantage of their position to raise themselves above our heads and save themselves at our expense.

ENQUIRER. The SPR. now denies completely the existence of the Mahatmas. They say that from beginning to end they were a romance which Madame Blavatsky has woven from her own brain.

THEOSOPHIST. Well, she might have done many things less clever than this. At any rate, we have not the slightest objection to this theory. As she always says now, she almost prefers that people should not believe in the Masters. She declares openly that she would rather people should seriously think that the only Mahatmaland is the grey matter of her brain, and that, in short, she has evolved them out of the depths of her own inner consciousness, than that their names and grand ideal should be so infamously desecrated as they are at present. At first she used to protest indignantly against any doubts as to their existence. Now she never goes out of her way to prove or disprove it. Let people think what they like.

ENQUIRER. But, of course, these Masters do exist?

THEOSOPHIST. We affirm they do. Nevertheless, this does not help much. Many people, even some Theosophists and ex-Theosophists, say that they have never had any proof of their existence. Very well; then Mme. Blavatsky replies with this alternative: If she has invented them, then she has also invented their philosophy and the practical knowledge which some few have acquired, and if so, what does it matter whether they do exist or not, since she herself is here, and her own existence, at any rate, can hardly be denied? If the knowledge supposed to have been imparted by them is good intrinsically, and it is accepted as such by many persons of more than average intelligence, why should there be such a hullabaloo made over that question? The fact of her being an imposter has never been proved and will always remain *sub judice*; whereas it is a certain and undeniable fact that, by whomsoever invented, the philosophy preached by the "Masters" is one of the grandest and most beneficent philosophies once it is properly understood. Thus the slanderers, while moved by the lowest and meanest feelings—those of hatred, revenge, malice, wounded vanity, or disappointed ambition—seem quite unaware that they are paying the greatest tribute to her intellectual powers. So be it, if the poor fools will have it so. Really, Mme. Blavatsky has not the slightest objection to being represented by her enemies as a triple Adept, and a "Mahatma" to boot. It is only her unwillingness to pose in her own sight as a crow parading in peacock's feathers that compels her to this day to insist upon the truth.

ENQUIRER. But if you have such wise and good men to guide the Society, how is it that so many mistakes have been made?

THEOSOPHIST. The Masters do not guide the Society, not even the Founders, and no one has ever asserted that they did: they only watch over and protect it. This is amply proved by the fact that no mistakes have been able to cripple it, and no scandals from within, nor the most damaging attacks from without, have been able to overthrow it. The Masters look at the future, not at the present, and every mistake is so much more accumulated wisdom for days to come. That other "Master" who sent the man with the five talents did not tell him how to double them, nor did he prevent the foolish servant from burying his one talent in the earth. Each must acquire wisdom by his own experience and merits. The Christian Churches, who claim a far higher "Master," the very Holy Ghost itself, have ever been and are still guilty not only of "mistakes" but of a series of bloody crimes throughout the ages. Yet, no Christian would deny, for all that, his belief in that "Master," I suppose? Although his existence is far more hypothetical than that of the Mahatmas, as no one has ever seen the Holy Ghost, and his guidance of the Church, moreover, their own ecclesiastical history distinctly contradicts. *Errare humanum est.* Let us return to our subject.

THE ABUSE OF SACRED NAMES AND TERMS

ENQUIRER. Then, what I have heard, namely, that many of your Theosophical writers claim to have been inspired by these Masters, or to have seen and conversed with them, is not true?

THEOSOPHIST. It may or it may not be true. How can I tell? The burden of proof rests with them. Some of them, a few—very few, indeed—have distinctly either lied or were hallucinated when boasting of such inspiration; others were truly inspired by great Adepts. The tree is known by its fruits, and as all Theosophists have to be judged by their deeds and not by what they write or say, so all Theosophical books must be accepted on their merits and not according to any claim to authority which they may put forward.

ENQUIRER. But would Mme. Blavatsky apply this to her own works—the Secret Doctrine, for instance?

THEOSOPHIST. Certainly, she says expressly in the Preface that she gives out the doctrines that she has learned from the Masters but claims no inspiration whatever for what she has lately written. As for our best Theosophists, they would also in this case far rather that the names of the Masters had never been mixed up with our books in any way. With few exceptions, most of such works are not only imperfect but positively erroneous and misleading. Great are the desecrations to which the names of two of the Masters have been subjected. There is hardly a medium who has not claimed to have seen them. Every bogus swindling Society, for commercial purposes, now claims to be guided and directed by "Masters," often supposed to be far higher than ours! Many and heavy are the sins of those who advanced these claims, prompted either by desire for lucre, vanity, or irresponsible mediumship. Many persons have been plundered of their money by such societies, which offer to sell the secrets of power, knowledge, and spiritual truth for worthless gold. Worst of all, the sacred names of Occultism and the holy keepers thereof have been dragged in this filthy mire, polluted by being associated with sordid motives and immoral practices, while thousands of men have been held back from the path of truth and light through the discredit and evil report which such shams, swindles, and frauds have brought upon the whole subject. I say again, every earnest Theosophist regrets today, from the bottom of his heart, that these sacred names and things have ever been mentioned before the public and fervently wishes that they had been kept secret within a small circle of trusted and devoted friends.

ENQUIRER. The names certainly do occur very frequently nowadays, and I never remember hearing of such persons as "Masters" till quite recently.

THEOSOPHIST. It is so, and had we acted on the wise principle of silence, instead of rushing into notoriety and publishing all we knew and heard, such desecration would never have occurred. Behold, only fourteen years ago, before the Theosophical Society was founded, all the talk was of "Spirits." They were everywhere, in everyone's mouth, and no one by any chance even dreamed of talking about living "Adepts," "Mahatmas," or "Masters." One hardly heard even the name of the Rosicrucians, while the existence of such a thing as "Occultism" was suspected even but by very few. Now all that is changed. We Theosophists were, unfortunately, the first to talk of these things, to make the fact of the existence in the East of "Adepts" and "Masters" and Occult knowledge known, and now the name has become common property. It is on us, now, that the Karma, the consequences of the resulting desecration of holy names and things, has fallen. All that you now find about such matters in current literature—and there is not a little of it—all is to be traced back to the impulse given in this direction by the Theosophical Society and its Founders. Our enemies profit to this day by our mistake. The most recent book directed against our teachings is alleged to have been written by an Adept of twenty years' standing. Now, it is a palpable lie. We know the amanuensis and his inspirers (as he is himself too ignorant to have written anything of the sort). These "inspirers" are living persons, revengeful and unscrupulous in proportion to their intellectual powers, and these bogus Adepts are not one but several. The cycle of "Adepts," used as sledgehammers to break the theosophical heads with, began twelve years ago, with Mrs. Emma Hardinge Britten's "Louis" of *Art Magic* and *Ghost-Land* and now ends with the "Adept" and "Author" of *The Light of Egypt*, a work written by Spiritualists against Theosophy and its teachings. But it is useless to grieve over what is done, and we can only suffer in the hope that our indiscretions may have made it a little easier for others to find the way to these Masters, whose names are now everywhere taken in vain, and under cover of which so many iniquities have already been perpetrated.

ENQUIRER. Do you reject "Louis" as an Adept?

THEOSOPHIST. We denounce no one, leaving this noble task to our enemies. The spiritualistic author of Art Magic, etc., may or may not have been acquainted with such an Adept—and saying this, I say far less than what that lady has said and written about us and Theosophy for the last several years—that is her own business. Only when, in a solemn scene of mystic vision, an alleged "Adept" sees "spirits" presumably at Greenwich, England, through Lord Rosse's telescope, which was built in, and never moved from, Parsonstown, Ireland (see "Ghost Land," Part I, pp. 133 ff.), I may well be permitted to wonder at the ignorance of that "Adept" in matters of science. This beats all the mistakes and blunders committed at times by the chelas of our Teachers! And it is this "Adept" that is used now to break the teachings of our Masters!

NOTE

1. Such as, for instance, Professor Bernheim and Dr. C. Lloyd Tuckey of England, Professors Beaunis and Liegeois of Nancy, Delboeuf of Liege, Burot and Bourru of Rochefort, Fontain and Sigard of Bordeaux, Forel of Zurich, Drs. Despine of Marseilles, Van Renterghem and Van Eeden of Amsterdam, Wetterstrand of Stockholm, Schrenck-Notzing of Leipzig, and many other physicians and writers of eminence.

3

ON THE MYSTERIES OF REINCARNATION

H. P. Blavatsky

PERIODICAL REBIRTHS

ENQUIRER. You mean, then, that we have all lived on earth before, in many past incarnations, and shall go on so living?

THEOSOPHIST. I do. The life-cycle, or rather the cycle of conscious life, begins with the separation of the mortal animal-man into sexes and will end with the close of the last generation of men, in the seventh round and seventh race of mankind. Considering we are only in the fourth round and fifth race, its duration is more easily imagined than expressed.

ENQUIRER. And we keep on incarnating in new personalities all the time?

THEOSOPHIST. Most assuredly so; because this life-cycle or period of incarnation may be best compared to human life. As each such life is composed of days of activity separated by nights of sleep or of inaction, so, in the incarnation-cycle, an active life is followed by a Devachanic rest.

ENQUIRER. And it is this succession of births that is generally defined as reincarnation?

From H. P. Blavatsky, *The Key to Theosophy* (New York: W. Q. Judge, 1889), section 11.

THEOSOPHIST. Just so. It is only through these births that the perpetual progress of the countless millions of Egos toward final perfection and final rest (as long as was the period of activity) can be achieved.

ENQUIRER. And what is it that regulates the duration or special qualities of these incarnations?

THEOSOPHIST. Karma, the universal law of retributive justice.

ENQUIRER. Is it an intelligent law?

THEOSOPHIST. For the Materialist, who calls the law of periodicity which regulates the marshaling of the several bodies, and all the other laws in nature, blind forces and mechanical laws, no doubt Karma would be a law of chance and no more. For us, no adjective or qualification could describe that which is impersonal and no entity but a universal operative law. If you question me about the causative intelligence in it, I must answer you I do not know. But if you ask me to define its effects and tell you what these are in our belief, I may say that the experience of thousands of ages has shown us that they are absolute and unerring equity, wisdom, and intelligence. For Karma in its effects is an unfailing redresser of human injustice and of all the failures of nature, a stern adjuster of wrongs, a retributive law which rewards and punishes with equal impartiality. It is, in the strictest sense, "no respecter of persons," though, on the other hand, it can neither be propitiated nor turned aside by prayer. This is a belief common to Hindus and Buddhists, who both believe in Karma.

ENQUIRER. In this Christian dogmas contradict both, and I doubt whether any Christian will accept the teaching.

THEOSOPHIST. No, and Inman gave the reason for it many years ago. As he puts it, while "the Christians will accept any nonsense, if promulgated by the Church as a matter of faith . . . the Buddhists hold that nothing which is contradicted by sound reason can be a true doctrine of Buddha." They do not believe in any pardon for their sins, except after an adequate and just punishment for each evil deed or thought in a future incarnation and a proportionate compensation to the parties injured.

ENQUIRER. Where is it so stated?

THEOSOPHIST. In most of their sacred works. In the "Wheel of the Law" (p. 57) you may find the following Theosophical tenet: "Buddhists believe that every act, word or thought has its consequence, which will appear sooner or later in the present or in the future state. Evil acts will produce evil consequences, good acts will produce good consequences: prosperity in this world, or birth in heaven (Devachan). . . in the future state."

ENQUIRER. Christians believe the same thing, don't they?

THEOSOPHIST. Oh, no; they believe in the pardon and the remission of all sins. They are promised that if they only believe in the blood of Christ (an innocent victim!), in the blood offered by Him for the expiation of the sins of the whole of mankind, it will atone for every mortal sin. And we believe neither in vicarious atonement nor in the possibility of the remission of the smallest sin by any god, not even by a "personal Absolute" or "Infinite," if such a thing could have any existence. What we believe in is strict and impartial justice. Our idea of the unknown Universal Deity, represented by Karma, is that it is a Power which cannot fail, and can, therefore, have neither wrath nor mercy, only absolute Equity, which leaves every cause, great or small, to work out its inevitable effects. The saying of Jesus: "With what measure you mete it shall be measured to you again" (Matt. 7:2), neither by expression nor implication points to any hope of future mercy or salvation by proxy. This is why, recognizing as we do in our philosophy the justice of this statement, we cannot recommend too strongly mercy, charity, and forgiveness of mutual offenses. Resist not evil and render good for evil are Buddhist precepts and were first preached in view of the implacability of Karmic law. For man to take the law into his own hands is anyhow a sacrilegious presumption. Human Law may use restrictive not punitive measures, but a man who, believing in Karma, still revenges himself and refuses to forgive every injury, thereby rendering good for evil, is a criminal and only hurts himself. As Karma is sure to punish the man who wronged him, by seeking to inflict an additional punishment on his enemy, he, who instead of leaving that punishment to the great Law adds to it his own mite, only begets thereby a cause for the future reward of his own enemy and a future punishment for himself. The unfailing Regulator affects in each incarnation the quality of its successor, and the sum of the merit or demerit in preceding ones determines it.

ENQUIRER. Are we then to infer a man's past from his present?

THEOSOPHIST. Only so far as to believe that his present life is what it justly should be, to atone for the sins of the past life. Of course—seers and great adepts excepted—we cannot as average mortals know what those sins were. From our paucity of data, it is impossible for us even to determine what an old man's youth must have been; neither can we, for like reasons, draw final conclusions merely from what we see in the life of some man, as to what his past life may have been.

WHAT IS KARMA?

ENQUIRER. But what is Karma?

THEOSOPHIST. As I have said, we consider it as the Ultimate Law of the Universe, the source, origin, and fount of all other laws which exist throughout Nature. Karma is the unerring law which adjusts effect to cause, on the physical, mental, and spiritual planes of being. As no cause remains without its due effect from greatest to least, from a cosmic disturbance down to the movement of your hand, and as like produces like, Karma is that unseen and unknown law which adjusts wisely, intelligently, and equitably each effect to its cause, tracing the latter back to its producer. Though itself unknowable, its action is perceivable.

ENQUIRER. Then it is the "Absolute," the "Unknowable" again, and is not of much value as an explanation of the problems of life?

THEOSOPHIST. On the contrary. For though we do not know what Karma is per se, and in its essence, we do know how it works, and we can define and describe its mode of action with accuracy. We only do not know its ultimate Cause, just as modern philosophy universally admits that the ultimate Cause of anything is "unknowable."

ENQUIRER. And what has Theosophy to say in regard to the solution of the more practical needs of humanity? What is the explanation which it offers in reference to the awful suffering and dire necessity prevalent among the so-called lower classes?

THEOSOPHIST. To be pointed, according to our teaching, all these great social evils, the distinction of classes in Society, and of the sexes in the affairs of life, the unequal distribution of capital and of labor—all are due to what we tersely but truly denominate Karma.

ENQUIRER. But, surely, all these evils which seem to fall upon the masses somewhat indiscriminately are not actual merited and *individual* Karma?

THEOSOPHIST. No, they cannot be so strictly defined in their effects as to show that each individual environment, and the particular conditions of life in which each person finds himself, are nothing more than the retributive Karma which the individual generated in a previous life. We must not lose sight of the fact that every atom is subject to the general law governing the whole body to which it belongs, and here we come upon the wider track of the Karmic law. Do you not perceive that the aggregate of individual Karma becomes that of the nation to which those individuals belong, and further, that the sum total of National Karma is that of the World? The evils that you speak of are not peculiar to the individual or even to the Nation, they are more or less universal, and it is upon this broad line of Human interdependence that the law of Karma finds its legitimate and equable issue.

ENQUIRER. Do I, then, understand that the law of Karma is not necessarily an individual law?

THEOSOPHIST. That is just what I mean. It is impossible that Karma could readjust the balance of power in the world's life and progress, unless it had a broad and general line of action. It is held as a truth among Theosophists that the interdependence of Humanity is the cause of what is called Distributive Karma, and it is this law which affords the solution to the great question of collective suffering and its relief. It is an occult law, moreover, that no man can rise superior to his individual failings, without lifting, be it ever so little, the whole body of which he is an integral part. In the same way, no one can sin, nor suffer the effects of sin, alone. In reality, there is no such thing as "Separateness"; and the nearest approach to that selfish state, which the laws of life permit, is in the intent or motive.

ENQUIRER. And are there no means by which the distributive or national Karma might be concentrated or collected, so to speak, and brought to its natural and legitimate fulfilment without all this protracted suffering?

THEOSOPHIST. As a general rule, and within certain limits which define the age to which we belong, the law of Karma cannot be hastened or retarded in its fulfillment. But of this I am certain, the point of possibility in either of these directions has never yet been touched. Listen to the following recital of one phase of national suffering, and then ask yourself whether, admitting the working power of individual, relative, and distributive Karma, these evils are not capable of extensive modification and general relief. What I am about to read to you is from the pen of a National Savior, one who, having overcome Self, and being free to choose, has elected to serve Humanity, in bearing at least as much as a woman's shoulders can possibly bear of National Karma. This is what she says:

> Yes, Nature always does speak, don't you think? only sometimes we make so much noise that we drown her voice. That is why it is so restful to go out of the town and nestle awhile in the Mother's arms. I am thinking of the evening on Hampstead Heath when we watched the sun go down; but oh! upon what suffering and misery that sun had set! A lady brought me yesterday a big hamper of wild flowers. I thought some of my East-end family had a better right to it than I, and so I took it down to a very poor school in Whitechapel this morning.

You should have seen the pallid little faces brighten! Thence I went to pay for some dinners at a little cookshop for some children. It was in a back street, narrow, full of jostling people; stench indescribable, from fish, meat, and other comestibles, all reeking in a sun that, in Whitechapel, festers instead of purifying. The cookshop was the quintessence of all the smells. Indescribable meat-pies at 1d., loathsome lumps of "food" and swarms of flies, a very altar of Beelzebub! All about, babies on the prowl for scraps, one, with the face of an angel, gathering up cherrystones as a light and nutritious form of diet. I came westward with every nerve shuddering and jarred, wondering whether anything can be done with some parts of London save swallowing them up in an earth-quake and starting their inhabitants afresh, after a plunge into some purifying Lethe, out of which not a memory might emerge! And then I thought of Hamp-stead Heath, and—pondered. If by any sacrifice one could win the power to save these people, the cost would not be worth counting; but, you see, *they* must be changed—and how can that be wrought? In the condition they now are, they would not profit by any environment in which they might be placed; and yet, in their present surroundings they must continue to putrefy. It breaks my heart, this endless, hopeless misery, and the brutish degradation that is at once its out-growth and its root. It is like the banyan tree; every branch roots itself and sends out new shoots. What a difference between these feelings and the peaceful scene at Hampstead! and yet we, who are the brothers and sisters of these poor crea-tures, have only a right to use Hampstead Heaths to gain strength to save Whitechapels. (Signed by a name too respected and too well known to be given to scoffers.)

ENQUIRER. That is a sad but beautiful letter, and I think it presents with painful conspicuity the terrible workings of what you have called "Relative and Distrib-utive Karma." But alas! there seems no immediate hope of any relief short of an earthquake or some such general engulfment!

THEOSOPHIST. What right have we to think so while one-half of humanity is in a position to effect an immediate relief of the privations which are suffered by their fellows? When every individual has contributed to the general good what he can of money, of labor, and of ennobling thought, then, and only then, will the bal-ance of National Karma be struck, and until then we have no right nor any rea-sons for saying that there is more life on the earth than Nature can support. It is reserved for the heroic souls, the Saviors of our Race and Nation, to find out the cause of this unequal pressure of retributive Karma, and by a supreme effort to readjust the balance of power, and save the people from a moral engulfment a thousand times more disastrous and more permanently evil than the like physical catastrophe, in which you seem to see the only possible outlet for this accumu-lated misery.

ENQUIRER. Well, then, tell me generally how you describe this law of Karma?

THEOSOPHIST. We describe Karma as that Law of readjustment which ever tends to restore disturbed equilibrium in the physical and broken harmony in the moral world. We say that Karma does not act in this or that particular way always, but that it always does act so as to restore Harmony and preserve the balance of equilibrium, in virtue of which the Universe exists.

ENQUIRER. Give me an illustration.

THEOSOPHIST. Later on I will give you a full illustration. Think now of a pond. A stone falls into the water and creates disturbing waves. These waves oscillate backward and forward till at last, owing to the operation of what physicists call the law of the dissipation of energy, they are brought to rest, and the water returns to its condition of calm tranquillity. Similarly all action, on every plane, produces disturbance in the balanced harmony of the Universe, and the vibrations so produced will continue to roll backward and forward, if its area is limited, till equilibrium is restored. But since each such disturbance starts from some particular point, it is clear that equilibrium and harmony can only be restored by the reconverging to that same point of all the forces which were set in motion from it. And here you have proof that the consequences of a man's deeds, thoughts, etc. must all react upon himself with the same force with which they were set in motion.

ENQUIRER. But I see nothing of a moral character about this law. It looks to me like the simple physical law that action and reaction are equal and opposite.

THEOSOPHIST. I am not surprised to hear you say that. Europeans have got so much into the ingrained habit of considering right and wrong, good and evil, as matters of an arbitrary code of law laid down either by men or imposed upon them by a Personal God. We Theosophists, however, say that "Good" and "Harmony," and "Evil" and "Dis-harmony," are synonymous. Further we maintain that all pain and suffering are results of want of Harmony and that the one terrible and only cause of the disturbance of Harmony is selfishness in some form or another. Hence Karma gives back to every man the actual consequences of his own actions, without any regard to their moral character, but since he receives his due for all, it is obvious that he will be made to atone for all sufferings which he has caused, just as he will reap in joy and gladness the fruits of all the happiness and harmony he had helped to produce. I can do no better than quote for your benefit certain passages from books and articles written by our Theosophists—those who have a correct idea of Karma.

ENQUIRER. I wish you would, as your literature seems to be very sparing on this subject.

THEOSOPHIST. Because it is the most difficult of all our tenets. Some short time ago, there appeared the following objection from a Christian pen: "Granting that the teaching in regard to Theosophy is correct, and that 'man must be his own saviour, must overcome self and conquer the evil that is in his dual nature, to obtain the emancipation of his soul,' what is man to do after he has been awakened and converted to a certain extent from evil or wickedness? How is he to get emancipation, or pardon, or the blotting out of the evil or wickedness he has already done?"

To this Mr. J. H. Conelly replies very pertinently that no one can hope to "make the theosophical engine run on the theological track." As he has it:

> The possibility of shirking individual responsibility is not among the concepts of Theosophy. In this faith there is no such thing as pardoning, or "blotting out of evil or wickedness already done," otherwise than by the adequate punishment therefor of the wrong-doer and the restoration of the harmony in the universe that had been disturbed by his wrongful act. The evil has been his own, and while others must suffer its consequences, atonement can be made by nobody but himself.
>
> The condition contemplated . . . in which a man shall have been "awakened and converted to a certain extent from evil or wickedness," is that in which a man shall have realized that his deeds are evil and deserving of punishment. In that realization a sense of personal responsibility is inevitable, and just in proportion to the extent of his awakening or "converting" must be the sense of that awful responsibility. While it is strong upon him is the time when he is urged to accept the doctrine of vicarious atonement.
>
> He is told that be must also repent, but nothing is easier than that. It is an amiable weakness of human nature that we are quite prone to regret the evil we have done when our attention is called, and we have either suffered from it ourselves or enjoyed its fruits. Possibly, close analysis of the feeling would show us that that which we regret is rather the necessity that seemed to require the evil as a means of attainment of our selfish ends than the evil itself.
>
> Attractive as this prospect of casting our burden of sins "at the foot of the cross" may be to the ordinary mind, it does not commend itself to the Theosophic student. He does not apprehend why the sinner by attaining knowledge of his evil can thereby merit any pardon for or the blotting out of his past wickedness; or why repentance and future right living entitle him to a suspension in his favour of the universal law of relation between cause and effect. The results of his evil deeds continue to exist; the suffering caused to others by his wickedness is not blotted out. The Theosophical student takes the result of wickedness upon the innocent into his problem. He considers not only the guilty person, but his victims.
>
> Evil is an infraction of the laws of harmony governing the universe, and the penalty thereof must fall upon the violator of that law himself. Christ uttered the warning, "Sin no more, lest a worse thing come upon thee," and St.

Paul said, "Work out your own salvation. Whatsoever a man soweth, that shall he also reap." That, by the way, is a fine metaphoric rendering of the sentence of the Puranas far antedating him—that "every man reaps the consequences of his own acts."

This is the principle of the law of Karma which is taught by Theosophy. Sinnett, in his "Esoteric Buddhism," rendered Karma as "the law of ethical causation." "The law of retribution," as Mdme. Blavatsky translates its meaning, is better. It is the power which "Just though mysterious, leads us on unerring/ Through ways unmarked from guilt to punishment."

But it is more. It rewards merit as unerringly and amply as it punishes demerit. It is the outcome of every act, of thought, word and deed, and by it men mould themselves, their lives and happenings. Eastern philosophy rejects the idea of a newly created soul for every baby born. It believes in a limited number of monads, evolving and growing more and more perfect through their assimilation of many successive personalities. Those personalities are the product of Karma and it is by Karma and re-incarnation that the human monad in time returns to its source—absolute deity.

E. D. Walker, in his "Re-incarnation," offers the following explanation:

Briefly, the doctrine of Karma is that we have made ourselves what we are by former actions, and are building our future eternity by present actions. There is no destiny but what we ourselves determine. There is no salvation or condemnation except what we ourselves bring about. . . . Because it offers no shelter for culpable actions and necessitates a sterling manliness, it is less welcome to weak natures than the easy religious tenets of vicarious atonement, intercession, forgiveness and death-bed conversions. . . . In the domain of eternal justice the offence and the punishment are inseparably connected as the same event, because there is no real distinction between the action and its outcome. . . . It is Karma, or our old acts, that draws us back into earthly life. The spirit's abode changes according to its Karma, and this Karma forbids any long continuance in one condition, because it is always changing. So long as action is governed by material and selfish motives, just so long must the effect of that action be manifested in physical re-births. Only the perfectly selfless man can elude the gravitation of material life. Few have attained this, but it is the goal of mankind.

And then the writer quotes from the Secret Doctrine:

Those who believe in Karma have to believe in destiny, which, from birth to death, every man is weaving, thread by thread, around himself, as a spider does his cobweb, and this destiny is guided either by the heavenly voice of the invisible prototype outside of us, or by our more intimate astral or inner man, who is but too often the evil genius of the embodied entity called man. Both these lead on the outward man, but one of them must prevail; and from the very beginning of the invisible affray the stern and implacable law of compensation steps in and takes its course, faithfully following the fluctuations. When the last strand is woven, and man is seemingly enwrapped in the network of his own doing, then he finds himself completely under the empire of this self-made destiny. . . . An Occultist or a philosopher will not speak of the goodness or cruelty of Providence; but, identifying it with Karma-Nemesis, he will teach that, nevertheless, it guards the good and watches over them in this as in future lives; and that it punishes the evil-doer—aye, even to his seventh re-birth—so long, in short, as the effect of his having thrown into perturbation even the smallest atom in the infinite world of harmony has not been finally re-adjusted. For the only decree of Karma—an eternal and immutable decree—is absolute harmony in the world of matter as it is in the world of spirit. It is not, therefore, Karma that rewards or punishes, but it is we who reward or punish ourselves according to whether we work with, through and along with nature, abiding by the laws on which that harmony depends, or—break them. Nor would the ways of Karma be inscrutable were men to work in union and harmony, instead of disunion and strife. For our ignorance of those ways—which one portion of mankind calls the ways of Providence, dark and intricate; while another sees in them the action of blind fatalism; and a third simple chance, with neither gods nor devils to guide them—would surely disappear if we would but attribute all these to their correct cause. . . . We stand bewildered before the mystery of our own making and the riddles of life that we will not solve, and then accuse the great Sphinx of devouring us. But verily there is not an accident of our lives, not a misshapen day, or a misfortune, that could not be traced back to our own doings in this or in another life. . . . The law of Karma is inextricably interwoven with that of reincarnation. . . . It is only this doctrine that can explain to us the mysterious problem of good and evil, and reconcile man to the terrible and apparent injustice of life. Nothing but such certainty can quiet our revolted sense of justice. For, when one unacquainted with the noble doctrine looks around him and observes the inequalities of birth and fortune, of intellect and capacities; when one sees honour paid to fools and profligates, on whom fortune has heaped her favours by mere privilege of birth, and their nearest neighbour, with all his intellect and noble virtues—far more deserving in every way—perishing for want and for lack of sympathy—when one sees all this and has to turn away, helpless to relieve the undeserved suffering, one's ears ringing and heart aching with the cries of pain around him—that blessed knowledge of Karma alone prevents him from cursing life and men as well as their supposed Creator. . . . This law, whether conscious or unconscious, predestines nothing and no one. It exists from and in eternity truly, for it is eternity itself; and as such, since no act can be coequal with eternity, it cannot be said to act, for it is action itself. It is not the wave which drowns the man, but the personal action of the wretch who goes deliberately and places himself under the impersonal action of the laws that govern the ocean's motion. Karma creates nothing, nor does it design. It is man who plants and creates causes, and Karmic law adjusts the effects, which adjustment is not an act but universal harmony, tending ever to resume its original position, like a bough, which, bent down too forcibly, rebounds with corresponding vigour. If it happen to dislocate the arm that tried to bend it out of its natural position, shall we say it is the bough which broke our arm or that our own folly has brought us to grief? Karma has never sought to destroy intellectual and individual liberty, like the god invented by the Monotheists. It has not involved its decrees in darkness purposely to perplex man, nor shall it punish him who dares to scrutinize its mysteries. On the contrary, he who unveils through study and meditation its intricate paths, and throws light on those dark ways, in the windings of which so many men perish owing to their ignorance of the labyrinth of life, is working for the good of his fellow-men. Karma is an absolute and eternal law in the world of manifestation; and as there can only be one Absolute, as one Eternal, ever-present Cause, believers in Karma cannot be regarded as atheists or materialists, still less as fatalists, for Karma is one with the Unknowable, of which it is an aspect, in its effects in the phenomenal world.

Another able Theosophic writer says ("Purpose of Theosophy" by Mrs. A. P. Sinnett):

Every individual is making Karma either good or bad in each action and thought of his daily round, and is at the same time working out in this life the Karma brought about by the acts and desires of the last. When we see people afflicted by congenital ailments it may be safely assumed that these ailments are the inevitable results of causes started by themselves in a previous birth. It may be argued that, as these afflictions are hereditary, they can have nothing to do with a past incarnation; but it must be remembered that the Ego, the real man, the individuality, has no spiritual origin in the parentage by which it is re-embodied, but it is drawn by the affinities which its previous mode of life attracted round it into the current that carries it, when the time comes for re-birth, to the home best fitted for the development of those tendencies. . . . This doctrine of Karma, when properly understood, is well calculated to guide and assist those who realize its truth to a higher and better mode of life, for it must not be forgotten that not only our actions but our thoughts also are most assuredly followed by a crowd of circumstances that will influence for good or for evil our own future, and, what is still more important, the future of many of our fellow-creatures. If sins of omission and commission could in any case be only self-regarding, the fact on the sinner's Karma would be a matter of minor consequence. The effect that every thought and act through life carries with it for good or evil a corresponding influence on other members of the human family renders a strict sense of justice, morality, and unselfishness so necessary to future happiness or progress. A crime once committed, an evil thought sent out from the mind, are past recall—no amount of repentance can wipe out their results in the future. Repentance, if sincere, will deter a man from repeating errors; it cannot save him or others from the effects of those already produced, which will most unerringly overtake him either in this life or in the next re-birth.

Mr. J. H. Conelly proceeds—

The believers in a religion based upon such doctrine are willing it should be compared with one in which man's destiny for eternity is determined by the accidents of a single, brief earthly existence, during which he is cheered by the promise that "as the tree falls so shall it lie"; in which his brightest hope, when he wakes up to a knowledge of his wickedness, is the doctrine of vicarious atonement, and in which even that is handicapped, according to the Presbyterian Confession of Faith.

> By the decree of God, for the manifestation of his glory, some men and angels are predestinated unto everlasting life and others foreordained to everlasting death.
>
> These angels and men thus predestinated and foreordained are particularly and unchangeably designed; and their number is so certain and definite that it cannot be either increased or diminished. . . . As God hath appointed the elect unto glory. . . . Neither are any other redeemed by Christ effectually called, justified, adopted, sanctified, and saved, but the elect only.
>
> The rest of mankind God was pleased, according to the unsearchable counsel of his own will, whereby he extendeth or withholdeth mercy as he pleaseth, for the glory of his sovereign power over his creatures, to pass by and to ordain them to dishonour and wrath for their sin to the praise of his glorious justice.

This is what the able defender says. Nor can we do any better than wind up the subject as he does, by a quotation from a magnificent poem. As he says: "The exquisite beauty of Edwin Arnold's exposition of Karma in 'The Light of Asia' tempts to its reproduction here, but it is too long for quotation in full. Here is a portion of it:—

> Karma—all that total of a soul
> Which is the things it did, the thoughts it had,
> The "self" it wove with woof of viewless time
> Crossed on the warp invisible of acts.
>
>   *   *   *
>
> Before beginning and without an end,
> As space eternal and as surety sure,
> Is fixed a Power divine which moves to good,
> Only its laws endure.
>
> It will not be contemned of anyone;
> Who thwarts it loses, and who serves it gains;
> The hidden good it pays with peace and bliss,
> The hidden ill with pains.
>
> It seeth everywhere and marketh all;
> Do right—it recompenseth! Do one wrong—
> The equal retribution must be made,
> Though Dharma tarry long.
>
> It knows not wrath nor pardon; utter-true,
> Its measures mete, its faultless balance weighs;

>Times are as naught, to-morrow it will judge
>Or after many days.
>
>   *   *   *
>
>Such is the law which moves to righteousness,
>Which none at last can turn aside or stay;
>The heart of it is love, the end of it
>Is peace and consummation sweet. Obey.

And now I advise you to compare our Theosophic views upon Karma, the law of Retribution, and say whether they are not both more philosophical and just than this cruel and idiotic dogma which makes of "God" a senseless fiend; the tenet, namely, that the "elect only" will be saved, and the rest doomed to eternal perdition!

ENQUIRER. Yes, I see what you mean generally, but I wish you could give some concrete example of the action of Karma.

THEOSOPHIST. That I cannot do. We can only feel sure, as I said before, that our present lives and circumstances are the direct results of our own deeds and thoughts in lives that are past. But we, who are not Seers or Initiates, cannot know anything about the details of the working of the law of Karma.

ENQUIRER. Can anyone, even an Adept or Seer, follow out this Karmic process of re-adjustment in detail?

THEOSOPHIST. Certainly: "Those who know" can do so by the exercise of powers which are latent even in all men.

WHO ARE THOSE WHO KNOW?

ENQUIRER. Does this hold equally of ourselves as of others?

THEOSOPHIST. Equally. As just said, the same limited vision exists for all, save those who have reached in the present incarnation the acme of spiritual vision and clairvoyance. We can only perceive that, if things with us ought to have been different, they would have been different; that we are what we have made ourselves, and have only what we have earned for ourselves.

ENQUIRER. I am afraid such a conception would only embitter us.

THEOSOPHIST. I believe it is precisely the reverse. It is disbelief in the just law of retribution that is more likely to awaken every combative feeling in man. A child, as much as a man, resents a punishment, or even a reproof he believes to be unmerited, far more than he does a severer punishment, if he feels that it is merited. Belief in Karma is the highest reason for reconcilement to one's lot in this life, and the very strongest incentive towards effort to better the succeeding re-birth. Both of these, indeed, would be destroyed if we supposed that our lot was the result of anything but strict Law, or that destiny was in any other hands than our own.

ENQUIRER. You have just asserted that this system of Re-incarnation under Karmic law commended itself to reason, justice, and the moral sense. But, if so, is it not at some sacrifice of the gentler qualities of sympathy and pity, and thus a hardening of the finer instincts of human nature?

THEOSOPHIST. Only apparently, not really. No man can receive more or less than his deserts without a corresponding injustice or partiality to others; and a law which could be averted through compassion would bring about more misery than it saved, more irritation and curses than thanks. Remember also, that we do not administer the law, if we do create causes for its effects; it administers itself; and again, that the most copious provision for the manifestation of just compassion and mercy is shown in the state of Devachan.

ENQUIRER. You speak of Adepts as being an exception to the rule of our general ignorance. Do they really know more than we do of Re-incarnation and after states?

THEOSOPHIST. They do, indeed. By the training of faculties we all possess, but which they alone have developed to perfection, they have entered in spirit these various planes and states we have been discussing. For long ages, one generation of Adepts after another has studied the mysteries of being, of life, death, and re-birth, and all have taught in their turn some of the facts so learned.

ENQUIRER. And is the production of Adepts the aim of Theosophy?

THEOSOPHIST. Theosophy considers humanity as an emanation from divinity on its return path thereto. At an advanced point upon the path, Adeptship is reached by those who have devoted several incarnations to its achievement. For, remember well, no man has ever reached Adeptship in the Secret Sciences in one life; but many incarnations are necessary for it after the formation of a conscious purpose and the beginning of the needful training. Many may be the men and women in the very midst of our Society who have begun this uphill work toward illumination several incarnations ago, and who yet, owing to the personal illusions of the present life, are either ignorant of the fact, or on the road to losing every chance in this existence of progressing any further. They feel an irresistible attraction toward occultism and the Higher Life, and yet are too personal and self-opinion-ated, too much in love with the deceptive allurements of mundane life and the world's ephemeral pleasures, to give them up; and so lose their chance in their present birth. But, for ordinary men, for the practical duties of daily life, such a far-off result is inappropriate as an aim and quite ineffective as a motive.

ENQUIRER. What, then, may be their object or distinct purpose in joining the Theosophical Society?

THEOSOPHIST. Many are interested in our doctrines and feel instinctively that they are truer than those of any dogmatic religion. Others have formed a fixed resolve to attain the highest ideal of man's duty.

THE DIFFERENCE BETWEEN FAITH AND KNOWLEDGE; OR, BLIND AND REASONED FAITH.

ENQUIRER. You say that they accept and believe in the doctrines of Theosophy. But, as they do not belong to those Adepts you have just mentioned, then they must accept your teachings on blind faith. In what does this differ from that of conventional religions?

THEOSOPHIST. As it differs on almost all the other points, so it differs on this one. What you call "faith," and that which is blind faith, in reality, and with regard to the dogmas of the Christian religions, becomes with us "knowledge," the logical sequence of things we know, about facts in nature. Your Doctrines are based upon interpretation, therefore, upon the second-hand testimony of Seers; ours upon the invariable and unvarying testimony of Seers. The ordinary Christian theology, for instance, holds that man is a creature of God, of three component parts—body, soul, and spirit—all essential to his integrity, and all, either in the gross form of physical earthly existence or in the etherealized form of postresur-rection experience, needed to so constitute him forever, each man having thus a permanent existence separate from other men and from the Divine. Theosophy, on the other hand, holds that man, being an emanation from the Unknown, yet ever-present and infinite Divine Essence, his body and everything else is imper-manent, hence an illusion, Spirit alone in him being the one enduring substance and even that losing its separated individuality at the moment of its complete reunion with the Universal Spirit.

ENQUIRER. If we lose even our individuality, then it becomes simply annihilation.

THEOSOPHIST. I say it does not, since I speak of separate, not of universal, indi-viduality. The latter becomes as a part transformed into the whole; the dewdrop is not evaporated but becomes the sea. Is physical man annihilated when from a fetus he becomes an old man? What kind of Satanic pride must be ours if we place our infinitesimally small consciousness and individuality higher than the universal and infinite consciousness!

ENQUIRER. It follows, then, that there is, de facto, no man, but all is Spirit?

THEOSOPHIST. You are mistaken. It thus follows that the union of Spirit with matter is but temporary, or, to put it more clearly, since Spirit and matter are one, being the two opposite poles of the universal manifested substance—that Spirit loses its right to the name so long as the smallest particle and atom of its manifesting substance still clings to any form, the result of differentiation. To believe otherwise is blind faith.

ENQUIRER. Thus it is on knowledge, not on faith, that you assert that the permanent principle, the Spirit, simply makes a transit through matter?

THEOSOPHIST. I would put it otherwise and say—we assert that the appearance of the permanent and one principle, Spirit, as matter is transient, and, therefore, no better than an illusion.

ENQUIRER. Very well; and this, given out on knowledge, not faith?

THEOSOPHIST. Just so. But as I see very well what you are driving at, I may just as well tell you that we hold faith, such as you advocate, to be a mental disease, and real faith, i.e., the *pistis* of the Greeks, as "belief based on knowledge," whether supplied by the evidence of physical or spiritual senses.

ENQUIRER. What do you mean?

THEOSOPHIST. I mean, if it is the difference between the two that you want to know, then I can tell you that between faith on authority and faith on one's spiritual intuition, there is a very great difference.

ENQUIRER. What is it?

THEOSOPHIST. One is human credulity and superstition, the other human belief and intuition. As Professor Alexander Wilder says in his "Introduction to the Eleusinian Mysteries," "It is ignorance which leads to profanation. Men ridicule what they do not properly understand. . . . The undercurrent of this world is set towards one goal; and inside of human credulity . . . is a power almost infinite, a holy faith capable of apprehending the supremest truths of all existence." Those who limit that "credulity" to human authoritative dogmas alone will never fathom that power nor even perceive it in their natures. It is stuck fast to the external plane and is unable to bring forth into play the essence that rules it; for to do this they have to claim their right of private judgment, and this they never dare to do.

ENQUIRER. And is it that "intuition" which forces you to reject God as a personal Father, Ruler, and Governor of the Universe?

THEOSOPHIST. Precisely. We believe in an ever-unknowable Principle, because blind aberration alone can make one maintain that the Universe, thinking man, and all the marvels contained even in the world of matter, could have grown without some intelligent powers to bring about the extraordinarily wise arrangement of all its parts. Nature may err, and often does, in its details and the external manifestations of its materials, never in its inner causes and results. Ancient pagans held on this question far more philosophical views than modern philosophers, whether Agnostics, Materialists, or Christians, and no pagan writer has ever yet advanced the proposition that cruelty and mercy are not finite feelings and can therefore be made the attributes of an infinite god. Their gods, therefore, were all finite. The Siamese author of the Wheel of the Law expresses the same idea about your personal god as we do; he says (p. 25):

> A Buddhist might believe in the existence of a god, sublime above all human qualities and attributes—a perfect god, above love, and hatred, and jealousy, calmly resting in a quietude that nothing could disturb, and of such a god he would speak no disparagement, not from a desire to please him or fear to offend him, but from natural veneration; but he cannot understand a god with the attributes and qualities of men, a god who loves and hates, and shows anger; a Deity who, whether described as by Christian Missionaries or by Mahometans or Brahmins,[1] or Jews, falls below his standard of even an ordinary good man.

ENQUIRER. Faith for faith is not the faith of the Christian who believes, in his human helplessness and humility, that there is a merciful Father in Heaven who will protect him from temptation, help him in life, and forgive him his transgressions, better than the cold and proud almost fatalistic faith of the Buddhists, Vedantins, and Theosophists?

THEOSOPHIST. Persist in calling our belief "faith" if you will. But once we are again on this ever-recurring question, I ask in my turn: faith for faith, is not the one based on strict logic and reason better than the one which is based simply on human authority or hero-worship? Our "faith" has all the logical force of the arithmetical truism that 2 and 2 will produce 4. Your faith is like the logic of some emotional women of whom Tourgenyeff said that for them 2 and 2 were generally 5 and a tallow candle into the bargain. Yours is a faith, moreover, which clashes not only with every conceivable view of justice and logic, but which, if analyzed, leads man to his moral perdition, checks the progress of mankind, and positively making of might, right—transforms every second man into a Cain to his brother Abel.

ENQUIRER. What do you allude to?

HAS GOD THE RIGHT TO FORGIVE?

THEOSOPHIST. To the Doctrine of Atonement; I allude to that dangerous dogma in which you believe, and which teaches us that no matter how enormous our crimes against the laws of God and of man, we have but to believe in the self-sacrifice of Jesus for the salvation of mankind, and his blood will wash out every stain. It is twenty years that I preach against it, and I may now draw your attention to a paragraph from *Isis Unveiled*, written in 1875. This is what Christianity teaches, and what we combat:

> God's mercy is boundless and unfathomable. It is impossible to conceive of a human sin so damnable that the price paid in advance for the redemption of the sinner would not wipe it out if a thousandfold worse. And furthermore, it is never too late to repent. Though the offender wait until the last minute of the last hour of the last day of his mortal life, before his blanched lips utter the confession of faith, he may go to Paradise; the dying thief did it, and so may all others as vile. These are the assumptions of the Church, and of the Clergy; assumptions banged at the heads of your countrymen by England's favourite preachers, right in the "light of the XIXth century,"

this most paradoxical age of all. Now to what does it lead?

ENQUIRER. Does it not make the Christian happier than the Buddhist or Brahmin?

THEOSOPHIST. No; not the educated man, at any rate, since the majority of these have long since virtually lost all belief in this cruel dogma. But it leads those who still believe in it more easily to the threshold of every conceivable crime, than any other I know of. Let me quote to you from *Isis* once more (see vol. 2, pp. 542 and 543):

> If we step outside the little circle of creed and consider the universe as a whole balanced by the exquisite adjustment of parts, how all sound logic, how the faintest glimmering sense of justice, revolts against this Vicarious Atonement! If the criminal sinned only against himself, and wronged no one but himself; if by sincere repentance he could cause the obliteration of past events, not only from the memory of man, but also from that imperishable record, which no

deity—not even the Supremest of the Supreme—can cause to disappear, then this dogma might not be incomprehensible. But to maintain that one may wrong his fellow-man, kill, disturb the equilibrium of society and the natural order of things, and then—through cowardice, hope, or compulsion, it matters not—be forgiven by believing that the spilling of one blood washes out the other blood spilt—this is preposterous! Can the results of a crime be obliterated even though the crime itself should be pardoned? The effects of a cause are never limited to the boundaries of the cause, nor can the results of crime be confined to the offender and his victim. Every good as well as evil action has its effects, as palpably as the stone flung into calm water. The simile is trite, but it is the best ever conceived, so let us use it. The eddying circles are greater and swifter as the disturbing object is greater or smaller, but the smallest pebble, nay, the tiniest speck, makes its ripples. And this disturbance is not alone visible and on the surface. Below, unseen, in every direction—outward and downward—drop pushes drop until the sides and bottom are touched by the force. More, the air above the water is agitated, and this disturbance passes, as the physicists tell us, from stratum to stratum out into space forever and ever; an impulse has been given to matter, and that is never lost, can never be recalled! . . .

So with crime, and so with its opposite. The action may be instantaneous, the effects are eternal. When, after the stone is once flung into the pond, we can recall it to the hand, roll back the ripples, obliterate the force expended, restore the etheric waves to their previous state of non-being, and wipe out every trace of the act of throwing the missile, so that Time's record shall not show that it ever happened, then, then we may patiently hear Christians argue for the efficacy of this Atonement,

and—cease to believe in Karmic Law. As it now stands, we call upon the whole world to decide, which of our two doctrines is the most appreciative of deific justice, and which is more reasonable, even on simple human evidence and logic.

ENQUIRER. Yet millions believe in the Christian dogma and are happy.

THEOSOPHIST. Pure sentimentalism overpowering their thinking faculties, which no true philanthropist or Altruist will ever accept. It is not even a dream of selfishness but a nightmare of the human intellect. Look where it leads to, and tell me the name of that pagan country where crimes are more easily committed or more numerous than in Christian lands. Look at the long and ghastly annual records of crimes committed in European countries and behold Protestant and Biblical America. There, conversions effected in prisons are more numerous than those made by public revivals and preaching. See how the ledger-balance of Christian justice (!) stands: Red-handed murderers, urged on by the demons of lust, revenge, cupidity, fanaticism, or mere brutal thirst for blood, who kill their victims, in most cases, without giving them time to repent or call on Jesus. These, perhaps, died sinful, and, of course—consistently with theological logic—met the reward of their greater or lesser offenses. But the murderer, overtaken by human justice, is imprisoned, wept over by sentimentalists, prayed with and at, pronounces the charmed words of conversion and goes to the scaffold a redeemed child of Jesus! Except for the murder, he would not have been prayed with, redeemed, pardoned. Clearly this man did well to murder, for thus he gained eternal happiness! And how about the victim, and his or her family, relatives, dependents, social relations; has justice no recompense for them? Must they suffer in this world and the next, while he who wronged them sits beside the "holy thief" of Calvary and is for ever blessed? On this question the clergy keep a prudent silence (*Isis Unveiled*). And now you know why Theosophists—whose fundamental belief and hope is justice for all, in Heaven as on earth, and in Karma—reject this dogma.

ENQUIRER. The ultimate destiny of man, then, is not a Heaven presided over by God but the gradual transformation of matter into its primordial element, Spirit?

THEOSOPHIST. It is to that final goal to which all tends in nature.

ENQUIRER. Do not some of you regard this association or "fall of spirit into matter" as evil and rebirth as a sorrow?

THEOSOPHIST. Some do and therefore strive to shorten their period of probation on earth. It is not an unmixed evil, however, since it ensures the experience upon which we mount to knowledge and wisdom. I mean that experience which teaches that the needs of our spiritual nature can never be met by other than spiritual happiness. As long as we are in the body, we are subjected to pain, suffering, and all the disappointing incidents occurring during life. Therefore, and to palliate this, we finally acquire knowledge which alone can afford us relief and hope of a better future.

NOTE

1. Sectarian Brahmins are here meant. The Parabrahm of the Vedantins is the Deity we accept and believe in.

"CHRISTIANIZED" THEOSOPHY

4

THE BIBLE AND WISDOM

Rudolf Steiner

It cannot he doubted that the influence of the Bible on Western culture has been greater than that of any other document. It may truly be said that as a result of the influence of the Bible, the human soul has for thousands of years maintained a hold on the most inward being of man—a hold which has extended to the life of feeling and also to the life of will. The influence in these two spheres of man's being has been stronger than in his thinking and conceptional life, although it may be said that all spiritual life, be it in the region of religion or of exact science, bears traces of the influence of the Bible. And it is evident to those who look more deeply into things, that the very arguments of men who today feel bound to attack the Bible—taking up in some cases the radical standpoint of downright denial—themselves show traces of its influence. There has never been any general recognition, and today there is practically none, of the extent of the influence of this document; but it exists nevertheless in actual fact to those who have an unbiased outlook. The attitude adopted toward the Bible by modern thought, feeling, and perception has for some time past changed very considerably from what it used formerly to be. The value of the Bible, the attitude adopted toward it by men who today take it seriously has altered essentially in the course of the nineteenth century. We must not of course undervalue in any

Lecture delivered in Hamburg, Germany, December 5, 1908, from shorthand report unrevised by the lecturer. English translation first printed by Rudolf Steiner Publishing Company, 1941. Second printing Steiner Book Centre, 1986. The original German text of this lecture can he found in the collected edition of Rudolf Steiner's works under the title: "Der Kreislauf des Menschen innerhalb des Sinnes, Seelen und Geisteswelt," No. 68 in the Bibliographical Survey, 1961.

sense the standpoint of many modern thinking men who feel themselves bound to take a firm stand on the ground of Science. There are others who hold fast to the Bible, who derive all their deepest convictions from this most significant record, and who prefer to pay no attention when the value of the Bible is under discussion. The attitude of such people is: "Others may think as they like; we find in the teachings of the Bible all that our souls need and we are quite satisfied." Such a point of view, however justifiable it may be in individual cases, is in a certain sense entirely egoistical and by no means without danger for spiritual evolution. That which in a given epoch has become a universal blessing to men—or, let us say, a universal belief and conviction—has always originated with the few, and it may well be that an ever-increasing stream of conviction may how out to become universal in no very distant future from the few who today feel themselves compelled to attack the Bible because of their desire to build up their world-conception conformably with their Science. For this reason to ignore such spiritual and mental currents and to refuse to listen because one is oneself satisfied is not without an element of danger. Anyone who really takes the evolution of mankind seriously ought rather to regard it as a duty to take notice of the objections brought by sincere seekers for Truth and to see what relation these objections have to the Bible.

I have said that the attitude adopted by men, and especially by leaders of intellectual and spiritual life, has changed. Today we shall do no more than point to this change. Were we to look back into the past we should find civilizations where men, especially when they stood at the summit of their spiritual life, doubted not at all that the very highest wisdom flowed from the Bible and that those with whom it originated were not just average men who were responsible for human errors in it but were under lofty inspiration and infused it with wisdom. This was a feeling of reverent recognition among those who stood on the heights of spiritual life. In modern times this has changed.

In the eighteenth century there was a French investigator who came to the conclusion that certain contradictions exist in the Old Testament. He noticed that the two Creation stories at the very beginning of the Bible contradict one another, that one story describes the work of the six or seven days including the creation of man and that then there is a further account with a different beginning, which ascribes quite a different origin to man. This investigator was specially disconcerted by the fact that at the beginning of the Bible two names of the God-head occur, the name of the "Elohim" in the narrative of the six days' creation and then later the name of Jehova. There is an echo of this in the German Bible. In the German Bible the name of the God-head is translated "Lord," "God," and then Jehova is translated by "God the Lord" or in some such way; at all events the difference is apparent. Upon noticing this the investigator suspected that something had given rise to the untenable statement that the Bible was written by a single individual, whether Moses or someone else, and that different accounts must have been welded together. And after much deliberation he came to the conclusion that all the existing accounts corresponding to the different traditions were simply welded together, one account being amalgamated with another and all the contradictions allowed to stand.

After, and as a result of this, there appeared the kind of investigation which might well be called a mutilation of the Bible. Today there are Bibles in which the various points of detail are traced back to different traditions. In the so-called Rainbow Bible it is stated for instance, how some portion or other that has come to be inserted into the collective statement has its origin in quite a different legendary tradition—hence it is said that the Bible must have been welded together from shreds of tradition. It became more and more general for investigators to proceed along this line in regard to the Old Testament, and then the same thing happened in the case of the New Testament. How could the fact be hidden that when the four Gospels are submitted to literal comparison they do not agree with each other? It is easy to discover contradictions in the Matthew, Luke, and John gospels. And so the investigators said: How can the single Evangelists have written their respective Gospels under lofty inspiration, when the accounts do not agree? The Gospel of St. John—that most profound writing of Christendom—was divested of all worth as an historical document in the minds of some investigators of the nineteenth century. Men came more and more to be convinced of the fact that it was nothing but a kind of hymn, written down by someone on the basis of his faith and not a historical tradition at all. They said that what he had written down could in no way lay claim to being a true description of what had actually taken place in Palestine at the beginning of our era. And so the New Testament was torn into shreds. The Old and New Testaments were treated just like any other historical document; it was said that bias and error had crept into them and that before all things it was necessary to show by purely historical investigation, how the fragments had been gradually pieced together. This is the standpoint which more and more came to be adopted by historical, theological investigation.

On the other side let us turn to those who felt compelled to stand firmly on the ground of the facts of Natural Science—who said, quite sincerely and honestly as a result of their knowledge: "What we are taught by Geology, Biology and the different branches of Natural Science flatly contradicts what the Bible relates. The Bible story of the development of the earth and living beings through the six days of creation is of the nature of a legend or a myth of primitive peoples, whereby they tried, in their childlike fashion to make the origin of the earth intelligible to themselves." And such men alienated themselves from the New Testament in the same degree as from the Old Testament. Men who feel compelled to hold fast to the facts of Natural Science will have nothing to do with all the wonderful acts performed by the Christ, with the way in which this unique Personality arises at the critical point of our history, and they radically oppose the very principle on which the Bible is based. Thus we see on the one hand the Bible torn to pieces by historical-theological investigation and on the other hand put aside, discredited by scientific research.

That may serve briefly to characterize the outlook of today; but if nobody troubled about this and simply persisted in the attitude: "I believe what is in the Bible"—that would be Egoism. Such men would only be thinking of themselves and it would not occur to them that future generations might hold as an universal conviction that which today is only the conviction of a few.

We may now ask: is there perhaps yet a further standpoint other than the two we have indicated? Indeed there is, and it is just this that we want to consider today. It is the standpoint of Spiritual Science, or Anthroposophy. We can in the first instance understand this best by means of comparison. The Anthroposophical standpoint with regard to the Bible era to our modern age is something similar to that which was accomplished three or four centuries ago by the mighty achievements of scientific research; Anthroposophy seeks to form a connecting link with what was achieved by such men as Kepler, Copernicus, Galileo.

Today we build upon the foundations of what was achieved by such personalities as these. When we look back to the relation which in former days existed between men and nature, we find that in the old Schools or Academics, certain books carried just as much weight as the Bible does with many people today. Aristotle, the ancient Greek scholar, whose achievements were by no means confined to the sphere of Natural Science, was looked upon by the widest circles both in the early and later Middle Ages as a far-reaching Authority. Wherever men were taught about nature the books of Aristotle were taken as the basis. His writings were fundamental and authoritative not only in spheres where men pursued the study of Nature in a more limited, philosophical sense, but also in spheres of definitely scientific thought. It was not customary in those days to look out at Nature with one's own eyes, and it was not a question of instruments, apparatus, and other things of that kind. In the time of Galileo a highly symptomatic incident occurred, and it has been handed down as a kind of anecdote. It was pointed out by a colleague to a man who was a convinced follower of Aristotle that many of the master's utterances were not correct; for instance that the nerves proceeded from the heart, this being contrary to the real facts. A corpse was placed in front of the man and it was demonstrated to him that this utterance of Aristotle did not agree with the facts. He said: "Yes, when I look at that myself it seems a contradiction, but even if Nature does show it to me I still believe Aristotle." And there were many such men—men who had more faith in the teachings and the authority of Aristotle than in their own eyes. Today men's point of view about Nature and also about Aristotle has changed. In our time it would be considered ridiculous to derive from ancient books the knowledge of nature which men ought to possess. Today the scientist confronts nature with his instruments and tries to explore her secrets in order that they may become a common good for all men. But circumstances were such that in the time of Galileo, those who were imbued with the teachings of Aristotle to the same degree as this above-mentioned follower did not understand the Greek Master in the very least; Aristotle meant something different, something very much more spiritual, than what we understand today by the nerves. And because of this we cannot do real justice to Aristotle—whose vision was in accordance with the age in which he lived—until we look into nature with free and impartial eyes.

That was the great change that took place three or four centuries ago—and we are experiencing such another now in reference to the Spiritual Science and those spiritual facts and processes which are the spiritual foundations of existence.

For centuries the Bible was taken by a very large number of men to be the only book able to give information about all that transcended the tangible, physical world. The Bible was the Authority so far as the spiritual world was concerned, just as Aristotle in the Middle Ages was the authority for the physical world.

How has it come about that today we are in a position to do greater justice to Aristotle? It is because we face the physical world from a position of greater independence. And what Anthroposophy has to give to man of modern times is the possibility of acquiring direct cognition of the invisible world, just as centuries ago the New Age began to acquire direct knowledge of the visible world. Spiritual Science states that it is possible for man to look into and perceive the spiritual world; that he need not be dependent upon tradition but can see for himself. This is what true Spiritual Science has to achieve for modern humanity—it has to convince man that slumbering powers and faculties exist within him; that there are certain great moments in life when these spiritual faculties awaken just as when a blind man is operated upon and is able to see color and light. To use Goethe's phrase: the spiritual ears and eyes awaken, and then the soul of man can perceive in its environment what is otherwise concealed. The awakening of the faculties slumbering in the soul is possible; it is possible for man to acquire an instrument whereby he call look into spiritual causes, just as with his physical instruments he looks into the physical world. We have all kinds of instruments for the perception of the physical world—and for perception of the spiritual world there is also an instrument—namely, man himself, transformed. From the standpoint of spiritual science the most important thing of all is that the word "Evolution" should be taken in all seriousness—"Evolution," which is a kind of magic word on many lips. It is not difficult today to perceive how the imperfect continually develops and evolves, and this evolution is carefully followed up in external Natural Science. To this conception Anthroposophy would not set up the slightest opposition where it remains in the region of scientific facts. But Anthroposophy takes the word "Evolution" in its full meaning—and so seriously that it points to those faculties which lie in the soul of man by means of which he can become aware of the Spiritual world. Spiritual beings are the foundation and basis of the physical world, and man only needs organs to be able to perceive them. I must here again lay stress upon the fact that today only a few men are in a position to transform their souls in this way. It requires a highly developed soul whose spiritual eyes are open before investigation of the spiritual world can be undertaken and information as to the events and beings there obtained. But if facts about the higher worlds are made manifest, then all that is necessary for the understanding of what is told by the spiritual investigator is healthy discernment, free from all bias pertaining to the intellect or to human logic. There is no justification for criticizing the use of spiritual investigation, because we cannot see for ourselves. How many men are able to form a clear conception of Ernst Haeckel's researches and follow them up? It is exactly the same in regard to research in the region of senselife, where what is illuminated by the understanding passes over into the consciousness, as it is in regard to what the spiritual investigator has to say about the information he has gained in the supersensible world. That which is known as the supersensible world through direct perception and human powers of cognition must pass over into the universal consciousness of mankind as a result of the Anthroposophical conception of the world.

On the one hand then, we have the ancient Bible bringing before us in its own way the secrets of the supersensible worlds and their connection with the sensible worlds, and on the other we have, in Spiritual Science, the direct experiences of the investigator in regard to the super-sensible world. This is surely a point of view similar to that which one finds at the dawn of modern Natural Science.

The question now arises: "What has Spiritual Science to say that is able to help us to understand the biblical truths?" We must here enter into details. We must above all point out that when as a result of the methods laid down by Spiritual Science, man awakens his soul faculties, he sees into the spiritual world and develops what in comparison to objective cognition is an Imaginative Knowledge. What is this Imaginative Knowledge? It has nothing in common with those vague fantasies readily associated with the word "Imagination" nor has it anything whatever to do with somnambulism and things of that nature, but fundamental to it is a strict discipline by means of which a man has to awaken these faculties. Let us proceed from external knowledge in order to make more intelligible what is really meant by "Imaginative Knowledge." What is characteristic of external objective cognition? There is, for example, the perception of a "table"; when the table is no longer before us there remains an idea, a concept of it, as a kind of echo. First, there is the object and then the image. Certain systems of philosophy affirm that everything is only image, conception. This is incorrect. Let us take, for example, the conception of red-hot steel or iron. The conception will not burn, but when we are faced by the reality the experience is different. The characteristic of objective cognition is that first the object is there and then the image is formed within us. Exactly the opposite process must take place in a man who wishes to penetrate into the higher world. He must first be able to transform his conceptual world in such a way that the conception may precede the perception. This faculty is developed by Meditation and Concentration, that is to say, by sinking the soul into the content of certain conceptions which do not correspond to any external reality. Just consider for a moment how much of what lives in the soul is dependent upon the fact of your having been born in a particular town on a particular day. Suppose that you had not been born on that day, and try to imagine what other experiences would then live within your soul and stream through it from morning to evening. In other words, make it clear to yourself how much of the content of the soul is dependent on your environment, and then let all that has stimulated you from outside pass away. Then try to think how much would still remain in the soul. All conceptions of the external world which flow into the soul must, day by day, be expelled from it and in their place there must live for a time the content of a conception that has not in any way been stimulated from without and that does not portray any external fact or event. Spiritual Science—if our search is sincere—gives many such conceptions and I will mention one as an example. I want to show you how the soul may gradually be led up into the higher worlds through certain definite conceptions. Such conceptions may be considered to be like letters of the alphabet. But in Spiritual Science there are not only twenty-two to twenty-seven letters but many hundreds, by means of which the soul learns to read in the spiritual world. Here is a simple example: suppose we take the well-known Rose Cross and in its simplest form, the black cross adorned with seven red roses. Very definite effects are produced if for a quarter of an hour each day the soul gives itself wholly up to the conception of this Rose Cross, excluding everything that acts as an external stimulus. In order to be able to understand what comes to pass in the soul as a result of this, let us consider intellectually the meaning of the Rose Cross. This is not the most important element, but we shall do it to show that it is possible to explain the meaning. I shall give it in the form of an instruction given by teacher to pupil. The teacher says to the pupil: "Look at the plant standing with its root in the ground and growing upward to the blossom. Compare the greater perfection of man standing before you, organized as he is, with the lesser perfection of the plant. Man has self-consciousness, has within him what we call an Ego, an "I." But because he has this higher principle within him he has had to accept in addition all that constitutes his lower nature, the passion of sense. The plant has no self-consciousness; it has no Ego; hence it is not yet burdened with desires, passions, or instincts. Its green beauty is there, chaste and pure. Look at the circulation of the chlorophyl fluid in the plant and then in man at the pulsation of the blood. That which in man constitutes his life of passions and instincts comes to expression in the plant as the blossom. In exchange for this man has won his self-consciousness. Now consider not only present-day man but look in a spiritual sense at a man of the far-distant future. He will develop, he will overcome, cleanse, and purify his desires and passions and will obtain a higher self-consciousness. Thus, spiritually, you can see a man who has once more attained to the purity of the plant-nature. But it is because he has reached a higher stage that his self-consciousness exists in this state of purity. His blood is as pure and chaste as the plant fluids. Take the red roses to be a prototype of what the blood will be at some future time, and in this way you have before you the prototype of higher man. In the Rose Cross you have a most beautiful paraphrase of Goethe's saying:—'The man who is without this dying and becoming is a sad stranger on this dark earth'! Dying and becoming—what does this mean? It means that in man there exists the possibility of growing out of and beyond himself. That which dies and is overcome is represented by the black cross which is the expression of his desires of senses. The blossoms in their purity are symbolical of the blood. The red roses and the black cross together represent the inner call to grow beyond oneself."

As I said, this intellectual explanation is not the most important element and it is only given in order that we may be able better to understand these things. In a Meditation of this kind the point is that we shall sink ourselves into the symbol, that it shall stand as a picture before us. And if it is said that a Rose Cross corresponds to nothing real, our answer must be that the whole significance lies not in the experience of something pertaining to the external world through the Rose Cross but that the effect of this Rose Cross upon the soul and its slumbering faculties is very real. No image pertaining to the external world could have the same effect as this image in all its varied aspects and in its nonreality. If the soul allows this image to work upon it, it makes greater and greater progress and is finally able to live in a world of conceptions that is at first really illusory; but when it has lived sufficiently long in this conceptual world with patience and energy, it has a significantly true experience. Spiritual realities, spiritual beings which otherwise are invisible emerge from the spiritual environment. And then the soul is able quite clearly to distinguish what is merely conception, illusion, from true and genuine reality.

Of course one must not be a visionary, for that is very dangerous; it is absolutely necessary to maintain reason and a sure foundation for one's experience. If a man dreams in a kind of fantasy, then it is not well with him, when the spiritual world breaks in upon his consciousness. But if he maintains a sense of absolute certainty in his perception of reality, then he knows how the spiritual events will be made manifest, and he ascends into the spiritual world. You will perhaps have surmised from what I have said that cognition of the spiritual world is quite different from that of the sense world. The spiritual world cannot be brought into the range of direct perception by means of conceptions having but one meaning, and anyone who thinks it possible to describe what he finds in the spiritual world in the same way as he would describe what he finds in the sense world simply has no knowledge of the nature of the spiritual world. The spiritual world can only be represented in pictures, and in imagery, which must be regarded merely as such. When the spiritual investigator looks into the spiritual world he sees the spiritual causes behind the physical phenomena, and he sees not only what underlies the present but what underlay the past. One thing above all else is manifest to him; namely, that man as he stands before us today as a physical being was not always a physical being. External Natural Science can only lead us back by way of physical phenomena to what man as a physical being once was, and the spiritual investigator has no objection to that. But what surrounds us physically has a spiritual origin. Man existed as a spiritual being before he became physical.

When the earth was not yet physical, it existed in the bosom of divine beings. As ice condenses from water, so did physical man condense from spiritual man. Spiritual Science shows that the physical is in perpetual contact with the spiritual. But what underlies the physical can only be expressed in pictures, if one wants to approximate to physical ideas.

What happens when a man has reattained the spiritual stage of evolution— what comes before him? In a certain sense the spiritual investigator rediscovers the Bible imagery, as given in the six or seven days of Creation. The pictures as given there actually appear before him. These pictures are not, of course, a description of physical occurrences, but the investigator who looks into the spiritual world sees in clairvoyant consciousness in how wonderful a way the writer of Genesis has portrayed in these pictures the formation of man from out of the Spirit. And it is marvelous how, point by point, agreement is established between what is so perceived by the spiritual investigator and the Bible imagery. The spiritual investigator can follow in just as unbiased a way as the Natural Scientist approaches the physical world. He does not derive his wisdom directly from the Bible, but he finds emphatic agreement with Bible imagery.

I will only mention one such point of agreement. When we go back to ancient times, it is seen that behind the evolution of man stand certain spiritual beings who are different from the beings who are there from a definite and later point of time onward. Many of you will know that man as he is today is a fourfold being, consisting of physical body, etheric body, astral body (the vehicle of joy, passions and so forth), and the Ego, the bearer of human self-consciousness. The three lower members, physical body, etheric body, and astral body, were in existence long before the Ego, which was incorporated into man last of all. Spiritual beings who are designated in the Bible as the Elohim worked on these three earlier principles. And when the Ego began to be incorporated into this threefold nature, another being from the spiritual world cooperated in the work of the Elohim. If we penetrate more deeply into the Bible we shall find that this Spiritual Being is given the name of Jehova, and rightly so. And in accordance with the inner principles of evolution itself we see that at a certain point in the narrative a new name is introduced in place of the old name of the God-head. We see, too, the circumstances surrounding the origin of man which is described in a twofold way in the Bible. For in point of fact man as a threefold being was dissolved into the universe: as a threefold being he came into existence afresh, and then from out of the transformed threefold man, the Ego developed. So that the cleft that would seem to lie between the first and second chapter of Genesis, and that has been the subject of so many false interpretations, is explained by spiritual investigation. It is only a question of rightly understanding the Bible and that is not very easy today. Spiritual Science shows that in the beginning higher Spiritual Beings were present; the descendants of these Beings are men; man has emerged from the bosom of Divine Spiritual Beings. We may speak of man as the descendant of the Gods in the same sense as we speak of the child being the descendant of his parents. From the standpoint of Spiritual Science we must look upon the human being standing before us as an Earth-man, the descendant of divine-spiritual beings.

Does the Bible tell us anything about this? Indeed it does, but we first must learn how to read it. The fourth sentence of the Second Chapter of Genesis runs: "These are the generations of the heavens" . . . and so on. This sentence is misleading, for it does not give what is really to be found at this place in the Bible. The text ought really to stand as follows: "What follow here and will now be described are the descendants of the Heavens and the Earth as they were brought forth by the divine power." And by the words "the Heavens and the Earth," divine spiritual beings are meant, divine spiritual beings whose descendant is man. The Bible describes exactly what the spiritual investigator rediscovers independently. Many of those who fight against the Bible today are directing their attacks against something of which they have no real knowledge. They are tilting against straws. The Anthroposophical view is exactly expressed in this fourth sentence. We might show verse by verse through the Old and New Testaments how man, when he ascends into the spiritual world through his own faculties, rediscovers the results of his investigation in the Bible. It would lead us too far now if we tried to describe the New Testament in a similar way. In my book *Christianity as Mystical Fact*, the Lazarus miracle among others is given in its real form. The manner of treating such subjects today makes it impossible for us to get at their real meaning, for modern commentators of the Bible are naturally only able to find what accords with their own personal knowledge. Their knowledge does not transcend sense-cognition, hence the many contradictory interpretations and expositions of the individual Biblical "Authorities." The only qualified expositor of the Bible is a man who, independently of the Bible, is able to reach the same truths as are there contained. Let us take for sake of example an old book—Euclid's Geometry. Anyone who understands something of Geometry today will understand this book. But one would of course only place reliance on someone who had really studied Geometry today. When such a man comes to Euclid he will recognize his teachings to be true. In the same sense a man who approaches the Bible with philological knowledge only can never be a real "Authority." Only a man who is able to create the wisdom from out of his own being can be a real Authority on the Bible.

It may be said then that the Bible is intelligible to a man who can penetrate into the spiritual world, who can receive its influences into himself. The Bible induces in such a man an absolute certainty that it is written by Initiates and inspired souls; a man who can today penetrate into the spiritual world understands the great Scribes of the Bible. He knows them to have been true Initiates, "awakened souls" who have written down their experiences from the levels of the spiritual worlds; if he knows this, he also knows what is hidden within their words.

I would like here to mention an experience of my own in reference to another matter. When I was engaged on special work in the Goethe Archives in Weimar, I tried to prove something quite externally. You all know Goethe's beautiful prose "Hymn to Nature," "Oh Nature we are encircled and embraced by thee," and so on. This hymn depicts in beautiful words that everything given to us by Nature is given in Love, that Love is the crown of Nature. This composition was lost sight of for a time by Goethe himself, and when he was an old man and what remained of his literary work was given over to the Duchess Amelia, it was found. Goethe was questioned about it, and said "Yes, I recognize the idea that came to me then." The composition was accepted as having been written by Goethe until certain hair-splitters refused to admit that he was the author and attributed it to someone else. My purpose was to investigate the truth about this composition. It had come to my knowledge that at an early period of his life Goethe had with him a young man called Tobler, who had an exceedingly good memory. During their walks together Goethe had elaborated his idea, Tobler had thoroughly assimilated it, and because of his marvelous memory he had been able afterward to write it down very nearly word for word. I tried to show that a great deal of what is to be found in Goethe's conceptions later on is intelligible in the light of this composition. The point is that someone other than Goethe had penned it on paper, but the idea itself in its phrasing and articulation was Goethe's—and that is what I tried to make clear. Later on, when my work was published, a celebrated Goethean scholar came to me and said: "We owe you a debt of gratitude for throwing light upon the subject, for now we know that this composition is by Tobler." You may well imagine how amused I was! This is how things present themselves to the minds of people who are at pains to prove that in the course of time some particular portion of the Bible was written by one man or another. Some people consider the most important thing to be who finally did the writing and not which Spirit was the origin and source. But with us the essential thing is to understand how the Bible was able to come into being from the Spirits of those who looked into the Spiritual World and experienced it.

And now let us examine whether there is in the Bible itself anything that explains this way of looking at things. The Old Testament lends itself to a great deal of controversy, for the events there have grown dim. But it will be clear to anyone who does not want to wrangle that the Old Testament faithfully describes the significant process of the penetration of the Ego into the entire nature and being of man. Anyone who from the point of view of Spiritual Science reads of the call to Moses at the Burning Bush will understand that in reality Moses was then raised into the Spiritual world. When God appeared to Moses in the Burning Bush, Moses asked: "Who shall I say to the people hath sent me?" God said: "Tell them that One Who can say 'I am' hath sent thee." And if we follow up the whole process of the incorporation of the Ego, step by step, then the Bible illuminates what is found in Spiritual Science independently.

But something else is evident as well, namely, that from a Christian point of view the Bible should not be considered from the same point of view as other historical documents. If we consider the figure of Paul we can learn a great deal that can lead us to this realization. When we study the earliest form in which Christianity was promulgated, from which all its later forms are derived, we shall find that none of the Gospel narratives are given by Paul at all but that he speaks of something quite different. What gave the impulse to Paul? How did this unique Apostle acquire his understanding of the Christ? Simply and solely as a consequence of the event of Damascus, that is, not as a result of physical but of supersensible truths. Now what is at the basis of the teaching of Paul? It is the knowledge that the Christ—although he was crucified—lives; the event of Damascus reveals Christ as a Living Being who can appear to men who ascend to him; it reveals moreover that there is in very truth a spiritual world. And Paul makes a parallel between Christ's appearance to him and His appearance to others. He says: "First He appeared to Cephas, then to the Twelve, then to five hundred Brethren at once, to James and then all the Apostles, and last of all to me also as to one born out of due time." This reference by Paul to "one born out of due time" is strange. But this very expression is evidence to experienced Initiates that Paul speaks with perfect knowledge of Spiritual Science. He says that he is "born out of due time," and from this we realize that his illumination is to be traced back to a certain fact. I will just hint at the meaning. He means to explain in these words that because he has been born out of due time he is less entangled in material existence. He traces back his illumination to his knowledge: the Christ lives and is here. He shows that he bases his Christianity upon this supersensible truth and that it is conviction acquired as the result of direct perception. The earliest form of Christianity as it spread abroad is based upon supersensible facts. We could show that what is contained in the John Gospel is based upon supersensible impressions which the writer of that Gospel gives as his own experience, and realizing that originally it was possible for Christianity to win belief on the basis of supersensible experiences of men who were able to look into the spiritual worlds, we can no longer imagine that it is right to apply to the Bible the same standard as we apply to other external documents.

Anyone who examines the Gospels with the same methods as he employs in the case of other documents is confronted by something whose inner contents he can never fathom. But a man who penetrates into the experiences of the writers of the Gospels will be led into the spiritual world and to those personalities who have built up their knowledge and their wisdom from out of the spiritual world and have given them to us.

We should realize that those from whom the Gospels proceeded were Initiates, awakened souls, taking into consideration as well that there may be different stages of awakening. Just imagine that different people are describing a landscape from a mountain; one stands at the bottom, another in the middle, and another at the summit. Each of these men will describe the landscape differently, according to his point of view. This is how the spiritual investigator looks at the four Gospels. The writers of the four Gospels were Initiates of different degrees. It is understandable that there may be external contradictions, just as there would be in the description of a landscape from a mountain. The deepest of all is the Gospel of John. The writer of the John Gospel was the most deeply initiated into the mysteries of what took place in Palestine at the beginning of our era because he wrote from the summit of the mountain.

Spiritual Science is able to elucidate the Gospels fully and to prove that the various contradictions in Genesis at the beginning of the Old Testament disappear. Direct perception, then, of the spiritual worlds brings us again to an understanding of the Bible which is a most wonderful document. A man who engages in spiritual investigation will find that there are four standpoints to be distinguished among men who approach the study of the Bible. The first is the standpoint of the naive believer, who has faith in the Bible as it stands and pays no attention to any other consideration; the second is that of "clever" people who stand neither on the ground of historical research, nor of Bible analysis, nor of Natural Science. They say: "We cannot recognize the Bible to be a uniform document." And when such men realize that Natural Science contradicts the Bible they become "Free Thinkers," so-called Free Spirits. They are in most cases honest, sincere seekers after truth. But then we come to something that transcends the standpoint of the "clever" people. Many Free Thinkers have held the point of view that the Bible is only suitable for a childlike stage of human evolution and cannot hold its own against Science. But after a time it strikes them that much of what is given in the Bible has a figurative sense, that it is a garment woven around experiences. This is the third standpoint—that of the Symbolist. Here a pure arbitrariness reigns, and the view that the Bible is to be understood symbolically.

The fourth standpoint is that of Spiritual Science. Here there is no longer ambiguity but in a certain sense literal interpretation of what is said in the Bible. We are brought back again to the Bible in order to understand it in a real sense. An important task of Spiritual Science is to restore the Bible to its real position. It will be a happy day when we hear in modern words what really is to be found in the Bible, different, indeed, from all that is said today.

We may pass from sentence to sentence and we shall see that the Bible everywhere contains a message to Initiates from Initiates; awakened souls speak to awakened souls. Spiritual investigation does not in any way alienate us from the Bible. A man who approaches the Bible by spiritual investigation experiences the fact that details become clear to him about which he formally had doubts because he could not understand them. It becomes evident that it was his fault when he was not able to understand. Now, however, he understands what once escaped him, and he gradually works through to a point of view where he says: "Now I understand certain things and see their deep content: others, again appear to be incredible. But just as formerly I did not understand what is now clear to me, so later I shall discover that it has a deep import." And then such a man will with gratitude accept what hashes up in him, leaving to the future what he cannot yet explain.

The Bible in all its depth will be revealed only in the future, when spiritual investigation, independently of any kind of tradition, penetrates into the spiritual facts and is able to show mankind what this document really contains. Then it will no longer seem unintelligible, for we shall feel united with what streamed into spiritual culture through those who wrote it down. In our age it is possible for us, through Initiation, again to investigate the spiritual world. Looking back to the past we feel ourselves united with those who have gone before us, for we can show how step by step they communicated what they had received in the spiritual world. We can promise that the Bible will prove itself to be the most profound document of humanity, the deepest source of our civilization. Spiritual Science will be able to restore this knowledge. And, however much bigoted people may say, "The Bible does not need such a complicated explanation—it is the very simplicity that is right,"it will be realized some day that the Bible, even when it is not fully understood, works upon every heart by virtue of its intrinsic mysteries. It will be realized too that not only is its simplicity within our grasp but that no wisdom is really adequate for a full understanding of it. The Bible is a most profound document not only for simple folk but also for the wisest of the wise. Wisdom, therefore, investigated spiritually and independently, will lead back to the Bible. And Spiritual Science, apart from everything else that it has to bring to humanity, will be the means of accomplishing a reconquest of the Bible.

5

CHRIST AND THE COMING NEW AGE

Alice Bailey

A s we come to an end of our consideration of the world today and its dominating rays, working through the nations and conditioning the people, there
is a final point which I would like to make; it lies in the realm of religion and
concerns the significance of Christmas. From the very night of time, as well you
know, the period wherein the sun moves northward again has been regarded as a
festival season; for thousands of years it has been associated with the coming of
the Sun-God to save the world, to bring light and fruitfulness to the Earth and
through the work of the Son of God to bring hope to humanity. The Christmas
season is regarded by those who do not know any better as uniquely the Festival
of the Christ, and this the Christian churches have emphasized and to this all
churchmen testify. This is both true and false. The Founder of the Christian
Church —God in the flesh—availed Himself of this period and came to us in the
dark of the year and initiated a new era in which light was to be the distinguishing note. This has been true from several angles, even from the purely physical, for today we have a lighted world; everywhere lights are to be seen and the
pitch dark nights of olden times are fast disappearing. Light has also descended
on the earth in the form of the "light of knowledge." Today, education whose
objective is to lead all men on to a "lighted way," is the keynote of our civilization and is a major preoccupation in all countries. The removal of illiteracy, the
development of a true culture, and the ascertaining of truth in all fields of thought

From Alice Bailey (Djwhal Khul), *The Destiny of the Nations* (New York: Lucis).

and of research are of paramount importance in all lands. Thus, when Christ proclaimed (as He assuredly did), along with all world Saviors and Sun-Gods, that He was the Light of the worlds, He inaugurated a marvelous period in which humanity has been widely and universally enlightened. This period dates from Christmas Day, two thousand years ago, in Palestine. That was the greatest of all Christmas Days and its emanating influence was more potent than was any previous arrival of a Bearer of Light, because humanity was more ready for the light. Christ came in the sign of Pisces, the Fishes—the sign of the divine Intermediary in the highest sense, or of the medium in the lower; it is the sign of many of the world Saviors and of those Revealers of divinity Who establish world relationships. I would have you note that phrase. The major impulse driving the Christ toward special work was the desire to establish right human relations; it is also the desire—realized or unrealized—of humanity, and we know that some day the Desire of all nations will come, that right human relations will be found everywhere and that goodwill will implement that fulfillment, leading to peace in all lands and among all peoples.

Down through the ages, Christmas Day has been recognized and kept as a season of new beginnings, of better human contacts, and of happier relations among families and communities. Yet just as the churches have descended into a profoundly materialistic presentation of Christianity, so the simple Christmas Day which would have pleased the heart of Christ has degenerated into an orgy of spending, of acquiring good things, and is regarded as a period which is "good for trade." We need, therefore, to remember that when any phase of life-inspired religion is interpreted entirely materially, when any civilization and culture loses its sense of spiritual values and responds mainly to the material values, then it has served its usefulness and must pass away, and this in the interests of life itself and progress.

The message of the birth of Christ rings ever new but is not today understood. The emphasis during the Aquarian Age, the age into which we are fast entering, will shift away from Bethlehem to Jerusalem and from the infant Savior to the Risen Christ. Pisces has seen, during two thousand years, the spreading light; Aquarius will see the Rising Light, and of both of these the Christ is the eternal symbol.

The ancient story of the Birth will become universalized and be seen as the story of every disciple and initiate who takes the first initiation and in his time and place becomes a server and a light-bearer. In the Aquarian Age two momentous developments will take place:

The Birth Initiation will condition human thinking and aspiration everywhere.

The religion of the Risen Christ, and not of the newly born Christ or of the crucified Christ, will be the distinctive keynote.

The purpose of Meditation Mount is to form groups of people around the world who med-itate on the 6 Laws and Principles of Soul inspired living that will help to create a new world and pave the way for the reappearance of the Christ. These Laws and Principles are: The Law of Right Human Relations & The Principle of Goodwill, The Law of Group Endeavor & The Principle of Unanimity, The Law of Spiritual Approach & The Principle of Essential Divinity.

It is seldom realized that hundreds of thousands of people in every land have taken, or are preparing to take, this first initiation, called the Birth at Bethlehem, the House of Bread. Humanity, the world disciple, is now ready for this. Indica-tions of the accuracy of the above statement can be seen in the reorientation of people everywhere to things spiritual, their interest in human good and human welfare, the perseverance they show in their search for light and their longing and desire for a true peace, based on right human relations, implemented by goodwill. This "mind as it is in Christ" can be seen in their revolt against mate-rialistic religion and in the widespread effort to be seen in Europe and elsewhere to return the land (Mother-Earth, the true Virgin Mary) to the people. It can be seen in the constant movement of people throughout the world from place to place, symbolized in the Gospel story by the journey of Mary with the infant Jesus into Egypt.

Then followed, as we are told in the New Testament, a cycle of thirty years wherein all we know is that the infant Jesus grew to manhood and could then take the second initiation, the Baptism in Jordan, and begin His public service. Today the many who in this life have taken the first initiation are entering the long silence of that symbolic thirty years wherein they too will grow to manhood and take the second initiation. This initiation demonstrates the complete control of the emotional nature and of all Piscean characteristics. The thirty years can be looked upon as a period of spiritual unfoldment during the three divisions into which Aquarius (and consequently the New Age now upon us) will be divided. I refer to what is technically known as the three decans of each sign. In this sign the waters of the Piscean age will, symbolically speaking, be absorbed into the water pot carried on the shoulder of Aquarius in the symbol which is distinctive of this sign, for Aquarius is the water-carrier, bringing the water of life to the people—life more abundantly.

In the Aquarian Age, the Risen Christ is Himself the Water-Carrier; He will not this time demonstrate the perfected life of a Son of God, which was His main mission before; He will appear as the supreme Head of the Spiritual Hierarchy, meeting the need of the thirsty nations of the world—thirsty for truth, for right human relations, and for loving understanding. He will be recognized this time by all and in His Own Person will testify to the fact of the resurrection and hence demonstrate the paralleling fact of the immortality of the soul, of the spiritual man. The emphasis during the past two thousand years has been on death; it has colored all the teaching of the orthodox churches; only one day in the year has been dedicated to the thought of the resurrection. The emphasis in the Aquarian Age will be on life and freedom from the tomb of matter, and this is the note which will distinguish the new world religion from all that have preceded it.

The Festival of Easter and the Feast of Pentecost will be the two outstanding days of the religious year. Pentecost is, as you must well know, the symbol of right human relations in which all men and nations will understand each other and—though speaking in many and diverse languages—will know only one spiritual speech.

It is significant that two important episodes are related in the final part of the Gospel story—one preceding and one following immediately after the apparent death of Christ. They are:

> The story of the upper chamber to which the man carrying the water pot and typifying Aquarius led the disciples, and in which the first communion service was held, participated in by all and foretelling that great relationship which will distinguish humanity in the coming age, after the tests of the Piscean Age. Such a communion service has never yet been held, but the New Age will see it take place.

> The story of the upper chamber in which the disciples met and arrived at a true recognition of the Risen Christ and at a perfect and complete understanding of each other in spite of the symbolic diversity of tongues. They had a touch of prevision, of prophetic insight, and foresaw a little of the wonder of the Aquarian Age.

The vision in men's minds today is that of the Aquarian Age, even if they recognize it not. The future will see right relationships, true communion, a sharing of all things (wine, the blood, the life and bread, economic satisfaction) and goodwill; we have also a picture of the future of humanity when all nations are united in complete understanding and the diversity of languages—symbolic of differing traditions, cultures, civilizations, and points of view—will provide no barrier to right human relations. At the center of each of these pictures is to be found the Christ. Thus the expressed aims and efforts of the United Nations will be eventually brought to fruition and a new church of God, gathered out of all religions and spiritual groups, will untidily bring to an end the great heresy of separateness. Love, unity, and the Risen Christ will be present, and He will demonstrate to us the perfect life.

6

THE GREAT INVOCATION

Alice Bailey

THE GREAT INVOCATION

From the point of Light within the Mind of God
Let light stream forth into the minds of men.
Let Light descend on Earth.
From the point of Love within the Heart of God
Let love stream forth into the hearts of men.
May Christ return to Earth.
From the center where the Will of God is known
Let purpose guide the little wills of men—
The purpose which the Masters know and serve.
From the center which we call the race of men
Let the Plan of Love and Light work out
And may it seal the door where evil dwells.
Let Light and Love and Power restore the Plan on Earth.

The above Invocation or Prayer does not belong to any person or group but to all humanity. The beauty and the strength of this Invocation lies in its simplicity, and in its expression of certain central truths which all men, innately and normally, accept—the truth of the existence of a basic Intelligence to Whom we vaguely

From Alice Bailey (Djwhal Khul), *The Destiny of the Nations* (New York: Lucis, 1949).

give the name of God; the truth that behind all outer seeming, the motivating power of the universe is Love; the truth that a great Individuality came to earth, called by Christians, the Christ, and embodied that love so that we could understand; the truth that both love and intelligence are effects of what is called the Will of God; and finally the self-evident truth that only through humanity itself can the Divine Plan work out.

SPIRITUALISM/
NEW THOUGHT

DECLARATION OF PRINCIPLES

National Spiritualist Association of Churches

THE SPIRITUALIST "DECLARATION OF PRINCIPLES"

1. We believe in Infinite Intelligence.

2. We believe that the phenomena of Nature, both physical and spiritual, are the expression of Infinite Intelligence.

3. We affirm that a correct understanding of such expression and living in accordance therewith constitute true religion.

4. We affirm that the existence and personal identity of the individual continue after the change called death.

5. We affirm that communication with the so-called dead is a fact, scientifically proven by the phenomena of Spiritualism.

6. We believe that the highest morality is contained in the Golden Rule: "Whatsoever ye would that others should do unto you, do ye also unto them."

Composed at the first meeting of the National Association of Spiritualists (now the National Spiritualist Association of Churches) in Chicago in the late nineteenth century.

7. We affirm the moral responsibility of the individual, and that he makes his own happiness or unhappiness as he obeys or disobeys Nature's physical and spiritual laws.

8. We affirm that the doorway to reformation is never closed against any human soul here or hereafter.

9. We affirm that the precept of Prophecy and Healing contained in the Bible is a divine attribute proven through Mediumship.

[The last three articles, which were added later, reflect the later move away from an emphasis on remarkable phenomena and toward an emphasis on philosophical development.—*Ed.*]

THE STATEMENT
OF BEING

Emma Curtis Hopkins

Let this mind be in you which was also in Christ Jesus.
—Philippians 2:5

There are twelve doctrines of Jesus Christ. This is to say that the one method of Jesus Christ is presented in twelve statements or settings. A diamond has many polished facets and it takes them all to make it shine in its full beauty. The truth has many ways in which it can be expressed and all are required if some people are to believe in its beauty and brightness. Each of the twelve lessons sets forth the whole doctrine in its own way.

We will consider the first lesson. It is the first idea with which mind everywhere, in all ages, has begun when proclaiming that outside of, and greater than any power exhibited by anything in nature, or in man, is a being called God.

The first lesson in Truth is the word "God." Have you ever heard that there is a marvelous power in every word? It contains its own potentiality. You can see that if every word contains its own potentiality, then that word which all the world agrees contains the greatest power must be the greatest word. Plotinus (250 AD) lost himself seven times in a trance of ecstasy by thinking over the word "God" in his mind. God was the beginning of all. God is the presence of all. The use of the word by Plotinus, Porphyr, and Spinoza did not solve the mystery of existence for them, however. They yielded to death and feebleness, even

From Emma Curtis Hopkins, chapter 1 in *Scientific Christian Mental Practice* (Marina del Ray, CA: DeVorss & Company, 1974).

falling into sickness sometimes, like other men and women. There was something lacking in their teaching, something lacking in their understanding of God, for the ideal of God is told as, "My words are life unto those that find them and health to all their flesh."

Jesus Christ had quite a different idea from these men, even though they loved the name of God so devoutly. "In my name preach the gospel, in my name heal the sick." "If a man keep my sayings he will never see death." What name was that which Jesus Christ used, which had such omnipotent energy that even when it was spoken it would heal the sick and raise the dead? The Name is within every mind.

If it is spoken it will be like letting loose the electricity which the physicist stored in batteries.

It has been taught from the remotest times that we have the Name stored within us as concealed energy. It can perform twelve great works, by our words, whenever we use it, even without very close relation to it. If we were to use that Name directly it would instantly work all the miracles recorded of all the mighty men of old. The speaking of words for performing cures is an ancient custom. The Zend-Avesta tells us that it is by the Divine Word that the sick are most surely cured. Sometimes the word is thought in the silent mind. It is not always by the repetition of our words that the cures are wrought. It is by the whole lines of reasoning. The study of the lines of reasoning which bring out your healing power is called the study of metaphysics. The word metaphysical means "above and away from the physical."

Thoughts are ideas. We study ideas. But ideas bear an important relation to each other. They make a course of reasoning. Some people study mathematics to train their mind to logical processes. But the study of mathematics does not make thoughts and words powerful to heal the sick. Some people have believed that there is a magical power in numbers just as there is great potency in words. Cornelius Agrippa of Cologne (1486) ascribed to numbers an efficacy. But no mathematician is a healer because of his mathematics. He must use the Healing Word or the reasoning which brings down somewhat of the power of the Healing Word.

You may be filled with wonder as to what the Healing Word or Name can be. It certainly is not the word "God," for these men who used that word continually were not mighty healers. Spiritual Science does not tell you the Name. It gives you the most direct reasoning which the word "God" brings out and consequently gives the best healing power of any line of reasoning in the world.

There are twelve points of doctrine put forth in these lessons in plain terms. All the time you can trace other points of the same doctrine, finer and more subtle, streaming under them like fires from purer altars of meaning than words can kindle. The very finest fires of meaning I cannot tell you in words; you must be of an esoteric or spiritual nature to read them while I am talking.

We call metaphysics the Science of Life, because to know pure metaphysics is to renew the life and make death and accident impossible.

We call metaphysics the Science of Health, because to know metaphysics is to be perfectly well and free from liability to sickness or disease of any kind.

We call metaphysics the Science of Strength, because to know metaphysics is to be strong beyond any strength you have ever dreamed of. Nothing is too hard for those who are strong with the strength of metaphysics.

We call metaphysics the Science of Support, because whoever studies the science finds his support coming to him in a new way, and he cannot come to actual want, no matter who would have failed if they had been put in his place. The prophecy of Jeremiah and of Isaiah comes to pass to whoever studies metaphysics without blundering in his reasonings. "Bread shall be given him, his waters shall be sure."

We call metaphysics the Science of Defense or Protection, for no ill can come nigh the dwelling of one who puts his trust in the principle taught by this science. "His place of defense shall be the munitions of rocks."

This science of Life, Truth, Love, Substance, and Intelligence is for all who look into it profoundly. Outside of metaphysics the world is seeking for for its life by physical performances; working at machinery, books, commerce, cooking, washing, eating, governing one another, employing one another, killing and using animals, wearing flesh and bones into the grave to make a living. But the whole system of living by material efforts is wrong. "Turn unto Me, for why will ye die?" said the Spirit. Death is the reward of hard effort to live by material actions. If you will look into the Science of Spirit you will see that your life is meant to be sustained by the Science of God and not by the science of matter. God is Spirit, therefore it is the Science of Spirit which we are to study when we open the reasoning with the word "God." God is the name for that Intelligence which out of its own substance bestowed upon you that intelligence you now have. Intelligence is Mind. Thus it is plain that by opening our study with the word "God" we are beginning the study of Mind.

By Mind alone we are taught we are to live and be strong. By Mind alone we are supported and defended. The further on we get in the Science, the more confident we become that it is by the words that proceed from the mouth of God that we are to live. Jesus Christ taught this. He was ministered by angels and said: "Man shall not live by bread alone, but by every word that proceedeth out of the mouth of God." This means that God has a way of giving freely from His Mind words that will make alive. Jesus Christ told the people that His words were Life. He spoke of the manna which the Jews had eaten while wandering forty years in the wilderness as being so far from the real bread that the Jews all died. He showed over and over again that the Word is a bread that will keep life in the body forever. "He that eateth of this bread shall live forever."

As nearly as possible, the twelve lessons which we now begin will take the

absolute meanings of the words of Jesus Christ. If we take the absolute meanings, dear friends, we are obliged to say that our life needs no material or physical effort to keep it forever. It needs only the true Word of God. It is not profitable to say that our life needs no material support. It is only profitable to say
that our life does need the Word of God. The Word of God *is* Truth. God works
only in Truth.

We may throw true words down into the arena of human life and their power
will be God's power. The power of God is freedom. Jesus Christ said that all who
knew Truth would be free. What do you want to be free from? Sin, sickness,
death; all the evil men fear is contained in these three words. From these the
Word of God sets absolutely free. Miracles of healing have been worked by thousands of men and women who taught true words concerning God in some of the
statements we find set forth in order by Spiritual Science.

Each lesson has this healing strength. Keep your mind open and free to
receive that lesson which fits your own disposition best. No matter what type or
character you are or what disposition of mind you have, I tell you that one of these
lessons strikes your keynote, and by speaking over and over the words which that
one lesson explains, you will let the fire of your own native healing gift from
Jehovah kindle health within your own body and in those of all your neighbors.

Elisha cured a terrible case of leprosy by one of these lessons. It was probably the second lesson. He raised the Shunamite woman's child to life by one of
these lessons. It was probably the third lesson. He increased the loaves of bread
to feed a hundred men. This was the fourth lesson. He would not have called it
the fourth lesson, but he would have felt in his mind all the strength of the fourth
lesson as we have it.

The first lesson finds out what your mind is seeking and names it. Can you
name now just exactly what your mind is seeking? You would soon be set on the
right track for finding what you are seeking if you could name what you want.
The naming of what the mind of the whole world is seeking is the first statement
of Jesus Christ and is the first lesson of Moses. It is the foundation thought even
in the minds of the insects. It is the Good.

Are you not seeking Good? Why do you move your right hand? You move
it to get your Good. Why do you breathe? You breathe to get your Good. Why do
the stones lie still and wait? They are waiting for their Good. Why does the fly?
It flies for its Good. Everything moves and waits for its Good. So you see that
the Good draws everything. The Good which you and I want governs everything
we do. Therefore the Good which you are seeking is your God.

Spinoza was called the God-intoxicated man, because he spoke the word
"God" so much. I am convinced that if he spoke the word Good, instead of the
word "God," he would have come into a nearer relation to his God.

Moses says that God (Good) created. The Good which you are seeking created you. Just that Good which you want is the combination of words which

brought you forth. The honest statement that "My Good is my God" has the power to set the mind to a key which is nearer to its normal tone than it is now thinking. John said that in the beginning was the Word, and the Word was God. He also said that out of the Word all things were made and without the Word was nothing made. Paul said that a veil is forever over the face when the Word is read because so many untruthful things have been spoken of God.

If you take the word "God" for your starting point, you will not start so near the foundation feeling of your mind as you will if you take the word *Good*. "I am seeking my Good, therefore I am seeking my God." The devout poet who wrote, "I was athirst for thee, the living God," would have found healing power beginning to stream forth into his life like a fine white fire if he had struck his lyre to the chord, "I seek my Good. My Good is my God." Therefore in the Science of Mind you may take for your first idea one word. It is the word "Good." In the science of words you may take the word "Good" and let it lie before you like a great white stone. It has a revealing power which the word "God" has not. John the Revelator speaks of the white stone. The white stone is a word. The word is Good. It is the name of what you want. It is the nearest approach to expressing what is in our mind that Science has thus far given us. It is evident that Science will give us the inner stone if we use the outer stone wisely. As we acknowledge that the Good we are seeking must be our God, because it pulls and pushes us all the time to see if we cannot come nearer to it, we must find ourselves better and better satisfied.

The acknowledgment that "I am seeking my Good, and my Good is my God" is telling a simple truth. It is so simple that the tiniest child can say, "I am seeking my Good, and my Good is my God, because it draws and pushes and moves me on." The child who tells this simple truth is telling aloud what the little stones are whispering without words, and the little baby who lisps this simple truth will be fed and clothed by the ever drawing closer and closer to him of his Good.

If I should take the unspoken sentence which lies like a hidden jewel under the jagged covering of your thoughts about the things you do not like, I would read it, "There is Good for me and I ought to have it." There is nothing but has in itself the conviction that there is Good belonging to it that it ought to have. The prince reels from the banquet hall, seeking the Good he believes he ought to have. The thief runs from the daylight, seeking the Good he thinks he ought to have. But none of them speaks the simple truth about his movements. If any one of them did he would come nearer to finding his Good. God, the Omnipotent Good, works through the word of Truth. Get to speaking the word of Truth from the first to the last statement and God will be found working for you and through you, with almighty power.

The first name of God is Good, and the first name of the Good is God. "There is Good for me and I ought to have it," says the unconscious instinct of the worm crawling at your feet. When you look at the worm and tell the truth about it, why it moves and why it keeps still, you will be in league with its life. It will feel your unity with it. When you look at a drunkard, or miser, you will say he is seeking his Good. His heart will be better satisfied the instant you speak out what his unspoken instinct is feeling. He does not say so. If he should say so his life would come nearer to being a satisfying one. The moment anybody speaks out the Truth of his life he has spoken the Omnipotent Principle. The unconscious truth is that there is Good for me and I ought to have it. Nothing can kill that unconscious feeling. It is indestructible. It is omnipotent. Thus the Omnipotent Truth is kept hidden in the stillness of the mind of man and the mind of the rocks. The Omnipotent Truth shall not be hidden in the stillness any longer, and the satisfaction of the living things will come when they are told that the reason they move, or do not move, is for one Good. In the Scriptures we read, "Prove me . . . and I will pour you out a blessing." "In all thy ways acknowledge Him and He will direct thy paths." To acknowledge God is to admit we are seeking our Good. It is well to give one day a week to acknowledging that we are seeking for our Good. We tell what our Good is. Is not our Good the free life we want? Do we want a burdened, obstructed, hampered life? Out of the word "Good" name a good which is Good to you.

The free life of the lily is the name of its Good. As the lily works out its life problem, it is telling as plainly as it can speak that its Good is its free life. You may name your Good as your free life. When you speak for yourself you speak for the world. It is the one chord to which, if you speak it, all nature will spring free. There will be no opposition to that truth when you speak it. You can name your Good as free health. All nature will say "Amen!" if you proclaim that the Good you are seeking is free health. Nothing wants its health interfered with; it wants unlimited health. There is a unity of feeling between you and the stones and the thief, when you tell aloud, or consiously, what they feel unconsciously about their health. The moment you feel this truth, and speak it, the chord between yourself and your neighbor chimes into one tone. You catch a new breath of health and your neighbor catches a new breath of health. Sometimes when you say to the sick man, mentally, that the Good he is seeking is his God, and God is free health, he will get well in five minutes. His mind was unconsciously groping around for the Divine Word that could heal him, and you spoke for him.

The prophet who felt there was something lacking in his life said: "We grope for the wall as the blind." It is better for us to speak our own words, but if somebody opens the door for us it will teach us to open the door ourselves. That is, if we do not speak our words and so are not satisfied with Good, another may speak, and our satisfaction will come.

When we say that the Good we are seeking is our free life, we certainly do feel the breath of new life blow through us. When we tell the lifeless plant that the Good it is seeking is its free life, and its Good is God, for God is its free life, we shall see the plant revive. Everything rises to acknowledge Truth. You see that is God, for Good is God. Sometimes you will feel the reviving life stream so hot, like a fine elixer, throughout your being, while you are naming God as free life, that whatever you touch will feel thrilled with a quick sense of pleasure. God works in Truth. Tell the Truth of God and the Omnipotent God is moving.

Nothing can resist the Very first proclamation of Truth if we let it be spoken through us. There are many names of our Good. They are all names to which all the universe of worlds nod their heads and oppose not when they are named. The irresistible name is Good. The irresistible name is God. It is an idea which is in everything, everywhere, and therefore you speak an omnipresent idea when you say: "I seek my Good; my Good is my God. My Good is my free life. My Good is my free health."

Another name of the Good we are seeking is strength. All things look for strength. They love strength. The baby laughs at every waft of strength through its little frame. The insect runs and rolls with speechless delight at every quiver of new strength. The Good it seeks is strength unlimited. It wants free, boundless strength. So do you. If you name your Good as unlimited strength, you will feel free and strong at once. As you look at some feeble woman and think further that the Good she is seeking is unlimited strength, she will let her mind shine with yours. She has felt that unconsciously. She will feel strength consciously. Everything you tell the Omnipotent Truth to, that its strength is God and God is its strength, will rise and be strong, and you will be stronger the more you proclaim the irresistible idea which all creation feels. It is only naming God. It is telling the truth of God.

Among the names of Good which we name, surely our heartstrings will chord with one which will bring satisfaction into our life. So hungry is the world for satisfaction that it has been set down that the problem of life is how to live and think so as to get satisfaction.

The sciences of man have not started their reasonings near enough to the foundation idea of mankind to obtain this end. At the word "God" many a mind rebels, because it has become bruised by trouble and disappointment. At the word that there is Good for everyone and everyone ought to have his Good, each mind agrees.

The principal point of truth is that satisfaction comes through Mind. Mind speaking truth through the lips, or thinking Truth consciously, can bring all the satisfaction to the world which the world is seeking. No material process can bring health. By a metaphysical process health will quicken and thrill mankind. Nothing material can strengthen people, but the Omnipotent Truth can strengthen them with all the power of Truth.

Another name for God is support. God is your support. You turn to the right or the left, you turn for sustaining. You breathe for support. You hope for support.

Thus one name for your Good is support. To tell any man who is poor that the Good which he is seeking is support is to tell him a truth which his mind has held unconsciously always. The chords of his mind chime when you speak the Truth that God is his support, and his support is his God, because it is Good. God works in Truth. That statement is Truth, therefore God works for that word. It is not Truth to say that man depends on any kind of work for his support. His work is not the Good he is seeking. God does not work in the lie which a man tells when he says he is seeking work. He must tell the Truth and God will work for him.

Support is another name for substance. Plato and Spinoza both called God the substance of the universe. All metaphysicians have called God the One Substance. The one support that man is looking for that will absolutely satisfy him is that kind of support which will not fail him. Let him sit down alone and tell the truth about what kind of support he is seeking. God works in Truth. Everybody, neatly, tries to cover up the main purpose of his life. He tells all kinds of stories to himself and others about what he is seeking. Often he tells that all he asks is just enough to feed and clothe and house his family. Let him tell the honest Truth—that he seeks for unlimited bounty. Nothing can possibly satisfy anybody short of unlimited supply. God is the idea of unlimited supply which men keep coverered so deeply within their minds. If you name your Good, do not fail to say: "My Good is my unlimited support, my unfailing support." The Good will soon bring you marvelous support. New provisions will be made for you. There is no limit to the bounty of Truth. The substance of Truth is shown by the happy prosperity which can come to you, and is sure to come, when you speak Truth.

Jesus Christ said that all who learned His doctrine would have a hundredfold more possessions in this life. Tolstoy, the Russian writer, declared that Christians do not have a hundredfold more than they would have if they were not Christians. But this is because they are not really Christians. In order to be a Christian one must tell the Truth of God. One Truth is that God the Good careth for us. We are told by Jesus Christ to take no care for ourselves. To sit down and proclaim to the universe that "My support is my Good, my Good is my God, thus God is my support" is to stir the air to work with mountains and seas to bring us our new provisions.

Jesus Christ said we would have tribulations while getting our Good support by telling the Truth, but he said: "Be not afraid, I have overcome." He meant He had come over all the worldly way of being supported by telling the Truth and that it would surely come out right with us. Tribulations are the oppositions which we meet by telling the world we get our support by thinking and speaking the Truth. Tribulations are the feelings we have when we first set forth as grown men and women into the way which is exactly opposite to out former way of thinking. It is a tribulation to attempt to cast away all anxiety. It is a tribulation to give up trying to get our living by our old mind.

After practicing the saying that your Good is your support, your old business will not be interesting to you. It will leave you, yet you will have your living. By and by you will have great and wonderful miracles of support come to you. Yet, for a long time, some of those who have told the Truth about their Good being unlimited supply may not have the faintest idea where their supplies are coming from. They need to say that their Good is Intelligence. This is a truth that will soon work out. There will come a time when they will know that their unlimited supplies are in certain places, and they need have no fear of ever losing sight of the rich provision of the Good. Good is God. God is Substance. God is Spirit. Therefore your supplies are to come from Spirit. Your supplies, coming from Spirit, are Spirit. It will not be a tribulation to practice providing for yourself by telling the Truth after a little while.

Another Good you are seeking is defense, protection. Another name of Good is defense. The movements of our bodies are all with the hope of being protected from evil. To be explicit in naming our Good, which we feel is for us, we should not forget to name the Good as defense. To every living creature we say, "God is your defense." It is another chord which the unconscious mind is glad to agree with. There is a bond of unity between us and all things. Fear leaves us. Fear leaves us by telling the Truth. Metaphysicians, in tracing the cause of evil conditions, have all agreed that fear of evil is the only evil. So, by telling the Truth that our Good is our defense, we see that in every place where we proclaim that defense, there is the Good we are seeking. That Good is our God, thus is our defense.

Love, Life, Truth, Substance, Intelligence, are names of our Good. We may tell that our Good is Truth. This will cause our lips to speak Truth. Pilate asked, "What is Truth?" The earliest Egyptians said, "Truth is God." The continual speaking for several years by the Christian metaphysicians that "Truth is God" finally brought them to where they could see exactly how Truth is God. It is because the telling of the exact Truth about what Good is, is an irresistible energy for bringing Good to pass.

Men formerly supposed it was truth to say sickness was good for them. They thought it was something sent of God. But God is Truth. Truth is a healing principle and not a sickening principle. They found much sickness following them up all the time. As soon as we say, "God is not the author of sickness; God is Good, Good is Truth, Truth is God," we are brought to where we cannot declare that sickness is Good. Good is God, therefore God is Health.

Love is the Good we are seeking. Love is the highest name of God. Love is the fulfilling of the law. At the height of our spiritual teachings we find God covering us with love. We find ourselves loving all things and all people. Edward Irvining put his hand on a dying boy's head and said, "God loves you." The boy lived.

It is well to say that God is unbounded, unlimited love. God is our love. There is an instinctive seeking of all things for love. Love is another name for life. Many a dying man has been saved by feeling his mother's soft kisses on his forehead. Many a woman has lifted her dying face and lived when sound of her son's voice was heard calling her name. Love is God. Do not forget to say,"The Good I am seeking is Love."

The heights and depths and splendors of Love have not been told. It is the name of God which Jesus Christ used. He said it so much that little children came close to His knees. Poor neglected women followed Him. Blind old beggars clung to His clothes. High dignitaries came by night to speak with Him. I do not suppose it would be possible to name the Good by the magic word Love too often. Love is not something which comes to us in any one man, woman, or child, and then goes away. That is only the sign of love. Love, that is God, is eternal, infinite.

The first lesson of the Science of Mind tells the foundation idea of Mind. It has been called the Statement of Being. Being is that which *is*. It is certain that the Good that is for us is the Good we ought to have. How shall we arrive at our Good? How shall we get hold of our Good? Not by working with our hands, for countless ages of labor have failed. It is by the Jesus Christ method only. The Jesus Christ method is the Truth method. Jesus Christ means Truth. The Jesus Christ method brings the fulfillment of all our expectations. "I know the thoughts that I think toward you, to bring you an expected end." This expectation of Good has been a long time waiting for us to declare what our expectations are. To expect Good and to be very definite in the mind that it *is* coming is to see it coming.

Many people would have their Good come instantly if they could name it and have a clear idea of how it ought to be. A little paralyzed girl heard the Paris doctor Bouchert praised so highly for his healing power that she went to see him, and by seeing him she was cured. A blind woman heard a shoemaker praised so highly for his power in prayer that she went to him, and she felt Jesus Christ's teachings so plainly that soon her eyes burst open. They both had a strong and clear idea of how it would seem to be well. They felt that those men could heal them.

If you have a clear idea of how sweet life, free and unburdened, must be, look to this Science to bring you this life. And declare very plainly that sweet, free life is your Good. It will come streaming through you like the elixir vitae of the ancients. Maxwell, the Scotch doctor, caught sight of this fine, fleet life-fire that streams through all the world.

If you think that health is Good, have a clear idea of how sweet, joyous health would feel. Name it as the name of Good. Have a clear idea of what is your Good. It will come and settle upon you. It will sift itself through you. It can be lapped up by all the little tongues of your system.

The word "Good" is the only word that can make all things. Good with its descriptions is as high as our mind and speech have ascended. There is no spot or place where the idea of Good as ours cannot come. It is the one conviction of animate and inanimate things. It has never been beaten out of anything. Being undefeated and never to be defeated, it is omnipotent. It always knows that it is right. It is omniscience. Know it, for it knows all things. Let the magic name Good be the name of all names in your mind. It is the name that Jesus Christ comes to be understood by. After speaking over the names of the Good, let your mind add the name of Jesus Christ. There was never any other character in history who gave orders to keep repeating his name. Many people will testify how wonderfully they have been led by repeating this name.

Another thing which the name of Jesus Christ teaches is humility and willingness. It is the meekness of character he manifested which brings us the victory over evil. He said, "The meek shall inherit the earth." Once a man who had become completely discouraged determined to let his dog lead him around, for he felt that his dog was more like God than he was. He went following the dog until it led him to a wise and good woman, who in turn led him to be a follower of Jesus Christ.

The meekness of obedience is the mystery of Godlines.

The Statement of Being was continually in the mouth of Jesus Christ. Let it be in your mouth also. Be definite when you give this statement of Good, which is the Statement of Being. Expect to see it work quickly. Truth is not slow. Truth is quick. With Truth, all is *now*. Jesus Christ said: "Now is the accepted time."

Truth does not have to make things new for you. In Truth it was so from the beginning, as the first verse of Moses reads. All Truth is waiting for you to say plainly what is your Good. The speaking out continuously what we have felt and thought intuitively is the first movement toward demonstration, toward manifestation, toward satisfaction.

Make now the statement of Good:

> The Good I am seeking is my God,
> My God is my Life.
> The Good I am seeking is my health,
> God is my health.
> The Good I am seeking is my strength,
> God is my strength.
> The Good I am seeking is my support,
> God is my support.
> The Good I am seeking is my defense,
> God is my defense. Life is God,
> Truth is God,
> Love is God.
> Substance is God.
> God is Intelligence,
> Omnipresent, Omnipotent, Omniscient.
> God is Life,

Omnipresent, Omnipotent, Omniscient.
God is Truth,
God is Love,
Omnipresent, Omnipotent, Omniscient.
God is Spirit,
Omnipresent, Omnipotent, Omniscient.

The name "OM" was a name of God which the ancient people of Asia used to repeat, and do even repeat now. They hold their breath while speaking it. It means: Good beyond Good. Far beyond even our ideas of Good, there is Infinite Good, awaiting our words.

Hosea exhorted Israel, "Take with you words and turn to the Lord." The first words we will take with which to go to the Lord are statements of our Good. That is as high as we can think or speak.

Have some special time to make the Statement of Being. This will make you a great thinker. The Mind of God will think through you. The words of God will speak through you. The joy of God will sing through you. The skill of Spirit will work miracles through you. The judgment and beauty of God will inspire you. The love of God will melt the hard lot of mankind before you. You will be so one with your words that you will be able to say with Jesus Christ, "I and the Father are one." You will drop off the garments of flesh. You will see that by speaking Truth you are Spirit and that by speaking Truth you are Omnipotent. God works through Truth.

If you give up your mind to Truth you are all God. Your substance being the Mind of God, by speaking Truth, you can see that no disease, neither death nor sin, can touch you anymore than disease or sin or death can touch God. It is through realizing this that so many strong young students have said that God had set his own name in their foreheads. They read where Moses was told to tell the Israelites that the name of the Good which was working for them was "I am that I am." If ever the name of this Good, which is your God, comes to you, do not hesitate to speak it. All the names of your Good which can name are right names. Write down the names of your Good which you are seeking. Think over the names of the Good which you are seeking. Speak aloud the names of the Good you are seeking. That will be naming God. And such a practice will be manifested in your life. God is not slow to come into the life of him who acknowledges the Good. God works only in Truth. All Truth is all God.

There are students arising who give all their mind, might, and strength to Truth. "If a man keep these sayings, he shall live forever."

9

LESSON ONE

Ernest Holmes

INTRODUCTION

In presenting these lessons in Mental Science to the public, it is my desire to make it possible for anyone, who cares to take the time to study them, to demonstrate the truths that will be discussed. It is, perhaps, hard to set down in writing a complete teaching in Mental Science that will not appear difficult to understand, but this could be said as well of any science, and the Science of Mind is no exception to the general rule.

SCIENCE

Science is knowledge of facts built around some proven principle. All that we know about any science is that certain things happen under certain conditions. Take electricity as an example; we know that there is such a thing as electricity; we have never seen it, but we know that it exists because we can use it; we know that it operates in a certain way and we have discovered the way it works. From this knowledge we go ahead and deduce certain facts about electricity, and, applying them to the general principle, we receive definite results. No one has ever seen the power or the energy that we call electricity, and the only proof we have that it really exists is that from it we receive light, heat, and motive power.

From *Science of Mind: A Complete Course of Lessons in the Science of Mind and Spirit* (New York: Robert M. McBride Co., 1926).

No one has ever seen any of the great causes that lie back of the manifestations of life, and perhaps no one ever will, but we know that such principles exist because we can use them.

HOW LAWS ARE DISCOVERED

The discovery of a law is generally made more or less by accident, or by someone who, after careful thought and observation, has come to the conclusion that such a principle must exist. As soon as a law is discovered experiments are made with it, certain facts are proved to be true, and in this way a science is gradually formulated; for any science consists of the number of known facts about any given principle. As more and more facts are gathered and proven, the science expands and gradually becomes accepted by all and used by those who understand it. In this way all of our sciences have been evolved until today we have the use of powers and unseen forces of which our ancestors never even dreamed.

PROOF OF MIND

This is true of the Science of Mind. No one has ever seen Mind or Spirit, but who could possibly doubt their existence? Nothing is more self-evident than that we live; and since we live, we must have life; yet who has ever seen this life? The only proof of life we have is that we live, and the only proof we have of Mind is that we can think; so we are perfectly justified in believing that we have a mind and that we live.

WHERE OUR THOUGHTS GO

As we watch the processes of thought we find that we think consciously, and we also find that something happens to our thoughts after we have thought them; for instance, they become memory. This proves that we have a deeper aspect of mind, which is called subjective, lying just below the threshold of the conscious. This subjective mind is the place where our thoughts go and from whence they eventually return to us again as memory. Observation proves this to be true; for it always happens this way.

Observation has proven that the subjective mind is the seat of memory and that it contains mental pictures, or impressions, of all that has ever happened to the individual. As these mental impressions come to the surface of the conscious mind they are called memories.

Moreover observation has shown that the subjective mind is the builder of the body. It has proven that it is not only the seat of memory; it is also the avenue through which Instinctive Man works. We mean by Instinctive Man that part of the individual which came with him when he was born, that inner something which makes him what he is. For instance, we do not have to consciously think to make the body function, so we say that the inner, or the Instinctive, Man, does this for us. This is true of most of the functions of the body; they appear to be automatic; they came with us and are nature's way of working through us. So we say that in the unconscious or the subconscious or the subjective, there is a silent process forever working away and always doing its duty, carrying on all of the unconscious activities of the body without effort on our part.

SUGGESTION BECOMES MEMORY

It has been observed that suggestions, planted in the subconscious, become memories, and eventually tend to externalize in the body. From this it has been deduced that the subconscious mind is the builder of the body and is the creative factor in man. It has also been proven that certain types of thought produce certain kinds of results. This shows that the subjective mind takes our suggestions and tends to act upon them, no matter what the suggestion may be.

While the Instinctive Man, or the Natural Man, must be perfect, it is known that the thoughts of the conscious man may hinder instinctive action through adverse suggestion. That is, conscious thought, acting as memory, may build a false condition in the body, which condition we call disease. Conscious thought may also erase this memory and thereby heal the disease.

Through observations such as these, a science of the subjective mind has gradually been formulated, many facts have been put together, and, today, these facts constitute what we call the science of the subjective life in its relationship to mental healing.

MENTAL MEDIUM THROUGH ALL

It has also been proven that thought operates in such a manner as to make it possible to convey mental impressions from one person to another, showing that there is a mental medium between all people. When we think of it, how could we talk with each other unless there were some kind of a medium through which we talked? We could not, and so we know that there really is such a medium. While there is a place where our bodies begin and leave off, as form, there does not appear to be a place where our thought leaves off. Indeed, the observations made and the facts gathered show that the medium between men's minds is omnipresent; that is, it seems to be everywhere present. Radio also shows this, for messages are sent out through some kind of a universal medium, and all that we can say of it is that we know the medium is there. So it is with Mind; all that we can say is that everything happens just as though it were there. We have a perfect right, then, to say that such a medium exists.

This opens up a far-reaching theory, for it leads to the conclusion that we are surrounded by a Universal Mind which is the Medium of the communication of our thoughts. Perhaps this is the Mind of God! Who knows? That It is there, we cannot doubt.

READING THOUGHT

Other observations have shown even more wonderful possibilities. It is known that certain people can read our thoughts, even when we are not aware of the fact, showing that thought operates through a medium which is universal, or always present. This also shows that the medium is subjective; for it retains our thoughts and transmits them to others. This leads to the conclusion that what we call our subjective mind is really the use that we, as individuals, make of something which is universal. Perhaps, just as radio messages are operative through a universal medium, our thoughts are operative through the medium of a Universal Mind. Indeed, this has been believed for thousands of years by some of the deepest thinkers.

MENTAL LAW

As we think of the medium of radio transmission in terms of law, so we should think of the Mental Medium in terms of law; for it must be the law of mental action. While we might think of it as the Mind of God, we surely could not think of it as the Spirit of God; for the Mental Medium is automatic, while the Spirit must be Self-Knowing. We could not call the Universal Medium of Mind God any more than we could call electricity God. It is but one of the many attributes of God or the Universe of Life. It is the avenue through which God operates as Law.

THE WORD OF GOD AS LAW

Since man has a self-conscious mind, a subconscious mind, and a body, we know that he is threefold in his nature. First, he is conscious mind or spirit; next, he is subconscious mind or mental law; and then, he is body. The conscious mind controls the subconscious, and in its turn, the subconscious controls the body.

It is evident that man comes from God, Life, or Nature, whichever we choose to call It. It is also evident that we can get from Life only that which is in It. Man must partake of the Divine Nature if he comes from It or is made out of It; for what is true of the Whole must also be true of any of Its parts. Something cannot come from nothing; something must come from something; for nothing comes from nothing and nothing is the result, but man is something, else he could not declare himself, and since he is something, he must be made from, or come out of, something, and that something must be what we call God.

THREEFOLD NATURE OF GOD

If we study the true nature of man, then, we shall have delved into the real nature of God, or First Cause, from which man springs, and as we have found that man is threefold in his nature, so we must also deduce that God is threefold in His Nature; that is, God is Spirit, or Self-Knowingness; God is Law and action; and God is Result or Body. This is the inner meaning of the teaching of "the Trinity." But let us elaborate: God, as Self-Knowing Spirit, means the Divine Being Whom we have always thought of and believed in; the Being to Whom we have prayed and Whom we have adored. God, as Law, means the way in which the Spirit works; and Law in this sense, would be the servant of the Spirit. God, as Body, means the manifestation of the Spirit. We might put it in another form and say, there is the Thing, the way that It works and the result of Its work. Still another form would be to say, Cause, Medium, and Effect.

TRINITY OF BEING

A trinity of being appears to run through all Nature and all Life; for instance, there is electricity, the way it works and its result, which is light or motive power. There is the seed, the creative medium of the soil, and the plant. Turn it as we may, we are confronted with the necessity of a trinity of being. There must always be the thing, what it does, and the way that it operates. Always a trinity runs through life and through everything in it. But through the Trinity of God and man there runs a Self-Conscious Spirit, and this is what distinguishes man from the brute, or from a purely mechanical creation, and is the only thing that could make God a Self-Knowing Power.

CONSCIOUS MIND IN GOD AND MAN

In God and in man there is a power that, while it may not transcend law, yet consciously uses it for definite purposes. In God this knowledge must be complete, but in man it is, of course, but dimly perceived. Jesus, the wisest Man who ever lived, said that God and man are One in real nature, and no doubt this understanding was what gave Him His marvelous power.

UNITY

It is well to remember that the enlightened in every age have taught that back of all things there is One Unseen Cause. In studying the teachings of the great thinkers we find that a common thread runs through all, the thread of Unity. There is no record of any deep thinker, of any age, who taught duality. One of the great teachings of Moses was, "Hear, O Israel, the Lord our God is One Lord"; and the saying "I AM that I AM" was old when Moses was yet unborn;

for it had been inscribed over the temple entrances for generations. We may go back much further than Moses and find the same teaching, for it crops out from the literatures and sayings of the wise of all ages. Jesus taught this when He said, "I and the Father are One," and in the saying, "The Father that dwelleth in me."

This teaching of Unity is the chief cornerstone of the Sacred Scriptures of the East as well as of our own Sacred Writings. It is today the mainspring of the teachings of the modern philosophies, such as Christian Science, Divine Science, the Unity Teachings, the New Thought Movement, the Occult Teachings, The Esoteric or Inner Teachings, and even of much that is taught under the name of Psychology. Without this basic teaching of Unity these movements would have but little to offer. Science has found nothing to contradict this teaching, and it never will, for the teaching is self-evident.

WORSHIP OF GOD

That there is a God or First Cause no one can doubt. That the Being Whom we call God really exists from eternity to eternity is self-evident. In every age people have worshiped some kind of Deity. It is true that as the evolution of man has progressed the idea of God has expanded, and the more that people have realized of life, and of nature and her laws, the clearer has been the concept of Deity, for this is the logical result of an unfolding mentality.

MANY GODS

The first stages of human thought brought out the idea that there were many gods, the natural outcome of a life which experienced many kinds of misfortune and difficulties. As there were many gods so there were many devils or evil powers; but as the understanding of man grew he began to realize that there could not be so many powers, since the Cause back of everything must be a Unity, else It could not exist. More than one power would indicate a universe divided against itself, and this kind of a universe could not hold together. However, it has taken a long time to come to this conclusion, and in the stages between many weird ideas have been formulated and believed in. At first there were many gods and many devils; but as thought progressed, this was narrowed down to One God and one devil or evil power. Duality has been believed in since time immemorial, and, indeed, is still believed in by many. By duality we mean a belief in more than One Power back of all things.

BELIEF IN DUALITY; ITS RESULTS

The belief in duality has robbed theology of power and has polluted philosophy with untruths; it has divided science against itself and has made countless thousands go through life with saddened hearts.

DUALITY IN THEOLOGY

The belief in duality has given rise in theology to the idea of a God and a devil, each with equal power to impose upon man a blessing or a curse, and men have worshiped a devil just as truly as they ever worshiped God. Even today this monstrous thought is robbing men of their birthright to happiness and a sense of security. Even today, and openly, men still teach that there is an evil power in the universe, that there is damnation to the souls of those who do not fall down and worship; they know not what. But the time is rapidly coming when such teachings will be thrown on the scrap heap and numbered among the delusions of a frantic mentality. It has been the habit of many religious teachers of all times to hold the crowd in awe before a mighty throne of condemnation and utter destruction, till the poor, ignorant population have rent the air with their lamentations of complete despair. This, indeed, was a good method to compel the attention with the hope of salvation through some sacred rites to be performed by those whom God had appointed. In justice to such an awful performance, we would better give to these religious teachers the benefit of the doubt and say that they themselves have believed in the atrocious teachings which they have so unhesitatingly given out.

Be this as it may, the time has now come for a clearer understanding of the true nature of the Deity, in Whom we all believe, and Whom we all seek to know and to understand. That there is a God no sane person would deny; that there could be a God of vengeance and hate, having all the characteristics of a huge man in a terrible rage, no person can well believe and keep his sanity. We will say, then, and without mincing matters in the least, that the most we had better believe about such a God is that there is no such being.

DUALITY IN PHILOSOPHY

As the belief in duality has robbed theology of its greater message, so it has robbed much of the philosophy of the ages of a greater truth; for in philosophy the belief in duality has created a confusion that is almost as great as that in theology. It has made a philosophy of good and evil in which men have come to believe. True philosophy in every age, however, has perceived that the Power back of all things must be One Power, and the clearer the thought of Unity, the greater has been the philosophy. It has shone forth as a beacon light toward which weary souls have traveled, hoping to find reality. To the great philosophers of all times we owe the advancement of the world, for they have been the great way-showers and helpers of mankind. In reverence, we humbly bow before them as Messengers of the Most High; for God has spoken through their lips and has told us that we are not creatures of the dust but that we are Divine Beings, made in the image of Perfection and with an endless destiny.

DUALITY AND SCIENCE

The belief in duality has robbed science, in that it has created Spirit and matter; i.e., a dual universe. However, modern science is rapidly giving out a different idea of the universe; for with the passing of matter into a hypothetical and theoretical ether there is but little left on which to hang any belief in materialism. We now are told that all matter is in a constant state of flow; that it all comes from one source; and that it will eventually return to that source.

AN AWAKENING

The world is waking up to the fact that things are not at all what they appear to be, that matter and form are but the one substance appearing and disappearing, and that form is simply used to express something which is formless but self-conscious life. What this life is, science does not attempt to explain. This has been left to theology, and whether or not it has been delegated to those competent to handle the problem time alone will tell.

PHILOSOPHY LEADS MAN'S THOUGHT

Philosophy has always transcended science and always will, for philosophy deals with causes while science deals with effects. A scientist observes the result of nature's work while a philosopher speculates as to its cause. Many things which philosophy has taught for thousands of years are today being demonstrated by science. The two should really go hand in hand, for one deals with causes and the other with effects. True philosophy and true science will some day meet on a common basis, and, working together, will give to the world a theology of reality. Then, indeed, will "God go forth anew into Creation."

A DEEP INQUIRY

The deep thinkers of antiquity as well as the philosophers of all ages have meditated long and earnestly on the nature of the Divine Being. Knowing that there could be but One Ultimate Reality back of all things, they have pondered deeply upon the nature of that Reality, and it is a significant fact that all of the greatest thinkers have come to about the same conclusion.

THE GREAT DIFFICULTY

The difficulty that has beset the path of true philosophy has been the necessity of explaining a multiplied Creation with a Unitary Cause. Nothing is more evident than that we live in a world of constant change. Things and forms come and go continuously; forms appear only to disappear; things happen only to stop happening; and it is no wonder that the average person, unused to trying to discover causes, is led to feel and to believe that there is a multiple cause back of the world of things.

The philosophers of all times have had to meet the difficulty of explaining how One Cause could manifest Itself in a multiplicity of forms without dividing or breaking up the One. This has not been easy, yet, when understood, the explanation becomes very apparent.

THE VOICE OF GOD IN CREATION

The argument has been something after this manner: The Ultimate Cause back of all things must be One, since Life cannot be divided against Itself; the Infinite must be One, for there could not be two Infinites. Whatever change takes place must take place within the One, but the One must be Changeless, for, being One and Only, It cannot change into anything but Itself. All seeming change, then, is really only the play of Life upon Itself, and all that happens must happen by and through It. How do these things happen through It? By some inner action upon Itself. What would be the nature of this inner action? It could not be physical, as we understand physics, but would have to be by the power of the inner Word of Life; that is, the Voice of God, God standing for the First Great and Only Cause of all that Is.

THE WORD OF GOD

It is impossible to conceive of anything other than the Word of God being that which sets power in motion. This is why the Scriptures announce that, "In the beginning was the Word, and the Word was with God and the Word was God. All things were made by Him, and without Him was not anything made that was made." God speaks and it is done.

It is evident that First Cause must be Self-Existent; that is, It must be Causeless. Nothing came before That Which was First; and, while it may be a little hard to understand this, yet we can all grasp the fact that whatever the Being is Whom we call God, It must be Self-Existent.

SPIRIT KNOWS ITSELF

God speaks and it is done, but if God speaks, His Word must be Law. The Word of God is also the Law of God. God is Word, God is Law, and God is Spirit; this is self-evident. We arrive at the conclusion that God, as Spirit, is Self-Conscious Life. That Spirit is conscious is proven by the fact that we have evidence of this consciousness strewn through all time and space. God must know that God Is.

This is the inner meaning of the teaching of the "I AM," handed down from antiquity. "The Spirit is the Power that knows Itself" is one of the oldest sayings of time.

LAW, SERVANT OF THE WORD

Spirit knows Itself, but the Law is the servant of the Spirit and is set in motion through Its Word. It is known that all law is some form of universal force or energy. Law does not know itself; law only knows to do; it is, therefore, the servant of the Spirit. It is the way that the Spirit works, and is the medium through which It operates to fulfill Its purpose.

Did God make law? As it is not possible to conceive a time when law did not operate, it is impossible to conceive that it was ever created; therefore, law must be coexistent and coeternal with Spirit. We might say that law is one of the attributes of Spirit.

The Spirit operates through law which is some part of Its own Nature; therefore, all action must be some action of Spirit as Law. The Word of Spirit sets Its purposes in motion through the law, and since the law must be as Infinite as the Spirit, we could not think of a time when it was not or a time when it would cease to be; neither can we imagine the law ever failing to operate when set in motion.

We have, then, an Infinite Spirit and an Infinite Law, Intelligence and the way that It works, God, working through Law, which is unfailing and certain.

FORMS OF SPIRIT OR CREATION

Next, we come to the forms of Spirit, which forms we call matter. But what is matter? Science tells us that matter is eternal and indestructible, that, at first, it is an invisible cosmic stuff, and that it gradually takes form through some law working within it. The worlds were formed by the power of His Word. We know that right now worlds are being formed in the vast reaches of space, and worlds are also ceasing to be; that is, they are gradually losing their form. In this way Creation is eternally going on. This proves a definite purposefulness and a definite law set in motion to work out this purposefulness, and a definite form as the result of the operation of this purposefulness. In other words, it shows that there is an Intelligence inherent in the universe which knows what It is doing, and how to do it, and which knows why It does it, and that there is a law obeying Its will. It also shows that there is something upon which It operates. This "something" we will call matter in its unformed state. Perhaps this is "the ether" of science; it is impossible to say, but surely there is something upon which the Spirit works.

The teaching of the great thinkers of all times is that we live in a threefold universe of Spirit, Soul, and Body; of Intelligence, Substance, and Form.

MEANING OF CREATION

With this in mind, we shall be better able to realize that Creation does not mean making something out of nothing but means the passing of Substance into form through a law which is set in motion by the Word of Spirit. Creation is eternally going on; for we could not imagine a time when the activity of Spirit would cease. It is "the same yesterday, today, and forever."

The whole action of Spirit must be within Itself, upon the Law, which is also within Itself, and upon the Universal Stuff, or matter, which is also within Itself. The three must in reality be One; hence, "The Trinity."

THE WORD ALONE IS CONSCIOUS

One of the main facts to bear in mind is that of the three attributes of Spirit, the Word alone is conscious of Itself. The Law is force, and matter is simply stuff ready to take form. Since law or energy is proven to be timeless, that is, not added to or taken from, and since matter is known to be of the same nature, we have a right to suppose that both matter and law are coexistent and coeternal with Spirit. But Spirit alone is Conscious. Law, of itself, is only a force, and matter has no mind of its own. Law is not a thinker but is a doer, while matter cannot think but is thought upon.

THE THOUGHT OF GOD

Just what is meant by the Word of God? This must mean the Inner Consciousness, or Self-Knowingness, of Spirit, the Thought of God. The word "thought" seems to mean more to us than any other word; it seems to cover the meaning better, for we know that thought is an inner process or consciousness. The Thought of God must be back of all that really exists, and, as there are many things that really exist, there must be many thoughts in the Mind of the Infinite. This is logical to suppose, for an Infinite Mind can think of an infinite number of ideas. Hence the world of multiplicity or many things. But the world of multiplicity does not contradict the world of Unity, for the many live in the One.

ETERNAL CREATION

There may be confusion in the minds of men but not in the Thought of God, and so we have a universe expressing the limitless Ideas of a Limitless Mind and without confusion. We have, then, a Cosmic World and an infinite and endless Creation. This is the inner meaning of those mystic words, "World without end." Creation always was and always will be. Things may come and things may go, but Creation goes on forever, for It is the Thought of God coming into expression. This is, indeed, a wonderful concept, for it means that there will always be a manifestation of the Divine Ideas. We need not worry about whether it will ever cease; it cannot cease so long as God exists, and since God will be forever, there will forever be some kind of manifestation.

THE UNIVERSE IS ALIVE

The universe is alive with action and power, with energy and life. We touch it only in parts, but from these parts we do catch a glimpse of the nature of the Whole. "He hath not left Himself without a witness." Modern science is revealing many things that the great thinkers of the ages have announced. One of them is that matter is in a constant state of flow; it is like a river flowing in, out, and on; it is operated upon by an unseen force or law and takes its form through some agency which science supposes to be the Will and Purpose of Spirit. This we call the Word. All things were made by the Word.

CONCLUSION

To sum up: There is a power in the universe which acts as though It were Intelligent and we may assume that It is. There is an activity in the universe which acts as law. We know this to be true. And there is a formless stuff in the universe, forever taking form, and forever changing its form; this also is self-evident. We have every right, then, to assume that there is a threefold nature of Being which we will call Spirit, Soul, and Body. We will think of the Spirit as the great Actor, the Soul as the medium of Its action, and the Body as the result of this action. We will think of Spirit as the only Conscious Actor, the only Power that knows Itself. We will think of Soul as a blind force, obeying the Will of Spirit, and we will think of Body as the effect of the Spirit, working through law, thus producing form. We will say that neither the Law nor the stuff from which form comes has any conscious intelligence but must, because of its nature, take the form of the Word. This simplifies the whole matter and enables us to see that in the entire universe One Power Alone really acts, the Power of the Word of God.

THE ASIAN INFLUENCE

10
THE FORCE CENTERS

Charles W. Leadbeater

THE MEANING OF THE WORD

The word "Chakra" is Sanskrit and signifies a wheel. It is also used in various subsidiary, derivative, and symbolical senses, just as is its English equivalent; as we might speak of the wheel of fate, so does the Buddhist speak of the wheel of life and death; and he describes that first great sermon in which the Lord Buddha propounded his doctrine as the *Dhwnmachakkappavattana Sutta* (*chakka* being the Paff equivalent for the Sanskrit *chakra*), which Professor Rhys Davids poetically renders as "to set rolling the royal chariot-wheel of a universal empire of truth and righteousness." That is exactly the spirit of the meaning which the expression conveys to the Buddhist devotee, though the literal translation of the bare words is "the turning of the wheel of the Law." The special use of the word "chakra" with which we are at the moment concerned is its application to a series of wheel-like vortices which exist in the surface of the etheric double of man.

PRELIMINARY EXPLANATIONS

As this book may probably fall into the hands of some who are not familiar with Theosophical terminology it may be well to insert here a few words of preliminary explanation.

From Charles W. Leadbeater, *The Chakras* (Adyar, India: Theosophical Publishing House, 1927).

In ordinary superficial conversation a man sometimes mentions his soul—implying that the body through which he speaks is the real man and that this thing called the soul is a possession or appanage of that body—a sort of captive balloon floating over him and in some vague sort of way attached to him. This is a loose, inaccurate, and misleading statement; the exact opposite is the truth. Man *is* a soul and owns a body—several bodies in fact; for besides the visible vehicle by means of which he transacts his business with his lower world, he has others which are not visible to ordinary sight, by means of which he deals with the emotional and mental worlds. With those, however, we are not for the moment concerned.

In the course of the last century, enormous advances have been made in our knowledge of the minute details of the physical body; students of medicine are now familiar with its bewildering complexities and have at least a general idea of the way in which its amazingly intricate machinery works.

The Etheric Double

Naturally, however, they have had to confine their attention to that part of the body which is dense enough to be visible to the eye, and most of them are probably unaware of the existence of that type of matter, still physical though invisible, to which in Theosophy we give the name of etheric.[1] This invisible part of the physical body is of great importance to us, for it is the vehicle through which flow the streams of vitality which keep the body alive, and without it as a bridge to convey undulations of thought and feeling from the astral to the visible denser physical matter, the ego[2] could make no use of the cells of his brain. It is clearly visible to the clairvoyant as a mass of faintly luminous violet-grey mist, interpenetrating the denser part of the body and extending very slightly beyond it.

The life of the physical body is one of perpetual change, and in order that it shall live it needs constantly to be supplied from three distinct sources. It must have food for its digestion, air for its breathing, and vitality in three forms for its absorption. This vitality is essentially a force, but when clothed with matter it appears to us as though it were a highly refined chemical element. It exists upon all planes, but our business for the moment is to consider its manifestation in the physical world.

In order to understand that, we must know something of the constitution and arrangement of this etheric part of our bodies. I have written on this subject many years ago in various volumes, and Colonel A. E. Powell has recently gathered together all the information heretofore published[3] and issued it in a convenient form in a book called *The Etheric Double*.[4]

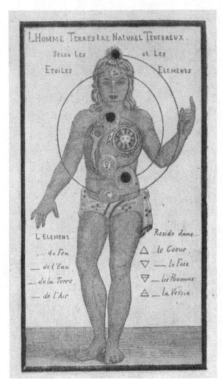

The chakras, according to Gichtel. *(Reprinted with permission of the American Religion Collection)*

The Centers

The chakras or force-centers are points of connection at which energy flows from one vehicle or body of a man to another. Anyone who possesses a slight degree of clairvoyance may easily see them in the etheric double, where they show themselves as saucerlike depressions or vortices in its surface. When quite undeveloped they appear as small circles about two inches in diameter, glowing dully in the ordinary man, but when awakened and vivified they are seen as blazing, coruscating whirlpools, much increased in size, and resembling miniature suns. We sometimes speak of them as roughly corresponding to certain physical organs; in reality they show themselves at the surface of the etheric double, which projects slightly beyond the outline of the dense body. If we imagine ourselves to be looking straight down into the bell of a flower of the convolvulus type, we shall get some idea of the general appearance of a chakra. The stalk of the flower in each springs from a point in the spine, so another view might show the spine as a central stem, from which flowers shoot forth at intervals, showing the opening of their bells at the surface of the etheric body.

The seven centers with which we are at present concerned are indicated in the accompanying illustration. Table 1 gives their English and Sanskrit names.

All these wheels are perpetually rotating, and into the hub or open mouth of each a force from the higher world is always flowing—a manifestation of the lifestream issuing from the Second Aspect of the Solar Logos—which we call the primary force. That force is sevenfold in its nature, and all its forms operate in each of these centers, although one of them in each case usually predominates over the others. Without this inrush of energy the physical body could not exist. Therefore the centers are in operation in every one, although in the undeveloped person they are usually in comparatively sluggish motion, just forming the necessary vortex for the force, and no more. In a more evolved man they may be glowing and pulsating with living light, so that an enormously greater amount of energy passes through them, with the result that there are additional faculties and possibilities open to the man.

Table 1. The seven chakras

ENGLISH NAME	SANSKRIT NAME	SITUATION
Root or Basic Chakra	Muladhara	At the base of the spine
Spleen or Splenic Chakra[5]	——	Over the spleen
Navel or Umbilical Chakra	Manipura	At the navel, over the solar plexus
Heart or Cardiac Chakra	Anahata	Over the heart
Throat or Laryngeal Chakra	Vishuddha	At the front of the throat
Brow or Frontal Chakra	Ajna	In the space between the eyebrows
Crown or Coronal Chakra	Sahasrara	On the top of the head

THE FORM OF THE VORTICES

This divine energy which pours into each center from without sets up at right angles to itself (that is to say, in the surface of the etheric double) secondary forces in undulatory circular motion, just as a bar-magnet thrust into an induction coil produces a current of electricity which flows round the coil at right angles to the axis or direction of the magnet. The primary force itself, having entered the vortex, radiates from it again at right angles, but in straight lines, as though the center of the vortex were the hub of a wheel and the radiations of the primary force its spokes. By means of these spokes the force seems to bind the astral and etheric bodies together as though with grappling hooks. The number of these spokes differs in the different force-centers and determines the number of waves or petals which each of them exhibits. Because of this these centers have often been poetically described in Oriental books as resembling flowers.

Each of the secondary forces which sweep round the saucerlike depression has its own characteristic wavelength, just as has light of a certain color; but instead of moving in a straight line as light does, it moves along relatively large undulations of various sizes, each of which is some multiple of the smaller wavelengths within it. The number of undulations is determined by the number of spokes in the wheel, and the secondary force weaves itself under and over the radiating currents of the primary force, just as basket-work might be woven round the spokes of a carriage wheel. The wavelengths are infinitesimal, and probably thousands of them are included within one of the undulations. As the forces rush round in the vortex, these oscillations of different sizes, crossing one another in this basket-work fashion, produce the flowerlike form to which I have referred. It is, perhaps, still more like the appearance of certain saucers or shallow vases of wavy iridescent glass, such as are made in Venice. All of these undulations or petals have that shimmering pavonine effect, like mother-of-pearl, yet each of them has usually its own predominant color, as will be seen from our illustrations. This nacreous silvery aspect is likened in Sanskrit works to the gleam of moonlight on water.

THE ILLUSTRATIONS

These illustrations of ours show the chakras as seen by clairvoyant sight in a fairly evolved and intelligent person, who has already brought them to some extent into working order. Of course our colors are not sufficiently luminous—no earthly colors could be, but at least the drawings will give some idea of the actual appearance of these wheels of light. It will be understood from what has already been said that the centers vary in size and in brightness in different people and that even in the same person some of them may be much more developed than the rest. They are drawn about life-size, except for the Sahasrdra or crown chakra, which we have found it necessary to magnify in order to show its amazing wealth of detail. In the case of a man who excels greatly in the qualities which express themselves through a certain center, that center will be not only much enlarged but also especially radiant, throwing out brilliant golden rays. An example of that may be seen in Madame Blavatsky's precipitation of the aura of Mr. Stainton Moses, which is now kept in a cabinet in the archives of the Society at Adyar. It is reproduced, though very imperfectly, on page 364 of volume 1 of Colonel Olcott's *Old Diary Leaves.*

These chakras naturally divide into three groups, the lower, the middle, and the higher; they might be called respectively the physiological, the personal, and the spiritual.

The first and second chakras, having but few spokes or petals, are principally concerned with receiving into the body two forces which come into it at that physical level—one being the serpent-fire from the earth and the other the vitality from the sun. The centers of the middle group, numbered 3, 4, and 5, are engaged with the forces which reach man through his personality—through the lower astral in the case of center 3, the higher astral in center 4, and from the lower mind in center 5. All these centers seem to feed certain ganglia in the body. Centers 6 and 7 stand apart from the rest, being connected with the pituitary body and the pineal gland, respectively, and coming into action only when a certain amount of spiritual development has taken place.

I have heard it suggested that each of the different petals of these force-centers represents a moral quality and that the development of that quality brings the center into activity. For example, in *The Dhyana-bindu Upanishad,* the petals of the heart chakra are associated with devotion, laziness, anger, charity, and similar qualities. I have not yet met with any facts which definitely confirm this, and it is not easy to see exactly how it can be, because the appearance is produced by certain readily recognizable forces, and the petals in any particular center are either active or not active according as these forces have or have not been aroused, and their unfoldment seems to have no more direct connection with morality than has the enlargement of the biceps. I have certainly met with persons in whom some of the centers were in full activity, though the moral advancement was by no means exceptionally high, whereas in other persons of high spirituality and the noblest possible morality the centers were scarcely yet vitalized at all, so that there does not seem to be any necessary connection between the two developments.

There are, however, certain facts observable which may be the basis of this rather curious idea. Although the likeness to petals is caused by the same forces flowing round and round the center, alternately over and under the various spokes, those spokes differ in character, because the inrushing force is subdivided into its component parts or qualities, and therefore each spoke radiates a specialized influence of its own, even though the variations be slight. The secondary force, in passing each spoke, is to some extent modified by its influence, and therefore changes a little in its hue. Some of these shades of color may indicate a form of the force which is helpful to the growth of some moral quality, and when that quality is strengthened its corresponding vibration will be more pronounced. Thus the deepening or weakening of the tint might be taken to betoken the possession of more or less of that attribute.

THE ROOT CHAKRA

The first center at the base of the spine has a primary force which radiates out in four spokes, and therefore arranges its undulations so as to give the effect of its being divided into quadrants, alternately red and orange in hue, with hollows between them. This makes it seem as though marked with the sign of the cross, and for that reason the cross is often used to symbolize this center, and sometimes a flaming cross is taken to indicate the serpent-fire which resides in it. When acting with any vigor this chakra is fiery orange-red in color, corresponding closely with the type of vitality which is sent down to it from the splenic center. Indeed, it will be noticed that in the case of every one of the chakras a similar correspondence with the color of its vitality may be seen.

THE SPLEEN CHAKRA

The second center, the splenic, at the spleen, is devoted to the specialization, subdivision, and dispersion of the vitality which comes to us from the sun. That vitality is poured out again from it in six horizontal streams, the seventh variety being drawn into the hub of the wheel. This center therefore has six petals or undulations, all of different colors, and is specially radiant, glowing, and sunlike. Each of the six divisions of the wheel shows predominantly the color of one of the forms of the vital force—red, orange, yellow, green, blue, and violet.

THE NAVEL CHAKRA

The third center, the umbilical, at the navel or solar plexus, receives a primary force with ten radiations, so it vibrates in such a manner as to divide itself into ten undulations or petals. It is very closely associated with feelings and emotions of various kinds. Its predominant color is a curious blending of several shades of red, though there is also a great deal of green in it. The divisions are alternately chiefly red and chiefly green.

THE HEART CHAKRA

The fourth center, the cardiac, at the heart, is of a glowing golden color, and each of its quadrants is divided into three parts, which gives it twelve undulations, because its primary force makes for it twelve spokes.

THE THROAT CHAKRA

The fifth center, the laryngeal, at the throat, has sixteen spokes, and therefore sixteen apparent divisions. There is a good deal of blue in it, but its general effect is silvery and gleaming, with a kind of suggestion as of moonlight upon rippling water. Blue and green predominate alternately in its sections.

THE BROW CHAKRA

The sixth center, the frontal, between the eyebrows, has the appearance of being divided into halves, one chiefly rose-colored, though with a great deal of yellow about it, and the other predominantly a kind of purplish-blue, again closely agreeing with the colors of the special types of vitality that vivify it. Perhaps it is for this reason that this center is mentioned in Indian books as having only two petals, though if we are to count undulations of the same character as those of the previous centers we shall find that each half is subdivided into forty-eight of these, making ninety-six in all, because its primary force has that number of radiations.

This sudden leap from sixteen to ninety-six spokes, and again the even more startling variation from ninety-six to 972 between this and the next chakra, shows us that we are now dealing with centers of an altogether different order from those which we have hitherto been considering. We do not yet know all the factors which determine the number of spokes in a chakra, but it is already evident that they represent shades of variation in the primary force. Before we can say much more than this, hundreds of observations and comparisons must be made—made, repeated, and verified over and over again. But meantime

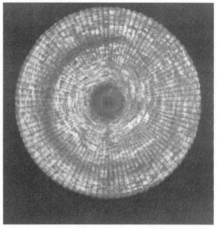

The brow chakra. (*Courtesy of the American Religion Collection*)

this much is clear—that while the need of the personality can be satisfied by a limited number of types of force, when we come to the higher and more permanent principles of man we encounter a complexity, a multiplicity, which demands for its expression a vastly greater selection of modifications of the energy.

THE CROWN CHAKRA

The seventh center, the coronal, at the top of the head, is when stirred into full activity the most resplendent of all, full of indescribable chromatic effects and vibrating with almost inconceivable rapidity. It seems to contain all sorts of prismatic hues but is on the whole predominantly violet. It is described in Indian books as thousand-petaled, and really this is not very far from the truth, the number of the radiations of its primary force in the outer circle being nine hundred sixty. Every line of this will be seen faithfully reproduced in our frontispiece [not shown], though it is hardly possible to give the effect of the separate petals. In addition to this it has a feature which is possessed by none of the other chakras—a sort of subsidiary central whirlpool of gleaming white flushed with gold in its heart—a minor activity which has twelve undulations of its own.

This chakra is usually the last to be awakened. In the beginning it is the same size as the others, but as the man progresses on the Path of spiritual advancement it increases steadily until it covers almost the whole top of the head. Another peculiarity attends its development. It is at first a depression in the etheric body, as are all the others, because through it, as through them, the divine force flows in from without; but when the man realizes his position as a king of the divine light, dispensing largesse to all around him, this chakra reverses itself, turning as it were inside out; it is no longer a channel of reception but of radiation, no longer a depression but a prominence, standing out from the head as a dome, a veritable crown of glory.

In Oriental pictures and statues of the deities or great men this prominence is often shown. In Fig. 2 [not shown] it appears on the head of a statue of the Lord Buddha at Borobudur in Java. This is the conventional method of representing it, and in this form it is to be found upon the heads of thousands of images of the Lord Buddha all over the Eastern world. In many cases it will be seen that the two tiers of the Sahasrara chakra are copied—the larger dome of 960 petals first and then the smaller dome of twelve rising out of that in turn. The head on the right is that of Brahma from the Hokke-do of Todai-ji at Nara in Japan (dating from 749 AD); and it will be seen that the statue is wearing a head-dress fashioned to represent this chakra, though in a form somewhat different from the last, showing the coronet of flames shooting up from it.

It appears also in the Christian symbology, in the crowns worn by the four-and-twenty elders who are forever casting them down before the throne of God. In the highly developed man this coronal chakra pours out splendor and glory which makes for him a veritable crown; and the meaning of that passage of Scripture is that all that he has gained, all the magnificent karma that he makes, all the wondrous spiritual force that he generates—all *that* he casts perpetually at the feet of the *Logos* to be used in his work. So, over and over again, can he continue to cast down his golden crown, because it continually re-forms as the force wells up from within him.

NOTES

1. Not to be confused with "aether," which some consider to be the medium for electromagnetic waves. (—*Ed.* of 1927 edition)

2. Individuality, not to be confused with the use of the term in psychology. (—*Ed.* of 1927 edition)

3. 1925.

4. The Theosophical Publishing House.

5. *The spleen chakra is not indicated in the Indian books; its place is taken by a center called the Svadhishthana,* situated in the neighborhood of the generative organs, to which the same six petals are assigned. From our point of view the arousing of such a center would be regarded as a misfortune, as there are serious dangers connected with it. In the Egyptian scheme of development elaborate precautions were taken to prevent any such awakening (See *The Hidden Life in Freemasonry*).

11
[HINDUISM]
Swami Vivekananda

Three religions now stand in the world which have come down to us from time prehistoric—Hinduism, Zoroastrianism, and Judaism. They have all received tremendous shocks, and all of them prove by their survival their internal strength. But while Judaism failed to absorb Christianity and was driven out of its place of birth by its all-conquering daughter, and a handful of Parsees is all that remains to tell the tale of their grand religion, sect after sect arose in India and seemed to shake the religion of the Vedas to its very foundations, but like the waters of the seashore in a tremendous earthquake it receded only for a while, only to return in an all-absorbing flood, a thousand times more vigorous, and when the tumult of the rush was over, these sects were all sucked in, absorbed, and assimilated into the immense body of the mother faith. From the high spiritual flights of the Vedanta philosophy, of which the latest discoveries of science seem like echoes, to the low ideas of idolatry with its multifarious mythology, the agnosticism of the Buddhists and the atheism of the Jains, each and all have a place in the Hindu's religion.

Where then, the question arises, where is the common center to which all these widely diverging radii converge? Where is the common basis upon which all these seemingly hopeless contradictions rest? And this is the question I shall attempt to answer.

Address to the World's Parliament of Religions, Chicago, September 19, 1893.

The Hindus have received their religion through revelation, the Vedas. They hold that the Vedas are without beginning and without end. It may sound ludicrous to this audience how a book can be without beginning or end. But by the Vedas no books are meant. They mean the accumulated treasury of spiritual laws discovered by different persons in different times. Just as the law of gravitation existed before its discovery, and would exist if all humanity forgot it, so is it with the laws that govern the spiritual relations between soul and soul and between individual spirits and the Father of all spirits were there before their discovery and would remain even if we forgot them.

The discoverers of these laws are called Rishis, and we honor them as perfected beings. I am glad to tell this audience that some of the very greatest of them were women.

Here it may be said that these laws as laws may be without end, but they must have had a beginning. The Vedas teach us that creation is without beginning or end. Science is said to have proved that the sum total of cosmic energy is always the same. Then, if there was a time when nothing existed, where was all this manifested energy? Some say it was in a potential form in God. In that case God is sometimes potential and sometimes kinetic, which would make Him mutable. Everything mutable is a compound and everything compound must undergo that change which is called destruction. So God would die, which is absurd. Therefore, there never was a time when there was no creation.

If I may be allowed to use a simile, creation and creator are two lines, without beginning and without end, zoning parallel to each other. God is the ever-active providence, by whose power systems after systems are being evolved out of chaos, made to run for a time, and again destroyed. This is what the Brahmin boy repeats every day: "The sun and the moon, the Lord created like the suns and the moons of previous cycles." And this agrees with modern science.

Here I Stand and if I shut my eyes and try to conceive my existence, "I," "I," "I," what is the idea before me? The idea of a body. Am I, then, nothing but a combination of material substances? The Vedas declare, No, I am a spirit living in a body: I am not the body. The body will die, but I shall not die. Here I am in this body; it will fall, but I shall go on living. I had also a past. The soul was not created, for creation means a combination, which means a certain future dissolution. If then the soul was created, it must die. Some are born happy, enjoy perfect health with beautiful body, mental vigor, and all wants supplied. Others are born miserable; some are without hands or feet; others again are idiots, and only drag on a wretched existence. Why, if they are all created, why does a just and merciful God create one happy and another unhappy, why is He so partial? Nor would it mend matters in the least to hold that those who are miserable in this life will be happy in another one. Why should a man be miserable even here in the reign of a just and merciful God?

In the second place, the idea of a creator God does not explain the anomaly but simply expresses the cruel Rat of an all-powerful being. There must have been causes, then, before his birth, to make a man miserable or happy and those were his past actions.

Are not all the tendencies of the mind and the body accounted for by inherited aptitude? Here are two parallel lines of existence—one of the mind, the other of matter. If matter and its transformations answer for all that we have, there is no necessity for supposing the existence of a soul. But it cannot be proved that thought has been evolved out of matter, and if a philosophical monism is inevitable, spiritual monism is certainly logical and no less desirable than a materialistic monism, but neither of these is necessary here.

We cannot deny that bodies acquire certain tendencies from heredity, but those tendencies only mean the physical configuration through which a peculiar mind alone can act in a peculiar way. There are other tendencies peculiar to a soul caused by his past actions. And a soul with a certain tendency would, by the laws of affinity, take birth in a body which is the fittest instrument for the display of that tendency. This is in accord with science, for science wants to explain everything by habit, and habit is got through repetitions. So repetitions are necessary to explain the natural habits of a newborn soul. And since they were not obtained in this present life, they must have come down from past lives.

There is another suggestion. Taking all these for granted, how is it that I do not remember anything of my past life? This can be easily explained. I am now speaking English. It is not my mother tongue; in fact, no words of my mother tongue are now present in my consciousness, but let me try to bring them up, and they rush in. That shows that consciousness is only the surface of mental ocean, and within its depths are stored up all our experiences. Try and struggle, they would come up and you would be conscious even of your past life.

This is direct and demonstrative evidence. Verification is the perfect proof of a theory, and here is the challenge thrown to the world by the Rishis. We have discovered the secret by which the very depths of the ocean of memory can be stirred up—try it and you would get a complete reminiscence of your past life. So then the Hindu believes that he is a spirit. Him the sword cannot pierce—him the fire cannot burn—him the water cannot melt—him the air cannot dry. The Hindu believes that every soul is a circle whose circumference is nowhere but whose center is located in the body and that death means the change of the center from body to body. Nor is the soul bound by the conditions of matter. In its very essence, it is free, unbounded, holy, pure, and perfect. But somehow or other it finds itself tied down to matter and thinks of itself as matter.

Why should the free, perfect, and pure be thus under the thraldom of matter is the next question. How can the perfect soul be deluded into the belief that it is imperfect? We have been told that the Hindus shirk the question and say that no such question can be there. Some thinkers want to answer it by positing one or more quasi-perfect beings and use big scientific names to fill up the gap. But naming is not explaining. The question remains the same. How can the perfect become the quasi-perfect; how can the pure, the absolute change even a microscopic particle of its nature? But the Hindu is sincere. He does not want to take shelter under sophistry. He is brave enough to face the question in a manly fashion, and his answer is: "I do not know. I do not know how the perfect being, the soul, came to think of itself as imperfect, as joined to and conditioned by matter." But the fact is a fact for all that. It is a fact in everybody's consciousness that one thinks of oneself as the body. The Hindu does not attempt to explain why one thinks one is the body. The answer that it is the will of God is no explanation. This is nothing more than what the Hindu says, "I do not know."

Well, then, the human soul is eternal and immortal, perfect and infinite, and death means only a change of center from one body to another. The present is determined by our past actions and the future by the present. The soul will go on evolving up or reverting back from birth to birth and death to death. But here is another question: Is man a tiny boat in a tempest, raised one moment on the foamy crest of a billow and dashed down into a yawning chasm the next, rolling to and from at the mercy of good and bad actions—a powerless, helpless wreck in an ever-raging, ever-rushing, uncompromising current of cause and effect—a little moth placed under the wheel of causation, which rolls on crushing everything in its way and waits not for the widow's tears or the orphan's cry? The heart sinks at the idea, yet this is the law of nature. Is there no hope? Is there no escape?—was the cry that went up from the bottom of the heart of despair. It reached the throne of mercy, and words of hope and consolation came down and inspired a Vedic sage, and he stood up before the world and in trumpet voice proclaimed the glad tidings: "Hear, ye children of immortal bliss! even ye that reside in higher spheres! I have found the Ancient One who is beyond all darkness, all delusion: knowing Him alone you shall be saved from death over again. "Children of immortal bliss"—what a sweet, what a hopeful name! Allow me to call you, brethren, by that sweet name—heirs of immortal bliss—yea, the Hindu refuses to call you sinners. We are the Children of God, the sharers of immortal bliss, holy and perfect beings. Divinities on earth—sinners! It is a sin to call a man so; it is standing libel on human nature. Come up, O lions, and shake off the delusion that you are sheep; you are souls immortal, spirits free, blest, and eternal; ye are not matter, ye are not bodies; matter is your servant, not you the servant of matter.

Thus it is that the Vedas proclaim not a dreadful combination of unforgiving laws, not an endless prison of cause and effect, but that at the head of all these laws, in and through every particle of matter and force, stands One, "by whose command the wind blows, the fire burns, the clouds rain and death stalks upon the earth."

And what is His nature?

He is everywhere, the pure and formless One, the Almighty and the All-merciful. "Thou art our father, Thou art our mother, Thou art our beloved friend, Thou art the source of all strength; give us strength. Thou art He that beareth the burdens of the universe; help me bear the little burden of this life." Thus sang the Rishis of the Veda. And how to worship Him? Through love. "He is to be worshiped as the one beloved, dearer than everything in this and the next life." This is the doctrine of love declared in the Vedas, and let us see how it is fully developed and taught by Krishna whom the Hindus believe to have been God incarnate on earth.

He taught that a man ought to live in this world like a lotus leaf, which grows in water but is never moistened by water; so a man ought to live in the world—his heart to God and his hands to work.

It is good to love God for hope of reward in this or the next world, but it is better to love God for love's sake; and the prayer goes: "Lord, I do not want wealth nor children nor learning. If it be Thy will, I shall go from birth to birth; but grant me this, that I may love Thee without the hope of reward—love unselfishly for love's sake." One of the disciples of Krishna, the then–Emperor of India, was driven from his kingdom by his enemies and had to take shelter with his queen in a forest in the Himalayas, and there one day the queen asked how it was that he, the most virtuous of men, should suffer so much misery. Yudhishthira answered, "Be hold, my queen, the Himalayas, how grand and beautiful they are; I love them. They do not give me anything but my nature is to love the grand, the beautiful, therefore I love them. Similarly, I love the Lord. He is the source of all beauty, of all sublimity. He is the only object to beloved; my nature is to love Him, and therefore I love. I do not pray for anything; I do not ask for anything. Let Him place me wherever He likes. I must love Him for love's sake. I cannot trade in love."

The Vedas teach that the soul is divine, only held in the bondage of matter; perfection will be reached when this bond will burst, and the word they use for it is, therefore, Mukti—freedom, freedom from the bonds of imperfection, freedom from death and misery.

And this bondage can only fall off through the mercy of God, and this mercy comes on the pure. So purity is the condition of His mercy. How does that mercy act? He reveals Himself to the pure heart; the pure and the stainless see God, yea, even in this life; then and then only all the crookedness of the heart is made straight. Then all doubt ceases. He is no more the freak of a terrible law of causation. This is the very center, the very vital conception of Hinduism. The Hindu does not want to live upon words and theories. If there are existences beyond the ordinary sensuous existence, he wants to come face to face with them. If there is a soul in him which is not matter, if there is an all-merciful universal Soul, he will go to Him direct. He must see Him, and that alone can destroy all doubts. So the best proof a Hindu sage gives about the soul, about God, is: "I have seen the soul; I have seen God." And that is the only condition of perfection. The Hindu religion does not consist in struggles and attempts to believe a certain doctrine or dogma but in realizing—not in believing, but in being and becoming.

Thus the whole object of their system is by constant struggle to become perfect, to become divine, to reach God, and see God; and this reaching God, seeing God, becoming perfect even as the Father in Heaven is perfect constitutes the religion of the Hindus.

And what becomes of a man when he attains perfection? He lives a life of bliss infinite. He enjoys infinite and perfect bliss, having obtained the only thing in which man ought to have pleasure, namely, God, and enjoys the bliss with God. So far all the Hindus are agreed. This is the common religion of all the sects of India, but then perfection is absolute, and the absolute cannot be two or three. It cannot have any qualities. It cannot be an individual. And so when a soul becomes perfect and absolute, it must become one with Brahman, and it would only realize the Lord as the perfection, the reality, of its own nature and existence, the existence absolute, knowledge absolute, and bliss absolute. We have often and often read this called the losing of individuality and becoming a stock or a stone.

"He jests at scars that never felt a wound."

I tell you it is nothing of the kind. If it is happiness to enjoy the consciousness of this small body, it must be greater happiness to enjoy the consciousness of two bodies, the measure of happiness increasing with the consciousness of an increasing number of bodies, the aim, the ultimate of happiness, being reached when it would become a universal consciousness. Therefore, to gain this infinite universal individuality, this miserable little prison—individuality must go. Then alone can death cease when I am one with life, then alone can misery cease when I am one with happiness itself, then alone can all errors cease when I am one with knowledge itself; and this is the necessary scientific conclusion. Science has proved to me that physical individuality is a delusion, that really my body is one little continuously changing body in an unbroken ocean of matter, and Advaita (unity) is the necessary conclusion with my other counterpart, Soul.

Science is nothing but the finding of unity. As soon as science would reach perfect unity, it would stop from further progress, because it would reach the goal. Thus chemistry could not progress further when it would discover one element out of which all others could be made. Physics would stop when it would be able to fulfill its services in discovering one energy of which all the others are but manifestations, and the science of religion become perfect when it would discover Him who is the one life in a universe of death, Him who is the constant basis of an ever-changing world, One who is the only Soul of which all souls are but delusive manifestations. Thus is it, through multiplicity and duality, that the ultimate unity is reached. Religion can go no further. This is the goal of all science.

All science is bound to come to this conclusion in the long run. Manifestation, and not creation, is the word of science today, and the Hindu is only glad that what he has been cherishing in his bosom for ages is going to be taught in more forcible language and with further light from the latest conclusions of science. Descend we now from the aspirations of philosophy to the religion of the ignorant. At the very outset, I may tell you that there is no polytheism in India. In every temple, if one stands by and listens, one will find the worshipers applying all the attributes of God, including omnipresence, to the images. It is not polytheism, nor would the name henotheism explain the situation.

"The rose, called by any other name, would smell as sweet." Names are not explanations. I remember, as a boy, hearing a Christian missionary preach to crowd in India. Among other sweet things he was telling them was that if he gave a blow to their idol with his stick, what could it do? One of his hearers sharply answered, "If I abuse your God, what can He do?" "You would be punished," said the preacher, "when you die." "So my idol will punish you when you die," retorted the Hindu.

The tree is known by its fruits. When I have seen among them that are called idolaters, men, the like of whom, in morality and spirituality and love, I have never seen anywhere, I stop and ask myself, "Can sin beget holiness?" Superstition is a great enemy of man, but bigotry is worse. Why does a Christian go to church? Why is the cross holy? Why is the face turned toward the sky in prayer? Why are there so many images in the Catholic Church? Why are there so many images in the minds of Protestants when they pray? My brethren, we can no more think about anything without a mental image than we can live without breathing. By the law of association the material image calls up the mental idea and vice versa. This is why the Hindu uses an external symbol when he worships. He will tell you, it helps to keep his mind fixed on the Being to whom he prays. He knows as well as you do that the image is not God, is not omnipresent. After all, how much does omnipresence mean to almost the whole world? It stands merely as a word, a symbol. Has God superficial area? If not, when we repeat that word "omnipresent," we think of the extended sky or of space—that is all.

As we find that somehow or other, by the laws of our mental constitution, we have to associate our ideas of infinity with the image of the blue sky, or of the sea, so we naturally connect our idea of holiness with the image of a church, a mosque, or a cross. The Hindus have associated the ideas of holiness, purity, truth, omnipresence, and such other ideas with different images and forms. But with this difference that while some people devote their whole lives to their idol of a church and never rise higher, because with them religion means an intellectual assent to certain doctrines and doing good to their fellows, the whole religion of the Hindu is centered in realization. Man is to become divine by realizing the divine. Idols or temples or churches or books are only the supports, the helps, of his spiritual childhood, but on and on he must progress.

He must not stop anywhere. "External worship, material worship," say the scriptures, "is the lowest stage; struggling to rise high, mental prayer is the next

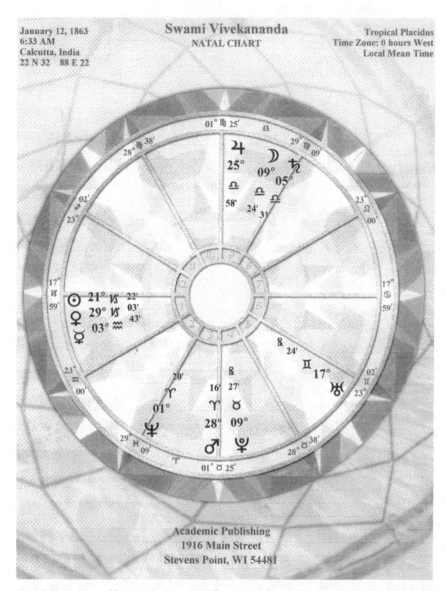

Astrological chart of Swami Vivekananda. (*Courtesy of Cosmic Patterns and created using the Kepler software program*)

stage, but the highest stage is when the Lord has been realized." Mark, the same earnest man who is kneeling before the idol, tells you, "Him the sun cannot express, nor the moon, nor the stars, the lightning cannot express Him, nor what we speak of as fire; through Him they shine." But he does not abuse anyone's idol or call its worship sin. He recognizes in it a necessary stage of life. "The child is father of the man." Would it be right for an old man to say that childhood is a sin or youth a sin?

If a man can realize his divine nature with the help of an image, would it be right to call that a sin? Nor, even when he has passed that stage, should he call it an error. To the Hindu, man is not traveling from error to truth but from truth to truth, from lower to higher truth. To him all the religions, from the lowest fetishism to the highest absolutism, mean so many attempts of the human soul to grasp and realize the Infinite, each determined by the conditions of its birth and association, and each of these marks a stage of progress; and every soul is a young eagle soaring higher and higher, gathering more and more strength till it reaches the Glorious Sun.

Unity in variety is the plan of nature, and the Hindu has recognized it. Every other religion lays down certain fixed dogmas and tries to force society to adopt them. It places before society only one coat which must fit Jack and John and Henry, all alike. If it does not fit John or Henry he must go without a coat to cover his body. The Hindus have discovered that the absolute can only be realized, or thought of, or stated through the relative, and the images, crosses, and crescents are simply so many symbols—so many pegs to hang spiritual ideas on. It is not that this help is necessary for everyone, but those that do not need it have no right to say that it is wrong. Nor is it compulsory in Hinduism.

One thing I must tell you. Idolatry in India does not mean anything horrible. It is not the mother of harlots. On the other hand, it is the attempt of undeveloped minds to grasp high spiritual truths. The Hindus have their faults, they sometimes have their exceptions; but mark this, they are always for punishing their own bodies and never for cutting the throats of their neighbors. If the Hindu fanatic burns himself on the pyre, he never lights the fire of Inquisition. And even this cannot be laid at the door of his religion any more than the burning of witches can be laid at the door of Christianity. To the Hindu, then, the whole world of religions is only a traveling, a coming up, of different men and women, through various conditions and circumstances, to the same goal. Every religion is only evolving a God out of the material man, and the same God is the inspirer of all of them. Why, then, are there so many contradictions? They are only apparent, says the Hindu. The contradictions come from the same truth adapting itself to the varying circumstances of different natures.

It is the same light coming through glasses of different colors. And these little variations are necessary for purposes of adaptation. But in the heart of everything the same truth reigns. The Lord has declared to the Hindu in His incarnation as Krishna: "I am in every religion as the thread through a string of pearls. Wherever thou seest extraordinary holiness and extraordinary power raising and purifying humanity, know thou that I am there." And what has been the result? I challenge the world to find, throughout the whole system of Sanskrit philosophy, any such expression as that the Hindu alone will be saved and not others. Says Vyasa, "We find perfect men even beyond the pale of our caste and creed." One thing more. How, then, can the Hindu, whose whole fabric of thought centers in God, believe in Buddhism which is agnostic or in Jainism which is atheistic?

The Buddhists or the Jains do not depend upon God, but the whole force of their religion is directed to the great central truth in every religion, to evolve a God out of man. They have not seen the Father, but they have seen the Son. And he that hath seen the Son hath seen the Father also.

This, brethren, is a short sketch of the religious ideas of the Hindus. The Hindu may have failed to carry out all his plans, but if there is ever to be a universal religion, it must be one which will have no location in place or time; which will be infinite like the God it will preach, and whose sun will shine upon the followers of Krishna and of Christ, on saints and sinners alike; which will not be Brahminic or Buddhistic, Christian or Mohammedan, but the sum total of all these, and still have infinite space for development; which in its catholicity will embrace in infinite arms, and find a place for, every human being from the lowest groveling savage, not far removed from the brute, to the highest man towering by the virtues of his head and heart almost above humanity, making society stand in awe of him and doubt his human nature. It will be a religion which will have no place for persecution or intolerance in its polity, which will recognize divinity in every man and woman, and whose whole scope, whose whole force, will be centered in aiding humanity to realize its own true, divine nature.

Offer such a religion and all the nations will follow you. Asoka's council was a council of the Buddhist faith. Akbar's, though more to the purpose, was only a parlor meeting. It was reserved for America to proclaim to all quarters of the globe that the Lord is in every religion.

May He who is the Brahman of the Hindus, the Ahura-Mazda of the Zoroastrians, the Buddha of the Buddhists, the Jehovah of the Jews, the Father in Heaven of the Christians, give strength to you to carry out your noble idea! The star arose in the East; it traveled steadily toward the West, sometimes dimmed and sometimes effulgent, till it made a circuit of the world, and now it is again rising on the very horizon of the East, the borders of the Sanpo,[1] a thousand fold more effulgent than it ever was before.

Hail Columbia, motherland of liberty! It has been given to thee, who never dipped her hand in her neighbor's blood, who never found out that the shortest way of becoming rich was by robbing one's neighbors, it has been given to thee to march at the vanguard of civilization with the flag of harmony.

NOTE

1. A Tibetan name for the Brahmaputra River.

12
SMOKEY THE BEAR SUTRA

Gary Snyder

Once in the Jurassic about 150 million years ago, the Great Sun Buddha in this corner of the Infinite Void gave a discourse to all the assembled elements and energies: to the standing beings, the walking beings, the flying beings, and the sitting beings—even the grasses, to the number of thirteen billion, each one born from a seed, assembled there: a Discourse concerning Enlightenment on the planet Earth.

> In some future time, there will be a continent called America. It will have great centers of power called such as Pyramid Lake, Walden Pond, Mt. Rainier, Big Sur, Everglades, and so forth; and powerful nerves and channels such as Columbia River, Mississippi River, and Grand Canyon. The human race in that era will get into troubles all over its head, and practically wreck everything in spite of its own strong intelligent Buddha-nature.
>
> The twisting strata of the great mountains and the pulsings of volcanoes are my love burning deep in the earth. My obstinate compassion is schist and basalt and granite, to be mountains, to bring down the rain. In that future American Era I shall enter a new form; to cure the world of loveless knowledge that seeks with blind hunger: and mindless rage eating food that will not fill it.

And he showed himself in his true form of

SMOKEY THE BEAR

A handsome smokey-colored brown bear standing on his hind legs, showing that he is aroused and watchful.

Bearing in his right paw the Shovel that digs to the truth beneath appearances, cuts the roots of useless attachments, and flings damp sand on the fires of greed and war;

His left paw in the mudra of Comradely Display—indicating that all creatures have the full right to live to their limits and that of deer, rabbits, chipmunks, snakes, dandelions, and lizards all grow in the realm of the Dharma;

Wearing the blue work overalls symbolic of slaves and laborers, the countless men oppressed by a civilization that claims to save but often destroys;

Wearing the broad-brimmed hat of the West, symbolic of the forces that guard the wilderness, which is the Natural State of the Dharma and the true path of man on Earth: all true paths lead through mountains—

With a halo of smoke and flame behind, the forest fires of the kali-yuga, fires caused by the stupidity of those who think things can be gained and lost whereas in truth all is contained vast and free in the Blue Sky and Green Earth of One Mind;

Round-bellied to show his kind nature and that the great earth has food enough for everyone who loves her and trusts her;

Trampling underfoot wasteful freeways and needless suburbs, smashing the worms of capitalism and totalitarianism;

Indicating the task: his followers, becoming free of cars, houses, canned foods, universities, and shoes, master the Three Mysteries of their own Body, Speech, and Mind; and fearlessly chop down the rotten trees and prune out the sick limbs of this country America and then burn the leftover trash.

Wrathful but calm. Austere but Comic. Smokey the Bear will Illuminate those who would help him; but for those who would hinder or slander him . . .

HE WILL PUT THEM OUT.

Thus his great Mantra:

> Namah samanta vajranam chanda maharoshana
>   Sphataya hum traks ham mam

> "I DEDICATE MYSELF TO THE UNIVERSAL DIAMOND
>   BE THIS RAGING FURY DESTROYED"

And he will protect those who love the woods and rivers, Gods and animals, hobos and madmen, prisoners and sick people, musicians, playful women, and hopeful children:

And if anyone is threatened by advertising, air pollution, television, or the police, they should chant SMOKEY THE BEAR'S WAR SPELL:

DROWN THEIR BUTTS
CRUSH THEIR BUTTS
DROWN THEIR BUTTS
CRUSH THEIR BUTTS

And SMOKEY THE BEAR will surely appear to put the enemy out with his vajra-shovel.

Now those who recite this Sutra and then try to put it in practice will accumulate merit as countless as the sands of Arizona and Nevada. Will help save the planet Earth from total oil slick. Will enter the age of harmony of man and nature. Will win the tender love and caresses of men, women, and beasts. Will always have ripened blackberries to eat and a sunny spot under a pine tree to sit at.

AND IN THE END WILL WIN HIGHEST PERFECT ENLIGHTENMENT

. . . thus we have heard . . .

(may be reproduced free forever)

OTHER FORERUNNERS

13

THE LIFE OF SAINT ISSA

Best of the Sons of Men

Nicholas Notovitch

CHAPTER I

1 The earth has trembled and the heavens have wept because of a great crime which has been committed in the land of Israel.

2 For they have tortured and there put to death the great and just Issa, in whom dwelt the soul of the universe,

3 Which was incarnate in a simple mortal in order to do good to men and to exterminate their evil thoughts.

4 And in order to bring back man degraded by his sins to a life of peace, love, and happiness and to recall to him the one and indivisible Creator, whose mercy is infinite and without bounds,

5 Hear what the merchants from Israel relate to us on this subject.

CHAPTER II

1 The people of Israel, who dwelt on a fertile soil giving forth two crops a year and who possessed large flocks, excited by their sins the anger of God,

2 Who inflicted upon them a terrible chastisement in taking from them their land, their cattle, and their possessions. Israel was reduced to slavery by the powerful and rich pharaohs who then reigned in Egypt.

3 These treated the Israelites worse than animals, burdening them with difficult

tasks and loading them with chains. They covered their bodies with weals and wounds, without giving them food or permitting them to dwell beneath a roof,

4 To keep them in a state of continual terror and to deprive them of all human resemblance.

5 And in their great calamity, the people of Israel remembered their heavenly protector and, addressing themselves to him, implored his grace and mercy.

6 An illustrious pharaoh then reigned in Egypt who had rendered himself famous by his numerous victories, the riches he had heaped up, and the vast palaces which his slaves had erected for him with their own hands.

7 This pharaoh had two sons, of whom the younger was called Mossa. Learned Israelites taught him diverse sciences.

8 And they loved Mossa in Egypt for his goodness and the compassion which he showed to all those who suffered.

9 Seeing that the Israelites would not, in spite of the intolerable sufferings they were enduring, abandon their God to worship those made by the hand of man, which were gods of the Egyptian nation,

10 Mossa believed in their invisible God, who did not let their failing strength give way.

11 And the Israelitish preceptors excited the ardor of Mossa and had recourse to him, praying him to intercede with the pharaoh his father in favor of their coreligionists.

12 Wherefore the Prince Mossa went to his father, begging him to ameliorate the fate of these unfortunates. But the pharaoh became angered against him and only augmented the torments endured by his slaves.

13 It happened that a short time after, a great evil visited Egypt. The pestilence came to decimate there both the young and the old, the weak and the strong; and the pharaoh believed in the resentment of his own gods against him.

14 But the Prince Mossa told his father that it was the God of his slaves who was interceding in favor of these unfortunates in punishing the Egyptians.

15 The pharaoh then gave to Mossa his son an order to take all the slaves of the Jewish race, to conduct them outside the town, and to found at a great distance from the capital another city where he should dwell with them.

16 Mossa then made known to the Hebrew slaves that he had set them free in the name of their God, the God of Israel, and he went out with them from the city and from the land of Egypt.

17 He led them into the land they had lost by their many sins, he gave unto them laws, and enjoined them to pray always to the invisible Creator whose goodness is infinite.

18 On the death of Prince Mossa, the Israelites rigorously observed his laws, wherefore God recompensed them for the ills to which he had exposed them in Egypt.

19 Their kingdom became the most powerful of all the earth, their kings made

themselves famous for their treasures, and a long peace reigned among the people of Israel.

CHAPTER III

1 The glory of the riches of Israel spread throughout the earth, and the neighboring nations bore them envy.

2 For the Most High himself led the victorious arms of the Hebrews, and the pagans dared not attack them.

3 Unhappily, as man is not always true to himself, the fidelity of the Israelites to their God did not last long.

4 They began by forgetting all the favors which he had heaped upon them, invoked but seldom his name, and sought the protection of magicians and sorcerers.

5 The kings and the captains substituted their own laws for those which Mossa had written down for them. The temple of God and the practice of worship were abandoned. The people gave themselves up to pleasure and lost their original purity.

6 Several centuries had elapsed since their departure from Egypt when God determined to exercise once more his chastisements upon them.

7 Strangers began to invade the land of Israel, devastating the country, ruining the villages, and carrying the inhabitants into captivity.

8 And there came at one time pagans from the country of Romeles, on the other side of the sea. They subdued the Hebrews and established among them military leaders who by delegation from Caesar ruled over them.

9 They destroyed the temples, they forced the inhabitants to cease worshiping the invisible God, and compelled them to sacrifice victims to the pagan deities.

10 They made warriors of those who had been nobles, the women were torn away from their husbands, and the lower classes, reduced to slavery, were sent by thousands beyond the seas.

11 As to the children, they were put to the sword. Soon in all the land of Israel naught was heard but groans and lamentations.

12 In this extreme distress, the people remembered their great God. They implored his grace and besought him to forgive them; and our Father, in his inexhaustible mercy, heard their prayer.

CHAPTER IV

1 At this time came the moment when the all-merciful Judge elected to become incarnate in a human being.

2 And the Eternal Spirit, dwelling in a state of complete inaction and of

supreme beatitude, awoke and detached itself for an indefinite period from the Eternal Being,

3 So as to show forth in the guise of humanity the means of self-identification with Divinity and of attaining to eternal felicity,

4 And to demonstrate by example how man may attain moral purity and, by separating his soul from its mortal coil, the degree of perfection necessary to enter into the kingdom of heaven, which is unchangeable and where happiness reigns eternal.

5 Soon after, a marvelous child was born in the land of Israel, God himself speaking by the mouth of this infant of the frailty of the body and the grandeur of the soul.

6 The parents of the newborn child were poor people, belonging by birth to a family of noted piety, who, forgetting their ancient grandeur on earth, praised the name of the Creator and thanked him for the ills with which he saw fit to prove them.

7 To reward them for not turning aside from the way of truth, God blessed the firstborn of this family. He chose him for his elect and sent him to help those who had fallen into evil and to cure those who suffered.

8 The divine child, to whom was given the name of Issa, began from his earliest years to speak of the one and indivisible God, exhorting the souls of those gone astray to repentance and the purification of the sins of which they were culpable.

9 People came from all parts to hear him, and they marveled at the discourses proceeding from his childish mouth. All the Israelites were of one accord in saying that the Eternal Spirit dwelt in this child.

10 When Issa had attained the age of thirteen years, the epoch when an Israelite should take a wife,

11 The house where his parents earned their living by carrying on a modest trade began to be a place of meeting for rich and noble people, desirous of having for a son-in-law the young Issa, already famous for his edifying discourses in the name of the Almighty.

12 Then it was that Issa left the parental house in secret, departed from Jerusalem, and with the merchants set out toward Sind,

13 With the object of perfecting himself in the Divine Word and of studying the laws of the great Buddhas

CHAPTER V

1 In the course of his fourteenth year, the young Issa, blessed of God, came on this side of Sind and established himself among the Aryas in the land beloved of God.

2 Fame spread the reputation of this marvelous child throughout the length of

northern Sind, and when he crossed the country of the five rivers and the Rajputana, the devotees of the god Jaine prayed him to dwell among them.

3 But he left the erring worshippers of Jaine and went to Juggernaut in the country of Orissa, where repose the mortal remains of Vyasa-Krishna and where the white priests of Brahma made him a Joyous welcome.

4 They taught him to read and understand the Vedas, to cure by aid of prayer, to teach, to explain the holy scriptures to the people, and to drive out evil spirits from the bodies of men, restoring unto them their sanity.

5 He passed six years at Juggernaut, at Rajagriha, at Benares, and in the other holy cities. Everyone loved him, for Issa lived in peace with the Vaisyas and the Sudras, whom he instructed in the holy scriptures.

6 But the Brahmans and the Kshatriyas told him that they were forbidden by the great Para-Brahma to come near to those whom he had created from his side and his feet;

7 That the Vaisyas were only authorized to hear the reading of the Vedas, and this on festival days only;

8 That the Sudras were forbidden not only to assist at the reading of the Vedas, but also from contemplating them, for their condition was to serve in perpetuity as slaves to the Brahmans, the Kshatriyas, and even the Vaisyas.

9 "'Death only can set them free from their servitude' has said Para-Brahma. Leave them then and come and worship with us the gods, who will become incensed against thee if thou cost disobey them."

10 But Issa listened not to their discourses and betook him to the Sudras, preaching against the Brahmans and the Kshatriyas.

11 He inveighed against the act of a man arrogating to himself the power to deprive his fellow beings of their rights of humanity; "for," said he, "God the Father makes no difference between his children; all to him are equally dear."

12 Issa denied the divine origin of the Vedas* and the Puranas. "For," taught he to his followers, "a law has already been given to man to guide him in his actions;

13 "Fear thy God, bend the knee before him only, and bring to him alone the offerings which proceed from thy gains."

14 Issa denied the Trimurti and the incarnation of Para-Brahma in Vishnu, Siva, and other gods, for said he:

15 "The Judge Eternal, the Eternal Spirit, comprehends the one and indivisible soul of the universe, which alone creates, contains, and vivifies all.

16 "He alone has willed and created, he alone has existed since all eternity, and his existence will have no end. He has no equal either in the heavens or on earth.

17 "The Great Creator has not shared his power with any living being, still less with inanimate objects, as they have taught to you; for he alone possesses omnipotence.

---

*Inasmuch as Jesus' closest disciple, John, begins his Gospel with a quotation from the Vedas, "In the beginning was the Word . . . ," the authenticity of this passage may be questioned.

18 "He willed it and the world appeared. In a divine thought, he gathered
together the waters, separating from them the dry portion of the globe. He is
the principle of the mysterious existence of man, in whom he has breathed a
part of his Being.

19 "And he has subordinated to man the earth, the waters, the beasts, and all
that he has created and that he himself preserves in immutable order, fixing for
each thing the length of its duration.

20 "The anger of God will soon be let loose against man; for he has forgotten
his Creator, he has filled his temples with abominations, and he worships a
crowd of creatures which God has made subordinate to him.

21 "For to do honor to stones and metals, he sacrifices human beings, in whom
dwells a part of the spirit of the Most High.

22 "For he humiliates those who work by the sweat of their brow to acquire
the favor of an idler seated at his sumptuous board.

23 "Those who deprive their brethren of divine happiness shall be deprived of
it themselves. The Brahmans and the Kshatriyas shall become the Sudras, and
with the Sudras the Eternal shall dwell everlastingly.

24 "Because in the day of the last judgment the Sudras and the Vaisyas will be
forgiven much because of their ignorance, while God, on the contrary, will
punish with his wrath those who have arrogated to themselves his rights."

25 The Vaisyas and the Sudras were filled with great admiration and asked
Issa how they should pray so as not to lose their eternal felicity.

26 "Worship not the idols, for they hear you not. Listen not to the Vedas, for
their truth is counterfeit. Never put yourself in the first place and never humiliate your neighbor.

27 "Help the poor, support the weak, do ill to no one, and covet not that which
thou hast not and which thou seest belongeth to another."

CHAPTER VI

1 The white priests and the warriors, becoming acquainted with the discourses
of Issa addressed to the Sudras, resolved upon his death and sent with this intent
their servants to seek out the young prophet.

2 But Issa, warned of his danger by the Sudras, left the neighborhood of Juggernaut by night, reached the mountain, and established himself in the country
of Gautamides, the birthplace of the great Buddha Sakyamuni, in the midst of a
people worshiping the one and sublime Brahma.

3 After having perfected himself in the Pali language, the just Issa applied
himself to the study of the sacred writings of the Sutras.

4 Six years after, Issa, whom the Buddha had elected to spread his holy word,
had become a perfect expositor of the sacred writings.

5 Then he left Nepal and the Himalayan mountains, descended into the valley of Rajputana, and went toward the west, preaching to diverse peoples the supreme perfection of man,

6 Which is—to do good to one's neighbor, being the sure means of merging oneself rapidly in the Eternal Spirit: "He who shall have regained his original purity," said Issa, "will die having obtained remission for his sins, and he will have the right to contemplate the majesty of God."

7 In crossing pagan territories, the divine Issa taught that the worship of visible gods was contrary to the law of nature.

8 "For man," said he, "has not been permitted to see the image of God, and yet he has made a host of deities in the likeness of the Eternal.

9 "Moreover, it is incompatible with the human conscience to make less matter of the grandeur of divine purity than of animals and objects executed by the hand of man in stone or metal.

10 "The Eternal Lawgiver is one; there is no other God but he. He has not shared the world with anyone, neither has he informed anyone of his intentions.

11 "Even as a father would act toward his children, so will God judge men after their deaths according to the laws of his mercy. Never would he so humiliate his child as to transmigrate his soul, as in a purgatory, into the body of an animal."

12 "The heavenly law," said the Creator by the mouth of Issa, "is opposed to the immolation of human sacrifices to an image or to an animal; for I have consecrated to man all the animals and all that the earth contains.

13 "All things have been sacrificed to man, who is directly and intimately associated with me, his Father; therefore he who shall have stolen from me my child will be severely judged and chastised by the divine law.

14 "Man is naught before the Eternal Judge, as the animal is naught before man.

15 "Wherefore I say unto you, Leave your idols and perform not rites which separate you from your Father, associating you with the priests from whom the heavens have turned away.

16 "For it is they who have led you from the true God and whose superstitions and cruelties conduce to the perversion of your soul and the loss of all moral sense."

CHAPTER VII

1 The words of Issa spread among the pagans in the midst of the countries he traversed, and the inhabitants forsook their idols.

2 Seeing which the priests exacted of him who glorified the name of the true God, reason in the presence of the people for the reproaches he made against them and a demonstration of the nothingness of their idols.

3 And Issa made answer to them: "If your idols and your animals are powerful and really possessed of supernatural strength, then let them strike me to the earth."

4 "Work then a miracle," replied the priests, "and let thy God confound our gods, if they inspire him with contempt."

5 But Issa then said: "The miracles of our God have been worked since the first day when the universe was created; they take place every day and at every moment. Whosoever seeth them not is deprived of one of the fairest gifts of life.

6 "And it is not against pieces of stone, metal, or wood, which are inanimate, that the anger of God will have full course; but it will fall on men, who, if they desire their salvation, must destroy all the idols they have made.

7 "Even as a stone and a grain of sand, naught as they are in the sight of man, wait patiently the moment when he shall take and make use of them,

8 "So man must await the great favor that God shall accord him in his final judgment.

9 "But woe unto you, ye enemies of men, if it be not a favor that you await but rather the wrath of the Divinity—woe unto you if ye expect miracles to bear witness to his power.

10 "For it will not be the idols that he will annihilate in his anger but those who shall have erected them. Their hearts shall be consumed with eternal fire, and their lacerated bodies shall go to satiate the hunger of wild beasts.

11 "God will drive the impure from among his flocks, but he will take back to himself those who shall have gone astray through not having recognized the portion of spirituality within them."

12 Seeing the powerlessness of their priests, the pagans had still greater faith in the sayings of Issa and, fearing the anger of the Divinity, broke their idols to pieces. As for the priests, they fled to escape the vengeance of the populace.

13 And Issa further taught the pagans not to strive to see the Eternal Spirit with their eyes but to endeavor to feel him in their hearts and by purity of soul to render themselves worthy of his favors.

14 "Not only," said he unto them, "abstain from consuming human sacrifices, but immolate no creature to whom life has been given, for all things that exist have been created for the profit of man.

15 "Do not steal the goods of your neighbor, for that would be to deprive him of what he has acquired by the sweat of his brow.

16 "Deceive no one, so as not to be yourselves deceived. Endeavor to justify yourself before the last judgment, for then it will be too late.

17 "Do not give yourselves up to debauchery, for that would be to violate the laws of God.

18 "You shall attain to supreme happiness, not only in purifying yourselves, but also in guiding others in the way that shall permit them to gain original perfection."

CHAPTER VIII

1 The neighboring countries resounded with the prophecies of Issa, and when he entered into Persia the priests became alarmed and forbade the inhabitants to listen to him.

2 And when they saw all the villages welcoming him with joy and listening devoutly to his sermons, they gave orders to arrest him and had him brought before the high priest, where he underwent the following interrogation:

3 "Of what new God dost thou speak? Art thou not aware, unhappy man, that Saint Zoroaster is the only just one admitted to the privilege of communion with the Supreme Being,

4 "Who ordered the angels to put down in writing the word of God for the use of his people, laws that were given to Zoroaster in paradise?

5 "Who then art thou to dare here to blaspheme our God and to sow doubt in the hearts of believers?"

6 And Issa said unto them: "It is not of a new God that I speak but of our Heavenly Father, who has existed since all time and who will still be after the end of all things.

7 "It is of him that I have discoursed to the people, who, like unto innocent children, are not yet capable of comprehending God by the simple strength of their intelligence or of penetrating into his divine and spiritual sublimity.

8 "But even as a babe discovers in the darkness its mother's breast, so even your people, who have been led into error by your erroneous doctrine and your religious ceremonies, have recognized by instinct their Father in the Father of whom I am the prophet.

9 "The Eternal Being has said to your people through the medium of my mouth: 'You shall not worship the sun, for it is but a part of the world which I have created for man.

10 "'The sun rises in order to warm you during your work; it sets to allow you the repose which I myself have appointed.

11 "'It is to me, and to me alone, that you owe all that you possess, all that is to be found about you, above you, and below you.'"

12 "But," said the priests, "how could a people live according to the rules of justice if it had no preceptors?"

13 Then Issa answered, "So long as the people had no priests, the natural law governed them, and they preserved the candor of their souls.

14 "Their souls were with God, and to commune with the Father they had recourse to the medium of no idol or animal, nor to the fire, as is practiced here.

15 "You contend that one must worship the sun, the spirit of good and of evil. Well, I say unto you, your doctrine is a false one, the sun acting not spontaneously but according to the will of the invisible Creator who gave it birth

16 "And who has willed it to be the star that should light the day, to warm the labor and the seedtime of man.

17 "The Eternal Spirit is the soul of all that is animate. You commit a great sin in dividing it into a spirit of evil and a spirit of good, for there is no God outside the good,

18 "Who, like unto the father of a family, does but good to his children, forgiving all their faults if they repent them.

19 "The spirit of evil dwells on the earth in the hearts of those men who turn aside the children of God from the strait path.

20 "Wherefore I say unto you, Beware of the day of judgment, for God will inflict a terrible chastisement upon all those who shall have led his children astray from the right path and have filled them with superstitions and prejudices;

21 "Those who have blinded them that see, conveyed contagion to the healthy, and taught the worship of the things that God has subordinated to man for his good and to aid him in his work.

22 "Your doctrine is therefore the fruit of your errors; for desiring to bring near to you the God of truth, you have created for yourselves false gods."

23 After having listened to him, the magi determined to do him no harm. But at night, when all the town lay sleeping, they conducted him outside of the walls and abandoned him on the high road, in the hope that he would soon become a prey to the wild beasts.

24 But, protected by the Lord our God, Saint Issa continued his way unmolested.

CHAPTER IX

1 Issa, whom the Creator had elected to remind a depraved humanity of the true God, had reached his twenty-ninth year when he returned to the land of Israel.

2 Since his departure the pagans had inflicted still more atrocious sufferings on the Israelites, who were a prey to the deepest despondency.

3 Many among them had already begun to abandon the laws of their God and those of Mossa in the hope of appeasing their savage conquerors.

4 In the face of this evil, Issa exhorted his compatriots not to despair because the day of the redemption of sins was at hand, and he confirmed them in the belief which they had in the God of their fathers.

5 "Children, do not give yourselves up to despair," said the Heavenly Father by the mouth of Issa, "for I have heard your voice, and your cries have reached me.

6 "Do not weep, O my beloved ones! For your grief has touched the heart of your Father, and he has forgiven you, even as he forgave your forefathers.

7 "Do not abandon your families to plunge yourselves into debauchery, do

not lose the nobility of your feelings, and do not worship idols who will remain deaf to your voices.

8 "Fill my temple with your hope and with your patience and abjure not the religion of your fathers; for I alone have guided them and have heaped them with benefits.

9 "You shall lift up those who have fallen, you shall give food to the hungry, and you shall come to the aid of the sick, so as to be all pure and just at the day of the last judgment which I prepare for you."

10 The Israelites came in crowds at the word of Issa, asking him where they should praise the Heavenly Father, seeing that the enemy had razed their temples to the ground and laid low their sacred vessels.

11 And Issa made answer to them that God had not in view temples erected by the hands of man, but he meant that the human heart was the true temple of God.

12 "Enter into your temple, into your heart. Illumine it with good thoughts and the patience and immovable confidence which you should have in your Father.

13 "And your sacred vessels, they are your hands and your eyes. See and do that which is agreeable to God, for in doing good to your neighbor you accomplish a rite which embellishes the temple wherein dwells he who gave you life.

14 "For God has created you in his own likeness—innocent, with pure souls and hearts filled with goodness, destined not for the conception of evil schemes but made to be sanctuaries of love and justice.

15 "Wherefore I say unto you, sully not your hearts, for the Supreme Being dwells therein eternally.

16 "If you wish to accomplish works marked with love or piety, do them with an open heart and let not your actions be governed by calculations or the hope of gain.

17 "For such actions would not help to your salvation, and you would fall into that state of moral degradation where theft, lying, and murder pass for generous deeds."

CHAPTER X

1 Saint Issa went from one town to another, strengthening by the word of God the courage of the Israelites, who were ready to succumb to the weight of their despair, and thousands of men followed him to hear him preach.

2 But the chiefs of the towns became afraid of him, and they made known to the principal governor who dwelt at Jerusalem that a man named Issa had arrived in the country; that he was stirring up by his discourses the people against the authorities; that the crowd listened to him with assiduity, neglected the works of the state, and affirmed that before long it would be rid of its intrusive governors.

3 Then Pilate, governor of Jerusalem, ordered that they should seize the person of the preacher Issa, that they should bring him into the town and lead him before the judges. But in order not to excite the anger of the populace, Pilate charged the priests and the learned Hebrew elders to judge him in the temple.

4 Meanwhile Issa, continuing his preachings, arrived at Jerusalem; and, having learned of his arrival, all the inhabitants, knowing him already by reputation, went out to meet him.

5 They greeted him respectfully and opened to him the gates of their temple in order to hear from his mouth what he had said in the other cities of Israel.

6 And Issa said unto them: "The human race perishes because of its lack of faith, for the darkness and the tempest have scattered the flocks of humanity and they have lost their shepherds.

7 "But the tempest will not last forever, and the darkness will not always obscure the light. The sky will become once more serene, the heavenly light will spread itself over the earth, and the flocks gone astray will gather around their shepherd.

8 "Do not strive to find straight paths in the darkness, lest ye fall into a pit; but gather together your remaining strength, support one another, place your confidence in your God, and wait till light appears.

9 "He who sustains his neighbor, sustains himself; and whosoever protects his family, protects the people and the state.

10 "For be sure that the day is at hand when you shall be delivered from the darkness; you shall be gathered together as one family; and your enemy, who ignores what the favor of God is, shall tremble with fear."

11 The priests and the elders who were listening to him, filled with admiration at his discourse, asked him if it were true that he had tried to stir up the people against the authorities of the country, as had been reported to the governor Pilate.

12 "Can one excite to insurrection men gone astray, from whom the obscurity has hidden their door and their path?" replied Issa. "I have only warned the unfortunate, as I do here in this temple, that they may not further advance along the darkened way, for an abyss is open under their feet.

13 "Earthly power is not of long duration, and it is subject to many changes. Of what use that man should revolt against it, seeing that one power always succeeds to another power? And thus it will come to pass until the extinction of humanity.

14 "Against which, see you not that the mighty and the rich sow among the sons of Israel a spirit of rebellion against the eternal power of heaven?"

15 The elders then asked: "Who art thou, and from what country dost thou come? We have not heard speak of thee before, and we know not even thy name."

16 "I am an Israelite," replied Issa. "From the day of my birth I saw the walls of Jerusalem, and I heard the weeping of my brothers reduced to slavery and the lamentations of my sisters who were carried away by the pagans.

17 "And my soul was filled with sadness when I saw that my brethren had forgotten the true God. As a child, I left my father's house and went to dwell among other peoples.

18 "But having heard that my brethren were suffering still greater tortures, I have come back to the country where my parents dwell to remind my brothers of the faith of their forefathers, which teaches us patience on earth to obtain perfect and sublime happiness in heaven."

19 And the learned elders put him this question: "It is said that thou deniest the laws of Mossa and that thou teachest the people to forsake the temple of God."

20 And Issa replied: "One cannot demolish that which has been given by our Heavenly Father, neither that which has been destroyed by sinners; but I have enjoined the purification of the heart from all blemish, for it is the true temple of God.

21 "As to the laws of Mossa, I have endeavored to establish them in the hearts of men. And I say unto you that you do not understand their real meaning, for it is not vengeance but mercy that they teach; only the sense of these laws has been perverted."

CHAPTER XI

1 Having hearkened unto Issa, the priests and the wise elders decided among themselves not to judge him, for he did harm to no one. And presenting themselves before Pilate, appointed governor of Jerusalem by the pagan king of the country of Romeles, they addressed him thus:

2 "We have seen the man whom thou accusest of inciting our people to rebellion; we have heard his discourses, and we know him to be our compatriot.

3 "But the chiefs of the cities have made thee false reports, for this is a just man who teaches the people the word of God. After having interrogated him, we dismissed him, that he might go in peace."

4 The governor then became enraged and sent near to Issa his servants in disguise, so that they might watch all his actions and report to the authorities the least word that he should address to the people.

5 In the meantime, Saint Issa continued to visit the neighboring towns, preaching the true ways of the Creator, exhorting the Hebrews to patience, and promising them a speedy deliverance.

6 And during all this time, many people followed him wherever he went, several never leaving him but becoming his servitors.

7 And Issa said: "Do not believe in miracles wrought by the hand of man, for he who dominates over nature is alone capable of doing that which is supernatural, while man is powerless to stay the anger of the winds or to spread the rain.

8 "Nevertheless, there is one miracle which it is possible for man to accomplish. It is when, full of a sincere belief, he decides to root out from his heart all evil thoughts, and when to attain this end he forsakes the paths of iniquity.

9 "And all the things that are done without God are but errors, seductions, and enchantments, which only demonstrate to what an extent the soul of him who practices this art is full of shamelessness, falsehood, and impurity.

10 "Put not your faith in oracles; God alone knows the future: he who has recourse to diviners profanes the temple which is in his heart and gives a proof of distrust toward his Creator.

11 "Faith in diviners and in their oracles destroys the innate simplicity of man and his childlike purity. An infernal power takes possession of him, forcing him to commit all sorts of crimes and to worship idols;

12 "Whereas the Lord our God, who has no equal, is one, all-mighty, omniscient, and omnipresent. It is he who possesses all wisdom and all light.

13 "It is to him you must address yourselves to be consoled in your sorrows, helped in your works, and cured in your sickness. Whosoever shall have recourse to him shall not be denied.

14 "The secret of nature is in the hands of God. For the world, before it appeared, existed in the depth of the divine thought; it became material and visible by the will of the Most High.

15 "When you address yourselves to him, become again as children; for you know neither the past, the present, nor the future, and God is the Master of all time."

CHAPTER XII

1 "Righteous man," said unto him the spies of the governor of Jerusalem, "tell us if we shall perform the will of our Caesar or await our speedy deliverance."

2 And Issa, having recognized them as people appointed to follow him, replied: "I have not said to you that you shall be delivered from Caesar. It is the soul plunged in error that shall have its deliverance.

3 "As there can be no family without a head, so there can be no order among a people without a Caesar; to him implicit obedience should be given, he alone being answerable for his acts before the supreme tribunal."

4 "Does Caesar possess a divine right?" further asked of him the spies. "And is he the best of mortals?"

5 "There should be no better among men, but there are also sufferers, whom those elected and charged with this mission should care for, making use of the means conferred on them by the sacred law of our Heavenly Father.

6 "Mercy and justice are the highest attributes of a Caesar; his name will be illustrious if he adhere to them.

7 "But he who acts otherwise, who exceeds the limit of power that he has over his subordinates, going so far as to put their lives in danger, offends the great Judge and loses his dignity in the sight of man."

8 At this juncture, an old woman who had approached the group, the better to hear Issa, was pushed aside by one of the spies, who placed himself before her.

9 Then Issa held forth: "It is not meet that a son should set aside his mother, taking her place. Whosoever respecteth not his mother, the most sacred being after his God, is unworthy of the name of son.

10 "Listen, then, to what I say unto you: Respect woman, for she is the mother of the universe, and all the truth of divine creation lies in her.

11 "She is the basis of all that is good and beautiful, as she is also the germ of life and death. On her depends the whole existence of man, for she is his natural and moral support.

12 "She gives birth to you in the midst of suffering. By the sweat of her brow she rears you, and until her death you cause her the gravest anxieties. Bless her and worship her, for she is your one friend, your one support on earth.

13 "Respect her, uphold her. In acting thus you will win her love and her heart. You will find favor in the sight of God and many sins shall be forgiven you.

14 "In the same way, love your wives and respect them; for they will be mothers tomorrow, and each later on the ancestress of a race.

15 "Be lenient toward woman. Her love ennobles man, softens his hardened heart, tames the brute in him, and makes of him a lamb.

16 "The wife and the mother are the inappreciable treasures given unto you by God. They are the fairest ornaments of existence, and of them shall be born all the inhabitants of the world.

17 "Even as the God of armies separated of old the light from the darkness and the land from the waters, woman possesses the divine faculty of separating in a man good intentions from evil thoughts.

18 "Wherefore I say unto you, after God your best thoughts should belong to the women and the wives, woman being for you the temple wherein you will obtain the most easily perfect happiness.

19 "Imbue yourselves in this temple with moral strength. Here you will forget your sorrows and your failures, and you will recover the lost energy necessary to enable you to help your neighbor.

20 "Do not expose her to humiliation. In acting thus you would humiliate yourselves and lose the sentiment of love, without which nothing exists here below.

21 "Protect your wife, in order that she may protect you and all your family. All that you do for your wife, your mother, for a widow or another woman in distress, you will have done unto your God."

CHAPTER XIII

1 Saint Issa taught the people of Israel thus for three years, in every town, in every village, by the waysides and on the plains; and all that he had predicted came to pass.

2 During all this time the disguised servants of Pilate watched him closely without hearing anything said like unto the reports made against Issa in former years by the chiefs of the towns.

3 But the governor Pilate, becoming alarmed at the too great popularity of Saint Issa, who according to his adversaries sought to stir up the people to proclaim him king, ordered one of his spies to accuse him.

4 Then soldiers were commanded to proceed to his arrest, and they imprisoned him in a subterranean cell where they tortured him in various ways in the hope of forcing him to make a confession which should permit of his being put to death.

5 The saint, thinking only of the perfect beatitude of his brethren, supported all his sufferings in the name of his Creator.

6 The servants of Pilate continued to torture him and reduced him to a state of extreme weakness; but God was with him and did not allow him to die.

7 Learning of the sufferings and the tortures which their saint was enduring, the high priests and the wise elders went to pray the governor to set Issa at liberty in honor of an approaching festival.

8 But the governor straightway refused them this. They then prayed him to allow Issa to appear before the tribunal of the ancients so that he might be condemned or acquitted before the festival, and to this Pilate consented.

9 The next day the governor assembled together the chief captains, priests, wise elders, and lawyers so that they might judge Issa.

10 They brought him from his prison and seated him before the governor between two thieves to be judged at the same time as he, in order to show unto the crowd that he was not the only one to be condemned.

11 And Pilate, addressing himself to Issa, said unto him: "O man! is it true that thou incitest the people against the authorities with the intent of thyself becoming king of Israel?"

12 "One becomes not king at one's own will," replied Issa, "and they have lied who have told thee that I stir up the people to rebellion. I have never spoken of other than the King of Heaven, and it is he I teach the people to worship.

13 "For the sons of Israel have lost their original purity; and if they have not recourse to the true God, they will be sacrificed and their temple shall fall into ruins.

14 "As temporal power maintains order in a country, I teach them accordingly not to forget it. I say unto them: 'Live conformably to your station and your fortune, so as not to disturb the public order.' And I have exhorted them also to remember that disorder reigns in their hearts and in their minds.

15 "Wherefore the King of Heaven has punished them and suppressed their national kings. Nevertheless, I have said unto them, 'If you become resigned to your destinies, as a reward the kingdom of heaven shall be reserved for you.'"

16 At this moment, the witnesses were brought forward, one of whom made the following deposition: "Thou hast said to the people that the temporal power is as naught against that of the king who shall soon deliver the Israelites from the pagan yoke."

17 "Blessed art thou," said Issa, "for having spoken the truth. The King of Heaven is greater and more powerful than the terrestrial law, and his kingdom surpasses all the kingdoms of the earth.

18 "And the time is not far off when, conforming to the divine will, the people of Israel shall purify them of their sins; for it has been said that a forerunner will come to proclaim the deliverance of the people, gathering them into one fold."

19 And the governor, addressing himself to the judges, said: "Dost hear? The Israelite Issa confesses to the crime of which he is accused. Judge him, then, according to your laws, and pronounce against him capital punishment."

20 "We cannot condemn him," replied the priests and the elders. "Thou hast just heard thyself that his allusions were made regarding the King of Heaven and that he has preached naught to the sons of Israel which could constitute an offense against the law."

21 The governor Pilate then sent for the witness who, at his instigation, had betrayed Issa. The man came and addressed Issa thus: "Didst thou not pass thyself off as the king of Israel when thou saidst that he who reigns in the heavens had sent thee to prepare his people?"

22 And Issa, having blessed him, said: "Thou shalt be pardoned, for what thou sayest does not come from thee!" Then, addressing himself to the governor: "Why humiliate thy dignity, and why teach thy inferiors to live in falsehood, as without doing so thou hast power to condemn the innocent?"

23 At these words the governor became exceeding wroth, ordering the sentence of death to be passed upon Issa and the acquittal of the two thieves.

24 The judges, having consulted together, said unto Pilate: "We will not take upon our heads the great sin of condemning an innocent man and acquitting thieves. That would be against the law.

25 "Do then as thou wilt." Saying which the priests and the wise elders went out and washed their hands in a sacred vessel, saying: "We are innocent of the death of this just man."

CHAPTER XIV

1 By the order of the governor, the soldiers then seized Issa and the two thieves, whom they led to the place of execution, where they nailed them to crosses erected on the ground.

2 All the day the bodies of Issa and the two thieves remained suspended, terrible to behold, under the guard of the soldiers; the people standing all around, the relations of the sufferers praying and weeping.

3 At sunset the sufferings of Issa came to an end. He lost consciousness, and the soul of this just man left his body to become absorbed in the Divinity.

4 Thus ended the earthly existence of the reflection of the Eternal Spirit under the form of a man who had saved hardened sinners and endured many sufferings.

5 Meanwhile, Pilate became afraid of his action and gave the body of the saint to his parents, who buried it near the spot of his execution. The crowd came to pray over his tomb, and the air was filled with groans and lamentations.

6 Three days after, the governor sent his soldiers to carry away the body of Issa to bury it elsewhere, fearing otherwise a popular insurrection.

7 The next day the crowd found the tomb open and empty. At once the rumor spread that the supreme Judge had sent his angels to carry away the mortal remains of the saint in whom dwelt on earth a part of the Divine Spirit.

8 When this rumor reached the knowledge of Pilate, he became angered and forbade anyone, under the pain of slavery and death, to pronounce the name of Issa or to pray the Lord for him.

9 But the people continued to weep and to glorify aloud their Master; wherefore many were led into captivity, subjected to torture, and put to death.

10 And the disciples of Saint Issa abandoned the land of Israel and scattered themselves among the heathen, preaching that they should renounce their errors, bethink them of the salvation of their souls and of the perfect felicity awaiting humanity in that immaterial world of light where, in repose and in all his purity, the Great Creator dwells in perfect majesty.

11 The pagans, their kings, and their warriors listened to the preachers, abandoned their absurd beliefs, and forsook their priests and their idols to celebrate the praise of the all-wise Creator of the universe, the King of kings, whose heart is filled with infinite mercy.

AUTHOR'S INTRODUCTION

Jane Roberts

It was February 29, 1968. I was holding one of my twice-weekly ESP classes. The large bay window was open, letting in the unusually warm night air. The lights were normally lit in my living room where classes are held. Suddenly I felt that we had a visitor. As always I went into trance easily, without preamble.

This class was composed of college girls. They had read my first book, knew about Seth, and had attended a few classes, but they had never witnessed a Seth session. My eyes closed. When they opened a few moments later, they were much darker. I began to speak for Seth. He had thrown my glasses to the floor in a quick characteristic gesture, yet now I scrutinized each student with sharp, clear focus. The voice that spoke was deep, quite loud, more masculine than feminine.

We were having a spontaneous Seth session. It served to introduce the students to Seth, and I will let a few excerpts from it serve the same purpose now, introducing Seth to those readers who have not heard of him:

> According to what you have been taught, you are composed of physical matter and cannot escape it, and this is not so. The physical matter will disintegrate, but you will not. Though you cannot find me, know that I am here. Your own parents seem to disappear before your eyes and vanish into nothingness forever. I can assure you that they will continue to live. I can assure you that death is

From Jane Roberts, *The Seth Material* (Manhasset, NY: New Awareness Network, 1970), pp. v–xii. Copyright © 2001 Robert Butts. Reprinted by permission of the New Awareness Network.

another beginning, and that when you are dead, you are not silenced. For is this voice that you hear now, silence? Is this presence that you sense within this room, death?

I am here to tell you that your joy is not dependent upon your youth, for I am hardly young. I am here to tell you that your joy is not dependent upon your physical body, for in your terms I have none. I have what I have always had, the identity that is mine. It is never diminished. It grows and develops.

You are what you are, and you will be more. Do not be afraid of change, for you are change, and you change as you sit before me. All action is change, for otherwise there would be a static universe, and then indeed death would be the end. What I am is also what you are: individualized consciousness.

Change with the seasons, for you are more than the seasons. You form the seasons. They are the reflections of your inner psychic climate. I came for one purpose this evening: so that you could sense my vitality, and sensing it, know that I speak to you from dimensions beyond those with which you are acquainted. The grave is not the end, for such a noisy one as I never spoke with the lips of death.

I am in this room, although there is no object within which you can place me. You are as disembodied as I. You have a vehicle to use, a body that you call your own, and that is all. I borrow Ruburt's [Seth's name for me; in addition, Seth always speaks of me as male] with his consent, but what I am is not dependent upon atoms and molecules and what you are is not dependent upon physical matter. You have lived before and will live again, and when you are done with physical existence, you will still live.

I come here as though I appeared through a hole in space and time. There are walks in space and time through which you can travel, and in dreams you have been where I am. I want you to feel your own vitality. Feel it travel through the universe and know that it is not dependent upon your physical image. In reality you project your own energy out to form the physical world. Therefore, to change your world, it is yourself you must change. You must change what you project.

You always were and you always will be. This is the meaning of existence and joy. The God that is, is within you, for you are a part of all that is.

Seth spoke through me for over two hours, so quickly that the students had trouble taking notes. His joy and vitality were obvious. The personality was not mine. Seth's dry, sardonic humor shone from my eyes. The muscles of my face rearranged themselves into different patterns. My normally feminine gestures were replaced by his. Seth was enjoying himself in the guise of an old man, shrewd, lively, quite human. When he spoke of the joy of existence, ringing even through such a voice as his, that deep voice boomed. Later one of the students, Carol, told me that although she knew the words were coming from my mouth, still she felt that they were coming from all over, from the walls themselves.

During a break, Carol read the notes that she had taken. Suddenly, without transition, I was Seth again, leaning forward, joking:

"If you are to be my stenographer, you must do better than that. You are a mad scribbler."

Then a give-and-take period began in which Seth corrected Carol's notes as she read them, added several remarks to clear certain sentences, and bantered back and forth with her. The students asked questions, and Seth answered them.

This was a very simple session. Seth addressed himself to the students for the first time, yet he touched upon several issues that appear often in the Seth Material: The personality is multidimensional. The individual is basically free of space and time. The fate of each of us is in our own hands. Problems not faced in this life will be faced in another. We cannot blame God, society, or our parents for misfortunes, since before this physical life we chose the circumstances into which we would be born and the challenges that could best bring about our development. We form physical matter as effortlessly and unselfconsciously as we breathe. Telepathically, we are all aware of the mass ideas from which we form our overall conception of physical reality.

As of December 1969, my husband, Rob, and I have held over five hundred Seth sessions over a period of five years. My first book in this field, *How to Develop Your ESP Power*, briefly explained the circumstances leading to my interest in ESP and the experiments that led to my introduction to Seth. Since then, Seth has demonstrated telepathic and clairvoyant abilities on occasions too frequent to mention. Through sessions he has helped friends, strangers, and students, and by following his instructions my husband and I are learning to develop our own psychic potentials.

Yet I was not a "born psychic" with a background of paranormal experience. Neither Rob nor I had any knowledge of such matters. Even after my first enthusiasm, I didn't accept these developments without serious self-questioning and intellectual analysis. I wanted to keep my experiences on as scientific a basis as possible.

"Yes," I said in effect. "I do speak in trance for a personality who claims to have survived death. Yes, you can develop your own extrasensory abilities. Yes, Seth does insist that reincarnation is a fact. But . . . but . . . but." I found the ideas presented in the Seth Material fascinating, but I was not about to accept them as the same kind of solid fact with which I accepted, say, the bacon I eat for breakfast. Now I know they are far more important.

To me it was tantamount to intellectual suicide to even admit the possibility that Seth actually was a personality who had survived death. Nowhere in my first book did I say that I thought Seth was exactly what he said he was: "an energy personality essence no longer focused in physical reality." Instead I studied the various explanations for such personalities given by psychologists and parapsychologists on the one hand and by spiritualists on the other. Nowhere did I find an explanation as logical and consistent as that given in the Seth Material itself.

I was so used to thinking of myself as a physical creature, bound to space and time, that I almost refused to accept the evidence of my own experience. While involved in the most intuitive work in the world, I tried to become more and more objective. I tried to step back into a world I had really left forever—a universe in which nothing existed except in physical terms, a world in which communications from any other realities or dimensions were impossible. Yet, we continued to have Seth sessions twice a week.

I began to have out-of-body experiences (astral projections) as I sat in the living room, speaking for Seth. Seth described what I saw while my own consciousness was miles away, perceiving locations and events in another town or state. Our files contain statements from two brothers in California, for example, asserting that Seth correctly described their home and neighborhood while I spoke for him in Elmira, New York, some three thousand miles away. I could hardly deny those facts.

Following publication of my earlier book, letters came from strangers asking for help or advice. Finally I agreed to hold a few sessions for those most in need, though the responsibility frightened me. The people involved didn't attend the sessions, since they lived in other parts of the country, yet they said the advice helped them; information given concerning individual backgrounds was correct. Seth often explained problems as the result of unresolved stresses in past reincarnational lives and gave specific advice as to how the individuals could use their abilities now to meet these challenges.

Before this I had suspected that the reincarnational data was a delightful dish of fantasy cooked up by my own subconscious. When all this began, in fact, I wasn't at all sure that we survived death once, much less over and over again.

Rob and I were hardly religious in conventional terms. We haven't been to a church in years, except to attend weddings or funerals; I was brought up a Catholic, but as I grew older I found it more and more difficult to accept the God of my ancestors. Irony whispered that He was as dead as they were. The heaven that had sustained me as a child seemed in my teens to be a shallow mockery of meaningful existence. Who wanted to sit around singing hymns to a father-God, even if He *did* exist, and what sort of intelligent God would require such constant adoration? A very insecure, appallingly human kind of God indeed.

The alternative, that of hellfire, was equally unbelievable. Yet the conventional God of our fathers apparently sat without a qualm with the blessed in heaven, while the devil tortured the rest of the unlucky dead. That God, I decided, was out. I would not tolerate Him as a friend. For that matter, He didn't treat His son too well, either, as the story goes. But Christ you could at least respect, I thought. He'd been here; he knew how it was.

Before I was twenty, then, I'd left behind me that archaic God, the Virgin, and the communion of saints. Heaven and hell, angels and devils, were dismissed. This particular group of chemicals and atoms I called "me" would fall into no such traps—at least none that I could recognize.

Rob's background was different. His parents' brand of religion was a sort of social Protestantism, rather delightfully innocent of dogma. In general, God loved little boys and girls with starched shirts, acceptable addresses, polished shoes, and fathers who made good money—it also helped if their mothers baked cookies for the PTA.

Neither of us was bitter about such a God's apparent injustices—we didn't pay Him that much attention. I had my poetry; Rob, who is an artist, had his painting. Each of us felt a strong sense of contact with nature. No one was more surprised than I was, then, to find myself quite abruptly speaking for someone who was supposed to have survived death. I berated myself at times, thinking that even my Irish grandmother would have found spirits in the living room rather hard to take—and I used to think *she* was superstitious! A surviving soul seemed part and parcel of the adults' nonsense I'd thought I'd escaped, thanks to a college education, a quick mind, and a fine dose of native rebelliousness. It took me a while to discover that I was being as prejudiced against the idea of survival as some others were for it. Now I realize that while I was priding myself on my open-mindedness, my mental flexibility extended only to ideas that fit in with my own preconceptions. Now I know that human personality has a far greater reality than we are usually prepared to give it. *Someone* has produced over fifty notebooks of fascinating material, and even at my most skeptical moments I have to accept the reality of the sessions and the material. The scope, quality, and theories of the material "hooked" us almost at once.

Rob and I are both convinced that the Seth Material springs from sources beyond my self and that it is much less distorted by pat, conventionalized symbolism than are other paranormal scripts we have encountered. Seth says this material has been given by himself and others in other times and places, but that it is given again, in new ways, for each succeeding generation through the centuries. The reader will have to make his own judgments, but personally I do accept his theories as valid and significant.

Moreover, the riddle of such personalities as Seth—call it "spirit possession," a "daemon" (as Socrates did)—has concerned mankind through the ages. The phenomenon is hardly new. Through telling my own story and presenting the material, I hope to throw some light upon the nature of such experiences and to show that human personality has abilities still to be tapped and other ways to receive knowledge than those it usually employs.

The Seth Material has completely changed my ideas of the nature of reality and reinforced my sense of identity. No longer do I feel as I did before, that man is the slave of time, illness, decay, and at the mercy of built-in destructive tendencies over which he has no control. I feel in control of my own destiny as never before, and no longer ruled by patterns subconsciously set during my childhood.

I don't mean to imply that I feel myself entirely released from every worry and fear, only that I now know we do have the freedom to change ourselves and our environment and that in a very basic manner, we ourselves form the environment to which we then react. I believe that we form our own reality—now, and after death.

The purpose of this book is to introduce you to Seth and the Seth Material. Though Seth has appeared only once in a physical materialization, Rob has seen him clearly enough to paint a portrait of him that hangs in our living room. Through me, Seth has produced a continuing manuscript that runs well over five thousand double-spaced typewritten pages, in not quite five years' time. I know many "living" persons who haven't produced that much in a lifetime. Yet my own work continues: Since the sessions began, I've written two books of nonfiction (not counting this one), two of poetry, and a dozen short stories. Seth certainly hasn't "stolen" any of my own creative energy for his own purposes.

1987

15

OPEN LETTER TO
144,000 RAINBOW
HUMANS

Jose Arguelles

Beginning at Dawn everywhere on the Earth on Sunday, August 16, 1987, 144,000 humans are being called upon to create a complete field of trust by surrendering themselves to the planet and to the higher galactic intelligences which guide and monitor the planet. At that time and continuing through Monday, August 17, the higher galactic intelligences will be transmitting a collective planetary vision as well as messages of personal destiny to and through these people, the rainbow humans.

These dates, August 16–17, 1987, represent a window of galactic synchronization, the first to occur since humans began testing atomic weapons, July 16, 1945. The testing and release of radiation into the atmosphere of the Earth set up a signal which drew the immediate attention of the higher galactic intelligences. The manifestation since that time of the higher galactic intelligences, which humans refer to as UFOs or flying saucers, has never been officially acknowledged in a positive public manner by the governments of the Earth. The messages of the higher galactic intelligences have been benign and compassionate, yet the dominant governments have chosen to use this information as a further instrument of fear. All that the higher galactic intelligences have wished for humans to learn on a planetary scale is this: the only way to break the cycle of fear and destruction to which they have made themselves hostage is by creating a complete planetray field of trust. The only acknowledgement the higher

---

Open letter written by Jose Arguelles, February 28, 1987, for Harmonic Convergence.

galactic intelligences wish for the humans is this creation of a complete planetary field of trust.

The optimum time for the creation of this complete planetary field of trust is August 16–17, 1987. The minimum number of humans required to create this field of trust and be with each other in conscious acknowledgement of their common act of surrender to the Earth is 144,000. By their coming together, wherever they may be, beginning at dawn, August 16, 1987, these 144,000 will establish a receptacle of galactic transmission. This will create a signal more powerful than the atomic signal at Los Alamos in 1945. In response, the higher galactic intelligences will stream communications in high frequency beams to and through these 144,000 rainbow humans, catalyzing the mental field of the planet. The integrity maintained by these 144,000 humans over the two-day period will be felt by virtually every other human being on the planet in one way or another. Everyone will know and, depending on their own mental and spiritual development, will respond accordingly.

The opportunity represented by these dates, August 16–17, is unprecedented. The vision of the Earth will be collective and common once again. Peace will come.

16
NEW AGE HARMONIES

A Strange Mix of Spirituality and Superstition Is Sweeping across the Country

Otto Friedrich

“**L**et us not walk the path of life in darkness but shed your light upon the path so that we may clearly see the power of your glory forever.” Those words of prayer are the last spoken by Bob Johnson, 54, a gentle, white-haired man who practices his spiritual arts in a modest apartment in mid-town New York City. Now his eyes are half shut, unseeing, and when he next speaks, in a strangely clipped Irish accent, he represents a “tutelage” of spectral beings from Alpha Centauri, the nearest of the stars.

“Greetings from the almighty form of God,” says the celestial tutelage. “Do you seek our counsel?”

“Yes,” says *Time* Correspondent Mary Cronin.

“Do you have an art?”

“I'm a reporter.”

“That is an art of sorts. Do you feel the vibrations now? It may be starting now.”

“I'm trying to find out more about the New Age.”

“Always the New Age!”

“Is all this interest in channeling and crystals a passing fad or something more?”

“It is both: a fad to some, a way of life to others. We would say there are more true spiritual seekers today.”

"What is my mission in life?"

"We feel you will be involved in the process of bringing the written thought about spirituality to man. This is a mission. People say there are accidents, but this is not an accident."

"Can you tell me about one of my past lives?"

"You have been a sailor. A man. You understand the Spanish Armada? You tried to attack England! You considered it to be a heathen country because they dropped Catholicism."

"What did I learn from that life?"

"To swim very well. You almost lost your life. Your ship was broken up around the northern coast of Ireland. You were in the water for days. It was very painful."

"How do you live up there on Alpha Centauri?"

"We don't have a day, a night. We have never been a human body. We don't speak like this. What is coming through is not our persona. We don't have a personality you could relate to. We manifest a personality so that you may relate to it. You see?"

So here we are in the New Age, a combination of spirituality and superstition, fad and farce, about which the only thing certain is that it is not new. Nobody seems to know exactly where the term came from, but it has been around for several decades or more, and many elements of the New Age, like faith healing, fortune-telling and transmigration of souls, go back for centuries. (Ages, in general, are an uncertain affair. The Age of Aquarius, celebrated in the musical *Hair*, may have started in the 1960s or at the turn of the century or may not yet have begun. Once under way, such astrological ages are supposed to last 2,000 years.)

Though it is hard to say exactly how many Americans believe in which parts of the New Age, the movement as a whole is growing steadily. Bantam Books says its New Age titles have increased tenfold in the past decade. The number of New Age bookstores has doubled in the past five years, to about 2,500. New Age radio is spreading, with such stations as WBMW in Washington and KTWV-FM in Los Angeles offering dreamy light jazz that one listener described as "like I tapped into a radio station on Mars." The Grammys now include a special prize for New Age music (latest winner: Swiss Harpist Andreas Vollenweider). Fledgling magazines with names like *New Age*, *Body Mind Spirit* and *Brain/Mind Bulletin* are full of odd ads: "Healing yourself with crystals," "American Indian magic can work for you," How to use a green candle to gain money," "The power of the pendulum can be in your hands," "Use numerology to win the lottery." And, perhaps inevitably, "New health through colon rejuvenation."

If some of those have a slightly greedy tone, the reason is that New Age fantasies often intersect with mainstream materialism, the very thing that many New

Age believers profess to scorn. A surprising number of successful stockbrokers consult astrological charts; a yuppie investment banker who earns $100,000 a year talks of her previous life as a monk. Some millionaires have their own private gurus who pay house calls to provide comfort and advice. Big corporations too are paying attention. "The principle here is to look at the mind, body, heart and spirit," says a corporate spokesperson, who asks that her employer be identified only as a "major petrochemical company." This company provides its employees with regular workshops in stress management; it has hired a faith healer to "read auras" for ailing employees and run her hands over their "fields of energy." Even the U.S. Army has commissioned a West Coast firm to explore the military potentials of meditation and extrasensory perception.

Now come to the ballroom of the New York Hilton, where 1,200 of the faithful have paid $300 apiece to get the word from the New Age's reigning whirling dervish, Shirley MacLaine. To the soothing accompaniment of crystal chimes and distant waterfalls, the star of *Terms of Endearment* leads her new acolytes in meditation on the body's various chakras, or energy points. First comes the spinning red wheel of the base chakra, then the sexual pulsation of the orange chakra, and finally upward to the solar plexus and the visceral emotions of the yellow chakra.

"Feel the cleansing power of the stream of life, the coolness of water . . ." MacLaine purrs. She is wearing a turquoise sweater, violet sweatpants and green ankle-high sneakers, and a sizable crystal dangles from her neck. "There is so much you need to know. . . . See the outer bubble of white light watching for you. It is part of you. Let it be. It is showing you itself, that part of God that you have not recognized."

A woman in the audience complains that she has suffered chronic physical pain since childhood. MacLaine is not fazed. "Sometimes people use pain to feel alive," she explains. "Pain is a perception, not a reality." That is a basic New Age doctrine: you can be whatever you want to be.

The doctrine is sometimes a little hard to apply. The woman in the audience (women outnumber the men two to one) does not feel healed. "No one else goes through what I do," she says.

From the back, another small voice says, "I do."

MacLaine moves into a visualization exercise aimed at cleansing the third eye (the one behind the forehead) of negative thought patterns. More questions:

"How do I deal with the vibration of joy and ecstasy that I get when I meet my higher self?" a woman wants to know. "Mine is a naked cupid."

"Ecstasy is a new frequency which we are just beginning to define," MacLaine says. "It is complete surrender and trust, the key words for this New Age."

"With all due respect," says another voice, "I don't think you are a god." (That is another New Age doctrine, that everybody is God, co-creator of the universe.)

"If you don't see me as God," says MacLaine, blithe as ever, "it's because you don't see yourself as God."

If this seems to make very little sense, it nonetheless pays handsome dividends. MacLaine's five books of self-exploration and self-promotion have run to more than 8 million copies. Her third volume, *Out on a Limb*, which tells how she discovered the spirit world, became a five-hour TV extravaganza that was aired earlier this year. Her fifth volume, *It's All in the Playing*, published last September and a best seller for more than two months, is mainly about the making of the TV version of Volume 3, including conference/séances on how her astral guides feel about being cast to play themselves on television. And so on.

MacLaine's New York Hilton session was part of a 15-city national tour (estimated earnings: $1.5 million) to spread the New Age gospel. Next year she plans to open Uriel Village, a 300-acre retreat in Baca, Colo., where customers will be able to get weeklong sessions of meditation, past-life regression therapy, and sound and color healing, among other things. "I want this to be all mine, my energy, my control," says MacLaine. "I want a big dome-covered meditation center and a series of dome-covered meeting rooms because spiritual energy goes in spirals. We'll grow all our own food and eat under another dome. I want to turn a profit with this so I can build another center and another. I want to prove that spirituality is profitable."

For all its popularity, the New Age is hard to define. It includes a whole cornucopia of beliefs, fads, rituals; some subscribe to some parts, some to others. Only on special occasions, like the highly publicized "harmonic convergence" in August, do believers in I Ching or crystals gather together with believers in astral travel, shamans, Lemurians and tarot readers, for a communal chanting of om, the Hindu invocation that often precedes meditation. Led on by the urgings of Jose Arguelles, a Colorado art historian who claimed that ancient Mayan calendars foretold the end of the world unless the faithful gathered to provide harmony, some 20,000 New Agers assembled at "sacred sites" from Central Park to Mount Shasta to—uh—provide harmony.

All in all, the New Age does express a cloudy sort of religion, claiming vague connections with both Christianity and the major faiths of the East (New Agers like to say that Jesus spent 18 years in India absorbing Hinduism and the teaching of Buddha), plus an occasional dab of pantheism and sorcery. The underlying faith is a lack of faith in the orthodoxies of rationalism, high technology, routine living, spiritual law-and-order. Somehow, the New Agers believe, there must be some secret and mysterious shortcut or alternative path to happiness and health. And nobody ever really dies.

Like other believers, many New Agers attach great importance to artifacts, relics and sacred objects, all of which can be profitably offered for sale: Tibetan bells, exotic herbal teas, Viking runes, solar energizers, colored candles for "chromotherapy," and a Himalayan mountain of occult books, pamphlets, instructions and tape recordings. Some of these magical products are quite imaginative. A bearded Colorado sage who calls himself Gurudas sells "gem elixirs," which he creates by putting stones in bowls of water and leaving them in the sun for several hours, claiming that this allows the water to absorb energy from the sun and the stone.

Most New Agers prefer the stones themselves, specifically crystals of all sorts. These are not only thought to have mysterious healing powers but are considered programmable, like a computer, if one just concentrates hard enough. (The most powerful crystals are buried deep under New England, some New Agers believe, because New England was once connected to Atlantis, the famous "lost continent.")

Tina Lucia, a self-styled therapist in Stone Mountain, Ga., uses crystals to treat patients, because "physical problems are manifestations of spiritual problems." Gallbladder ailments, she says, come from a bitterness toward God, and lung trouble from a hatred of one's own body. "All you have to do is release these problems," she says. She uses amethyst, rose and blue quartz, and even black onyx and obsidian. One of her satisfied customers is Annette Manders, who wields a crystal wand that Lucia gave her. "I healed a fungus under my toenail with my wand," says Manders, "and I had a stomach problem that doesn't bother me anymore. The energy is subtle. It's not like you're being zapped."

Another favorite New Age cure for the misfortunes of the body is the therapeutic touch, again an ancient method newly back in fashion. While nobody knows exactly how these quasi-medical techniques work, people generally turn to them because conventional medicine seems so impersonal, costs so much and fails so often. Greg Schelkun, for example, graduated from Dartmouth and was working for a Boston publisher when he got a chance to go to the Orient with his mother, who was suffering from chronic chills and fevers. In the Philippines she met a healer who laid his hands on her and cured her. The healer also cured Schelkun of migraine headaches, which he had suffered for 15 years. "At the time, I didn't know what was going on," says Schelkun. "All I knew was that the headaches stopped."

Schelkun subsequently spent two years studying with another healer in the Philippines, and now practices his arts in Marin County. A burly, mustachioed man who likes to wear pink oxford-cloth button-down shirts, Schelkun hardly looks like a wizard. "I don't see disease written on a body with flashing neon lights saying 'Here! Here! Here!'" he says. "I place my hands to connect them to their healing source. My hands are able to feel hot spots, cold spots, pain and symptoms of problems in the body. We're not rocks. We're taught in this society to see only reflected light, instead of radiant or inner light."

There is always a danger of quackery in such unorthodox approaches, as orthodox doctors repeatedly warn. But some New Age healers have perfectly

Couple engaged in a "dyadic mediation." (*Author's collection*).

standard medical training. Bernie Siegel, for example, is a surgeon who teaches at Yale and has written a new best seller, *Love, Medicine & Miracles*. After years of treating cancer patients, he believes "all disease is ultimately related to a lack of love, or to love that is only conditional, for the exhaustion of the immune system thus created leads to physical vulnerability." Dolores Krieger, an R.N. and a Ph.D., teaches the art of therapeutic touch to nurses at New York University. "The best thing that happens," she says, "is rapid relaxation, the eradication or lessening of pain and the beginning of healing processes."

Another practitioner is a slight, intelligent, no-nonsense woman of 63, who treats ailments as varied as cancer, AIDS and multiple sclerosis in a cluttered studio apartment in Manhattan. A onetime bacteriologist, she had no psychic experiences until after the death of her husband, when she began hearing voices and seeing visions and thought "I was losing my mind." When she began to study these phenomena, she became convinced that unseen doctors were working through her. "I am not a mystical person," she says, "but I have learned to accept many, many things. I know my doctors are geniuses." She has applied her touch to 14 AIDS patients in the past few years and has lost only three so far. "I haven't found any disease that we can't do something for," she says. "Some people have disease for a reason, to learn a lesson in this life or from a past life."

There is no unanimity of New Age belief in anything, but many New Agers do believe in unidentified flying objects, crewed by oddly shaped extraterrestrials who have long visited the earth from more advanced planets, spreading the wisdom that created, among other things, Stonehenge and the pyramids of Egypt. Government officials keep announcing that there are no such things as UFOs, but the National Science Foundation reported last year that 43% of the citizenry believe it "likely" that some of the UFOs reported "are really space vehicles from other civilizations." (And where *did* those airstrip-like markings in the Peruvian Andes come from?)

If one can place any faith in Steven Spielberg films like *E.T.* and *Close Encounters of the Third Kind*, the visitors from outer space are benign and friendly folk. But several recently reported episodes have been more sinister. High on the best-seller lists this past summer stood *Communion* by Whitley Strieber, previously known mainly as a writer of fantasies (*The Wolfen*, *Warday*), who vehemently describes as a "true story" his chilling account of being spirited onto a spaceship by a pack of 3-ft. high "visitors." When they proposed sticking a needle into his brain, he recalls, one of them casually asked him, "What can we do to help you stop screaming?" More scare stories came from *Intruders* by Budd Hopkins, a chronicle of 130 people who claim to have been abducted by extra-terrestrial visitors and tell tales of being subjected to various degrading medical experiments. On the other hand, the extraterrestrials who turn up the course of channeling—one of the most popular New Age sports—appear almost unfailingly wise and benevolent.

Come to the rocky meadow on California's Mount Shasta, where a New Zealander named Neville Rowe tells the encircling crowd of 200 (admission: $10) that he speaks with the voice of Soli, an "off-planet being" who has never actually lived on earth. Dressed in a white-peaked cap, purple shirt and purple shoes, Rowe clutches a bottle of Evian water as the voice emerges from him in a rather peculiar British accent. "You are here to express who you are," says Soli. "You are here to search for yourself. The highest recognition you can make is that I am what I am. All that is, is. You are God. You are, each and every one, part of the Second Coming."

Somebody wants to argue. What about murderers? Are they God too?

"Your truth is your truth," says Soli, while his helpers start trying to sell videotapes of his latest incarnation. "My truth is my truth."

Not all the channeled voices are from outer space. Come to the Phoenix Institute in Lexington, Ky., for example, and hear Lea Schultz speak with the voice of somebody called Samuel. "What Lea does," says Tripp Bratton, an official at the institute, "is she calms herself and tunes in to a signal. Everything has a vibration, even if it doesn't have a physical form. Then she becomes animated by the energy on the other end of the 'line.' It's direct telepathic communication." Samuel usually discusses problems he feels are present in the audience and then takes questions: What happened to Atlantis? What happened to the *Challenger*?

Jach Pursel, a former Florida insurance agent living in Los Angeles, squints his eyes and speaks with the voice of Lazaris, a spiritual entity of uncertain origins.

"How old are you?" he is asked.

"In our reality, we have no time," says Lazaris.

"Why are you making your presence known to man?"

"Because you are ready now . . ."

"Is the world about to end?"

"No. In a word, no. This is not the ending. This is the beginning."

Pursel charges customers an average of $700 a year, and he has quite a few customers. "Lazaris is so popular," he says, "that, yeah, a lot of money gets made." But Pursel makes his real money as an art dealer and is opening a second gallery, on Rodeo Drive in Beverly Hills. As for channeling, "it's not a business; it's a labor of love." He adds a dark warning that others are less worthy. "There's some loony tunes out there," he says.

Probably the most celebrated of all current channelers is J. Z. Knight, a handsome ex-housewife in Yelm, Wash., who has performed for thousands at a price of $150 each per session. She speaks for Ramtha, a 35,000-year-old warrior who reports that he once lived on Atlantis. He has even dictated a book, *I Am Ramtha*, published in Portland, Ore., by Beyond Words Publishing and illustrated with photographs of Knight going into a trance on *The Merv Griffin Show*. Sample words of Ramthan wisdom: "Who be I? I am a notorious entity. I have that which is called a reputation. Know you what that is? Controversial, and I do what I say I do. What I am here to do is not to change people's minds, only to engage them and allow the wonderments for those that desire them to come to pass. I have been you, and I have become the other side of what you are . . ."

The sayings of Ramtha have brought Knight substantial rewards, including a luxurious mansion complete with spa, swimming pool and Arabian horses. A spokesman deprecates talk of her wealth, however, by noting that she pays a staff of 14 and that the tax collectors are insatiable.

Jo Ann Karl is a tall blond who says she was an up-and-coming business executive until she discovered the supernatural seven years ago. She was on a business trip in the Midwest when she first felt herself drifting through space outside her body. She tried to ignore the experience, but it kept recurring. Now she gets $15 a customer for channeling the archangel Gabriel and a spirit named Ashtar.

"The lesson I learned in one of my past lives was about taking risks," says Karl. "I was married to St. Peter. We traveled widely with Jesus, teaching with him. After he was crucified, we continued to teach and travel for several more years, until we were caught by the Romans. Peter was crucified, and I was thrown to the lions, after being raped and pilloried. Now I understand why I've always been afraid of big animals."

Karl's spirit guides had been advising her to go to the Incan empire's sacred Lake Titicaca in Bolivia (the Andes seem to be a favorite way station for UFOs). "They sort of told us we would meet *them*," she says. "I won't believe it until I

J. Z. Knight channeling Ramtha. (*Courtesy of Ramtha School of Enlightenment*)

see them and talk to them and feel the panel on the spaceship. But maybe it is time for people to know they have help." And so, starry-eyed and full of hope, Karl headed southward, and she did catch a distant glimpse of what she took to be a spaceship. "It looked like a whole lot of orange light," she says. "A blast of light spherical in shape. It was big and far away."

This kind of thing inspires some observers to mockery. Garry Trudeau's *Doonesbury* ridiculed the harmonic convergence as an "age where . . . the heavens are in perfect alignment, and finally, after years of anticipation, where Sean Penn is in jail." Some New Age people admit that the movement is so full of eccentrics and profiteers that they even dislike applying the term New Age to their own activities. New York City's Open Center, for example, studiously avoids the label. Founded four years ago by Wall Street Lawyer Walter Beebe, the center runs on a budget of $1.7 million and enrolls 3,000 students a month for a range of 250 one- and two-day workshops and such courses as Aspects of Zen Practice, Internal Kung Fu and Jungian Symbolism in Astrology.

"We see this movement as a different perspective on life, a holistic view of life," says Ralph White, who teaches philosophy at the center. "It encompasses an enormous spectrum involving the body, mind and spirit, including an increased awareness of nutrition, the rise in ecological thinking, a change in business perspectives, greater emphasis on preventive medicine, a shift to Jungian philosophy, an emphasis on the individual's intuition. Many people see themselves as living in a pretty meaningless world, and there is a profound cry for meaning. We've seen that tendency in churches, because the way religion is presented traditionally has spoken to our inner selves less and less. People want a living, feeling experience of spirituality. They yearn to get in touch with the soul."

This relatively level-headed approach to spirituality has its attractions in the world of commerce, particularly in the important area of management training. Innovation Associates of Framingham, Mass., charges $15,000 for a four-day seminar designed to strengthen executives' commitment to a common purpose. "We tell them to imagine themselves walking on a beach or a meadow," says the firm's director of consulting services, Joel Yanowitz. "Once we get them in the relaxed state, we ask them to pay attention to new thoughts and to test them against rational information about a situation. We teach them the art of holistic systemic thinking." One major engineering laboratory on the East Coast has established a program, run by a small New York City firm named Hoy Powers & Wayno, that is using meditation, imaging and techniques of intuitive thought to instill more creativity and leadership in some 400 corporate managers and executives.

Social Psychologist Michael Ray invokes Zen, yoga and tarot cards when he teaches his course Creativity in Business at the Stanford Graduate School of Business—but he groans at any mention of a New Age. "Our assumption is that creativity is essential for health and happiness in a business career," he says. Business executives have always developed their own methods of clearing the mind. J. P. Morgan used to play solitaire before making an important business decision, Ray points out. Conrad Hilton claimed he relied on intuition to help him decide what prices to bid for properties. "It's not that unusual these days," says Ray, "to see enormously successful, hard-core corporate types doing biofeedback and using crystals." Among those who have participated as guest speakers in Ray's course: Apple Computer Co-Founder Steven Jobs and Discount Broker Charles Schwab.

And what does make the stock market rise and fall? Mason Sexton graduated from Harvard Business School in 1972, went to Wall Street, and decided that all the traditional ways of making predictions were "at best hit or miss." Then he learned of the Fibonacci Ratio, based on the work of a 13th century Italian mathematician, and a modern development of it known as the Elliott Wave Theory, which declares that all advancing markets have five waves up and three waves down.

"But the key to the timing of when these waves will bottom or crest depends very much on astrology," says Sexton, "which is simply the science of understanding the nature of time, since our sense of time depends on the relationship of the earth to the sun and moon. We are getting very close to the end of the primary wave-three rally, which has been in effect since July 1984. Then we will have a primary-wave correction, which will take eight months, representing a decline of 400 to 600 points."

That is what Sexton was saying last August, when he predicted the market would hit its peak late that month. On Oct. 2, he warned: "Any Dow close below 2387 would be a signal to sell all stocks." And he took his own advice, not only selling but also going short.

Incredible? Sexton has 1,500 subscribers who pay $360 a year for his biweekly newsletter of predictions, and many have written to thank him for saving them from Black Monday. Says Marc Klee, who helps manage the $200 million American Fund Advisors: "His techniques are unconventional, to say the least, but I've been working with him three years or so, and his track record is well above average."

One of the most go-getting New Age entrepreneurs is Chris Majer, 36, president of SportsMind, Inc., based in Seattle. As the corporate name indicates, Majer originally worked mainly on athletic training, though his current clients include not only AT&T but also the U.S. Army. Majer started his military efforts in 1982 with an eight-week, $50,000 training program at Fort Hood in Texas. Traditional calisthenics were replaced by a holistic stretching-warm-up-aerobics-cool-down routine. Soldiers practiced visualizing their combat tasks. The results in training test scores were apparently so good that the Army expanded Sports-Mind's assignment into a yearlong $350,000 program to help train Green Berets. "They wanted the most far-ranging human-performance program we could deliver," Majer says.

The Green Berets were taught meditation techniques so that they could spend long hours hidden in enemy territory. "They have to be comfortable at a deep level with who they are," Majer says, "not make mental mistakes or they'll give away their position and get killed. People say all this New Age stuff is a bunch of hoo-hoo, but it gets results."

While the idea of New Age Green Berets meditating in the jungle can inspire laughter, it can also inspire a certain concern about the political and social implications of the whole movement. Is it some kind of neoleftist response to the Age of Reagan, or is it an ultrarightist extension of Reaganism? The answer depends somewhat on the answerer's politics. While some see in the New Agers' chants and nebulous slogans a revival of the shaggy '60s, others see the devotion of many New Agers to moneymaking as simply a new variant of yuppieism.

Whether leftist, rightist or none of the above, the New Age has attracted a fair amount of criticism on philosophical and ethical grounds. "A lot of it is a cop-out, an escape from reality, an anti-intellectual movement denying rationality," says Alan Dundes, a professor of anthropology and folklore at the University of California, Berkeley. "The New Age movement reflects anxieties of one sort of another—the threat of nuclear warfare, the President running a vigilante action out of the White House, nurses accused of killing patients. People look at all this and say, 'If this is the Establishment, then I don't want this. I want something else, something I can trust.' It's people latching onto a belief system to get certainty where there is no certainty."

It's a religion without being a religion, says Robert J. L. Burrows, publications editor of the evangelical Spiritual Counterfeits Project in Berkeley. "Humans are essentially religious creatures, and they don't rest until they have some sort of answer to the fundamental questions. Rationalism and secularism don't answer those questions. But you can see the rise of the New Age as a barometer of the disintegration of American culture. Dostoyevsky said anything is permissible if there is no God. But anything is also permissible if everything is God. There is no way of making any distinction between good and evil."

Douglas Groothuis, a research associate at a Christian think tank called Probe Center Northwest and author of *Unmasking the New Age*, raises a similar objection. "Once you've deified yourself," he says, "which is what the New Age is all about, there is no higher moral absolute. It's a recipe for ethical anarchy. I see it as a counterfeit religious claim. It's both messianic and millennial."

Though Groothuis is now writing a second book, *Confronting the New Age*, about the movement's inroads into business and education, it is probably wise to remember that phenomena like the New Age have to some extent been a part of the American scene every since there was an American scene. Remember the 18th century Shaker leader, Mother Ann Lee, whose followers believed she represented the Second Coming of Christ. Remember Mary Baker Eddy, severely injured by a fall on the ice, who became cured while reading a passage in St. Matthew and thereafter taught the unreality of all physical ills. Spiritualism was the rage of the 1850s, and a heroine of Henry James' *The Bostonians* went into mesmeric trances to gather recruits for the cause of feminism. Walt Whitman believed in transmigration of the soul—"And as to you Life I reckon you are the leavings of many deaths, / (No doubt I have died myself ten thousand times before.)"—and so did the practical-minded Thomas Alva Edison.

Remember Madame Blavatsky who founded the Theosophical Society and revealed the secrets of the universe in *Isis Unveiled*. There were sightings of spaceships in the 1890s, at a time when no American had ever seen an airplane, much less an Apollo rocket, but then as now a century was coming to an end. Mars was once widely believed to be inhabited by little green men, so when Orson Welles declared on the radio in 1938 that space invaders had landed, much of the nation went into a panic. And do not forget *The Search for Bridey Murphy*. Or the fad of talking to plants. *Plus ca change . . .*

"It's important to point out the moral imbecility of what the New Age people are trying to do," says United Methodist Clergyman J. Gordon Melton, director of Santa Barbara's Institute for the Study of American Religion. "But at the same time I wouldn't see it as a threat." Even that, though, is perhaps too harsh a condemnation to serve as the final word on an essentially harmless anthology of illusions.

But Shirley MacLaine is accustomed to slings and arrows. "I think the thrust of this article, aside from bemused sarcasm, is going to be that a lot of people are getting rich on all this," she says, in a fairly successful venture into prophecy. "That seems to be a concern of many journalists. But I would say we all have to decide what we're worth . . . I think journalists who are investigating belief in the unseen have to adjust the way they are judging the issue of materialism in relation to spirituality. Anything you want to learn costs money in this world."

MacLaine is working hard these days. Aside from all her New Age activities, she is in London to shoot a new John Schlesinger film about a domineering piano teacher. "This character makes Aurora Greenway in *Terms of Endearment* look like a day at the beach," she says. "I'm on the set by 8, and we work till 8, and then I have lines to learn." She has also written a new book, tentatively titled *Going Within.* "It's techniques of meditation, visualization, color therapy, sound therapy, how to work with crystals, how to work with colored jewelry, acupuncture, acupressure, things that have been helpful to me. I can only write about what's happened to me."

In many ways, her life remains much the same as ever. "I live a kind of nomad existence. I like to travel light. I don't wear a lot of jewelry. I travel with one suitcase because I always end up carrying it." In other ways, though, her life is quite different from what it was in her early days of singing and dancing on Broadway, which seem, if one may say so, several lifetimes ago. "It's me that makes things happen to me," she says. "I'm not the leader of this movement. I'm not a high priestess of New Age concepts. I'm just a human being trying to find some answers about what we're doing here, where we came from and where we're going. That search is equal to finding a good script, and maybe it even helps."

So let the final word on the New Age be: om.

NEW AGE
CONCEPTS

17
"THE HUNDRETH MONKEY" REVISITED

Elaine Myers

THE STORY OF "The Hundredth Monkey" has recently become popular in our culture as a strategy for social change. Lyall Watson first told it in *Lifetide* (pp. 147–48), but its most widely known version is the opening to the book *The Hundredth Monkey* by Ken Keyes (see page 606). The story is based on research with monkeys on a northern Japanese Island, and its central idea is that when enough individuals in a population adopt a new idea or behavior, there occurs an ideological breakthrough that allows this new awareness to be communicated directly from mind to mind without the connection of external experience and then all individuals in the population spontaneously adopt it. "It may be that when enough of us hold something to be true, it becomes true for everyone." (Watson, 148)I found this to be a very appealing and believable idea. The concept of Jung's collective unconscious and the biologists' morphogenetic fields (*In Context* 6) offer parallel stories that help strengthen this strand of our imaginations. Archetypes, patterns, or fields that are themselves without mass or energy could shape the individual manifestations of mass and energy. The more widespread these fields are, the greater their influence on the physical level of reality. We sometimes mention the Hundredth Monkey Phenomenon when we need supporting evidence of the possibility of an optimistic scenario for the future, especially a future based on peace instead of war. If enough of us will just think the right thoughts, then suddenly, almost magically, such ideas will become reality. However, when I went back to the original research reports cited by Watson, I did not find the same story that he tells. Where he claims to have had to improvise details, the research reports are quite precise, and they do not support the "ideological breakthrough" phenomenon. At first I was disappointed, but as I delved deeper into the research I found a growing appreciation for the lessons the real story of these monkeys has for us. Based on what I have learned from the Japan Monkey Center reports in *Primates* 2, 5, and 6, here is how the real story seems to have gone.

Up until 1958, Keyes's description follows the research quite closely, although not all the young monkeys in the troop learned to wash the potatoes. By March 1958, fifteen of the nineteen young monkeys (aged two to seven years) and two of the eleven adults were washing sweet potatoes. Up to this time, the propagation of the innovative behavior was on an individual basis, along family lines and playmate relationships. Most of the young monkeys began to wash the potatoes when they were one to two and a half years old. Males older than four years, who had little contact with the young monkeys, did not acquire the behavior.

By 1959, the sweet potato washing was no longer a new behavior to the group. Monkeys that had acquired the behavior as juveniles were growing up and having their own babies. This new generation of babies learned sweet potato washing behavior through the normal cultural pattern of the young imitating their mothers. By January 1962, almost all the monkeys in the Koshima troop, excepting those adults born before 1950, were observed to be washing their sweet potatoes. If an individual monkey had not started to wash sweet potatoes by the time he was an adult, he was unlikely to learn it later, regardless of how widespread it became among the younger members of the troop.

In the original reports, there was no mention of the group passing a critical threshold that would impart the idea to the entire troop. The older monkeys remained steadfastly ignorant of the new behavior. Likewise, there was no mention of widespread sweet potato washing in other monkey troops. There was mention of occasional sweet potato washing by individual monkeys in other troops, but I think there are other simpler explanations for such occurrences. If there was an Imo in one troop, there could be other Imo-like monkeys in other troops.

Instead of an example of the spontaneous transmission of ideas, I think the story of the Japanese monkeys is a good example of the propagation of a paradigm shift, as in Thomas Kuhn's *The Structure of Scientific Revolutions*. The truly innovative points of view tend to come from those on the edge between youth and adulthood. The older generation continues to cling to the worldview it grew up with. The new idea does not become universal until the older generation withdraws from power, and a younger generation matures within the new point of view.

It is also an example of the way that simple innovations can lead to extensive cultural change. By using the water in connection with their food, the Koshima monkeys began to exploit the sea as a resource in their environment. Sweet potato washing led to wheat washing, and then to bathing behavior and swimming, and the utilization of sea plants and animals for food: "Therefore, provisioned monkeys suffered changes in their attitude and value system and were given foundations on which precultural phenomena developed" (M. Kawai, *Primates* 6, no. 1 [1965]).

What does this say about morphogenetic fields and the collective unconscious? Not very much, but the "ideological breakthrough" idea is not what Sheldrake's theory of morphogenetic fields would predict anyway. That theory would recognize that the behavior of the older monkeys (not washing) also is a well-established pattern. There may well be a "critical mass" required to shift a new behavior from being a fragile personal idiosyncrasy to being a well-established alternative, but creating a new alternative does not automatically displace older alternatives. It just provides more choices. It is possible that the washing alternative established by the monkeys on Koshima Island did create a morphogenetic field that made it easier for monkeys on other islands to "discover" the same technique, but the actual research neither supports nor denies that idea. It remains for other cultural experiments and experiences to illuminate this question.

What the research does suggest, however, is that holding positive ideas (as important a step as this is) is not sufficient by itself to change the world. We still need direct communication between individuals, we need to translate our ideas into action, and we need to recognize the freedom of choice of those who choose alternatives different from our own.

THE HUNDREDTH MONKEY

by Ken Keyes

The Japanese monkey, *Macaca fuscata*, has been observed in the wild for a period of over thirty years.

In 1952, on the island of Koshima, scientists were providing monkeys with sweet potatoes dropped in the sand. The monkeys liked the taste of the raw sweet potatoes, but they found the dirt unpleasant.

An eighteen-month-old female named Imo found she could solve the problem by washing the potatoes in a nearby stream. She taught this trick to her mother. Her playmates also learned this new way and they taught their mothers, too.

This cultural innovation was gradually picked up by various monkeys before the eyes of the scientists.

Between 1953 and 1958 all of the young monkeys learned to wash the sandy sweet potatoes to make them more palatable.

Only the adults who imitated their children learned this social improvement. Other adults kept eating the dirty sweet potatoes.

Then something startling took place. In the autumn of 1958, a certain number of Koshima monkeys were washing sweet potatoes—the exact number is not known.

Let us suppose that when the sun rose one morning, there were ninety-nine monkeys on Koshima Island who had learned to wash their sweet potatoes.

Let us further suppose that later that morning the hundreth monkey learned to wash potatoes.

THEN IT HAPPENED!

By that evening almost everyone in the tribe was washing sweet potatoes before eating them.

The added energy of this hundredth monkey somehow created an ideological breakthrough!

But notice.

A most surprising thing observed by these scientists was that the habit of washing sweet potatoes then jumped over the sea—

Colonies of monkeys on other islands and the mainland troop of monkeys at Takasakiyama began washing their sweet potatoes!

18

THE MEANING
OF GAIA

David Spangler

Irecently was invited to a worship service and celebration in which Gaia was specifically incorporated as a source of spiritual nourishment and help. In ritual and song, the participants called upon the "Spirit of Gaia" to heighten their awareness of their connections with the earth and to fill them with love and compassion for all creatures and for the physical environment as a whole.

The idea of a "Spirit of Gaia" is definitely alien to the original Gaia Hypothesis as developed by James Lovelock and Lynn Margulis. Though it does conceive of the earth as a living entity, such a being, if conscious at all, has (in the words of Margulis) the sentiency "of an amoeba"—hardly the stuff of myth and spiritual invocation. On the other hand, the idea of a world soul, an *anima mundi*, a planetary Logos, is an ancient one found in both Eastern and Western culture. This world soul is usually conceived as a "formative force," an active, intelligent, purposeful spiritual presence at work in the material world to guide and guard the course of planetary evolution. It is generally not accorded the status of being the ultimate source or Creator but might be looked upon as a great angelic or archangelic being presiding over the well-being of the world, or as the gestalt, the wholeness of all the lives and patterns that manifest upon, and as, the earth.

It is this tradition that Gaia reinvokes in our culture. However, a reinvocation is not the same as a reincarnation. The sense of a living earth enjoyed and practiced by earlier, nonindustrial cultures grew out of living experience and a closeness to nature that our culture has set aside. It was woven into the fabric of life and culture. This is not true for us. Furthermore, the Judeo-Christian tradition arises from the Semitic spiritual perspective of God and creation being separate and distinct, as well as from patriarchal social structures. In such a context, sacredness has overtones of authority, power, distance, and maleness that would have been alien to the spirituality of, for instance, the ancient Celts or the Native Americans, two cultures that incorporated a sense of the living earth. This means that when we strive to imagine the sacredness of the earth, we do so in a very different cultural context than did those who took for granted an immanent, accessible sacred presence pervading all things.

Can we simply adopt and graft on their notion of a living, sacred earth? I don't think so, at least not without distortion. We have to deeply think into and live out this idea in a modern context. Until we do, Gaia, the spirit of the living earth, is an idea to think about rather than an idea to think with. It is a novelty rather than a tacit assumption, and as a spiritual idea it can be superficial. It lacks the overtones and undertones, the deeper connections with our everyday life and with the mysteries of creation, that it possessed in earlier cultures. As an idea, it becomes a suit to try on rather than a body to inhabit and live through.

In this respect, some current images of Gaia are to the ancient mythic idea of the living earth what a Disney cartoon version of a fairy tale, such as *Sleeping Beauty* or the current hit, *The Little Mermaid*, is to the original folk story. The cartoon is witty, bright, colorful, delightful, fun, and very superficial. It lacks the depth, the resonances, the hidden meanings, and undertones of the original. The appearance, the skin of the story is there, but the bones and muscle have been removed.

THE "TOP LINE"

When we talk about the spirit of Gaia, the spirit of a living earth, or even of the earth as being alive, just what do we mean in our time? Do we even have the same sense of life, of what being an entity means, as did our ancestors? We are the products of a materialistic, technological, rational, male-oriented culture that over two hundred years ago set aside the medieval notions of the Great Chain of Being in which each and every life had a purpose, a place, and a meaning. The importance of the bottom line has made us forget that there is also a "top line" that gives the spiritual value, the holistic value, of a person, a plant, an animal, or a place. If at worst the bottom line represents how entities can be exploited and used for profit, the top line represents how entities can empower and must be empowered for the good of the whole.

It is this sense of the whole as a component of life and of the individual as an expression of the whole that we do not have. We have a sense of incarnation but not of co-incarnation, of the many ways in which the fabric of our identities is interwoven and interdependent in ways extending far beyond just the human milieu. Thus our definitions of life become very reductionist, individualized, and utilitarian. What, then, does it mean to us to speak of the earth as a living being, not in a biological sense but in a metaphysical sense?

Accepting Gaia simply as a "return of the Goddess" or jumping on the bandwagon of a new planetary animism, without thinking through the implications of just what Gaia might mean in our culture, can lead to sentimentality rather than spirituality. It leads to what William Irwin Thompson's daughter Hilary calls "the Gooey-Gaia Syndrome."

If Gaia is an important spiritual idea for our time, then we must remember that a spiritual idea is not something we think about but something that inhabits and shapes us. It is like a strand of DNA, organizing and energizing our lives. A spiritual idea is not just another bit of data to be filed away. It is incarnational in a profound way, coming alive only when incorporated (made flesh) in our lives through work, practice, effort, skill, and reflection. It becomes part of the foundation and the architecture of our lives. Being a new icon for worship is not enough. Invoking the spirit of Gaia is insufficient unless we understand just how we shape and participate in that spirit and how we in turn are shaped and participated in by it.

DO WE REALLY NEED GAIA?

However, a deeper question is whether we really need Gaia as a spiritual image. Do we need another spiritual source, another presence to invoke? If there is a true spirit of the earth, a planetary Logos, is it hierarchically superior to humanity? That is, does it stand somewhere between ourselves and God? If so, we run the risk of interposing yet another image between ourselves and divinity. Or if the earth is seen as sacred, just what does that mean? Why should the earth be conceived of as sacred simply because it is alive? Do we extend the same privilege to other living things? Is life alone the criterion for sacredness? Or does something become sacred when it is living and powerful, big and capable of doing us either harm or good? Does Gaia become a substitute for God? What would such a substitution mean? Does it bring God closer to us, or does it further muddy the meaning and nature of God, making it yet more difficult to clearly determine just what the sacred is and what our relationship is to it?

These are important questions, and unfortunately, exploring them in the manner they deserve would far exceed the space I have in this article. Still, they need to be raised. There is a strong tendency as new planetary and religious paradigms emerge in our time to affirm the sacredness of all life and of the earth as a whole. However, the object of this excercise, it seems to me, is not to come up with new images of divinity, but to affect behavior. What we really want is to relate to ourselves, to each other, and to the world as a whole as if we all have ultimate value apart from utilitarian considerations. If something is sacred, it is assumed to have value beyond its form, usefulness, duration, and products. It is valuable; it is precious. It is worthy of respect and honor, love and compassion; it is worth entering into communion with. Its very being is its only justification; it needs no other.

As things stand, before we can manipulate or exploit something or someone, we must first devalue it, making it lower than ourselves. That which is sacred cannot be devalued, and by naming the earth and all upon it as sacred, we seek to protect it and ourselves from ourselves. Yet, if we must call something "sacred" before we can extend ourselves to it with love, empathy, communion, honor, and compassion—if something must be alive and have spirit before we can relate to it as having value—then we dishonor and devalue the spirit within us that sets no such preconditions. We devalue the meaning of the sacred itself, which is not a status but a function: it manifests when there is a sharing of love and being in order to empower, uplift, and liberate that to which the sharing is directed. The sacred does not pick and choose what it shall love. It is love given freely and unconditionally, just as in the Christmas celebration, Christians honor the mystery of a God who "so loved the world" (even though, in traditional Christianity, that world is not "sacred") that He made the ultimate sacrifice of Himself through His only Son on that world's behalf.

Paradoxically then, we seem to need to call something sacred in order to make it worthy of receiving our highest values and noblest relationships, while in the Judeo-Christian tradition God appears under no such constraint, giving Himself freely and totally to creation whether it is seen as "sacred" or not. To bring sacredness into the world, should we not be more like the God many of us worship? We should not need to make either ourselves or the earth "sacred" in order to love it and ourselves and to get on with doing what needs to be done to heal and protect the biosphere. Turning Gaia into a mythic or spiritual idea may be inappropriate or premature, leading both to misplaced concreteness and misplaced spirituality. On the other hand, Gaia can be an inspirational idea. Such an idea, to me, is like an enzyme. It is not important in itself except as it catalyzes a process. An enzyme is a means toward something else, a component of a larger emergence. In this context, Gaia would be an enzyme of consciousness, promoting and aiding a process of expanding our awareness in at least five areas important to our time.

The first of these is the most obvious: The idea of Gaia heightens our awareness of ecological and environmental necessities and responsibilities. It inspires us to translate theory and concern into practical strategies to preserve the environment and to meet ecological crises.

The second area of awareness follows from the first: Gaia focuses our attention on issues of life. It shifts our operating paradigm from a mechanical one based on classical physics to an ecological one based on biology. It puts the phenomenon of life itself back into center stage in our culture. It inspires us toward a reformation that produces a culture that is truly life-affirming and life-centered.

Third, because the phenomenon of life as expressed through organisms and ecologies of organisms manifests more than the sum of its parts, it cannot be understood using solely analytical and reductionist techniques or modes of thought. Thus, Gaia represents an epistemology as well, a way of learning, seeing, and knowing. It inspires us to develop modes of thinking and acting that are holistic, systemic, symbiotic, connective, and participatory. We must learn to see the world in terms of patterns and not just positions and points; in terms of networks and lattices, not just centers and peripheries; in terms of processes, not just objects and things. We are encouraged to develop and practice an "ecology of mindfulness," to paraphrase Bateson, as well as a mindful ecological practice. It inspires us to act toward each other as well as toward the environment in ways that serve and nourish the whole of which we are all participants—in ways that are compassionate and cocreative, cooperative, and co-incarnational.

Fourth, Gaia does inspire us to think of the spirituality of the earth and to explore an "eco-theology." Such a spirituality is important, for beyond ecology and conservation lies a deeper dimension of spiritual interaction and communion with our environment that is mutually important for ourselves and for nature. Within that dimension we will also find new insights into the meaning of the divine that cannot help but aid us in the emergence of a healthy and whole planetary culture.

My earlier comments are not meant to belittle or discourage this search, only to suggest that its importance warrants the best of our thinking and contemplation. We cannot simply take up the mindsets of our ancestors nor wear their myths as if we have not changed in the interim between their world and time and ours. We cannot assume the sacredness nor spiritual livingness of the earth or accept it as a new ideology or as a sentimentally pleasing idea. We must experience that life and sacredness, if it is there, in relationship to our own and to that ultimate mystery we call God. We must experience it in our lives, in our practice, in the flesh of our cultural creativity. We must allow it to shape us, as great spiritual ideas have always shaped those who entertain them, and not expect that we can simply use the image of Gaia to meet emotional, religious, political, or even commercial needs without allowing it to transform us in unexpected and radical ways. The spirituality of the earth is more than a slogan. It is an invitation to initiation, to the death of what we have been and the birth of something new.

Finally, Gaia provides a mirror in which to see ourselves anew. It inspires us to reflect on our own natures, on the meaning and destiny of humanity. Lovelock paved the way for this in his book *Gaia* in which he first presented the Gaia Hypothesis. In the last chapter, he suggested that humanity might be the evolving nervous system of the earth, the means by which Gaia achieves self-awareness. At a time when our society seems motivated by no higher purpose than endless expansion and the making of money and when humanity seems to have no purpose beyond itself, this image is striking and refreshing. It would seem to suggest a direction, a connection, a role that we can play in a world that is more than just the sum total of human desires.

Paradoxically, this image of humanity as nervous system is itself very un-Gaian in that it is not systemic enough. If by nervous system we mean the wiring that carries the sensations and thoughts of a larger being, then that is not a very participatory image, reducing humanity to being simply the instrumentality for the transmission and execution of the thoughts of the earth.

On the other hand, if by nervous system we mean the whole system that governs, guides, and controls the organism through reception and integration of sensation and the transmission of thought, then such a nervous system is more than just wiring. As modern medicine and biochemisty increasingly show, the whole body is an integrated sensing/directing organism. Glands, hormones, blood, circulation, physical structure, and interrelationships between organs play as much a role in structuring and transmitting "thought" as does the nervous system itself. Thus, to be the "nervous system" of the earth really means to be integrated with all the systems of the earth, from wind and weather to tidal flows and the growth of plants, from the ecology of watersheds to the migration of birds and insects from one bioregion to another, and so on. It means being Gaia in a way that transcends and enlarges our humanity. Just what that really involves is what we have to discover, but surely it goes beyond accepting without reflection pat slogans about Gaia and the sacredness of the earth.

I do not see Gaia itself as an image of human destiny, but it enlarges our vision of human purpose and activity beyond the personal and the local and puts it into a planetary and cosmic context. At the same time, the actions of Gaia are very local and specific, so that we are made more aware, not less, of our interactions with the particular places we inhabit. This is an important shift in our time.

Gaia is an important idea, both as a scientific hypothesis and as a spiritual image. However, I see it as a transitional idea. It is not so much a revelation in itself as a precursor to revelation or to new insights that can come when that idea is examined and lived with and given a chance to settle into our bones. Its meaning now lies in what it can inspire us to discover about ourselves and the nature of life, in rallying our energies to meet the needs of our environment, and through these processes of discovery and healing, to become a truly planetary species, blessed in ways we can now only imagine.

MATERIAL FROM SELECT CONTEMPORARY GROUPS

19

SOME EXPRESSIONS OF CHRISTIAN BELIEF

Familiar Traditional	**Contemporary Alternatives**

A. THE BIBLE AND REVELATION

	Familiar Traditional	**Contemporary Alternatives**
1.	God has given us a full and final Revelation of Himself, to be guarded against corruption.	Humanity is still evolving, so our understanding of God is always in the process of developing.
2.	The Bible is the sole source of God's Revelation.	The Universe and our inner experience constitute the primary sources of Revelation.
3.	The Bible is the once-and-for-all statement of Divine Truth.	Each age needs to reinterpret afresh the biblical message if its underlying Truth is to be our inspiration.
4.	There are truths that we could not have known except for God's Revelation.	"Revelation" is born out of human experience and can only be understood and expressed within the bounds of human experience.

From Adrian B. Smith, *Exploring Ways Forward for Christianity into the Twenty-First Century: A Paper for Dialogue* (Oxford, UK: Christians Awakening to a New Awareness, 1999).

Familiar Traditional	Contemporary Alternatives
5. Revelation reaches its climax in Jesus.	"Revelation" is ongoing; it cannot be totally possessed by any one religion.
6. Jesus' actions and words are accurately recorded in the Gospels.	Jesus is the person of whom the Gospels speak: a product of memory, reflection, revision, and community experience.
7. Faith is belief in doctrine.	Faith is the framework that gives our life direction and out of which we make our judgments.

B. GOD

Familiar Traditional	Contemporary Alternatives
8. The Holy Trinity is defined as "Three Persons (Father, Son, and Holy Spirit) in one God."	The relational nature of God can be understood in many different ways. E.g., the Trinity symbolizes the three elements in God's relationship with all things in Creation, namely, God, Creation, and the love that flows between them.
9. The Holy Spirit distributes God's grace through the Church.	The Spirit of God inspires all people of good will in different ways and through different events throughout history.
10. "We believe in one God, the Father Almighty, Creator of Heaven and Earth."	We experience the Ground of Being as the creative, loving, and wise Reality that underlies our ultimate concerns. This we name God.
11. Creation was an act of God done once and for all at the beginning of time.	Creation is the continuing action of God holding all things in existence.
12. God is the all-powerful, all-knowing Lord of all creation, the loving Father who sent his Son to reveal the mysteries of Divine Grace.	God is the Divine presence in, and creative energy of, this world whom we discover through our relationships with people, things, events, and concepts.

Familiar Traditional	Contemporary Alternatives
13. Our understanding of God is in the context of looking back to the Fall-Redemption story.	Our understanding of God is in the context of the unfolding creation story.

C. JESUS THE CHRIST

14. Starting from our knowledge of God we discover who Jesus is as the Christ. We know the qualities of Jesus because we know the attributes of God.	Starting from what we know of the historical man, Jesus, we learn from him what we can of the mystery of God. We know some of the attributes of God because we see the sort of person Jesus was.
15. God "sent" his Son "down" to Earth and Jesus ascended "up" into Heaven.	We do not think of the Incarnation or the Ascension as physically down or up. We understand them as metaphors.
16. Jesus is God-made-man who came down from Heaven to save us.	Jesus is perceived as the icon of God who lived among us to show and empower us to live by higher values— which he called "The Kingdom of God." This perception was a radical step forward in humanity's under standing of its call to At-one-ment with the divine nature.
17. The accounts of Jesus' birth given in the Bible, in particular "he came down from Heaven by power of the Holy Spirit and became incarnate from the Virgin Mary," are literally true.	Jesus was conceived naturally and born as a human baby to a young woman (the proper translation of "virgin"). The accounts of his birth were constructed later to explain his divine nature in mythological terms.
18. The emphasis is on the divinity Jesus.	The emphasis is on the humanity of Jesus and his God-consciousness.
19. Jesus equals God, a Divine Being who took on human nature.	Jesus, in his humanity, does not equal God but is a human being who is transparent to the Divine. God was as fully present and active in Jesus as is possible in human form.
20. Jesus is worthy of unconditional worship as God.	We worship God as revealed in Jesus.

Familiar Traditional	**Contemporary Alternatives**
21. Jesus was omniscient and omnipotent from his conception.	Jesus was limited by his humanity. His understanding of himself, of his mission, of God, and of other people developed in his lifetime.
22. Everything Jesus did and said is done and said by God. He had supernatural powers because he was God.	Jesus acted and spoke as a human being. All his powers issued from his potential being fully realized because he was fully aware of his unity with God.
23. From Jesus' words, "I am the way, the truth and the life" (John 14:6), we understand that Jesus alone is the key to our salvation: he is the only way to God.	The Way revealed by Jesus is also found in other faiths, but for Christians its manifestation in Jesus is the most accessible, powerful, and inspiring.
24. Jesus brought us "Salvation"; variously described as Ransom, a price paid, Justification, Satisfaction, Reparation.	Jesus brought about the possibility of At-one-ment: a step forward in humanity's evolution toward our becoming one with the Divine.
25. Redemption is an act of rescue an external, Divine agent.	Redemption is the transformation process by which the life-giving Spirit within us moves us from human-centeredness to Divine-centeredness.
26. The "Resurrection" is the belief that God raised Jesus to bodily life on the third day after he died on the cross.	The "Resurrection" is the way in which the Gospel writers affirm that the spirit of Jesus is still among us, thus demonstrating the power of divine love over material limitations.

D. HUMAN BEINGS

27. Humanity became enslaved to Satan by Adam and Eve's sin (the event known as "The Fall") but has been set free by the blood of Christ.	The world is part of an essentially good creation and God chooses to share his creative activity with us to make it even better. The Genesis story is an expression of humanity's "rise" to consciousness of the Self; it describes a step in human evolution.

Familiar Traditional	Contemporary Alternatives
28. Sin is an offense against God.	Sin is a failure to grow in wholeness, within ourselves, with others and in relation to the whole of creation. It is to ignore the Divine within us.
29. We obey the Commandments in order to receive our reward in the next life.	We try to be loving people because we believe this leads to our own and all Creation's fulfillment.
30. The human being is at the pinnacle of Creation, for whom all else was created.	The human being is the most evolved species to appear on this planet. Evolution is continuing.
31. Human beings were granted dominion over the Earth to use the natural world for human benefit.	We human beings are not above the natural world but embedded within it. As evolved creatures with intelligence we have a duty to care for it.

E. THE CHURCH

Familiar Traditional	Contemporary Alternatives
32 The Church is an organization superior to civil society because matters spiritual are superior to matters temporal.	The Church is called to be the expression on Earth—the sign or witness—of what it means to live by the values of what Jesus called "the Kingdom of God."
33. The Church is hierarchical in structure. Members relate according to their authority roles.	The Church is a community. The fundamental relationship of all Christians is as sisters and brothers in a common humanity.
34. Christianity alone holds the true Revelation and key to Salvation. All other religions are false or inadequate.	Christianity is the religion in which the role of Christ is most clearly understood. Other religions have different perspectives on the One Truth. Each is a path to ultimate union with God for its followers.
35. Christians alone can bring about the Kingdom of God.	The Kingdom of God is promoted by all who act unselfishly for others, whether Christian or not.

Familiar Traditional	Contemporary Alternatives

F. THEOLOGY AND WORLDVIEWS

36   When we die our souls enter Heaven or Hell: eternal reward or eternal punishment. We know this by Revelation.

We cannot know what happens when we shed our earthly bodies but trust that we continue on a journey toward the fullest union with God.

37.   Theology is the "queen of sciences"; it gives us knowledge of all else, because it comes through Revelation.

All human knowledge is tentative and interrelated. Theology needs to co-operate with all other disciplines to develop a holistic worldview.

20
HOW THE
JOURNEY BEGINS
John Roger Hinkins

In the beginning of time, God was in all places in an absolutely pure state. And in this purity, It was a void—without specific consciousness. In essence, God did not know Itself, in awareness, in Its greater beingness. So God instituted patterns of creation. It created universes, within which was what appeared to be solid objects (which we call planets) and less solid material (which we call space). All of it is God in Its different manifestations. And God instituted the plan that every part would know every other part—through experience. Thus the Soul, which is more directly the spark of God, was evolved and was given the opportunity to experience all levels, layers, planes, and realms of experience and being. A Soul can inhabit any form it wishes. Its job, its reason for being, is to experience all it can on every level it can—thereby growing in awareness of its own divine nature. The Soul that has experienced all is God and is one with God. This experience of God is incomprehensibly large and complex, so the Soul spends tremendous time evolving through the realms of experience back into the awareness and knowledge of its divine nature.

Let me give you an idea of this by telling you a story about a Soul that decided it would leave heaven—the Soul realm. It got a little bored one day so it said to itself "Thou are a rock." And sure enough, it was a rock. It got in a little

From John Roger Hinkins, *The Journey of a Soul*, Peace Theological Seminary and College of Philosophy, 1975, 2001. Copyright © 1975, 2001 by Peace Theological Seminary and College of Philosophy. Reprinted by permission of Peace Theological Seminary and College of Philosophy.

bit of trouble because it found itself isolated; there weren't any other rocks nearby, and it couldn't move around very much. But this Soul was pretty happy anyway because the nature of the Soul is joyful. The rock was heavier than anything else around it, so it kept sinking into denser areas until it came to the place called Earth. It settled down with a slight jolt and said, "Oh, wow, I really am this rock." It didn't know what to do next, so it said, "I think I'll learn patience." And it sat there for a long time.

Over the course of thousands of years, the rock slowly eroded and broke apart. Then the Soul said, "That's interesting. I'm freer now." But it wasn't too free because it found out that it had been absorbed into the

John Roger Hinkins, founder of the Movement of Spiritual Inner Awareness. (*Courtesy of the Movement of Spiritual Inner Awareness*)

land, and now it was being absorbed into a tree. That was a little better than being the rock. At least it could play in the sun and enjoy the breeze—and it really felt fantastic. It thought, "This is great; I'm really having a wonderful experience. I think I've learned patience being a rock. Now I think I'll learn gradualness." So it was part of the tree for a long time, until one day it decided to become the fruit on the tree.

The fruit became ripe in its time, and it fell down and decayed. Then there appeared a worm who lived off the fruit, and pretty soon the worm sprouted wings and discovered it could fly. And the Soul said, "Wow, that's pretty good. I've learned patience and gradualness, and now I just have to learn elevation." So it flew around, but as it flew, it found out that a bird came along and absorbed it. And the Soul said, "This is fine. Now I'm a bigger bird and I can fly higher." But before long, an animal came along and consumed the bird. The animal couldn't fly, but it could run very fast. So the Soul said, "I think I'll learn mobility on the earth." It discovered that the new form was strong, and it lived a long time in this form. Eventually, though, the form passed from the earth, and the Soul discovered itself in a new form—in the form of a man.

Through many lifetimes in human form the Soul discovered it had greater freedom than ever, even though it couldn't fly in this physical form. It realized the reality of itself. It realized that it had always been a Soul and that it had had all these other experiences. It realized that it had experienced all these other things but never really been any of them, that it had always been just what it was—a Soul, a part of God. It discovered that the strength of the Soul is far greater than the physical strength of the beast, and it found that its beingness is far more magnificent than the most magnificent earthly monarch. It discovered that its kingdom is neither on nor of the earth. So after many lifetimes it said, "I don't belong here," and it just dropped that physical form and moved directly into the Soul realm—its home. And the Soul was greeted regally; it entered royally and sat on the throne because it was the king of its own principality. That is the allegory of the Soul's evolvement.

The reality of the Soul's evolvement is more complex, but the story tells the essence of it. Within our universe, there are five planes, or realms, which we call the lower planes or negative planes. In this sense negative does not mean "bad," but rather, negative like the pole of a battery. A battery has negative and positive poles, and together they create the charge that is the power. In a similar way, the planes of existence have negative and positive poles.

The "negative" planes or realms are as follows:

The etheric realm—related to the unconscious level of man's consciousness
The mental realm—related to the mind of man;
The causal realm—related to the emotional level of man;
The astral realm—related to the imaginative level of man; and
The physical realm—related to the material substance of man's experience.

The physical level is the densest level. The Soul, expressing through various forms, may incarnate on any of these realms at various points in its journey. The Soul's experience on any negative realm other than the physical is more restricted or limited to that particular realm. But through the form of the human on the physical realm, the Soul's awareness is multidimensional and it has the unique opportunity of experiencing all negative realms simultaneously.

Not only can the Soul, through the human form, experience all the negative realms, but it also can directly experience the positive realms that exist beyond the negative. The first of the positive realms is the Soul realm. This is the first level where the Soul is consciously aware of its true nature, its pure beingness, and its oneness with God. There are also many ascending realms of pure Spirit above the Soul realm. They are all involved in the greater, more conscious realization of Soul and Spirit and God, until the Soul eventually dissolves its individuality into its greater oneness with the supreme God of all. These realms of pure Spirit really defy explanation in physical vocabulary; they must be experienced to be known. There are no words—it can only be said that they do exist and that it is everyone's potential and everyone's heritage to someday know of them in direct, conscious experience.

The Soul has its home in the Soul realm. That is the realm from which it has come. In many senses, it is a stranger to the lower or negative realms, and there is always within it the thrust to return to its home, to return to the realm of positive Spirit. The Soul incarnates in the lower/negative realms to gain the experience of those parts of God. Coming down through the lower levels, it picks up the form or "body" of each realm: etheric, mental, casual, astral, and physical. Each form is heavier and denser than the one before. The physical form is the final body that is picked up and is also the densest. With the physical form come several levels of consciousness:

- An unconsciousness (where memory is stored, where dreams may originate, and where many behavior patterns become automatic habits);
- A mind (used to record events and record and play back information);
- Emotions (where energy is generated and stored to be used as directed); and
- An imagination (the expressions of which may be positive or negative and may enhance or block one's experience).

As the Soul takes on these different aspects, which are all reflections of the negative realms, it remains as the one positive aspect among all the negative (again, not bad, but negative). The Soul becomes the weakest part in the physical form because its job is to experience the lower realms through the physical form.

The physical form also comes equipped with:

- A conscious self (which gets up in the morning, drives the car to work, reads the newspaper, studies the reports, talks to friends, etc.);
- A basic self (which controls the bodily functions, directs the body in well-learned habit patterns, and much like a four or five-year-old child, asserts its desires and wishes upon the conscious self); and
- A high self (which functions much like a guardian, directing the conscious self toward those experiences which will be for its greatest good, having knowledge of the life destiny of the physical form and attempting to fulfill it).

The conscious self is the "captain of the ship" and can ignore or override both basic self and high self. For the most part the high self will act in the best interests of the Soul's progression and evolvement; it will direct the human consciousness into those experiences it needs for its "education." The basic self will act primarily to preserve the body. It will resist anything that will harm or hurt the body or cause destruction to itself. The conscious self is the part that is most apt to get caught up in the illusions of the imagination, mind, emotions, and glamour of the physical world, creating situations that delay the Soul's evolvement.

When the human consciousness inflicts itself upon another human consciousness—when it creates harm, hurt, pain, and so on, through physical action, thought patterns, verbal expression, dishonesty, deceit, financial fraud, emotional control patterns, or any other way—it is held accountable for that and will be given the opportunity to clear the action and bring it into balance. No one has the right to harm or hurt another, in any way. When that happens, the action must be balanced; it is the law of cause and effect. If you cause imbalance, the effect is that the imbalance is returned to you, as its creator, and you get to make it right. This, in essence, is the action of karma. It is a just and fair action. And it is the creation of karmic situations that institutes the action of reincarnation.

As a human, a Soul starts by incarnating once onto the physical realm, into a physical form. If that form could walk through its life here in perfect balance, creating only peace and love and harmony, it might complete and free itself from this realm and earn the opportunity to continue its evolvement on higher realms. But when the Soul incarnates into physical form, it is usually inexperienced in the ways of this world. The consciousness sees all the glamour, the illusions, the attractions of the world—the pleasures—and gets sidetracked. It is all a part of learning. So as it goes through its life plan, it is apt to create imbalance. Then when the time comes for the body to die, there are often karmic situations that have never been cleared or balanced. Thus, the Soul, at a later time, embodies again onto the physical realm so that it can clear its debts, right the wrongs, and bring balance and harmony. But if the consciousness again gets caught up in the illusions and the glamour, it may end up creating more karmic situations so that the Soul must again embody to clear them. And so on.

At some point in time, the consciousness will come into an understanding of this process, will learn to be a responsible creator, and will learn to place its value and its concern on those things that are positive and spiritual in nature rather than on the materiality of this world. In this way the consciousness begins its evolution back toward God, fulfills its past karma, stays free of accruing more karma, and liberates itself from this world. It is everyone's heritage to know the divine nature, to experience the joy and freedom and perfection of the Soul.

The Soul, in itself, is both positive and negative. It is complete in its energy pattern, just like its Creator is complete. But, when it decides to come into a physical form, it orients itself more toward one or the other polarity, male or female. It may say, "I'm going to come into the earth this time as a male." The high self, then, who works with the Soul, will go to the repository of basic selves and get a basic self that will be able to bring a body into the correct form. The basic self will begin to form the male body. The Soul will embody, at the time of birth, into the form as a male expression, but its energy cycles are still complete within itself because the Soul is perfect and complete.

The polarity of the body may feel the need for the balance of the opposite polarity and so it will seek out a mate, a companion, someone with whom it can exchange energy and feel complete. The male form expresses primarily a positive polarity; the female expresses a negative polarity. When male and female come together in the sexual encounter, the energies are exchanged; in essence, the battery is charged. People who are working with the high spiritual energies recognize the completeness of the Soul—and that recognition is their "Soul mate."

When you recognize that the Soul is perfect and complete, you have found your "Soul mate." The Soul does not look for a mate; it is perfect. It is the lower levels of consciousness that look for a mate, that seek to complete themselves. When you recognize that you are complete, then you will really have no need for the boundaries of this world. And this is what is often called self-realization. It is freedom!

All Souls were created at one "time." In God's "time" they have always been, but they have chosen different occasions to incarnate on this planet and gain their experiences. So each Soul is not equal in its progression and development, even though all are equal in the higher reality. Also, the time patterns between incarnations (or embodiments—you incarnate on the planet only once; your next lifetimes here are re-embodiments) may vary. There is no true average time between embodiments. So, although all Souls were created simultaneously, one may have experienced physicality more than another. One person may be experiencing his fiftieth lifetime here while another may be experiencing her hundred and ninety-fifth. That will make considerable difference in each one's awareness of Spirit and in each one's expression.

Over the eons of time on the planet, there have been many races of people. Each race is a different experience, a different consciousness. It is all "one" spiritually, but there is a separate consciousness within each race. You may not acquire the experience to know all of God in all his dominion unless you incarnate through all races. You may incarnate as a red man or woman one lifetime and learn it and never need to come back into that consciousness, or you may come in one lifetime as black or brown or white or yellow and learn it and never need to come back in that consciousness. It would be rare, however, to complete those experiences in one lifetime. When you get down here on the planet in all the levels of karmic fulfillment, it becomes difficult to fulfill all conditions in one lifetime.

Before you incarnate on the planet, you are in consciousness on some other realm living another existence. Then, for whatever reason, it becomes time for you to incarnate on the physical realm. Keep in mind that it is the nature of the Soul to experience all levels and conditions of God. Thus, the earth experience is part of the Soul's evolution into the greater consciousness of God. Before you re-embody you meet with karmic counselors or masters (known as the karmic board) to plan your life on the planet within high degrees of possibility and probability.

At this time of planning you choose your parents, you choose the talents and abilities you will have, and you choose those things that you and the karmic counselors decide will be best for you to further your spiritual progression. You also set up the situations that will bring you together with people in relation-

John Morton, John Roger's spiritual heir.
(*Courtesy of the Movement for Spiritual Inner Awareness*)

ships that will give you the opportunity to fulfill karmic debts from your past existences.

It is the Soul's nature to incarnate onto the physical plane to gain experience, but it is the action of karma—the creation and the releasing of karma—that perpetuates the action of re-embodiment. Many people have lived hundreds of lives on earth and are still in the process of attempting to gain an understanding of karma so they can release themselves from the wheel of incarnation or embodiment, realize the freedom of their Soul, transcend this realm, and know the higher realms.

Before incarnation/re-embodiment you have free will and you exercise it; after you incarnate, you have free choice. Before you incarnate, you set up many possibilities; after you incarnate, you choose which of the possibilities you wish to follow. It is very complex and complicated to lay out all the variables that you can possibly enter into in your lifetime. It is so complex that if you attempted it with a computer, it would probably be inadequate to do what can be done by the masters of the karmic board who know, down to the most minute detail, what has happened through all of your existences. They sit with you, and then they sit with the Souls of your potential parents and family, and these patterns of your existence are worked out through many generations.

One metaphysical group says that an incarnation pattern is one hundred and forty-four years. They are setting forward a generalization that you will live on the planet for about one hundred years, and then, at your physical death, you will live about forty-four years in another realm before you re-embody back to earth again. The plan is approximately one hundred and forty-four years; however, within that cycling, you may break free much sooner; you may fulfill and work through your karma more quickly. But usually the karmic reactions that you set in motion will proceed for about one hundred and forty-four years.

Within your karmic pattern, for example, the counselors may set up actions whereby you work with the pattern of patience. In a former situation, you may have been very impatient with people and cut them off short, possibly by way of their heads. Because you created this action, you're going to have to enter into situations where you won't necessarily lose your head physically, but you will be experiencing impatience and be losing your head in other ways, maybe through emotions or temper. The action may be symbolic rather than physical. You will enter into these situations to learn to become patient. It may be set up so that the one person who keys this off for you is someone from a previous lifetime who was a receiver of your action. Perhaps he will be your father this time. Before you re-embody you agree to the action and the conditions because it is fair that he gets the chance to balance the action.

In situations of this sort, it is possible that when the child incarnates, the father will see the child and experience a recall (not often on the conscious level) of the past life and kill the child. This has happened. Usually, though, it doesn't happen because the "father" will give the "child" the opportunity to balance and fulfill the action. He must allow the action. These opportunities are so perfect. If you ever do something that is inflicting on another and play the little mental game of "Oh, nobody knows; I can get away with it," think again. You're not getting away with anything. The Soul records it all and holds itself responsible for it all—in perfection and in justice.

Reincarnation is not negative, as a lot of people would like to believe. It's a very positive, progressive philosophy: if you don't make it now, you get another chance. What could be better than that? Everyone is working for awareness of the inner consciousness, seeking first the kingdom of God within and then seeking God in the outer reality. And everybody wants to reach heaven. But if you were told you were going to die in two weeks, you'd probably say, "Oh, God, no, I don't want to die. I want to stay in this misery." With that attitude you will, either now or later. You must be extremely careful of how you place things toward yourself because, being a creator and having divine essence within you, that which you create will be returned to you. You will be held responsible, as the author of the creation. It comes back to you.

The interesting thing is that within the Movement of Spiritual Inner Awareness, through its teachings, you can break the incarnation wheel. There are specialized techniques that are known to the people in MSIA who are courageously and consciously seeking for the uplifted experience. It can be difficult because often people may do their meditations, their spiritual exercises, their contemplation, or their upliftment of themselves for five minutes of the day, and for the other twenty-three hours and fifty-five minutes of the day put themselves down and lock themselves into the bondage of what we call the planet earth.

The temptation to focus on the negative of this level is very strong. However, with the inner support that comes from doing spiritual exercises and other spiritual practices, people are redirecting their focus to going back home to God.

21
OVERVIEW OF RAMTHA'S SCHOOL OF ENLIGHTENMENT

Greg Simmons

Ramtha's School of Enlightenment is a school of ancient wisdom founded in 1988 by an American woman, J. Z. Knight, channel of Ramtha. Born in Roswell, New Mexico, in March 1946, Knight was living in Tacoma, Washington, when she first encountered Ramtha in February 1977. Describing that event, she said, "I blinked and to my utter shock and amazement there stood a giant man at the other end of my kitchen—just standing there aglow." He told her, "I am Ramtha the Enlightened One. I have come to help you over the ditch." Initially she was not able to comprehend the experience, but Ramtha continued, "Beloved woman, the greatest of things are achieved with a light heart. It is the ditch of limitation and fear." Over the next months, Knight was taught by Ramtha and allowed him to speak through her. In November 1978, she first channeled Ramtha to a small group of people in Tacoma, Washington.

Ramtha has said that he lived on earth some 35,000 years ago. He was one of the despised Lemurian minority who had fled with his mother and brother to the Atlatian port of Onai, after massive geological changes that were happening at the time. He became a powerful warrior who outwitted and conquered his enemies on every occasion except one. After being betrayed, run through with a broadsword, and given up for dead, his battles shifted to the dimensions of his own consciousness, where with his powerful mind he eventually became enlightened and conquered death. During a lengthy recovery period he had time to contemplate the Unknown God. He contemplated the powerful unseen wind, free of boundaries, limits, or form, and after several years of such contemplation he discovered the ability to separate his consciousness from his body. Further contemplation led to further change and he was able to raise his frequency and change his entire body. Ramtha never died; instead, with his mind, he learned to take his body with his consciousness into the other dimensions.

The term "channel" was initially coined by Ramtha and subsequently adopted by the New Age movement from which Ramtha has distanced himself. The word "channeling" refers to the process of his consciousness flowing through Knight's brain to facilitate his spoken teachings. By voluntarily abdicating her body, she allows his consciousness to surround and operate her physical body. Knight's channeling of Ramtha is one of the greatest anomalies that scholars of neurophysiology and parapsychology have studied.

For two years, 1996–1997, scientists studied Knight, Ramtha, and a group of his students. The results of their findings were given at a conference, titled In Search of the Self, held in February 1997. Baffled by the unexpected results of their tests taken while Knight was channeling, confirmed and reconfirmed at different times, they were amazed to admit that Knight's body functions as if it were in a normal waking state while the most sophisticated polygraph equipment showed that it should be asleep. Although her neocortex is emitting the delta waves of deep sleep, her eyes are open and her body talks, walks, eats, drinks, or dances while Ramtha teaches profound knowledge throughout the long hours that he engages his students. Compounding the mystery are the test results that show it is her subconscious brain, the lower cerebellum, that facilitates the body when Ramtha is being channeled.

Knight enjoyed great success traveling throughout the United States and Europe channeling Ramtha's teachings and having them released in written and audio form. She culminated her first decade as Ramtha's channel in 1987 with the publication of her autobiography, A State of Mind. At this time she recognized that the format of the Dialogues (the name given to the teachings in those days) that made Ramtha very popular did not allow for the natural evolution of his teachings and was limiting the progress of his most sincere students. Through the Dialogues and resultant books and tapes, Ramtha was able to engage students with ideas, but for those ideas to become a reality, the students needed a domain in which to do the necessary work.

Thus in May 1988, Knight established Ramtha's School of Enlightenment (RSE) in Yelm, Washington, a place where students would come, learn, and practice the spiritual disciplines required for personal change and mastery.

BELIEFS AND PRACTICES

At the school, Ramtha expanded the ideas of his early Dialogues into a coherent system of thought and implemented his program of spiritual disciplines. The per-

J. Z. Knight. (*Courtesy of the Ramtha School of Enlightenment*)

spective of his system was to some degree gnostic in that he takes on the role of a Master Teacher and Hierophant, a teacher who has the power to initiate his students into direct experience. However, unlike Gnosticism—which emphasizes the struggle between good and evil, light and darkness, sin and righteousness—the material world, the densest plane of existence, which Ramtha calls the plane of demonstration, and the human body are never regarded as evil, undesirable, or intrinsically bad. What becomes an undesirable condition is to remain in a state of ignorance and denial to our true nature and destiny.

The work of the school, the Great Work, as Ramtha terms it, is the combining of scientific knowledge with the esoteric understanding of consciousness. This is coupled with the mastery of personal limitations, thus mastering the storms that divide the individual against the unity that manifests God as self.

At RSE, Ramtha began to teach that what we know as the universe originated in a "sea" of pure potentiality called the Void, a dimension in which no material thing exists; rather it is the fountainhead pouring forth the thoughts from which everything is created. In the timeless past, the Void in an unimaginable contemplation created a principal point of consciousness called Point Zero. Point Zero received the command from the Void to make known all unknown potentials of the Void.

To simplify this understanding, Ramtha explains this concept with imagery. He uses a pyramid, with Point Zero at the apex and divided horizontally into seven levels below. The levels equate with the creative potentials issuing from Point Zero and the Void. These levels represent, on one hand, the creation and involution of consciousness down from Point Zero, through seven levels of frequency and time, into gross material existence at the base of the pyramid.

From the reverse perspective, once the consciousness of beings began to manifest at the material level, the slowest level of frequency, they began the process of creating and evolving. The evolutionary path of humanity is the return journey back up through the seven levels, "home," to Point Zero.

The four cornerstones of Ramtha's teachings are God Lives within each of us; Consciousness and Energy Create the Nature of Reality; We are here to Make Known the Unknown; We are here to become God In Human Form. These teachings are not a new religion nor are they the building blocks of a new church. They are a coherent system of thought that contains within its approach to reality the elements and mechanisms that allow the individual to engage the teachings and verify and experience their content firsthand. Leaving nothing to blind faith, Ramtha stresses that his teachings are merely philosophy until they are experienced by the student. However, knowledge of that philosophy is a necessary precondition for the student to experience and verify for himself what is being taught.

At Ramtha's School of Enlightenment, students study biology, neurophysiology, neurochemistry, and quantum physics to illustrate how their very consciousness creates their reality (their life). In learning to *know thyself,* they learn how to redefine God, the creator, to be experienced within themselves.

Ramtha's curriculum provides a series of spiritual disciplines which, when practiced correctly, provide direct experience. Each student creates a greater reality and thus owns the philosophy and knowledge as personal truth and wisdom.

The key spiritual discipline and mechanism for manifestation at RSE is known as Consciousness and Energy. In this practice students learn to move energy within the body by means of focused concentration. It is the foundation for the additional disciplines which Ramtha has devised for multiple, specific goals to be accomplished by each individual.

Ramtha tells his students, "This work doesn't ask you to die; this work asks you to live. This work celebrates life. It asks you to have knowledge—enough knowledge—that in common reasoning we can see the reason for our life, genetically as a predisposition of the soul." "So knowledge is a goal, a goal of pursuit in which to grow into."

ORGANIZATION

Ramtha's School of Enlightenment is organized as an esoteric academy with students advancing through a progressive curriculum. Individuals can begin to study at home with Ramtha's teachings available in books and on audiotapes and videotapes. New students can begin by viewing at home *Creating Personal Reality,* a five-tape video course comprising some nine hours of Ramtha's teachings which give the fundamentals of what students will further learn and practice when they enroll at RSE. The next step is a Beginner's Retreat. Here they will be given more knowledge, taught additional disciplines, and begin to master what they have learned on the tapes. Over the next year, they have the opportunity to attend additional events. To retain their status as a current student, individuals are required to attend two events a year: one in the spring and one in the fall. There are a number of additional classes, workshops, and retreats that students may attend. Many of those who reside close to the school take advantage of these opportunities.

In 1999 Knight channeled Ramtha in the first of what has become an annual world tour. She has made selected visits to Australia, South Africa, Scotland, Japan, Italy, Spain, Germany, and Mexico. The world tour, in its fourth year in 2002, now encompasses international introductory evenings and retreats that are presented by selected advanced students. In addition, there are regular showings of Ramtha's teachings on video in over forty cities in seventeen countries.

MEMBERSHIP

As of 2002, there are approximately thirty-five hundred current students, about half of whom live in the northwest corner of the state of Washington. The others are scattered across North America, Europe, South Africa, Australia, New Zealand, and Japan.

Ramtha's teachings have been documented in fourteen current book titles. *Ramtha: The White Book*, one of the first to be published by JZK, Inc., has been translated into thirteen languages.

22
DAMANHUR

THE FEDERATION OF DAMANHUR

Founded in 1977, Damanhur is an internationally renowned center for spiritual research. Situated in Valchiusella Valley, in the Alpine foothills of northern Italy, Damanhur is a federation of communities with over eight hundred fifty citizens; a social and political structure; a constitution; its own currency, called "Credit"; schools; and a daily paper. Damanhur is a way of living and thinking based upon experimentation, play, and transformation and solidarity.

Damanhur's people have established over forty business and services, which form the economic basis of Damanhur. They are all privately owned and organized on a cooperative basis. Their profits are shared among the business partners, which can then choose how to invest them. Often, companies choose to support the building of the Temple of Humankind by commissioning works of art to the different workshops.

Real estate is owned by co-ops, of which all Damanhur's citizens own shares, according to how much money they invested in it. Damanhur has doctors, lawyers, teachers, nurses, civil servants, computer consultants, farmers . . . living in Damanhur does not require working only inside of Damanhur.

Besides paying Italian taxes, all Damanhur's citizens contribute economically on a monthly basis to the development and the growth of the Federation with

From http://www.damanhur.org. Reprinted by permission of the Federation of Damanhur.

a small percentage of their income. Public money is then invested in the sectors of public interest such as the schools, the arts, the acquisition of new territories.

Damanhur's society is interested in creating a sustainable way of living. Damanhur's people consider our planet as a living being to respect and preserve. In Damanhur nobody smokes and smoking is not allowed even outdoors as a form of respect not only for humans but also for plants, animals, and the natural environment.

Since the very first day of its foundation, Damanhur has being recycling its wastes, starting organic agriculture, and looking for eco-compatible ways of living, of producing, and of developing its settlements.

Damanhur's people are also actively involved in the valley councils: thirteen of Damanhur's citizens have been elected on Damanhur's own list and now sit in four different village councils cooperating with ideas and projects to the social and economic development of the whole valley. In the town of Vidracco, the mayor is a Damanhurian citizen, elected by a majority of non-Damanhurian residents. Damanhur has a specific office to coordinate work both at local and national level. The main fields of action are eco-compatible planning and development, tourism development, bio-architecture, and alternative energies.

Damanhur's lawyers and experts are also actively involved at national level, cooperating with many other organizations to promote the recognition of nonprofit organizations and communities as important subjects for future sustainable development.

Damanhur's society invests many resources to give children not only a happy and healthy environment to live in but also the best possible education. Damanhur has internal schools for boys and girls from one to thirteen years of age. The official Italian curriculum is complemented by subjects such as music, theater, computer sciences, several foreign languages. Teaching methods combine "classic" classroom lessons with frequent trips for hands-on observation of the topics under study.

Dozens of Damanhurian citizens are trained as volunteers for the Italian Red Cross and Damanhur has its own civil protection teams, officially recognized by the Italian authorities. They are two teams, based in two different geographical regions and composed of about fifty people, all well trained and experienced in extinguishing fires in the woods and emergency situations, such as floods and earthquakes.

Damanhurians like to call their society a "university of the spirit" where everything offers the individual an opportunity to discover his or her own hidden talents and potential, a live laboratory in which to put that potential into practice and make it grow, not only for oneself but also for others.

In Damanhur we have abolished the word "must" from our vocabulary— because all our actions derive from a conscious choice—and also the word "impossible"—to remind themselves of the endless potential of human beings.

In our research we push beyond the limitations imposed by conventional ways of thinking and those of contemporary science aiming at the union of beauty and science, the marriage of the spirit with the material, the mind and the heart, the soul and the hands. Research in all fields is very important—from social models to alternative energies, from the arts to physics. The first and most important principle of Damanhurian philosophy is that everything changes. Life itself is continuous transformation and Damanhur is above all change, growth and renewal, building new roads for the future upon experience already acquired. After almost thirty years since its foundation, Damanhur today is a reference point for thousands of people all over the world; spiritual and material researchers who are not satisfied with just the "search" but want in the end to be able "to find." And having found, they want to build from then on with passion and altruism, creating something different on the planet, aware that true conquests of the spirit always correspond to practical results in the material world.

Change has been an important factor also in Damanhur's social and political systems. They have had to evolve throughout the years, from the first single community to the complex organization of today's federation. Likewise, Damanhur's model of decision making has evolved creating an efficient democratic system with elected representatives and elective bodies and the lively participation of its citizens in the public debate.

The Federation now numbers over five hundred full-time citizens and three hundred fifty others who live nearby and take part in its activities. Damanhur offers different kinds of citizenship, according to the level of involvement each person decides upon. It is possible to be a full-time resident but also to live in other parts of the world and visit regularly.

The homes and the companies of the federation are not concentrated in one single area but are scattered all over the Valchiusella Valley. They include one hundred twenty hectares of woods, five hectares of urban surface, sixty hectares of farmland, and over seventy buildings including private homes, studios, laboratories, and farms. Since the very first day of its foundation, Damanhur has been engaged in creating a sustainable way of life, which is also reflected in its commercial prodution and in the development of its settlements. Our planet is considered as a living being to be respected and preserved.

The federation has many centers in Italy and Europe and maintains contact with spiritual groups worldwide. Every year thousands of people visit Damanhur to explore its social model and study its philosophy. They also come to meditate in the Temple of Humankind, the great underground building carved by hand out of the rock by Damanhur's citizens and defined by many as the "Eighth Wonder of the World." Art is in fact Damanhur's preferred instrument for growth and transformation; it is used to translate that which shines inside individual into real changes in the world of Forms. In Damanhur it is believed that the objects and the environment that surround us influence our ideas and our ability to elaborate, and Damanhurian citizens are striving to create a very beautiful and stimulating place in which art makes it possible to open up to intuition and images that arrive from the outside. Damanhur is a place of inspiration, where spirit and form are no longer separate and where spiritual aspirations are verified through the work of our hands, because they manifest in the material plane.

The Synchronic Lines

The choice to establish Damanhur in Valchiusella, and to build the Temple of Humankind there, was not made by accident. The valley presents unique features: it has the highest concentration of different minerals on the planet, and in Valchiusella four "Synchronic Lines" meet; they are energy rivers that surround the Earth and link it to the universe. These energy flows are able to catalyze the great forces present in the cosmos. The lines can modify events and carry ideas, thoughts, and moods, thereby influencing all living creatures. A stay in Damanhur, a visit or a meditation in the Temple of Humankind creates the opportunity to take advantage of the extraordinary energy of the synchronic lines and to use them to help one's inner growth.

The Temple of Humankind

The Hall of Water, of the Earth, of the Spheres, of Mirrors, of Metals, the Blue Temple, the Labyrinth: The Temple of Humankind is an underground work of art, a great three-dimensional book built entirely by hand and dedicated to the divine nature of humanity and to the narration of the history of humankind through all forms of art. The Temple of Humankind is a pathway toward the Divine inside and outside of oneself. Here it is possible to enter into contact with the Forces which are cooperating with humankind to create a new future. Just as in the Renaissance, the construction of the Temple of Humankind has given impulse to the creation of artistic studios and craft workshops for which Damanhur is appreciated all over the world.

The Temple is a large laboratory where art and science, technology and spirituality are united in the search for new paths of evolution and growth for all humanity.

The temple has been built entirely by hand. It stretches for over four thousand cubic meters, on five different levels, connected by hundreds of meters of corridors. The Temple rises where the Eurasian continental plate meets the African one, creating breakthroughs of a rare mineral, over 300 million years old. It is called mylonite. It is a rock characterized by the faculty of transporting the physical energies of the earth.

The Temple of the Humankind is built inside a vein of this particular mineral, whose presence follows perfectly the flow of the synchronic lines. Over twenty years from the start of the building, official scientific researches confirm that there is only one point of energy such as the one where the Temple is built.

The Temple of Humankind symbolically represents the inner rooms of every human being. Walking along its halls and corridors corresponds to an inner journey deep inside oneself.

At each bend the Temple seems to come to an end, but it goes on behind secret doors and opening walls to reveal more halls and chambers, just as in each one of us are secret parts one has to discover by oneself.

In the Temple everything can be read like a book: every color, measure, step has a meaning; they follow a precise code of forms and proportions. Every Chamber has its own specific resonance, its own sound.

Hall of Water

The Hall of Water, an island twenty meters below ground, is dedicated to the feminine principle, to birth, to death, to the cycles of life.

One of the functions of the temple of Humankind is as a sophisticated healing device. This chamber is connected to the throat, the uterus, the sense of sight.

The dome is made of Tiffany glass, lit from behind; the walls are painted with circuits and signs activated with water circulating within.

The window with the blue sphere is dedicated to the moon, another feminine symbol.

Hall of Earth

The photograph on page 640 shows the Hall of the Earth, thirty meters underground.

The precious painted ceiling is a mandala created by the interlacing of signs of Damanhur's sacred language. It is an ancient, ancestral language that can be expressed through sound, sign, and dance. The embroidery of the ceiling repeats sixty-six times the ideogrammatical transcription of the song we are listening to, and which the dancer is interpreting.

The paintings on the walls, still an ongoing work, tell the history of humankind through time, from the creation of the universe to the present. This is the battle every one of us has to fight against one's own negative parts—a battle to win through joy, laughter, sense of humor.

In the lower part of the walls are represented the Ways of Damanhur.

The floor is a labyrinth traced with signs in sacred language. The stones composing it have been picked up from beaches all over the world to symbolize the link of this Hall with our planet.

The doors represent the Sun and the Moon.

For healing this room is used to intervene on the liver, the spleen, the reproductive apparatus. The eight columns in china and gold resound on the different chakras of the human body.

The Hall of the Earth. (*Courtesy of Damanhur*)

Labyrinth

The Labyrinth is dedicated to the unity of the Divine Forces of our planet. Each window represents a god or a goddess.

The mosaic on the floor presents symbols and signs linked to the correspondent window.

Hall of Metals

The Hall of Metals is a very rich and complex room, both from the symbolic and the artistic point of view.

The terracotta ceiling is the largest in the world. Knights and dancers are engaged in defending every human being's spiritual fire. In opposition, on the dark green marble floor, stand out the allegories of six common vices of the human beings. They are composed of over thirty thousand pieces of marble each.

The columns are trees to remind us of the wood twenty meters above us and of the bond between the human beings and the plant world. They are trees of knowledge, symbol of the wholeness humankind must recover.

The windows are dedicated to eight metals, the main theme of this room, and to eight ages of the human being. The lower part in Tiffany glass of each window

The Hall of Metals. (*Courtesy of Damanhur*)

describes the human and spiritual achievements every age should conquer. This window, composed of over three thousand pieces, represents tin, the autumn of life, the wisdom of seniority. This is lead, childhood, the thoughtlessness of the years of play, the Spring of life. This is the age where we create the basis of the human being we are going to be.

Room of Spheres

The Room of the Spheres is covered in gold leaf. It hosts nine spheres containing alchemical liquids. We are in the heart of the Temple and from here, through the spheres, we can contact all the points of our planet, through the network of the synchronic lines. The ancient Chinese called it "the back of the Dragon." It is the great energetic net surrounding our planet and linking it to the universe. The Temple of the Humankind has been built following the flow of these large rivers of energy transporting ideas, dreams, and thought. Here as many as four synchronic lines meet and intertwine.

Hall of Mirrors

The dome in Tiffany glass is the largest in the world, one hundred square meters, thousands of small pieces of glass. This room is dedicated to light, air, spirituality. In the human body it is connected to the heart and the head.

The glass mosaics on the walls right under the cupola present symbolic elements of the other halls of the Temple and link them to the seasons of the year. In the four corners minute pieces of mirror reproduce the constellations visible from our latitude at the four moments of seasonal passage: the Solstices and the Equinoxes.

The floor is in red granite adorned with a central mosaic enclosing a round slab of precious black marble. The dandelion flower, symbol of Damanhur, stands out among signs in sacred language.

On the four sides of the floor open four niches devoted to the elements: Earth, Air, Fire, Water.

INTERVIEW WITH LUIGI BERZANO

University Professor, Faculty of Political Sciences, Turin University

Since my first studies on Damanhur, in 1989, the dimension which has interested and surprised me most was precisely that of the "social experiment." Studying Damanhur I got the perception of what the Carthusian monasteries and the abbeys represented in the Middle Ages. Establishing themselves inside agricultural valleys, they brought benefits and revitalized entire valleys. And, in fact, I believe this is partly what has happened with Damanhur. In a valley which had all the economical and social indexes of depression and aging, Damanhur has represented a resource in many aspects. Damanhur has revitalized the valley in demographic terms, has reactivated the interest for many ancient trades, has brought back the pleasure for artistic production in many sectors. And since the beginning, Damanhur has represented this element of social innovation. Damanhur, in spite of the objective diversity it represents to mainstream culture, and in spite of the many innovations it has brought about, has never had a lasting and significant dispute with the Italian State. Damanhur, unlike some religious movements, has never gone through phases of conscientious objection toward the Italian normative systems. This datum of a cultural, economical, and social integration inside the Italian context is no doubt an element to keep on studying, for it represents the possibility and the conciliation of areas of innovation, which are radical without being revolutionary and represent forms of conciliation inside the Italian state. The only area of tension is the one which presented itself some-times with some religious institutions, but this was very transitory, and I think that today it is not as significant as it has been in the past.

CONSTITUTION OF THE FEDERATION OF DAMANHUR

Damanhur is a school of thought founded by Oberto Airaudi and inspired by his teachings: it is expressed through the three bodies called Meditation, Game of Life, and Social. They represent respectively ritual tradition; experimentation and dynamics; and the social realization of such teachings.

The aims of Damanhur are: the freedom and reawakening of the Human Being as a divine, spiritual and material principle; the creation of a self-sustaining model of life based on ethical principles of good communal living and love; harmonic inte-gration and cooperation with all the Forces linked to the evolution of Humankind.

The Constitution is the fundamental Charter regulating the Social Body, formed by Damanhur's citizens.

Damanhurian citizens dedicate their life to the application of the principles and aims indicated in the Constitution, and they make a commitment to respect and apply it in all its norms.

The act of becoming a citizen takes different forms, corresponding to the choice and commitment of the individual.

The Communities represent the ideal form of union and communal living. They are inspired by principles of solidarity and sharing. The Communities as a whole are organised as a Federation.

Communities belonging to different schools of thought may affiliate with the Federation, even though they do not originate from Damanhur's school of thought, as long as they are inspired by the same aims.

Out of the creation of a Tradition, a Culture, a History and common ethics, the People is born.

1. The citizens are brothers and sisters who help one another through reciprocal trust, respect, clarity, acceptance, solidarity, and continuous inner transformation. Everyone is committed to always giving others opportunities to aim higher.

2. Each citizen makes a commitment to spread positive and harmonious thoughts and to direct every thought and action toward spiritual growth. Each person is socially and spiritually responsible for every action they take, as everybody is aware that each act is multiplied and reflected through the Synchronic Lines all over the world.

3. Through community life, Damanhur aims at developing individuals whose reciprocal relations are regulated by Knowledge and Consciousness. Fundamental rules of life are common sense, thinking well of others and the welcoming and exaltation of diversity.

4. Work has spiritual value and is understood as a gift of oneself to others. Through it everyone takes part in the material and spiritual progress of the people, carrying out assignments as they become necessary. Each citizen offers a proportion of their work in activities of common interest (*Terrazzatura*). Every task is precious and carries the same dignity.

5. Those who take on roles of social responsibility carry out their tasks in a spirit of service, without looking for personal advantage or serving the private interests of others. Only Citizens residing in the Communities may be elected or nominated for positions of social responsibility, in the forms and modes provided for by the federal laws.

6. Spirituality, research, and ecology inspire all relationships with the environment, also through the use of appropriate technologies, useful in improving the quality of life. Every Citizen lives in communion with nature and the subtle forces which inhabit it. Everyone is committed to respect and preserve resources and avoid as far as possible forms of pollution and waste.

7. Each Citizen respects their own body, takes care of it, and nourishes it harmoniously, refraining from any form of substance abuse. Citizens put into practice rules of life suitable for harmonious physical, mental, and spiritual development; they ensure the orderliness and cleanliness of their environment. Each individual is expected to be capable of self-control, of making mature choices, and of manifesting purity in thought and action.

8. Damanhur promotes and supports research both in science and art; it fosters and encourages continual experimentation of both the physical and the nonphysical, as long as it is expressed in a harmonious form. All Citizens constantly improve their education and widen and deepen their knowledge in the fields of research, art, work, and leisure activities.

9. The People is a single body in constant evolution, the organic sum of all the single individualities; it holds and synthesizes all the experiences, thoughts, and feelings expressed within itself and makes them a common cultural, ethical, and spiritual wealth.

10. Damanhurian citizens contribute with their own resources, their work, and in every way to their own economic maintenance and to that of the whole Federation. Communal funds participate in investments of general interest, in harmony with the principle of solidarity. Individuals who leave the People may not make any financial claims against, and have no right to be reimbursed by the People.

11. Those Citizens residing in the Communities who wish to engage in a recognized relationship as a couple make a public announcement to their fellow Citizens. The couple, by means of a public ceremony, commit themselves to establish a union that is solid and useful to the community. Damanhur's citizens choose to plan the birth of children.

12. All citizens educate children in order to encourage them to become autonomous and free individuals, giving them all the necessary instruments to express and develop their own characteristics, applying common pedagogical guidelines. All resident citizens participate in the education of children and in their care and maintenance.

13. Whosoever wishes to become a citizen of Damanhur must present a written request outlining their reasons. If the applicant possesses the basic qualities to become a Citizen, the person will be allowed to begin the probationary period. During this period the applicants agree upon how they will participate in Community life. They are expected to observe this Charter and other Community rules. The request for admission will be accepted only after the applicant has demonstrated a knowledge of the principles and cultural heritage of the People. This is called the "Concession of Citizenship."

14. An individual will cease to belong to the population by withdrawal or by exclusion. If serious cases of misconduct make it impossible to continue the relationship, the decision to exclude can be made only after giving the individual in question the possibility to exercise their defense.

15. The highest authority of Damanhur is represented by the Guides. They guarantee a constant pursuance of the ideal aims and spiritual goals in every manifestation of social life, supervising the three Bodies. They direct and coordinate all choices and emanate laws on those subjects of interest to all Damanhurian citizens. They are periodically elected by the members of the body of Meditation according to the rules determined within it. The unanimous opinion of the Guides is binding for every individual, group, or organization of the People. In serious cases of need or emergency they may adopt any kind of measure or procedure.

16. Within the People, any group of two or more resident Citizens who have a socially useful function, may obtain recognition. A Group is a new entity formed from the interaction among different and complementary individuals. Therefore, it develops a greater ability to confront and propose, in relation to its aims.

17. The functions regarding control of the observance of the regulations are carried out by the College of Justice. Every Citizen has to respect its decisions. The College of Justice may suspend and annul the illegitimate acts issued by other bodies of the People. It instructs and defines disciplinary procedures in cases of violation of constitutional norms. It carries out functions of appeal in case of disciplinary procedures emanated by other bodies in the modes and forms provided for by the federal laws. Any controversy whatsoever among citizens and between citizens and Damanhur and its bodies will be subject, with the exclusion of any other jurisdiction, to the competence of the College of Justice, which will judge fairly, without formality of procedure and its ruling will be final.

18. Those citizens who choose to live together organize themselves into communities. Every community has its own territory, its own population and autonomy within the forms and limits established by the federal laws. Each community aims at reaching complete self-sufficiency and its population must not exceed 200–220 individuals. The provisions relating to the organization, administration, functioning of each community, and the coordination of its activities are adopted by the periodically elected local Government. The Community may set up bodies and put forward any rules that it regards necessary to function better, having regard to the Tradition and to the superior interests of the whole population. All citizens of Damanhur commit themselves to respect the laws of each community, when they are present on its territory. The citizens residing in Damanhurian communities and those who are present in a territory recognized as Damanhurian by an act of the Guides do not smoke, do not abuse alcohol and do not use drugs.

19. Communities or groups inspired by principles and aims compatible with those expressed in this Charter can affiliate with the Federation of Damanhur. The modalities of affiliation with the Federation are established by the Guides.

20. The norms of execution of the present Charter must not contain measures that are contrary to it. The discipline of all the matters relating to the whole population is carried out by means of Laws which must be observed by all the citizens. Any revision of rules contained in this Charter is to be approved by those who belong to the body of Meditation, according to rules decided within it. In every case where the interpretation of the existing norms is questioned, the resolution is adopted

by the Guides, expressed according to the principles of the Tradition, after having consulted the College of Justice.

Damanhur 14 December 1998

THE MAGIC ARCHITECTURE OF THE TEMPLES OF HUMANKIND

Even before the advent of writing, humankind was able to leave traces of its levels of civilization through well-defined and enduring signs: cave paintings, standing stones, and terracotta figurines in burial grounds. Each of these testimonies speaks and allows us to reconstruct a pathway, thanks to the interpretation of these objects which have been constructed or sited in such a way as to provide absolutely clear evidence of human intervention.

Architecture is that which provides the connecting thread, able to unite through time intelligence, strength, science, and human art.

Architecture can therefore be considered the principal art from which all the others derive because it creates the perfect "container" that exalts and completes every other form of human expression. When planning and construction are released from merely functional needs, those, for example, pursued in house building and urbanism, the architectonics assume a valence that touches significant aspects of human existence. These include philosophical and scientific thought and the interaction with other planes of reality, ending in contact with the Divine. Architecture can therefore become the intermediary between the spiritual and material planes.

The ancient cathedrals, just as the temples of the oriental tradition, contain scientific and mathematical information, along with esoteric knowledge. For thousands and thousands of years sacred buildings have been used as a method of transmitting something: knowledge is encoded in the building through the creation of surfaces, angles, curves, empty and filled spaces. There are elements that serve to distract and others, positioned in certain prearranged points that serve to hand down information or to open inner keys in whoever finds themselves in front of them. In magic architecture, logic and invention can live alongside rationality and emotionalism, multiple logic and the level of interpretation.

The Temples of Humankind, constructed by the citizens of the Federation of Damanhur in Italy, are examples of contemporary magic architecture that reflect and exalt the artistic, social, and spiritual realizations of their creators. The Temples aim to represent the union of beauty and science, the marriage between the spirit and the material, between the heart and the mind, between the soul and the hands. In this difficult and fascinating challenge, architecture and art are the privileged instruments for translating into real changes in the world of form that radiance each one of us creates inside.

Human beings think with objects, their environmental surroundings influence their ideas and their capacity to elaborate. Damanhur has constructed the Temples as a place of inspiration, so that spirit and form be no longer separate and the spiritual planes, be real because they are also created inside matter through physical work. The complex of the Temples is a living creature in constant transformation and evolution, able to speak to the heart and the soul through all the expressions of art it contains. The pathway that takes you from one Hall of the Temple to another symbolically represents the journey that every human being makes to the source of his or her own soul.

The Temples rise on a very active energetic point of the planet. In Valchiusella four synchronic lines meet; they are the energy lines that surround the Earth and connect it to the universe. The ancient Chinese called them the "Back of the Dragon." Nine horizontal lines and nine vertical lines that knot at the center of the Earth and again at the Poles to connect the planet to the galaxy. These subtle roads transport ideas, thought, intuition, dreams, and ways of thinking winding around all the planets and stars. Where there is a large amount of life the network is dense and pulsating; where there is none they thin out and disappear.

The Temples of Humankind were constructed to allow whoever visited them to enter in contact with these extraordinary energies and to use them for their own spiritual growth. The spatial development of the Temples follows the flow of a "shining knot" of synchronic lines—given by the intersection of two vertical and two horizontal lines—and makes the underground complex a real gateway to the entire network of the Lines.

This shining knot corresponds to the zone in which the Euro-Asian continental plate meets the African, creating outcrops of a rare mineral called mylonite. It is a rock more than 300 million years old, characterized by its capacity to transport the physical energies of the Earth. The complex of the Temples of Humankind has been entirely constructed inside a seam of this particular mineral whose presence perfectly follows the flow of the Synchronic Lines.

The logic behind the construction of the Temples can be understood only considering the need to reach these flows of energy, which flow at different depths underground. The Temples extend for thousands of cubic meters on many levels, linked by hundreds of meters of corridors.

Thanks to the energy that they contain and transform, the complex is a great alchemical laboratory, a sophisticated healing instrument and a means of contacting divine forces inside and outside of the human being. The logic behind its construction therefore makes constant reference to the link between microcosm and macrocosm. The geometry of planes always starts from the supposition that the human being is the unit of measurement for all the dimensions. For this reason during the excavation of the Temples straight lines were avoided, because Nature's lines are always curved and never straight.

The angles inside the Temples are used to activate the energies contained in different parts of the building and to interact with the energetic centers of the human body. All geometric forms are present, from circle, to square, to spiral, the latter also being included by the addition of spiral staircases.

In the Temples according to the classical canons of esoteric architecture, architectonic forms are connected to the elements of nature: air, earth, fire, water, and ether. The earth is the womb that creates and nourishes. The air is a crystal with mobile form in which the complexity of life is immersed. Water represents the living cycle, transmits life, and preserves memories. Fire represents life. Ether, the spiritual element par excellence, is linked to thought and creation.

To understand the Temples of Humankind it is therefore necessary to study how these elements can be read inside of them. Fire, for example, becomes light and the light becomes heat. Certain substances descend from high toward low, while others rise from low to high. It is interesting to observe how technical necessity and magical needs can find the same solution; as in the case of the collection of waste water, from condensation and seepage, or the channeling of air and heat.

The circulation of the air is based upon a natural system that takes advantage of the existing gradient inside the Temples and the consequent difference of pressure between the highest and lowest points. Besides having a function linked to the health of the people who find themselves in the Temples, air intervenes in an essential way in the process of dehumidifying the building's mass. If one thinks of the Temple complex as a living creature, then the air that circulates becomes its respiration.

In the same way, the flow of excess water can be compared to blood circulation. Water is collected and channeled, following an opposite pathway to that of the air. Air touches the deepest areas first then rises, while water touches the highest areas first then descend before being diverted into a small lake outside the Temples. Then it is absorbed by the earth, joins a river, and acts as an extension of the Temples.

Air and water also interact with the presence of people. The air moved in the corridors by the passage of people is energized, the human breath interacts with that of the Temples; the liquids present in the human body mirror that of the circulation of water. And fire is present in the Temples not only in the braziers and candles but also as intellectual fire and vital energy.

Another indispensable key for reading the great book of knowledge represented by the Temples of Humankind is that of the Damanhurian sacred language. It is an ideogrammatic language that is based on ancient signs stratified in the race mind of the human species. It is called "sacred" because these signs have a precise respondence inside the human being and can be used as a means of communication with the divine. This sacred language can be represented in the form of signs, sounds, or dance. The graphic elaboration of its ideograms is the basis of many of the artworks inside the Temples. To those with an untrained eye they may seem simple decorations but to the careful observer they represent prayers, instructions, and information on multiple levels of reading.

The great complexity of elements, decorations, colors, and shapes in each Hall of the Temples—combined with the perfumes and sounds that are always present—creates complete sensory saturation in those who find themselves there. This is not a casual effect but the result of careful research. It allows the user to completely fill every known perceptive channel and allows the surfacing of other less-used and hidden senses closely linked to the soul. In the East, this result is often searched for through contemplation, but to the Western mind it is simpler to "put the self aside" through the saturation of the normal senses. This includes a holistic and not just a linear understanding of the work, a game of respondence between those who create it and those who use it. The Temples of Humankind are also in this sense alive and subject to constant change because every person who enters there—with their emotions and interpretation—is also in part their artist and creator.

THE TEMPLE AS A LABORATORY

Another very important element in understanding the Temples of Humankind is Selfica. It is a discipline which makes possible the concentration and direction of vital and intelligent energies. It was widely used in Atlantis and traces can be found of its use in the cultures of the ancient Egyptians, the Etruscans, the Celts, and the ancient Arabs until the eighth century BC. Selfica, introduced in Damanhur through the research of Oberto Airaudi, creates structures which are able to host intelligent energies. These structures are based upon the spiral and on the use of metals, color, special inks, and crystal structures of different kinds. This discipline allows more complex forms to possess simpler ones: the complexity of living beings is superimposed upon less complex structures made of metals, specific geometric systems, and substances. The particular energies that are called "Selfs" are living forms, border forces that can move from one reality to another, linking different planes of existence. Selfic energies belong to a sector of our universe characterized by ultralight speed, and when they are called inside an object they undergo a sort of deceleration. Building a selfic structure is like giving the "Self" a body to use.

The specific energy, which controls the physical selfic structure, can be defined as "intelligence." It uses the laws of its plane of existence to act upon ours. The interaction of a self with a human being is based upon reciprocal advantage. The self deviates or attracts conditions that are useful for the physical life of the individual, linking to their aura through the "microlines," i.e., the energy lines of the human body. Selfs and human forms do not live all aspects of their existence in reciprocal interaction but "meet" only in those specific fields in which they can both take advantage of this relationship.

Selfs can be considered as specialized symbionts, because they carry out functions that are useful to us—for instance, linked to health—and in exchange they experience a different world from the one in which they originated.

The largest selfic structure on the planet, which weighs hundreds of tons, is hosted in the Temples of Humankind. Among its many functions, one of the most important is that of correcting, balancing, and codifying sounds, rhythms, and time. The Temples, seen in the context of a laboratory, provide the ideal location and optimum conditions in which to talk and interact with superior forces. The use of the selfic structures in the Temples has allowed the development of new fields of research, linked both to therapy and the exploration of time and space.

LIGHT AND GLASS

Even though an underground building, the Temples of Humankind are rich in light and color. The luminosity of the Halls is the result of careful research in order to symbolically represent the conquest of the Inner Light in every human being. Light represents the first act of creation: in the All/nothingness that is the primordial earth, untouched by human presence, the construction of the Temples carries with it the desire to direct and fill with transcendent meanings the presence of humankind itself on the planet.

According to Damanhurian philosophy every human being contains a divine principle. The work of humankind is to reawaken its inner god with the aim of deifying the material world and making the universe a conscious part of God. The search for the self and God coincides because the human being is a bridge-Form between the material and spiritual planes. Every human has this completeness inside and can use the inner self as a transforming crucible to direct matter toward the spirit. The Temples of Humankind are built to be a collective crucible in which the results of this growth are transformed into works and art: it is in glass that this metaphor is mostly manifest.

The luminous white rays that go through the surface of the glass fragment into a thousand colored reflections just as the divinity enters the universe and fragments into a myriad forms. And just as every single form has its own function, its perfect place in the unity of creation. Light is divided through magic signs and precise colors so that it takes on significance and direction. Art is not just for decoration but an instrument for transmitting values and knowledge. The senses and the mind are thus solicited to respond and the surrounding light becomes the spark able to turn on the Inner Light. The original fragmented source can thus be recomposed inside the self.

The symbol par excellence of this reunification is the mirror, which is often used on its own or together with glass. An ancient myth, dear to Damanhurian tradition, describes the divinity as a mirror which in order to enter the material world must shatter into an infinite number of fragments. Each fragment maintains its ability to reflect the absolute but no longer contains the whole. Each person who sees themselves reflected in the glass of the Temples is reminded of their divine origin and that all that surrounds them in the Temples corresponds to that which they have inside. The true Temple is inside every human being, to be constructed inside the self with beauty, love, and altruism. The splendor of the halls of the Temples speaks to the heart. By respondence the Temples make all of this "shine" inside every person who passes there, if they are open to hearing its voice.

HOW IT ALL BEGAN

The first pick struck the rock on a warm August night. It was a Saturday evening in 1978. Oberto and about ten other Damanhurians sat around a fire. It was in a clearing behind a house in the shelter of Vidracco hill.

A large star fell across the sky, a sight rarely ever seen, bright and slow. It left behind a trail of visible gilded stardust that fell to Earth. It was a positive sign; a good moment to begin to dig a tunnel into the mountain, toward the heart of Earth, to create a synchronic contact, to build a temple the like of which had not existed for a thousand years or more. Everything would have to be created by hand and will power, in a job of work that nobody at the time could possibly conceive of.

These unexpected words of Oberto Airaudi had been so vital and full of expectation that, as soon the meeting was finished, two of those present began to dig at the designated point. They had only a hammer and a pick, but they continued to dig with great fervor all night until the morning and when others came to take over, they had already dug over a meter inside the mountain. The turns continued nonstop with groups of people working for four hours at a time, for fifteen days, then the pace relaxed a little, but they never stopped, and everyone participated with equal ardor. The digging was done with only a hammer and chisel, shovel and pick, and a curved pick which was bought specially. The tunnel continued to be dug on into the side of the mountain.

For the fifteen busy people involved in the work, digging inside the mountain was synonymous with digging inside of the self: The enjoyment and the serious importance of the work strengthened their union and friendship.

The digging would in any case be useful in the case of a nuclear alarm or natural catastrophe. In fact, the first corridor was dug in an "S" shape to constitute a barrier against possible outside radiation. Many different self-sufficiency measures had always been envisaged as a part of the philosophical principles of Damanhur; like homemade bread, woven fabrics, and wild plants, the underground shelter was perfectly consistent with these ideas, in an epoch characterized by the fear of catastrophe.

The Damanhurians worked intensely, tenaciously aroused by an enthusiasm that united all in the pleasure of group activity and the taste for secrecy. Secrecy because at this point they did not have permission to excavate. The permission would never have been granted for a project that seemed impossible to realize and in that region there were no laws to control such a construction. It was also secret because this kind of shelter must not be known about by too many people. It was also confidential because the group was animated by the spiritual idea of contact with the universe through Mother Earth. This in a place, that had never before seen the light of day, or welcomed the presence of humankind.

Whenever the moon was full, those leaving the corridor being dug behind the house would lie down on the ground and gaze at the stars, in an atmosphere that seemed totally unreal.

Meanwhile a group of diggers, alternating with the others, brought the earth out in buckets to fill the numerous holes along the roads of the mountain leading to the house.

Pick and shovel, buckets, pick and shovel, chisel and hammer, buckets. . . . The earth fell in small muddy blocks. It was at once clay, then rock, then earth of millennia, never before touched by human microlines. A primeval element.

To enter the corridor it was necessary to bend over and the tunnel seemed very long and narrow, but working there gave the diggers an inexhaustible supply of energy of primordial strength. All those participating always wanted to return and continue the progress, to conquer new spaces. And the mountain permitted the penetration, ever maternal and ever kind.

After many long days of digging, over a couple of months, the first phase was completed and a recess was dug in the side of the corridor to make contact with the Earth in meditation practice.

Now that the symbolic ritual of digging with only with human strength had been completed, it was possible to acquire an electric hammer. Sometime afterwards a second one was bought and from two opposite sides they began to dig two large semicircles, following very precise calculations and without any room for error.

The moment at which the semicircles met was celebrated euphorically by the diggers. And after the celebrations the job of work began, with even more fervor, to dismantle the central column of earth, attacking it from all sides simultaneously.

A large circular cavern was formed, where many people could be present at the same time. The place was damp and dark and it produced intense feelings.

Along the corridor and in the walls some small niches were dug in the shape of a pyramid base, in which were positioned some candles to illuminate the room.

Everything was quiet. Big drops of water found their way down the clammy clay of the jagged walls.

The walls were plastered directly onto wet earth. The mortar was mixed by hand outside; nobody had any experience in construction work but nevertheless began to build the walls and the semispherical ceiling. Some parts of the particularly unstable corridor were strengthened with masonry bricks.

Finally, a mosaic floor was prepared and created with large Luserna stones.

When the work was completed fruits from the garden and homemade bread cooked in the wood oven were taken inside. Everything was shared between those who had worked and in the center of the room some herbs were offered to the fire.

It was the beginning of what was to become the greatest magic and artistic work of the New Millennium, a temple dedicated to the reawakening of the divine in every human being.

OLAMI DAMANHUR UNIVERSITY

Olami Damanhur University is the University of Damanhur. Its seminars and schools are based on the teachings of Oberto Airaudi (Falco), the experience of life in the federation, and on the continuous study and research of its citizens. The instructors are Damanhurians who have all undergone specific theoretical preparation and have years of experience working in the field. Many of these seminars can also be held outside of Damanhur for interested parties abroad.

Seminars and Courses

Learning to Guide the Emotions
(Seminar with successive levels)

Two days and one night; intense, amusing, moving, and unpredictable learning to distinguish between emotion and emotional reactions. An inner voyage beyond normal expectations toward the pleasure of recognizing yourself in others. Emotions and feelings are fundamental personal values that can make us feel happy and satisfied or unrewarded and sad. Our emotions are like a river that flows, and we can learn how to navigate its waters without being capsized and use its incredible energy to our advantage. The aim of this seminar is to help participants recognize and enjoy a wide range of emotions, to make their personal "map of emotions" as rich and as flexible as possible. We can learn how to guide our emotional flow in a positive manner so that they can become a source of wealth and personal growth, instead of unease and difficulty. The basic course can be completed with a second level. Every course is a "full immersion" in which to play, experiment, live practical experiences, deepen theoretical concepts, and let your own rich emotional inner world emerge and flow.

Duration of seminar: two days. Meals and overnight stay are an integral part of the seminar.

Personalities Within
(Seminar with successive levels)

Every human being is a complex reality of desires, thoughts, dreams, and ideas. Often, though, we have contrasting desires, different wishes, as if we were composed of multiple parts, even multiple personalities, and each one with a well-defined character. If this contrast becomes too strong we become ill, but very often these inner "conversations" are at the basis of our most intense creative moments, of our most important choices. They create the necessary tension to apply our Free Will; they give us the possibility of being masters of our life.

Because of our cultural conditioning and genetic inheritance we are accustomed to considering ourselves as one unique person, but our physical body is actually shared by many personalities, many "individuals." The objective of this seminar is to make a real voyage inside and outside of the self in order to contact the different personalities of which we are composed. During the course evidence and "traces" of the parts that comprise our complex internal "me" are collected and a new and more functional balance is created by instituting "order" at a higher and more complex level of awareness.

Duration of seminar: two days. Meals and overnight stay are an integral part of the seminar.

Reawakening the Inner Senses
(Seminar with successive levels)

This seminar is an exciting pathway inside our most extraordinary potential and it represents an essential step toward the reawakening of our internal Divinity. It is an inner voyage beyond the limits of what we normally call reality, safely guided with sweetness and humor by selfic beings. A pathway that moves our most forgotten senses and more importantly opens new doors of understanding and participation in life. We discover that what we think of as our confines are in fact only dictated by the mind and that there is something true and profound that unites us to one another and the whole of creation.

The "training" of the inner senses during the seminar is a direct and different experience for every participant, because the selfic beings are able to provide the most appropriate and effective contact for each person. The seminar includes phases in the Temples of Humankind.

Duration of seminar: two days. Meals and overnight stay are an integral part of the seminar.

Discover Your Inner Artists
(Seminar with successive levels)

The most imaginative and amusing seminar that you have ever done! The perfect complement to the seminars of Emotions and Re-awakening the Inner Senses. Painting, dance, theater, song, scenography, photography, sculpture and drawing are just some of the techniques that are proposed at a fast pace, so that participants can experiment with many forms of artistic expression. Art as a pathway into spirit and matter to create the inner terrain for inspiration and to leave on reality a trace of our most beautiful aspects: this is a seminar for letting go of shyness and the fear of others, for discovering hidden talents and learning to use them, transforming your own life into a work of art.

Duration of seminar: two and a half days. Meals are an integral part of the seminar.

The Art of Lateral Thinking

A seminar aimed at helping you create reality according to a new logic.

Multiply the quantity and quality of your creative thoughts, discover how to apply many more "logics" than you normally use daily, learn how to draw on humor to solve difficulties and to activate different parts of the brain contemporaneously in order to develop more coordinated activities. These are just some of the objectives of this course which works through individual and group dynamics.

Intense creative moments await you. Discover new horizons of thought that will integrate with all you have learned in reawakening your inner artist.

Duration of seminar: two days.

The Dream Path
(Seminar with subsequent levels)

We always dream, even when we are awake and the Sense of Dream is one of our most important dormant faculties. This course teaches us to train this precious inner sense which allows us to participate in different and contemporaneous realities to the one in which we normally seem to live.

This seminar explores the magic dimension of the dream, not the psychological or psychoanalytical one. It furnishes participants with techniques and exercises to learn to dream lucidly, interpreting and actively guiding the dreams themselves. The stone circuits, the spirals, and the great opportunity to sleep and dream in the Temples of Humankind are some of the instruments which make this course very effective. It is accessible to everybody, even those who do not believe they have specific abilities in this field.

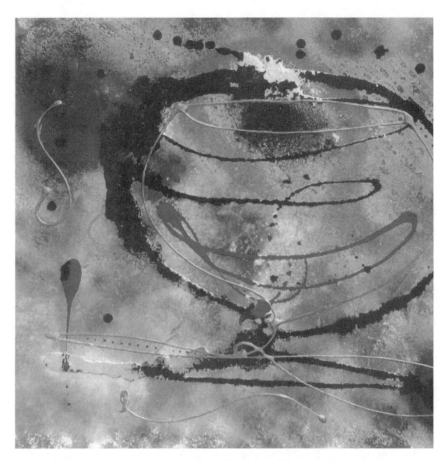

Selfic painting by Alberto Airaudi, founder of Damanhur. (*Courtesy of Damanhur*)

Duration of seminar: two days. Meals and overnight stay are an integral part of the seminar.

Past Lives Research
(Seminar with subsequent levels)

A pathway of several levels to rediscover the past and understand many aspects of your present life. These seminars are lucid and practical experiences to bring to conscious awareness the memory of talents and possibilities still present inside of us. The information on past lives is traced by a specialist Damanhurian group in the "Way of the Oracle." Their research is unique of its genre and consists of a sensitive comparative survey, which reveals the essential elements of past lives.

Hypnotic regression techniques are not used during the seminars: this is a safe, effective, and accessible course for everyone. The seminar is the culmination of a process of connection to past memories that starts from the moment in which the person chooses to participate. Do not expect to discover that you were Napoleon or an Egyptian Pharaoh, because this is not the purpose of these seminars. You will perhaps indeed have an extraordinary history to discover, but the true treasure lies in understanding how many of the emotions, riches, and possibilities of the past are still alive inside of you today.

Duration of seminar: two days. Please note: The information about past lives that is collated through the delicate and careful research of the Way of the Oracle requires two photographs of participants, one recent and the other taken ten to fifteen years ago, including full name and place and date of birth. For this reason, participants are requested to register at least twenty days before the commencement of the seminar in order for the initial research to be undertaken (exceptions must be discussed with Olami University).

Inner Harmonizing
(Seminar with subsequent levels)

Harmonizing is one of the techniques of Damanhurian meditation dynamics. Through simple movements of the body, sounding the vowels, the use of colored light, and a connection with the frequency of the race mind of animals and plants, it is possible to achieve a good internal equilibrium. The technique is useful in combating stress; the internal harmonization rebalances energy and loosens tension. Inner Harmonizing can be used as a preparatory technique before therapy and is a very effective supportive technique for seminars and in the creation of working groups. It is a useful technique for people of all ages, and it is particularly recommended for therapists and trainers.

Duration of seminar: two days.

Spiritual Physics
(Seminar with subsequent levels)

Spiritual Physics is a course that leads to the heart of Damanhurian philosophy. Studies and research in this field allow the student to explore the mysteries of the universe and the human being with the aim of harmonizing the scientific vision of reality with that of the spiritual. Elaborating on these themes creates a wider perception of the self and of life.

The seminar includes research on many different subjects: cosmology, the mysteries of space-time, the subtle and spiritual structure of the human being, the spiritual and divine eco-systems, the inner senses, the awakening of inner divinity, and magic technology.

The seminar is accessible to all, even those who do not profess to have any technical knowledge. Experts will find the course exciting inspiration for their own personal research.

Duration of seminar: two days.

Damanhurian Rituality

A mystical immersion into contact with the Divine, in the most sacred places of Damanhur, an extraordinary occasion, unique in the world, to enter into the heart of mystical Damanhurian practice and research, a contact with Theurgic Magic.

The program is conducted entirely in the Temples of Humankind and the Baita Temple—until now a reserved and sacred place open exclusively to Damanhurian citizens. It is an immersion into the most sacred places of Damanhur that speak to the heart and the soul, a first-hand participation in the Ritual Magic that brings us closer to the Divine and reawakens it inside of us.

This experience begins on Friday at 3 p.m. and ends on Sunday toward 10 p.m.

Astrology

Understanding the meaning of the configuration of the stars in the night sky has always been the desire of many students and researchers. Astrologers have always maintained that the stars do not determine events but influence their direction.

In Damanhur, astrological studies focus on planet Earth and the analysis of the geographical place of birth. This method relates the personal horoscope to the Damanhurian theory of Personalities and promotes a clear understanding of how to use these fundamental tools in the application of astrological rules. The atmosphere of research and experimentation that characterizes this course makes it suitable for both beginners and experts in the field.

Duration of seminar: two days

Upon registration, please supply the following information: name, date of birth, time of birth, place of birth. They will be required for charting your personal "Map of the Sky."

Inner Beauty

Our body is a Temple and beauty is a reflection of our divine essence. Beauty does not depend upon age or physical appearance: a mouth is beautiful that speaks sweet words, eyes when they shine, a smile when it is warm. . . . When we make contact with our deeper self, we can find the precious treasure that is concealed inside of us and reawaken the subtle body of Beauty. This seminar is an instrument for transformation, a path of joy to discover inside the key to internal light, that will make you and the world beautiful. Dance, guided meditations, perfume, sound, and selfic instruments are just some of the tools used in this course devoted to well being and harmony. During the seminar, every participant will receive an application of specific Prana for beauty.

Duration of seminar: one or two days.

Know the Tarot

The Tarot is linked to a book of knowledge that is believed to symbolically contain the entire history of Humankind. The Tarot is a tool for enhancing the intuitive abilities we all possess. The use of the Tarot allows us to make temporal forays in order to widen our possibilities of choice and provides useful indications about how to act in order to reach our goals in life.

This course helps you to understand the symbolism contained in the cards and teaches you how to use them for personal research and as a guide for others. The Damanhurian method is unique in that it uses the divination for actively constructing one's future, exploring one's choices in order to intervene on their probable development in time.

Duration of seminar: two days.

Astral Travel

All the techniques for learning to travel with the consciousness. Practical and guided exercises for exploring a new dimension of reality. For some people the separation of the emotional self from the physical body is instinctive, but nevertheless it is still difficult to guide and use experientially. This seminar teaches the student effective techniques in order to leave the body and travel with just the consciousness. The aim of this experimentation is to contact a dimension that is normally only known through dreams. This course provides the philosophical foundation for understanding the mechanisms and potential of astral projection and includes tried and tested practical experiences that are suitable for everyone. Each session is conducted by highly experienced instructors.

Duration of seminar: two days.

Art Courses

Work side by side with the artists who have created the Temples of Humankind and learn the ancient techniques and new innovations, which have grown out of the continuous research of the Damanhurian studios and workshops: glass-painting, fusion, Tiffany technique; mosaic and stone inlay; ceramic art and sculpture; art restoration; portrait painting: drawing and technique.

... And Craftmanship

Weaving and natural dyes, basketmaking, embossed copperwork, art metalwork, and pottery.

Olami Damanhur University also organizes residential courses, seminars, weekly meetings and lessons on the following: widening one's perceptions, chiromancy and the study of the hand, contact with the plant world, sacred dance, graphology, hypnosis, sacred language, numerology, new societies and community life, natural childbirth, dowsing, pre-Atlantidean history and mysteries of the past, and development of ESP faculties. Personal tuition is available in all subject areas. Olami University also organizes personal and certified courses of study.

The Schools

The School for Spiritual Healers

Founded in 1975 by Oberto Airaudi, the Damanhur School for Spiritual Healers is open to healers who wish to increase their knowledge as well as to those people who have no experience in the field.

The Damanhur School for Spiritual Healers guides people on an inner journey to develop their intuitive faculties. The transformation induced through individual and group experiences promotes self-healing by opening up one's channels to cosmic healing energies (Prana). The technical knowledge that the School has acquired in over twenty-five years of experience constitutes a precious cultural background for the support of the student/healer in the art of healing.

The School for Spiritual Healers is structured as a three-year course. Each level (or year) consists of sixteen residential days in July. Lessons are translated into English. They start at about 10 a.m. and go on until late in the evening.

Even though there is a timetable, the course ideally has no interruptions, and lunch breaks are used for further discussion.

For these intensive weeks, students are expected to arrive on Sunday and settle in before starting the course on Monday morning. The course finishes the following Sunday with a final supper.

At the end of the third year there are examinations, and a thesis must be submitted, on the date established by the School, usually within three months.

First year: The first year's study leads to the students' activation, which symbolically represents a spiritual birth. The healer's path begins with a process of inner transformation. The activation is the central moment of this process, and the whole program of study and the practical experiences of these three weeks are centered upon it. The healer is able to acquire knowledge, extend the use of energies, and become a channel for Prana energy.

Second year: In this second level, having acquired some healing experience, students are given all the necessary tools to begin healing on a more intense and regular basis. Students learn to consider and use Prana as a basic element for their own personal inner growth. At this level, if necessary, students address personal problems that might impede the free flow of energy and interfere with the rapport with their patients.

Third year: The third year leads to an important goal: the acquisition of healing maturity. The more conscious use of energies and the experience acquired during the previous two years makes it possible for the healers to deepen their study of prana-healing techniques. New methods for working with the hands and other integrative systems of healing are studied.

After the degree, the School still remains a reference point for those who desire it. Weekends are organized for perfecting personal preparation and specializing in therapy and diagnostics. Healers are assisted in energetic discharging techniques and are given an opportunity to compare different clinical experiences.

The Director of the School is Orango Riso (Michele Scapino). He has been working as a spiritual healer since 1978 and living in Damanhur since 1977, the year of its foundation. After ten years of research in cybernetics and artificial intelligence, he became a healer and assistant to Oberto Airaudi, the founder of Damanhur and its School for Spiritual Healers. He is an expert in communication techniques, hypnosis, and sound and color therapy. He has worked as a consultant in the use of color therapy for the World Health Foundation and is the author of several books on healing. He gives seminars on healing all over the world.

The School of Color Therapy

The course is structured as four units totaling sixty hours. It provides practical tools for healing and diagnosis through color that can be immediately applied. Every level is organized as a residential weekend. The teaching is not only tuned to therapists who wish to widen their scope but also to people looking for an effective and practical healing method to have at their disposal.

First level: Color: its significance and symbolic value; the relationship between light, energy, and matter; the influence of color vibrations on the physical body, on the psyche, and on the vital aura. Practical exercises.

Second and third level: The practical use of color in therapy and methods of application: painting, use of material and light baths, short-term therapy, sound and color therapy, visualizations.

Fourth level: Color diagnostic techniques using the Luscher test, Rorschach test, dowsing map of Benedetto Lavagna, oriental diagnosis, chromatic intolerance, color balancing.

The School of Color Therapy is directed by Aythya (Lea Ghedin), a graduate of the III Liceo Artistico of Rome and specialist in art restoration from the Central Institute for Restoration. In 1995 Aythya graduated from the School of Color Therapy and the School of Spiritual Healers in Damanhur. Since then, besides working as a healer and chromotherapist, she has become a stylist and architectural consultant on interior decoration, specializing in the employment of color at a therapeutic level in the environment.

Duration of the course: four weekends.

Association card: Olami Damanhur University's seminars and Schools are one of the services offered by the Olami Damanhur Association. To take part in all such activities it is necessary to apply for membership in the Olami Damanhur Association. The cost is 6,000 Liras per year.

Staying in Damanhur: room and board are not included in the cost of the seminars. If you so wish, you can stay in one of Damanhur's guesthouses. We'll be happy to help you with reservations. Please bring casual and comfortable clothes, including outdoor clothing.

Please note: in Damanhur smoking is forbidden indoors and out. If you need to smoke, you must go outside the main gates.

Application: to subscribe to seminars and Schools, advance payment of the association membership fee plus 20 percent of the seminar fee is required as a deposit.

The School of Hypnosis and Self-Hypnosis

This is a one-year course, consisting of six weekends and four days in summer that provides all students with a complete training in hypnosis. The teaching techniques applied by Olami Damanhur University are based upon direct experimentation.

Since 1979, the University of Damanhur has trained more than two thousand hypnosis practitioners and has provided specialist instruction for more than fifteen hundred doctors, psychologists, herbalists, managers, and sport instructors.

This school is open to practitioners in the field requiring further specialization and to those who approach this subject for the first time.

The program includes exercises and techniques appropriate to everyone's needs.

Program

- Self hypnosis and creative visualization
- Experimental hypnosis
- Hypnosis and self-healing
- Hypnosis with induction schemes
- Hypnosis and verbal and nonverbal communication
- Hypnosis and the paranormal
- Hypnosis and memory

The director of the School of Hypnosis is Setter Gordon Juta (Antonino Furfaro). Spiritual healer, teacher of hypnosis and global communication, Setter Juta works with the National Guild of Hypnosis of Turin, in the field of N.L.P. He is a specialist in Superlearning, memorization techniques, and studying methods. He has been living in Damanhur for over twenty years.

ACCOMMODATION AND FOOD

Damanhur has two pleasant guesthouses with dormitory-style rooms and shared bathrooms. Single or double rooms are available on request. Damanhur also has two camping sites, one right in the heart of the Sacred Wood and the other open to agri-tourism for tents, caravans, and motor homes.

If you do not want to take advantage of our guesthouse services, we can book you into a local hotel which offers special rates for Damanhurian guests.

Damanhur is not vegetarian, but Italian cuisine offers many dishes perfectly suited to nonmeat eaters. Damanhur has a restaurant which is open for lunch and dinner seven days a week, a pizzeria in the heart of the wood, and a trattoria which offers its own organically grown food.

There is also a small café, which is open all day for snacks and coffee and an organic food store which also sells basic items for daily use.

The nearest supermarket and automatic banking facilities are in Castellamonte, five kilometers from Damanhur's central site. The closest town is Ivrea, thriteen kilometers from Damanhur's central site, and Turin is thirty kilometers away. In Ivrea there is a shopping mall with a comprehensive range of shops and services. Ivrea's market is on Friday from 8 a.m. to 4 p.m. Public transport exists but is infrequent. If you plan to move around the area, it is useful to have a car.

And again: All over Damanhurian territory, indoors and outdoors, smoking is absolutely forbidden!

If you are coming to Damanhur for the first time, we advise you to choose one of the welcome programs outlined below.

There is a short three-day program and one for seven days, which allows for a more in-depth exploration. If then you have a specific area of interest we can design a special program for you which can include any of the courses introduced.

Three-Day Visit

Thursday—Arrival. Welcome and presentation of the visit.

Friday—Morning and afternoon: guided visit to the Federation, to the art workshops and studios. Questions and answers on Damanhurian philosophy and research.

Saturday—Preparation and visit to the Temples of Humankind. Exercises to widen the perception:
- Inner harmonizing
- Sacred Dance
- Stone Circuits in the Sacred Wood
- Selfic paintings gallery

Visit to the Temples.

Sunday—Morning:

The Damanhurian path of Transformation. Action, Meditation, Game of Life: principles, theories, and practice of the Damanhurian spiritual and social path. Afternoon: Festival of Communities.

Seven-Day Visit

Sunday—Arrival. Welcome and presentation of the visit.

Monday—Morning and afternoon: guided visit to the Federation, to the art workshops and studios. Questions and answers on Damanhurian philosophy and research.

Tuesday—Visit to the Sacred Wood: Contact with the Plants World. Direct experiences in the stone Selfic Circuits of the Wood.

Wednesday—Preparation and visit to the Temples of Humankind. Exercises to widen the perception:
- Inner harmonizing
- Sacred Dance
- Stone Circuits in the Sacred Wood
- Selfic paintings gallery

Visit to the Temples

Thursday—Art workshop: sculpture. Art as a means of creative expression and self-knowledge.

Friday—Magic Turin: Fun in the city discovering the symbols and messages that speak of its secret history and the magic world connected to it. Visit to the Egyptian Museum, treasure house of ancient esoteric knowledge.

Saturday—The Damanhurian path of Transformation. Action, Meditation, Game of Life: principles, theory, and practice of Damanhur's spiritual and social path.

Sunday—Free morning. Afternoon: Festival of Communities. Conclusion of the visit.

Work Exchange

If you'd like to come to Damanhur to study and would like to offer voluntary work in exchange for your accommodation, here is how you can do it.

For the first week, besides room and board, the exchange includes free entrance to evening lectures. The second week also includes the visit to the Underground Temples. If you stay for three weeks, you can also participate in one of Olami Damanhur University's seminars.

If you want to stay in Damanhur for over three weeks, a special program can be devised for you.

Health Regulations

For all stays of over seven days, you are requested to present the following medical examinations: TPHA (throat swab), Hepatitis markers (B, C), and salmonella (stool culture).

CITTADINI DI DAMANHUR

Damanhur is based upon diversity and change. Change applies to everything in the community, including the social and political systems, which have changed many times throughout the years. Likewise, Damanhur's model of decision making has evolved creating an efficient democratic system with elected representatives and elected bodies. Citizens play a major part in the public debate. From the first single community, Damanhur has grown into today's federation, offering different levels of citizenship, according to personal choice. To be a Damanhurian citizen you do not have to live in Damanhur full-time, you can live nearby and participate in its activities, or even live on the other side of the world.

Resident Citizens

Resident citizens are people who choose to fully live the experience of Damanhur, both spiritually and socially. They live in a Damanhurian community and actively contribute their time and resources to the growth of the federation. To become a resident citizen requires precise choices and time to get to know Damanhur as outlined in article 13 of the Damanhurian Constitution: "Whoso-ever wishes to become a citizen of Damanhur must present a written request out-lining their reasons. If the applicant possesses the basic qualities to become a Cit-izen, the person will be allowed to begin the probationary period. During this period the applicants agree upon how they will participate in Community life. They are expected to observe this Charter and other Community rules. . . ."

Supporting Citizens

Supporting citizens recognize the importance of the Damanhur project and choose to contribute even though they may live in other parts of the world. They participate in those parts of the Damanhurian experience they have most interest in without living in a Damanhurian community. Their contribution to the growth of the federation can take many forms, according to individual wishes and cir-cumstances.

DAMANHUR IN THE WORLD

The Damanhurian Centers are cultural associations that promote and offer the experience of Damanhur in many cities throughout Italy and Europe. They are real embassies, brothers and sisters of the federation, places full of vitality where people meet together to enjoy art, culture, and research.

All the first Damanhurian Centers were born out of spiritual healing clinics, and today this continues with a strong emphasis being placed upon the practice of harmonious, traditional, and innovative healing therapies. Every center holds lectures, exhibitions, celebrations, courses, and seminars; organizes research trips to Damanhur and other interesting places around the world; and offers con-sultation and services.

In other parts of the world, where Centers do not yet exist, Damanhur has wonderful friends who help organize seminars and events, presentations, and trips to Damanhur. . . .

We invite you to collaborate with us on bringing events to your area.

CREATING COMMUNITIES

Today the Federation of Damanhur wishes to put at everyone's disposal the results of all its years of work, research, and experience. For Damanhur, participating in the process of planetary change means to create new societies, societies able to plan the future with imagination and wisdom, implementing politics inspired by a respect for life and growth through diversity. If you want to create such a community, we will be happy to help you by sharing our social and spiritual experience.

We believe that in the future on our planet there will be many small communities unified in a federation. Different communities, with their own culture and their own customs creating a world where respect for diversity is held sacred. Maybe in that moment, who knows, humanity will be invited to participate in a grander assembly and looking up at the stars we will finally feel at home. . . .

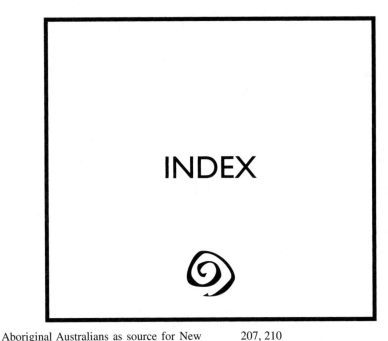

INDEX